T0319531

# COMMERCE IN CULTURE

*The Sibao Book Trade in the
Qing and Republican Periods*

Harvard East Asian Monographs 280

Publication of this book was partially underwritten by the Mr. and Mrs. Stephen C. M. King Publishing and Communications Fund, established by Stephen C. M. King to further the cause of international understanding and cooperation, especially between the China and the United States, by enhancing cross-cultural education and the exchange of ideas across national boundaries through publications of the Harvard University Asia Center.

# COMMERCE IN CULTURE

*The Sibao Book Trade in the Qing and Republican Periods*

Cynthia J. Brokaw

Published by the Harvard University Asia Center
Distributed by Harvard University Press
Cambridge (Massachusetts) and London 2007

Printed in the United States of America

The Harvard University Asia Center publishes a monograph series and, in coordination with the Fairbank Center for East Asian Research, the Korea Institute, the Reischauer Institute of Japanese Studies, and other faculties and institutes, administers research projects designed to further scholarly understanding of China, Japan, Vietnam, Korea, and other Asian countries. The Center also sponsors projects addressing multidisciplinary and regional issues in Asia.

Library of Congress Cataloging-in-Publication Data

Brokaw, Cynthia Joanne.

Commerce in culture : the Sibao book trade in the Qing and Republican periods / Cynthia J. Brokaw.

p. cm. -- (Harvard East Asian monographs ; 280)

Includes bibliographical references and index.

ISBN-13: 978-0-674-02449-6 (acid-free paper)

ISBN-10: 0-674-02449-4 (acid-free paper)

1. Book industries and trade--China--Sibao--History. 2. Publishers and publishing--China--Sibao--History. 3. Booksellers and bookselling--China--Sibao--History. 4. Sibao (China)--Imprints. 5. China--Intellectual life--1644–1912. 6. China--Intellectual life--1912–1949. I. Title.

Z462.86.S53B76 2007

381'.450020951--dc22

2007003139

Index by Mary Mortensen

⊗ Printed on acid-free paper

Last figure below indicates year of this printing

17  16  15  14  13  12  11  10  09  08  07

*For Joe*

# *Acknowledgments*

MY GREATEST DEBT is to the people of Wuge and Mawu, who welcomed me to their communities and tolerated my repeated questions and requests for materials with patience and good humor. This work is the fruit of their generosity and forbearance, and I regret that I cannot here thank individually all the many members of the Zou and Ma lineages who contributed to it. My special thanks to Zou Risheng, who introduced me to both communities and served as my guide to the history of Sibao publishing; to Bao Fasheng, who, as head of the Sibao Cultural Center, helped me locate Sibao imprints; and to Zou Jiangrui, whose calmness and excellent judgment were of great help during my visits. I have learned, to my sorrow, that two of my most helpful informants died since I left Sibao: Ma Jiashu, who advised me on the history of publishing in Mawu; and Ma Xunjian, whose superb recall of the details of early twentieth-century publishing-bookselling provided the foundation for my understanding of the Sibao trade. In addition, I thank Zou Hengchen, Zou Hongqiang, Zou Junfu, Ma Huogen, Ma Wenlin, and Ma Yushan for their kindly assistance. Zou Hongji of Zhangzhou, Zou Shuming of Nanning (Guangxi), Zou Shimu of Lingyun (Guangxi), and Zou Qingsheng of Bose (Guangxi) all provided valuable information about the operation of Sibao branch bookstores.

I first learned of Sibao's publishing history from the work of Chen Zhiping and Zheng Zhenman of Xiamen University in the course of a visit to Xiamen in 1991. I am grateful to these scholars for their willingness to share their materials with me during the preliminary stage of my research and for their support of my work. Zeng Ling, also of Xiamen University, accompanied me on my first visit to Sibao; her assistance, by introducing me to the community and demonstrating the method of historical fieldwork pioneered by her teacher Fu Yiling, was of crucial importance to the completion of this project. I was also extremely fortunate to have the assistance of Liu Yonghua during most of my longest visits to Wuge and Mawu. A graduate student at the time (and now Assistant Professor of History at Xiamen University), Mr. Liu generously shared his knowledge of lineage society, considerably enriching my understanding of Sibao social history. (He has since produced his own study of Sibao society, an examination of the role of ritual in lineage formation, economic growth and competition, and religious and social life.) Discussions with Hou Zhenping, of the Institute for the Study of Ancient Texts at Xiamen University, enhanced my understanding of Sibao imprints. I have benefited from the written work of all these scholars, as the references throughout the book indicate. I also thank Wu Shideng of the Fujian Xinwen chubanju, whose fieldwork in Sibao overlapped with mine, and who shared some of his materials on Sibao publishing with me; and Qiu Rongzhou of Longyan and Xie Jiangfei of Xiamen, both for generously showing me their private collections of Sibao imprints.

Xiamen University was my unit for all my research trips to China. I am grateful to the staff of the Foreign Affairs Office and the Overseas Education Center for their assistance, both in welcoming me to Xiamen and in arranging research and fieldwork in Guangdong, Sichuan, Guangxi, Jiangxi, Shanghai, and Beijing. My work in Wuge and Mawu was possible only with the cooperation of the local governments; I am particularly grateful to Zhang Changming, head of the Liancheng County Foreign Affairs Office, and Wu Gonghe, head of Wuge township in 1995–96, for their support and tact.

An attempt to put Sibao publishing in a larger context required fieldwork and library research at several other sites. In Jiangxi, Professor Liang Hongsheng of Jiangxi Normal University provided much needed assistance in gaining access to the Jiangxi Provincial Library, not to mention permission to conduct interviews in Xuwan and Jinxi. I am

grateful to Zhao Shuiquan and Xu Zhengfu for taking time to introduce Xuwan and for sharing their scholarship on Xuwanzhen publishing. In Sichuan, my work was facilitated by Yang Lin of the Sichuan Institute of Minority Nationalities and Cheng Wanhui of the Yuechi
Overseas Chinese Office. In Guangdong, Huang Guosheng and Li Xubo freely shared their knowledge of Guangzhou and Magang publishing;
I am also grateful to Feng Tianye, who kindly arranged several interviews with residents of Magang. I also thank Wu Ge, curator of rare
books at the Fudan University Library, and the staff of the Changting
County Archives, the Fujian Provincial Library (in particular Mr. Liu
Dazhi), the Jiangxi Provincial Library, and the Shanghai Library.

In shaping the manuscript that has resulted from this research, I owe
a particular debt to Bryna Goodman and Daniel Gardner. Professor
Goodman took precious time away from her own work to give my unwieldy manuscript a fine critical reading; throughout this long project,
she has been a source of encouragement—I am very grateful for her
help. Professor Gardner offered sharp criticisms of certain crucial sections of the work, forcing me to rethink and (I hope) refine and
strengthen my arguments. I have benefited a great deal from many discussions with him about education, literacy, and reading in China.

Many other scholars read and offered comments on the manuscript
at different stages. Lucille Chia, author of a fine study of another Fujian
publishing industry, that of Jianyang, read the whole draft manuscript
with scrupulous care and made helpful suggestions for improvement.
Geoffrey Parker and Evelyn Rawski also read the whole manuscript
and had penetrating (and difficult to answer) questions and recommen-
dations for the reorganization of the material. Valerie Hansen helped
me to define more precisely the goals of the work. Martin Heijdra,
Thomas Lyon, and Joseph McDermott asked detailed questions about
the socioeconomic history of the Sibao trade. I regret that I have not
been able to respond to most of these searching questions, yet this
work benefited greatly from their readings. Christopher Reed gave useful criticisms of the chapter on Sibao's place in the late imperial economy. Benjamin Elman provided invaluable guidance, both through his
written work on the examination system and through comments on the
manuscript at various stages. Patricia Sieber greatly improved my understanding of late imperial *xiaoshuo* and other forms of "fiction" in late

imperial China; I am grateful to her and Paize Keulemann for their advice on this topic. Harvey Graff helped me rethink my conclusion with stimulating comments on my argument about literacy. I have also learned much from comments by and conversations with Sören Edgren, David Johnson, Susan Naquin, Kenneth Pomeranz, Richard von Glahn, and Thomas Wilson.

Ron McLean made the maps and genealogical tables; I thank him for his patience and persistence. I am grateful to Bao Ying, Xu Yan, and Wu Xiaonan, who assisted in the compilation of the appendixes. Readers of the work should be grateful to Naomi Richard for her efforts to clarify and sharpen the prose of the initial draft.

Funding for this project came from a variety of sources. I thank the National Endowment for the Humanities and the Committee for Scholarly Communication with China for their generous support of archival research in the United States and China and fieldwork in China in 1995–96. Grants from the Center for Asian and Pacific Studies, the Humanities Center, and the Summer Research Fellowship program at the University of Oregon supported brief visits to Fujian and several quarters of writing time. The Oregon Humanities Council also provided summer support for fieldwork in Sichuan (1997). A year at the School of Historical Studies, Institute for Advanced Study, in Princeton (1999–2000) allowed me time to work steadily on analyzing and writing up my data; I was able to complete the draft manuscript thanks to a leave from the Ohio State University.

Portions of the manuscript have appeared in "Reading the Best-Sellers of the Nineteenth Century: Commercial Publishing in Sibao" in *Printing and Book Culture in Late Imperial China* (University of California Press, 2005); and in "Fieldwork on the Social and Economic History of Chinese Print Culture: A Survey of Sources" (*East Asian Library Journal* 10, no. 2, Autumn 2001). They are reprinted here with permission of the Regents of the University of California and the editor of the *East Asian Library Journal*.

C.J.B.

# Contents

*Tables, Maps, and Figures*                                    xv

*Notes to the Reader*                                          xxi

1   Introduction: The Sibao Book Trade and Qing Society          1
    The Expansion of Commercial Publishing in the Qing 8/
    Sources for the Study of Sibao Publishing-Bookselling 20

*Part I*
*The Business of Book Publishing and Bookselling in Sibao*

2   The Setting: Minxi and Sibao                                35
    Minxi 35/   Sibao and the Zou and Ma Lineages 57

3   The Origins of Publishing and the Production of Books
    in Sibao                                                    79
    The Beginnings of Publishing in Wuge and Mawu 79/   The
    History of the Zou and Ma Publishing houses: An Overview 84/
    Producing Books in Sibao 93/   Conclusion 124

4   The Structure of the Sibao Publishing Industry             126
    Publishing Houses as Household Industries Within the Zou
    and Ma Lineages 127/   The Income from Publishing-
    Bookselling 145/   The Use of Earnings 149

5    "We are all brothers": Household Division, the Proliferation
of Publishing Houses, and the Management of Competition    159
Family Division and the Development of New Publishing
Houses 161/    Managing Intra-Lineage Competition Among
Publishing Households: Customary Rules and Practices 177/
Managing Inter-Lineage Competition 186

6    Sibao Bookselling Routes    189
The Book Market in Sibao 190/    Bookselling Networks
Outside Sibao 192/    The Pattern of Sibao Bookselling:
Why They Went Where They Went 206/    Conclusion 230

7    Sojourning Bookselling and the Operation of the
Branch Shops    235
Life on the Road: Itinerant Bookselling 236/    Branch
Bookstores 252

8    Sibao's "Confucian Merchants" in Minxi Society and the
Late Imperial Economy    268
"Confucian Merchants": The Image of the Sibao Publisher-
Booksellers 269/    The Zou and Ma Publishing Families as
Local Gentry 275/    The Sibao Publisher-Booksellers in the
Late Imperial Economy 287

*Part II*
*Sibao Imprints*

9    The Nature and Sources of Sibao Imprints    305
Overview of Sibao's Output 306/    The Sources of Sibao
Texts 309

10    Educational Works    321
Primers and Glossaries for Beginning Students 326/    Beyond
"Primer Literacy": Supplemental Texts for Elementary
Education 349/    Textbooks for Composition 358/    Poetry
Anthologies and Manuals 367/    The Heart of the Curriculum:
The Classics 374/    Beyond the Four Books and Five
Classics 396/    Conclusion 402

11    Guides to Good Manners, Good Health, and Good Fortune    410
Household Encyclopedias and Guides to the Rituals of Daily
Life 411/    Medical and Pharmaceutical Manuals 428/    Guides

to Good Fortune: Almanacs, Fengshui and Divination Manuals, and Morality Books 449/ Conclusion 470

12   Fiction and Belles-Lettres                                                      476
     Fiction 478/ Drama and Songbooks 499/ The Elite Arts:
     Poetry Collections and Calligraphy and Painting Albums 506/
     Conclusion 510

13   Sibao's Customers and Popular Textual Culture in the Qing   513
     Audience and the Prices of Sibao Imprints 513/ The Production
     Quality of Sibao Imprints 519 Sibao and Popular Textual
     Culture 523/ The Stability of Sibao's Popular Canon 529

14   The Diffusion of Print Culture in Qing China                  535
     Sibao in Context: Other Commercial Publishing Sites of the
     Qing 536/ The Circulation of Texts in the Qing 548/ The
     Book Cultures of the Qing 553/ Literacy, Social Status, and
     Political Power 559

*Appendixes*

A   Transport Routes Within the Min-Gan-Yue Region            573
B   Value of Woodblocks from the Juxian tang and Dawen
    tang, 1897                                                    577
C   Genealogical Charts                                          578
D   Sibao Publishing Houses and Publisher-Booksellers*
E   Sites of Sibao Bookselling and the Zou and Ma Booksellers*
F   Sites of Zou and Ma Migration in the Qing*
G   List of Sibao Imprints*

*Reference Matter*

*Works Cited*                                                   603
*Index*                                                         637

---

*These appendixes are available online on the website of the Harvard University Asia Center at www.fas.harvard.edu/~asiactr. They can be downloaded and printed out for free.

# Tables, Maps, and Figures

## Tables

5.1    Rental prices for woodblocks from the Wenhai lou, 1894    182

5.2    Rental prices for woodblocks from the Yijing tang, Guangxu era    183

13.1    Estimated retail prices of some Sibao imprints    516

B.1    Value of woodblocks    578

D.1    Sibao publishing houses (tentative)*

D.2    Other Sibao publishers and publisher-booksellers*

E.1    Sites of Zou and Ma bookselling and booksellers in Fujian province*

E.2    Sites of Zou and Ma bookselling and booksellers in Guangdong province*

E.3    Sites of Zou and Ma bookselling and booksellers in Guangxi province*

E.4    Sites of Zou and Ma bookselling and booksellers in Jiangxi province*

*Available online on the website of the Harvard University Asia Center at www.fas.harvard.edu/~asiactr. They can be downloaded and printed out for free.

E.5    Sites of Zou and Ma bookselling and booksellers in
       Hunan and Hubei provinces*

F      Sites of Zou and Ma migration in the Qing*

G      List of Sibao imprints*

### Maps

2.1    Tingzhou prefecture in Fujian province                    36

2.2    Sibao in the late Qing                                    59

6.1    Zou and Ma bookselling sites in Fujian                   198

6.2    Zou and Ma bookselling sites in Guangdong                200

6.3    Zou and Ma bookselling sites in Guangxi                  203

6.4    Zou and Ma bookselling sites in Jiangxi                  204

6.5    Zou and Ma bookselling sites in Hunan and Hubei          206

6.6    Comparison of Zou and Ma migration and bookselling
       sites in south China                                    215

### Figures

1.1    Page from the property-division document of the
       Zaizi tang                                                22

1.2    Page from the Wenhai lou account book                     24

1.3a   Sibao woodblocks                                          27

1.3b   A block containing the cover pages for two different texts  27

3.1    Zhongtian Wu                                               88

3.2a   Wind and fire wall                                        104

3.2b   Cross-section of the wind and fire wall                   104

3.3a   Printing rooms along the wall of a courtyard              106

3.3b   Ink tub                                                   107

3.4    Brushes used to ink the woodblocks                        108

3.5a   Book press                                                110

---

*Available online on the website of the Harvard University Asia Center at
www.fas.harvard.edu/~asiactr. They can be downloaded and printed out for free.

| | | |
|---|---|---|
| 3.5b | Book press with cutting edge | 110 |
| 7.1 | Book boxes used to carry Sibao imprints | 243 |
| 7.2 | Cover page of the *Duilian daquan* | 253 |
| 10.1 | *Zengzhu Sanzi jing* | 329 |
| 10.2 | *Xinke zhengzihua Qianzi wen* | 331 |
| 10.3a | Cover page of *Zengguang zhengwen* | 334 |
| 10.3b | Title page of the *Zengguang zhengwen* | 334 |
| 10.3c | Title page of the *Zengguang zhengwen*, published by the Yingwen Tang | 334 |
| 10.4a | Cover page of *Longmen caofa* | 336 |
| 10.4b | Pages from the *Longmen caofa* illustrating seal script | 336 |
| 10.5 | The glossary *Xinke Siyan zazi* | 338 |
| 10.6a | Cover page of *Xinzeng zazi Renjia riyong* | 340 |
| 10.6b | Page from *Renjia riyong* | 340 |
| 10.7 | Page from *Suanfa cuoyao* | 343 |
| 10.8a | Cover page of *Zhushi San Bai Qian Zengguang heke* | 346 |
| 10.8b | The first text page of *Zhushi San Bai Qian Zengguang heke* | 346 |
| 10.8c | Illustrations and text of *Ershisi xiao* | 347 |
| 10.8d | Preface to *Zhushi San Bai Qian Zengguang heke* | 347 |
| 10.9a | Cover page of *Xinzeng Youxue gushi qionglin* | 350 |
| 10.9b | Title page of *Xinzeng Youxue gushi qionglin* | 350 |
| 10.10 | *Xinzha/Zibian* | 356 |
| 10.11 | Editorial marks in *Zengding Guwen xiyi hebian* | 360 |
| 10.12 | *Tiegang shanhu sanji xinbian* | 363 |
| 10.13 | *Zhupi Xiaoti zhenggu* | 366 |
| 10.14 | *Zhong Bojing xiansheng dingbu Qianjia shi tuzhu* | 369 |
| 10.15 | *Xinke Qianjia shi* | 370 |
| 10.16 | *Sishu yizhu* | 377 |
| 10.17 | From the *Mencius,* in *Wenhai lou jiaozheng jianyun fenzhang fenjie Sishu zhengwen* | 379 |
| 10.18 | Page layout of the *Yuanben Erlun qiyou yinduan* | 383 |

| | | |
|---|---|---|
| 10.19 | From the *Mencius*, in *Sishu buzhu beizhi tiqiao huican* | 384 |
| 10.20 | Title page of a late Qing edition of *Wujing beizhi* | 390 |
| 10.21a | Title page of *Liji jinghua* | 392 |
| 10.21b | Page from *Liji jinghua* | 392 |
| 10.22 | Title page of the *Shijing zengding jujie* | 394 |
| 10.23a | Cover page of *Xuanjin zihui* | 400 |
| 10.23b | Page from *Xuanjin zihui* | 400 |
| 10.24 | Page from *Sishu renwu leidian chuanzhu* | 402 |
| 11.1a | Cover page of *Xinjian Choushi jinnang* | 415 |
| 11.1b | List of contents of *Xinjian Choushi jinnang* | 415 |
| 11.2a | A mourning chart from *Huizuan Jiali tieshi jiyao* | 420 |
| 11.2b | Illustrating the proper forms for invitations, from *Huizuan Jiali tieshi jiyao* | 420 |
| 11.3a | Cover page of *Zhinan chidu shengli yaojue* | 425 |
| 11.3b | "Admonitions to beginning students" from *Xinke chidu* | 425 |
| 11.4 | Couplets for different months from *Qiaozi xiulin* | 427 |
| 11.5a | Cover page of Sibao edition of the *Yuzuan Yizong jinjian waike* | 430 |
| 11.5b | Comparison of pages from two different Sibao editions of the *Yuzuan Yizong jinjian waike* | 431 |
| 11.5c | Page from the Siku quanshu edition of the *Yuzuan Yizong jinjian* | 431 |
| 11.6 | Page from the prescription-recipe book *Shifang gekuo* | 434 |
| 11.7 | Page from *Yixue sanzi jing* | 437 |
| 11.8 | Portrait of Zhang Zhongjing from a Sibao edition of *Yaoxing fu* | 440 |
| 11.9a | Cover page of *Baochi zhinan che yishu* | 444 |
| 11.9b | Illustrations from *Baochi zhinan che yishu* | 444 |
| 11.10a | Block of the cover page of *Yuan Heng liao niu ji* | 447 |
| 11.10b | Illustrations from *Yuan Heng liao niu ji* | 447 |
| 11.11a | Illustrations from the almanac *Zengbu zhujia xuanze guang Yuxia ji* | 454 |

11.11b   Illustration of the ox spirit from *Zengbu zhujia xuanze guang Yuxia ji*   455

11.11c   Illustration of the ox spirit from *Xinjuan Xu Zhenjun Yuxia ji zengbu zhujia xuanze riyong tongshu*   455

11.12a   Cover page of *Luojing jie*   458

11.12b   Page from *Luojing jie*   458

11.13a   Configurations of graves illustratred in *Dili He Luo jingyi*   460

11.13b   Illustration of the "earthly compass" from *Dili He Luo jingyi*   460

12.1   Page from the Sibao edition of the *Narrative of the Three Kingdoms*   480

12.2   Block for *Xinke Liang Shanbo Zhu Yingtai*   501

12.3   From a Sibao songbook, *Qin Xuemei zhuanwen*   502

12.4   From a Sibao songbook, *Zhao Yulin*   503

12.5a   Cover page of *Shuhua tongzhen*   508

12.5b   Portrait of Zou Shengmai from *Shuhua tongzhen*   508

12.5c   Calligraphy by Zou Shengmai from *Shuhua tongzhen*   509

12.5d   Calligraphy by Zou Shengmai from *Shuhua tongzhen*   509

13.1a   Cover page of Xuwan edition of *Shennong bencao jingdu*   520

13.1b   Cover page of Sibao edition of *Shennong bencao jingdu*   521

13.1c   Page of Sibao edition of *Shennong bencao jingdu*   521

14.1   Page from the *Analects* from a Yuechi edition of *Sishu pangyin*   543

14.2   Yuechi edition of *Xun younü ge*   544

C.1   Simplified genealogy of publisher-booksellers in the line of Ma Yipiao   579

C.2   Simplified genealogy of publisher-booksellers in the line of Zou Dianmo   585

C.3   Simplified genealogy of publisher-booksellers in the line of Zou Zhaoxiong   589

C.4   Simplified genealogy of publisher-booksellers in the line of Zou Fuguo   594

# Notes to the Reader

## Abbreviations

FYZSZP      *Fanyang Zoushi zupu* 范陽鄒氏族譜 (editions of 1947 and 1996)

MSDZZP      *Mashi dazong zupu* 馬氏大宗族譜 (editions of 1945 and 1993)

MTLZXZSZP      *Minting Longzuxiang Zoushi zupu* 閩汀龍足鄉鄒氏族譜 (editions of 1911 and 1994)

## Measures and Currencies

Since there was considerable variation over space and time in weights, measures, and currency usages, the following equivalencies are approximate.

### AREA

1 *mu* 畝 = 0.077 hectare

1 *tiao* 挑 = 1/3 of a *mu* = 0.23 hectare

CAPACITY

1 *dan* 石 (also pronounced *shi* or written 擔 in the Qing), "bushel" = 67 liters (by some measures, as much as 104 liters)

1 *dou* 斗, "pint" = 6.7 liters

WEIGHT

1 *dan* 擔 (used interchangeably with *shi* 石 in the Qing), "picul" = 60.5 kilograms

1 *jin* 斤, "catty" = 605 grams

LENGTH AND DISTANCE

1 *li* 里 (or *huali* 華里, "Chinese mile") = 0.5 kilometer

1 *chi* 尺, "foot" = 32 centimeters

CURRENCIES

Multiple currencies were used in the Qing and Republican periods; three (indicated below under "A," "B," and "C") were commonly mentioned by Sibao informants.

A.

1 *liang* 兩, "ounce" = 37.8 grams of silver = 10 *qian*

1 *qian* 錢 = 10 *fen* 分

1 *fen* 分 = 10 *li* 釐 or 10 *wen* 文 (10 copper cash), and thus roughly equivalent to 1 *tongban* 銅扳 (see below)

B.

1 *yuan* 圓 (員, 元) or 1 dollar = approximately 7/10 of 1 *liang* = 10 *mao* 毛

1 *mao* 毛 = 10 *fen* 分 or 10 cents

1 *tongban* 銅扳, copper dollar = 10 cash or 10 *wen*

*C.*

I *huabian* 花邊錢, originally Flower Border Coins or Doubloon silver coins minted in Mexico City, the term comes to be used for silver dollars

## Place-names

Whenever possible I use the Qing-dynasty place-names (dating from 1820) in Tan Qixiang's *Zhongguo lishi dituce* (Historical atlas of China), vol. 8, since these reflect most closely the sites of Zou and Ma migration and bookselling throughout most of their history. The current name of each place, if different from that in use in the Qing, is given in parentheses after the first mention of the place in the text. Late Qing and Republican-era sites are identified by their modern names (and are underlined on maps).

## Imprint Measurements

The measurements of texts are in centimeters and give the height and width of the woodblock (and thus of a full folio page). The bound book would be slightly higher than the height measurement and a little more than half as wide as the width measurement, since the page was always larger than the block, with a space at the top (the "heavenly head," *tiantou* 天頭) and bottom ("foot," *dijiao* 地腳). The extra paper at the sides was necessary for binding.

## Qing Dynasty Reign Periods

Shunzhi, 1644–61
Kangxi, 1662–1722
Yongzheng, 1723–35
Qianlong, 1736–95
Jiaqing, 1796–1820
Daoguang, 1821–50
Xianfeng, 1851–61
Tongzhi, 1862–74
Guangxu, 1875–1908
Xuantong, 1909–11

COMMERCE IN CULTURE

*The Sibao Book Trade in the Qing and Republican Periods*

# ONE

## *Introduction: The Sibao Book Trade and Qing Society*

SIBAO TOWNSHIP 四堡鄉 today is a cluster of impoverished villages in the mountains of western Fujian (Minxi 閩西).[1] With too many people for the available arable land and few alternative resources, the township has, despite efforts to start rural industries, failed to benefit from the freer economic structures that have recently enriched better-endowed villages on the Fujian coast. Sibao has no valuable mineral deposits, and the hills surrounding its villages have long since been deforested. Nor does it enjoy an advantageous location. Isolated in the poorest part of the province, Sibao is not a commercial center of any importance (although Wuge 霧閣, the administrative center, is the site of a periodic market). As in the old days, many of Sibao's able-bodied men seek jobs as sojourning laborers elsewhere, while their wives work the fields or oversee shops at home; the ambitious young are eager to move away.

Yet Sibao has not always been this poor. Throughout most of the Qing, two of its villages, Wuge and Mawu 馬屋, were sites of a flourishing publishing industry, in the form of dozens of separate household-

---

1. On the different characters used to write "Sibao," see Li Shengbao, "Sibao diming kao," pp. 79–80; Wang Rongguang, *Minxi diming*, p. 112; and *Liancheng xianzhi* (1993), p. 985.

based publishing houses (*shufang* 書坊).[2] Founded in the late seventeenth century—the first recorded publishing house was established in 1663—and continuing throughout the last dynasty and into the Republican era, this industry supplied much of south China, through itinerant booksellers and branch bookshops managed by Sibao natives, with educational texts, household guides, medical handbooks, and fortune-telling manuals. The industry reached a peak in the Qianlong (1736–95) and Jiaqing (1796–1820) eras; then, "the extremely wealthy lined up like beads on a string as far as the eye could see."[3]

Although the business peaked in the eighteenth and early nineteenth centuries, it survived into the early twentieth century. The 1854 *Changting xianzhi* 長汀縣志 (Changting county gazetteer) notes that Sibao made "not insignificant" profits from "printing books and selling them throughout half the empire."[4] And the industry enjoyed a considerable revival late in the century. Yang Lan 楊瀾 (*jr* 1789), writing in the Daoguang era (1821–50), praised the Sibao book industry not only for the benefits it brought to literati of the empire but also for the economic support, "the stable assets," it provided the households of the township. "Great wealth is stored up, and [the publisher-booksellers] are able to nurture their ancestral legacy of virtue—they can do no greater service to their forbears."[5] The industry was snuffed out by a series of blows: the development of lithographic and letterpress printing in Shanghai in the last quarter of the nineteenth century, the abolition of the examination system in 1905 (which made much of Sibao's stock

---

2. I translate *shufang* as "publishing house," rather than the more literal "bookshop" or "printshop." "Bookshop" in English suggests a shop that only sells books, a printshop, a factory that only prints books. *Shufang*, however, were book-producing and -selling units. "Publishing house," although not ideal, at least encompasses both the publishing and the wholesale bookselling activities of the *shufang*. I use "publishing house" and *shufang* interchangeably throughout the manuscript. When I discuss the *shudian* (literally, "bookstore") that the Sibao *shufang* established in Fujian and the surrounding provinces, I identify these as bookshops or bookstores to emphasize that they were established primarily as outlets for the sale of Sibao texts (although some did, indeed, engage in printing and publishing).

3. *FYZSZP* (1947), 33.99a.

4. *Changting xianzhi* (1854), 31.69b.

5. Yang Lan, *Linting huikao* (preface dated 1878), 4.8ab. A Changting native, Yang Lan was quite familiar with the Tingzhou area; see *Changting xianzhi* (1993), p. 962.

irrelevant), and the political and social disorders of the early twentieth century. The last publishing house stopped printing in the late 1940s, and the last Sibao bookstore closed in the mid-1950s (although by that time its link to Sibao was tenuous). The 1940 *Changting xianzhi* tersely notes, "Formerly Sibao township made book [production] its primary industry. [Residents] cut, printed, edited, and distributed texts rather widely. Now lithographic and lead- [movable-]type books have become popular, and the surviving blocks have been lost."[6]

But from the early eighteenth through the early twentieth centuries, the Zou and Ma lineages of Sibao ran one of the largest regional publishing and bookselling operations in south China. The literary scholar Zheng Zhenduo 鄭振鐸 (1898–1958) ranked the township with Xu-wanzhen 滸灣鎮 (in Jiangxi), Hankou, and Beijing as one of the four largest publishing centers of the Qing.[7] Sibao booksellers established routes and outlets in as many as ten different provinces—Fujian, Jiangsu, Zhejiang, Hubei, Hunan, Jiangxi, Guangdong, Guangxi, Yunnan, and Guizhou (although their most important bookselling networks were in Fujian, Jiangxi, Guangdong, and Guangxi). A tattered account book, surviving from the early twentieth century, records the wholesale distribution, over the course of one year, of more than 8,000 copies of roughly 250 titles. This volume of sales by just one publishing house, at a time when the industry had passed its peak, suggests something of the magnitude of the business.

Yet Sibao remains almost unknown in the Chinese book world. Few contemporary references to Sibao publishing (outside of the Zou and Ma genealogies and celebratory articles by lineage members and Sibao residents) survive[8]—I have summarized above almost all the brief gazetteer references to the business.[9] Modern scholars of the Chinese book have

6. *Changting xianzhi* (1940), 10.21a.
7. Zou Risheng, "Zhongguo sida diaoban yinshua jidi zhi yi," p. 102.
8. See, e.g., ibid., pp. 102–15; Qiu Rongzhou, "Sibao diaoban yinshua suoyi"; Ma Kadan, "Sibao diaoban yinshuaye chutan"; Ma Liwen, "Minxi Sibao fangke de xingshuai ji qi yuanyin"; Mao Xing, "Sibao guji diaoban de zuihou quchu"; and Bao Fasheng, "Sibao diaoban yinshuaye de qingkuang diaocha."
9. The 1922 *Fujian tongji* merely reproduces Yang Lan's brief description of the industry, cited above; see vol. 3, "Banbenzhi" 版本志, 4a.

paid little attention to the subject; Zhang Xiumin, in his magisterial study
of Chinese publishing, *Zhongguo yinshua shi* (History of Chinese printing;
1989), devotes one sentence to Sibao—and that consists largely of a
citation of Yang Lan's brief, Daoguang-era statement about Sibao publishing.[10] Economic historians have touched on Sibao, using the Zou
and Ma publishing industry as an example of a lineage merchant (*zushang* 族商) group tied to "traditional" social and economic practices
and thus ultimately unable to transcend the limits of a "natural economy."[11] Only recently, after the central government's Press and Publication Bureau (Xinwen chubanju 新聞出版局) directed provincial bureaus to compile histories of publishing, have Chinese scholars of the
book developed an interest in Sibao as a publishing center; Xie Shuishun and Li Ting's *Fujian gudai keshu* (Traditional publishing in Fujian;
1997) includes a section on the industry.[12]

Several factors explain the virtual neglect, in both contemporaneous
commentary and secondary works on Chinese printing and book culture, of this large regional publishing center. First, Sibao today, as I
have indicated above, bears only scant and faint marks of its earlier
prosperity—a few crumbling mansions built by wealthy publishers,
some small and scattered stores of rapidly decaying woodblocks, texts,
printing tools, and so forth. Distant from the major highways through
the Qing and most of the twentieth century, Sibao was also difficult of
access from the cities of the southeast (only new road construction now
makes it possible to travel from Xiamen to Wuge in one day). Until
very recently, study of the industry was limited to local historians celebrating their native place.

Sibao suffers, too, from a larger scholarly neglect—of commercial
woodblock publishing concerns generally and, more particularly, of
commercial publishing in the Qing. Despite the early attention of men
like Thomas Carter, Paul Pelliot, Denis Twitchett, Tsuen-hsuin Tsien,

<hr/>

10. Zhang Xiumin, *Zhongguo yinshua shi*, p. 558.

11. Chen Zhiping and Zheng Zhenman, "Qingdai Minxi Sibao zushang yanjiu." For
a brief but insightful discussion of the Sibao industry, see Zeng Ling, *Fujian shougongye
fazhan shi*, pp. 206–9.

12. Xie Shuishun and Li Ting, *Fujian gudai keshu*, pp. 453–72. See also the report on
Sibao by Wu Shideng, "Qingdai Sibao keshuye diaocha baogao."

Sören Edgren, and Jean-Pierre Drège,[13] there has been little sustained study of Chinese publishing and book history in the West. The recent work of Ellen Widmer, Lucille Chia, and Kai-wing Chow suggests that this might change,[14] but it will certainly be some time before we have, in Western languages, a body of work that explores this topic in depth. Chinese and Japanese scholars have compiled extensive bibliographies of works on Chinese book culture, but these generally focus on technology or the study of editions (*banbenxue* 版本學):[15] for example, the invention of printing in the late Tang, the transmission of fine and rare editions (often the products of official or private literati printing) in the Song, Yuan, and Ming; and the development of modern printing techniques in the late nineteenth and early twentieth centuries.

Qing commercial publishing has received little attention. Commercial woodblock publishers of the Qing produced no technological innovations that we are aware of. Nor did they, generally speaking, produce many "fine" or "rare" editions (*shanben* 善本) in any sense of the term. Although the criteria for the identification of a book as "fine" or "rare" vary,[16] works of Qing date do not arouse the excitement or enjoy the value of rare books from the Song, Yuan, or even the Ming. And Qing commercial imprints, especially those produced from the beginning of

---

13. See, e.g., Carter, *The Invention of Printing in China and Its Spread Westward* (1925; 2d ed. rev. L. Carrington Goodrich, 1955); Pelliot, *Les débuts de l'imprimerie en Chine* (1953); Twitchett, *Printing and Publishing in Medieval China* (1983); Tsien, *Paper and Printing* (1985); Edgren, ed., *Chinese Rare Books in American Collections* (1984); and Drège, *Les bibliothèques en Chine au temps des manuscrits* (1991) and "Des effets de l'imprimerie en Chine sous la dynastie des Song" (1994).

14. Widmer, "The Huanduzhai of Hangzhou and Suzhou" (1996) and "*Honglou meng ying* and Its Publisher, Juzhen tang of Beijing" (2002); Chia, *Printing for Profit* (2002); and Chow, *Publishing, Culture, and Power in Early Modern China* (2004).

15. One exception is the recent work of Inoue Susumu, *Chūgoku shuppan bunkashi—shomotsu sekai to chi no fūkei* (2002); this volume surveys the relationship between the circulation of texts, both as manuscript copies and as woodblock imprints, and Chinese intellectual life and reading patterns through the Ming. For a brief overview of the scholarship on Chinese book culture, see Brokaw, "On the History of the Book in China," pp. 3–54; and Tsien, *Paper and Printing*, pp. 19–23. For bibliographies of works in all languages, see Tsien, *Paper and Printing*, pp. 389–450, and Tsien, "Zhongguo yinshua shi jianmu."

16. For a discussion of the different criteria that might be considered in a definition of *shanben*, see Mao Chunxiang, *Gushu banben changtan*, pp. 3–7.

the nineteenth century on, are often dismissed as specimens of declining skill and artistry in block cutting. For Tsien, the great achievements of Qing printing are the works produced by the Imperial Printing Office in the Wuying Palace 武英殿 and individual bibliophile-publishers. Generally, however, he comments that "the printing industry . . . degenerated in quality if not in quantity in both official and private sectors."[17]

It is certainly not surprising that scholars have preferred to focus on the high points of Chinese publishing and book culture. This preference, however, has led them to neglect technologically and aesthetically less remarkable, but still important, imprints and their producers. And it has encouraged a somewhat narrow focus on the publication and circulation of texts for the elites of late imperial China.

Why do Sibao imprints deserve notice? Even by the modest standards of commercial publishers in the mid- and late Qing, Sibao texts are not of compelling interest. Most surviving Sibao imprints are not particularly well produced; they tend to small formats and cheap paper, and—at least according to one nineteenth-century critic—a profusion of errors.[18] And the Zou and Ma publishers, concerned first and foremost with profitability, wisely chose to publish "best-selling" texts of assured popularity rather than interestingly esoteric works of scholarship or literature. In short, Sibao imprints, being neither "rare" works nor fine examples of the block cutter's art, are unlikely to attract the attention of either book collectors and bibliophiles or modern book scholars.

But it is precisely the ordinariness of the Zou and Ma operations' booklists and the shabbiness of their imprints that makes them interesting and valuable for the study of the organization of commercial publishing, the commercial production process, and the geographical and social expansion of book culture in late imperial society. How rapidly did woodblock publishing spread after the publishing boom of the late Ming? How was the technology transmitted, and what forms did the publishing industry take? What impact did these forms—the structure and organization of publishing and bookselling in different locations—have on the production of texts and on the types of texts printed? How

---

17. Tsien, *Paper and Printing*, pp. 184–88.
18. Huang Junyuan, *Zhizhai yishu*, 13.9a; cited in Xie and Li, *Fujian gudai keshu*, p. 471.

widely did texts circulate throughout the Chinese countryside, particularly in rural hinterlands distant from urban cultural, commercial, and administrative centers? How deeply did they penetrate socially in these areas—did they make it into peasant villages or stop at the level of the market town or county seat? What sorts of texts were sold, and what sort of knowledge and information did they disseminate? What impact did the widespread distribution of these texts have on cultural integration? What were the social implications of the broader and deeper circulation of texts achieved through the operation of businesses like those of the Zou and the Ma? What impact did this circulation have on the shape of Chinese book culture and on the spread of literacy?

This study, in attempting to answer these questions, addresses a level of publishing activity and book culture, as well as a period, that have heretofore received little attention from historians of the book: rural, lower-level publishing-bookselling operations at the end of the imperial period.[19] Sibao, a hinterland site close to the bottom of the publishing-bookselling hierarchy, yet serving most of southern China throughout the Qing and Republican periods, provides an almost ideal subject for research. There are factors that make the Sibao industry distinctive. The Hakka identity of the Zou and Ma publisher-booksellers shaped the configuration of their distribution networks and even, to a much lesser extent, the nature of their publications. And the poverty and isolation of Sibao necessitated a bare-bones approach to publishing and bookselling, an approach reflected not only in the poor quality of most Sibao texts but also in the hard lives on the road of most Sibao booksellers.

In other important ways, however, I will argue that Sibao was by no means atypical of publishing trends in late seventeenth-, eighteenth-, and nineteenth-century China. Sibao's publishing industry reveals two major trends in Qing print culture: the geographical extension of commercial woodblock publishing concerns to rural hinterland and frontier

---

19. Evelyn Rawski's pioneering study of popular literacy, *Education and Popular Literacy in Ch'ing China*, published in 1979, treats some of these questions but focuses not so much on the production of texts as on the availability of education. Lucille Chia's study of the great Jianyang publishing industry of northwestern Fujian, *Printing for Profit*, treats a different period, ending with the decline of the Jianyang industry in the very early Qing, just around the time when the Sibao publishers were establishing themselves.

regions hitherto largely untouched by commercial book culture; and the related social penetration of texts to lower-status levels of the population in these regions.

## The Expansion of Commercial
## Publishing in the Qing

In the most general and summary terms, woodblock publishing during the Qing might be seen simply as an extension of the publishing boom of the late Ming.[20] In other words, the expansion in the commercial book trade that began in the sixteenth century simply continued, after a relatively brief downturn in the first decades after the dynastic transition, throughout the next dynasty. Certainly no one doubts the productivity of Qing publishers; Tsien notes that there was such a surge of printing in the Qing "that the products of no previous period can be compared with it for quantity and the magnitude of the works produced."[21]

But on closer inspection, Qing publishing was not simply a continuation or intensification of the Ming boom. The Qing-period diffusion of commercial printing into the hinterlands and through all social and educational strata, from highly literate elites to petty merchants and peasants, exhibits a pattern of production different from that of the late Ming. The boom in publishing from the sixteenth century to the fall of the Ming dynasty was dominated at the point of production, by just a handful of extremely important commercial publishing sites: the Jiang-

---

20. Miao Yonghe (*Mingdai chubanshi*, pp. 41–42), analyzing catalogues of *shanben* collections, estimates that as many as 30,366 imprints were published in the Ming. Yang Jialuo ("Zhongguo gujin zhuzuo ming shu zhi tongji," p. 27; cited in Tsien, *Paper and Printing*, p. 190, note f), relying on dynastic and other bibliographies from the Han dynasty (206 BCE–221 CE) to the 1930s, concludes that at least 126,649 imprints (almost half of all titles) were produced during the Qing. These figures are at best rough estimates, but they do give some sense of the magnitude of the late Ming–Qing publishing boom.

On the late Ming publishing boom, see Zhang Xiumin, *Zhongguo yinshua shi*, pp. 334–543; Tsien, *Paper and Printing*, pp. 172–83; Rawski, "Economic and Social Foundations of Late Imperial Culture," pp. 17–28; Ko, *Teachers of the Inner Chambers*, pp. 29–67; Chia, "*Mashaben:* Commercial Publishing in Jianyang from the Song to the Ming," pp. 302–6; and Chia, "Counting and Recounting Chinese Imprints," pp. 66–70.

21. Tsien, *Paper and Printing*, p. 190; see also note 20 to this chapter.

nan cities of Nanjing, Hangzhou, and Suzhou (and to some extent Yangzhou, Huzhou, and Huizhou); and Masha 麻沙 and Shufang 書坊 in Jianyang 建陽 county in northern Fujian. Although there were commercial printing establishments in almost all regions of China by the early seventeenth century,[22] none came close to rivaling either Jianyang or Jiangnan, the two sites with the greatest concentrations of publishers. The imperial capital itself, Beijing, boasted only thirteen commercial publishing houses in the late Ming.[23]

The disorder attendant on the Manchu conquest of China in 1644 caused a depression in the publishing trade from which some of the late Ming centers never fully recovered. Most notable here is Jianyang, which for no obvious reason sank into obscurity in the early Qing.[24] So too, at the high end of the publishing scale, Huizhou, famous for its production of expensive, illustrated, "art" editions in the late Ming, ceased to be a printing site of special importance.[25] Nanjing and Hangzhou suffered at least temporary setbacks. Although they eventually recovered enough to become regional centers, they lost the leading position they had enjoyed, along with Jianyang. According to Zhang Xiumin's admittedly preliminary figures, the number of publishing

---

22. Rawski, "Economic and Social Foundations," pp. 24–27.

23. If we look simply at numbers of *shufang* alone, as calculated by Zhang Xiumin, Nanjing ranked at the forefront of production, with ninety-three shops. Jianyang had eighty-four shops, and Suzhou thirty-seven (thirty-eight, if we count Mao Jin's 毛晉 Jigu ge 及古閣, in Changshu, Suzhou prefecture), Hangzhou twenty-four, and Huizhou ten. Of course, numbers of *shufang* serve as only a crude indicator of publishing importance, since they do not reveal volume of output or significance in the market. But Zhang's rough estimate of volume of production by commercial publishers approximates this general ranking of numbers of *shufang*; see *Zhongguo yinshua shi*, pp. 343–48, 359–60, 365–66, 369–72, 378–83, 400–401, and 550–51.

None of the figures given here should be taken as definitive; future research will almost certainly revise Zhang's count. (Chia, for example, has provided a count of surviving Jianyang imprints: 1,664. This suggests that Zhang's figure of "roughly over a thousand" for Jianyang underestimates production; see Chia, "Counting and Recounting Chinese Imprints," pp. 64–65.) Until more extensive research is done on Ming publishing, however, these figures, with the equally problematic estimates of output, can serve as a rough index of the relative importance of different regions.

24. Chia, *Printing for Profit*, pp. 247–50.

25. Ju Mi and Ye Xian'en, "Ming Qing shiqi Huizhou de keshu he banhua," pp. 6–7.

houses in Nanjing fell from thirty-eight in the late Ming to seven in the early Qing, and in Hangzhou, from twenty-five to five.[26]

The decline of these earlier centers did not signal a decline in commercial publishing or a decline in printing as a whole, however. The boom continued, but spread throughout the eighteen provinces of China Proper. To be sure, certain sites rose to genuine prominence— Beijing, for example, became the largest commercial publishing center in the empire. Zhang Xiumin lists 112 publishing houses for Qing Beijing, almost nine times the Ming figure of thirteen. And it was, of course, during this time that Liulichang 琉璃廠 in Beijing became the most famous symbol of the vitality of the Chinese book market.[27] Suzhou, too, among the cities of Jiangnan, managed to maintain and even increase its production.

But the rise to prominence of Beijing and the continuing importance of Suzhou did not bespeak a new centralization of the commercial book trade. A number of provincial capitals (usually important sites of government printing) as well as regional cities emerged as centers of commercial publishing. In Sichuan, for example, Chengdu, after recovering from the destruction of Zhang Xianzhong's 張賢忠 (1605–47) rebellion in the late Ming and from the Manchu invasion, became in the late Kangxi (1662–1722) and early Qianlong eras the site of at least ten large commercial publishing houses.[28] Chongqing never rivaled Chengdu in numbers, but it was a site of several important publishing houses, most notably the Shancheng tang 善成堂, founded during the Kangxi era.[29] Guangzhou provides another example; it became a noted commercial publishing center in the mid-Qing and then flourished in the late Qing as a site for the production of local writings on statecraft.[30] During the peak of commercial publishing in Guangzhou, from the

---

26. Zhang Xiumin, *Zhongguo yinshua shi*, pp. 343–48, 365–72, 550–51, 553–54, and 558. The only late Ming site to hold its own was Suzhou, where the number of *shufang* actually increased, from thirty-seven in the late Ming to fifty-three in the Qing.

27. Ibid., pp. 550–51.

28. Wang Gang, "Qingdai Sichuan de yinshuye," pp. 62–63; and Wang Xiaoyuan, "Qingdai Sichuan muke shufang shulue," pp. 44–45.

29. *Sichuan shengzhi—chuban zhi*, 1: 19–20.

30. Xu Xinfu, "Guangzhou banpian jilue"; and *Guangdong shengzhi—chuban zhi*, pp. 58–61 and 63–72.

1850s through the first decade of the twentieth century, the city had at least twenty-three shops.[31]

With the spread of commercial publishing to the major provincial and regional centers came the rise of new intermediate-level publishing centers. The best two examples are Foshanzhen 佛山鎮 in Guangdong, one of the "four great market towns" of the Qing, and Xuwanzhen in Jiangxi. By the late nineteenth century, Foshanzhen was the site of twelve commercial publishing houses (two of which may have been branches of Guangzhou shops); by the dynasty's end, there were over twenty, specializing in vernacular fiction and popular medical manuals.[32] Xuwanzhen, a market town on the upper reaches of the Xu River 盱江, about twenty-five kilometers from Fuzhou 撫州, developed a publishing industry in the eighteenth century. At its peak, the two-street publishing district of Xuwanzhen had forty-seven different publishing houses; another thirteen shops were scattered throughout the town. These shops together produced, according to the estimate of one nine-teenth-century scholar, more texts than any other woodblock publishing site (with the possible exception of Magang 馬崗, Guangdong, the home of a pool of female block cutters).[33] Although this outward spread of publishing industries was most notable in south China, per-haps because of the greater accessibility of paper, examples can be found in north China as well. Ji'nan and Liaocheng 聊城, both in Shandong province, benefited, like Xuwanzhen, from their strategic location near an important waterway; their increasing importance during the Qing as printing and publishing centers owed a great deal to their access to the Grand Canal.[34]

Influential publishing industries could be found at even lower levels of the central-place hierarchy in the Qing, at times in places quite dis-tant from major transport routes. In addition to Sibao, Yuechi 岳池 county in eastern Sichuan provides another example. Yuechi county

---

31. Zhang Xiumin, *Zhongguo yinshua shi*, p. 556.

32. Ibid., p. 557.

33. Jin Wuxiang, *Suxiang sanbi*, 4.10b, cited in Nagasawa Kikuya, *Wa Kan sho no insatsu to sono rekishi*, p. 84.

34. For other northern sites, see Zhang Xiumin, *Zhongguo yinshuashi*, p. 559; reports on field research by Lucille Chia, in Brokaw, ed., "Mapping the Book Trade: The Ex-pansion of Print Culture in Late Imperial China," for 1998–1999: 6, and 1999–2000: 1–4.

seat and the villages around it developed block cutting as a subsidiary handicraft in the eighteenth and nineteenth centuries. Although most of Yuechi's block cutters supplied commercial publishers in Chengdu and Chongqing, a local publishing industry also arose by taking advantage of the local expertise.

Book trade networks also became more comprehensive at this time. Even relatively minor publishing centers established surprisingly far-reaching bookselling routes in the Qing. Sibao, as noted above, sent book merchants to ten provinces in south China. Some of these merchants were following well-worn trade routes, but others, advancing into central and western Guangxi, Guizhou, and Yunnan, opened up new book markets in what were essentially frontier regions in the early and mid-Qing. It is, indeed, in this period that the Yunnan-Guizhou region was finally incorporated into the empire-wide book trade.[35] Provincial publishers also began to develop branch shops in several locations—for example, the Shancheng tang eventually established nineteen different branches, although its major publishing sites were Chongqing, Chengdu, Beijing, and Liaocheng.[36] The Xuwanzhen publishers sold their texts at outlets in Nanchang, several Yangzi port cities—Jiujiang 九江, Wuhu 蕪湖, Anqing 安慶, Changsha, and Nanjing—and the imperial capital.[37] Sojourning booksellers from Baoqing 寶慶, Hunan, brought textbooks and folk prints (*nianhua* 年畫) to Guiyang 貴陽 and Anshun 安順, Guizhou, and some stayed to establish bookstores. In the Guangxu era (1875–1908), He Youlian 何友蓮, for example, founded the Baojing tang 抱經堂, a sales outlet for woodblock texts published in Baoqing, his native place, and shipped by water to Zhenyuan 鎮遠, Guizhou, and then by land to Guiyang.[38] By the late nineteenth century, then, all parts of China Proper were integrated into a

---

35. Block cutters from Sichuan and booksellers from Fujian and Jiangxi established publishing houses and/or distribution routes in this heretofore isolated region, thus drawing it into the national network. See Rawski, "Economic and Social Foundations," p. 24.

36. *Sichuan shengzhi—Chuban zhi*, p. 19.

37. Zhao Shuiquan, "Xuwan yu muke yinshu," p. 52; *Jiangxisheng chuban zhi*, p. 178.

38. Interview 1 (Anshun, 9/1/04); see also He Mingyang, *Guizhou banshi yanjiu*, pp. 14–15.

comprehensive hierarchy of book-producing centers and bookselling markets and distribution routes.

Why this shift in the distribution of publishing industries and this proliferation of often interconnected industries at intermediate and lower levels of the central-place hierarchy? To some extent, as mentioned above, the expansion of publishing in the Qing is simply the natural progression of a trend begun in the late Ming. Crucial to this progression was the simplicity and portability of the dominant print technology, xylography. It is difficult to overstate the importance of this fact: had the tools of block cutting and printing been more complicated, cumbersome, or expensive, the spread of printing operations would not have been as rapid, thorough, and easy. Consider W. H. Medhurst's assessment of Chinese print technology and the impact it had on the availability of books in the early decades of the nineteenth century:

The whole apparatus of a printer, in that country, consists of his gravers, blocks, and brushes; these he may shoulder and travel with, from place to place, purchasing paper and lamp-black, as he needs them; and borrowing a table anywhere, he may throw off his editions by the hundred or the score, as he is able to dispose of them. Their paper is thin, but cheap; ten sheets of demy-size, costing only one half-penny. This connected with the low price of labour, enables the Chinese to furnish books to each other, for next to nothing.[39]

By the mid-Qing, the simplicity and low costs of publishing technology had facilitated the spread of print culture beyond the larger centers of the late Ming.

Medhurst is, of course, stating an extreme case; he seems to be imagining an itinerant publisher. But the relatively low capital investment[40] and limited skills required by xylography also facilitated the establishment of settled publishing operations more or less anywhere, as long as hardwood for the printing blocks and paper were readily available.

---

39. Medhurst, *China*, pp. 105–6.

40. William Medhurst ("Typographus Sinensis"), in his comparison of the expenses of different kinds of publishing in the 1830s, remarks of xylographic publishing: "The expense of starting such an establishment is much less than would be required for either lithography or typography" ("Estimate of the Proportionate Expense of Xylography, Lithography, and Typography," p. 248).

Clearly the most expensive part of the publishing process was the labor of block cutting. On limited evidence, however, it appears that block cutting was not necessarily costly, particularly for cheap popular productions.[41] Certainly the "machinery" required for cutting was negligible—just a set of easily portable cutting and scooping handtools. Nor, apparently, was great skill or literacy a prerequisite for block cutting. In the Southern Song (1127–1279), religious institutions engaged nonprofessional labor—"religious devotees, women and idle peasants"—to cut blocks for little or no pay;[42] this practice suggests that intelligible, if not beautiful, characters could be cut by people with little or no training. For professional cutters, the training period varied considerably. Interviews of surviving cutters in Yuechi county, Sichuan, reveal that they might study for as little as three years and as many as four to five, beginning as early as ten *sui*.[43]

Moreover, although literacy may have been desirable in block cutters, since it enabled them to work with more confidence and to catch erroneous characters, it was not necessary: since the characters were first written on a sheet of thin paper, which was then pasted face-down on the block, leaving (once the paper was rubbed away) the ink impression of the characters on the block, the cutter had only to carve out the wood around the character-shape. William Milne, comparing the costs of European mechanized printing to those of xylography in 1820, claims that the wages of compositors, who had to be literate, would have to be much higher than those of "block cutters whose only business is to follow their copy." He adds, "Of this latter sort there are many in China, females particularly (for they also cut as well as men),

---

41. Rawski, *Education and Popular Literacy*, pp. 120–22 and 237–38, nn. 64–73. Although acknowledging that it is very difficult to get comprehensive evidence on this point, Joseph McDermott ("The Ascendance of the Imprint in China," pp. 79–80) states that the payment for cutting one hundred characters in 1600 was about 35 *wen*, a relatively modest amount.

42. Edgren, "Southern Song Printing at Hangzhou," p. 50.

43. Interviews 6 and 11, 7/13/97, 7/17/97 (Yuechi); 17, 7/23/97 (Dashi); 19 and 21, 7/24/97 (Zhenlongxiang [Yixingxiang]). Most informants identified three years as the typical period of apprenticeship, though an anonymous unpublished report on the Yuechi block-cutting craft states that four to five years was the norm ("Kanke hangye yuanqi he biange").

who cannot read a single word; and yet they earn their daily bread at this work."[44] And the *Shunde xianzhi* 順德縣志 (Shunde county gazetteer) of 1835, referring to the female block cutters of Magang, notes dismissively that the skill required was so minimal that "all women and children could do it."[45] In Yongzhou 永州, Hunan, block cutting was practiced by men, women, and children as a subsidiary craft, done "while watching oxen at pasture, grasping a chisel and cutting while leaning against a tree."[46] To be sure, the very best carvers, like the famous craftsmen of the Huang 黃, Wang 汪, Qiu 仇, and Liu 劉 lineages of Huizhou, responsible for some of the most finely carved illustrated texts of the late Ming,[47] might be both literate and highly skilled—and thus able to command high wages—but the production of a legible text did not *require* their degree of knowledge or skill. There was, in short, a considerable range in acceptable levels of block-cutting skill.

One other aspect of xylography made it easily adaptable to a variety of economic contexts: the publisher-printer's ability to adjust print runs to demand. Once the blocks for a title were carved, the publisher could tailor the size of the run to his estimate of the market. When demand outstripped supply, new copies could simply be printed off the original blocks. This is one of the great advantages of woodblock printing; in letterpress publishing, a "reprinting" of a work meant that the entire text had to be retypeset from scratch, a considerable investment of labor. The Chinese publisher, unlike his Western counterpart, did not have to guess at the popularity of a new text, risking, if he overestimated, overstocking and a very slow return on his original investment;

---

44. Milne, *Retrospect of the First Ten Years of the Protestant Mission to China*, pp. 259–60.

45. *Shunde xianzhi* (1853), 3.50a, cited in Xu Dixin and Wu Chengming, eds., *Chinese Capitalism, 1522–1840*, p. 238. For a similar comment about block cutting in Xuwan, see *Jiangxi sheng* (Minguo era), cited in Zhao Shuiquan, "Xuwan yu muke yinshu," p. 54: "The men and women of Xuwan, in Jinxi county, are all good at cutting characters. In former times most of the texts found throughout the province were produced there."

46. Xu Ke, "Gongshu lei," *Qingbei leichao*, 5: 2397. This entry explains that blocks cut in Magang were especially cheap because they were cut by young girls of age ten or so "who are paid little and work fast," but whose blocks are not as accurately cut as those done by the Yongzhou cutters. Cited in Xu Dixin and Wu Chengming, eds., *Chinese Capitalism, 1522–1840*, p. 238.

47. Bussotti, *Gravures de Hui*, pp. 275–82.

or, if he underestimated, the cost of a new, time-consuming, and labor-intensive setting of the text. Thus woodblock printing enabled Chinese publishers to keep capital costs down somewhat (although they still had to make the original investment in the cutting of the blocks) and to respond rapidly and sensitively to fluctuations in demand. It is this very flexibility that impressed Matteo Ricci in the early seventeenth century:

> Their method of printing has one decided advantage, namely, that once these tablets are made, they can be preserved and used for making changes in the text as often as one wishes. . . . [W]ith this method, the printer and the author are not obliged to produce here and now an excessively large edition of a book, but are able to print a book in smaller or larger lots sufficient to meet the demand at the time. . . . The simplicity of Chinese printing is what accounts for the exceedingly large numbers of books in circulation here and the ridiculously low prices at which they are sold.[48]

Block-cutting costs were thus only occasional—unless, of course, the popularity of a text occasioned so many reprints that the first set of blocks wore out, in which case profits would probably defray the cost of touching up the original blocks or cutting a whole new set.[49]

---

48. Gallagher, *China in the Sixteenth Century*, p. 21; cited in Rawski, "Economic and Social Foundations," p. 17.

49. There is debate over two relevant points here: the size of most woodblock print runs and the durability of the blocks. Estimates of the former range from a high of "hundreds" to a low of twenty-five; most likely the number of copies in a run varied considerably, a variation that doubtless depended on the resources of the publisher and his estimate of the demand for a given title. Some publishers just printed on demand, advertising this service in their imprints.

As for the durability of the blocks, the difference in estimates is astonishing. One scholar claims that a set of blocks could yield as many as 25,000 impressions (an initial 15,000, and another 10,000 after the blocks, made of pear wood, had been slightly "touched up") (Tsien, *Paper and Printing*, p. 201). Contemporary block cutters put the figure much lower, at as few as 2,000 to 3,000 for the initial printing (Chia, *Printing for Profit*, p. 331, n. 37). Medhurst ("Typographus Sinensis"), in a communication to the *Chinese Repository*, states that after 10,000 impressions, blocks "are no longer capable of giving good impressions" ("Estimate of the Proportionate Expense of Xylography, Lithography, and Typography," p. 249). In a study of Japanese publishing, Peter Kornicki (*The Book in Japan*, p. 137) suggests that 8,000 is a reasonable figure. Of course this variation can be explained by differences in the woods or other materials used for the blocks (unfortunately sources rarely indicate which material corresponded to which figure), the care taken in block preparation, and the quality of the cutting, but the range in

It also seems to have been quite easy to find at least minimally qualified block cutters and to engage them in a variety of different employment relationships. A small-scale publisher who could not afford to maintain a permanent crew of workers could simply turn to a local "character-cutting shop" (*kezi dian* 刻字店, *kezi pu* 刻字舖) or to a band of itinerant carvers working on commission. Or he might cut costs by hiring distant peasants to cut blocks. Such workers, usually impoverished and practicing block cutting as a subsidiary craft, could be paid so little that it was worth the cost of transporting the blocks—often considerable distances—to employ them.[50] Thus blocks cut by peasant craftsmen in Yuechi were often shipped down river to Chongqing or carried overland to Chengdu (a journey of over two hundred kilometers) for printing. Finally, the employment of female labor could very significantly reduce costs; Ye Dehui estimated that women cutters in Hunan, Jiangxi, and Guangdong were paid between one-fourth and one-third of the wages of male cutters in the late nineteenth century.[51]

If the costs of block cutting could be kept low, the costs of the other steps in the publishing process were even easier to limit. Printing and binding did not necessarily demand high skills or expensive materials; indeed, these tasks were commonly left to women and children (often family members who need not be paid),[52] a sure sign that they were perceived as work requiring no or little skill. Access to a steady supply of cheap paper may have been the greatest constraint on the spread of commercial printing. But paper, which was made from a wide range of easily available materials, most notably bamboo but including mulberry tree bark, rattan, and other plant fibers, was relatively inexpensive in the

---

numbers of impressions still seems remarkable. See Rawski, *Education and Popular Literacy*, p. 120.

50. Indeed, it seems that blocks were more commonly transported from cutter to publisher, and from publisher to publisher, than has previously been assumed. The recent work of Joseph Dennis on the production of gazetteers in the early Ming supports this conclusion; see, e.g., "The Production and Circulation of Early Ming Gazetteers."

51. Ye Dehui, *Shulin qinghua*, p. 186.

52. I do not mean to suggest that this labor was free to the publishers; the printing and binding work of the women in the household diverted their labor from other occupations. Yet, particularly within large households, this system was more cost efficient than hiring wage laborers from outside the family.

south.[53] It is probably primarily for this reason that commercial publishing spread more rapidly and pervasively in south China, where bamboo paper was abundant and cheap, than in the north, where paper making was not as widespread. In sum, depending on the aesthetic aspirations and location of the publisher, neither the initial investment nor the continuing labor costs for publishing needed to be considerable, and thus it was possible for those with limited access to capital to imagine publishing-bookselling as a livelihood.[54]

Thus the portability and relative cheapness of xylography shaped the geography of printing in China and allowed considerable mobility and decentralization.[55] These characteristics in turn encouraged, first, a diffusion of printing operations throughout the empire and, second, the proliferation of operations of varying sizes and configurations, at different levels of the central-place hierarchy. These developments are not particularly surprising. Given the simplicity of the technology and the importance of books in Chinese society, both as aids to power, prestige, and wealth through the examination system and as emblems of elite culture, it is logical that the publishing "explosion" of the late Ming would continue and intensify.

But it was not simply the easiness and flexibility of Chinese print technology and the steady market for books that supported the spread of publishing. Other catalysts, distinctive to the Qing, were at work as well. The growing prosperity of China and the demographic explosion of the eighteenth century (just the time when most of the smaller publishing industries mentioned here got their start) spurred an expansion in publishing, creating greater demand and wider markets for texts. The population increased from 155 million in 1500 to 268 million in 1650, rising through the Qing to roughly 400 million by the 1840s.[56] Surely it is

---

53. Tsien, *Paper and Printing*, pp. 52–64.

54. See Chapter 5 for a description of how one Sibao publisher, Ma Quanheng, established a business with very slender means—just twenty ounces (*liang* 兩) of silver. See also Rawski, *Education and Popular Literacy*, pp. 119–23.

55. Rawski, "Economic and Social Foundations," pp. 21–22.

56. Martin Heijdra ("The Socio-economic Development of Rural China During the Ming," p. 438) provides three sets of population figures in his study of population growth over the mid- to late Ming, and I have chosen the middle estimate.

no coincidence that the boom in publishing, begun in the sixteenth century and persisting, with only a brief interruption over the Ming-Qing transition, parallels this long-term expansion in population.

At the same time, the migrations of the early and high Qing diffused the demand for books, creating markets in newly settled areas; the opening of hinterland and frontier regions encouraged the wider distribution of publishing sites throughout the empire. Migration worked on the supply side as well, to spread block cutting, printing, and managerial skills throughout China Proper. The major Qing-era publishing houses of Chengdu were founded by immigrants from Jiangxi province. Similarly, block-cutting techniques were introduced to isolated Yuechi county by Jiangxi and Fujian migrants to eastern Sichuan. Yuechi carvers in search of higher wages in turn migrated to or sojourned in the frontier areas of Gansu, Yunnan, and Guizhou, where their skills were still rare, and passed along a craft previously learned from Jiangxi and Fujian immigrants.[57]

In sum, the expansion in geographical scope, the growth in number of publishing and bookselling sites, and the greater complexity of intra- and interregional links among these sites that characterize the Qing book trade, coupled with the increased prosperity and expanding population of the eighteenth century, made possible not only a broader but also a deeper dissemination of texts, socially as well as geographically. Many of the new publishing sites, like Sibao, served both the larger book market and a smaller, rural demand for relatively inexpensive texts. The expansion of bookselling networks made possible the distribution of printed texts to even quite isolated peasant communities, to members of the lower rungs of the social order heretofore largely excluded from printed book culture. It was in the context of these trends that the Sibao book industry unfolded.

---

57. Wang Gang, "Qingdai Sichuan de yinshuye," pp. 62–63. For the sojourning and migration of Yuechi block cutters, see Interviews 6, 7/13/97 (Yuechi); 17, 7/23/97 (Dashi); 19 and 21, 7/24/97 (Zhenlongxiang [Yixingxiang]). As yet we do not understand the pattern of migration, or the degree to which links established through migration integrated commercial publishing concerns into regional or even national networks. This is clearly a question requiring further study if we are to understand the spread of Chinese publishing.

## Sources for the Study of Sibao
## Publishing-Bookselling

Since full and detailed business records, accounts, and correspondence do not survive for the Sibao industry—as they do not for most Chinese business operations before the nineteenth century—it is necessary to draw on a wide range of other sources to reconstruct the history of Sibao publishing.[58] The sources a Qing historian might first turn to—memorials, local gazetteers, and the writings (both the casual "jottings," or *biji* 筆記, and the more polished literary collections, or *wenji* 文集) of local literati and officials—provide little information about Sibao publishing, although of course they (especially the gazetteers) are useful sources of information about the context in which the industry evolved. These sources are used in this study primarily to describe the socioeconomic and cultural development of western Fujian and the major market areas of the Zou and Ma booksellers in Guangdong, Guangxi, and Jiangxi.

The richest sources for the study of Sibao publishing are to be found on site, in Wuge and Mawu. Genealogies of several Zou branch lineages and one Ma branch lineage make possible the reconstruction of relationships among some of the most prominent publishers; they also provide relatively detailed information about the origins and development of the business and even, to some extent, about the titles the Zou and Ma published (and edited).[59] They are virtually the only primary sources for the first century of the Sibao book trade. The genealogies also supply essential information about the migration patterns of lineage members and about the bookselling routes and bookselling outlets they established, often on the basis of these patterns. Biographies and commemorative essays in honor of the publishers, both by local Minxi

---

58. For a fuller discussion of the sources available in Sibao (and in some other sites) and their interpretation, see Brokaw, "Fieldwork on the Social and Economic History of Chinese Print Culture."

59. In this case, the failure of the Zou and Ma to earn much distinction through the examination system works to the historian's advantage, for it seems to have freed them to be more open and communicative about their business activities, at least in comparison with the Jianyang publishers studied by Chia.

literati and officials and by business contacts from surrounding provinces, reveal a great deal about the social networks publisher-booksellers
developed. And, of course, the genealogies help us to trace the growth of
the lineage and the scope of its educational and religious practices and to
link these to the growth of the local publishing industry.

To be sure, the genealogies present many difficulties for interpretation. As texts designed to define membership in the lineage unit and to
assert allegiance to approved ritual and ethical values, they do not present a clear or necessarily reliable account of family history—and they
devote little attention to the evolution of the publishing-bookselling
business. The biographies of leading lineage members are written not
so much to convey the distinctive character of their subjects as to present a series of exemplary lives, both to exalt the lineage by demonstrating that its members conformed to accepted standards of good conduct
and to provide models for future generations. Thus there is a sameness
to many of the biographies: a strikingly high number of subjects (except,
of course, for the virtuous women of the families, who were held to a
different standard) were brilliant students in youth, devoted to the recitation of the Classics and poetry and the practice of calligraphy; filial
sons and responsible and loving brothers, protectors of family harmony;
selfless contributors to community charities; and recipients of rewards
for their virtue in old age, not to mention the progenitors of many accomplished descendants. Of course, these ritual elements and rhetorical
flourishes are in themselves useful historical evidence of a sort. Although they tell us little about the real behavior of specific individuals,
they reveal much about the economic concerns and social and moral
preoccupations of the Zou and Ma publisher-booksellers. But a reader
must search hard for specific references to the business activities of
lineage members, and such information, when included in a biography
at all, is often delivered in an offhand and, for a historian, frustratingly
vague fashion. The genealogies constitute, nonetheless, the most significant historical record of the Sibao industry; they provide, however
spottily and accidentally, the only roughly contemporary narrative we
have of the development of the Zou and Ma book trade in the Qing.

Valuable, too, are some scattered property-division documents (*fenguan* 分關 in the local parlance), dating from 1773 to the Guangxu era,
recording the distribution of property (including woodblocks and print

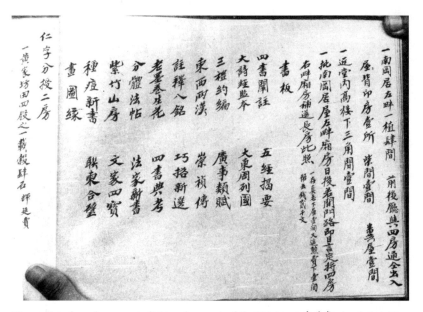

Fig. 1.1 Page from the property-division document of the Zaizi tang 在茲堂, dated 1839. Note that, in addition to woodblocks, the text refers to the division of printing rooms. Photograph by the author.

rooms, *yinfang* 印房, where the blocks were printed) among a man's sons (see Fig. 1.1). These records tell us something not only of the numbers but also of the works produced by Sibao publishing houses. They also explain one of the mechanisms by which publishing houses proliferated in Sibao—inheritance—and, in the rules they include for the sale and rental of blocks, some of the regulations that governed relations both within and between publishing houses. Since most of the extant property-division documents date from the nineteenth century, they are particularly useful for an overview of the industry at that time, providing what amount to publishing house inventories of titles available for printing.

Several valuable, but difficult-to-date, sources provide information about Sibao's output and, in some cases, the prices of Sibao texts and bookselling strategies. The most extensive list of Sibao titles, with 860 separate entries, records the amount of paper required to print each text; there are a few duplicate titles with different trim sizes ("large," "medium," and "small"). This list was probably used by a group of publishing houses to calculate the amount of paper they needed to order. [60] Two ledgers survive as well from Wuge. The first is an account book kept by the manager of the Wenhai lou 文海樓, a Wuge concern that flourished in the late nineteenth and early twentieth centuries (see Fig. 1.2). This ledger records sixty-seven different lots of texts to be distributed to different bookshops and lists, after abbreviated titles, the numbers of copies of each title per lot and the wholesale price for each; it also includes some information about the income of the various branch shops operating within the Wenhai lou bookselling chain. Unfortunately, like the two book lists mentioned above, this ledger is not dated. Since the paper in the ledger is a type not in common use until the early twentieth century, this source provides information about only the later years of the industry, at the earliest the first decade of the twentieth century. Another ledger records the activities of itinerant booksellers Zou Weinan 位南 (1860–1933), Zou Xiyao 希堯 (1866–1926), and Zou Xinfeng 新豐 (fl. late 19th c.), who peddled primers, correspondence guides, novels, geomancy manuals, stationery supplies, and simple medicines to lineage or village schools and bookstores in over forty different villages. There are also a few single-page documents recording transactions (the sale or purchase of woodblocks or texts) between Sibao *shufang* and other publishing houses in Foshan or Guangzhou; given what we know of Sibao publishing and bookselling history, these can be dated to the late Qing. Finally, there are a few contracts that record the pawning or mortgaging of woodblocks; the earliest are dated 1822, the latest 1863. The fragmentary nature of many of these sources—the Wenhai lou ledger in particular has been severely damaged by damp and worms—presents considerable challenges for interpretation. But the extreme rarity of such

---

60. This inventory is in the possession of a descendant of the family that operated the Cuiyun tang 萃蕓堂 publishing house (founded in 1816?); see *FYZSZP* (1996), *shang*, p. 180. It is possible that it lists all the titles published by this shop in a year, but 860 seems an extraordinary number of titles for one shop to have produced. The account book from the Wenhai lou lists 251 different titles (since many titles are illegible, the original number was probably higher); and the longest of the property-division documents lists only 107. Thus it seems likely that this list was a kind of reference, including all titles for which woodblocks had been cut and that thus might be produced either by a group of Wuge printshops or by the Cuiyun tang over several years. Two other much shorter book lists, untitled and undated, appear to be the inventories of the Sibao publishing houses.

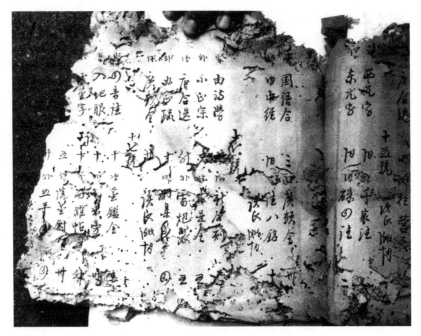

Fig. 1.2 Page from the Wenhai lou 文海樓 account book, listing the wholesale prices, titles, and numbers of copies of texts sold by the publishing house. Photograph by the author.

sources for commercial woodblock publishing also makes them particularly precious, at least as evidence for roughly the last century of the Sibao industry. (Throughout I refer to all these sources collectively as the Sibao "book lists.")

Surviving Sibao imprints are, of course, one of the most reliable and fruitful sources for this study, since they supply not only information about titles published but also material evidence about the production quality of Sibao texts. I have photocopied, photographed, or recorded as many Sibao editions as I could on site in Wuge and Mawu and, of course, visited library collections (and at least two private collectors) throughout south China in an effort to collect as much evidence as possible from Sibao imprints.

I should note here the difficulties in interpreting what at first glance might seem unassailably concrete sources. First, many of the cheaper Sibao editions do not record the name of the publishing house (*tangming* 堂名) or the date of publication (that is, the date the blocks were cut), making it difficult to date works or to associate them with a particular publishing house. In part because of these omissions, it has been im-possible to develop a definitive list of Sibao publishing houses.[61]

Furthermore, many of the titles extant in Wuge and Mawu, because of the detrimental conditions in which they have been kept, survive only in part, as isolated volumes or even, sometimes, as loose, rotting, worm-eaten pages, without either *fengmian* 封面 (cover pages) or title pages (the first half-folio page of the first *juan*), much less prefaces or tables of contents. In these cases it is difficult to get a sense of the tar-get audience for a text (often this is defined or suggested in a preface) or even the full extent of the text. As indicated above, Sibao produc-tions are not, generally speaking, of fine quality and thus are often not to be found in libraries; the ephemeral nature of many Sibao publica-tions, too, has limited their preservation. Finally, since the Zou and Ma publishers employed numerous block cutters, whose styles and tech-niques varied, it is difficult to identify their texts by a distinctive cutting style, a criterion that can be used, for example, to identify some late Ming Jianyang editions.

Nonetheless, a large enough store of Sibao imprints—roughly 160— has survived intact or sufficiently so to permit an analysis of their pro-duction quality, contents, prefaces, and format—and thence some con-clusions about their intended audiences and often about their sources and circumstances of publication. In addition, we have records of Sibao publication of over eleven hundred additional titles from surviving property-division documents, book lists, and ledgers; although these are clearly not as useful as the surviving texts, they nonetheless help flesh out our picture of Sibao's stock in the last century of its publishing history. In the discussion of Sibao's output in Part II, when possible I restrict my comments to surviving titles known to have been produced by the Zou and Ma.[62]

---

61. Nor are publishing house names listed in the genealogies or other written pri-mary documents. Contemporary residents of Wuge and Mawu have compiled lists of *shufang* names of variable reliability and completeness. Here I refer to publishing-house names only when the evidence seems to support the identification, but the reader should be aware that all identifications, except those drawn from Sibao imprints them-selves, are tentative. See Appendix D.1 for a tentative list of Sibao *shufang*.

62. One problem I encountered in collecting texts on site is that many informants presented any old woodblock text (or lithographic text) in their possession as a Sibao

Other physical evidence of the publishing-bookselling business survives in Wuge and Mawu. It is still possible to find woodblocks (see Figs. 1.3a and b), although most of these have been destroyed or lost in the decades since the decline of the printing industry in the 1930s and 1940s. A large publishing house would have devoted several rooms to block storage, and once book publication ceased to be profitable, this was a waste of space. Poor households began to use woodblocks—bulky and by that time useless—for fuel. The Cultural Revolution also took its toll; in fearful anticipation of the arrival of the Red Guards, the residents of Wuge and Mawu incinerated many of the remaining woodblocks and imprints in a huge bonfire that burned, it is said, for over a month. The few blocks that remain do, however, provide visual evidence of the quality of cutting, of methods of repairing blocks, and of the efficient practice of cutting both sides of some blocks. Examples of printing and binding tools (brushes, ink basins, a book press) and other paraphernalia (book boxes, bamboo baskets for the transport of ink, and so forth) also survive. It is possible, too, to get some sense of the physical arrangement of the printing process by visiting the courtyard units that functioned as small printing factories within the larger mansions. And these mansions themselves, albeit now worn and crumbling, testify to the profits earned by the publishers.

Finally, oral histories have also provided much useful information, particularly about the sources of raw materials for printing, customary regulations governing relationships among the Zou and Ma publishing houses, the establishment of branch outlets, the relationships between branch outlets and the Sibao headquarters, transportation networks, texts published, and the nature of Sibao's markets. Over the course of roughly eight months' residence in Wuge (between 1993 and 2004) and visits to Zhangzhou (Fujian) and Nanning, Lingyun, and Bose (Guangxi), I conducted over ninety interviews with members of the Zou and Ma lineages, either those at one point directly involved in the

---

imprint. The recently opened exhibition hall in Wuge includes in its display of Sibao imprints many texts that were not in fact produced in Sibao. See Appendix G for a list conflating all the titles from the property-division documents, account books, other book lists, and private collections; I have excluded doubtful texts from this list.

Fig. 1.3 (a, *top*) Sibao woodblocks. (b, *bottom*) A block containing the cover pages for two different texts: *Xinke Siyan zazi* 新刻四言雜字 (Newly published *Four-Word Glossary*) and *Zengzhu Sanzi jing* 增註三字經 (*Three-Character Classic,* with expanded commentary), both published by the Linlan tang 林蘭堂 in the Tongzhi era. Photographs by the author.

early twentieth-century publishing industry and book trade or descendants of late nineteenth- and early twentieth-century publishers and
booksellers. Comparative information on other contemporary publishing sites was collected in part through interviews in Yuechi (Sichuan),
Xuwan (Jiangxi), and Magang (Guangdong).[63] The interview material
varies widely in evidential quality and has to be carefully assessed. I
have tried, whenever possible, to verify information by reference to
printed sources; relied most heavily on reports for which there is a
broad consensus (and have recorded divergences from the consensus in
the notes); and weeded out clearly prejudiced or unlikely responses. Finally, I indicate where in the text I am relying primarily on interview
materials, so that readers can recognize interpretations based on this
kind of evidence. Notwithstanding the obvious problems inherent in
this type of source, I found that the interviews and oral histories greatly
illuminated my understanding of the operation of the Sibao publishing-
bookselling trade.

Although the Zou and Ma genealogies provide information on the
early development of the publishing industry, fuller sources are available beginning only in the Daoguang era—unfortunately just at the
time the industry was beginning its slow (but by no means linear) decline. Thus the story of the last century of Sibao publishing-bookselling
is inevitably more detailed than that of its first century and a half. And
even for this portion of the story, readers in search of certitude and
precision may be frustrated by my reluctance to provide statistics for
the numbers of booksellers at work at any one time, the number (and
names) of Sibao *shufang*, the number of titles they produced, and so
forth. Awareness of the incompleteness of the sources has led me to be
cautious about supplying figures that could easily mislead. As a result,
this work presents more a general picture of the sorts of relationships
and practices that shaped the Sibao book trade and of the texts the Zou
and Ma publishers produced than an exact and detailed history.

---

63. The precise breakdown is: eighty-seven interviews with Sibao (Wuge and Mawu)
residents; three with Changting residents with connections to Sibao; one with a Sibao
bookseller in Zhangzhou; four with Sibao booksellers in Guangxi (two in Nanning, one
in Lingyun 凌雲, one in Bose); one with a papermaker in Shangchicun, Anjie, Changting; twenty-seven in Yuechi, Sichuan; five in Xuwan, Jinxi, Jiangxi; and four in Magang,
Shundeshi, Guangdong.

❖

This study is divided into two parts, the first ("The Business of Book Publishing and Bookselling in Sibao") on the structure and organization of the publishing-bookselling businesses of Sibao; the second ("Sibao Imprints") on the texts that these businesses printed and sold and their place in Qing and early Republican society. Understanding the role of the Sibao book trade in Chinese society and culture requires study both of the context and process of book production and sale *and* of the contents and material quality of the books produced. My goal is twofold: to describe and analyze the organization of the *business* of publishing in Sibao and the influence it had on what books were produced and how they were produced; and to characterize as fully as the evidence allows the *products* of Sibao publishing and the impact they had on Chinese book culture and society.[64]

Since the history of Sibao publishing is inextricably bound to the location of Wuge and Mawu in western Fujian, I begin Part I with a description of the environment, economy, culture, and society of Minxi and Sibao. Contemporary visitors to Sibao usually express astonishment

---

64. Western scholars have suggested a variety of strategies for studying the history of the book. Robert Darnton, in "What Is the History of the Book?," an essay that established the early guidelines for the field, outlined a "communications circuit" that linked authors, publishers, printers and their suppliers, shippers, booksellers, and readers (in their appropriate intellectual, economic, social, political, and legal contexts), emphasizing the need to understand the relationships between all these factors and agents. In "A New Model for the Study of the Book," Thomas Adams and Nicolas Barker challenge Darnton's model, but their revision (which emphasizes the role of the book rather than that of people in the book trade) also emphasizes the interconnections among socioeconomic context; intellectual, political, and legal influences; and the publication, manufacture, distribution, reception, and survival of texts. Finally, William St Clair, in *The Reading Nation in the Romantic Period* (p. 449), suggests yet another model, "the commercial and political model," which focuses on the strategies of publishers (and political, ecclesiastical, and commercial interest groups) in selecting and packaging texts and the impact their strategies have on authors and editors, the market, readers, and ultimately textual culture. My approach is closest to St Clair's (after making allowances for the considerable differences between the British and the Chinese book worlds); I show how the socioeconomic organization of the Sibao publisher-booksellers and their business choices influenced the nature of Sibao's imprints and then speculate about the impact that Sibao's bestsellers had on Chinese society and book culture.

that so isolated and poor a place was once a publishing center. Chapter 2 ("The Setting: Minxi and Sibao"), by outlining Minxi's long history of violence and poverty, serves to reinforce this astonishment. But, by describing the social and economic strategies developed by the Sibao lineages to survive in an inhospitable terrain, it also explains how the Zou and Ma created and maintained, "in the middle of nowhere," a publishing industry that endured for at least two and a half centuries. Chapter 3 ("The Origins of Publishing and the Production of Books in Sibao") continues this explanation by discussing the origins of the publishing business, providing an overview of its history, and focusing on the physical production of texts in Sibao. Here I describe both the natural resources that supported the business and the organization of the book-manufacturing process.

The Sibao book trade was to a considerable extent shaped by the distinctive structure of the publishing operations and the mechanisms that governed *shufang* relationships. The next two chapters treat these topics: Chapter 4 ("The Structure of the Sibao Publishing Industry") describes and analyzes the structure of the Zou and Ma *shufang*; Chapter 5 ("'We are all brothers': Household Division, the Proliferation of Publishing Houses, and the Management of Competition") explains how *shufang* multiplied and how the publishers managed competition (both inter- and intralineage) among publishing houses as they proliferated in the eighteenth and early nineteenth centuries.

The Zou and Ma were, like most Chinese publishers of the day, booksellers as well as publishers. Chapters 6 and 7 deal with the bookselling aspect of their business and its interaction with the publishing industry. Chapter 6 ("Sibao Bookselling Routes") traces the elaborate sales networks that the Zou and Ma book merchants developed to market their texts in the surrounding provinces of southern China. Chapter 7 ("Sojourning Bookselling and the Operation of the Branch Shops") describes the life of itinerant book merchants and the series of branch shops established by booksellers in Fujian, Guangdong, Guangxi, Jiangxi, Zhejiang, Hunan, and Hubei. It ends with a brief account of the disintegration of the Sibao publishing-bookselling networks as the industry declined in the Republican era.

The conclusion to Part I, Chapter 8 ("Sibao's 'Confucian Merchants' in Minxi Society and the Late Imperial Economy") places the Zou and

Ma publisher-booksellers in the context of late imperial society and economy, describing their own understanding of this place, assessing their social standing in the Minxi area, and, by comparing their operations to other businesses, pointing up what is distinctive about the Sibao concerns.

To understand the full social and cultural significance of the Sibao book trade, it is necessary to analyze, in some detail, the products of that trade. As the works of Western historians of the book such as D. F. McKenzie and Roger Chartier have shown,[65] it is not enough to know generally what titles or types of books a publisher produced. Equally important is the presentation of the text—the prefatorial notes, editing, commentary, formatting, production quality, and so forth. Part II thus both describes the range of texts that the Sibao publishers produced and sold and analyzes the contents and paratexts of a selection of these texts. This material, together with scattered information about the prices of Sibao imprints, also provides some indication of the audience for Sibao's products. After a brief discussion in Chapter 9 of the sources of Sibao's imprints and the roles that the Zou and Ma publishers themselves played in compiling and editing these texts ("The Nature and Sources of Sibao Imprints"), I focus in Chapter 10 ("Educational Works") on the texts that, throughout Sibao's history, were the staples of the business: texts for education, including primers, editions of the Four Books and Five Classics, poetry and *guwen* 古文 (ancient-style prose) collections, model "eight-legged essays" (*baguwen* 八股文), and reference works. Although these were the works that brought the Zou and Ma publishers their initial success and, I would argue, sustained the industry through its long history, they were quickly supplemented with a wide range of other popular texts, the subjects of Chapters 11 ("Guides to Good Manners, Good Health, and Good Fortune") and 12 ("Fiction and Belles-Lettres")—practical guides for family management and correct ritual practice, rhymed-couplet and letter-writing manuals, household encyclopedias, medical handbooks, and fortune-telling guides as well as a large store of fiction and songbooks. Chapter 13

---

65. See, e.g., McKenzie, *Bibliography and the Sociology of Texts*, pp. 9–30; and Chartier, *Forms and Meanings*, pp. 6–24.

("Sibao's Customers and Popular Textual Culture in the Qing"), the conclusion to Part II, presents a profile of the audience for Sibao imprints and constructs a "Sibao model" of popular textual culture.

Finally, in Chapter 14 ("The Diffusion of Print Culture in Qing China"), I return to a theme presented in this introductory chapter and discuss how Sibao fits into the general trends I have defined here for commercial publishing in the Qing: an extension of commercial operations outward geographically into hinterland and frontier areas, and a penetration socially downward in these areas to the lowest levels of the rural population. Here I draw in comparative material from fieldwork and library research on other Qing commercial publishing (or block cutting) sites—Xuwanzhen, Yuechi, and Magang. Finally, I suggest, very generally, what a preliminary analysis of the types of texts produced at all these sites—an analysis of what I would call the "book cultures" of the Qing—suggests about the relationship between print and the educational and social order, and what implications these various book cultures have for our understanding of the constitution of reading publics and literacy in late imperial China.

The unusual richness of the Sibao primary sources (no other woodblock commercial publishing site, to my knowledge, offers similar quantity and variety) makes possible an in-depth study of the structure and operations of an important commercial publishing industry in rural China in the Qing and Republican periods. They allow as well for a detailed survey and analysis of Sibao's publications. My hope, then, is that this work can serve as a baseline or foundational reference for future research in the field of the social history of the Chinese book, a field still in its early stages.

PART I

_____

*The Business of Book
Publishing and Bookselling
in Sibao*

# TWO

## The Setting: Minxi and Sibao

### Minxi

Sibao township is, at first glance, an unlikely site for the development of a flourishing printing business, the sort of industry we might more naturally associate with heavily populated and culturally advanced centers such as Beijing and the great Jiangnan cities of Nanjing, Suzhou, Hangzhou, and Yangzhou. Located in Tingzhou 汀州 prefecture, the westernmost of the nine prefectures and two departments that constituted administrative Fujian in the Qing, within the poorest region of the province, Minxi or western Fujian, Sibao was isolated geographically from the major urban centers along the coast.[1] (See Map 2.1.) Robert Gardella, in his description of Fujian's socioeconomic landscape, remarks dismissively that "West Fukien, the least developed area . . . , can be passed over quickly,"[2] and most scholars have followed this suggestion: Minxi, "a wild area of innumerable rivers zigzagging between seemingly endless mountains,"[3] is by far the least studied of the province's

---

1. The eight counties of Tingzhou prefecture in the Qing—Yongding 永定, Shanghang 上杭, Wuping 武平, Liancheng 連城, Changting 長汀, Guihua 歸化, Ninghua 寧化, and Qingliu 清流—are the area at the heart of Sibao's history and therefore focus of my inquiry.

2. Gardella, "Fukien's Tea Industry and Trade in Ch'ing and Republican China," p. 21.

3. Dai Yifeng, "West Fujian's Rural Society, Economy and Politics in the First Half of the Twentieth Century," p. 24.

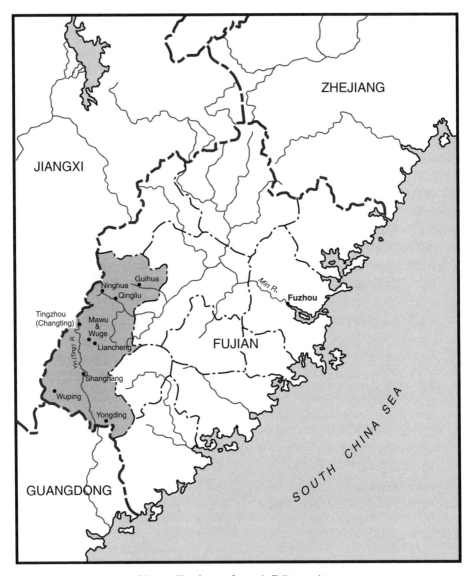

Map 2.1 Tingzhou prefecture in Fujian province

four regions. The geography and the cultural and socioeconomic history of the region were, however, important factors in the development of the Sibao publishing industry and the choices made by the Zou and Ma publishers.

## Western Fujian and
## the Hakka Heartland

Topographically, Minxi is dominated, like most of Fujian outside the coastal plain and the Fuzhou valley, by mountains. These mountains increase in height toward the west, to maximum elevations of about thirteen hundred meters along the southwestern border with Jiangxi.[4] Interrupted only by small V-shaped valleys, these mountains have made interprovincial—and, for that matter, intraprovincial—transportation and communication difficult. As late as the 1920s one foreign observer noted, "With inland waterways made dangerous by shallows and frequent rapids; and with a land topography characterized by a series of rugged mountain ranges, traversed by the crudest of footpaths, the problem of moving persons, goods or information from one place to another within [Fujian] or from the province to other parts of the world is a serious one."[5]

The configuration of the provincial river system reinforced Minxi's isolation from the other regions of the province. The major Minxi river system, that of the Yin 鄞江, or Ting 汀江, River,[6] Fujian's only southward-flowing river,[7] supplied transport from west-central

---

4. Zhao Zhaobing, *Fujiansheng dili*, pp. 10–12; Lacy, "Geography," p. 3; Sun Ching-chih, ed., *Economic Geography of South China*, p. 342; Hurlbut, *The Fukienese*, pp. 3–4; and Chen Jiayuan, ed., *Fujiansheng jingji dili*, pp. 12–18. The province has been described as "perhaps the only extensive mountainous region in the world without a main mountain range distinct by elevation and continuity, without extensive table land, or without interruption of larger plains" (von Richtofen, *Letters*, p. 63; cited in Hurlbut, *The Fukienese*, p. 3).

5. Price and Wiant, "Transportation and Public Works," p. 72; cited in Gardella, "Fukien's Tea Industry and Trade in Ch'ing and Republican China," p. 19. See also Lacy, "Geography," in *Fukien*, p. 3. Human failure to create, until recently, effective overland roads meant that such problems limited communication within Fujian well into the twentieth century. In 1959 western Fujian was still "relatively backward in transportation," with the lowest density of highways in the whole province (Sun Ching-chih, *Economic Geography of South China*, p. 462).

6. This river is also called Tingshui 汀水 or Changtingxi 長汀溪 (*Linting zhi*, pp. 7, 9). These names seem to have been interchangeable even in the Song, although the Qing volume of Tan Qixiang, ed., *Zhongguo lishi ditu ji* (8: 42), identifies the river as the Yin.

7. *Minshu*, 1: 495–96; see also Feng Lin and Zi Bing, "Min, Yue, Gan bian congqian zhuyao hangdao—Tingjiang."

Tingzhou to northeastern Guangdong and the city of Chaozhou, but
not to any other region of Fujian itself. Unlike Minbei 閩北, the region
of the upper drainage basin of the Min River 閩江 (the dominant river
system of the province, which flows from the northwest into the sea at
Fuzhou), Minxi enjoyed no direct links to eastern Fujian and the
Fuzhou valley, the political and cultural core of the province.[8] Nor were
there easy transportation routes to the southern coastal plain, Minnan
閩南, the most prosperous region of the province, although the upper
reaches of the Jiulong River 九龍江 provided a tenuous connection
between Minxi and the port city of Xiamen. The steep hills surrounding the many small valleys that constitute Minxi created barriers that
made land travel to all these regions—Minbei, the Fuzhou valley, and
Minnan—particularly difficult.[9]

Of the four regions of Fujian, Minxi was the most isolated from the
other three. Geographically and, as we shall see later, culturally, the area
more logically formed a unit, not with Fujian, but with portions of two
contiguous provinces, northeastern Guangdong and eastern Jiangxi.[10]
These three areas, forming the Min-Gan-Yue 閩贛粵 border region,
were interconnected by a web of overland and river networks that
served both as administrative post roads and commercial trade routes.[11]
Not surprisingly, both emigrants and sojourning merchants from western Fujian, among them the Sibao booksellers, settled or marketed their
wares in eastern Jiangxi and northeastern Guangdong. Migrants and
merchants looked beyond this region as well; Sibao book merchants,
despite the transportation difficulties, extended their routes to Zhangzhou in Minnan and through Minbei (via Pucheng 浦城 county in Jianning 建寧 prefecture) into southern Zhejiang province to the seaport
of Wenzhou. Nonetheless, the Min-Gan-Yue border region formed an
important economic and cultural unit, the focus of migration and trade

---

8. It was possible to reach the Minjiang from Minxi first via the Qing River 清溪 (or
Zheng River 正溪) and then the Sha River 沙溪, but this route was not much traveled
by Minxi merchants.

9. Hurlbut, *The Fukienese*, pp. 4, 8.

10. There is, of course, an argument for making this point about all the regions of
Fujian; see Vermeer, "Introduction: Historical Background and Major Issues," p. 14;
and Chia, "Debatable Land."

11. See Appendix A for a description of these routes.

for its residents, and the access route to markets in Hunan, Hubei, Guangxi, and even Yunnan. This migration and trading network developed exclusively within a peripheral area. It contains no important core city that directed the flow of trade within the network.[12]

This Min-Gan-Yue network cohered as a cultural as well as a geographical and economic unit because of one important demographic fact: it encompassed a region heavily settled, indeed dominated, by Hakka (*kejia* 客家), the "guest people." Han migrants, the ancestors of the Hakka, had come to this region, the so-called Hakka heartland, in the late Song and early Yuan,[13] settling first, it is believed, in Tingzhou and then spreading into eastern Jiangxi and northeastern Guangdong. Not surprisingly, the arrival of thousands of immigrants disrupted Tingzhou society—the new Han settlers inevitably came into conflict with the original settlers, as they competed for the area's meager amount of farmable land.

Life in Minxi was hard, for the region was not only the most peripheral but also the poorest in the province, with little arable land. Only 5 to 10 percent of western Fujian's total acreage was cultivated.[14] The new residents struggled to feed themselves, practicing subsistence agriculture in the scattered basins and on the terraced hills that supplied what little farmland the region enjoyed. The depression that stalled the economy of south China from the thirteenth through the fifteenth centuries limited opportunities for further migration, and the new settlers, the guest people, were trapped in a struggle with the local population, composed of earlier Han migrants and the She 畲 subgroup of the Yao 瑤.[15] The ensuing centuries of conflict, exacerbated by the widespread banditry and disorder of the late Yuan, earned the people of the region a reputation for "taking life lightly and fighting seriously";[16] Minxi, with

---

12. This pattern calls into question the macroregional divisions defined by G. William Skinner. For his discussion of the problem, see his "Introduction," in Sow-theng Leong, *Migration and Ethnicity in Chinese History*, pp. 3–5.

13. Leong, *Migration and Ethnicity in Chinese History*, pp. 29, 33–34.

14. Gardella, "Fukien's Tea Industry and Trade in Ch'ing and Republican China," p. 21.

15. Leong, *Migration and Ethnicity in Chinese History*, pp. 33–36.

16. *Linting zhi* (Song), p. 16. Well before the Yuan, Zhu Xi (1130–1200) painted a gloomy picture of life in Tingzhou: the limited arable land was monopolized by the

the rest of the Min-Yue-Gan border region, was known as a "region of bandits" throughout most of the Ming.[17] She revolts against the more recent Han migrants persisted through the mid- and late Ming; Wang Yangming 王陽明 (1472–1529) suppressed one such uprising in 1517–18, and others occurred in 1553, 1566–67, 1572–73, and 1653.

In four centuries of intraregional conflict, the newer immigrants succeeded in suppressing the earlier settlers and taking over much of their land. But at the cultural and economic level the assimilation of the older settlers, including the She, by the newer, "guest" people transformed the economic practices, social relations, and even the language of the stronger group. From the She and the earlier Han settlers of the area, the Hakka learned upland agricultural techniques (including the slash-and-burn method of preparing fields) and forestry, mining, and stone-carving technologies. And from the language of their new home, they developed a dialect, Hakka (*kejia hua* 客家話), derived from Old Southern Chinese. Possibly by this time, too, they had borrowed from the earlier residents certain social customs—most notably, "natural feet" and field work for women—and religious practices that later came to distinguish these guest people from other Han settlers in the south.[18] Tensions between the more recent Han arrivals and the original settlers eased somewhat in the mid-sixteenth century, as Hakka started migrating out of the Minxi area in search of unexploited uplands near rivers or seaports, "whose location minimized cost-distance to the market,"[19] in the hope of profiting from the economic boom that brought prosperity to much of the Yangzi delta region and southeast China. This period of migration, while extending the immigrant society of the Hakka heart-

---

wealthy; local officials neglected their duties while exploiting the local population; banditry and violence were endemic; and many, unable to earn a living, sought to flee the area ("Yu Zhang Tingsou shu" 與張定叟書, in *Zhu Wengong wenji*, 27.21a–22a; cited in Su Jilang, *Tang Song shidai Minnan Quanzhou shidi lungao*, p. 175).

17. See Tang Lizong, *Zai "daoqu" yu "zhengqu" zhi jian*. For a good summary of the long history of violence and ethnic conflict that afflicted Tingzhou from the Song through the Ming, see Liu Yonghua, "The World of Rituals," pp. 32–60.

18. Leong, *Migration and Ethnicity in Chinese History*, pp. 32–36. See also Chen Zhiping, *Kejia yuanliu xinlun*, pp. 76–77; Chen Zhiping, *Fujian zupu*, pp. 252–53; and Liu Yonghua, "The World of Rituals," pp. 53–60.

19. Skinner, "Introduction," pp. 3–4.

land to new regions, also eventually stimulated the formation of a distinct Hakka identity. When the new migrants from Min-Gan-Yue came into contact, often violent, with other Han settlements, they became aware of the distinctiveness of their dialect and customs.[20] Sow-theng Leong has identified "peripherality" as the key to Hakka cultural difference: centered in their homeland, the uplands of southeastern Jiangxi, western Fujian, and northeastern Guangdong, the Hakka had "no drainage basin," no core or major urban center of their own. Driven by economic necessity, they developed traditions of mobility and sojourning and unorthodox gender roles (male sojourning required women's agricultural labor). Since they could not identify with a significant core area or economic center, in their migrations they asserted the primacy of ethnic over territorial bonds.[21]

Given the poverty and isolation of western Fujian, it is not surprising that, once the agricultural and commercial boom of the late Ming and Qing created opportunities outside the region, migration, sojourning commerce, and the development of handicraft industries became the Hakkas' major strategies for economic advancement. Leong identifies two major waves of Hakka out-migration, the first from the mid-sixteenth century to the early seventeenth, and the second from the 1680s through the 1730s (although new migration to already established Hakka settlements continued through the nineteenth century). Some of this migration was within the Min-Gan-Yue border region, but many peasants moved farther afield: northeast to the port of Wenzhou (Zhejiang); northwest into Hunan (through western Jiangxi), and south and southwest into coastal and central Guangdong and ultimately Guangxi, seeking new work opportunities as miners, cash croppers, migrant field laborers, and construction workers. As we shall see, the Sibao publishing industry, in its nature and reach, was profoundly shaped and conditioned by the networks of Hakka settlers established in these series of migrations.

For those Hakka who remained in Minxi, economic diversification was essential to survival. The commercialization of southern China's economy stimulated the development of commercial agriculture, handi-

---

20. Leong, *Migration and Ethnicity in Chinese History*, pp. 35–36.
21. Ibid., p. 63; and Skinner, "Introduction," pp. 10–11.

craft industries, and commerce to some extent within Minxi as well. By the early sixteenth century, the prefectural capital of Tingzhou had developed specialized markets for salt, iron, indigo, bamboo, and timber and for imports from Jiangxi and Guangdong, a clear indicator of a growth in regional commerce.[22] There is evidence of some occupational diversification in the area as well. Writing roughly a century later, He Qiaoyuan 何喬遠 (1557–1631), compiler of the *Minshu* 閩書 (Book of Min, 1628–31?), provided a rough survey of the variety of handicraft and service occupations, in addition to farming, practiced in Minxi. The men of Qingliu were noted for their skill in hauling boats along the Jian 建, Jian 劍, Shao 邵, and Yin, the major rivers of Minxi and Minbei— "penetrating rapids and passing through gorges, amid rumbling thunder and lightning flashes, they are known as the best" in the water transport trade. The people of Liancheng, "where the soil is barren," practiced handicrafts, and the men often went to other counties as construction workers. In Shanghang, where "all the necessities of life are available," people produced bamboo mats and other bamboo products for the market. And in Yongding, "in addition to farming, the people practice crafts and trade."[23]

Minxi suffered—as did all parts of Fujian province and its southern neighbor, Guangdong—from the fall of the Ming in 1644 through the early 1680s,[24] as the area was successively a center of Southern Ming re-

---

22. *Tingzhou fuzhi* (1527), 3.15ab; cited in Liu Yonghua, "The World of Rituals," p. 68.

23. *Minshu*, 1: 945; see also Alger, "Skill, Silence, and Speed." Other sources suggest that the diversification He describes did not extend to industry. Wang Shimao, a vice-intendant of education for Fujian, writing several decades earlier, about 1580, described a rather static agricultural economy in Minxi: "In the prefectures of western Fujian, all the people support themselves from their labor in the mountains. To raise their children, they do not seek any other profession, particularly not in industry" (Wang Shimao, *Minbu shu*, 23a [p. 49]).

24. In *Koubian ji*, Li Shixiong provides a catalogue of the violent uprisings and disturbances that afflicted his native county, Ninghua, and Tingzhou prefecture from the 1630s through the Ming-Qing transition. Many of these disturbances had little to do with the change in dynasty, originating rather from socioeconomic tensions. Li attributes much of the disorder to bandits and rabble-rousers from eastern Jiangxi and northeastern Guangdong, who either traveled within the Min-Gan-Yue region deliberately fomenting trouble or, by inciting peasant uprisings at home, inspired turmoil throughout the region (pp. 32–46).

sistance to the Manchus,[25] then a site of rebellion during the Revolt of the Three Feudatories, and finally the indirect victim of some of the more draconian consolidation policies of the Qing state.[26] But by the end of the century, there were signs that the region was beginning to recover. The crisis of the early Kangxi years was followed by a long period of relative peace, from 1684 to the mid-nineteenth century, which supported the development of the agrarian economy, as did the efforts of the Yongzheng emperor (r. 1723–35) to free peasants from onerous labor-service burdens. Minxi began producing crops for export and developing handicraft industries. Tobacco became an important commercial crop in the early Qing.[27] Timber, too, was a common Minxi export.[28] By the late nineteenth century, the commerce in pine and *shanmu* 杉木 (a type of China fir locally called *shamu* 沙木) was in the hands of local merchants, who cut and processed the wood and floated it down the Yin River for sale in Chaozhou, Foshanzhen, and Guangzhou.[29] In addition, Minxi bamboo shoots, valued for their tenderness and fine flavor, were harvested from all parts of the prefecture, although this crop was limited by the demands of the paper industry for bamboo. Vegetable oils, particularly *tong* 桐 and rapeseed oil, were specialties of Liancheng county; Ninghua alone produced some textiles for export, most famously cloth made from ramie fiber.

Paper, made largely from the *mao* bamboo (*maozhu* 貓 or 毛竹, *Phyllostachys pubescens*), which flourished in the Tingzhou mountains, had been

---

25. Struve, *The Southern Ming*, pp. 84–86, 95–99.

26. Although Minxi did not suffer directly from the closure of the Minnan coast to trade and the ruthless evacuation of the coastal population inland (both measures designed to weaken the dominance of the Zheng family on Taiwan), it was hurt indirectly by the falling-off in commercial activity that naturally resulted from the termination of overseas trade and the dislocation of the population.

27. Wang Jian'an, the prefect of Tingzhou in the late seventeenth century and the author of *Linting kaoyan* (prefaces dated 1699, 1700), estimated that tobacco was planted on 30–40 percent of the arable land of the prefecture (Wang, *Linting kaoyan*, 6.9b; cited in Miki Satoshi, "Kōzo to sobei," p. 35).

28. Pine and a type of China fir "grew everywhere" in Tingzhou and at one point were such valuable commodities that a Huizhou merchant purchased a whole mountain in Ninghua county from which he harvested *shamu* (Yang Lan, *Linting huikao*, 4.5b–6a).

29. Ibid., 4.6a; *Changting xianzhi* (1940), 18.78a–79a.

an important handicraft product even in the late Ming.[30] Produced in every Tingzhou county, paper became an increasingly important export in the Qing, and by the late nineteenth century, according to Yang Lan, it had become the most widely sold export of the area: "Of all the products of Tingzhou, it is paper that penetrates to all four corners [of the world]."[31] Small-scale operations in Liancheng, Ninghua, Shanghang, and Changting 長汀 supplied publishing ventures both in the Min-Gan-Yue region, such as those of Sibao and Xuwanzhen,[32] and in more distant markets, including Jiangnan, with paper. As late as the Republican era, Hangzhou publishers were purchasing paper from Ninghua county.[33] And by the early twentieth century Tingzhou came to dominate the growing export of paper from Fujian to Southeast Asia (see Chapter 3).

Through the late seventeenth and eighteenth centuries, particularly during the Qianlong era, western Fujian seems to have enjoyed a period of relative prosperity, in striking contrast to the once more-prosperous coast, then suffering a period of economic contraction.[34] The Liancheng gazetteer presents a picture of active commerce:

Sojourning merchants and resident dealers bustle about, coming and going, covering the whole empire. How could the people of Liancheng stubbornly stick to their corner? Although those who make their living from the land are fewer than before, there are many who sell paper, trade in timber, market grain, and buy tea. Moreover, they travel to Wuyi 武夷 and into Baiyue 百粵 [Guangdong]; travel to Jiangxi is particularly common. As for the production of silver from mines, the skill [of Liancheng natives] is matchless—the area these workers have traveled covers almost half the empire.[35]

---

30. See Tomasko, "Chinese Handmade Paper," p. 24 and *passim*, for descriptions of papermaking in three different southern Chinese sites; and Mao Xing, "Jianguo qian Changting shangye maoyi linzhao," p. 35.

31. Yang Lan, *Linting huikao*, 4.15a.

32. Zhao Shuiquan, "Xuwan yu muke yinshu," p. 53.

33. Interview 1, 7/99 (Hangzhou).

34. Vermeer, "Introduction," pp. 10–11.

35. *Liancheng xianzhi* (1751), *j.* 17, "Fengsu"; cited in Chen Zhiping and Zheng Zhenman, "Qingdai Minxi Sibao zushang yanjiu," p. 105.

Periodic markets multiplied,[36] and merchant networks developed within western Fujian and the whole Min-Gan-Yue border region. Liancheng merchants traded oil; Yongding merchants, tobacco. Shanghang merchants specialized in the indigo trade, establishing guilds (*huiguan* 會館) throughout Jiangxi, Zhejiang, Hubei, and Guangdong.[37]

Others were in effect transport merchants, exporting local products and importing necessities not produced locally into western Fujian. Tingzhou benefited from its strategic location at the center of the important transport circuit linking western Fujian to Guangdong and Jiangxi, becoming an entrepôt for essential imports of rice and salt and for the export of tobacco, paper, and timber.[38] These three commercial products were shipped, in return for rice and salt, in both directions, south to Chaozhou, where these products (and surplus rice from Jiangxi) were traded for salt; and north and west to Jiangxi, where, with salt, they were traded for rice. Tingzhou's role as both an inter- and intraprovincial commercial center brought employment to transport workers not only in the prefectural seat, but also in the small river ports, such as Wuping, Shanghang, Ninghua, and Qingliu, along the way.[39]

Thus, by the high Qing, the western Fujian area was more fully integrated than ever before into the trade and market networks of Min-Gan-Yue, Minbei, and the other regions of Fujian. Contemporary observers frequently remarked on the easy mobility characteristic of workers and merchants from Minxi. When Tingzhou *ren* appear in the written record at all, it is usually as workers outside of Tingzhou (although still within Fujian), as tea cultivators and pickers in Jianning and Yanping 延平, or as iron mongers and indigo processors in Yongan

36. Zhu Weigan, *Fujian shigao*, 2: 471.

37. Xu Xiaowang, "Ming Qing Min Zhe Gan bianqu shanqu jingji fazhan de xin qushi," pp. 198–99. See also Fu Yiling, "Mingmo Qingchu Min Gan pilin diqu de shequ jingji yu diannong kangzu fengchao," p. 350.

38. Defu, *Minzheng lingyao* (1767), *j.* 2, "Suichan migu" 歲產米穀; cited in Miki, "Kōzo to sobei," p. 42. See also Chen Zhiping, "Qingdai qianqi Fujian de feizheng-chang mijia."

39. *Changting xianzhi* (1854), 30.3b–5b; Wang Yeh-chien, "Food Supply in Eighteenth-Century Fujian," p. 98.

永安.[40] But in the late eighteenth century there were signs of a reverse trend: economic development within Tingzhou itself in the form of outside investment. Guangdong merchants established paper factories in Liancheng and purchased mountains for the cultivation of bamboo. Noncommercial agriculture flourished as well; by the mid-nineteenth century, gazetteers begin to report double-cropping as common: peasants in Minxi, following a pattern first established in the more fertile Fuzhou area, were harvesting a first crop of early-ripening rice and/or wheat, and a second of either rice, wheat, or various beans and vegetables (soybeans, sweet potatoes, and rape).[41]

This increase in commercial and industrial activity and in market integration did not necessarily or easily lead to unproblematic prosperity and social stability for the region, however. Merchants and landlords benefited, many using their profits to obtain land or increase their landholdings. But despite the apparent opportunities offered by the cultivation of cash crops such as tobacco, peasants and tenant farmers had to struggle harder to maintain a subsistence livelihood. These peasants also tended to suffer from the region's dependency on imported rice;[42] the counties of Changting, Shanghang, and Yongding experienced regular rice shortages throughout the eighteenth and early nineteenth centuries, as did Liancheng and Guihua in the early nineteenth century.[43] The early Qing in particular was marked by unprecedented concentration of land in the hands of a few landlords and growth in the amount of corporately owned lineage land under the management of the wealthier lineage members. Landlord-tenant relations became increasingly tense, as landlords—many of whom now lived not on their land but in the cities and thus had no firsthand knowledge of conditions on their estates—attempted to extract as much rent as possible from their

---

40. Chen Keng, "Lun shijiu shiji shangbanye Fujian de jingji xingtai," pp. 242–43.

41. Zhu Weigan, *Fujian shigao*, 2: 431–37, 484–85; Liu Yonghua, "The World of Rituals," pp. 62–71.

42. As early as the 1690s, Wang Jian'an complained about the impact that the spread of commercial tobacco farming was having on the social and economic landscape, particularly as it discouraged rice planting (see *Linting kaoyan*, 6.8ab; cited in Miki, "Kōzo to sobei," p. 35).

43. Wang Yeh-chien, "Food Supply in Eighteenth-Century Fujian," pp. 82–84; and Chen Keng, "Lun shijiu shiji shangbanye Fujian de jingji xingtai," p. 240.

tenants.[44] Local gazetteers record fifteen different incidents of landlord-tenant conflict from 1646 to 1746. A series of rent-resistance incidents throughout the Qianlong period earned the people of Ninghua county, at least, the description "violent, fierce, and difficult to govern."[45] Western Fujian thus maintained its reputation for disorder, but by the late Ming and Qing ethnic conflicts and competition between "original settlers" and "guests" were replaced as the primary causes of tension by socioeconomic landlord-tenant struggles.

Minxi also continued, through the early twentieth century, to be a battleground in empirewide political and military conflicts. The Qing government became increasingly suspicious of the spread of popular religious sects and secret societies in the area,[46] particularly that of the Tiandihui 天地會, and urged officials to watch for signs of secret organizations. By the 1830s, there were in fact several Tiandihui associations, as well as a miscellaneous cluster of other secret brotherhoods subscribing to an overlapping mixture of religious beliefs and practices, in the Min-Gan-Yue area. But these groups, rather than forming the nuclei of rebellion, served to offer people living on the socioeconomic edge the protection of magic talismans and the assurance of mutual assistance.[47] Promises of protection and aid were, of course, particularly

---

44. Although the "one-field two-masters" (*yitian liangzhu* 一田兩主) system, in which the land was divided into "skin" (*pitian* 皮田, the cultivated surface, which was the tenant's charge) and "bone" (*gutian* 骨田, land owned by the landlord), was common in Fujian, it apparently did not benefit tenants there as it did in the Jiangnan area. See the brief account by Shi Hongbao, a magistrate's secretary in the province from 1845 to 1858, in his *Min zaji*, p. 128; and Liu Yonghua, "Shiqi zhi shiba shiji Minxi diannong de kangzu, nongcun shehui yu xiangmin wenhua," pp. 141–45.

45. Miki Satoshi, "Qingdai qianqi Fujian nongcun shehui yu diannong kangzu douzheng," p. 50. See also the accounts of rent-resistance struggles in the Tingzhou area in *Kang Yong Qian shiqi chengxiang renmin fankang douzheng ziliao*, 1: 96–105, 114–15; for rice riots, see 1: 303–4.

46. Local officials had, as early as the mid-eighteenth century, taken action against at least one local cult, the Luojiao 羅教 in Ninghua (*Kang Yong Qian shiqi chengxiang renmin fankang douzheng ziliao*, 2: 654–57).

47. Owenby, *Brotherhoods and Secret Societies in Early and Mid-Qing China*, pp. 130, 139–44. See also Lian Lichang, *Fujian mimi shehui*, pp. 192–206. Fan Qilong, "Taiping jun sici xia Tingzhou," p. 17, refers to several different secret societies in the Tingzhou area: the Jianghu hui 江湖會, the Qiandao hui 千刀會, and the Jiandao hui 尖刀會. By the late nineteenth century at the latest, the Tiandihui had spread to several sites of Sibao

appealing to people trying to get by in the harsh and highly mobile society of Minxi. In particular, they offered migrant workers and sojourning merchants and peddlers some security against the everyday uncertainties and dangers they faced while away from the assistance afforded by family and village associations.

It took the very significant achievements of the Taiping rebels to spark genuine political rebellion by secret societies in western Fujian. When the Taipings took Nanjing in 1853, some secret societies in Minxi rose in support, but did not succeed in overthrowing the local government. In 1857 Taiping troops under the leadership of Shi Zhenji 石 鎮吉 (?–1860) and later Shi Dakai 石達開 (1831?–63), fleeing the chaos caused by the Taiping leadership struggles in Nanjing and hoping to restore the fortunes of the rebellion, stimulated a series of attacks by secret brotherhoods on local governments. The next several years saw intermittent fighting, as the Taiping troops moved in and out of the area, at times supporting the activities of the local rebels, but as often deserting the locals in order to pursue an advantage in some other part of the Min-Gan-Yue border region. The Taiping campaigns in western Fujian brought widespread economic disruption as commercial networks and markets were blocked or destroyed by the warring armies. Social conflict increased as well, as local elites, benefiting from the victory of Zuo Zongtang 左宗棠 (1812–85) over the rebels in 1865,[48] took vengeance not only on Taiping and secret society followers but also on the hapless peasants who had taken advantage of the rebellion to rectify what they perceived as long-standing socioeconomic inequities. The rebellion also brought greater government surveillance and exactions. The *likin* (*lijin* 釐金), an internal customs duty on commercial transactions, the revenue from which was to pay for the costs of suppressing the Taiping rebellion, was imposed in the late 1860s, and ruthlessly— and often corruptly—collected throughout the rest of the century. In Fujian "each prefecture has established a customs house, and all ap-

---

bookselling in Guangxi (and into Guizhou as well): Guixian 貴縣, Lingshan 靈山, Sanjiang 三江, and Nanning 南寧 (see Xu Ge, *Qingmo Guangxi Tiandihui fengyun lu*, pp. 19– 30, 44–85).

48. *Changting xianzhi* (1940), 2.22b–24a; and Lian Lichang, *Fujian mimi shehui*, pp. 228– 33. On the Taiping rebellion in western Fujian, see Fan Qilong, "Taiping jun sici xia Tingzhou"; and Zhu Weigan, *Fujian shigao*, 2: 587–641.

point braves (*yong* 勇) to guard the offices, men who abuse their authority. From even small peddlers they always extract a heavy payment, all of which enters their own pockets. Should anyone protest, the same braves beat them without sanction."[49] Since much of the population of Minxi was at least partially dependent on sojourning commerce for its livelihood, the new and vigorously collected *likin* meant considerable hardship.[50]

The intrusion of foreign missionaries into Tingzhou in the 1890s became another source of local disorder in the form of intermittent attacks on the mission and popular resistance to missionary teachings.[51] The founding of the Republic in 1911, far from stabilizing the troubled region, instead introduced new sources of disorder. From 1918 through 1926 the Northern and Southern armies fought for control of Fujian, and Minxi was one of their battlegrounds. After the victory of the Southern army, competition among local warlords, weak Guomindang officials, Communist activists, and the usual complement of bandits produced a level of continuing chaos unusual even for western Fujian.[52] Minxi's isolation and poverty apparently spared it invasion by

---

49. "Sanshan qiaosou" 三山樵叟, *Minsheng jinshi zhuzhi ci* 閩省近事竹枝詞 (manuscript edition); cited in Xie Shuishun and Li Ting, *Fujian gudai keshu*, p. 472.

50. See Xie Shuishun and Li Ting, *Fujian gudai keshu*, p. 472, for more evidence of the economic suffering brought by the *likin*.

51. In 1901 the mission church was destroyed by a mob of angry Tingzhou residents and the visiting missionary, E. S. Dukes, was forced to flee (London Missionary Society, Report no. 106 [1901], p. 56).

52. One mission report, dated 1923, mourned: "The province has again been the plaything of reckless political adventurers, to the sorrow of the helpless population" (London Missionary Society, Report no. 128, p. 60). As early as the second decade of the century, the mission reports began emphasizing the increase in violence, not just from the larger political-military struggle, but also from "the prevalence of robbery and clan fights, accompanied by murder" (London Missionary Society, Report no. 124 [1919], p. 40; and Report no. 120 [1915], p. 159).

For more on Minxi under the Republic, see Fan Qilong, "'Yiyi.jiu' qiyi—Xinhai geming zai Fujian," p. 145; and Chen Nengnan, "Fujian difang junfa de xingwang he tedian," pp. 166–73. Lloyd Eastman (*The Abortive Revolution*, pp. 97–102) describes the efforts of the Nineteenth Route Army to develop the economy of Minxi, the most chronically impoverished part of the province, after its arrival in Fujian in 1932. The rebellion of the army against the Nationalist government late in 1933—and its almost immediate suppression—brought an abrupt end to this program of reform and the

Japanese troops, however. Indeed, it became a kind of refuge for residents of more prosperous and strategically important areas—Tingzhou, for example, in 1938 became the wartime home of Xiamen University.[53] But the region nonetheless continued to be a site of constant internal fighting between the Red Army and Republican troops until the Communists' final victory in September and October 1949.[54]

## EDUCATION AND CULTURE

Not surprisingly, given its long history of isolation, poverty, and disorder, western Fujian was considered among the most culturally backward areas of the province. It never enjoyed the association with Zhu Xi 朱熹 (1130–1200), the great Confucian scholar of the Song, and his school that Minbei, the next most isolated and poverty-stricken region, could boast. Nor was it home to any of the more adventuresome thinkers produced by the province: both Lin Zhao'en 林昭恩 (1517–98), founder of the "Three Teachings are One" movement, and Li Zhi 李贄 (1527–1602), perhaps the most notorious of late Ming iconoclasts, were from the coast. And Minxi never participated in the debates over reform that preoccupied scholars in the provincial capital and along the coast in the late nineteenth century. Even by the crude and conventional measure of rate of success in the civil-service examinations, it consistently lagged behind the wealthier and more populous areas of Fuzhou and the coast in the production of *jinshi*.

Yet the situation was not entirely bleak. Indeed, on the last point at least, we might conclude that Minxi, given its physical and economic

---

Western Fujian Reconstruction Council (Minxi shanhou weiyuanhui 閩西善後委員會) that had been established to effect it.

53. Hu Shanmei, "Changting–Xiamen Daxue–Sa bendong."

54. For a laudatory account of the Communist movement, see *Minxi geming genjudi shi*, pp. 11–33, 58–89, 106–30, 154–201. The report of the Tingzhou mission for 1929, on the other hand, emphasizes the destruction and disruption of communications brought by the revolutionaries: "In every place their policy has been to capture any wealthy people who did not flee and execute or hold them to ransom, destroying and looting their homes"; and, "the state of the country is still so disturbed that it is a matter of very great difficulty to travel between Amoy [Xiamen] and Tingchow [Tingzhou]" (London Missionary Society, Report no. 135 [1930], p. 82).

limitations, performed rather well. Although the lack of reliable population statistics and, in some cases, *jinshi* figures, makes any exact comparison impossible, it seems that Tingzhou's share of the highest degree-holders did at least increase over the later imperial period. In both the Northern and Southern Song, when Fujian's number of *jinshi* degree-holders was high relative to that of other provinces, it placed last among the eight regions of the province, with 80 *jinshi*, less than half the number of the next lowest area, Shaowu jun 邵武郡, with 195.[55] Tingzhou's performance improved significantly in the Ming; it moved up to sixth place out of ten. Most striking, however, is its ranking in the Qing: it produced the fourth-highest number of *jinshi*, 86, of thirteen different regional units, although, to be sure, it still lagged far behind the more heavily populated areas that outranked it, Fuzhou (with over 727 *jinshi*), Quanzhou (241), and Zhangzhou (132).[56]

Tingzhou's modest achievement in the examination competition peaked between 1719 and 1818, when 57 *jinshi* were produced. This period, roughly the Yongzheng through the Jiaqing eras, corresponds to the period of relative economic prosperity in Minxi, as well as the "golden age" of Sibao publishing and bookselling. Greater economic security led to the establishment of new schools, most notably academies devoted to training students for the examinations. There were at least eight academies in Tingzhou prefecture during the Ming; over the course of the first century and a half of Qing rule, no fewer than fourteen new academies were established, mostly by county magistrates

---

55. As evidence, of course, these figures are only of rough value, in part because they are taken from local gazetteers. The major problem is that they are not calculated relative to the whole population of each region (a statistic that is not reliably known). The low figure for Tingzhou could simply reflect its low population density.

56. The figures for *juren* degree-holders express the same ranking; see Liu Haifeng and Zhuang Mingshui, *Fujian jiaoyu shi*, pp. 73, 160, 212, 220; and Hans Bielenstein, "The Regional Provenance of *Chin-shih* During the Ch'ing," pp. 30–31, 77–78. The reform of the quota system in 1702, because it gave some advantage to the provinces of the southeast (Fujian, Guangdong, and Guangxi) and shifted competition to the intra-provincial arena, may have helped Tingzhou somewhat. See Bielenstein, pp. 13–15. Liu Yonghua ("The World of Rituals," pp. 49–50) reports slightly different *jinshi* figures for the Qing (84, not 86, for Tingzhou; and 723 for Fuzhou, not 727), but these differences do not significantly affect the argument here.

serving in Minxi.[57] Although there seems to have been little change in the number of prefectural and county schools in the area (these, in any event, did not offer schooling, serving rather as examination sites), Tingzhou may have benefited as well from the improved quality of the provincial educational administration.[58] At a more elementary level, Tingzhou could boast sixty-nine active community and/or charitable schools in the early nineteenth century, and only one fewer, sixty-eight, in the second half of the century. In the comparison of thirty-eight different areas conducted by Evelyn Rawski, Tingzhou ranked fourth in the number of such schools.[59] Increased prosperity led to the establishment of more private or family schools (*sishu* 私塾, *jiashu* 家塾), where most students got their primary schooling and began study of the Four Books, their introduction to examination studies. Certainly one of the direct consequences of the growth of the publishing industry in Sibao, as we shall see, was the creation of *jiashu* in Wuge and Mawu.

Tingzhou's relative examination success and the proliferation of schools there did not, however, signify lively intellectual debate or the development of new trends in thought. Most of the academies taught the examination curriculum, implicitly accepting the orthodox Cheng-Zhu interpretation of Confucianism on which the examinations were based. And most of western Fujian's leading thinkers—none seemed to arise until the Qing—were, in fact, explicit supporters of this school; they are noted, if at all, for their defense and elaboration of orthodoxy.

In this they were following the ideology that dominated the province until the late nineteenth century. Fujian's leading thinkers of the early Ming were explicators of Zhu Xi's philosophy. Yang Rong 楊榮 (1371–

57. Liu Haifeng and Zhuang Mingshui, *Fujian jiaoyu shi*, pp. 128, 187. Here Tingzhou led a provincial trend; over one hundred new *shuyuan* were established in Fujian in the Qing (Xu Xiaowang, *Fujian sixiang wenhua shigang*, p. 199). But in nineteenth-century Tingzhou, only one new academy was established, the Minxiu shuyuan 敏秀書院, founded in Ninghua in 1882.

58. Liu Haifeng and Zhuang Mingshui, *Fujian jiaoyu shi*, pp. 179–83.

59. Rawski, *Education and Popular Literacy*, pp. 89–92. Tingzhou trailed behind Zhengding 正定 prefecture, Zhili, with 133 schools; Quanzhou prefecture, with 116; and Xi'an prefecture with 113; and was at roughly the same level as Yanping prefecture (68). The number declines to 45 (Xiangyang 襄陽 prefecture, Hubei), 42 (Fengxiang 鳳翔 prefecture, Shaanxi), and then to 27 and 23; the remaining areas had between 1 and 20 schools.

1440) was one of the editors of the great compendia of Cheng-Zhu teachings that profoundly influenced examination study, the *Wujing daquan* 五經大全 (Great compendium of the Five Classics), *Sishu daquan* 四書大全 (Great compendium of the Four Books), and *Xingli daquan* 性理大全 (Great compendium on nature and principle). When Wang Yangming's challenges to many of Zhu Xi's ideas began to attract favorable attention in the Jiangnan area, they met consistent opposition in Fujian. The Huian 惠安 literatus and official Zhang Yue 張岳 (1492–1552) debated Wang over his famous essay on Zhu Xi's mature thought.[60] In the early Qing, Fujian produced one of the leading proponents of the renewed Cheng-Zhu school (and a grand secretary from 1705 to 1718), Li Guangdi 李光地 (1642–1718), editor of the *Zhuzi quanshu* 朱子全書 (Complete works of Master Zhu), *Xingli jingyi* 性理精義 (Essential meaning of nature and principle), and *Yuzuan Zhouyi zhezhong* 御纂周易折中 (Imperially sponsored Balanced discussion of the *Classic of Changes*). In 1707, the founding of the Aofeng shuyuan 鰲峰書院 in Fuzhou by Zhang Boxing 張伯行 (1651–1725), then the governor of Fujian, created a center for the teaching of Zhu Xi's thought in the province.[61]

It is into this line of thinkers that Minxi scholars fit. Tong Nengling 童能靈 (1683–1745)[62] from Liancheng, Lei Hong 雷鋐 (1697–1760; *js* 1733) and Yin Chengfang 陰承方 (1715–91) from Ninghua, and their contemporary Lan Dingyuan 藍鼎元 (1675–1733) from nearby Zhangpu all ardently supported Cheng-Zhu teaching. As a modern scholar has noted, they contributed little that was new to the teaching, choosing rather to reiterate its major tenets—"be attentive and truthful in order to establish what is fundamental, study and investigate principle in order to extend knowledge, accumulate righteousness and enlarge upon it in order to make one's actions sincere, examine and discipline the self

60. Other prominent defenders of orthodoxy were Zhou Ying 周瑛 (1430–1518), Cai Qing 蔡清 (1453–1508, author of *Sishu mengyin* 四書蒙引 and *Yijing mengyin* 易經蒙引), Chen Chen 陳琛 (1477–1545), and Lin Xiyuan 林希元 (1482–1566) (Xu Xiaowang, *Fujian sixiang wenhua shigang*, pp. 209–22). There were exceptions to the rigid orthodoxy of the province's thinkers: Huang Daozhou 黃道周 (1585–1646), the Donglin adherent and Ming loyalist, followed a moderate version of Wang Yangming's philosophy.

61. Xu Xiaowang, *Fujian sixiang wenhua shigang*, pp. 222–27.

62. *Liancheng xianzhi* (Minguo), 21.24b–25a.

in order to guard against loss"—and continue what had become a more or less moot attack on the Wang Yangming school.[63] To be sure, the most original thinkers of the day, the scholars of "empirical research" (*kaozheng* 考證), were also enemies of the Wang school, but they advocated new critical study of the Classics, not a tired return to Confucian orthodoxy.

Thus the leading philosophers of Tingzhou were conservative, devoted to the perpetuation—without much in the way of adaptation to changing times—of the Cheng-Zhu orthodoxy. To the end of the imperial period, the region remained essentially outside the major intellectual currents of the day—there is no evidence that Tingzhou scholars engaged in, or even knew of, *kaozheng* scholarship or the later statecraft movement. Even after the modern educational system was established in the early years of the Republic, there are few signs that students were touched by the nationalist sentiments or informed of the array of reform ideas that transformed intellectual life in the coastal cities of the southeast after May 4, 1919. As one Tingzhou missionary teacher noted thankfully in 1923, "Whereas schools at the coast have had big troubles owing to the new spirit among students, we have escaped."[64] Communist youth study societies were formed as early as 1921 in the southern Minxi counties of Shanghang and Yongding,[65] but the Communist movement would not have a strong impact on the area until later in the decade.

Minxi remained, then, in terms of intellectual trends and educational development, largely outside the mainstream and, from the late nineteenth century through the early 1920s, outside even the mainstream within Fujian. The region did produce a few noted scholars and artists: Li Shixiong 李世熊 (1602–86) of Ninghua produced what is considered one of the finest, most carefully researched local gazetteers of the late imperial period, the *Ninghua xianzhi* (Ninghua county gazetteer) of 1684,

---

63. Yin Chengfang, *Yin Jingfu xiansheng yiwen*, j. 2; cited in Xu Xiaowang, *Fujian sixiang wenhua shigang*, pp. 227–28. Lei Hong, for example, in his *Xiaoshi ou cun* (1ab), repeatedly denounced Wang Yangming and his followers for their distortion of Mencius, Zhu Xi, and early Ming Confucians such as Wu Yubi 吳與弼 (1392–1469) and Xue Xuan 薛瑄 (1389–1464).

64. London Missionary Society, Report no. 129 (1924), p. 70.

65. Xu Xiaowang, *Fujian sixiang wenhua shigang*, p. 388.

as well as a series of other historical works and a useful account of the Ming-Qing transition in western Fujian. Li Shihong 黎士弘 (ca. 1626–ca. 1705; *jr* 1654) of Changting was a poet and essayist of some note, admired by Qian Qianyi 錢謙益 (1582–1664), and the author of several collections (*Renshu Tang biji* 仁恕堂筆記, Random notes from the Renshu Tang; *Xichui wenjian lu* 西陲聞見錄, Record of things seen and heard on the western frontier; *Tuosu zhai wenji, shiji* 托素齋文集, 詩集, Literary collection, Poetry collection from the Tuosu zhai; and *Lixin cungao* 理信存稿, a text on Confucian ethics). And in the Qing, the three painters Shangguan Zhou 上官周 (1665–after 1749) of Changting, Hua Yan 華嵒 (1682–1756) of Shanghang, and Huang Shen 黃慎 (1687–after 1768) of Ninghua attained reputations beyond the borders of Minxi. But, as these scattered examples suggest, these impressive individuals did not emerge from a regional society that produced or could sustain new schools of thought or a critical mass of important writers and innovative artists who had a wide-ranging influence on late imperial or modern society.[66]

The nature of Minxi publishing to a large extent reflected the limits of local intellectual and cultural circles. As we shall see, the commercial publishing business of Sibao operated within this context of intellectual conservatism and education geared to the examinations. Publishing by other commercial houses, officials, academies, and literati also reveal some of the limits of the regional culture. First, with the exception of Sibao, there was little publishing in late imperial Minxi. Xie Shuishun and Li Ting, in their study of Fujian printing, rank the area well behind Minbei and the more prosperous capital and coastal areas in the production of both governmentally and privately published texts. Second, the few works that were produced in places other than Sibao were of largely local interest and utility. Thus in 1689 the Shanghang magistrate had a text entitled *Keshi lu* 課士錄 (Examination records), a collection of examination essays, cut and printed in order to aid students in the

---

66. Xie Shuishun and Li Ting, *Fujian gudai keshu*, p. 450; and Xu Xiaowang, *Fujian sixiang wenhua shigang*, pp. 279–80. Li Bingqian's useful bibliography of writings by Fujian authors through the Republican era, *Fujian wenxian shumu*, lists only forty authors (including artists) from the Tingzhou area, representing fewer than a hundred titles out of a total of almost 5,100 for the whole province.

local academy; in 1889, the Changting magistrate, seeing that the calligraphy of local scholars lacked refinement, had a calligraphy manual,
the *Zixue juyu* 字學舉隅 (Beginning the study of characters),[67] published, and so on. A few publishing houses (or perhaps *kezi dian*) in
the county seats cut texts on a commission basis: in 1754 a Fan Taiyuan 范泰元 had his father's poetry printed through just such a shop.
And presumably it was a similar shop in Shanghang that produced the
medical texts *Suwen* 素問 (Plain questions) and *Lingshu* 靈樞 (Efficacious pivot; together these formed the *Huangdi neijing* 皇帝內經, or
Yellow Emperor's classic of internal medicine) for a Li Shikui 李世奎,
who then distributed the texts as an act of charity. The Jijin zhai
剞錦齋, a publishing house established by Shanghang native Zhou
Weiqing 周維慶 in Changting in the Kangxi era, published a few literary collections, including, in 1725, a collection of poetry and essays from
Tingzhou called *Minting wenxuan* 閩汀文選 (Selected writings from
Tingzhou).[68]

Such works of local literary interest made up the bulk of publication,
whether government or private. In 1874 Yang Lan's *Tingnan jincun ji*
汀南廑存集 (Collection from a hut in southern Tingzhou) was
published by a Zheng Rulian 鄭汝廉, and the same author's gazetteer,
*Linting huikao* 臨汀彙考 (Collected investigations of the Tingzhou
area), was printed by the Changting local magistrate four years later, in
1878. The works of famous native sons were also popular. In 1684
the magistrate of Ninghua county had Li Shixiong's fine *Ninghua xianzhi*
cut and printed. In 1745, after the death of the Liancheng Cheng-
Zhu scholar Tong Nengling, his descendants collected his writings into
a volume, the *Guanzhai shantang quanji* 冠豸山堂全集 (Complete collection from the Guanzhai shantang); and in 1845 a collaboration
between the prefect and the gentry of Tingzhou produced a new edition of Li Shihong's literary collection *Tuosu zhai wenji, shiji*.[69] But
another common source of publications was absent in Tingzhou:
although academies proliferated in Tingzhou during the Qing, there is

---

67. Literally, "raising a corner in the study of characters," an allusion to *Analects* 7.8.
68. Xie Shuishun and Li Ting, *Fujian gudai keshu*, pp. 451–52.
69. For a fuller listing of official and private publishing in Qing Minxi, see ibid., pp.
438, 449–53.

little evidence of publishing on their part until the early twentieth century.[70]

For the most part, then, publishing in western Fujian—with the exception of Sibao—was limited to local officials printing gazetteers, writings of well-known local authors, and educational works for the local academies; literati transmitting the works of family members; and the occasional publishing house turning out a very small number of literary collections, scholarly texts, or primers.[71] Only after the new, state-mandated school texts were introduced under the early Republic did Minxi book culture reflect modern educational change. And not until the late 1920s and 1930s were the nonofficial texts of the New Culture—that is, the fiction of the May Fourth writers, the essays of public intellectuals on China's problems, and the propaganda of rival political factions—published.[72]

## Sibao and the Zou and Ma Lineages

Tingzhou, then, provided little in the way of economic opportunities, social order, or cultural and intellectual stimulation throughout the late imperial period and the Republic. Within this isolated and impoverished prefecture, the situation of the Sibao community, site of the Zou and Ma businesses, was about equally bleak. The history of Sibao, to the extent that it can be reconstructed, echoes many of the conditions identified above as typical of western Fujian.

During the Qing and earlier, Sibao consisted of a cluster of over seventy hamlets and villages concentrated for the most part within a

---

70. In 1902 the Ninghua Yunlong shuyuan 雲龍書院, under the sponsorship of a member of the Lei lineage, published an edition of Lei Hong's *Jingsi Tang wenchao* 經笥堂文鈔 (ibid., p. 483).

71. Ninghua county seat had, in the late Qing and early Republican period, two printshops producing primers, ledger forms, and stationery (Liu Zhenbang and Qiu Hengkuan, "Jiefangqian Ninghua gongye gaishu," p. 33; and Qiu Hengkuan, comp., "Ninghua shudian shihua," p. 89). It is likely that most county seats in the area did have such shops, serving a local readership.

72. These developments did not occur simultaneously throughout Minxi. Shanghang and Yongding, perhaps because they are more easily accessible from the coast and from cities like Zhangzhou, seem to have encountered the New Culture movement and Communist organizers earlier than the northern part of the region, where Sibao is located.

narrow basin stretching westward from the Aofeng 傲峰 Mountains and straddling the border areas of four counties, Changting, Ninghua, Liancheng, and Qingliu (see Map 2.2).[73] The inhabitants of the Sibao basin developed a strong sense of their separate identity. Even today, residents speak of themselves as "Sibao *ren*" 四堡人, rather than as "Changting *ren*" or "Liancheng *ren*." Isolation from the prefectural city and the major towns of Minxi doubtless helped to create this notion that Sibao was a cultural and territorial unit apart. No navigable rivers linked the basin to the rest of the region. And although a courier route provided transport to the northern counties of Ninghua and Qingliu and the southern county of Liancheng, there was no safe and easy road to the prefectural capital, roughly a day's walk away. Thus Sibao was a "periphery of a periphery," isolated from the major center even within the peripheral region of Minxi.[74]

The origins of Sibao as a distinct social, economic, and cultural unit remain somewhat mysterious. Settled by a variety of different descent groups later identified as Hakka, the villages of Sibao were perhaps most securely linked by marriage networks. The Zou and Ma genealogies, for example, reveal certain patterns of wife-selection from among the various settlements within Sibao as early as the late Ming. The preferred marriage partners for the Zou (of Wuge, Shuangquan 雙泉, and Shangbao 上保 villages) came from the Ma (of Mawu) and vice versa,[75] although each descent group also frequently formed marriage alliances with the Jiang 江 of Jiangfang 江坊, the Li 李 of Changxiao 長校 and Shapingcun 沙平村, and the Zhang 張, Lai 賴, Xie 謝, Tong 童, Wang 王, Wu 吳, Bao 包, Yang 楊, or Yan 嚴 of other settlements within Sibao. Landholding patterns and burial sites also suggest something of the economic ties that bound the community together. Both lineage

---

73. During the Qing, forty-four Sibao villages were located in Changting county (which until 1951 administered Sibao), twenty-two in Qingliu, several in Liancheng, and one in Ninghua. Today Sibao, designated a township (*xiang* 鄉) and considerably reduced in size, is under the jurisdiction of Liancheng county (Liu Yonghua, "The World of Rituals," pp. 71–77).

74. Ibid., p. 71.

75. Modern estimates of Zou-Ma intermarriage put the rate at a high 60 percent (Ma Chuanyong, "Lianchengxian Sibaoxiang Mawucun minjian xisu," p. 338).

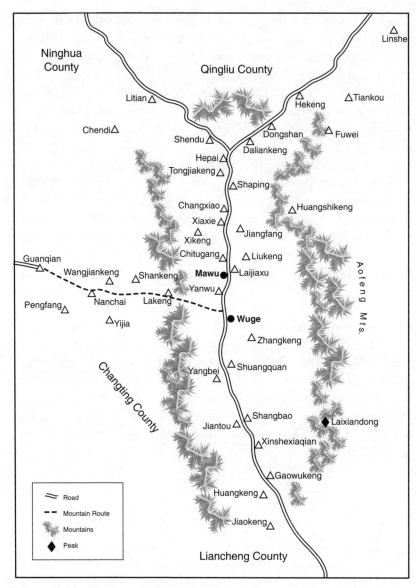

Map 2.2  Sibao in the late Qing

landlords and private landlords frequently held scattered plots of land in as many as three or four different locations—often even in different counties—within the Sibao area. Burial sites were equally scattered; it was not uncommon for a resident of Mawu or Wuge to be buried in

Qingliu or Ninghua county, at family gravesites quite distant from the deceased's native village but within the borders of Sibao. Shared religious practices also helped to create a distinctive Sibao culture. In addition to widely revered gods like Tianhou 天后 and Guangong 關公, Sibao residents honored many locally specific spirits. The Liuyue miao 六月廟 in one Sibao village, for example, contained spirit places for the founding ancestors of the Zou, Ma, Lai, Yan, Wang, and Yang, all Sibao lineages.[76]

We are primarily concerned here, however, not with all of Sibao, but with just two of the villages, Mawu and Wuge, among the dominant settlements and market towns of Sibao in the late Ming and Qing. Although some smaller villages—Shangbao, Jiantou 梘頭, and Yanwu 嚴屋—participated to a limited extent in the Sibao printing trade, these two large contiguous settlements were unquestionably the center of the industry.[77] Each settlement was dominated by a single descent group, the Ma in Mawu and the Zou in Wuge. Both descent groups claim that they settled in their respective villages during the Song; Ma Qilang 七郎, founding ancestor of the Ma, is believed to have moved to Laijiayu 賴家圩 (a portion of what is now Mawu) from Majiawei 馬家圍, Anle 安樂 township, Ninghua county, some time during the Jianyan and Shaoxing eras (1127–63), the period of the great flight south after the Jurchen conquest of north China. Zou Liulang 六郎, the founding ancestor of the Zou family in Wuge, moved from Shangbao to Wuge roughly a century later, it is said, during the reign of Song Duzong 宋度宗 (r. 1265–74).[78]

---

76. Ibid., pp. 329–30; see also *MSDZZP* (1945), *Liezhuan*, 1.3b.

77. I am grateful to Liu Yonghua for materials about the participation of Shangbao, Jiantou, and Yanwu in the publishing industry. Liu, in his study of Sibao as a ritual unit, has divided the villages in the Sibao basin into three types: "super-lineage" villages with populations over 3,000; villages at the periphery of the Sibao basin, with populations of 1,000 to 3,000; and small villages with populations of several dozen to several hundred. Wuge and Mawu, with populations of over 5,000, fit into the first category; Shangbao and Jiantou into the second; and Yanwu into the third. See Liu Yonghua, "The World of Rituals," pp. 76–89.

78. *MSDZZP* (1993), 1.6b; for a legendary account of the founding of the Ma line, which reveals something of She-Han tensions, see Ma Chuanyong, "Lianchengxian Sibaoxiang Mawucun minjian xisu," p. 305. For the Zou origin story, see *FYZSZP* (1947), *j. shou,* "Yuanliu xingai" 源流新改, 6a–8b.

The first Ma lineage—that is, the first line of descendants from Ma Qilang to be defined as a distinct lineage through the compilation of a genealogy and the construction of an ancestral temple[79]—was formed in the early fifteenth century under the leadership of Ma Hetu 河圖, who achieved tribute-student (*gongsheng* 貢生) status (that is, he was a student under the Directorate of Education) in 1438 and held the position of prefect of Cizhou 磁州 subprefecture in Henan. He completed the genealogy that defined membership in the "upper shrine" lineage within the Ma descent group, established in the sixth generation from Ma Qilang,[80] and constructed an ancestral hall in Mawu the very year he passed the tribute-student examination. Half a century later, the lower-shrine descendants followed suit. At the initiative of Mawu's most distinguished native son, the *jinshi* and high official Ma Xun 馬馴 (*zi* Deliang 德良 1421–96; *js* 1445), the lower-shrine lineage first established an ancestral hall and in 1496 completed its genealogy.[81] Both the upper-shrine and the lower-shrine efforts, led by members of the descent group who had achieved some official distinction, seem to have been aimed in part at enhancing the status of their respective lineages. They were very much part of a larger regional trend toward the formation of lineages by ambitious gentry.[82]

-------

79. I use the terms "descent group," "lineage," and "branch" lineage as defined in Ebrey and Watson, "Introduction," pp. 4–9; see also Ebrey, "The Early Stages in the Development of Descent Group Organization."

80. The Ma descent group divided into two branches or lineages, the "upper shrine" (*shangci* 上祠; or the left branch) and "lower shrine" (*xiaci* 下祠; or the right branch). *MSDZZP* (1945), 1.1b–2b; *Changting Sibaoli Mashi zupu* (10th edition, 1913), *j. shou*, 1ab.

81. Ma Xun was first secretary, later director, of the Board of Revenue. He seems to have been particularly skilled at suppressing rebellion, most notably as administrative vice commissioner of Sichuan, and eventually as provincial administrative commissioner of the same province. His highest appointment was as right vice-censor-in-chief in the Huguang region. There he was noted for the development of aid policies (and successful appeals for tax reduction) that contained famine in Hubei and Hunan. See Jiao Hong, comp., *Guochao xianzheng lu*, 60.75a, "Ducha yuan youfu duyushi Ma Xun zhuan" 都察院右副都御史馬馴傳.

82. See Liu Yonghua, "The World of Rituals," pp. 188–216, for a more detailed account of lineage building among the Ma. Liu suggests that Ma Xun aimed not only to elevate the status of his family but also to create a stronger sense of group identity and stability in the face of the rebellions in mid-Ming Fujian (pp. 215–16). Hilary Beattie

Ma Hetu and Ma Xun accomplished the "first wave" of lineage building in Sibao. Roughly a century later, the Zou, following the Ma model, initiated the "second wave" of lineage formation, and established two Zou lineage organizations. By this time the Zou descent group had already divided into two branches, the "lower-shrine" branch of Yesheng gong 葉勝公 (1336–1407) in Longzu 龍足 hamlet,[83] and the "upper-shrine" branch of Dingfu gong 定敷公 (1349–1417) in Tiancha 田茶 hamlet.[84] Zou Xiong 雄, a successful geomancer of the upper-shrine branch, began the formal process of lineage building by constructing an ancestral hall during the early Wanli era (1573–1619). The first genealogy of this lineage was completed a few decades later, in 1598, under the leadership of several subofficials and Imperial Academy students (*jiansheng* 監生).[85] Shortly thereafter, the lower-shrine lineage completed its genealogy, also under the sponsorship of an Imperial University student.

Within the next hundred years, all the major agnate groups within Sibao and even the smaller descent groups of the peripheral settlements had established lineage organizations.[86] Throughout the eighteenth and nineteenth centuries, the more prosperous Sibao lineages, including the Zou and Ma, updated their genealogies. New branches were formed within each lineage, with separate ancestral halls, genealogies, and branch-lineage corporate estates. Leading lineage members also frequently established family schools to educate promising boys and prepare them for the examinations.

Like most residents of Minxi, the Ma and Zou chose, once the economic boom of the late Ming made it possible, to diversify their sources of revenue. The family instructions written by Ma Xun in the late fifteenth century already acknowledged the sojourning handicraft and commercial activities of lineage members: "Most lineage members farm and study, but among them there are also those who work as

(*Land and Lineage*, chap. 4) describes a similar process of lineage building for the Yao and Zhang families of Tongcheng county, Anhui, roughly one century later.

83. *MTLZXZSZP* (1911), 1.2b–4b.
84. *FYZSZP* (1947), 1.3b–4b.
85. Ibid., *j. shou*, "Lijie bianxiu gaikuang" 歷屆編修概況, 9a.
86. Liu Yonghua, "World of Rituals," pp. 216–32.

laborers and merchants outside [Sibao]." As long as these merchants did not "hurt the family's reputation by cheating people, forcing purchases or sales," or using counterfeit money (misdeeds for which they should be reported to the local official), there was no harm in earning profit in these occupations. [87] By the end of the Ming and the beginning of the Qing, the biographies in each of the genealogies reveal increasing commercial activity. Both Zou Yanglu 仰魯 (1568–1634) and Zou Shilu 仕魯 (1568–1640) were sojourning merchants, Yanglu to eastern Guangdong and Hangzhou, his cousin Shilu to unidentified places "a thousand *li* from home."[88] Ma Liangfeng 良鳳 (1540–84) chose to be a scholar, "even though all his uncles and nephews were merchants."[89] And Ma Mengji 孟吉 (1645–1724?) "devoted himself to Confucian studies when young and did not sell, [but then] abandoned his studies and became a merchant, accumulating great abundance." [90] Ma Lüe 馬略, of the same generation, "pulled a cart, serving as a merchant" (*qian che fu gu* 牽車服賈) in order to support his family.[91] By the late seventeenth century, so many lineage members had become sojourning merchants that an editor revising the Ma genealogy complained:

Seventy to 80 percent of our lineage exhaust themselves as merchants in other regions, and so it is difficult at any given time to revise the genealogy. One has to ask women and children for the names of the wives of the previous generation, examine them about the virtuous deeds of the previous generation, and ask them to get the posthumous writings of the previous generation from their storage boxes. Thus even though one has the will [to complete the genealogy], it is not possible to follow through.[92]

But few households relied solely on sojourning merchants or laborers for support. The preferred strategy was to encourage or require occupational diversification, to combine farming, study, handicraft

---

87. *MSDZZP* (1945), *ji* 2.1.16ab.

88. *FYZSZP* (1947), 1.13ab, 1.52ab, 34.6ab, 34.25ab.

89. *MSDZZP* (1945), 1.36b–37a; *ji* 7, 1.18b–19a.

90. Ibid., 3.52a; *ji* 7, 1.22b–23a. See Chen Zhiping and Zheng Zhenman, "Qingdai Minxi Sibao zushang yanjiu," pp. 93–94, for discussion of the cases cited in notes 88 through 90 to this chapter.

91. *MSDZZP* (1945), *ji* 7, 1.22ab.

92. Ibid., 1.22b.

production, and commerce "under one roof"—doubtless to maximize economic security while optimizing earning power. Ma Yuanlu 元祿 (Wanli era?), *de facto* head of a family consisting of himself and seven brothers, sons, and nephews,

> divided occupations among his sons and nephews, saying, "This one will farm; this one will be a merchant; this one a craftsman." To each he assigned an occupation in accordance with the person's talent and knowledge. Thus everyone was suited to his task, and each task was successfully accomplished. This is the best method of ordering a family, for the family industries flourished, making myriad profits. The seven were commonly known as the "seven heroes," and Ma Yuanlu as their leader.[93]

It seems that the development of large households practicing a social division of labor, which was not uncommon in economically more advanced parts of China,[94] was a strategy ideally suited to underdeveloped areas such as western Fujian as well. As one scholar of Fujian lineages explains, "Given the stalemate between the subsistence and the commercial economies, maintaining a large family on a considerable scale facilitated the expansion of financial resources and improved the family's economic structure by creating opportunities to participate in both economies."[95]

---

93. Ibid., *ji* 7, 1.15b–16a; cited in Chen Zhiping and Zheng Zhenman, "Qingdai Minxi Sibao zushang yanjiu," p. 94. In the late eighteenth century, Zou Hongyi 洪益 (1715–91) employed a similar approach with his seven sons: "He had the talented study, those who were not talented farm, the strong work hard, and the weak stay at home." The genealogy credits this wise management with the prosperity of his family: "Although his family had no ancestral profession and very few savings, Zou Hongyi worked out an arrangement that gradually enriched the family" (*FYZSZP* [1947], 5.93b–94a, 33.27a). See also the biographies of Ma Dingce 定策, *MSDZZP* (1945), *ji* 7, 1.59a–b; Zou Qicui 啓萃, Zou Biaoguo 表國, and Zou Kongai 孔愛, in *FYZSZP* (1947), 33.9ab, 33.20ab, 33.60b, respectively.

94. For examples, see Rankin, "Rural-Urban Continuities," pp. 70–74; Ho Ping-ti, *The Ladder of Success in Imperial China*, pp. 73–86; and Bergère, *The Golden Age of the Chinese Bourgeoisie*, p. 23.

95. Zheng Zhenman, *Family Lineage Organization and Social Change in Ming and Qing Fujian*, p. 44. Zheng goes on to use the Zou and Ma of Sibao as examples of this strategy, developed to deal with the mixed, "semisubsistence and semicommercial economy" of western Fujian, where "overpopulation and the shortage of arable land made it objectively difficult for the natural subsistence economy to be sustained, while on the other hand low productivity inhibited the full development of a commercial economy. In this

Agriculture was the foundation of this approach—most families included at least one member who farmed the land (and perhaps was in charge of "family governance," *jiazheng* 家政), to ensure at least a baseline security for all. But in an area where arable land was scarce and the population growing, most families saw the need for at least one other source of income. Civil service in the imperial bureaucracy was, at least until the early twentieth century, an attractive occupational option, but study for it was a gamble, removing the student from the workforce over an extended period of time for a very slight chance of success— although success, if achieved, amply repaid the earlier sacrifice.[96] For the most part this choice did not bring either the Zou or the Ma much profit, however, for throughout the Ming and Qing, although the genealogies record dogged efforts at examination study, the Ma could boast only one *jinshi* and four *juren* degree-holders, the Zou only one *juren*. The Ma were much more successful at the lower levels of the civil hierarchy: twenty-five Ma—but only three Zou—earned some form of tribute-student status, entitling them to permanent *shengyuan* status (and thus to repeated opportunities to take the provincial examinations) and to admission to the Imperial University. If the lineages contributed at all to Tingzhou's improved standing in the Fujian examination results (see above), it was only at the *juren* or lower levels, and largely the work of the Ma. The Zou excelled, rather, in the less prestigious military examinations—sixteen lineage members (and only one Ma) earned the military *juren* degree between the late eighteenth and late nineteenth centuries.[97] To a great extent the examination record of both lineages

---

deadlock . . . , a certain social division of labor existed but full specialization was still impossible. As a result, occupational diversification of labor within the family was seen as the ideal strategy" (pp. 45–46). See also Chen Zhiping and Zheng Zhenman, "Qingdai Minxi Sibao zushang yanjiu," p. 94.

96. See Cole, *Shaohsing*, pp. 25–30, for a discussion of this strategy as it was practiced in Shaoxing.

97. This count does not include purchased degrees and includes only the highest degree of each degree-holder. The exact breakdown was, for the Ming: one Ma *jinshi*, nine Ma *suigong* 歲貢; for the Qing: three Ma *juren*, one Zou *juren*, five Ma *engong* 恩貢, one Ma *bagong* 拔貢, one Ma *fugong* 副貢, seven Ma *suigong*, one Ma *yougong* 優貢, two Zou *suigong*, sixteen Zou military *juren*, and one Ma military *juren*. The *bagong* and *yougong*, in addition to enjoying permanent status as graduates or *shengyuan*, could also be

reflects the low social mobility that characterized not only Fujian but also, during the Qing, most southeastern provinces, as a consequence of the demographic increase and greater examination competition.[98] Their modest successes—clustering in the Qianlong and Jiaqing eras, when the lineages enjoyed their greatest prosperity—led at most to lower official or suboffical postings and were neither striking enough nor sustained enough to enrich either lineage significantly. And the professional alternatives—the practice of medicine or *fengshui*—occasionally chosen by failed Zou and Ma examination candidates were apparently not lucrative enough to provide steady support for the lineages. Commerce and crafts were more attractive choices because they entailed less lengthy training and a much greater likelihood of gain, albeit at the expense of prestige and status.

In fact, by the early Qing, although most families continued to practice occupational diversification, crafts and particularly commerce had clearly become the favored occupations of most Zou and Ma households. Nor did they work and deal in books alone. Although printing and bookselling were the dominant businesses of Wuge and Mawu in the eighteenth and nineteenth centuries, members of the Zou and Ma lineages also worked in the tin, carpentry, and construction crafts (often as itinerant laborers),[99] or in processing and/or trading timber, bamboo shoots, tobacco, oil, tea, paper, lacquer, indigo, and medicinal herbs.[100] Ma Dafang 大芳 (1625–83), for example, made a fortune selling oil in Jiangxi and paper in Guangdong. During the turmoil of the Ming-Qing transition, when "bandits and thieves rose up, traveling was very dangerous and few people dared travel afar to trade," Ma was virtually the only trader to the south and west. With no competitors, he "earned great profits and returned home."[101] Sibao residents might also work as rice peddlers, managing the transport of the rice surplus from the

---

selected for immediate low-level official appointments (*Changting xianzhi* [1940], 14.58b–69b, and Liu Yonghua, "The World of Ritual," p. 252).

98. Ho Ping-ti, *The Ladder of Success in Imperial China*, p. 242.

99. Interview 26, 11/11/95 (Wuge).

100. Chen Zhiping and Zheng Zhenman, "Qingdai Minxi Sibao zushang yanjiu," pp. 105–6; see also *MSDZZP* (1945), *ji* 7, 1.34a–36a.

101. *MSDZZP* (1945), *ji* 7, 1.35ab.

northern Tingzhou counties to the rice-poor southern counties.[102] As the example of Ma Dafang suggests, many merchants, including some of the more prosperous printer-booksellers, traded in a variety of goods. Ma Dingbang 定邦 (1672–1743) traded in timber, and Zou Bingchun 秉椿 (1755–1805) in textiles and porcelain as well as books.[103] Thus printing and bookselling were simply the foremost among a range of handicraft industries and commercial enterprises that supported the Sibao economy in the late Ming and Qing.

The importance of commerce in the household economies of Wuge and Mawu gave village society a distinctive character. Given Sibao's isolation, its commerce almost automatically entailed sojourning. Thus, most Zou and Ma merchants spent much of their time away from home, returning at best once a year, or settled at a key business site, returning only infrequently or never at all. Family patriarchs tried to marry their sons to women from the Sibao villages before they embarked on their commercial travels, hoping that a family in Sibao would motivate them to return.[104] Some merchants, however, married women from their sojourning sites, without their father's permission or knowledge. Ma Daguang 大光, for example, married a woman from Longnan 龍南 county, Jiangxi province, where he did business. After his sudden death, Miss Zhong 鍾, with her two sons, carried her husband's coffin back to Mawu for burial, an act for which she received a glowing biographical tribute in the *Mashi zupu* 馬氏族譜 (Genealogy of the Ma lineage).[105] Other men took a Sibao wife and then established a second household in their place of business, returning only occasionally to the first wife and family back home. For all these reasons, marrying a daughter to a man of Wuge and Mawu became increasingly unattractive to local Minxi families, for fear that their daughters might in effect be abandoned by their sojourning husbands: "Don't marry your daughter to a Zou—he will go off to Guangxi" (*you nü bujia Zou—zou Guangxi* 有女不嫁鄒—走廣西) became a common Sibao

---

102. Liu Yonghua, "The World of Rituals," pp. 82–83.
103. *MSDZZP* (1945), *ji* 7, 1.75ab; interview 32, 11/13/95 (Wuge); *FYZSZP* (1947), 9.71b–73a, 33.38b–41a.
104. Interview 10, 4/26/95 (Wuge).
105. *MSDZZP* (1945), *Liezhuan*, 1.42ab, 51b–52b.

warning. [106] This reluctance to marry into the two families could explain the high incidence of intermarriage between the Zou and Ma; as neighbors sharing a sojourning tradition, these families might have been able to provide both understanding and material support to ease the emotional and economic tensions created by long-term separation of men from their families.[107]

Although sojourning over the short run placed heavy economic burdens on the wives of Wuge and Mawu and in the long run undermined the unity and threatened the continuity of some family lines, this form of commerce was essential to the economic survival of many Zou and Ma households. The new handicraft and commercial opportunities might divide individual families, but the relative wealth they brought to

---

106. Sojourning imposed a heavy economic burden on a man's wife and family. In larger joint families, where income was shared, a wife would be expected to contribute to the household, although she could also rely on support from the larger family for herself and her children. In poorer small families, if the man failed to return, the woman was often left destitute—"without food when hungry, without clothing when cold"—forced to eke out a bare living for herself and her children by textile weaving (*MSDZZP* [1945], *Liezhuan*, 1.54b–57a). The Zou and Ma genealogies are full of biographies of faithful wives raising their families virtually alone in Wuge or Mawu, either while their husbands were traveling on business or after their husbands had settled elsewhere or had died on the road. (See, e.g., *MSDZZP* [1945], *Liezhuan* 1.42a, 47b, 49a, 60a, 61a; *FYZSZP* [1947], 33.15ab, 16ab, 23b–24a, 38ab, 51ab; and *MTLZXZSZP* [1911], 20.6ab, 12b–13b, 44ab, 46b–47b, 60ab.) Some widows took over the management of the household (and perhaps the management of *shufang*) while their sons continued the sojourning commercial life of their fathers (*MSDZZP* [1945], *Liezhuan*, 1.62a–64b). See Mann, "Women, Families, and Gender Relations," pp. 456–66, for a discussion of the impact of sojourning on women and the family.

107. Wives' dissatisfaction with their husbands' long absences from home is clear from one legend explaining the failure of the Ma lineage to produce any distinguished officials after the first centuries of the Ming. According to this tale, the early academic success of the Ma meant that many of the men took up official posts outside Minxi, leaving their wives and concubines behind. When one of these wives had to call in a geomancer for advice on a new gravesite, she asked that he find a way to improve her lot and that of the other lonely women. The geomancer had the new grave and two wells dug near the site of the ancestral temple and, sure enough, this action disrupted the lineage's good *fengshui*, causing consistent examination failure and, temporarily, a more stable male presence in Mawu. Ultimately the effort backfired, for the men of Mawu took to the road again, not as officials but as less-distinguished sojourning merchants (Ma Chuanyong, "Lianchengxian Sibaoxiang Mawucun minjian xisu," pp. 300–303).

Sibao nonetheless helped to support and strengthen the Zou and Ma lineage organizations. Successful merchants used their profits first to promote the welfare of their own immediate family by buying land, building new houses, and establishing schools for the education of their descendants. But they might also donate land for the creation or expansion of ancestral estates (*zutian* 祖田) or lineage trusts. Such lands were held by a sublineage or segment (*fang* 房) within the lineage, and the income they generated was used to support sacrifices to the sublineage founder, fund a school, or supplement the incomes of the member-households. Ancestral estates were also frequently formed or augmented by donations of land made when property was divided among family members.

Insufficient information on landholdings makes it difficult to estimate the significance of these lineage holdings, considered "public land" (*gongtian* 公田), throughout most of Sibao's history. We do know that by the mid-twentieth century a little more than half (51.12 percent or 6,789 *mu*) of all cultivated land in the township was corporate, "public," land; some evidence suggests that the bulk of these lineage estates were formed in the seventeenth and eighteenth centuries.[108] This public land was managed by the elite of the lineage, or, as one informant put it, the lineage "gentry" (*shenshi* 紳士), who were in charge of selecting tenants and collecting rents. Lineage estates were composed of small, scattered plots of land; the Zou and Ma lineage landlords might own plots in several of the villages and hamlets within those portions of Ninghua, Qingliu, Liancheng, and Changting counties that Sibao encompassed. In renting lineage land, managers favored members of their own lineage.

---

108. The lower-shrine branch of the Zou descent group, whose land records survive in part, owned thirty-three separate lineage estates, comprising 725 plots of land (equivalent to at least that many *mu*) by the late nineteenth century. We have an account of size and date of purchase for only 331 of these plots (equaling 333.372 *mu*); it suggests that estate formation began in the 1570s, but that public land grew most rapidly between 1623 and 1772—a total of 300.1729 *mu* was added during that 150-year period. Then came a precipitous falling-off: from 1773 to 1897 only 15.751 *mu* were donated. If the other lineages of Wuge and Mawu followed the same level and pattern of estate formation, then it is likely that roughly half of the cultivated land in these two villages was lineage land by the late eighteenth century (Liu Yonghua, "The World of Rituals," pp. 258–65, esp. 264; for a comparison, see Rubie Watson, *Inequality Among Brothers*, pp. 68–69).

Although no rental statistics survive from earlier periods, contemporary informants claim that a lineage member might pay as little as 30 percent of the harvest to a lineage landlord, whereas a tenant from another lineage would be charged 50 percent.[109] In addition, all tenants might also have to pay a small fee for the delivery of the rice rent and to contribute to a communal meal (*hefan* 合飯), at which managers and tenants would meet to arrange rental contracts for the coming year. Because of the relatively low rental rates and the assumption that lineage landlords were more likely to reduce rents during times of crisis, Zou and Ma tenants much preferred to rent land from ancestral estates rather than from private landlords.[110] Indeed, contemporary informants report that some peasants found renting lineage land more profitable than farming land they owned. One explained that his father had told him, "It is more profitable to rent from the ancestral estate than to cultivate your own land, for tenants do not have to pay taxes on land they rent. Once you are able to rent some plots of the ancestral estate, never give up the tenancy rights."[111] Many landowners thus chose to rent land from the ancestral estates while renting their own land out to others to farm. One such family, for example, in the early twentieth century rented out 27 to 30 *mu* (2.1–2.3 hectares) of its 40 to 43 *mu* (3.1–3.3 hectares), at the same time farming several plots rented from the ancestral estate.[112]

Sibao—in the heart of an area noted for high rates of rent resistance throughout the eighteenth century—appears to have remained remark-

---

109. Interview 26, 11/11/95 (Wuge). Information about rents varied rather widely. Other informants claimed that the rent, even for lineage members, was 50 percent of the harvest; yet others explained a more complicated system, whereby the lineage received 60 percent of the harvest for high-quality land (*shangtian* 上田), and 40 percent for low-quality land (*xiatian* 下田). No matter what the figures, however, all seemed to agree that it was better to rent lineage land than private land. Interviews 64, 12/5/95 (Wuge); 59, 12/2/95 (Wuge); and 28, 11/12/95 (Wuge).

110. Interviews 25, 11/9/95 (Wuge); and 84, 4/21/96 (Wuge). Even if paying a higher rate of rent, nonlineage tenants, too, might prefer to rent ancestral estates, largely because of greater flexibility in the rental arrangements. Zhong Qisheng ("Lun Fujian zongzu tudi," pp. 4–6) argues that lineage land, owned collectively, was not managed as closely as private, individually owned land, making it easier for the tenant to extend the terms of tenancy indefinitely.

111. Interview 85, 4/23/96 (Mawu).

112. Interview 28, 11/12/95 (Wuge). In the informant's terms, the figures were 80 to 90 of 120 to 130 *tiao* of land. One *tiao* was roughly one-third of a *mu*.

ably free of this particular form of conflict. Some scholars have argued that the dominance of lineage estates and the intrafamilial tenancy system they produced served to reduce social and economic tensions in Sibao.[113] It is possible, too, that the occupational diversification and commercial activities of much of the township population—their trade in lumber, oil, textiles, porcelain, and tea as well as books—provided income that relieved some of the pressure for agricultural production and access to arable land.

There is also evidence that lineages within Wuge and Mawu cooperated in establishing certain associations and commercial operations that strengthened intralineage relationships by creating a web of interlocking interests and at the same time benefited the village communities. One such action is the contractual agreement forged between branches of two Zou lineages to establish a periodic market in Wuge. The Zou genealogy records that in 1778 the "Gongping xu" 公平墟, or "fair market"—a name clearly chosen to denigrate the presumably "unfair" Laijia market (Laijia xu 賴家墟) near Mawu[114]—was founded by five branches within the Zou descent group. Each of the five branches contributed a portion of the land on which the market was built as well as funds toward the construction of stores and a warehouse; in return, each branch-shareholder received a share of rents from the market in proportion to its original input.[115]

Investment in the "fair market" linked several branches of the Zou descent group in Wuge in a project that, by creating a periodic market, brought added commercial benefits to the village at large. Other contractual associations, such as the Longxiang hui 龍翔會 (Soaring dragon association), established within the Tianhou temple 天后廟 to support the annual celebration of the birthday of the Sagely Mother in Heaven

---

113. Liu Yonghua, "Kangzu yu bukangzu."

114. Probably the "unfairness" of the Laijia market related to the requirement that all brokers at this market be Ma; brokers were able to charge traders a fee for permission to sell their goods at the market. Interview 85, 4/23/96 (Mawu). Quite possibly the Laijia market was founded on the same kind of contractual agreement as the Gongping market, but no record of this agreement survives.

115. The agreement is recorded in the *FYZSZP* (1947), 29.2a–6a, and translated by Michael Szonyi in Zheng Zhenman, *Family Lineage Organization and Social Change in Ming and Qing Fujian*, p. 124; see also Liu Yonghua, "The World of Rituals," pp. 426–35.

(Tianshang shengmu 天上聖母),[116] or the host of temple and loan associations formed within the Ma lineage in the Republican era, had a somewhat narrower scope, but they did operate to forge ties across branch lineage lines even as they served the religious or economic needs of the community. Indeed, both Wuge and Mawu seem to have been crisscrossed by such associations, forming collectively a network of religious, economic, and possibly territorial connections. Ancestor worship bound members of each lineage together in reverence to their common ancestors; the creation of branch lineages also helped unify smaller units within the lineages. The corporate estates were both economic and territorial units that supported, in very practical ways, the cohesion of these groups. Extra-lineage religious beliefs and practices, by cutting across family lines, could also serve to unify the community. Neighborhoods within the village were symbolized in altars to Tudi bogong 土地伯公, the earth god, or to Shegong 社公, believed to oversee the affairs of each particular neighborhood.[117] Both Wuge and Mawu—for that matter, all of Sibao—honored Zougong 鄒公 in his guise as the deified Tang official who had protected settlers from barbarian invasion.[118]

In addition to these local deities, well established in the area by the late Ming, in the eighteenth century Wuge and Mawu residents began to worship a range of gods and spirits well known throughout southern China as bringers of good fortune and wealth. Tianhou or Mazu 馬祖, popular throughout Fujian among seafarers and sojourning merchants, was perhaps the most important god. During the Qianlong era a temple

---

116. For a fuller discussion of this association, see Zheng Zhenman, *Family Lineage Organization and Social Change in Ming and Qing Fujian*, p. 127; and Liu Yonghua, "The World of Rituals," pp. 432–35. The contract defining the fields providing the income for this association appears in *FYZSZP* (1947), 29.45b–46a.

117. Interview 25, 11/9/95 (Wuge); Liu Yonghua, "The World of Rituals," pp. 385–410. Imposed in the early Ming as part of Ming Taizu's system of local control, the altars to the gods of *she* and *li* were ultimately appropriated by the people, who, ignoring the state-established altars, began in the mid-Ming to set up *shetan* 社壇 and *litan* 里壇 of their own.

118. The Zou lineage has conflated this Zougong with their ancestor, Zou Yinglong 應龍 (1173–1245), a noted Song official and said to have been the father of Liulang, the founding ancestor of the Wuge Zou. Thus the Zougong temple in Shangbao honors both the god Zougong and the Zou lineage's purported ancestor (see Liu Yonghua, "The World of Rituals," pp. 372–85).

was constructed in Mawu in her honor near the Laijia market, right next to the Magong temple 馬公廟, the shrine to the founder of the Ma lineage.[119] As we have seen, a second temple in her honor was built in Wuge in 1792. Guandi 關帝 (or Guangong 關公), the god of war, literature, or riches, depending on the worshipper's needs, was also a popular figure, with his own temple in Wuge, supported by a society organized to manage his worship.[120] Informants consistently mentioned Caishen 財神 (Zhao Gongming 趙公明), the god of wealth, as a common object of worship among Zou and Ma merchants, although he was honored within their homes, not in a place of communal worship.[121] Although there are few references to formal Buddhist practices in the genealogies, due perhaps to the general decline suffered by Buddhist institutions in Minxi through the Qing[122] (or perhaps to

---

119. Ma Chuanyong, "Lianchengxian Sibaoxiang Mawucun minjian xisu," p. 328. On the spread of Mazu worship among merchants from the Fujian coast to the western and northern portions of the province, see Zhang Guilin and Luo Qingsi, "Fujian shangren yu Mazu xinyang," p. 108.

120. *FYZSZP* (1947), 29.5b–6a.

121. Interviews 7, 4/21/95 (Liancheng); 14, 4/28/95 (Wuge); 26, 11/11/95 (Wuge); 30, 11/13/95 (Wuge); and 94, 5/13/96 (Bose). In Sibao the god of wealth was identified with Zhao Gongming 趙公明, originally a plague god and a character in the sixteenth-century novel *Fengshen yanyi* 封神演義 (Investiture of the gods) (see von Glahn, *The Sinister Way*, pp. 247–48).

122. Apparently the prosperity of Buddhist institutions worked against them in late Ming and early Qing Fujian. Their rather large landholdings, in a land-poor province, made them natural targets of antagonism and attack from officialdom and local gentry alike. And, since the relative wealth of the monasteries and temples offered a comparatively easy life, these institutions, despite government efforts at regulation, became swollen with illiterate or semiliterate and feckless monks and nuns. Their popular support declined considerably, and they were eventually deprived of much of their property. But this decline in both the wealth and the religious authority of Buddhist institutions did not undermine the attractiveness of Buddhist gods and beliefs. Lay Buddhist societies and popular beliefs and practices—including the worship of such perennial favorites as Guanyin and Maitreya—continued to flourish outside formal, "elite," institutional structures. See Xu Xiaowang, *Fujian sixiang wenhua shigang*, pp. 249–56; and Ju-k'ang T'ien, "The Decadence of Buddhist Temples in Fu-chien in Late Ming and Early Ch'ing." Minxi, in any event, was never one of the livelier of Fujianese Buddhist centers—it lacked famous temples and monasteries and did not produce any notable Buddhist leaders. Although the depth and breadth of popular belief is very difficult to measure, it appears that the area also did not participate, at least in formal institutional

Buddhism's association with women worshippers),[123] members of the
Ma lineage were the major patrons of a Buddhist temple, the Fengrao
Temple 豐饒寺, in Sibao.[124] The bodhisattva Guanyin was honored in
a small convent in Mawu, the Dafo an 大佛庵, and in a temple built in
her honor on a hill overlooking the villages.

Thus the Sibao villages, lineages, and branch lineages were interconnected through a complex hierarchy of religious and economic practices. Ancestral rites and lineage associations were of primary importance, but those communities and families were also linked through a
dense, eclectic, and interlocking network of festivals, associations, and
rituals devoted to the avoidance of bad fortune and the procurement of
good fortune and profit for the individual, the family, the branch lineage, lineage, descent group, village, and township.

This is not to say, of course, that the communities of Sibao were free
of internal conflict—intra-familial, intra-lineage, and inter-lineage—or
that the associations and ritual practices described above did not create
points of contention. Although detailed information is difficult to
gather on this sensitive topic, both the Zou and the Ma genealogies reveal, usually indirectly, the existence of such conflict.[125] Property divi-

---

terms, in the Buddhist revival of the late Qing. See Chen Zhiping, ed., *Fujian zongjiao
shi*, pp. 251–96.

123. Buddhism is mentioned infrequently in the genealogies and almost always in the
biographies of women; see, e.g., *MSDZZP* (1945), *Liezhuan*, 1.46b, and *MTLZXZSZP*
(1911), 20.4b, 12b. One of these biographies also praises a woman for refusing to "be
deceived by Buddhist delusions" (*MSDZZP* [1945], *Liezhuan*, 1.54ab). One contemporary informant claimed that 80 to 90 percent of the Buddhist worshippers in the villages were women. This same man also pointed out that Buddhist practice aided the
family, by encouraging the accumulation of merit and thus good fortune (interview 20,
5/1/95 [Mawu]).

124. *Changting xianzhi* (1879), 27.4a.

125. For example, the Ma genealogy makes much of Ma Dingyi 定一 for refusing to
cheat his brothers in the sale of the family's mountain forest property. Offered a bribe
of one hundred ounces of silver if he would agree to a reduced price for the mountain
land, he indignantly refused, saying, "I dare not selfishly cheat my younger brothers.
The amount my younger brothers receive cannot be reduced, and I do not want the
amount I receive to be increased." This same man was plagued with lawsuits after the
death of his father; as the Ma genealogy explains, "All the villagers observed that he had
inherited, and many rushed to bring suit against him. He had to go back and forth to
Changting and Qingliu in order to respond to the charges, so that he had no peace"

sion frequently kindled bitter family disputes, even lawsuits. Within the lineages, the rules developed to regulate the ancestral sacrifices, recorded in the genealogies, served to exclude as well as unite—certain members of the lineage were not allowed to participate. Presumably the religious associations formed to manage the rituals and festivals in honor of specific spirits might have the same effect: conflicts over the disposition of temple-association resources, leadership struggles, and competition for the favor of the gods could divide as much as commitment to a specific deity or festival could unite.

And, of course, the simple fact of socioeconomic difference—of "inequality among brothers"—within the lineages also created tensions and at times outright conflict.[126] As Zheng Zhenman has pointed out, the very associations that originally defined "equal" contractual relationships between lineage branches, tended over time to devolve into what he identifies as "control-subordination lineages," in which certain branches dominated others.[127] Most seriously, the system of corporate landholding, despite the relatively easy landlord-tenant relationships it appears to have promoted, served to exacerbate socioeconomic divisions within the villages. Managers of the ancestral estates—as mentioned above, drawn from the "gentry" of the villages—had considerable discretionary power over the disposal of the estates in their care. Since rental of lineage land was considered highly desirable, managers could easily extract special fees and services from aspiring tenants. And since rental contracts appear to have been rather easily renewed, certain

---

(*MSDZZP* [1945], *ji* 7, 1.51b). Another biography celebrates Ma Dafang for using a propitious plot for his brother's grave rather than saving it for his own burial (*MSDZZP* [1945], *ji* 7, 1.34b). Contests over family property, then, were one of the primary sources of tension within the village. Indeed, this genealogy records the prefaces from a few property division documents—most of them emphasizing harmonious property division—presumably to provide later lineage members with models for what was known to be a delicate and often highly contested procedure (*MSDZZP* [1945], *ji* 9, 1.60a–62b, 70a–71a).

126. See Rubie S. Watson, *Inequality Among Brothers*, particularly chap. 6, for a description of some of the kinds of issues that divided lineage villages like Mawu and Wuge. Watson also points out that the assertion of lineage harmony is not necessarily just a Confucian piety but a very practical expression of the dangers of open protest against class inequities within a lineage.

127. Zheng Zhenman, *Family Lineage Organization and Social Change*, pp. 127–28.

families were able to hold on to their tenancies for generations, while other families were more or less permanently excluded from rental opportunities. After the late eighteenth century, when little land appears to have been added to ancestral estates, the division between those favored with lineage rental contracts and those forced to rent from private landlords grew sharper.[128]

Interlineage tensions shaped Sibao society and relations within the publishing industry as well. Today both Zou and Ma informants emphasize the blood ties that link the two lineages (and the two villages of Wuge and Mawu)—"we are all brothers" is the pious phrase commonly used to sum up relations between the two families. Yet it is clear that, despite the strong marriage connections between the two communities, their relationship, at least throughout much of the Qing and the early twentieth century, was characterized at best by a strong sense of economic and cultural competition and at worst by violent conflict. The greater success of the Ma in the civil examinations, although not impressive in absolute terms, was a point of irritation for the Zou. It is perhaps partly for this reason that the Zou emphasize, even today, their leading role in printing and bookselling. More directly, the two descent groups competed to control the local periodic market; the "fair market" established by the Zou in Wuge in the late eighteenth century was a direct challenge to the dominance of the Laijia market, which was under the charge of the Ma lineage. The Wuge market's increasing popularity and eventual dominance by the end of the Republican era signaled the greater economic and, to some extent, political centrality of Wuge within Sibao.[129]

---

128. Sometimes economic jealousy exploded into a conflict whose trigger—or pretext—was some trivial incident. For example, Ma Jingyan 景燕 (active early 19th c.), the manager of a *shufang* in Sibao and of the Huixian tang 會賢堂 bookstore in Jiayingzhou 嘉應州 (Guangdong), accumulated enough wealth to purchase over 300 *mu* of land, build a sizable mansion, and hire eight long-term workers (*changgong* 長工) and purchase nine oxen to farm his family's holdings. A quarrel between one of these hired workers, from Wuge, and another Mawu family over a trespassing flock of ducks resulted ultimately in a lawsuit that ruined Ma Jingyan's family (interview 54, 11/28/95 [Mawu]). This oral account doubtless omitted many contributing enmities, but the story does suggest that inequalities in wealth inspired considerable jealousy and tension.

129. Ma Chuanyong, "Lianchengxian Sibaoxiang Mawucun minjian xisu," pp. 311–12. Interviews 24, 11/8/95 (Wuge); 50, 11/25/95 (Mawu); 54, 11/28/95 (Mawu); 84, 4/21/96

And at least one long-standing feud (deserving the name of "feud," or *xiedou* 械斗, because it did entail two outbreaks of violence involving both lineage organizations) over *fengshui* siting also undermined intervillage relations. In the late sixteenth century, the Ma complained that a Zou Shiliang 時良 had dug a ditch through the grave site of a Ma ancestor, disrupting its favorable *fengshui*. The Tingzhou prefect ruled against Zou, and eventually a stele was erected at the gravesite, warning against further desecration. More serious conflicts arose over the gravesite of the same ancestor's wife, which bordered on Wuge land. The prosperity of the Ma line over the centuries was credited to the excellent siting of this grave. During the Jiaqing era, the Zou built a temple to Tianhou (and a market) in front of the grave and several houses on the "dragon line" in an attempt to block and disrupt the Ma family's good *fengshui*—or so the Ma argued. Once again the Tingzhou prefect intervened, erecting a stele prohibiting building on the site. But this conflict continued to undermine inter-lineage harmony well into the twentieth century.[130]

This, then, was the context in which Sibao publishing-bookselling developed: in the "periphery of a periphery," in the most isolated and impoverished area of the most isolated and impoverished region of Fujian. Part of the Hakka heartland and geographically and economically within the Min-Gan-Yue border region, Sibao required for survival

---

(Wuge); and 85–86, 4/23/96 (Mawu). See *MTLZXZSZP* (1911), 20.7b, 8b–10b, for another account, from the late seventeenth century, of a conflict between the Zou and a neighboring village over water rights.

130. In 1938 and as recently as 1962, fighting erupted between the two lineages over the issue. The 1962 broil, which lasted ten days and engaged partisans from other Sibao villages, was so serious that the local government called in the People's Liberation Army. The dispute was settled when the Ma agreed to move the grave, and both sides promised not to dig up one another's graves (Ma Chuanyong, "Lianchengxian Sibaoxiang Mawucun minjian xisu," pp. 313–14). Although the reticence of the sources makes it difficult to know for sure, the tensions between the Zou and the Ma seem less persistent and less violent in expression than in the notoriously strife-ridden prefectures of Zhangzhou and Quanzhou; see Lamley, "Lineage Feuding in Southern Fujian and Eastern Guangdong Under Qing Rule."

hard work at a variety of different occupations—farming, handicraft industries, and sojourning commerce. Those who could not make a living simply left, joining the waves of Hakka migrants who helped fill up the hinterland areas of Jiangxi, Hunan, and Guangdong, and the frontier provinces of Sichuan, Guangxi, Guizhou, and Yunnan in the late Ming and Qing. Those who remained survived through occupational diversification, combining handicraft industries, sojourning commerce, and agriculture. The strong lineage societies of Mawu and Wuge provided a clear structure for the formation of household industries and networks of sojourning merchants, both of which defined the ambitions and shaped the organization and operation of the Zou and Ma business enterprises.

# THREE

## The Origins of Publishing and the Production of Books in Sibao

### The Beginnings of Publishing in Wuge and Mawu

At what point did the people of Mawu and Wuge turn to publishing-bookselling? The precise origins of the Zou and Ma publishing businesses are difficult to determine. Local informants provide two competing accounts, neither of which is supported in any of the genealogies. The Ma argue that Ma Xun, the early Ming *jinshi* and official responsible for creating the early lineage identity, introduced block printing to his native place as a means of strengthening local schools and ensuring the continuing examination success of his line. This explanation, if true, dates the origins of printing in Sibao to the late fifteenth century, just about the time the book trade in Jianyang and the Jiangnan area was gaining fresh momentum after the economic stagnation of the early Ming.[1]

The upper branch of the Zou lineage has produced a rather polished, but textually unverified, account that naturally places a Zou at center stage. This legend has it that Zou Xuesheng 鄒學聖 (1523–98) was the true father of Sibao publishing. One of the more successful members of the Zou family, he was director of granaries in Hangzhou, Zhejiang,

---

1. For claims that the industry was established even earlier, see Brokaw, "Commercial Publishing in Late Imperial China," p. 54, n. 16.

a subofficial post.[2] In 1580, as his term of office expired, he planned to return home to Sibao to care for his aged father and invalid mother. But his young wife, Shao Miaozheng 邵妙正, a native of Hangzhou, protested; she was reluctant to leave the sophisticated pleasures and high culture of Hangzhou for life in an isolated mountain village. And she was particularly concerned about her three sons (aged three, six, and twelve *sui*) and the limits that an upbringing in a place like Sibao would impose on their education and future prospects. She relented only after her husband promised to master the techniques of wood-block printing and to bring back to Sibao woodblocks that could be used to print textbooks for her sons.[3]

Since Hangzhou was, by the late sixteenth century, one of the major publishing centers of China, famous for its fine editions, this story has a certain attractive plausibility. As we have seen, the relative easiness of woodblock-print technology made it a simple matter, once one had the cut blocks, to print texts. This story would also help to explain the initial capitalization of the business in Sibao: presumably it consisted of woodblocks purchased in Hangzhou from the profits of Zou Xuesheng's office. Unfortunately there is no solid evidence either that Zou imported printing blocks to Sibao from Hangzhou or, if he did, that he used them for any purpose other than printing up a limited number of textbooks for his own family. Nothing in the Zou genealogy suggests that he engaged in the commercial production of books.

Biographies of the next generation are more promising. Zou Xuesheng's sons, Zou Yanglu and Zou Weizong 維宗 (1578–1643), and his nephew Zou Shilu 什魯 (1568–1640) did take up commerce as a livelihood. Whereas Zou Shilu traveled "all over" as a merchant,[4] Zou Yanglu traveled to eastern Guangdong, ultimately becoming "as successful as Tao Zhu 陶朱 [a Zhou-dynasty figure famous for his great wealth] in his skiff, doubling his fortune, so that he was widely known as 'untitled nobility.'"[5] Zou Weizong traveled to all the academies in the local

2. *FYZSZP* (1947), 1.12b–14a.
3. Zou Risheng, "Zhongguo sida diaoban yinshua jidi zhi yi," p. 103.
4. *FYZSZP* (1947), 34.6b.
5. Ibid., 34.5a, 25a. "Untitled nobility" is an allusion to the chapter on "money-makers" in Sima Qian's 司馬遷 *Shiji* 史記; see Burton Watson, trans., *Records of the Grand Historian of China*, 2: 492; on Tao Zhu, see 2: 481.

area, and "his name became known at all the schools, and his wealth was first among the region's cities and townships."[6] The genealogy never states explicitly what these men were selling, but Zou Weizong's frequent rounds to the local schools suggests that he, at least, was selling educational texts, possibly produced from his father's blocks.

Not until the next generation, however, with Zou Mengchun 孟純 (1619–72), is there a clear textual reference to the establishment of printing in Sibao. The grand-nephew of Zou Xuesheng, Zou Mengchun worked in his youth as a sojourning merchant, "earning considerable profits" in Xingning 興寧 county, Guangdong—just the area where his father's cousin, Zou Yanglu, had been active as a trader. Eventually he married and settled in Xingning, and there he started to "cut blocks and print the Classics for sale," presumably using his mercantile profits to finance the purchase or cutting of woodblocks. In 1663 he returned to Wuge, purchased a house and land, and settled down to manage his extended family. He also continued his book business, and the genealogy proudly notes that "the first publishing house (*shufang*) in Sibao of Tingzhou, Fujian, was established by him." His biographer credited him with bringing education and general enlightenment to the Sibao area: "His abundant merit and great achievement rest entirely in the printing of the Classics, for since he has been publishing books, many have advanced in their studies. He has, in fact, spread civilization throughout the area."[7]

The origins of the printing industry in Mawu are equally uncertain. Although there are references to Ma families in commerce during the late Ming, there are none to bookselling or printing until the early Qing. Ma Weihan 維翰 (1639–1700), a contemporary of Zou Mengchun, was apparently the first Ma to publish as well as sell books; he is said to have established the first Mawu publishing house, the Wanzhu lou 萬竹樓. The description of his entry into the world of publishing is similar to many found in the Zou and Ma genealogies:

When a child, Ma Weihan studied for the examinations. But, as every day he saw his father weary from the management of the family, he was troubled. He

---

6. *FYZSZP* (1947), 34.5a–b.

7. Ibid., 34.9a. One informant supplied some weak support for this account in claiming that the publishing industry was founded in Sibao when a Zou from Guangdong settled there (Interview I, 10/27/93, Wuge).

asked his father, "My younger brother is still young; you, my father, are already old. It would be better for my younger brother to study and for me to become a merchant [literally, "plow as a merchant," *geng shang* 耕商] than for you alone to be exhausted by the difficulties of supporting the family. May I aid you in this way?" His father agreed. Thereupon Ma Weihan took over the management of the family; at the same time he sold books in Jiangxi and Guangdong. For altogether fourteen or fifteen years he worked at this profession, earning great profits.

During that period Ma Weihan established a bookshop in Chaozhou, Guangdong. Eventually, to fulfill his filial obligations, he returned permanently to Mawu: "He did not return to selling books in Guangdong, but he had workmen cut woodblocks, and he printed books to sell wholesale in the Sibao area. His profits were two to five times higher than when he was a traveling merchant, and he was able to be by his parents' side to serve them day and night."[8] This pattern—learning the bookselling trade, accumulating capital, and then using that capital to establish a publishing house in Sibao—was followed by most of the pioneer publishers in Sibao.[9]

The lower-shrine branch of the Zou lineage also claims a place in the early development of the Sibao book trade. Certainly its genealogy records a tradition of sojourning commerce that began quite early. Zou Weidi 惟棣 (1587–1638) and his two elder sons, Qing 清 (1607–76) and Shu 淑 (1610–?), and his grandson Zhaoxiong 兆熊 (1626–73) were sojourning merchants in Jiangsu, Zhejiang, Jiangxi, and Guangdong provinces—and Zhaoxiong was said to have sold texts to scholars in the Hangzhou–Suzhou area.[10] But not until the next generation, with Zhaoxiong's son Funan 撫南 (1650–1738), is it clear that the family was

---

8. *MSDZZP* (1945), *ji* 7, 1.38a–b.

9. Zou Risheng ("Zhongguo sida diaoban yinshua jidi zhi yi," p. 106) states that remittances sent to Sibao by Zou and Ma lineage members who had migrated to Southeast Asia also helped to capitalize the industry, but there is little written evidence to support this claim.

10. *MTLZXZSZP* (1911), 20.1a–4b. Editors of the fifth edition of the genealogy claim that Zou Ding 錠 (1639–1720) was also a publisher, but I find no textual evidence in the genealogy for this assertion (see "Longzuxiang Yesheng Gong houyi diaoban yinshua zhi xunli" 龙足乡叶胜公后裔雕版印刷之巡礼, *MTLZXZSZP* [1994], *j. shou*, pp. 44–45).

publishing and selling texts; Funan "abundantly printed the Classics, histories, and Qin and Han writings, distributing them widely, enriching the minds of contemporary men of the Way."[11] By this time, as we have seen, at least two other publishing houses had been established in Wuge and Mawu. Whatever the precise date of origin of publishing in the two villages, clearly it caught on very quickly—by the 1670s all three lineages were engaged in the business.

In describing the origins of Sibao publishing, the genealogies— the only sources of information about the early development of the industry—emphasize the link between education and bookselling-printing, which first appears in the legend of Zou Xuesheng. Zou Wei-zong made a living selling texts to local schools, and Zou Mengchun and Zou Funan were praised, as publishers, for bringing the basic texts of Chinese education, the Classics, to Minxi. The link is more directly expressed in the biography of Ma Qibing 馬其炳 (1624–1705), a local teacher whose son, Ma Kuanyu 寬裕 (1670–1754), was one of the early Sibao compiler-publishers and founder of the Wenhui lou 文匯樓: Ma Qibing's "son sold books; thus the family profession was like waves un-folding from a rushing stream"—that is, the son's occupation, book-selling (which the rhetoric of the Zou and Ma genealogies equates with the spread of culture and learning), was a natural extension of his fa-ther's career in education.[12]

There is some evidence, then, that members of the Zou and Ma lineages were sojourning booksellers—and perhaps printers of school texts as well—in the late sixteenth and early seventeenth century. The founding of true publishing houses in both Wuge and Mawu can be firmly dated only to a somewhat later period, the sixth decade of the seventeenth century. The idea of printing-bookselling as a business and the technology of woodblock printing seem to have been introduced to the villages by sojourning merchants (if we discount the legend of Zou Xuesheng) with experience of such businesses in Xingning and Chaozhou, Guangdong. These men returned to Sibao in the 1660s and 1670s, according to the genealogies out of filial obligation, but perhaps

---

11. *MTLZXZSZP* (1911), 20.7b–8a. Zou Funan may have learned the publishing business from his elder brother, Zou Kuinan 魁南 (1648–1709).

12. *MSDZZP* (1945), *ji* 7, 1.32b–33a.

also because of the widespread economic depression and disruption of trade that afflicted Guangdong during the early years of the Kangxi era (see Chapter 6); quite possibly poor business drove both Zou Meng-chun and Ma Weihan back home to make a living printing and selling books within a well-known area. For, although the genealogies' account of the cultural and educational services performed by the early publish-ers may in large part be rhetoric, it is likely that the most profitable markets for these early publishing houses were local family schools, and their primary products, educational primers and the Classics. These, whatever their contributions to the local culture, were books guaran-teed to sell as long as the examination system remained in place. In a place like Sibao, where economic survival was precarious, a publishing industry centered on these texts and free of stiff competition promised a steady and stable income.

### The History of the Zou and Ma
### Publishing Houses: An Overview

Once established in Wuge in 1663 and in Mawu shortly thereafter, the printing industry and book trade seem to have expanded rapidly, both contributing to and benefiting from the boom in commerce and handi-craft industries (lumber, paper, tea, and cloth, in particular) that charac-terized the economy of western Fujian from the late Ming through the eighteenth century.[13] As book publishers whose primary product was school texts—primers, editions of the Four Books, and examination aids—it seems likely that the Zou and Ma publisher-booksellers bene-fited even more directly from the proliferation of schools, from lineage schools to academies, in the Tingzhou area. As noted above, one of the earliest of the Sibao booksellers, Zou Weizong, was said to have traveled around to schools to sell texts in the late Ming. In the second half of the seventeenth century, four new academies were established in the prefec-ture, and by the middle of the following century nine more had been cre-ated, providing the Zou and Ma with an expanded local market.[14]

------

13. See Chen Zhiping and Zheng Zhenman, "Qingdai Minxi Sibao zushang yanjiu," pp. 104–5.

14. Liu Haifeng and Zhuang Mingshui, *Fujian jiaoyu shi*, p. 187.

The Zou and Ma publisher-booksellers thus benefited from superb timing. They established their businesses in the late seventeenth century—just as south China was beginning to recover from the devastation of the dynastic transition period and the consolidation policies of the Manchus. At first they relied exclusively on the local demand for school texts, an outgrowth of the isolation of Sibao. Absent competition from outside the area, they profited handsomely from the increased demand for educational works generated by the newly forming lineages of the area and the construction of new academies. But the expansion and continued growth of the Sibao industries throughout the eighteenth and early nineteenth centuries depended on the increased regional, as opposed to local, demand for texts. Population increase and migration during the eighteenth century in Guangdong, Jiangxi, Hunan, and the frontier regions of Guangxi, Guizhou, and Yunnan created new communities (or enlarged old ones), which naturally expanded the market for books. The Sibao publisher-booksellers, relying heavily (though not exclusively) on their Hakka identity—the Hakka, after all, were among the most active of the migrant populations—became chief purveyors of books to these new migrant communities.

The late seventeenth and early eighteenth centuries saw a steady increase in the number of publishing houses and lineage members engaged in bookselling in Wuge and Mawu. As we have seen, in the first stage of Sibao's printing history the capital for founding publishing houses came from sojourning merchants, often book merchants, who returned to Sibao and sank their accumulated profits into the cutting of woodblocks and the purchase of paper, the primary initial investments required. This method of capitalization continued throughout the long life of the industry. New publishing houses were also frequently capitalized by one other means: the inheritance of either woodblocks or funds—that is, the division of these forms of property among heirs on the death or "retirement" of a *shufang* manager (see Chapter 5). Wealthier lineage members might on occasion supply capital to relatives to start and manage a business, although whether the transaction was a loan or an investment against a share of profits is never reported in surviving texts.[15] All

---

15. Zou Han 瀚 and his brother, both left in poverty on the death of their father, relied on contributions from ten relatives and friends to "piece together" a bit of silver to

informants emphasize that woodblocks were never given as dowries,[16] but possibly dowry funds could be used as well, at the discretion of the wife, to help found or support a *shufang*. Once a *shufang* was established, however, inheritance of blocks seemed to have been the major means of capitalization of new shops; property division thus was largely responsible for the proliferation of *shufang* in Sibao.

Although the reticence of the sources makes it difficult to identify publishing houses precisely by date of founding and name, by the end of the seventeenth century, there appear to have been at least thirteen publishing houses in Sibao, eight in Wuge, and five in Mawu. The Qianlong and Jiaqing eras represent the golden age of Sibao printing.[17] Over the course of the eighteenth and early nineteenth centuries, forty-six new *shufang* were founded (thirty-one in Wuge, fifteen in Mawu). These houses doubtless varied widely in publishing output, but the largest of them had extensive book lists. At the time of property division, the Zaizi tang had a woodblock stock of 107 titles, the Xiangshan tang, 87; each figure represents a respectable publishing output. Even more impressive is the figure from the Wenhai lou account book, which lists 251 titles (in multiple copies, for a total of 8,440 copies)—and this at a time when the industry was in decline. The absence of reliable statistics on the output of other contemporary publishing concerns makes it difficult to interpret this evidence, but we can attempt a brief comparison with figures from Jianyang, one of the largest (if not the largest) publishing centers of the Ming. Lucille Chia, in the statistics she has compiled on extant Jianyang publications, lists the Yu family, the most prolific of the Jianyang publishers, as the producers, through the Ming dynasty, of 371 imprints; this figure refers to the extant texts printed by forty-nine Yu publishers between the Jiajing era and the end of the

---

start a business. They flourished, soon earning profits of several tens of pieces of silver (*jin* 金) (*FYZSZP* [1947], 33.34a).

16. A few informants reluctantly admitted that once upon a time—just once—a Zou patriarch had included some woodblocks in the dowry he provided for his daughter's marriage to a Ma. Most informants, however, repudiated even the possibility of such an event. Presumably the competition between the Zou and Ma publishers made this practice unthinkable or at least very rare (Interview 16, 4/29/95 [Wuge]).

17. *FYZSZP* (1947), 33.99a.

dynasty (1522–1644). By far the largest publisher on the list is Yu Xiang-dou 余象斗, who can be identified as the producer of over seventy texts; the second highest output for a single publishing house is fifty-seven texts; the third, a mere sixteen. Since these are numbers of sur-viving texts, we must assume that the actual output of the Yu family was considerably larger.[18] Furthermore, the significant expansion of woodblock printing during the Qing makes it difficult to extrapolate from the late Ming figures to the late eighteenth and early nineteenth centuries.

Nonetheless, the 107-title stock of the Zaizi tang, the 87-title stock of the Xiangshan tang, and certainly the 251-title stock of the Wenhai lou—each representing just one household *shufang* at one specific point in its history (not the total output of a multi-generational family busi-ness persisting through at least a century and a half)—is impressive. Moreover, these figures represent just a portion of Sibao's output, as property-division documents and account books survive for only a handful of publishing houses and bookstores. Sibao publishing was at the very least a significant regional business.

So successful were the Zou and Ma publishing concerns, it is said, that even in the early decades of the business they attracted book merchants from other provinces—Hunan, Guangdong, Guangxi, and Jiangxi—to out-of-the-way Sibao to purchase texts at an annual whole-sale book market. Publishing houses also sent out sojourning book merchants who sold Sibao imprints in almost all the provinces of south China; many established branch bookstores devoted to the sale of Sibao texts. From this golden period in the township's economic his-tory, doubtless, comes the popular saying, "Carry out a load of books and return with a load of silver" (*yidan shu tiaochuqu, huan yidan yin huilai* 一擔書挑出去, 換一擔銀回來).[19] Such a saying is not a reliable rec-ord of the real progress of the Sibao concerns, but there are other, more concrete indicators of Sibao's former prosperity. Surviving in both Wuge and Mawu today are the remains of the large compounds, the "mansions" (*dasha* 大廈) as the genealogies term them, built by

---

18. Chia, *Printing for Profit*, pp. 155–61, 298–302.
19. Zeng Ling, *Fujian shougongye fazhan shi*, p. 208.

Fig. 3.1 Zhongtian wu 中田屋, the mansion built by Ma Dingbang 馬定邦 in the early eighteenth century with the profits from publishing. Photograph by the author.

the wealthiest publishers both to house their printing shops and families and to display their success (see Fig. 3.1). Throughout the Qianlong and Jiaqing eras, publishing-bookselling seems to have been the dominant and most lucrative occupation of the populations of Mawu and Wuge.

The early decades of the nineteenth century show little sign of decline. At least fifteen new publishing houses were founded in the first half of the century, apparently to meet the increasing demand for books from the ever-growing populations of Jiangxi, Guangdong, and Guangxi. The first significant setback came in mid-century, when the Taiping rebellion and the smaller uprisings and disturbances associated with it brought widespread disorder and devastation to south China. As we have seen, Taiping troops were active in the Minxi area between 1857 and 1865 and even marched through Wuge and Mawu in 1858 on their way to Liancheng city. It is difficult to assess the extent of the damage to the publishing industry. Only one publishing house, that managed by the line of Zou Boan 伯安, was recorded as lost in the genealogies: "During the Xianfeng era [1851–62], when the hairy rebels [the Taipings] brought disaster, the fires set by the soldiers torched the stored woodblocks and all the precious books collected by the family were destroyed."[20] Another shop almost suffered the same fate; the Mawu Zaizi tang 在茲堂 was reportedly spared only because the rebels spotted a plaque engraved with the characters *shanqing* 善慶, "virtue celebrated," and dared not burn the property of a worthy household.[21] Most informants suggest that, although the Taipings destroyed much property in the two villages, the publishing industry was not entirely devastated. Many *shufang* managed to survive and, by the end of the century, new *shufang* had emerged to replace those destroyed by the rebels.[22]

But the rebellion also disrupted Sibao trade routes and devastated its markets. Indeed, it is the genealogy biographies of sojourning booksellers, men working and living temporarily outside Sibao, that most frequently refer to the dangers of the rebellion and banditry. Often these references are not precise enough to identify specific incidents or rebel groups, but the significant increase in references to the troubles of the late Daoguang (1821–50), Xianfeng, and early Tongzhi (1862–74) eras certainly suggests that the book traders were hurt by the Taiping rebellion and/or by rebel and bandit groups that arose in their wake. The Red Turban rebellions of 1854–56 and the Hakka-Punti War of 1856–68 (between the Hakka and the "original settlers" or *bendiren* 本地人, Punti) that ravaged portions of Guangdong must also have limited Zou and Ma bookselling activities. The final battles between the Taipings and Zuo Zongtang's army in south China centered on the Hakka heartland—Minxi, eastern Jiangxi, and northern and eastern Guangdong—just the area where the Zou and Ma book merchants had established their most important sale routes and branch shops.

Recovery was slow, dependent not only on the restoration of secure transport and communication links but also, more important, on the revival of demand in a population devastated by war. The strong reassertion of government control and particularly the now vigorous—and often arbitrary and corrupt—imposition of a tax on commercial transactions, the *lijin*, presumably cut into profits (although the genealogies do not complain of the *lijin* or any other commercial taxes). As Hakka,

---

20. *MTLZXZSZP* (1911), 20.109a.
21. Interview 50, 11/25/95 (Mawu).
22. Interviews 7, 4/21/95 (Wuge); 10, 4/26/95 (Wuge); 24, 11/8/95 (Wuge); and 25, 11/9/95 (Wuge).

the Zou and Ma doubtless had to be particularly cautious in their actions, in the wake of both the empire-threatening Hakka-led Taiping rebellion and the more restricted Hakka-Punti conflicts in Guangdong province, although on this subject, too, the genealogies are silent.

Troubles not withstanding, the Sibao industry did survive. Once the Taiping and other threats were past, the Wuge and Mawu publishers seem to have maintained a steady, though not spectacular business. As the *Fanyang Zoushi zupu* 范陽鄒氏族譜 (Genealogy of the Fanyang Zou lineage) explains:

In our township the book industry reached its height in the Qianlong and Jiaqing eras—the extremely wealthy lined up like beads on a string as far as the eye could see. But then, from the Xianfeng and Tongzhi eras on, the industry was no longer that successful. Of the new businesses that started [after that], many succeeded by practicing frugality and accumulating profits. None of them equaled any of the earlier successes, however.[23]

New publishing houses continued to be established, perhaps as many as fifteen between 1850 and 1900, and some shops, like the Wenhai lou, enjoyed a revival that lasted from the last decades of the nineteenth century into the twentieth. A few proprietors even succeeded on the old scale: Zou Jianchi 建池 (1848–98) established a small empire of bookstores in Fujian, Guangdong, and Guangxi—although it is telling that he seems to have flourished by focusing on careful management of branch shops outside Wuge, rather than (like the most successful of his predecessors) by devoting himself to book production in Sibao. The mid- to late nineteenth century, then, was a period of leveling off for the Sibao industry and trade; book publishing could no longer offer riches, and those who wished to enter the trade did best to establish shops outside Wuge or Mawu, in the growing hinterland communities of Guangdong and Guangxi.

Had the book business not been subject to a series of new technological and cultural challenges, the Zou and Ma might have recovered fully from the turmoil and economic exactions of the mid- to late nineteenth century, perhaps even regaining the economic heights they had reached during the business's glory days in the Qianlong and Jiaqing

---

23. *FYZSZP* (1947), 33.99a.

eras. But, in fact, the book industry was confronted with a succession of dramatic changes and new demands, changes and demands that the Sibao book publishers in particular were ill equipped to adopt or meet.

Toward the end of the century, at the same time that the Zou and Ma were struggling to revive their business in the aftermath of the Taiping rebellion, a very new kind of technological competition threatened the two-century-long stability of the Sibao woodblock printing industry. Lithographic and letterpress machines could quickly and easily turn out much larger quantities of any text, often at a higher level of quality, than the woodblock method. But unlike woodblock printing, lithography and especially letterpress printing were not easily portable and learnable; letterpress required complex machines and skilled workmen to operate and repair them. Shanghai was the port of entry for these new technologies and rapidly rose to new prominence as *the* publishing capital, first of the fading Qing empire and then of the new Republic.[24] Sibao, at the periphery of a periphery, without easy access to the new technology and skills of mechanized printing, could not hope to compete.

But perhaps the blow that most dramatically hastened the decline of the Sibao industry came in 1905, with the abolition of the examination system. This act rendered the staple texts of the Sibao publishers—the Classics and the whole large cluster of texts that explained them and taught the tricks of the eight-legged essay—if not worthless, at least worth far less than a mere year before. Reform of the educational system and the introduction of new textbooks—whose production was quite easily monopolized by the more efficient, mechanized publishing houses of Shanghai, many of which enjoyed excellent contacts with the central educational bureaucracy[25]—further undercut the value of Sibao's stock of suddenly old-fashioned primers. Chapter 1 emphasized the advantages of woodblock printing for places like Sibao; in the new circumstances, however, reliance on woodblocks was a huge disadvantage—the blocks could not be broken down like matrices of movable type and reset to suit the very different demands of a new educational system and, indeed, a growing new reading public.

---

24. Reed, *Gutenberg in Shanghai*, chaps. 1–4.
25. Ibid., chap. 5.

It would be a mistake to exaggerate the speed of the change. Certainly the educational reforms of the early twentieth century accelerated the demise of Sibao as a publishing center, but its decline was by no means immediate. The slowness of educational reform measures in the hinterland—just the area that the Sibao publisher-booksellers served—ensured a continued, albeit shrinking, market for Sibao's textbooks well into the century. And even after new schools had been established and new textbooks mandated, some people adjusted only gradually to the new system; others were reluctant to accept or believe in the changes. The demand for the Classics and old school primers behind Sibao's original success did not vanish overnight, and Shanghai texts only gradually came to dominate the countryside.[26] In sum, Sibao's woodblocks did not suddenly lose all worth; rather, during the 1920s, 1930s, and 1940s, they steadily declined in value, finally becoming useful more as fuel than as tools for printing.

By the second decade of the twentieth century, then, the business was beginning its final decline: the range of texts produced became increasingly limited, branch shops drifted away from the control of their parent publishing houses in Wuge or Mawu, and booksellers were forced to seek out ever more distant and isolated markets in the mountain villages of Guangdong and Guangxi. The civil and military tensions within Sibao during the 1920s and 1930s—the genealogies repeatedly refer to banditry and the rise of village gangs—further weakened the industry, and the depredations of warlord armies again disrupted the major trade routes to Jiangxi and through Guangdong and Guangxi. A few publishing houses supplying primers for largely local consumption held on almost to the end of the Republican era; according to local informants, as late as 1946 two such houses, one Zou and one Ma, were still in operation, albeit on a very small scale.[27] Branch shops operated by members of the Zou and Ma descent groups in Fujian, Guangdong, and Guangxi survived through the Republican period to 1949—one even to 1957. Nonetheless, it is clear that by the early twentieth century at the latest, the Sibao publishing industries (and their branches outside

---

26. See Chapter 13.

27. Zou Risheng, "Zhongguo sida diaoban yinshua jidi zhi yi," p. 114; Interview 33, 11/14/95 (Wuge).

Sibao) had lost their vitality. They were reduced to reprinting basic educational texts or exercise books for use in local schools or to the retail
sale of "foreign-style" (*yangban* 洋版) books published in Guangzhou
or Shanghai.

## Producing Books in Sibao

As we have seen, the establishment of the Zou and Ma publishing-
bookselling industry owed much to the tradition of sojourning labor
and commerce that characterized the economy of Sibao (and, for that
matter, Minxi). The industry was founded by Wuge and Mawu natives
who worked as sojourning booksellers in Guangdong in the mid- and
late seventeenth century, then returned to their villages and applied the
knowledge and skills they had learned as migrants to set up their own
businesses. The portability of the tools required for block cutting and
the simplicity of the printing process, as described in Chapter 1, made
this technology transfer feasible. The flexibility that woodblock printing
offered in allowing publishers to adjust print runs to known demand,
thus making large capital investments in slow-selling stock unnecessary,
also made it a suitable industry for poor rural villages like Wuge and
Mawu. Finally, the Zou and Ma were fortunate (or shrewd) in the timing of their enterprises: they began publishing at a time when local demand was high in consequence of the "civilizing" educational activities
of the prefectural and county governments and local lineages, and they
expanded their operations, extending their sales routes and establishing
branch stores, in step with the population growth of the late seventeenth and eighteenth centuries and population migration to the frontier regions of the south.

Nonetheless, for all the convenience of the existing print technology
and for all the expanding market for books, it seems unlikely that the
Zou and Ma would have succeeded—or even thought of publishing as
a source of income—if the Sibao area had not been rich in the raw materials necessary for woodblock printing. Given Sibao's isolation and
the poor transportation links between the area and the outside world,
for the industry to be cost effective the publishers had to be able to rely
on local resources. What these materials were and how the Sibao publishers used them to produce books are the subjects of the remainder of
this chapter.

## NATURAL RESOURCES FOR PUBLISHING

Wuge and Mawu had easy access to almost all the materials, raw and manufactured, required for woodblock book production. Western Fujian, in the "mixed deciduous and evergreen broadleaf" forest zone that dominates south China, produced all the forest products necessary for cutting blocks and printing texts. Local hardwood trees like camphor (*zhang* 樟), pear (*li* 梨), catalpa (*zi* 梓), and jujube (*zao* 棗), all flourishing in the area through the late nineteenth century,[28] could be used to produce woodblocks. Informants claim that camphor (*Cinnamonum camphora*), particularly the "small-leaf" variety, was especially popular for this purpose in Sibao, in part because it grew in such abundance that even its use in manufacturing medicine and furniture did not limit the supply. As the 1940 *Changting xianzhi* explains, camphor "is everywhere in the area. There are two types—large-leaf and small-leaf. The grain of the small-leaf camphor is very fine, and its odor particularly strong. It is the best material for making tools and cutting (*diaolou* 雕鏤)." Although pear was not as common, a certain variety called "mountain pear" (*shanli* 山梨 or 橘), "fine of grain and strong," was also listed in the 1940 gazetteer as "suitable for use in cutting [blocks]" (*juanke* 鐫刻). Finally, catalpa, so closely associated with woodblock printing that *zi*, "catalpa," was a common synonym for woodblocks, and jujube also grew in the area—although they appear to have been used less commonly than pear or camphor for that purpose.[29]

---

28. Almost all regions of Fujian were suffering from deforestation by the late nineteenth century; only Tingzhou seems, perhaps because of its remoteness, to have retained considerable forest resources. Norman Shaw, in his 1914 study of Chinese forests, notes that almost all other parts of the province had been cleared of forests, but "in the more remote parts, where transport is difficult, there are still probably forests, and towards the west, in the Tingchow [Tingzhou] prefecture, large forests still exist, especially on the Tachin [Dajin] Range along the Kiangsi border" (*Chinese Forest Trees and Timber Supply*, pp. 52–53, 54). On camphor, see Culver, "The Lumber Industry of Fukien," p. 138.

29. *Changting xianzhi* (1940), 10.13a; *Changting xianzhi* (1879), 31.19ab, 21b; see also *Tingzhou fuzhi* (1867), 8.8a–10a, and Yang Lan, *Linting huikao*, 4.4ab. Camphor also flourished in Qingliu, Ninghua, Liancheng, and on the Jiangxi-Fujian border; see the 1829 *Qingliu xianzhi* in (*Jiajing Daoguang*) *Qingliu xianzhi*, pp. 351, 357–60; *Qingliu xianzhi* (Republican era), pp. 335–37, 338; *Ninghua xianzhi* (1684), pp. 117, 119, 122, and 125; *Ninghua xianzhi*

Minxi also produced plenty of pine (*song* 松; the major variety is *Pinus massoniana*), the primary raw material in the manufacture of printing ink. All eight counties of Tingzhou prefecture were noted for their montane pine forests—with the northern Fujian prefectures of Yanping, Jianning, and Shaowu, Tingzhou remained a major producer of pine well into the early twentieth century. Most of this timber was transported to Fuzhou and Minnan for shipbuilding, with the remainder used locally to make printing ink.[30] Tingzhou is just far enough south to produce some tropical plants as well; and the fibers of one of these, the coir palm (*Tachycarpus excelsus*, H. Wendl., *zong* 棕), "with leaves as large as cart wheels," were used to make printing brushes.[31] Each tree produced, on average, a catty (about 605 grams) of fiber, valued for its ability to "last for a long time, even under water"[32]—and thus suitable material for the manufacture of frequently inked printing brushes.

But for a publisher-printer, by far the most important requisite was raw material for the production of paper. Fortunately, northern and western Fujian, with their abundant bamboo forests, lay in the heart of one of the most prolific paper-producing areas of south China, encompassing the Min-Gan-Yue border area. Song Yingxing 宋應星 (1587–ca. 1665; *jr* 1615) identified Fujian in particular as the major source for bamboo paper in his *Tiangong kaiwu* 天工開物 (Exploitation of the works of nature; 1637).[33] Although Minbei had become a noted production center even earlier, Minxi developed a booming paper industry in the late Ming and by the mid-nineteenth century rivaled Minbei in the manufacture and export of bamboo paper (called *zhuzhi* 竹紙 or *kouzhi* 扣紙).[34] The 1940 *Changting xianzhi* lists no fewer than twenty-nine different varieties of bamboo, three of which—*maozhu* 貓竹, *fenzhu* 粉竹, *kuzhu* 苦竹—are described as suitable for the manufacture of

---

(1869), 2.93a, 95a, 98a. *Liancheng xianzhi* (1938), 11.4a; and Shaw, *Chinese Forest Trees*, p. 75. The *Changting xianzhi* of 1879 and 1940 both list "mountain pear" as a local tree.

30. Cannon, "Forestry," pp. 49–51.

31. *Changting xianzhi* (1940), 10.13a; and Culver, "The Lumber Industry of Fukien," p. 139.

32. Shaw, *Chinese Forest Trees*, p. 306.

33. Sung Ying-hsing, *Chinese Technology in the Seventeenth Century*, p. 224. Modern scholars support this claim as well; see Xu Jianqing, "Qingdai de zaozhiye."

34. Guo Bocang, *Minchan luyi* (1886), 1.17b.

paper.[35] Indeed, *maozhu* and *kuzhu* (particularly favored because it repels insects) were heavily cultivated in all the four counties linked in Sibao—Ninghua, Changting, Qingliu, and Liancheng—and provided the raw material for the increasingly important paper industry of the area throughout the Qing.[36]

Publishing concerns in the cities of Jiangnan, superbly located at the heart of extensive transportation and market networks, could import paper, hardwood, and ink.[37] Isolated Sibao could not depend on such imports, but did not have to: all the raw materials plus the essential supporting industry of papermaking were locally available. The combination of available materials and a simple and portable technology of block cutting would have been strong inducement for Zou Mengchun and Ma Weihan, having learned the publishing trade as sojourning merchants in Guangdong, to bring the publishing business to Sibao.[38]

## OBTAINING THE WOODBLOCKS
## AND HIRING BLOCK CUTTERS

How did the Zou and Ma publishers organize the process of producing books? Whom did they employ to prepare and cut the blocks, make the ink and paper, print and bind the texts? Other scholars and observers have described the general method of Chinese woodblock printing; here, relying on brief references in the genealogies, interviews with former Sibao printers, and some surviving print tools, I recon-

---

35. *Changting xianzhi* (1940), 10.13b. Guo Bocang, in *Minchan luyi* (1.17a), lists *huangzhu* 篁竹, *mazhu* 麻竹, *mianzhu* 綿竹, and *chijianzhu* 赤梘竹 as also suitable for paper-making. See also Tomasko, "Chinese Handmade Paper," p. 24.

36. See (*Jiajing Daoguang*) *Qingliu xianzhi* (1545; 1991 reprint), p. 28; *Ninghua xianzhi* (1989 reprint of 1684 edition), *j.* 2, p. 125; *Ninghua xianzhi* (1869), 2.101ab; and Huang Ma-jin, *Changting zhishi*, pp. 9–11. See also Daniels, "Jūroku–jūshichi seiki Fukken no take-gama seizō gijutsu," pp. 252–56.

37. Li Bozhong, "Ming Qing Jiangnan de chuban yinshuaye," pp. 106–7.

38. Daniels ("Jūroku–jūshichi seiki Fukken no takegama seisō gijutsu," p. 266) suggests that, for both Jianyang and Sibao, the existence of nearby sources of paper production, offering stable output and stable prices, was essential to the development of the publishing industries.

struct, as fully as possible, the manufacture of texts as it was practiced in Sibao.[39]

The first step in the printing process—the one that required both the heaviest investment of capital and labor and the highest level of skill—was the preparation and cutting of the woodblocks. This all-important task the Sibao publishers seem to have accomplished in various ways: using specialists within the two lineages, hiring professional cutters outside the Zou or Ma lineages, hiring cutter-monks from local temples (or itinerant cutters residing at a local temple), and purchasing blocks from other publishers.

If the legend of Zou Xuesheng is true, then the first blocks to be used in Wuge were, in fact, blocks purchased from other publishers—Zou was said to have brought blocks for children's educational texts from Hangzhou back to his village in 1580. Zou Mengchun, the founder of the first publishing operation in Sibao, is said to have mastered the craft of block cutting in Xingning; on his return to Wuge, he taught the skill to members of his household and other relatives. Ma Weihan, the first publishing-house owner of the Ma lineage and a contemporary of Zou Mengchun, might have brought back with him to Mawu the blocks he had used in his publishing house in Chaozhou, Guangdong; or, like Zou Mengchun, he might have learned the craft himself and taught it to others in Sibao.[40]

Certainly within two decades of the establishment of the first Sibao publishing house, the Ma genealogy reveals a considerable number of block cutters in the Sibao area (apparently not members of the Ma lineage itself) available for hire. Ma Long 龍 (1702–81), in his account of the cutting of the *Sishu jicheng* 四書集成 (Collected commentaries on the

---

39. For a description of xylography, see Tsien, *Paper and Printing*, pp. 196–201. Chia (*Printing for Profit*, chap. 2) provides much useful information about woodblock printing in general and, more specifically, the manufacture of texts in Jianyang. Western observers have left several very interesting accounts of Chinese block cutting and printing in the nineteenth century. For example, see Milne, *Retrospect of the First Ten Years of the Protestant Mission to China*, pp. 222–67; Medhurst, *China*, pp. 103–6; Williams, *The Middle Kingdom* (1882 ed.), vol. 1, part 2, pp. 599–603; and Hunter, *Bits of Old China*, pp. 213–15.

40. For a description of the block-cutting process and the cutting tools, see Barker, *Traditional Techniques in Contemporary Chinese Printmaking*, pp. 26–34.

Four Books),[41] an essential text for examination study, in his grandfather's *shufang* in the late seventeenth century, suggests that the cutters—often a considerable number of them—were "invited" to live and eat with the family while they were working, probably as a means of reducing costs:

That year [1683], at Dongshengzhai 東昇寨, the blocks for the *Sishu jicheng* were carved and the family provided food for several dozen block cutters. Once the rice for the meal was put in the pot, no one was strong enough to lift it, so they had to put the pot on the cooker and then put the rice in, scoop by scoop. When it was cooked, then the workmen were ordered to lift it together. Each dawn, after breakfast, my father [Ma Dingbang, at that point only 12 *sui*] and the old family servant, Laifu 來福, would carry provisions down to Dongshengzhai; Laifu carried a *dan* 石 [picul, about 70 kilograms] of rice, my father a *dan* of vegetables. Then in the afternoon, Laifu carried a *dan* of firewood, and my father a *dan* [about 67 liters] of wine.[42]

This passage suggests that block cutters were easy enough to find in the Sibao area, but does not indicate whether these laborers were hired through a character-cutting shop in one of the four county seats close to Sibao, a band of itinerant cutters who routinely worked in the Sibao area, or members of a local lineage able to specialize in the craft because of the high demand from the Sibao publishing business. Local informants claim that such lineages did much of the cutting for the Sibao publishers. For example, the Wu 巫 lineage of Ninghua was named as a source of professional block cutters; in particular, one Wu Fuduan 巫復端 is said to have worked in Wuge as a cutter before becoming a teacher and frequent contributor to the Zou genealogy.[43]

The *Sishu jicheng* block cutters might also have been hired from a local temple. Ma Quanheng 權亨 (1651–1710), the publisher who commissioned the cutting of that text, had the blocks for another one of his

---

41. This may be the *Sishu jicheng* of the Song scholar Wu Zhenzi 吳眞子; see *Zhongguo guji shanben shumu, Jingbu*, 1: 3.45b (p. 324).

42. *MSDZZP* (1945), *ji* 7, 1.74ab.

43. Interview 10, 4/26/95 (Wuge). I have not been able to find independent evidence that households within this lineage specialized in cutting or that they worked for the Sibao publishers. There is evidence, however, that some lineages specialized in cutting in the early twentieth century; see the reference below to the Shanghang cutting shop staffed by workers from the Jiang and Ding lineages.

most profitable examination texts, the *Sishu beizhi* 四書備旨 (Full purport of the Four Books), carved at Fengrao Temple 豐饒寺 (a temple heavily patronized by the Ma lineage),[44] perhaps by monks who took on outside work in addition to cutting their own temple's religious publications or by a group of itinerant cutters who were lodging at the temple. Here again the employer, as Ma Long notes, was responsible for providing the workers' food.[45]

Contemporary informants state that Zou and Ma publishing houses also employed household members to do the block cutting for their publications. "Both *bendiren* 本地人 and *waidiren* 外地人 would carve; often a publishing house manager himself would help with the cutting of blocks. It was never difficult to find block cutters, either in Sibao or in the surrounding counties."[46] Pointing to the carved rhymed couplets, landscape and ornamental reliefs, and screens that decorate the old eighteenth-and nineteenth-century mansions in the villages, they claim that most *shufang* included some workers who were highly skilled cutters.[47] Many publishing houses apparently included household members who specialized in block cutting. Indeed, some informants claimed that the writing of the *diben* 底本, the manuscript that was pasted on the blocks to be cut, and the cutting of the blocks were important jobs reserved exclusively for the "elders" in the household, and the rest of the labor—printing and binding—was left to the women, children, and hired help. Informants also described some more fluid arrangements, whereby the publishing-house manager himself might contribute his labor to the cutting process and, if the shop got very busy, might ask his poorer relatives to help out with the cutting, paying them at least in part

---

44. According to the 1879 *Changting xianzhi* (27.4a), this temple was moved to Sibao after Ma Ziren 子仁 (Ming) made significant contributions of land to the temple. See also *MSDZZP* (1945), *ji* 7, 1.21ab; and *MSDZZP* (1993), 5.137–39.

45. *MSDZZP* (1945), *ji* 7, 1.74b.

46. Interview 25, 11/9/95 (Wuge).

47. Interview 24, 11/8/95 (Wuge). Some textual evidence suggests that cutting was a valued local craft: the Ma family history contains biographies of two lineage members noted for their skill, although these men are praised for their ability to carve lively and beautiful figures, landscapes, and plants in relief. No mention is made of block cutting, a craft that requires a somewhat different skill. I am grateful to David Barker of the University of Belfast for explaining the different skills required in carving and block cutting.

with room and board.[48] There was a sense that cutting was simple enough that almost anyone could be drafted into service—"The cutting of blocks was quite easy," claimed one man; "it was the sale of books that was hard."[49] Some Sibao texts reveal the involvement of more than one *diben* scribe and cutter, suggesting that tasks were shared out just as these informants claim. (Note, for example, the disparity between the clear and well-cut characters and the crude illustrations in the Sibao editions of *Sanzi jing* [Fig. 10.1] and *Renjia riyong* [Fig. 10.6a]. Surely the characters were written and cut separately from the illustrations, which were probably drawn and cut later by less skilled workers.)

As the industry grew over the course of the late seventeenth and eighteenth centuries, it seems likely that the publishers continued to turn to non-family cutters available in the Sibao area and that the high demand from the Sibao publishers in turn ensured the existence of a large pool of such workers. Indeed, local informants assured me repeatedly that "it was not hard to find block cutters—they were scattered all over," so scattered in fact that "it was hard to remember where they came from."[50] To ease the costs of room and board, several publishing houses might join together to hire several outside cutters to cut titles for each shop. Reliance on in-house cutters or local professionals persisted to the end of Sibao's publishing history. The Linlan yiji tang 林蘭儀記堂, founded in Mawu in the early twentieth century, at first relied on Ma workers to transcribe texts and prepare and cut the blocks. But when the shop moved to Shanghang, they turned to a local cutting-and-printing shop (*keyin dian* 刻印店) which regularly employed men from the local Jiang 蔣 and Ding 丁 lineages. These men were hired on a title-by-title basis, whenever the need for their services arose. The blocks for cutting would either be purchased locally or processed in Mawu and then transported to Shanghang, via the Yin river, a distance of roughly 90 kilometers. The transcription of the text to be carved was supplied by Ma publishing-house scribes.[51]

---

48. Interviews 24, 11/8/95 (Wuge); and 26, 11/11/95 (Wuge).
49. Interview 24, 11/8/95 (Wuge).
50. Ibid.
51. Interviews 4, 10/30/93 (Mawu); 44 and 45, 11/23/95 (Mawu); and 46, 11/24/95 (Mawu).

By the early nineteenth century at the latest, however, when the publishers had to rely more and more on sojourning booksellers to sell their books, other means of obtaining woodblocks were employed as well. Informants claim that these same sojourning booksellers, while working their routes to sell Sibao imprints, often bought already cut woodblocks from publishers in Guangdong and Guangxi for use back home. A descendant of the founder of the Linlan tang 林蘭堂, one of the most successful of the Mawu publishing houses, reported that both his grandfather and his father often exchanged woodblocks with other publishers—on one occasion they procured the blocks for a Linlan tang publication of the *Sanguo tongsu yanyi* 三國通俗演義 (Narrative of the Three Kingdoms) from a commercial publisher in Foshanzhen, Guangdong.[52] Foshanzhen, a publishing center and market town in the late nineteenth and early twentieth century, specialized in the production of popular editions of fiction and medical manuals,[53] both genres that constituted an important part of Sibao's output. The Suwei tang 素位堂 also followed this practice, purchasing blocks cut by publishers in Guangdong or Guangxi. This was why, my informants explained, the house or *tang* name listed on the cover page of many Sibao texts is different from the house name that appears on the text pages—the Zou and Ma publishers, on purchasing these blocks, would cut the seller's house name from the cover block and cut in their own, but would neglect to make the change on the text blocks.[54]

By this time, too, some Sibao publishers had turned for their supply of blocks to a group of professional cutters well outside the Sibao area. These were the craftswomen of Magang, Shunde 順德 county, Guangdong. Managed by a male "boss" (*laoban* 老板), the daughters and wives of local peasants worked at block cutting to supplement the meager returns from farming in this poverty-stricken area. Publishers as distant from Magang as Suzhou commissioned these workers to carve blocks for them; because female labor was inherently less valuable, the blocks were relatively cheap, so cheap that it was worth transporting

---

52. Interview 44, 11/23/95 (Mawu).
53. Zhang Xiumin, *Zhongguo yinshua shi*, p. 557.
54. Interview 10, 4/26/95 (Wuge).

them long distances.[55] Magang was not a market for Sibao publications, but was relatively close to Sibao and to the routes most commonly traveled by the Zou and Ma book merchants. As early as 1809 Zou Kongjia 孔嘉 (1760–1838) and his paternal first cousin Zou Pibin 丕彬 (1767–1845) were traveling to Magang to purchase carved blocks for their household publishing house.[56] Some Zou publishers continued to purchase blocks from Magang throughout the nineteenth and into the early twentieth century.[57]

## CUTTING THE BLOCKS

When the blocks were cut in Sibao or nearby (in, for example, Shanghang), the uncut blocks seem to have been supplied by the publishers, who either purchased blocks ready for cutting or had them prepared by household labor. As mentioned above, the Zou and Ma printers, at least by the late nineteenth century, relied most on camphor wood, indigenous to the area, for their blocks; some informants report, more precisely, that the wood of the "small-leaf camphor" was used for large blocks, and that of pear or jujube—also available locally, at least still in the late nineteenth century—for smaller blocks. Descriptions of the block-preparation process are quite simple: after the large chunks of wood were split and peeled, they were soaked in water and then left to dry slowly in the shade (to avoid warping in the sun). Once dry, they were cut into blocks of the appropriate size, planed flat, and lightly oiled.[58] At this point the block was deemed ready for cutting. The tran-

---

55. Huang Guosheng, "Guangdong Magang nüzi keshu kaosuo." Ye Dehui (*Shulin qinghua, j.* 7, p. 186) claims that male workers were paid 50–60 *wen* per 100 characters in 1875 and 80–90 *wen* later in the century, but the female cutters of Guangdong, Hunan, and Jiangxi were paid as little as 20–30 *wen*. Although the blocks cut by Magang women were disparaged, the few Magang texts that I have seen were quite well cut.

56. Ibid.; *FYZSZP* (1947), 33.63b, 77b.

57. Interviews 25, 11/9/95 (Wuge); and 10, 4/26/95 (Wuge).

58. Interviews 25, 11/9/95 (Wuge); 4, 10/30/93 (Mawu); 85, 4/23/96 (Mawu); and 86, 4/23/96 (Mawu). Tsien, in *Paper and Printing*, describes a similar process: the blocks, after they are cut, are "usually soaked in water for about a month before use but, if they are needed for immediate use, they can be boiled instead; they are then left to dry in a shaded place before being planed on both sides. Vegetable oil may be spread over the block surface, which is then polished with the stems of polishing grass" (pp. 196–

script of the text to be published was written out on thin paper by a *shufang* member, using a "sticky" ink, and then pasted onto the block with *mitang* 米湯, a paste made of rice and water, and smoothed over the block with a flat brush. Once the paste had dried, the paper was scraped off the block, leaving the characters inked in reverse. Then the worker would cut away the wood around the characters, leaving them in relief. Most cutters could cut at least one hundred characters a day; and hired cutters were paid by hundred-character units.[59]

Since the Zou and Ma publishers handled the production of the transcript, they thus controlled the design of the book—the size of the page (consequently the size of block required), the number of columns and characters per page, the use and placement of illustrations—as well. When not in use, blocks were stored at home by the publishing household, placed vertically upright on bookshelves. Although only several hundred blocks survive today, villagers in both Wuge and Mawu can recall a time, early in the twentieth century, when households might hold several storerooms full of woodblocks; a descendant of the Wenhai lou publishing house related that one whole courtyard (*ting* 庭) in his family's house had been devoted to the storage of blocks.[60] The walls of these storerooms and of the publishers' homes—even the walls that lined the streets of both villages—were built extra-thick to protect the blocks and the whole printing operation from fire. In Mawu in particular, some of these "wind and fire walls" or "wind and fire rooms" (*fenghuo qiang* 風火墙, or *fenghuo wu* 屋) still remain (see Figs. 3.2a and b).[61]

---

97). But Chia, in *Printing for Profit* (p. 30), suggests a much longer procedure; blocks were often seasoned "for up to several years" before use. The simpler and shorter process described by my informants may reflect either the lower quality of Sibao woodblocks by the very late nineteenth century—the very earliest period for which my informants could provide reliable information—or simply the loss of any detailed understanding of the process, given the fact that Sibao was producing few new blocks by the second or third decade of the twentieth century, when my informants would have been small children. A few of these informants suggested that the soaking or boiling stage was skipped, but since this step was essential, its omission seems unlikely.

59. Interview 26, 11/11/95 (Wuge). Unfortunately there are no records of what Sibao publishers paid block cutters.

60. Interview 12, 4/27/95 (Wuge).

61. In a survey conducted in 1993, the Committee of the Mawu Ancestral Hall (Mawu Zongci weiyuanhui 马屋宗祠委员会) determined that of the more than 10,000

Fig. 3.2 (a, *left*) "Wind and fire wall" (*fenghuo qiang* 風火牆). (b, *right*) Cross-section of the wall. Photographs by the author.

In summary, Sibao publishers obtained the cut woodblocks for their publications from a variety of sources. When introducing publishing to Wuge and Mawu, the first publishers cut their own blocks (and taught the skill to their family members); they may also have imported cut blocks from established publishing venues. As the industry developed, it is possible, as claimed by local informants, that some Zou and Ma *shufang* households included skilled cutters. But mainly the publishers seem to have hired "outside" professional cutters. These laborers might be drawn from local lineages unrelated to the publishers, whose members specialized in the woodblock-cutting craft—certainly the Sibao publishers could offer them steady employment—or from character-cutting shops located in the market towns and county seats of Minxi. By the early nineteenth century some publishing houses began in addition to purchase cut blocks from other publishers or to hire the women of Magang to cut for them, at least in part to supply the expansion of

---

rooms (*jian* 間) in Mawu today, roughly 40 percent are *fenghuo wu* from the old days (Zeng Ling, *Fujian shougongye fazhan shi*, p. 207).

the Sibao book trade. Extension of the bookselling routes also introduced the Sibao merchants to new suppliers of cut blocks, either the
Foshanzhen publishers or the Magang cutters. The growth of the marketing area thus engaged the Sibao publishers in more impersonal business relationships, in negotiations with distant outsiders rather than the
employment of local craftsmen and family members. Of course, distant
suppliers also meant considerably less control over the most important
part of the production process: the Sibao publishers could neither prescribe the precise format of a text nor supervise the quality of the cutting.

## PRINTING AND BINDING

Once the woodblocks were prepared, the actual printing of the book—
inking the blocks, pressing the paper onto the block, taking the impression by smoothing the paper over the block with a brush—required little skill. It was a task that might be performed by anyone, male or female, adult or child, within the household. Presumably printers learned
on the job, imitating more experienced workers and simply practicing
until they were able to print cleanly and quickly. By the early Qianlong
era one Zou ancestral hall included a structure called a "book-printing
school" (*yinshu xuetang yisuo* 印書學堂一所)—perhaps where novice
block cutters, printers, and binders practiced their crafts—but we do
not know precisely what this phrase meant.[62]

The physical organization of printing in Wuge and Mawu reflects the
household focus of the industry, for the printing "factories" were usually embedded physically in the home. Printing was sometimes done in
ancestral halls; the hall mentioned above also included "two large printing rooms" (*yinfang er dajian* 印房二大間) in the back, with a nearby
small room for preparing printing ink.[63] But more commonly books
were printed within the household.[64] Still today one can see in the

---

62. *FYZSZP* (1947), 29.26b. This was the hall to Huazhong gong 華中公, Zou Shilu.

63. Ibid. The date of this information is not clear, though it appears that the description refers to the arrangement of the hall in 1743.

64. The arrangement in Sibao contrasts with that in Xuwanzhen, where publishing
and bookselling were less tightly linked to the household. There, since printing operations were located in rooms behind bookstores, producing books was physically linked

Fig. 3.3 (a, *above*) Printing rooms along the wall of a courtyard. (b, *opposite*) The ink tub in the center of the courtyard. Photographs by the author.

mansions of former publishing families the "factory" courtyards once devoted to printing: rows of small, dark printing workrooms built around a rectangular courtyard open to the sky (see Fig. 3.3a). A large stone tub in the center of the courtyard held the prepared ink, just a few convenient steps from the printing rooms (Fig. 3.3b).

As the publishing business expanded, however, the larger houses had to construct separate buildings for printing.[65] Thus Zou Kongai 孔愛 (1755–1827) used the profits from his book trade to construct a separate printing building near the family mansion in Wuge;[66] and the 1839 property division record of Ma Cuizhong 萃仲 (1770–1848), manager of the Zaizi tang, refers to a "printing building" (*yinfang yisuo*) "behind the house." (Perhaps the "book-printing school" at the Wuge ancestral temple was another such printing "factory.")

---

to selling them, and both were separate from the family dwelling. See Brokaw, "Fieldwork on the Social and Economic History of Chinese Print Culture," pp. 43–44.

65. Zou Risheng, "Zhongguo sida diaoban yinshua jidi zhi yi," p. 108.

66. *FYZSZP* (1947), 33.60ab.

According to contemporary descriptions of the printing process,[67] the printer would stand inside a workroom at a rectangular table, with a long, thin hole cut a few centimeters from its far edge. A stack of paper, cut so that each sheet was somewhat larger than the dimensions of the woodblock surface, was fixed to the far edge with a wooden bar tied or screwed onto the table; the paper was folded over the far edge of the table, so that it hung below the table surface. The woodblock was fixed between nails in front of the printer. An ink pan was placed to the right of the woodblock and periodically replenished as needed from the ink tub outside. With a round brush made of coir-palm fibers, a *shuapa* 刷耙 (Fig. 3.4), the printer would ink the relief characters on the block evenly, in three or four strokes, and then lift up the first sheet of paper, pull it tight, and lay it over the block, pressing it over the block with a rectangular brush or "print burnisher" (in appearance rather like a long blackboard eraser), a *shuazi* 刷子 or *cazi* 擦子, made by attaching a pad of woven coir-palm fibers to a rectangular piece of

---

67. This summary is based on Interviews 29, 11/12/95 (Wuge); and 44, 11/23/95 (Mawu). See also Zou Risheng, "Zhongguo sida diaoban yinshua jidi zhi yi," p. 108.

Fig. 3.4 Brushes used to ink the woodblocks. Photograph by the author.

hardwood.[68] Then the sheet was folded down into the rectangular hole to dry, leaving the second sheet available for printing.[69] (The ink dried very quickly, so there was little danger that the printed paper would stick together.) To add a little distinction to Sibao's more expensive texts, the cover page might be stamped with a block consisting of a flowered border around a hollow center.

A block did not need to be inked for every page—only after printing two or "a few" pages. To keep track of the number of pages printed, the printer would mark every hundredth page.[70] Estimates of the number of pages that a worker could print in a day vary considerably, from

---

68. Interview 85, 4/23/96 (Mawu). See Barker, *Traditional Techniques in Contemporary Chinese Printmaking*, pp. 46–47, for a description of this tool. Medhurst (*China*, p. 105) also refers to "rubbers" made of "the fibrous parts of a species of palm"; Tsien (*Paper and Printing*, p. 200), perhaps describing a more upscale operation, mentions a brush made of horsehair.

69. Alternatively, a second table was placed beyond the printing table, with a gap left between the two tables. The stack of paper was clamped to the near edge of the second table and the printed paper was dropped between the two tables to dry. See Barker, *Traditional Techniques in Contemporary Chinese Printmaking*, pp. 58–59, for illustrations of how the tables might be set up. My informants suggested that the tables would be aligned front to back, not side to side, as shown in Barker's figures.

70. Interviews 70, 12/6/95 (Wuge); 61, 12/3/95 (Wuge); and 44, 11/23/95 (Mawu).

several hundred up to five or six thousand (the informant who mentioned this last figure emphasized that it would require a *very* hard day's work).[71] A likely estimate for an experienced printer, working steadily, would be two to three thousand pages.[72]

Printing was typically done by the women of the household, although children might also participate—one informant recalled that his job, as a young boy, had been to ink the blocks in between printings.[73] Once the sheets of paper had dried, they had to be separated, the folio pages folded in half with the printed side facing out, and assembled into *juan* 卷 (scrolls, or chapters) and then whole *ce* 冊 (volumes). The stacks of pages would be put into a book press (*shuzha* 書榨) and compressed as tightly as possible; a large press was used for texts that were to be transported for sale, so that they would be as compact as possible, allowing the book merchants to carry as many texts as they could; a smaller one was used for books sold locally. While still fixed in the press, the pages might also be trimmed—the one book press surviving in Sibao today includes a sliding blade for this purpose (see Figs. 3.5a and b). Removed from the press, the stack of pages was then pierced with an awl in two places along the border of the cut edge, and one paper twist, a strip of paper twisted into the shape of nail, with one end left untwisted (the head of the "nail"), was inserted into each hole to keep the pages together—the head of the "paper nail" (*zhiding* 紙釘) kept the twist from falling out (see Figs. 10.2 and 10.5). Covers made of heavier paper, often a vermilion-colored paper that was insect repellent, were placed at the top and bottom of each *ce*, the volume was pressed

---

71. Interviews 26, 11/11/95 (Wuge); and 44, 11/23/95 (Mawu).

72. Here I am following Tsuen-hsuin Tsien's estimate in *Paper and Printing* (p. 201). Tsien cites Matteo Ricci's estimate of 1,500 and John F. Davis's similar figure of 2,000 sheets per day but also mentions that "others" have suggested 6,000–8,000 sheets per ten-hour day. Medhurst (*China*, p. 105) gives 3,000 sheets a day, but Harold E. Gorst (*China*, p. 102) gives a startlingly high figure, stating that "a skilled artisan can turn out 10,000 copies of the same sheet in one day." All these estimates assume the use of more than one block in the course of a day, because the blocks held up longer if allowed to "rest" for several hours after the printing of 200–300 sheets; see Chia, *Printing for Profit*, pp. 30–31.

73. Interview 36, 11/14/95 (Wuge).

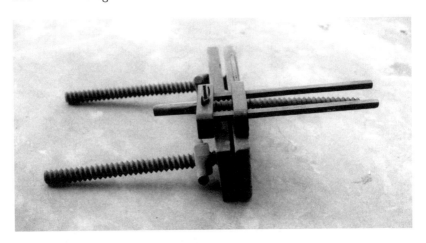

Fig. 3.5 (a, *top*) Book press. (b, *bottom*) The press included a cutting blade used to trim the edges of the books. Photographs by the author.

again, and then the whole was sewn together with thread.[74] A label bearing the title of the book was then pasted on the front cover. Binding, like printing, was largely women's work. Several informants recalled that their mothers or grandmothers, after completing their work around the house, would devote evenings to the folding and arranging of pages and the binding of *ce*.[75]

The tools for printing and binding were all, according to present-day informants, made locally. Fibers of the indigenous coir palm were easily and cheaply available in the local village markets, and members of the *shufang* made the brushes. The book presses, the most complex bit of machinery required, were made either by *shufang* members or by local craftsmen and were passed down through the family just like the printing workrooms, woodblocks, and brushes.[76]

## INK

Ink was obviously required in abundance. Two different types were used: a relatively high-quality ink reputedly from Huizhou, Anhui, and printing ink. The "Huizhou ink" (*huimo* 徽墨) was used to write the manuscripts of the texts to be pasted on the blocks; its slightly oily texture made it stick more firmly to the block. Sticks of this ink could be purchased from sojourning merchants or, most recently in the late nineteenth century, at the market in Shanghang county seat, conveniently located on the Sibao southern bookselling route.[77] Printing ink (*yinmo* 印墨), of lower quality, was required in much larger quantities. According to contemporary informants, many of the Sibao publishing houses, at least in the late nineteenth century, produced their own printing ink; one member of the family would be assigned to make it for the shop. Sibao seems to have developed a group of households specializing in the production of ink for the printing industry.

---

74. Some informants claimed that Sibao imprints were covered in silk, specifically *huxiang* 湖緗, a kind of silk imported from Hunan. Although this silk was a common import into Minxi in the Qing, I have never seen a Sibao imprint covered in silk; all extant volumes are covered with paper and sewn with cotton thread.

75. Interview 26, 11/11/95 (Wuge).

76. Interviews 24, 11/8/95 (Wuge); and 44, 11/23/95 (Mawu).

77. Interviews 14, 4/28/95 (Wuge); and 4, 10/30/93 (Mawu).

Pine, the necessary raw material for printing ink, grew abundantly on the hills of Sibao until as recently as the middle of this century. According to an informant who had worked in the printing industry in the early twentieth century, one cut a hole in the trunk as close to the roots as possible and placed a lamp or torch (*songming* 松明 or *songguang* 松光) against it, to draw out the resin. The tree then would be felled and chopped and the slabs placed on a low platform over which an old wok or empty oil tin was suspended. The pine wood was set on fire and the smoke caught in the wok or tin. Alternatively, a pine-wood fire was set under a stove with one burner blocked, so that the smoke would be forced into an overturned wok placed above a second burner. The caked soot (*songyan* 松煙) thus collected would then be scraped off and ground to a powder with a stone mortar and pestle. This soot, or ink-black (*moyan* 墨煙), was the basic ingredient of printing ink and could be stored in powder form.[78] When needed for printing, it was mixed with thin rice paste or glue made of ox tendons, to make it somewhat adhesive. For more expensive texts only, a "panful" of tea oil (*chayou* 茶油, a local product)[79] and a little hot boiled water (about 2–3 *liang* 兩, roughly a tenth of a liter or a little more) might be added to the solution for extra glossiness and smoothness.[80]

To be sure, the ink-making process described above would not have produced enough to supply the Sibao publishing industry or even a single publishing house in its prime. It contrasts sharply with the more elaborate method described in Song Yingxing's *Tiangong kaiwu*, in which a bamboo chamber of over one hundred *chi* 尺 (roughly 32 meters) was constructed to catch the soot from burning logs.[81] The procedure de-

---

78. Since the Minxi area produced *tong* and rapeseed oil as well as pine, ink might also have been made from lampblack produced in roughly the same way, although none of my informants mentioned the use of oil. For the production of lampblack, see Tsien, *Paper and Printing*, pp. 241–42.

79. Wang Shimao, *Minbu shu*, 32b (p. 48).

80. Interview 46, 11/24/95 (Mawu). See also Tsien, *Paper and Printing*, pp. 242–43; and Chia, *Printing for Profit*, pp. 29–30.

81. Sung Ying-hsing, *Chinese Technology in the Seventeenth Century*, pp. 285–87; and Tsien, *Paper and Printing*, p. 241. The process described by Song—and indeed the processes described in most texts on ink—was primarily for the production of high- or medium-quality ink used in painting and calligraphy or ordinary writing. Song states that it was only

scribed by Sibao informants was likely used by smaller publishing houses with limited output or was practiced only when the industry was in decline and the demand for ink had shrunk. Perhaps, too, it was employed by some publishing houses to supplement other supplies of ink.

Most publishing houses appear to have purchased ink soot in bulk from producers outside Wuge and Mawu, frequently from the same factories that supplied their paper. One informant explained that paper factories, in particular those in Guihua county and Shankeng 珊坑 (in Changting), often made printing ink on the side;[82] both the process and the equipment were simple, and the pine logs easily available to papermakers. The making of inkblack could be conveniently combined with the longer and slower process of papermaking—it could be done many times over, for example, while workers were waiting for the bamboo fibers to steep in lime. Inkblack produced by papermakers might be sold at the Wuge periodic market, but more often publishing-house workers would transport it themselves, in large woven bamboo baskets, *lou* 簍, from its point of manufacture. Each basket could hold five to six (at the very most, ten) *jin* 斤 of soot; one man could carry four to five *lou* or twenty to fifty *jin* (12.1 to 30.3 kilograms) on a shoulder pole at one time. At the publishing house the ink soot was powdered and combined with the rice paste or glue. [83] The ancestral hall dedicated to Zou Shilu, also the site of a "book-printing school," included "one small room for pounding ink soot" (*lei moyan yi xiaojian* 擂墨煙一小間), where this process was completed.[84]

## PAPER AND THE SIBAO PUBLISHING INDUSTRY

Paper was one of the few materials that had to be purchased ready-made by the publishing houses. Fortunately, as mentioned in Chapter 2, Sibao was in the heart of a paper-producing area; by the Qing Tingzhou

---

the "low-grade soot" from the first two sections of the bamboo chamber that would be "further pounded and ground by printers and used [in printing books]."

82. Interviews 19, 5/1/95 (Mawu); and 44, 11/23/95 (Mawu).

83. Interviews 38, 11/15/95 (Wuge); and 44, 11/23/95 (Mawu).

84. *FYZSZP* (1947), 29.26b.

was a major exporter of paper. According to the 1879 *Changting xianzhi*: "People of the county rent mountains, plant bamboo, and establish factories to manufacture paper; it is considered the best of all Ting products."[85] Many of the smaller paper factories were probably handicraft operations that supplemented the agricultural income of peasant households, but the much larger concerns, run by managers and staffed by outside laborers, were devoted exclusively to paper manufacture.[86] Among the villages in four different counties that constituted Sibao were numerous papermaking sites: Shankeng, Maluowei 馬羅尾, Zhuangxia 莊下, Nanchaikeng 南柴坑, Jingkou 井口, and Shibei 石背 in Changting county; Daohu 到湖, Dakengyuan 大坑原, and Zhangdijing 張地井 in Liancheng; and Hucun 湖村, Anle 安樂, Caofang 曹坊, Liufang 劉坊, and Zhiping 治平 in Ninghua. Beituan 北團, on the western border of Sibao, was also a papermaking center.[87] Many of these sites were home to numerous papermaking concerns—the Sibao informants estimated that there were over eighty paper mills (*zhicao* 紙槽) in Anle and over one hundred in Hucun in the late Qing and early Republican period.[88] They also suggest that, by the later decades of Sibao printing history at least, the Zou and Ma printers favored paper produced in Shankeng (Changting); Hucun, Anle, Zhiping, and Shaxian (Ninghua); and Gutian 姑田 (Liancheng). Certain sites specialized in certain types of paper—Gutian and Zhiping were sources of the

---

85. *Changting xianzhi* (1879), 31.69b.
86. See Xu Jianqing, "Qingdai de zaozhiye," pp. 141–42. The manager of a factory in Changting that still makes paper in the traditional fashion described his family's Republican-era paper factory as just such an operation: the thirteen laborers were hired from outside the household, and the family derived its income from the factory. The family owned one mountain; if that failed to supply sufficient bamboo, they would rent a mountain or purchase prepared materials (interview in Shangchi cun 上赤村, Anjie xiang 庵杰鄉, Changting county, 12/18/95).
87. Interviews 14, 4/28/95 (Wuge); and 24, 11/8/95 (Wuge). Mao Xing, "Ning Ting zhiye lishi yuanyuan," pp. 72–73; Liu Zhenbang and Qiu Hengkuan, "Jiefangqian Ninghua gongye gaishu," pp. 32–33; Mao Xing, "Jianguo qian Changting shangye maoyi linzhao," pp. 35–36; Mao Xing, "Changtingxian gailiang zhi manhua," pp. 92–93; Zou Zibin, "'Lianggong zaozhi Tingzhou fu,'" pp. 102–6; and "Liancheng shougong zaozhiye de qiyuan, fazhan he zhanwang," pp. 100–103.
88. On the Anle paper industry, see Liao Shiyao, "Anlexiang de chuantong zaozhi yu xushi jingji."

higher-quality *xuan* 宣 and *yukou* 玉扣 papers, respectively; Anle was the source for the cheaper *maobian* 毛邊 paper used most commonly in Sibao printing.[89]

Methods of procuring the paper varied. The biography of Ma Ding-bang in the Ma genealogy states that, as a young man (15 *sui*) starting a household publishing house, he "went to the mountains to buy paper, which he carried back himself," suggesting that publishers with little capital acted as their own purchasing and shipping agents. During the period of prosperity for the Wuge book market in the late eighteenth century, paper was sold in the market there by paper brokers (*zhihang* 紙行) who had purchased it from paper factories in Changting county.[90] Contemporary informants, reporting more recent nineteenth- and early twentieth-century practice, relate that *shufang* heads ordered paper from paper brokers in four places "where there were plenty of paper brokers"—Liancheng,[91] Beituan, Gutian,[92] and Changting—or, less frequently, in Shanghang.[93] Or, as one informant explained, a publishing house might order directly from a paper factory; his father, manager of the Yijing tang 翼經堂 in the early twentieth century, would simply "write a letter ordering the paper, either *maobian* or *yukou*, and the factory would send it."[94] In other words, either buyer or seller might undertake the shipping.[95] One informant reports that his family's publishing house hired porters to carry the paper from Anle to Mawu; each carrying a load of up to one *dan* 擔 (one thousand sheets, weighing about 60.5 kilograms), a porter could complete the round-trip journey of roughly eighty *li* (40 kilometers) in a day.[96] Local branch publishing

---

89. Interviews 1, 10/27/93 (Wuge); 42, 11/19/95 (Wuge); and 4, 10/30/93 (Mawu). See notes 104 and 107 to this chapter for a discussion of the terminology.

90. Interviews 24, 11/8/95 (Wuge); and 26, 11/11/95 (Wuge).

91. An entire street of Liancheng county seat was devoted to the shops of paper brokers or *zhihang* (Lin Shuimei, "Shufang yong zhi zhi yi," p. 30).

92. Interview 36, 11/14/95 (Wuge).

93. Interviews 33, 11/14/95 (Wuge); and 44, 11/23/95 (Mawu).

94. Interview 55, 12/1/95 (Mawu).

95. Interviews 25, 11/9/95 (Wuge); 33, 11/14/95 (Wuge); 36, 11/14/95 (Wuge); and 55, 12/1/95 (Mawu).

96. Interview 4, 10/30/93 (Mawu). Two other sources support the considerable variation in purchasing and delivery arrangements described by my Sibao informants. The *Fujian Changting zaozhi diaocha*, a 1946 report by Chen Zhikun on the Changting

houses, established in the early twentieth century in Changting and Shanghang, had perhaps the easiest access to paper. The Linlan yiji tang used paper from Zhiping; it was shipped by river to a Linlan branch shop in Changting and thence to the Linlan yiji tang in Shanghang. Each boat typically carried thirty "loads" (*tiao* 挑 or *dan*) of paper (that is, about 30,000 sheets, weighing 1.82 metric tons). [97] In more distant Zhangzhou, the Suwei shanfang 素位山房 bought its paper in the city from a paper shop whose primary trade was the export of paper from Liancheng county to Singapore, Malaysia, and the Philippines.[98]

It is probable that printers developed special relationships with specific paper factories or paper brokers very early in the development of the publishing industry. Certainly such arrangements obtained at other, roughly contemporaneous, commercial publishing sites in south China.[99] When Sibao publishing began to decline in the twentieth century, members of *shufang* households occasionally found work in the paper industry, either as merchants or laborers, to pay in part for the paper needed by their publishing houses. "When Sibao was wealthy," one informant claimed, "we bought paper from the paper-manufacturing areas, but when the publishing business declined, there were too many people and not enough work. So about 20 percent of the population went to work in the paper factories."[100] One informant, when his family's publishing house, the Fuxing tang 福興堂, was failing, became a paper broker, buying paper from factories in Maluowei and selling it in Changting;[101] two others in a similar situation worked for a paper factory in Anle that

---

paper industry, describes a range of relationships between paper-factory owners (*zhi caohu* 紙槽户) and sojourning merchants and brokers but suggests that the paper brokers dominated the trade at least through the Republican period. The manager of the Xiantong Paper Factory 賢通纸厂 in Shangchi village, Anjie township, Changting, also described a flexible system in which paper factories might sell either to brokers or directly to merchants or printers (interview in Shangchi, Anjie, Changting, 12/18/95).

97. Interviews 45, 11/23/95 (Mawu); and 46, 11/24/95 (Mawu).

98. Interview 68, 12/5/95 (Wuge).

99. This practice was reported in Longhui 隆回, Hunan, a paper-producing area that supplied local publishing and *nianhua* 年畫 industries (Interview 10, 8/30/2000 [Longhui]).

100. Interview 1, 10/27/93 (Wuge).

101. Interview 26, 11/11/95 (Wuge).

supplied their family publishing houses, the Yijing tang and the Shizhong chang 時中昌, with paper.[102] Sibao paper workers might take 40 or 50 percent of their wages in cash and the balance in paper for the publishing houses back home.[103]

The bamboo paper used for Sibao imprints, at least by the late nineteenth and early twentieth centuries, was of relatively low quality—coarse, quick to yellow and to crumble, with many impurities. Paper types are difficult to categorize, for, as Guo Bocang pointed out in his late nineteenth-century study of Fujian products, "The names for different types [of bamboo paper] vary from factory to factory."[104] Sibao informants consistently referred to the following different types of paper: *xuan, dalian* 大連 (or *lianshi* 連史, *liansi* 連四, "fourfold"), *maobian, yukou*, and, occasionally, *changhang* 長行. The finer *xuan* and *dalian* papers, processed ("boiled") papers produced most notably in Gutian in Liancheng (although Gutian also produced lower-quality paper),[105] were not used to print texts. Instead, Sibao publishing houses almost always purchased the cheaper, lower-quality *maobian*, or unprocessed ("raw," i.e., unboiled), paper, commonly seen as suitable for "popular" (*minjian* 民間) use.[106] Sibao informants generally used the term *maobian* to refer to the cheaper unprocessed paper, suitable for primers and children's texts, and the term *yukou* to designate the (relatively) higher-quality paper appropriate for finer texts, like novels or editions of the Classics. In fact, however, *yukou* and *changhang* papers are types of *maobian*, differing by weight and size of sheet, *yukou* being heavier,

---

102. Interviews 38, 11/15/95 (Wuge); and 39, 11/15/95 (Wuge).

103. Interview 1, 10/27/93 (Wuge).

104. Guo Bocang, *Minchan luyi*, 1.17b. The terms that Guo lists in fact bear no relationship to those used by the Sibao informants. He states that another name for bamboo paper is *kouzhi* 扣紙, but makes no reference to either *maobian* or *yukou* paper. What he identifies as "the category of *dakou* 大扣 [papers], all of which are inferior—thick and susceptible to insects" may include the *maobian* and *yukou* papers named by Sibao residents. *Dakou* papers are "used by contemporary *shufang* [possibly in Sibao] to print school books" (1.17b).

105. Wu Hongyou, "Lüetan Liancheng tuzhi he dalianzhi ji qi jingying qingkuang," p. 81.

106. "Liancheng shougong zaozhiye de qiyuan, fazhan he zhanwang," p. 101; and Mao Xing, "Liancheng 'gonghe' zaozhi shihua," p. 55.

thicker, and larger; and *changhang* lighter, thinner, and smaller in sheet size.[107]

In any case, neither *yukou* nor *changhang* (in Sibao parlance, *maobian*) unprocessed papers are of particularly high quality, reflecting a general trend in bamboo paper–making, at least in much of south China in the nineteenth century. Christian Daniels, in his study of bamboo-paper manufacture, has stated that, as early as the sixteenth century, paper-makers developed methods to shorten and simplify the process, largely by decreasing the number of times the fibers were "cooked" to elimi-nate impurities, or by eliminating that step altogether. Notwithstanding the scantiness of the evidence about paper manufacture in the seven-teenth and eighteenth centuries, it appears that this shortened and sim-plified method was not widely employed until the nineteenth century, when greater demand provided a strong economic incentive to simplify and shorten the manufacturing process.[108] Yang Lan describes a pro-cess including only one boiling of the pulp—in contrast to the two boilings in Song Yingxing's seventeenth-century *Tiangong kaiwu*[109]—in his account of Tingzhou papermaking in the late 1870s:

This is the method [of making paper]: First, cut the bamboo and peel away the skin, leaving the white fibers. Place these in a pool and add lime. After leaving it for a long time, remove the fibers and dry them in the sun. If the fibers are left in the sun for a long time, they will become white and fine; if for a short time, they will become coarse and oozing. These fibers are popularly called

---

107. *Kou* 扣 is the local measure term for the width of the paper. Interviews 24, 11/8/95 (Wuge); 14, 4/28/95 (Wuge); and 50, 11/25/95 (Mawu); Huang Majin, *Changting zhishi*, pp. 82–91. The confusion seems to derive from the fact that, over time, the size of *changhang* paper sheets—originally smaller than *yukou* sheets—was increased to match that of *yukou* paper. At that point, the name of the *changhang* paper was changed to *da-guang* 大廣. Then, however, the term *daguang* fell into disuse, and that kind of paper—thinner and lighter than *yukou* paper, but now cut in roughly the same size sheets—came to be called *maobian* paper. See Mao Xing, "Ning Ting zhiye lishi yuanyuan," p. 72; and Guan Ming, "Fujian Changting zaozhi jishushi chukao," pp. 149–50.

108. Daniels, "Jūroku–jūshichi seiki Fukken no takegama seisō gijutsu," pp. 273–85.

109. Sung, *Chinese Technology in the Seventeenth Century*, pp. 224–26. In the process Song describes, the bamboo is first soaked for one hundred days in water, then pounded and mixed with a lime solution, then cooked over boiling water for eight days. The fibers are then washed and subjected to another few rounds of cooking, straining, and wash-ing before being pounded into pulp.

*zhuma* 竹麻. When it comes time to make the paper, pile up stones to a height of about 2.5 meters and a width of about 3.2 meters and place a large pot within the stones. Place the bamboo fibers in the pot and mix in lime and boil, so that the bamboo fibers are softened. In a nearby stream, use stones to divide the flow into two channels. Speed up the flow on one side [by using a water wheel], making the water circulate. Pound the fibers with a water mill (*shuique* 水碓) and pestle to separate the fibers. Lift the pulp up from the water in a filter, at the same time mixing the solution [so that the fibers are evenly distributed] and float to the top. While grasping a bamboo screen, push and pull with your hands so that the paper forms a sheet. Overturn the screen onto a board, piling up the paper. Crease a corner of each sheet, so as to make the sheets easy to separate and place on the fire to dry. For the paper-drying oven, dig a hole in the ground and then build two walls, leaving a hole between them for the warm air to pass through [when the two sides are warmed by the fire]. Stick the paper on the wall to dry—it will dry quickly.[110]

But the 1879 edition of the *Changting xianzhi* outlines an even briefer process, entailing no cooking at all:

The people of the county cut bamboo and put it into a pool, steeping it in a solution with lime for several tens of days. After the bamboo has been softened, they remove the skin, take out the fibers, and stamp on them until they have liquefied. Then they put [the pulp] in a trough of clean, clear water, and with a filter screen draw the pulp out of the water to make a sheet of paper. There are two different sizes of paper; the large size is called *qianbian* 乾邊 or *maobian*. The raw materials for it are not boiled.[111]

This description corresponds roughly to that provided by two Wuge residents who worked in Anle paper factories in the early twentieth century;[112] and it is the process described in the 1946 report on paper-

---

110. Yang Lan, *Linting huikao*, 4.15a–16a; and Daniels, "Jūroku–jūshichi seiki Fukken no takegama seisō gijutsu," p. 279.

111. *Changting xianzhi* (1879), 31.69b; cited in Daniels, "Jūroku–jūshichi seiki Fukken no takegama seisō gijutsu," p. 283.

112. Another Wuge resident and former paper-factory worker reiterated: "First, the bamboo was cut and peeled, then placed in a 'lime pool' (*shihui chi* 石灰池). After forty days the bamboo was rinsed and the pool cleaned, and then the bamboo was put back in the pool, not now in a lime solution but in clear water. After it soaked for another forty days, two workers stamped it into pulp. The pulp was put into a large wooden tub and left again for forty days. Using a bamboo screen (*lian* 簾), a worker lifted up the sheets of paper, then stacked them two to three *cun* 寸 (5 to 7.5 cm) high. Then the

making in Fujian by the Chinese Industrial Cooperative Association (Zhongguo gongye hezuo xiehui 中國工業合作協會).[113] Indeed, this same process—including the workers trampling the bamboo to separate the fibers (rather than pounding the fibers apart by machine), a method distinctive to Changting—is followed today in paper factories in the county.[114]

It seems that the heightened demand for paper encouraged the reduction or omission of "boilings," an expedient that made for coarser, quicker-to-produce, hence more abundant and cheaper paper.[115] It is likely that the Sibao publishers themselves, their business growing over the eighteenth and nineteenth centuries, pressured papermakers to increase productivity. And by the second half of the nineteenth century, paper had become an important export, for Changting county in particular. As the overseas Chinese population expanded significantly in Southeast Asia in the decades of the 1870s, 1880s, and 1890s, the demand for bamboo paper skyrocketed; between 1892 and 1901 Tingzhou paper production increased fourfold in response to heightened demand from Hong Kong, Macao, Thailand, Burma, Singapore, and the Philippines (through the port of Shantou 汕頭 in Guangdong).[116] A brisk domestic trade in Minxi paper also passed through Shantou and thence to the river ports of Shicheng 石城 or Guangchang 廣昌 in Jiangxi.[117] These demands, plus the popular nature of Sibao publications, may help to explain the diminishing quality of the paper used to print Sibao editions.

The number of boilings was not the only determinant of paper quality: also critical were the age of the bamboo stalks, the amount of lime in the solution, the care taken to expel impurities in the "trampling"

---

water was pressed out of the stack, the sheets were peeled off, and baked dry." It was the informant's task to "bake" the paper (*bei zhi* 焙紙) by hanging the wet sheets on a heated wall (Interview 39, 11/15/95 [Wuge]).

113. Chen Zhikun, *Fujian Changting zaozhi diaocha*, pp. 29–30. Cf. note 62 to this chapter.

114. Interview: Shangchi cun, Anjie xiang, Changting, 95/12/18.

115. Daniels, "Jūroku–jūshichi seiki Fukken no takegama seizō gijutsu," p. 281.

116. Ibid., p. 284; for the trade in *lianshi zhi*, made in Liancheng and sold in Southeast Asia, see Lin Shuimei, "Shufang yong zhi zhi yi," p. 31.

117. Zheng Guangchang, "Ninghua mingyou techanpin," p. 46. On the production of *maobian* paper in Fujian today, see Polastron, *Le papier*, p. 37.

process, and the thickness of the sheets. One modern scholar of the Changting paper industry has identified twelve different grades of *yukou* paper and eight of *maobian* paper.[118] Extant Sibao imprints from the nineteenth and early twentieth centuries show considerable variety in the quality of paper used by the Zou and Ma printers. Some texts, mostly editions of the Classics, were printed on paper that has remained relatively white. But other texts, most notably the more recent imprints of children's primers like *Sanzi jing*, were printed on brittle and coarse paper that has yellowed severely—"browned," even—over the years.

Paper was purchased in large sheets the size of a door leaf (*menshan zhi* 門扇紙), by the *dao* 刀, a unit of one hundred sheets,[119] the *ming* 命 (500 sheets), or the *tiao* or *dan* (1,000 sheets). One *dao* of the lightest, most commonly used paper, the *maobian* paper, weighed about eight *jin* 斤 (about 4.8 kilograms, although there were different qualities and presumably different weights within this category), whereas an equal measure of the heavier, better-quality paper (*yukou* paper) was about ten *jin* (6 kilograms).[120] One informant, who had worked at his family's small publishing house in the early twentieth century, estimated that *maobian* paper ranged in price from two to four dollars (*yuan*) per *dao*; his publishing house, the Linlan tang, at that point could not afford to purchase the higher-quality *yukou* paper.[121]

In the publishing houses workers would cut the large sheets, a *dao* at a time, into eight, twelve, eighteen, or twenty-four sections (*kai* 開) depending on the size of the page required.[122] This task required a special knife, a folded sheet as a model, and considerable strength; one former publishing-house worker described it as the hardest of the printing jobs,

---

118. Huang Majin, *Changting zhishi*, pp. 85–91.

119. Huang Majin (ibid.) identifies a *dao* as two hundred sheets of paper, but he is referring to a modern measure. As with the names of paper types and measurement of paper sizes, there seems to have been a great deal of variation in terminology over both space and time. I report here the definitions used by the Sibao informants.

120. Interview 26, 11/11/95 (Wuge).

121. Interview 44, 11/23/95 (Mawu).

122. Interviews 26, 11/11/95 (Wuge); and 44, 11/23/95 (Mawu). These differences are generally reflected in the paper inventory for the later Sibao printshops, which notes after most titles the size of the paper ("large," *da* 大; "medium," *zhong* 中; or "small," *xiao* 小) to be used.

and it was always assigned to men.[123] The twenty-four-cut paper, which made a page measuring roughly 11 cm wide by 16 cm high, seems, at least by the late nineteenth century, to have been the most popular size, although some examples survive of eighteen- and twelve-cut texts and one of an eight-cut text, this last being one of Sibao's finer productions (see Fig. 12.5).[124]

## THE PUBLISHING SEASON

One of the major tasks of the *shufang* manager was to coordinate the printing process, from the production of blocks and purchase of paper and ink to the final printing, pressing, and binding of the texts. In Sibao the timing of most of these tasks was dictated by the strong seasonal nature of the demand for texts, or, rather, for the sorts of texts that dominated Sibao's stock. Since the staples of the Zou and Ma publishers were school texts and examination materials, most of their books had to be ready for wholesale and retail sale before the beginning of the school year, after Chunjie 春節 (Spring Festival or New Year's).

To be sure, the publishing houses, particularly the larger ones, printed year-around; certainly works of fiction, fortune-telling manuals, medical guides, and household encyclopedias, also important parts of Sibao's output, enjoyed a steady, consistent demand.[125] But most informants agreed that the tenth, eleventh, and twelfth months were the busy season for publishers as they rushed to meet the demand for primers and other educational texts to supply both local schools and sojourning book merchants who would shortly return for New Year's before setting out again on their sales routes. Fortunately, the busy season for printing dovetailed nicely with the peak periods of paper production in Minxi; papermaking was completed in late fall and early winter. Woodblocks had to be cut well before this time, of course, but with many different pools of cutters available, the Sibao printers were

---

123. Interview 46, 11/24/95 (Mawu).

124. See the discussion of Zou Shengmai's *Shuhua tongzhen* in Chapter 12.

125. Interview 29, 11/12/95 (Wuge). This informant said that children's books were printed toward the end of the year, and "more sophisticated" texts for literati once the school rush was over.

unlikely to have trouble getting prepared blocks. The heaviest pressure fell on the workers doing the printing and binding. Informants report, in fact, that their New Year's celebration was often quite abbreviated; and the Wenhai lou routinely postponed the celebration to ensure that all the printing was done in time.[126]

It is impossible to discover what constituted an adequate stock of school texts in the early periods of Sibao publishing. One informant describing the Republican-era book trade, however, suggested that just before the beginning of the schoolyear, his shop, the Linlan zhunji shuju 林蘭准記書局 in Changting (which specialized in school texts), wanted to have 2,000–3,000 copies of *Sanzi jing*, several thousand copies of *Renjia riyong* 人家日用 (Everyone, everyday), a glossary for the use of Hakka communities, and 800–1,000 copies total of a variety of other primers and textbooks—and this at a time when these old-style books were supposedly competing with modern textbooks.[127] This same man claimed that his small publishing house, relying on household members and two hired female laborers, could print and bind one hundred copies of the *Sanzi jing* in a day.[128] Presumably, then, this labor force would have put in several months of hard work to produce a full stock of primers in time for the school season. By about the third month of the year, the pressure would have eased, and the publishing houses could return to a reduced production schedule, conveniently just when the labor supply was shrinking, as agriculture demanded the attention of the printshop workers.

---

126. Interview 29, 11/12/95 (Wuge).

127. Interview 86, 4/23/96 (Mawu). The Linlan zhunji tang, because it specialized in the production of school texts, probably had to stock an unusually high number. The Wenhai lou account book, because it divides its inventory into lots, each of which might have been designed for a different location (and because it is not clear whether or not the lots are supplementing existing bookstore inventories), is an ambiguous source for the size of a bookstore's stock. But its evidence is nonetheless suggestive: the largest number of copies (300 each) pertain to two examination preparation guides, and the next largest (100 copies) to *Zengguang xianwen* 增廣賢文, a very popular primer.

128. Interview 44, 11/23/95 (Mawu). If the edition in question is the cheap, 11-folio pamphlet-like version common in early twentieth-century Sibao, then 1,100 folio pages would have to be printed fairly early in the day, to allow time for binding. Presumably the printers would work on another text while the binders did their work.

## Conclusion

The process of book manufacture in Wuge and Mawu, from the preparation of the blocks to the binding of the volumes, conforms, at least in its general outlines, to the very few descriptions of woodblock printing that survive from the late Ming and Qing. Zou and Ma informants insisted that there were no changes in technology or printing procedures over the course of their families' printing history. If that is so, then the relatively simple procedures described by contemporary informants for block preparation and ink manufacture and the preference for a labor force of family members or cheap female hirelings probably reflect a considered system for keeping production costs low[129] and time of production relatively short, natural goals for commercial publishers with little capital to invest.

In sum, the Zou and Ma publishers "specialized" in the manufacture of cheap texts, profiting from their ability to keep labor costs down through the employment of household members as well as from the assured popularity of their offerings and the lack of competition in poor hinterland areas. It may well be that the quality of Sibao texts declined over the last century of the industry and that the surviving texts—almost all from that period and poorly produced—are not representative of Sibao at its height. We have seen that paper quality almost certainly declined, which would, of course, have affected the look and durability of Sibao's imprints. And the slow overall decline in the publishing industry in the mid- and late nineteenth century might have made burdensome even meager labor costs, thus encouraging greater compromises in block preparation and cutting quality.

Striking here are the extraordinary efficiencies of Sibao book production in the nineteenth and early twentieth centuries. Efforts to reduce costs were made at virtually every stage of production, by simpli-

---

129. Reliable information about production costs is hard to come by, but informants knowledgeable about the early twentieth-century Sibao book trade suggest that the publishers were able to profit by keeping these costs (*chengben* 成本) down. One informant reported that, once the blocks for the *Sanzi jing* were cut, for example, each copy could be produced at a cost of 2 *fen* 分, or roughly 20 copper cash. Similarly, the *Zengguang xianwen* cost 5 *fen* (50 copper cash) (Interview 44, 11/23/95 [Mawu]). See Chapter 4 of this book for a discussion of production costs relative to wholesale and retail prices.

fying processes and by relying heavily on household labor (and, if that was not available, cheap hired labor, like that of the Magang cutters) and on the hard practice of sojourning. Born of economic desperation and fortuitous access to key raw materials, the publishing industry remained profitable only as long as production costs could be kept down. The struggle to do so shaped not only the organization of the trade but also the very nature of the texts the Zou and Ma produced.

# FOUR

---

## *The Structure of the Sibao*
## *Publishing Industry*

THE PRECEDING CHAPTER summarized what little is
known about the physical manufacture of books in Sibao, about the
sources of the materials used, the organization of the printing process,
and the nature of the labor force. This chapter examines the management of the Sibao publishing houses, in particular how the family or
household nature of the business and the need for occupational diversity within the household influenced the organization of publishing and
bookselling responsibilities, management strategies, profitability, and
the use of the profits. Here and in the following chapter, I focus on
the operations of the publishing houses in Sibao, the headquarters of
the industry, and thus largely on the publishing, rather than bookselling,
activities of the Zou and Ma. The organization of the business in
Sibao—and the constraints imposed by doing business in a place like
Sibao—shaped not only the publishing choices of the *shufang* managers
but also the methods and geography of Sibao bookselling as well as the
depth, extent, and nature of the industry's impact on Qing book culture
and society.

## Publishing Houses as Household Industries Within the Zou and Ma Lineages

### THE ORGANIZATION OF *SHUFANG*

The Zou and Ma publishing houses were for the most part household industries—that is, they were usually centered on either nuclear, stem, or joint-family households. (By "household" I mean any family unit sharing living space and property. Household size ranged widely, from small groups of five to six persons to large units of seventy to eighty people.)[1] The household patriarch, the *jiazhang* 家長, either the founder or the inheritor of the shop, presided over shop business, employing most or all of the household members in the work of printing and selling books. Only if the patriarch were illiterate (that is, if his "cultural level was not high enough") or not adept at business management would a son take charge.[2] While remaining the nominal manager, the household head might, however, also work primarily as a sojourning book merchant, delegating the day-to-day management of the publishing house to a son or wife and returning to manage the publishing house only after a son or nephew replaced him in the field.

The division of responsibilities within the household seems to have been highly flexible and to have depended on the size of the household, the skills of its members, and the importance of publishing to the household income. One informant, in describing his family's work in the book trade, outlined a situation that probably became increasingly common in the early twentieth century, as the trade declined: his grandfather operated a publishing house in Sibao, assigning his youngest son (the informant's father) the task of operating the family bookstore in Hengzhou, Guangxi. But the real mainstay of the household was farming: the two other sons farmed land rented, at very favorable terms, from two lineage estates. By the early twentieth century, lineage control of this land had weakened so much that, as the informant explained, "my family virtually owned it." Like other cottage industries, the profits

---

1. Informants claimed that once a household reached eighty people, division of the property and a breakup into smaller households were inevitable. See Chapter 5.

2. Interviews 1, 10/27/93 (Wuge); 3, 10/28/93 (Wuge); and 4, 10/30/93 (Mawu).

from publishing-bookselling simply supplemented the family's agricultural income.[3]

In the eighteenth and nineteenth centuries, when the demand for Sibao's texts was still great, publishing-bookselling was more often the major source of household income. Of the five surviving sons of Zou Yongzhe 永哲, the manager of the Suwei tang in the late nineteenth century, two farmed the land, while three had varied careers—all linked at some point to the book trade—shifting as necessary between bookselling, *shufang* management, and household oversight.[4] Even clearer on this score is the report of an informant whose great-grandfather was the manager of the Yingwen tang 應文堂, also in the late nineteenth century. He ran the publishing house with the assistance of his eldest son, and his two other sons sold books in Jiaying department, Guangdong. The family landholdings, roughly 40–50 *mu*, had to be farmed by long-term hired laborers, because all the men of the household were preoccupied with the publishing house and bookselling—"and these were seen as more important than farming."[5]

The largest and most prosperous publishing houses often absorbed the managerial talent and bookselling labor of all adult males within the household, requiring either that their land be rented out to tenants or that they hire short- and long-term laborers to farm for them. For example, the household of Zou Bingjun 秉均 (1718–96), a descendant of Zou Mengchun, reputedly Wuge's first publisher, was organized primarily as a publishing house: the older males wrote the *diben* and carved the woodblocks, the younger adult males sold books (as did Zou Bingjun himself), and the women, children, and some hired workers (included in the household total) printed texts. One of the largest and most successful publishing households, Bingjun's family also owned considerable landed property as well as a forested mountain, all scattered within the Sibao area. When printing was slow, they farmed the land themselves; when the demand for texts was high, they rented the land to others. Never, apparently, did any household, however lucrative its publishing operation, consider selling its land and devoting all its en-

---

3. Interview 39, 11/15/95 (Wuge).
4. Interview 34, 11/14/95 (Wuge).
5. Interview 42, 11/19/95 (Wuge).

ergies to publishing and bookselling. Every household held on to its land, even if it had to rent its fields out or pay laborers to farm for them.[6] Indeed, the first expenditure of a newly prosperous publishing-house manager was invariably the initial or additional purchase of land for his family, presumably because land was seen as a secure investment, whereas commerce of any sort was subject to the vagaries of supply and demand.

Although the multi-occupational household headed by a patriarch who assigned each member an economic role was by far the most common pattern for Sibao publishing, in certain circumstances publishing businesses and ultimately households were established by brothers or by uncles and nephews, often through efforts to pool capital. For example, the orphaned Zou Shuwen 述文 (1692–1756) and his four brothers together established both a publishing house and their own distribution route in the early eighteenth century.[7] Successful older brothers also funded the business enterprises of younger siblings: Ma Longheng 龍珩 (fl. early eighteenth c.?), for example, provided his younger brother with the capital to purchase books for sale. The business failed, and Ma Longheng had to pay off several hundred pieces of silver (*jin*) in debts incurred by his brother. Longheng remained optimistic and lent his brother money to start up a bookstore; because of the incompetence of the store manager, this too failed, and Ma Longheng once more rescued his brother by paying his debt of five hundred pieces of silver. The indulgent older brother agreed to a third loan; this time his patience and generosity were rewarded, and his brother finally succeeded as a merchant.[8]

The circle of obligation and assistance seemed to extend, at least at times, to the uncle-nephew relationship, particularly if a nephew had no father to assist him. Ma Dafang, a wealthy merchant, aided his brother's

---

6. Interview 32, 11/13/95 (Wuge). My informant, a descendant of Zou Bingjun, stated that the household reached the size of 130 members. This seems a very high figure and is not substantiated in any text. See also *FYZSZP* (1947), 33.40a–41a; and *Fanyang Zouzhi zupu* (1996), 3: 85–87.

7. *FYZSZP* (1947), 33.30b–31a.

8. *MSDZZP* (1945), *ji* 7, 1.60b–61a; cited in Chen Zhiping and Zheng Zhenman, "Qingdai Minxi Sibao zushang yanjiu," p. 95.

orphaned sons until they were able to establish themselves in publishing.[9] And Zou Huaichuan 懷川 (1729–88) was a poor orphan who eked out a living collecting firewood or hiring himself out as a shepherd until his uncle came to his aid, rounding up funds from relatives to provide Huaichuan with capital to start up his own bookselling business. Within a year, "with profits of several tens of pieces of silver, he . . . managed to pay his debts to all who had helped him . . . and was able to live comfortably."[10] The wording here is vague, but the arrangement between Huaichuan and his benefactors may have resembled a kind of partnership: the relatives supplying the capital and Huaichuan the management and labor for the enterprise.[11]

Once a publishing house and household had been established, however, the relatively centralized model of management by the household head was the norm. The family patriarch and other adult males in the household performed certain tasks exclusively: publishing; household management; book sales; writing of the *diben* or carving of the template; and block cutting. But as we saw in Chapter 3, almost any member of the household, male or female, young or old, might participate in the work of printing and binding. The larger households numbered as many as seventy to eighty people and included four generations, making for a large pool of potential labor. The biggest publishing houses might require the labor of twenty to thirty workers (or, as one informant claimed, "several tens" of workers), between one-quarter and almost one-half of the members in one of these larger households.[12] At their busiest—for example, during the pre–Spring Festival rush—family

---

9. See Chapter 2 and Chapter 5, pp. 66–67, 164.
10. *FYZSZP* (1947), 33b–34a; (1996), 2: 377–79.
11. Chen Zhiping and Zheng Zhenman, "Qingdai Minxi Sibao zushang yanjiu," p. 95. The arrangement between Ma Longheng and his brother might also fall into this category. For a general description of such "partnerships," see Wang Shixin, "Ming Qing shiqi shangye jingying fangshi de bianhua," pp. 27–28. In Wang's terms, Ma Huaichuan's arrangement would have been a *hegu* 合股 arrangement (funded by a group of investors and managed by a person who is himself not an investor), whereas Ma Longheng's arrangement would have been a *hehuo* 合夥 (one investor and two non-investing managers).
12. Interviews 3, 10/28/93 (Wuge); 15, 4/29/95 (Wuge); 9, 5/1/95 (Mawu); 25, 11/9/95 (Wuge); and 28, 11/8/95 (Wuge).

labor might not be enough, and workers from other Ma or Zou households would be employed to help with the printing and binding. At the other extreme, the smallest publishing houses might get by with a labor force of only five to six members of a small joint family, possibly supplemented by hired workers.

The preference was to draw these hired workers from among the lineages in Wuge and Mawu, from the neighboring hamlets of Shuangquan and Shangjian, or at least from the Sibao area; as one informant put it, from "places like Jiantou [a Sibao village] and Tiancha 田茶 [a hamlet within Wuge], but never from as far away as Changting or Jiangxi."[13] Unfortunately we have no information on wages until the end of Sibao's publishing history, but the evidence from that period suggests that printers and binders were paid very little, particularly if they were female. In the 1930s printers at the Linlan yiji tang in Shanghang were paid 2 *mao* 毛 (20 cents) for every 1,000 sheets printed,[14] thus earning perhaps 6 *mao* (60 cents) a day. At the same time, the Benli tang 本立堂 hired between two and five printers from within Wuge, paying each 4–5 *mao* (40–50 cents) a day.[15] Lineage members from outside the publishing household might be paid even less or not at all, receiving only room and board in exchange for their labor.[16]

Household labor, supplemented as necessary by hired workers from within the lineage or the Sibao sociocultural unit, assured the publishing houses of low labor costs (assuming that the hired workers did not include block cutters). So too, the existence of this fairly stable pool of laborers allowed publishing houses considerable flexibility in production: when demand was high, they could call on members of the extended family for work; when it was low, their workers took up other occupations but remained available.

---

13. Interview 25, 11/9/95 (Wuge).

14. Interview 44, 11/23/95 (Mawu).

15. Interview 28, 11/12/95 (Wuge). Another informant suggested that female printers were paid even less, between 1 and 2 *mao* a day, in the first decade of the twentieth century (Interview 25, 11/9/95 [Wuge]).

16. Interview 46, 11/24/95 (Mawu).

## GENDER DIVISIONS AND HOUSEHOLD
## ECONOMIES IN THE PUBLISHING INDUSTRY

One of the greatest sources of this labor flexibility was the pool of female (and to some extent child) labor that the household could call on. Although ignored in the written record (their work in Sibao publishing is revealed only in oral histories), the labor of women, both as household members and hired laborers, was crucial to the success of this industry. They provided the relatively unskilled labor needed for printing and binding, the "technologies" consistently associated with women in the publishing trade, freeing their husbands and fathers for the tasks of management and bookselling, both of which required interaction with the outside world and thus were more or less closed to women.[17] But this divide derived not simply from the separation of the inner and outer spheres; it rested, too, on the different abilities of the learned and the unlearned. As one informant explained, "It was the men with a high level of education who went out to sell books, because they had to talk to literati (*wenren* 文人) and readers. Others in the family would stay at home and print books, because this was work that anyone could do, including women and children."[18] As was often the case with women's work,[19] women's contributions to the publishing industry were dismissed, their work seen as unskilled and on a par with that of children. But however uneducated, women afforded their household considerable flexibility in meeting its labor requirements: capable of a multitude of different tasks, depending on household needs, they could print and bind, but during the slow season for publishing, they could also weave and farm.

As hired laborers within the lineage, women provided a large source of cheap labor, performing the same printing and binding tasks as men for much lower wages. As one informant noted, in explaining why his father, manager of a Mawu bookshop in Changting in the early twentieth century, hired female printers, "printing was unskilled work, and

---

17. See Bray, *Technology and Gender*, pp. 369–80, on "female technologies" in the late imperial period.

18. Interview 62, 12/3/95 (Wuge).

19. See Bray, *Technology and Gender*, pp. 43–44.

female workers (*nügong* 女工) could be paid less than men."[20] The female carvers of Magang, Guangdong—who supplied some Zou publishers with blocks in the nineteenth century—were successful largely because, though skilled, they worked for less than men did.

In exceptional cases, women also played managerial roles in publishing. One informant proudly recounted the business career of his grandmother, who took charge of the household publishing house when her husband was out selling books. This redoubtable lady not only managed the shop, hiring and supervising workers, but also defended the shop against the physical attack of a competitor, driving the man off with her superior martial skill (*gongfu* 功夫)—or so her grandson claims. Another informant from a Zou lineage reported that his grandmother, née Zhang, managed his family's small publishing house, with some help from her brothers-in-law, while his grandfather sold books (and took a second wife) in Guixian 貴縣, Guangxi; in the absence of the household patriarch, she hired four or five printers, either relatives or older women, and oversaw the printing of texts.[21] So, too, Ma Chuancui 傳粹 (fl. late nineteenth c.) left his wife, née Tong 童, in Mawu to manage the household and run the publishing house, while he sold books in Jiangxi, taking with him a second wife he had married earlier while selling books in Guangxi.[22] These women *shufang* managers, in effect the heads of their Sibao households and unlikely to see much of their husbands, had considerable control over the conduct of the family industry.

But for the most part women's roles in publishing were limited by custom: society valued women's labor per se less than that of men and looked askance at women working outside the household. In Wuge and Mawu, women for the most part worked at low-skill jobs within their household printshops. Only poverty would drive a woman to work as a printer or binder outside her household (and normally not outside the lineage organization to which their family be-

---

20. Interview 44, 11/23/95 (Mawu).
21. Interview 38, 11/15/95 (Wuge).
22. Interview 56, 12/2/95 (Mawu). Only one other informant reported such an arrangement; in the early twentieth century, his mother oversaw a hired printer, sometimes two, at home in Wuge, while his father sold the books they produced in the Hakka villages of northern Guangdong (Interview 67, 12/5/95 [Wuge]).

longed),[23] and she would be paid less than male printers and binders. Only the absence of a responsible male allowed his wife to exercise authority over the publishing house. Although the labor of women (and children) was essential to book production in Wuge and Mawu, it was rare for a woman to participate overtly in managing a printshop.

My point here is not simply to celebrate the heretofore hidden contributions of women to this industry (nor to lament the constraints on their contributions) but to highlight the centrality of the household unit in this system. All members of the household were drawn into production for the household, to perform a series of seasonal tasks or to change tasks (from bookselling to family management, from examination study to bookselling, from printing to weaving) as the population, constitution, economic circumstances and opportunities, and goals of the household as a unit changed. Within this structure, women, children, and younger, less skilled males generally performed the least-skilled jobs and shifted among tasks frequently as household needs changed.[24]

## THE TRAINING OF THE ZOU AND MA PUBLISHER-BOOKSELLERS

Women and children were by no means the only flexible laborers in this system. To be sure, the separation between the agricultural laborers and the publishers, booksellers, and other "men with a high level of

23. The absence of footbinding, the practice of female field labor, and the employment of women outside the household have led some scholars to argue that women had a higher status or more freedom in Hakka communities than in neighboring lowland settlements (see Leong, *Migration and Ethnicity*, pp. 35–36, 78–79). I am not persuaded that this was the case (although clearly they enjoyed a greater degree of physical mobility). These different practices reflect a desperate need to maximize labor resources in an impoverished environment, where, because of male sojourning, there was often a shortage of male labor. For a similar argument about non-Hakka communities, see Philip Huang, *The Peasant Family and Rural Development*, pp. 55–56. Huang explains that in the Yangzi delta area, where there was a strong social stigma attached to women working in the fields, there was considerable variety in practice, depending on the economic status of the family. Prejudices against female agricultural labor "could be overcome when there was an economic imperative for women's participation in farmwork" (p. 56).

24. See Pomeranz, "Women's Work and the Economics of Respectability," p. 257; and Philip Huang, *The Peasant Family and Rural Development*, pp. 49–57, 306–8.

education" within a household seems to have been fairly rigid. In households large enough to practice a strategy of labor division, once designated a farmer, a male appears to have remained a farmer. But non-farming males might rotate among a variety of tasks. The biographies in both the Ma and the Zou genealogies suggest that households tried first to provide sons with some education, in hope that at least one would show sufficient scholastic talent to justify his continuing studies for the examinations. This was a luxury poorer households could not afford; the genealogies are full of biographies of men who as boys "could memorize a text after reading over it just once" or "deeply penetrated the meaning of the Classics and histories" but had to give up their studies to help support their impoverished families.

Indeed, from the very earliest of the Zou and Ma biographies, one common theme runs through all the discussions of family occupational strategy: a hope for success in the examinations. Each descent group put great stock in educating its sons; most males took up the book trade only after several years of examination study and perhaps one or more attempts to pass the examinations. Thus Zou Bingchun

studied when young, since he was intelligent and talented by nature. But he had no father or elder brothers to care for him, and thus he had to abandon his Confucian studies and travel to Guangxi as a merchant, eventually becoming wealthy through trade. Since he was not studying, his talent and intelligence had no outlet; so he used them to manage his property and amass wealth. At the age of fifteen he married a woman from the Ma family, and, having gained her wise assistance at home, he made his trade the family occupation.[25]

So, too, in the early Qing, the orphaned Ma Quanwen 權文 (1663–1743) was at first supported in school in the Changting county seat by his uncle. Although "he thoroughly comprehended the teachings of the ancient sages and worthies," he was forced to give up his studies when a decline in the family fortunes necessitated his taking up the book trade.[26] Zou Shengmai 聖脈 (1692–1762), one of the better known of the Sibao publishers, was groomed for success in the examinations—his father even built a special study, the Meiyuan 梅園 (Plum Garden,

---

25. *FYZSZP* (1947), 33.38b–39a; *Fanyang Zouzhi zupu* (1996), 3: 928–30.
26. *MSDZZP* (1945), *ji* 7, 1.45a; and (1993), 5.145–47.

remains of which survive), for his use. But local lore explains that his distaste for the eight-legged essay hindered his scholarly career. In his last attempt at the examinations, he ranked 101, but the examiner passed only the first one hundred candidates. Thoroughly disgusted with what he perceived as the corruption and arbitrariness of the system, Zou Shengmai returned home and devoted his talents to editing and publishing.[27] The biographies cited above explain in some detail the circumstances under which their subjects left their schooling for publishing; many biographies simply repeat the cliché *qi ru jing shang* 棄儒經商 ("[he] abandoned Confucian studies to practice commerce") as a shorthand explanation of their subjects' entry into business.[28]

As we saw in Chapter 2, the very low success rate of both the Zou and the Ma in the Qing civil-service examinations helps to explain the frequency of this choice. They participated most actively at just the time that the examinations were becoming increasingly competitive in two ways: the population increase of the eighteenth and early nineteenth centuries meant that more people were competing for a relatively fixed number of places; and from the late Qianlong era on the examinations demanded the mastery of more texts and skills,[29] which meant that fewer people were likely to pass. The isolation and relative indigence of Sibao made it difficult for the families to employ skilled teachers and to participate in the culture of examination preparation. No wonder the Sibao families found it more sensible to turn to other forms of livelihood.

Occasionally the genealogies hint at such a calculation, as in the biography of Zou Hongchun 洪春 (1721–86), one of the more successful publishers of Wuge. Hongchun, too, started on the course of study common to all Sibao schoolboys, but

had little ambition in his studies. He read just to get the main idea, refusing to make extracts from the texts or to examine closely the meaning of the passages,

---

27. On Zou Shengmai's work as a publisher and compiler of texts, see Chapter 9. Interviews 1, 10/27/93 (Wuge), and 2, 10/27/93 (Wuge); *MTLZXZSZP* (1911), 5.56a–57b. See also Zou Chunsheng, "*Youxue qionglin* zengbuzhe Zou Shengmai," pp. 114–15.

28. This formula is by no means unique to the Sibao publisher-booksellers. Almost the same phrase—*qi ru cong shang* 棄儒從商—is used in the biographies of Huizhou merchants (Ye Xian'en, *Ming Qing Huizhou nongcun shehui yu dianpu zhi*, p. 126). See also Chapter 8.

29. Elman, *A Cultural History of Civil Examinations*, p. 544. See also Chapter 10.

supposing that he could get by with a superficial knowledge of the Classics. Thus his learning was vague and crude. What better, then, but for him to print the whole store of the ancients' writings and quickly disseminate them, so that everyone could understand the spirit of the writings of the sages and worthies and devote themselves in turn to spreading their teachings. Moreover, he could thereby earn profits to support his family members.[30]

Certainly the readiness with which most Zou and Ma publishers "abandoned their studies to take up commerce" suggests that they or their fathers, like Zou Hongchun or his father, saw the clear economic advantages of this choice. Those who did persist in study for the examinations rarely profited significantly—they usually ended up teaching in the family schools established by their more successful publisher-relatives or managing the household. To be sure, their modest successes added to the cultural capital of their families—the genealogy biographies faithfully note their low-ranking degrees and honors. Many, with *jiansheng* degrees purchased with the profits of publishing, became community leaders.[31] But they contributed little to the economic well-being of their households.

Although for the Zou and Ma the chance of examination success was slight, education in the examination curriculum was important for business reasons. In fact, it is quite possible to interpret examination study by most Zou and Ma males—the rhetoric of the genealogies to the contrary—as preparation for publishing rather than real ambition for official status. Most obviously, publishers and book merchants had to be broadly (if not highly) literate simply to conduct their business. But since the examination system ensured a good and steady market for educational texts (including elementary guides to literacy, editions of the Classics, and aids to examination study), publishers needed to know the best titles to publish, and booksellers needed to be familiar with the usefulness of these titles. How better to learn than through participation in the examination curriculum? And certainly it was in these males' interests to claim a sincere desire for "Confucian study" and its approved goal, official service, while pursuing a more secure and practically rewarding career in

---

30. *FYZSZP* (1947), 33.27b–28a; cited in Chen Zhiping and Zheng Zhenman, "Qingdai Minxi Sibao zushang yanjiu," p. 100.

31. Liu Yonghua, "The World of Rituals," pp. 228, 434. See Chapter 8.

publishing-bookselling. It seems likely, then, that the *qi ru jing shang* pattern repeated over and over in the Zou and Ma genealogies reflects an understanding that knowing the examination curriculum was essential to publisher-booksellers, for it ensured their familiarity with the most important of Sibao's imprints, a sensitivity to changes in the examination curriculum that might affect business, and the ability to talk knowledgeably to customers about much of their stock. The Sibao trade survived for roughly two and a half centuries in large part because of its symbiotic relationship to the examination system.

Once the decision to enter the publishing trade was taken, a young man would typically start by working as a traveling merchant, usually under the tutelage of his father, elder brother(s), or an uncle, but on occasion alone. Ma Dinglüe 定略 (1680–1718), for example, operating on his own, established a bookselling route through the provinces of Jiangxi, Guangdong, and Guangxi.[32] Ma Qian 謙 (1722–96) worked with his three brothers to learn the trade in Jiangxi, but then sent his sons to Guangdong and Guangxi to sell books.[33] Zou Kongmao 孔茂 (1752–1829) accompanied his father and paternal grandfather, Zou Hongyou 鋐猷 (1723–72), on business trips to Zhangshuzhen 樟樹鎮 in Jiangxi. Zou Hongyou seems to have been, in fact, a particularly popular teacher of the book trade in the early nineteenth century. He also took his nephew, a grand-nephew, and other grandsons with him on trips to Zhangshuzhen, Suzhou, Hangzhou, and Huguang.[34] As late as the early twentieth century, this kind of apprenticeship was a common beginning to a successful career in publishing and bookselling: Zou Jianbao 建保 (1879–1933) "as a young man accompanied his uncle and older brother to sell books in Guangdong and Guangxi," until he was familiar enough with the business and the distribution routes to work on his own, "accumulating texts broadly across all the four categories of books and distributing them throughout the empire. His reputation for trustworthiness radiated ever more widely, and as a result, the family business flourished." Eventually he established a *shufang* of his own (or perhaps inherited a family shop), which he then passed on to his sons, who

---

32. *MSDZZP* (1945), *ji* 7, 1.61a–b.
33. Ibid., 1.69b.
34. *FYZSZP* (1947), 33.42a–43b, 59a, 60a, 61a, 61b, 62b.

"sold books everywhere in the great cities of Guangdong and Guangxi, displaying both Chinese and foreign books (*luozhi Zhong wai tushu* 羅置中外圖書), thereby bringing enlightenment to the area."[35]

Presumably this early experience selling books on the road was invaluable to those who hoped someday to manage their own printing shop. Direct contact with the book markets of the south provided essential information about demand and markets: what books would sell steadily, what books might offer high profits but only briefly, what books were likely to sell most briskly in a given area and to a given sector of the population—in other words, to learn the best distribution practices for Sibao texts. Additionally, such travels enabled future booksellers and publishers to make important contacts with book wholesalers and retailers and, more important, with local literati, probably their best customers and possibly a rich source of new texts.

After an apprenticeship as a traveling book merchant, a young man might establish his own bookstore (*shudian* 書店) somewhere along the routes he had covered. He might also, as indicated above, marry a second wife and establish another household at this site, in effect settling there and returning to Wuge or Mawu increasingly seldom, largely for important ritual occasions. Or he might return to Sibao to take over a family firm or to establish his own *shufang*, like Zou Jianbao. Ma Dinglüe, after his success as a bookseller in Jiangxi, Guangdong, and Guangxi, opened a printing shop in Mawu with the help of his brothers, but continued to work his old sales routes, returning home once a year to replenish his stock.[36] Ma Qian and his three brothers returned from selling in Jiangxi with the capital to start their own printing shop; they then sent their sons and grandsons out as traveling booksellers.[37]

The pattern outlined here—a period of "apprenticeship" as a traveling merchant, followed by the management of a *shufang* in Sibao or a bookstore along one of the book distribution routes—was by no means fixed. At different times, a Sibao publisher might experience all aspects of the book trade: as a child, he might help in the printing process,

---

35. *FYZSZP* (1947), 33.101a; cited in Chen Zhiping and Zheng Zhenman, "Qingdai Minxi Sibao zushang yanjiu," p. 97.

36. *MSDZZP* (1945), *ji* 7, 1.61a–b.

37. Ibid., 1.69b.

mixing ink or pressing pages. As a young man, he might peddle books or, with more capital to invest, be a traveling wholesale dealer, selling Sibao texts and perhaps texts produced by other printers. Eventually, he might establish a publishing house in Sibao and devote himself exclusively to cutting and printing texts, or he might also open a bookstore outside Sibao as a retail outlet for Sibao and other imprints. Or, in cooperation with family members, he might alternate among these various functions.

## ACCOUNTING AND THE
## HOUSEHOLD ECONOMY

As the household worked as a unit, so, too, it profited as a unit. Some informants reported that, in the smaller publishing houses, there was no separation of household accounts and *shufang* accounts from other household business accounts or domestic accounts. The publishing house was simply one element in the household economy. The larger, more complex *shufang* might separate the publishing business accounts from other household expenses and income, but in other ways these, too, subordinated the book business to the economy of the household.[38] All earnings from publishing and bookselling were handed over to the family patriarch (probably also the manager of the publishing house) to support the household (and publishing house) as a whole.[39] Booksellers, one informant told me, "would not have dared" to withhold money for themselves or their nuclear families; failure to hand over all earnings on return to Wuge and Mawu would result in the division of the household property—in essence, the separation of the offending book merchant and his family from the publishing household.[40]

To some extent this principle of a unified household economy is, of course, embedded in the ideals of lineage organization. Certainly both Zou and Ma lineage rules contain general proscriptions against selfishness, greed, and competition among family members. The Ma genealogy, for example, warns against *pianai* 偏愛 (favoritism) and *zicang* 自藏 (selfish hoarding) of goods within nuclear families and explicitly

---

38. Interviews 59, 12/2/95 (Wuge); and 63, 12/5/95 (Wuge).
39. Interview 15, 4/29/95 (Wuge).
40. Interview 18, 4/30/95 (Wuge).

cautions men not to listen to wives or sisters-in-law who try to stir up household jealousies and compete for household resources.[41]

The biographies of lineage members provide more vivid and persuasive counsels of economic cooperation. As mentioned in Chapter 2, all the genealogies repeatedly emphasize the importance of this principle to the economic security of the household; lineage members are praised for their scrupulous refusal to "hold back anything for their private use, not even one cash." The biographies celebrate as models of virtue those who furthered the fortunes of their household or extended family even at the expense of their nuclear family. Ma Dinglüe, for example, helped manage the family publishing house and also sold books in Jiangxi and Guangdong, "traveling back and forth by boat and cart every year, suffering this hard labor in order to serve his father and elder brothers." Exhausted by this taxing schedule, he fell ill of consumption at the age of 39 *sui* and, on his deathbed, apologized to his brother for his inability to continue helping to support the extended household. Then he ordered his wife to turn over to this brother the fifty pieces of silver he had earned on his travels. Lest the reader miss the point, the biographer comments:

After working in commerce for over twenty years, on the verge of death, he still could not bear to cheat his older brother in order to benefit his wife. If those of the current generation, who accumulate private wealth and fatten their purses without paying any attention to their families, who are selfishly complacent when they are lucky enough to become rich, could learn of Ma Dinglüe's outstanding character and understand his rectitude, how could they not be ashamed?[42]

Similar models appear in the Zou genealogies. There is Zou Zhuguo 洙國 (1650–89) who, like Ma Dinglüe, quite literally sacrificed himself to the economic good of the household: his family's poverty forced him to give up his studies and find a livelihood that would bring quick returns. He wore himself out "rushing about, without leisure, struggling to make a living" to support his parents and his younger brothers. His health ruined, he also died at 39 *sui*, while his younger brothers, thanks

---

41. "Chengdao Gong xunci" 呈道公訓辭, in *MSDZZP* (1945), *j. shou*, 43b. See also "Jiaxun sitiao" 家訓四條, 1a, in *FYZSZP* (1947), *j. shou*.

42. *MSDZZP* (1945), *ji* 7, 1.61ab.

to his labors, were prospering, with families of their own.[43] But most of the stories emphasize the happy endings that result from selfless devotion to the household good: Zou Hongcai 鴻才 (1760–1846) was sent off to Guangdong as a young man to learn the bookselling trade from his elder brother. He increased *shufang* revenues "from three [hundred] to one thousand pieces of silver" (*san*[*bai*] *zhi qian jin* 三[百]致千金) and scrupulously turned over all his earnings to his father on his yearly returns home—"he kept nothing for his own family."[44] After his father's death, he became the household head presiding over a harmonious extended household of over fifty people, including seven brothers and their families, four generations under one roof.

RELATIONS BETWEEN THE
SIBAO *SHUFANG* AND THE
ZOU AND MA BOOKSELLERS

These exemplars delineate the model for the good bookseller: he delivers all his earnings to the household head. Other, more practical—and probably more effective—safeguards—of the communal household economy were employed as well. One such mechanism was the careful selection of itinerant booksellers, either to encourage a sense of unity or to provide checks against cheating. Sending the sons of the *shufang* manager's younger brother(s) out to sell books was a means, one informant explained, "of creating a sense that the whole family was involved in the business" and thus of discouraging cheating.[45] A more cynical approach had booksellers travel in pairs or groups whose members came from the different nuclear families within a joint household. Thus a publisher might go on the road with his brothers or with his nephews; or his sons might travel with their uncles and/or their cousins. Certainly these arrangements were means of teaching newcomers the book trade and of ensuring the continuity and expansion of the business, but they also worked to ensure that no one held profits back from

43. *FYZSZP* (1947), 33.13b–14a. See also the biography of Zou Tingyue 廷月 (1752–1810) in *MTLZXZSZP* (1911), 13.82ab, 20.43b.
44. *FYZSZP* (1947), 33.51b.
45. Interview 26, 11/11/95 (Wuge).

the common store.[46] Finally, most publishing houses used a system of matched accounting: the *shufang* manager recorded each book and its price before consigning it to one of his booksellers (booksellers from outside a *shufang* purchased texts wholesale from a publisher). The latter was then required to note the sale price of each text. On his return, the two records would be compared (*jiao zhang* 較帳), and the money handed over to the *shufang*.[47]

Even more potentially disruptive of household economic unity than itinerant bookselling were the branch bookstores at some distance from Wuge or Mawu, managed by brothers, sons, nephews, or cousins sent out from the "headquarters" household. Although the establishment of branch stores reflected the prosperity of a publishing house, stable markets, and the expectation of strong and steady profits, it also created a potential threat to the centrality and authority of the Sibao *shufang* managers, not to mention the financial unity of the household. The publishing houses thus took measures to emphasize their central authority. Branch bookstores were forbidden to publish; they were to serve as outlets for Sibao publishing, not to set themselves up as competitors (although this prohibition was not thoroughly enforced).[48] Management of the branch shops was rotated among family members, from father to son to brother and so on, so that no single figure came to dominate the branch business. As with itinerant bookselling, the management of branch shops was often assigned to uncle-nephew or cousin-cousin pairs, a means of combining reasonably close affective relationships with some mutual surveillance and a check against rampant economic individualism (or nuclear familism).

Efforts were made to bind the booksellers and branch shop managers to their native place and the Zou and Ma lineages by marrying them to women from the Sibao area (who usually remained at home with their children while their husbands went off to sell books or manage a branch bookstore). A warning proverbial among Sibao *shufang* managers,

---

46. Informants repeatedly gave this explanation for decisions made within each household about whom to designate as booksellers. For example, Interviews 15, 4/29/95 (Wuge); and 26, 11/11/95 (Wuge).

47. Interview 26, 11/11/95 (Wuge).

48. Interview 13, 4/27/95 (Wuge). See Chapter 7.

"Never allow your son to marry a woman from Guangxi," was a straight-forward acknowledgment of the importance of marriage ties as a means of strengthening loyalty to Sibao. Marriages to women from outside the Sibao area were also viewed with misgivings because they invited possible interference from a distant and unknown family.[49] Bookstore managers were not generally identified as migrants in the genealogies; their settlement away from Sibao was seen as temporary, and they were expected to return in retirement. If they died away from Sibao, their bodies were, ideally, to be transported back home for burial.[50]

Shop managers (as well as itinerant booksellers) were expected to return regularly to Sibao at least for the New Year's celebrations, to reaffirm their links to the ancestral line—and to present their accounts to the *shufang* manager. Each side kept its own account: the publishing house, an inventory of books shipped; and the branch stores, a *shoushu danzi* 收書單子, "a list of books received," consisting of the quantities of each title and the wholesale price. Each branch store also kept a daybook or cashbook, a *liushui zhang* 流水帳, or "flowing water" record, in which all expenses and gross earnings were listed in chronological order.[51] At the end of every month, this running account of receipts and expenditures was tallied, so that the booksellers had some idea of their profits and could calculate the amounts due the household *shufang*. If bookstore managers failed to report to Sibao as frequently as desired, then *shufang* managers from Sibao might visit these branch shops to

---

49. Interview 7, 4/27/95 (Wuge). Some "outsider" wives submitted to the control of the lineages. See, e.g., the account of the wife of Ma Daguang, née Zhong, in Chapter 2, p. 67; and *MSDZZP* (1945), *Liezhuan*, 1.42ab, 51b–52b.

50. This was not always possible; at least three booksellers (Zou Kongshu 孔書, Zou Kongqu 孔衢, and Zou Pikang 丕康, d. 1793, 1798, and 1816, respectively) were buried near the Fujian *huiguan* in Nanning; and Zou Tingrong 廷榮 (1801–63), his son Lianyang 聯颺, and his grandson Jianchi were buried in Lingshan, Guangdong, the site of a branch store.

51. Interviews 25, 11/9/95 (Wuge); 85, 4/23/95 (Mawu); and 61, 12/6/95 (Wuge). See Gardella, "Squaring Accounts," p. 326; and Otte, "The Evolution of Bookkeeping and Accounting in China," pp. 169–70. For a discussion of the relationship between the rather basic, single-entry *liushui zhang* and other forms of accounting in the Qing, see Fu Jianmu, "Qingdai minjian kuaiji fushi jizhang gaishu," pp. 73–75; and Chien Ming Li, *The Accounting System of Native Banks in Peking and Tientsin*, pp. 48–55.

check these accounts as well as to establish a stable stock of titles and solicit suggestions for new titles.

Models of exemplary branch shop management were highlighted in the genealogies as lessons for booksellers. The two brothers Zou Shangqing 尚清 (1835–88) and Zou Fuqing 福清 (1848–1906), for example, divided their slender patrimony "exactly in half, so that no amount went unfairly into a private purse," in order to establish separate stores in Yanqian 巖前 and Shibazhai 十八寨 (both in Yongan county, Fujian), respectively. Although by then the heads of separate nuclear families, each still considered himself part of a common household, for each continued to send silver home for the purchase of land and a large family compound in Wuge.[52] Most *shufang* managers seemed to fear that few branch store operators would follow this model, however, probably with good reason. As we shall see in Chapter 7, the growing independence of branch shops from centralized oversight in Wuge and Mawu is one of the signs of decline in the industry.

## *The Income from Publishing-Bookselling*

What were the likely profits from publishing-bookselling? Exactly how profitable was the book trade? It is possible to provide only an impressionistic response, since what little evidence survives is fragmentary and difficult to interpret and dates largely from the late nineteenth or early twentieth century, when the industry was in decline.

Contemporary informants, reporting on production costs and prices in the 1920s, 1930s, and 1940s, suggest that, even then, publishers could profit from sure-fire sellers. One of the more reliable Mawu historians reported that, once the blocks for the *Sanzi jing* were cut, for example, each text could be produced at a cost of 2 cents (2 *fen* 分), which included the costs of the paper,[53] the inkblack, oil, *mitang*, and binding materials. A copy would sell for 3 cents wholesale and 5 cents retail. *Zengguang xianwen* 增廣賢文 (Expanded words of wisdom), another very

---

52. *MTLZXZSZP* (1911), 20.108ab.

53. The paper cost was calculated at 3 dollars (*yuan* 圓) for 200 sheets, 180 of which would typically be usable. But the *Sanzi jing* required only two-thirds of one sheet, since it was only eleven–twelve folio pages, and the paper cost for one copy would be roughly 1 *fen*.

popular primer, cost 5 cents to produce, but sold for 7–8 cents whole-sale and at least 10 cents (1 *mao* 毛) retail.[54] Another informant reports that the production cost for the *Sanzi jing* and *Renjia riyong* was 2–3 cop-per dollars (*tongban* 銅扳), and the price was 5–6 copper dollars. This same informant argued that, since the publishing house relied on un-paid family labor, the difference between the cost of materials and the sale price, wholesale or retail, was pure profit.[55] (Of course the *shufang* did pay something for family labor in the form of opportunity costs, but given the overpopulation and paucity of economic opportunities in Si-bao, these were negligible.)

The profits suggested in these two accounts range from 50 percent to over 100 percent of production costs, but it is important to remem-ber that the highest cost, the price of block cutting, is not included in the calculations. Evelyn Rawski has demonstrated that, for inexpensive popular texts like those favored by the Sibao publishers, the cost of cut-ting blocks was quite modest in the late nineteenth and early twentieth centuries, particularly when cheap female labor was employed. And since "the relative expense of a book fell as the number of copies to be printed rose," the Zou and Ma publishers could count on a rising profit margin, given the steady, heavy demand for their texts.[56] Nonetheless, the cost of the block cutting—even the blocks for the brief *Sanzi jing*— would have to be factored in to obtain an accurate production cost.

---

54. Interview 44, 11/23/95 (Mawu).

55. Interview 60, 12/3/95 (Wuge).

56. Rawski, *Education and Popular Literacy in Ch'ing China*, pp. 118–24. Rawski, relying on statistics from Shanghai in the 1840s, concludes that it was "possible to produce books for well under a hundred cash" (p. 121). Unfortunately, very little evidence sur-vives from Sibao for the cost of block cutting. The 1897 document dividing the prop-erty of the household that ran the Juxian tang 聚賢堂 *shufang* and the Dawen tang 達文堂 *shudian* lists the value of nine titles (see Table B1 in Appendix B). Without a count of the numbers of blocks for each title, however, this information is of limited use. Infor-mants suggested that the blocks for even a small text like *Sanzi jing* were worth a great deal (Interview 44, 11/23/95 [Mawu]), although the estimate of 1,000 ounces (*liang* 兩) of silver provided by one informant seems impossibly high for a text that could be printed on eleven folio pages, particularly in light of the more modest sums listed in the table. Somewhat more credible is the claim that the blocks for the lengthy and very popular *Kangxi zidian* were so valuable that they could "support an entire family in com-fort" (Interview 26, 11/11/95 [Wuge]).

Even if the publishers were able to make profits of from 50 to 100 percent of production costs, all the books mentioned were so inexpensive that in absolute terms the profit from them was probably rather insignificant: the wholesale profit on two to three thousand copies of the *Sanzi jing* (the number, according to the informant, that would be in stock at the beginning of the school year) would be only 20–30 *qian* 錢. The publishing house in question would have had to stock an impressive range of texts before its earnings would be significant.

The Wenhai lou account book, dating from the early twentieth century, indicates a total income of 3,074.937 ounces (*liang* 兩) of silver from wholesale book sales at nine different shops. This total includes 1,800 ounces "from last year's [sales]," leaving 1,274.937 ounces as the total for the current year (and 326.421 ounces worth of stock left in warehouses). The income for the Wenhai lou might range, then, between 1,275 and 1,800 ounces a year. It is difficult to interpret these figures. They appear to represent gross income, and without information about production costs, it is impossible to calculate net profit. Nor do we know how large a household these sums were to support (or what other sources of income this household might enjoy). But we can say, cautiously, that it represents a respectable income. It cannot compare, to be sure, to the high profits made in more sophisticated and more lucrative industries; it pales beside the 7,308 ounces net profit (22,836 gross profit) made by a Zigong salt merchant from a single brine well in early twentieth-century Sichuan.[57] And it is considerably less than the 5,000 ounces Chang Chung-li estimates as the average annual gross income of an officeholder in the late nineteenth century. But it is roughly equivalent to the sum a high-ranking educational official (1,500 ounces) or a well-paid Fujian district magistrate (1,645 ounces) could expect; a poorly paid magistrate would receive 645 ounces. And it is far more than the 100 ounces a teacher and the 250 ounces a secretary to a district magistrate (both common employments for men who had earned licentiate or purchased *jiansheng* status) might earn in a year.[58]

---

57. Zelin, *The Merchants of Zigong*, p. 70. This is the estimated net income from one brine well in 1916. As Zelin explains, brine wells, unlike book production, required heavy capital investment and entailed high risk.

58. Chung-li Chang, *The Income of the Chinese Gentry*, pp. 14, 33, 42, 85, 101, 197–98. If we rely on the annual per-capita income statistics Chang calculates (90 ounces for a

If accurate, this calculation reveals that the most successful Sibao publisher-booksellers were, by the early twentieth century, earning respectable sums from the book trade; the less successful might find it necessary to supplement their income with earnings from farming and perhaps other trades.[59] But it should not be taken as representative of Sibao earnings, for by the 1900s the industry was in decline. Presumably the business brought in considerably larger sums in its heyday, the Qianlong and Jiaqing eras. Taking into account the investment that official service required, the gamble that examination study represented, and the relatively low wages and the uncertainty of the two professions most open to lower degree–holders, it is easy to see why many of the Zou and Ma chose the path of publishing-bookselling even in the late Qing.

The genealogies suggest that in the eighteenth and early nineteenth centuries at least some of the publisher-booksellers earned substantial sums, enough to earn them the designation "wealthy as untitled nobility." These sources distinguish loosely between two different degrees of publishing success. There were the very wealthy entrepreneurs, invariably compared either to "untitled nobility" ("his wealth multiplied so that he became as rich as an untitled noble," *zhi zi bei rao ru sufeng* 致貲倍饒如素封) or to Tao Zhu ("he mastered [the methods of] Tao

---

member of the gentry, 5.7 ounces for a commoner; p. 328), it is likely that the Wenhai lou business could support a medium-sized household (of 30 people) at a per-capita level (42.5 ounces) well above the average for commoners, although also well below that for *juren* and *jinshi* degree-holders.

59. Chung-li Chang (*The Income of the Chinese Gentry*) provides evidence, however, that men earning an income of as little as 300 to 400 ounces a year were able to accumulate respectable amounts of cash or landed property. He provides several examples of teachers and secretaries who were able to support their families "according to the average gentry standard of living" on their salaries. Wu Yun, who supported his parents and his own family and aided his six brothers on his teacher's salary, managed to increase the amount of land he had inherited by "several tens of times"—that is, from 30 *mu* (2.3 hectares) to 600 to 900 *mu* (46 to 69 hectares). Wu Zhaoyuan supported his family and distributed land worth 1,000 ounces to his poor relatives on a teaching salary (p. 97). Hou Xun was a secretary and holder of minor offices (from a purchased *jiansheng* degree); he could afford to repair twenty ancestral halls, collect paintings, and still leave his family 3,000 ounces (pp. 80–81). Thus it is possible that those publishing households earning only one-half or one-third of the Wenhai lou's income were nonetheless able to maintain themselves on the profits from publishing-bookselling alone.

Zhu," *xue Tao Zhu gong* 學陶朱公).[60] These men could profit indirectly as well as directly from the publishing trade, being rich enough to lend money out at interest. Thus Zou Ming 明 (1732–1819) and his successors, managers of the Wanjuan lou 萬卷樓, amassed considerable landed property through profits earned from publishing-bookselling and moneylending;[61] the profits from publishing supplied the capital for investment in moneylending.

Below these magnates were those who simply made enough to support their households, indicated by the more prosaic phrase "he earned profits" (*quan zimu* 權字母).[62] The genealogies say little about the less successful publisher-booksellers, but even for them the trade seems to have provided a steady, if not spectacular, living throughout most of the nineteenth century. In the late 1860s, Thomas Cooper, reporting an encounter with an itinerant Jiangxi bookseller, observed that "the book . . . trade throughout China, is a safe one, returning small but sure profits, and is one of the very few exempt from duty."[63] That seems to be a fairly accurate characterization of the Sibao trade as well: after the golden days of the eighteenth and early nineteenth century, profits generally leveled off but remained fairly steady. Only in the 1920s and 1930s did the changes in the educational system, book culture, print technology, and government extractive policies (commerce in books was taxed under the Republic) severely undermine the stability of the trade.

## The Use of Earnings

In the end, anecdotal evidence about the uses to which the Sibao publishing houses put their earnings is probably the most useful source for assessing the economic and social value of the business. These uses reveal, too, the dominance of communal household goals in the opera-

---

60. These phrases are also used to describe Huizhou merchants; see Ye Xian'en, *Ming Qing Huizhou nongcun shehui yu dianpu zhi*, p. 126.

61. Liu Yonghua, "The World of Rituals," p. 279.

62. This phrase also means "to compound interest." But the context in which it is used in the genealogy biographies suggests that it is best translated here as "to earn profits."

63. Cooper, *Travels of a Pioneer of Commerce*, pp. 73–74. The Qing government, at least until the late nineteenth century, did not tax commerce on cultural products like books.

tion of the Sibao publishing industry. Earnings from the book trade had to be devoted first to the immediate maintenance of both the business and the household. Naturally it was necessary to cover the operating costs of book production and sale—payment for the repair of old blocks, the purchase of paper and ink, hired workers, and the expenses of book transport and booksellers' travel.

Household maintenance could, depending on the time and the size of the household, be a considerable burden. By the second and third decades of the twentieth century, when the business was in decline, the meager profits from the book trade might be used to supplement income from agricultural labor. Thus one bookseller, head of a three-generation household of six or seven people, worked as an itinerant book peddler in a desperate effort to add to the harvest from his tiny plot of 10 to 13 *mu* (0.77 to 1.0 hectare). But in the Qianlong and Jiaqing eras, at the height of the trade, publishing-bookselling was often the primary support of large households including as many as seventy to eighty people. Even the support of a medium-size household of thirty was costly.

Once publishing houses and household heads had provided for the material needs of the household, they had some flexibility in the use of whatever disposable income remained. The more ambitious publishers used at least some of their profits to expand their business, after calculating carefully the advantages of reinvestment and expansion, balancing potential profits against the size of the available workforce (especially the unpaid household workforce), costs of paper and ink, demand for texts, and the possible loss of control that came with expansion. Informants mentioned that reinvestment, in particular the cutting or purchase of new blocks, was one of the uses to which profits might be put, at least until it became clear, in the early twentieth century, that the returns did not justify such a costly investment.[64]

The written sources hint, too, at reinvestment in the business, through the purchase of new blocks, the expansion of printing facilities,

---

64. Interviews 50, 11/25/95 (Mawu); and 44, 11/23/95 (Mawu). See also Interviews 25, 11/9/95 (Wuge); and 26, 11/11/95 (Wuge). *Fenguan* documents from the less prosperous late nineteenth and early twentieth centuries reveal a decline in the woodblock stock: the 1839 document lists 107 titles; 1894, 21; 1897, 17; 1937, 46.

or the careful planning of publishing strategies. The biography of the bookseller Zou Jun 濬 (1762–?) notes his efforts to accumulate wood-blocks "in order to increase production, the source of expanding wealth."[65] In the late eighteenth century, Zou Kongai, presumably to accommodate an expansion of publishing, used some of the earnings of his family's flourishing publishing house to construct a new printshop behind the family home. By 1839, Ma Cuizhong, the manager of the Zaizi tang, had woodblocks for 107 titles, an achievement that suggests both careful planning and substantial outlays of capital. And Ma Quan-heng and Ma Dingbang, the father-and-son managers of one of Mawu's most successful publishing businesses, judiciously developed a long-term publishing schedule that allowed them to build up a store of popular and lucrative texts. They began with texts that were both proven best-sellers and relatively short (annotated editions of the Four Books, the *Shijing*, and some children's primers), requiring relatively lit-tle capital investment while promising good returns. They invested the profits from these in cutting an important, quite lengthy (and thus ex-pensive to cut), examination guide to the Four Books. Their investment paid off: the popularity of this work secured the family fortunes.[66]

Tellingly, however, once Ma Dingbang became successful, he de-voted at least a portion of his profits to the construction of a mansion, Zhongtian wu 中田屋 (see Fig. 3.1), still much admired today, and the purchase of land. Houses and land appear to have been the ultimate de-siderata of the Sibao entrepreneurs.[67] In the genealogies, phrases such as *gou dasha mai yutian* 構大廈買腴田 (he built a mansion and bought fertile fields) function as markers of publishing or other commercial success. The relative wealth of Sibao publishing-bookselling operations seems, in fact, to have been calculated roughly according to the mag-nificence of the main house and the size of the landholdings their man-agers could control. That Zou Hongchun (the publisher who had little use for examination study) was able to build his first "mansion" by the

---

65. *MTLZXZSZP*, 20.75a.
66. See Chapter 5, pp. 164–65, for a more detailed account of this strategy.
67. Interviews 1, 10/27/93 (Wuge); and 3, 10/28/93 (Wuge). One successful Ma publishing family reputedly built a house with a hall that could hold 120 banquet tables (Interview 19, 5/1/95 [Mawu]).

age of 16 *sui* was cited as a clear sign of his commercial brilliance.[68] So, too, the descendant of one of the most prosperous later Wuge publishers used the fact that his great-uncle was able to build "the finest house in Sibao" as proof of his business success.[69]

Lack of exact records makes the magnificence of these "mansions" and the size of the landholdings purchased with publishing profits difficult to calculate, but estimates suggest that the achievement of some of the *shufang* could be impressive within the local context. A "mansion" seems to have been the equivalent of a house of nine halls and eighteen skywells (*jiu ting shiba jing* 九廳十八井), which would have required several thousand *liang* of silver to construct in the late nineteenth century.[70] Wuge boasted three such "mansions"; two belonged to publishing households.[71] But by that time most publisher-booksellers lived more modestly.

Accounts of land purchases range widely. At the top end, the Wanjuan lou publishing house, managed by Zou Ming, yielded profits that paid for 150 *mu* (11.55 hectares) of land between 1776 and 1843 (some of the purchase money came from interest on moneylending).[72] One informant reported that, in his great-grandfather's generation (the midnineteenth century), the family *shufang*, the Huixian tang, had so prospered from the sale of books in Jiaying department, Guangdong, that the family was able to purchase over 100 *mu* (7.7 hectares) of land in Mawu: "Their ducks never drank other people's water."[73] In a landpoor area where a middling landlord was someone owning roughly 25 to 30 *mu* (1.93 to 2.3 hectares), this was a considerable achievement.[74] By

---

68. Interview 30, 11/13/95 (Wuge).

69. Interview 68, 12/5/95 (Wuge).

70. Interviews 1, 10/27/93 (Wuge); 3, 10/28/93 (Wuge); 49, 11/25/95 (Mawu); and 66, 12/5/95 (Wuge).

71. Interview 66, 12/5/95 (Wuge). These were Hengfen li 橫分里, another structure of "nine halls and eighteen skywells," and, the largest of the three, Ziyun wu 子雲屋.

72. Liu Yonghua, "The World of Rituals," p. 279. The account book (dated 1822) that records these purchases was apparently written by Zou Ming's heirs. The Benli tang also funded the purchase of about a hundred *mu* (7.7 hectares) in the late nineteenth century (Interview 28, 11/12/95 [Wuge]); and the Yijing tang, a purchase of 67 *mu* (4.2 hectares) (Interview 55, 12/1/95 [Mawu]).

73. Interview 54, 11/28/95 (Mawu).

74. Interview 59, 12/2/95 (Wuge); and see note 76 to this chapter.

the late nineteenth century, the amount of land typically bought from publishing-bookselling profits had sharply declined, either because falling profits reduced purchasing power or because the concentration of land in lineage estates had created a land shortage. For that period and the early twentieth century, most informants report much more modest purchases, ranging from 8 *mu* (0.62 hectare) to 13 or 27 *mu* (1.0 or 2.1 hectares), usually combined with the construction of a house.[75] But these plots, if added to existing holdings and/or supplemented by land rented from the lineage estates (as explained in Chapter 2, at favorable rates), were still not insignificant in the context of the landowning patterns of the area.[76]

Purchase of land and construction of houses were not the only ways in which publishing profits were used to enhance the welfare of the extended-family household. Many *shufang* owners also devoted some of their profits to educating male family members, usually by establishing a family school. Zou and Ma informants speak of two types of family schools: *mengguan* 蒙館, in essence primary schools (literally, "halls for untaught children") where boys learned to read and write; and *jingguan* 經館, "halls of the Classics," for students selected for examination study. Needless to say, the former greatly outnumbered the latter; one informant estimated that mid-Qing Mawu held over twenty *mengguan* but only two or three *jingguan*.

Publishing families had a vested interest, as we have seen, in producing educated successors, men who could at least understand the literature of the examination system well enough to publish and sell it. The

---

75. Interviews 34, 11/14/95 (Wuge); 44, 11/23/95 (Mawu); and 50, 11/25/95 (Mawu).

76. Liu Yonghua has estimated, on the basis of figures recorded at the time of land reform in Sibao, that the average holding among landlords was 22.175 *mu* (1.71 hectares); in neighboring Beituan, the average was 28 *mu* (2.2 hectares), and in the area around Liancheng city, 19.614 *mu* (1.51 hectares). As Liu points out, these averages are quite low, probably because much of the land was lineage-owned (see "Kangzu yu bukangzu," unpublished manuscript, pp. 7–8.) Liu's figures correspond roughly to those provided by John Buck for Lianjiang 連江, near Fuzhou in eastern Fujian, in the early 1920s, where the average holding was 23.58 *mu* (1 hectare by Buck's measure), the median, 14.01 *mu* (0.6 hectare). The greater productivity of the soil in this area of the province, as well as different socioeconomic conditions for landholding, make it difficult to extend these figures to Sibao, but they do suggest at least that landholdings in Fujian tended to be rather small (see Buck, *Chinese Farm Economy*, pp. 46, 102, 103).

link between education and business success was clearly understood by Ma Quanwen, one of the early successes of the Mawu book trade. After building up his store of titles and "building a house and buying some extra land," he "built a study (*jingshe* 精舍), hired a noted Confucian scholar, and practiced the rites of reverence to him. He then assembled all his talented heirs and had their lessons supervised by this teacher."[77] A rough contemporary of Ma Quanwen's, Zou Funan, manager of an important *shufang* and one of Wuge's more distinguished publishers— he was honored by the local magistrate with the title *binxiang* 賓鄉 (local guest) in 1720—also established a school, the Wugang shuwu 梧岡 書屋, "in order to nourish talent" among his sons and nephews.[78] Zou Shengmai, Funan's son, in couplets honoring the establishment of a Moxiang shuwu 墨香書屋 by the other Zou branch in Wuge, pointed up the long-term financial benefits of setting funds aside for schools: "Several *mu* of 'book' land preserves good fortune for generations; a store of a thousand *juan* of texts perfumes the family line with the scent of ink, without the need to pay taxes year after year."[79] Throughout the nineteenth and early twentieth centuries, the publishing households continued this practice of establishing family schools.[80]

Some publishers, in establishing schools for their heirs, seem to have cherished real hopes of examination success. Zou Hongchun, the only publisher to state explicitly his preference for business over study (or the only one with a biographer willing to record this choice), tellingly devoted some of his profits to the construction of a school ("book room" 書屋) for his younger brothers, which later became a school for his sons: "He invited noted teachers and called on his good friends to instruct them deep in the mountains and distant valleys," not permitting them to get involved in the management of the business.[81] To some degree, the Zou and Ma followed the strategy outlined by Wang

---

77. *MSDZZP* (1945), *ji* 7, 1.45a.

78. *MTLZXZSZP* (1911), 20.8b.

79. *FYZSZP* (1947), 35.29b.

80. For other examples, see the biographies of Zou Tingming 廷明, a military *juren* of 1786 (*MTLZXZSZP* [1911], 20.49ab); and Zou Qing 青 (1741–1826) (*FYZSZP* [1947], 33.35a–36a; and [1996], 2: 622–24). See Chapter 13 for a discussion of schools in Republican-era Sibao.

81. *FYZSZP* (1947), 33.28a.

Daokun 汪道昆 (1525–93) in his description of the alternation between study and trade among the Huizhou merchants of the late Ming: "It is not until a man is repeatedly frustrated that he gives up his studies and takes up trade. After he has accumulated substantial savings, he encourages his descendants, in planning for their future, to give up trade and take up studies. Trade and studies thus alternate with each other."[82]— although it must be said that the Huizhou merchants were more successful at both parts of this strategy than were the Zou and Ma.

Schools for the education of male household members,[83] fine houses, and land were leading goals of the publishing families, a three-pronged strategy for long-term economic stability and improved local social status. Once these three goals were met, wealthy publishing households might contribute to their lineage, funding the building or repair of ancestral halls, or creating a lineage trust or donating land to an existing trust. Or they might undertake charitable activities within the community at large. In short, they might pursue all the activities widely deemed the responsibility of local gentry in late imperial society.

The biography of Ma Dingbang, for example, provides a kind of blueprint or schedule of benevolence beginning with the family and then extending to the larger community: at 42 *sui* he organized a community group to fund repairs to the Zougong Temple in Mawu; at 48 he led his extended family in rebuilding the lower-shrine ancestral hall; at 52 he financed, with other family members, the construction of two bridges that linked Mawu to Ninghua (and the main route to Jiangxi) and Changting (and thus access to the Yin river); at 53 he organized repairs of the shrine to Zhongcheng gong 中丞公, one of the more distinguished Ma ancestors; at 56 he again funded a stone bridge that would facilitate travel and trade to Jiangxi, Guangdong, and Guangxi as well as to the nearest prefectural seat; at 71, when Sibao suffered from

---

82. Wang Daokun, *Taihan ji*, 42.10b–15a; cited in Ho, *The Ladder of Success in Imperial China*, p. 73; see also Zurndorfer, *Change and Continuity in Chinese Local History*, p. 55.

83. There is no explicit reference to the education of women in Wuge or Mawu. A few scattered comments indicate that some women might have had at least basic literacy: for example, the *MSDZZP* (1945), in a biography of the virtuous widow Jiang, explains that she taught her three sons to recite the *Sanzi jing* and *Baijia xing* 百家姓 (Myriad family names); *MSDZZP* (1945), *ji* 7, 1, *you* 9b. But such evidence is not conclusive, since it is possible that she had learned the text orally.

famine, he ordered his family to sell rice at reduced prices to women of the community whose husbands worked as traveling merchants and thus could not provide for them. Amid this history of charitable activities, the local magistrate in 1732 bestowed the title of "great guest" (*dabin* 大賓) on Ma, in recognition of his contributions to his village.[84]

Generally speaking, Sibao—or, more narrowly, the boundaries of branch-lineage settlements within Sibao—seems to have defined the limits of Zou and Ma charity. Ma Yangguang 揚光 (fl. nineteenth c.?) was praised for "happily contributing, without either stinginess or pride, several *jin* or several tens of *jin*" to build ancestral halls, shrines, bridges, fords, and roads within the *li* (*fan lizhong* 凡里中)—that is, within Sibao. In Sibao, of course, where most villages were single-surname units, community or public welfare was often either descent-group or branch-lineage welfare, and thus the funding of family concerns like the revision of the genealogy or the repair of an ancestral hall is identified in the genealogies as "public" charity.[85] Presumably Ma Yangguang's contributions to ancestral halls and shrines were limited to those of his branch lineage and perhaps the descent group, whereas his support of public works benefited the Sibao community.

The pull of native place and family was strong, even for those who settled elsewhere in pursuit of commerce: Zou Bingjun, although he made his wealth selling books and other products in Chongan county in northern Fujian, resettled in Sibao in his old age both to display his good fortune and to share it with his extended family. As the genealogy explains, he returned home after his sixtieth birthday, believing that "if the wealthy and high of status do not return home to ornament their native place, they are 'wearing brocade to walk at night'" (i.e., they are needlessly concealing their achievements). He collected small sums of money from members of his lineage branch, invested this money for them, and then used the profits to buy land and build an ancestral hall

---

84. *MSDZZP* (1945), *ji* 7, 1.77b–78b; *Changting xianzhi* (1879), *j.* 24, "Renwu xiangxing" 人物鄉行, 3a. Ma Dingbang earned this honor specifically for his relief work during a flood in Tingzhou city in 1706 and during the famine of 1726. Such activities were common among well-to-do merchants; see Rankin, "Rural-Urban Continuities," *passim*, for several examples.

85. *MSDZZP* (1947), *Liezhuan*, 1.72b–73a; see also "Jiaxun sitiao," 4b–5a, in *FYZSZP* (1947), *j. shou.*

and lineage shrines. For the larger "public" good, he also repaired roads, built a tea pavilion, and donated aid to the poor of Sibao.[86]

Many publisher-bookseller philanthropists focused on contributions, in or beyond Sibao, closely linked to and supportive of the book trade that had enriched them: the establishment of schools and the building and repair of roads, fords, bridges, and pavilions for weary travelers.[87] Ma Dingbang's building of bridges easing travel between Sibao and the Zou and Ma bookselling routes into Jiangxi and Guangdong, mentioned above, clearly fits into this category. So, too, does the charity work of the publisher Ma Lüzhi; he funded and organized a society to provide sacrifices to orphaned souls in Xufang 許坊, a village lying on the road between Sibao and Liancheng county seat. Victims of drowning, these orphan spirits were believed to cause the calamities that frequently beset Xufang;[88] Ma's society, by appeasing the restless spirits, made travel through the village safe again. And Zou Guoguang's 國光 (1814–93) repair of the Minting huiguan 閩汀會館 in Jiayingzhou with profits earned from his bookstore in that area might well have benefited Zou's own business as well as the larger community.[89] Zou Jiazhao 嘉兆 (fl. early nineteenth c.) was noted for his aid to distressed travelers; he donated free medicine to merchants poisoned by unscrupulous innkeepers and restaurateurs plotting to steal their goods—according to the genealogy, a common occupational hazard for merchants (like himself) sojourning in Fujian.[90] Several publishers also made use of their easy access to block cutters and printers, commissioning the printing and free distribution of morality books (*shanshu* 善書).[91]

---

86. *FYZSZP* (1947), 33.40b–41a. A few successful book merchants cast their bounty more widely. Zou Zhaomin 兆敏 (1744–1818), for example, helped fund the construction of a shrine to Zhu Xi in Tingzhou prefectural city, earning a place on the public list of sponsors and thus a name for himself and his family outside of Sibao. Ibid., 33.96b–97a.

87. For other examples, see *FYZSZP* (1947), 33.44a (Zou Hongxing 鋐興), 73b (Zou Xun 勳), 83a (Zou Jiming 際明); *MTLZXZSZP* (1911), 20.54b–55a (Zou Rong 榮), 65ab (Zou Danxuan 淡軒), 66b (Zou Lianfang 聯芳); and *MSDZZP*, *Liezhuan*, 1.82ab (Ma Xianfu 賢輔), 91ab (Ma Chaojin 朝縉), and 93a–94b (Ma Congbin 從彬).

88. *MSDZZP* (1993), *ji* 5, 83; cited in Liu Yonghua, "The World of Rituals," pp. 392–93.

89. *MTLZXZSZP* (1911), 20.89a.

90. Ibid., 20.68b.

91. See biographies of Zou Guoliang 國良 (ibid., 20.96a) and Ma Kekuan 克寬 (*MSDZZP*, 1945, *ji* 7, 1 *you* 4a–5a).

In sum, the Zou and Ma publishing households used the profits from their publishing enterprises to support the household economy, social standing, and future development of their families, whether nuclear, stem, joint, or extended. This support might take many forms, depending on the size and configuration of the household (the number of generations and distribution of members among these and between the two sexes), the kind and size of labor force it presented, its material needs, existing landholdings and resources, and business prospects. A first priority might be expanding the publishing operation and book trade; or acquiring land; or building a house large enough to hold, and thus help to preserve, the extended family; or providing education for future publisher-booksellers—or for talented boys who might become officials and thus make the family's fortunes. Philanthropies transcending the household or family might help the family business, while consolidating the family's standing in the community, identifying them collectively as part of the elite of Sibao or even of a wider locale. According to the genealogies, good works also contributed to the household's store of merit, helping to ensure continuation of the family line and an increase in family wealth and fame. Since the divisions of labor and contributions to the publishing and book trades were made, in essence, by the household unit, so, too, the disposition of profits, the fruits of this labor and these contributions, were also calculated, dispersed, and reinvested to advance the goals of the household as a unit.

---

# FIVE

# "We are all brothers": Household Division, the Proliferation of Publishing Houses, and the Management of Competition

THE IDEAL OF household unity—all members working harmoniously for the economic and demographic aggrandizement of the whole unit—was achieved only rarely in Sibao society and, when achieved, proved difficult to maintain. Tensions within the household—among brothers, among sisters-in-law, between father and sons—often led to a decision, usually by the sons but at times by the father or his widow, to divide the family property. But histories of family conflict in Sibao are difficult to uncover, for informants deny and genealogies ignore conflict, preferring to assert the normative value of family harmony. "We are all brothers," all informants claimed indignantly at any attempt to introduce the topic of family differences.

Yet the relentless emphasis in the genealogies on the importance of family harmony—of working for the good of the household as a whole, of sharing all resources equally, and of returning all profits to the household head—is in itself a sign that competition over material resources, among nuclear families in particular, was a common source of household disunity and division. Presumably this competition was usually behind the decision to divide the household and its property—possibly that is what is meant when a genealogy declares that a joint family had become "too troublesome" to remain a single communal unit. Evidence from both the genealogies and the informants suggests that the natural limit of a functioning household was roughly seventy or eighty persons; any larger and the household became too unwieldy for efficient management, and its members more susceptible to interpersonal conflicts.[1] Greater numbers, and perhaps more diffuse bonds as a result, seem to have intensified competition within a household for resources and resentment over real and imagined inequities.

This chapter examines the ways in which the practice of household division and, most important, the distribution of household property that accompanied it, influenced the Sibao publishing-bookselling business. The tradition of partible inheritance has been seen as a problem for China's agrarian economy, since it led to continual diminution in the size of household landholdings during periods of demographic increase. I would argue that it had quite a different effect on the book trade in Sibao. Although it discouraged the development of monolithic publishing houses, it stimulated—indeed, forced—the creation of new houses.[2] Since the book trade, unlike landownership in western Fujian, was at the time quite susceptible to expansion, particularly in the hands of ambitious merchants willing to sojourn some distance from their native place, one could argue that it was partly household division and the resulting proliferation of publishing houses that drove Sibao publishing and created a network of Sibao bookselling routes extending throughout most of southern China. Competition among *shufang* led publishers to search for new texts to print and book merchants to seek out new markets. At the same time, other forces modified the impact of *shufang* proliferation. The maintenance of business ties between "related" publishing houses— that is, *shufang* created by brothers at family division—allowed the formation of loosely connected *shufang* clusters that provided some protection against competition within the isolated and rather tightly lineage-based societies of Wuge and Mawu. And customary rules developed to regulate *shufang* relationships and ease competition.

---

1. For a fuller discussion of the motives for family division, see Wakefield, *Fenjia: Household Division and Inheritance in Qing and Republican China*, pp. 34–39.

2. See Chen Zhiping and Zheng Zhenman, "Qingdai Minxi Sibao zushang yanjiu," pp. 94–95.

*Family Division and the Development*
*of New Publishing Houses*

Property division had a profound impact on the development of the publishing trade in Sibao, for a household's store of woodblocks and its printing workrooms (and the stock of any branch bookstores) were considered part of the property and thus subject to the rules of partible inheritance that governed such arrangements. We saw in Chapter 3 that the first publishing houses in Sibao were founded on capital derived from the earnings of Zou and Ma sojourning merchants, often book merchants; presumably this continued to be one source of capital throughout Sibao's printing history. But inheritance, either of woodblocks or imprints, or of silver and other property, could also provide capital for the establishment of new shops. Thus property division, rather than disrupting *shufang* activities and scattering resources, might well have enabled the creation of new publishing houses. The 87 sets of blocks belonging to the Xiangshan tang 湘山堂 in 1773 were divided, for example, among the six heirs of Ma Lie 烈 (1709–52), the *shufang* manager, in lots of 19, 14, 12, 16, 17, and 9, along with land and portions of the household's buildings. At the time of this first division, the printing building of the Xiangshan tang, the Nanshan tang *yinshufang* 南山堂印書房, along with a storage building, remained common property, still to be shared by the brothers, presumably to print texts from their separate stores of blocks.[3] But a second division document, dated just four months after the first, divided this facility among the three heirs who had inherited the largest number of titles. In this case, seemingly, the division of one publishing house's property resulted in the creation of at least two new *shufang* (assuming that one of the branches, presumably that of the eldest son, continued to manage the Xiangshan tang) and possibly as many as five (if the brothers who did not receive rooms in the family "printing building" had access to other work areas).

---

3. The third heir was also given a building identified as the Nanshan Nan'ailu *shuguan* 南山南愛廬書館; it is not clear what this structure was—probably a school, possibly a storehouse for books printed by the family or another printing area.

The principle underlying household division in Sibao—and, indeed, everywhere[4]—was equal shares of household property to each family. Presumably, then, differences in the numbers of titles (or amounts of land or numbers of rooms) received by each branch were intended to compensate for the diverse values of the titles—indeed, it is easy to see that the blocks for a text like the *Dizi gui* 弟子規 (Regulations for students), a short primer, were probably less valuable than those for the *Sishu jianben* 四書監本 ("Directorate of Education" edition of the Four Books). What is striking, then—given the existence of clearly accepted ways of adjusting the types of property distributed, so that each heir got the same total value—is that, at least in the extant complete property-division records from publishing households in Wuge and Mawu, each heir usually received some share of each type of property being divided. As we have seen above, the titles of the Xiangshan tang were divided among six branches; the document that distributed the blocks of the Zaizi tang in 1839 listed 107 titles, to be divided also among six heirs (19, 16, 18, 22, 15, 17);[5] the 46 titles of the Yunshen Chu 雲深處 were divided in the Daoguang era among five heirs (9, 10, 8, 9, 10); the 21 titles of the Wenhai lou among five heirs in 1894;[6] and the 31 titles of the Juxian tang into five lots (6, 5, 6, 5, 9) in 1897. Even when there were only a few titles to divide, each branch received a portion, though often in what might appear to be negligible numbers. The 1897 property-division document for the household that operated the Wanjuan lou, for example, divided 17 titles among four heirs in such a way that two heirs received only 3 titles, one got 5, and another, 6.[7]

These numbers hint at the flexibility of the Sibao industry as a whole, in particular at the ways in which the local economy and the variety of sources of livelihood allowed for and even encouraged considerable variation in size and rate of growth of Sibao publishing houses. Long-

---

4. Wakefield, Fenjia: *Household Division and Inheritance*, pp. 56–58.

5. This document also disposes the books in the Guangdong branch bookstore among the heirs.

6. This document does not provide a clear breakdown of which titles go to which branch.

7. The three titles in each case are also not noticeably more valuable than the titles given to the other branches; presumably the inequity here was made up in distributions of more valuable land or buildings.

established houses might produce as many as 107 titles. New houses opened with a "seed" supply of as many as 22 or as few as 3 titles' worth of blocks (for an average of 11.5 per heir); this number, supplemented by land and some living (and perhaps working) space, might have been enough to set up a new branch household. The division of woodblock property, in a context in which almost all households welcomed opportunities to diversify their sources of income, encouraged the expansion of the publishing industry by multiplying *shufang* of different sizes, rather than by merging and consolidating them.

There were exceptions. All the blocks of a publishing house might be left to one branch family. As we shall see below, Ma Quanwen, the youngest heir within his household, received all of his father's woodblocks during the property division. But this arrangement was made as a means not of consolidating the business and putting it under the control of the most talented and ambitious manager but of furnishing a livelihood to the weakest and youngest member of the family. Informants mentioned the practice of selecting one heir to inherit woodblocks: "The house name and woodblocks would be given to the son who wished to continue publishing."[8] But this might have been a strategy more common when a publishing house was either just getting started or in decline, when its titles were too few to enable all the heirs to start up separate shops. Ma Quanheng, Quanwen's elder brother and an experienced publisher-bookseller, received no woodblocks at the family division but got three *mu* (0.23 hectare) of land and twenty ounces of silver. He used the silver as capital to acquire his own blocks and paper, and he and his enterprising son Dingbang built one of the most successful Sibao *shufang*.

Division of the woodblocks, however, seems to have been the usual choice, intended to give each heir a start—in some cases, a slender, three-title start—at building his own store of blocks. Possibly, too, a small number of titles was seen not as a start in publishing but as a commodity that could be sold or rented out to supplement the household income. The method of property division, in tandem with household occupational diversity, by and large prevented or at least discouraged the consolidation of publishing houses and the evolution of household

---

8. Interview 25, 11/9/95 (Wuge).

monoliths specializing exclusively in publishing (although, as mentioned in Chapter 3, individual Sibao publishing houses did achieve what was, by premodern Chinese publishing standards, considerable size). The continuity of the industry was ensured by a process that repeatedly reduced the size of the publishing-bookselling unit. At the same time, however, certain customary regulations encouraged the formation of close business alliances among related *shufang.*

## CONTINUITY WITHIN THE
## PUBLISHING HOUSEHOLDS:
## TWO CASES

The histories of a few Zou and Ma household publishing concerns will illustrate the flexibility and elasticity distinctive of the structure and development of these household businesses, as well as the particular kind of continuity that contributed to the almost three-century life span of the Sibao enterprises. The remarkably prolific line of Ma Dafan 大蕃 (1629–63) provides an impressive first case study (see Appendix C1, beginning with Dafan's father, Ma Yipiao 一驃). From the late seventeenth through the early twentieth century, over eight generations, descendants of Ma Dafan were active in the printing industry. Like many publishing families in the Zou and Ma genealogies, their story began in desperation, with the loss of the family head and resulting threat of destitution for his family. When Ma Dafan died, his oldest son, Ma Quanheng, was only thirteen *sui*, and his wife was still pregnant with his youngest son, Ma Quanwen.[9] Fortunately Ma Dafan's elder brother, Ma Dafang, one of Mawu's more enterprising and successful non-publishing merchants,[10] was able to assist the destitute family, "giving them capital and teaching them [the skills of] trading."[11] Ma Quanheng invested some of this capital in the cutting of woodblocks for popular textbooks such as *Sishu jizhu* 四書集註 (or 注) (Collected commentaries on the Four Books; which contains the orthodox Cheng-Zhu inter-

---

9. *MSDZZP* (1945), *ji* 7, 1.42ab; (1993), 5.137–38.
10. See Chapter 4, p. 129.
11. *MSDZZP* (1945), *ji* 7, 1.34b; (1993), 5.130–31.

pretation of these central examination texts), *Sishu jicheng*, and *Sishu beizhi*. The genealogy laconically announces that "these blocks were very popular, and after four years [in 1685] the brothers divided the family property."[12]

In the division, Ma Quanheng, who by this time had long since established his own family, received three *mu* of land and twenty ounces of silver. All the woodblocks (and printing workrooms) went to the youngest brother, Ma Quanwen. With these blocks Quanwen established a publishing house (the Benli tang 本立堂), which prospered so well that "the blocks they accumulated reached to the ridgepole of the house, and they became as gloriously wealthy as an untitled noble."[13] Even greater success attended the line of Ma Quanheng. With some of his twenty ounces of silver, he hired workers to cut blocks for the *Sishu* 四書 (Four Books), *Shijing zhu* 詩經註 (*Classic of Songs* with commentary), and two popular primers, *Youxue gushi qionglin* 幼學故事瓊林 (Treasury of allusions for young students) and *Zengguang xianwen*, in effect establishing his own publishing house.[14] In 1687, he set off to sell these texts in Guangdong, entrusting the management of the family to his son, Ma Dingbang, who, "though young [sixteen *sui*], was rich in talent."[15] Ma Quanheng left behind

---

12. Ibid., *ji* 7, 1.42b–43a, 74a. It is impossible to know exactly what texts these titles represent, since the texts themselves do not survive. The biography of Ma Quanheng lists the text titles as *Sishu jizhu beizhi* 四書集注備旨, which I have taken to mean the *Sishu jizhu* and the *Sishu beizhi* (possibly an abbreviated title, referring to one of a large number of study aids for the Four Books; see Chapter 10). But it might refer to a single title (Full purport of the *Collected Commentaries on the Four Books*). The biography of Ma Dingbang adds another title: the *Sishu jicheng*. A *Sishu jicheng* is attributed to a Song dynasty author, Wu Zhenzi 吳真子 (see *Zhongguo guji shanben shumu, Jingbu*, 1: 3.45b, p. 324), but all that we can deduce from the title here is that it was a collection relevant to the Four Books.

13. *MSDZZP* (1945), *ji* 7, 1.45b.

14. Ibid., *ji* 7, 1.74b. The text lists *Youxue Zengguang*; I am assuming that *Youxue* refers to a child's primer or beginning textbook (probably the *Youxue gushi qionglin*, a very popular children's encyclopedia of *chengyu* 成語), and *Zengguang* to the very common primer *Zengguang xianwen*, the title of which was frequently abbreviated in this fashion.

15. Ibid., *ji* 7, 1.43a.

two reels (*gu* 箍) of "small paper" (*xiaozhi* 小紙)[16] as capital to supply the daily needs of the family. This paper was worth three *qian* 錢. [Ma Dingbang] used it to print texts. When all of these had been sold, he went into the mountains to buy more paper, which he carried back himself and again used to print up texts. He continued this cycle, and the family never suffered hunger or cold, all on the strength of those two reels of paper. Later, as a result of his labors, his younger brother was able to marry. Thus those two reels of paper were made into ten million [*qian*]. [Ma Quanheng], distant from home, could begin to feel no anxiety about his family.[17]

Ma Dingbang, obviously an enterprising young man, later supplemented the family's income from printing: with his brother-in-law Zou Wenguang 文光 and Ma Linjiu 林舅, he also traded in timber.[18] But printing-bookselling seems to have been the mainstay of the household. Once the two eldest of his younger brothers were old enough, he left them in charge of the family and began traveling in Guangdong and Guangxi to sell books. The fourth brother, Ma Dinglüe, branched out into Jiangxi.[19] Eventually Ma Dingce 定策 (1677–?), the younger of the two brothers left behind to manage the family, also began selling, working the family's routes in all three provinces.[20] Finally, the youngest of the brothers, Ma Dingtao 定韜 (1688–1729), after studying for several years, also went out to sell the family's texts in Jiangxi, Guangdong, Zhejiang, and Jiangsu ("Wu Yue 吳越"), where "all the literati welcomed him."[21] The family continued producing books. In 1707 Ma Dingbang cut (or commissioned) the blocks for the *Sishu zhu daquan* 四書注大全 (Compendium of the Four Books with commentary). This long work must have required considerable capital outlay, but it alone set the family finances on a stable foundation: "This book was so popular that it made the family

---

16. The precise meanings of *gu*, "hoop," "band," or "to wind around," and *xiaozhi* are uncertain.

17. *MSDZZP* (1945), *ji* 7, 1.75a.

18. Ibid., *ji* 7, 1.75b.

19. Ibid., *ji* 7, 1.61ab; see Chapter 4.

20. *MSDZZP* (1945), *ji* 7, 1.59a.

21. Ibid., *ji* 7, 1.64b.

circumstances more comfortable, and providing daily necessities ceased to be a hardship."[22]

At the height of the joint family's prosperity, Ma Dingbang headed a household of about fifty people: his mother, his four younger brothers (three after Ma Dinglüe died in 1718), and their families. In 1722, he turned fifty-one *sui*, and at the insistence of his mother, née Zou, the family divided. The property was apportioned among the brothers, with, according to the genealogy, scrupulous attention to equality.[23] The woodblocks appear to have been divided among the three brothers most active in the book trade: Ma Dingbang, Ma Dingce, and Ma Dingtao. The family of the deceased Ma Dinglüe shared the portion of blocks given to Ma Dingtao. Each of the three living brothers then established his own shop, which in turn passed to his descendants.

Descendants of all three brothers continued publishing and bookselling for at least another two generations. Ma Dingbang's shop (the Wencui lou 文萃樓) was managed by his second son, Ma Jiu 就 (1704–

---

22. Ibid., *ji* 7, 1.75b. The Chinese text reads 四書汪大全. I read *wang* 汪 as an error for *zhu* 注, but the character may refer to a "complete compendium" of the Four Books and their commentaries compiled by an author with the surname Wang. Or this title may be the great compendium of commentaries on the Four Books produced at the command of the Yongle emperor (r. 1402–24), the *Sishu daquan* (Complete compendium of the Four Books, 1415)—"whose purpose was to define and print for use the sources candidates should use to prepare for the civil examinations in all government schools down to the county level" (Elman, *Cultural History of the Civil Examinations*, p. 114). This text, with the *Xingli daquan* 性理大全 (Compendium on nature and principle), standardized the contents of examination study through the rest of the imperial period; see Wilson, *Genealogy of the Way*, pp. 161–67.

Most likely, however, the *Sishu zhu daquan* is yet another compendium of commentaries to the Four Books, for these compendia, all offered as "comprehensive" guides to examination success (capitalizing on the title of the *Sishu daquan*), proliferated in the late Ming and Qing. (See Chia, *Printing for Profit*, pp. 221–22, 230; I am grateful to Thomas Wilson for guidance on this point.) Whatever the exact identity of this Ma-family best-seller, two points can be made: its popularity was ensured because it promised guidance in the study of the Four Books; and since such *daquan* were usually long and cut in multiple text registers or levels, the publication of this work was quite expensive.

23. *MSDZZP* (1945), *ji* 7, 1.77ab. Ma Dingbang's mother ordered the family division after she became severely ill. No explicit reason is given for her decision, if it was in fact her decision. We might guess that, aware that the family had reached a size that made division attractive, she wanted to ensure that all arrangements were made before her death.

89), while his eldest son, Ma Long 龍 (1702–81), studied for the examinations (eventually earning or purchasing *jiansheng*, or Imperial Academy, student status).[24] Following Ma Jiu, management of the shop passed to Ma Lüzhi, Long's son and Jiu's nephew. At least some blocks from Ma Dingtao's shop, the Jinglun tang 經綸堂, went to his second son, Shu 恕 (1711–82), who used them to establish the Tongwen tang 同文堂 and marketed his books in the area of southwestern Guangdong. From Shu, the blocks went to his eldest son, Ma Lügong 履恭 (1729–71).[25]

By far the most impressive achievements in family publishing were made by the descendants of Ma Dingce, the middle son and founder of the Xiangshan tang 湘山堂. His second son, Lie, inherited this shop and sold its books in southeastern Guangdong.[26] Lie's six sons continued to manage the shop cooperatively until 1773, when the household property was divided. The printing workrooms (*yinshu fangwu* 印書房屋) were apportioned among three of Lie's six heirs, including the household of the eldest son, who had died in 1765, well before the division. The other households were compensated with portions of another family building, a granary. Although not all six households inherited printing workrooms, all received woodblocks, with the workrooms going to those who received the largest number of titles (nineteen, seventeen, and sixteen).[27]

Ma Dingce's elder son, Guang 光 (1702–66), seems to have entered the book trade rather late, after a protracted period of study. We know nothing of his publishing or bookselling career. But two of his grandsons, Ma Cuida 萃大 (1768–1858) and Ma Cuizhong 萃仲 (1770–1848),

---

24. Ibid., *ji* 7, 1.80a–81a, 1.95a–96b, 21.1a–4a.

25. Ibid., *ji* 7, 1.99a–100a, 22.15a; Ma Jiashu, "Mawu diaoban yinshuaye chayue ziliao."

26. Ibid., *ji* 6, 1.50b, 21.72a–73a.

27. The printing workrooms were apportioned as follows. The first household received "the first hall and the main hall to the right side near the road, a total of three *jian* 間 [a room; literally, the space between walls]; a privy one *jian* in area; and the printing workroom on the left that is one large *jian*." The fourth household got "the five rows of printing workrooms on the left and the one-*jian* room by the side of the small gate"; and the fifth, "the three-*jian* printing workroom on the right of the Nanshan tang, the back hall, and the three-*jian* room on the left." See also *MSDZZP* (1945), 21.72a–83b.

were active in the trade. Cuida sold books in Fujian, Guangdong, Guangxi, Hunan, and Hubei; Cuizhong was a sojourning book merchant in Fuzhou and Guangzhou and the manager of a thriving publishing house, the Zaizi tang, quite possibly founded on woodblocks inherited through his father and grandfather. This shop, like the Xiangshan tang, was a cooperative family business, staffed by all six of Ma Cuizhong's sons, until the family property was divided in 1839. Once again the woodblocks were distributed, by title, among all Ma Cuizhong's sons, whereas the printing workrooms were divided, less evenly, between two of the sons.[28] Among them, Ma Cuizhong's sons and grandsons had at least four shops, prosperous enough to establish branches outside of Sibao: the Zaizi tang (first son); the Nianzi tang 念茲堂 (second son), with bookstores in Wuzhou, Guangxi; the Wenzi tang 文茲堂 (third son), with a store in Yanping prefecture, Fujian; and the Wenlin tang 文林堂 (heir of the fourth son) in Xingning county, Guangdong.[29]

Similarly long and complex family publishing and bookselling traditions can be found in the Zou lineage as well. Five generations descending from Zou Shuwen were engaged in the book trade, from the early eighteenth century through the early twentieth century (see Appendix C2). Zou Shuwen's father, Dianmo 殿謨 (1649–1710),[30] may have begun the family book business, since we learn from Shuwen's biography that, after abandoning his studies, Shuwen joined his father and four elder brothers as a merchant sojourning in Zhangshuzhen

---

28. Thus the first son, Ma Yuhui 玉暉 (1791–1876), the heir to the Zaizi tang, was given nineteen titles and the "one printing room (*yinfang yisuo* 印房一所) behind the house"; Ma Yulan 玉蘭 (1797–1829), who established the Nianzi tang 念茲堂 with his patrimony, received sixteen titles; Ma Yuzhang 玉章 (1801–52), the founder of the Wenzi tang 文茲堂, got eighteen titles and "the Fujian woodblocks"; and the fourth son, Ma Yutang 玉堂 (1806–39), founder of the Wenlin tang 文林堂, had died before the property division, but Yutang's son was given twenty-two titles. The fifth and sixth sons, Ma Yuming 玉鳴 (1808–?) and Ma Yuting 玉廷 (1812–69), combined their inheritance of fifteen and seventeen titles, respectively, to form a separate shop (*tangming* unknown); they continued to print books in the "publishing house on Nanshan" left to Ma Yuming. See *MSDZZP* (1945), 21.59a–68a; Zaizi tang property-division document (1839), unpaginated ms.

29. Interview 53, 11/28/95 (Mawu).

30. *FYZSZP* (1947), 10.13a–14a.

樟樹鎮, Linjiang 臨江 county, Jiangxi. After his father's death (when Shuwen was nineteen *sui*), he continued to work with his brothers, and within a few years they had "a large house and were rich in fields and gardens"—in short, "a middling degree of wealth." After the death of all four brothers, Shuwen continued on alone, supporting his nephews as well as his sons, sending some to school and some to train as book merchants.[31] When his second son, Hongyou, was thirteen *sui*, he began training him in the bookselling business; in 1755 Shuwen returned to Sibao to manage the household and publishing house (the Zushu tang 祖述堂), leaving Hongyou, then thirty-three *sui*, in charge of the shop in Zhangshuzhen.[32] Zou Hongyou's two younger brothers, Hongqi 鋐起 (1726–62) and Hongxing 鋐興 (1732–1816), worked with him as "Confucian merchants" (*rugu* 儒賈) in Zhangshuzhen.[33] At some point the brothers appear to have diversified their trade routes, for Hongxing, after training with his father and brothers in Jiangxi, worked as a sojourning merchant in Chongan (in northern Fujian), Suzhou, Hangzhou, and Hanchuan 漢川 (Hubei), "establishing a series of bookstores in order to sell the Classics."[34]

After Zou Hongqi died in 1762, it appears that Zou Hongyou and Zou Hongxing continued working together for roughly another decade, with Hongyou managing the store in Zhangshuzhen while Hongxing sold books on the road. All of Hongyou's sons ended up working in the trade. His eldest, Zou Kongshu 孔書 (1745–93), at first devoted himself to study for the examinations, but at age twenty-four, when his father became ill, he abandoned his aspirations to office and took over the bookstore in Zhangshuzhen. A few years later, his younger brother Zou Kongai began his training; at age fifteen, he went on his first bookselling trip with his father into Hubei, to Wuchang 武昌 prefectural city.[35]

At least four of Zou Hongxing's eight sons were trained in the trade by their uncle; Zou Kongmao, the eldest, first worked with his uncle in

---

31. Ibid., 10.23a–24b, 33.30b–31a.
32. Ibid., 10.24a–26a, 33.43ab.
33. Ibid., 10.31b–32b, 10.34a–36a, 33.44ab, 33.45ab.
34. Ibid., 34.42b; see also 10.24a–26a, 10.34a–36a, and 33.42a–45b.
35. Ibid., 10.24a–29b, 33.59a–60b.

Zhangshuzhen and then together with his next three brothers as book merchants in Guangdong and Guangxi. Zou Hongyou eventually summoned his nephew Kongmao home to manage the household in Sibao, then numbering about thirty, while Hongyou took his son Kong-ai on the road. Zou Kongyin 孔音 (1764–1820), Kongmao's fourth brother, continued to sell books in Guangxi after his second and third elder brothers died. Hongqi's two orphaned sons, Zou Kongchun 孔椿 (1747–1832) and Zou Kongjia, sixteen and three *sui*, respectively, on the death of their father, were at first also taken under the wing of Zou Hongyou. The elder, Kongchun, started work with Hongyou as a book merchant in Zhangshuzhen immediately after his father's death, while Kongjia devoted himself to study.[36]

At or just before the death of Zou Hongyou in 1772, the family property was divided among each of the three lines of descent from Zou Shuwen: Zou Hongyou and his heirs, Zou Hongqi's heirs, and Zou Hongxing and his heirs. Hongxing's line appears to have abandoned the book trade after the second generation; there is no further reference to publishing or bookselling activities among his descendants in the genealogy. Hongqi's heirs stayed with the business—in fact they inherited the Zushu tang and presumably some of its blocks—although their position seems to have been a little precarious. By the time of his uncle's death, Kongchun had acquired some training in the book trade, but Kongjia, only twelve and still a student, had no experience in business at all. The genealogy laconically notes that "the family affairs became more difficult." As a result, Kongjia abandoned his examination studies to work with his older brother as a book merchant, again in Zhangshuzhen. Both later diversified their sojourning routes, Kongchun elaborating on the pattern established by his uncle Hongxing, traveling to Suzhou, Hangzhou, Hanchuan (Hubei), and "all different places in Hunan and Hubei," while his younger brother worked routes into Guangdong and as far west as Guixian 貴縣, Guangxi.[37] Apparently none of Kongchun's or Kongjia's sons continued in the trade.

It is Zou Hongyou's line that enjoyed the longest-lasting success in the book business. All three of Hongyou's sons remained active in the

---

36. Ibid., 10.31b–39a, 33.61b–64a.
37. Ibid., 33.61b–62a, 33.63a–64a.

publishing-bookselling trade. Zou Kongai returned to Sibao to manage the family publishing house, "taking the printing of texts as his occupation." His elder brother, Kongshu, continued selling books in Zhangshuzhen, as well as in Guangdong and Guangxi; he died on the road, aged forty-nine, in the Fujian *huiguan* in Nanning, Guangxi. Zou Kongchang 孔昌 (1770–1834), the youngest brother and only three at the time of his father's death, was also raised to the trade; he traveled with Kongshu to Guangxi and, on Kongshu's death, spent several years as a sojourning merchant in Ganzhou, Zhangshuzhen, and Wuchengzhen 吳城鎮 (Jiangxi), Yunnan, and Annam or Vietnam.[38]

The household labor pool was augmented by several members of the next generation, the sons of Kongshu, Kongai, and Kongchang. Zou Kongshu's eldest son, Zou Pibin 丕彬 (1767–1845), like so many other booksellers, studied for the examinations when a boy, but "family members had become so numerous" and providing for all of them so onerous that at age eighteen he took up bookselling. "At first he traveled to Meizhou [Jiaying department], and then on to Nanning—he traversed all the famous mountains and noted regions of the two Yue 粵."[39] He continued to work in Guangdong and Guangxi while his uncle Kongai managed the publishing house and the extended family back in Sibao. His youngest brother, Zou Pihuang 丕煌 (1785–1865), moved to Rongxian 容縣, Wuzhou prefecture, Guangxi province, to set up a bookstore.[40]

Zou Pibin's cousin, Zou Pikang 丕康 (1776–1816), the second son of Zou Kongai, "had gone, ever since he was young, with the men of his father's and uncles' generation to Beiliu, Nanning, and other places in Guangxi" as a book merchant; he died en route in the Fujian *huiguan* in Nanning.[41] His younger brother, Zou Pirong 丕融 (1782–1866), began as a student, but "too many mouths to feed" turned him to the "arts of calculation" (*xi jiran zhi shu* 習計然之術)—traveling with his father and older brother on their bookselling routes in Guangdong and Guangxi.[42]

---

38. Ibid., 33.59a–61b; Interview 14, 4/28/95 (Wuge).
39. *FYZSZP* (1947), 22.10a–11b, 33.77b–78a.
40. Interview 57, 12/2/95 (Wuge); *FYZSZP* (1947), 22.55ab, 34.65ab.
41. *FYZSZP* (1947), 22.61a–63a, 33.78b–79a.
42. Ibid., 22.66a–69a, 33.79a–80a.

This cooperative arrangement worked well; the publishing house flourished under Zou Kongai's management, and Zou Kongchang, Zou Kongshu, and selected members of the next generation returned enough in sales to support the growing household, estimated at fifty, comfortably and to fund the expansion of their publishing enterprise. Zou Pibin's biography refers pointedly to his "bitter" labor "several thousand *li* from home for several decades" and its contribution to the household fortunes. Although Pibin never diverted "even one *qian* 錢 or one *chi* 尺 of cloth to his own family's funds"[43] out of joint household profits, Zou Kongai was able to build a large mansion, purchase several hundred *mu* of high-quality land, and build a new publishing building (*shufang yisuo* 書坊一所). He also established a family school, hiring a teacher to instruct his sons and nephews.[44] Imperial Academy student degrees were purchased for Kongai himself in 1795, Kongchang in 1801, Pibin in 1806, Pihuang in 1820 (and another brother, Piqing 丕清 [1775–1848], in 1825),[45] Pirong in 1818, Pikang in 1821, and Kongchang's only son, Jiyu 際虞 (1795–1859), in 1832.[46] By the time Zou Pirong, Kongai's third son, returned home from bookselling to take over management of the household from his father, it had grown to seventy members, making it one of the larger joint households in Wuge at the time.[47]

In keeping with the common lineage strategy of diversification, not all the male household members worked in the book trade. Some members of the family were directed to long-term study in the family school that Zou Kongai had established. Even the most promising failed the household's hopes. Kongshu's third son, Zou Jitang 際唐 (1781–after 1824), managed to achieve only the status of a supplementary licentiate (*xianxue fusheng* 縣學附生) at the age of forty-three.[48] His cousin, Zou Jiyu, studied at the Longshan shuyuan 龍山書院 in 1820, but, as noted above, eventually purchased Imperial Academy student status.[49]

---

43. Ibid., 33.78a.
44. Ibid., 33.60b.
45. Ibid., 22.33b–36a.
46. Ibid., 10.27a–31b, 22.10a–11b, 22.55ab, 22.61a–63a, 22.66a–69a, 22.95b–96b.
47. Ibid., 33.79b–80a.
48. Ibid., 22.49a–51a.
49. Ibid., 22.95b–96a.

By the third generation from Zou Hongyou (the twenty-second generation in the genealogical listing), the prosperity of the line, which had peaked in the early nineteenth century, was beginning to decline, apparently fairly precipitously. One of the problems may have been the dramatic increase in household size—the twenty-second generation counted forty sons, compared to only ten in the previous generation. Yet the book trade seems to have remained lucrative enough to retain several of this generation. Zou Xifu 希福 (1823–89), a son of Piqing, together with his cousin Zou Xidao 希道 (1815–84), son of Jitang, moved to Wenzhou (Zhejiang) to establish a bookstore, and Xifu's descendants settled there permanently.[50] Zou Pihuang and six of his seven sons eventually moved to Wuzhou (Guangxi) to work in the book trade.[51] One of Pirong's nine sons, Zou Xicheng 希程 (1817–90), worked as a book merchant in Guangdong.[52] Two of Jiyu's four sons, Zou Xiting 希廷 (1819–61) and Zou Xihuai 希槐 (1836–66), sold books in Guangdong and Guangxi.[53]

With the next generation, however, references to the book trade peter out; the genealogy states that two or three sons of Xifu were selling books in Wenzhou,[54] and Xihuai's son Cunxuan 存軒 (1858–84) worked his father's routes in Guangdong.[55] But references to family poverty appear more frequently in the genealogy biographies, and most members of this generation seem to have been seeking other means of livelihood—subofficial service, farming, tin working, and medicine—a sign that publishing-bookselling offered diminishing profits.

As these two extended examples indicate, there was considerable flexibility and changeability, synchronically and diachronically, in any household's commitment to the publishing business and thus to the size and scope of the Zou and Ma publishing operations. Once a publishing house had proven profitable enough to support a household, its labor force could easily be expanded by drawing more household members into production and bookselling. The household of fifty

---

50. Ibid., *j. shou*, 21b, 22.48a–49b, 22.50b–51b.
51. Ibid., 22.55a–60a.
52. Ibid., 34.69a.
53. Ibid., 22.95b–97a, 22.108b–9b.
54. Ibid., 22.48a–49a.
55. Ibid., 22.108b–9b; Interview 57, 12/2/95 (Wuge).

headed by Ma Dingbang in the early eighteenth century constituted one of the most successful of Mawu's publishing concerns. With four younger brothers, Dingbang was able to train two to manage the publishing house, so that he could join the other two in bookselling; these five men, aided in printing by their wives and offspring, and in bookselling by their sons and nephews, supported a household of at least three generations. So, too, Zou Kongai, head of an extended family of fifty, managed a publishing house that was able to employ five of his sons and nephews as booksellers in the late eighteenth and early nineteenth centuries; by the late 1820s, the household numbered seventy people.

Division of large households partitioned the publishing houses that supported them. In some instances a single son—like Ma Quanwen, the youngest son of Ma Dafan—inherited the publishing-house name and all the woodblocks and printing workrooms associated with it. Usually, however, the division of the household meant the division of the publishing house into smaller, potentially competing publishing houses. Too small a family or one lacking a strong head would encounter difficulty in maintaining or building up a *shufang*. Witness Zou Kongchun and Zou Kongjia, the two orphaned sons of Zou Hongqi, who at ages twenty-five and twelve, respectively, inherited a portion of the publishing house headed by their uncle, Zou Hongyou. Although they managed to keep the business going, they were never able to achieve a level of activity and profit even close to that of their cousin Zou Kongai, who had a larger pool of family workers at his disposal at the time of the property division. A shortage of household workers might even lead to the formation of partnerships. In the late nineteenth century, for example, the manager of the Benli tang, Ma Qiming 啓明, invited members of the lower-shrine Zou lineage to form a partnership, because his household lacked the numbers of workers necessary to sustain the publishing business.[56]

Indeed, access to a supply of labor seems to have been key, as the success of Ma Quanheng, Quanwen's older brother, suggests. Despite inheriting none of the family woodblocks, he was able to start his own publishing house, relying on his own previous experience and, perhaps

---

56. Ma Jiashu, "Mawu diaoban yinshuaye chayue ziliao"; *MSDZZP* (1993), 3.160–64; and *MTLZXZSZP* (1994), *j. shou*, "Longzuxiang Yesheng gong houyi diaoban yinshua zhi xunli," p. 53.

even more important, on the work of his eldest son, Ma Dingbang, and eventually his four other sons. Certainly, too, the striking publishing-bookselling success of the descendants of Zou Zhaoxiong 兆熊 (1626–73) of the lower-shrine Zou lineage owed at least something to the extraordinary fertility of that line (see Appendix C3).

Up to a point, then, the location of the publishing houses in multi-generational joint households was a boon to business. The large population of such households provided a pool of labor for the publishing house. Since printing did not for the most part require much skill, there was some flexibility in the ways in which this workforce could be employed. Jobs could be rotated among family members, including women and children, particularly when household tasks or agricultural work was particularly demanding. Cooperation among brothers allowed one household to manage both production and sales. It also enabled family members to trade jobs as expediency dictated. Finally, cooperation between generations meant that the labor force could be steadily renewed; the relative ages of descendants tended to ensure that by the time the sons of the youngest brother were ready to manage production or to go on the road, the grandsons of the oldest brother were old enough to be trained in the business. Certainly the households did not lack for instructors; each of the publishing houses discussed above provided multiple examples of managers and booksellers teaching both sons and nephews the intricacies of the trade.

Of course, at the same time that the growth of the joint family encouraged the expansion of the publishing enterprise embedded in the household, it also increased the risk of division and the consequent proliferation of competing publishing houses of different sizes. Some of the smaller of these might focus exclusively on printing, selling their texts wholesale to book merchants outside the household. Or, on the contrary, they might abandon any effort to establish a publishing house in order to concentrate on bookselling, marking out a new route for themselves, either by branching off established routes (as Zou Kongjia did in pushing on to Guixian, Guangxi, extending a route long set through Guangdong and eastern Guangxi) or by forging into completely new territory (as his brother Kongchun attempted in traveling to "all different places in Hunan and Hubei"). Some of the smaller households might participate in the publishing trade as a sideline, perhaps hiring out family members on an ad hoc basis to the larger publishing houses or renting out their small store of blocks. Although these smaller efforts rarely yielded the high profits enjoyed by the larger joint-family shops, they did serve both to support and to extend the reach of the Sibao publisher-booksellers as a group.

## Managing Intra-Lineage Competition Among Publishing Households: Customary Rules and Practices

We have discussed the competition for resources that inevitably arose within household publishing operations and the mechanisms used to discourage the conflict that might result—the relentless preaching of the genealogies in support of the principle of household unity, the prohibition against publishing by branch bookstores, the close scrutiny of records by the household head, and, perhaps most effective, the effort to pair natural competitors, brothers, uncles and nephews, and to some extent fathers and sons, in bookselling work in order to create a system of natural checks. But what about the competition inevitably engendered by the proliferation of publishing houses, encouraged by family division and partible inheritance? In addition to tensions within a given *shufang*, in particular between its publishing and bookselling arms, Sibao publishers had to deal with competition among an ever-expanding number of publishing houses, many headed by brothers who had formerly worked (and competed) within the same household shop.

Over the years certain customary rules of business conduct evolved to regulate relations among the publishing houses. The managers of the various publishing houses agreed on the practice of *suiyi shua xin* 歲一刷新 (at the first of the year printing the new),[57] a method of ensuring, at least in theory, that publishing houses did not publish the same titles and thereby undercut each other's business. At the end of every year, each publishing house printed a sample cover page of each new work it planned to print in the coming year and posted these on the gate to its *shufang*. In this way, in the course of paying the traditional New Year's

---

57. Yang Lan, *Linting huikao*, 4.8a.

day visits, publishers would learn what texts other shops planned to print, although presumably there had been some previous discussion with booksellers over what titles were needed and some negotiation among the *shufang* managers over titles.[58] (Faint evidence of this practice can be found still on the gate of the Wenhai lou, where a worn copy of the cover page of *Shennong bencao jingdu* 神農本草經讀 [Reading the *Materia medica* classic of Shennong] can still be seen.) These postings effectively claimed the titles for the publishing house in question; participation in this end-of-the-year ritual as custom prescribed gave it the right to publish the titles it posted. Should conflicts arise at this point, the leading *shufang* managers would intervene, either getting the two sides to reach an agreement or, if that proved impossible, imposing a settlement. These conflicts were contained as much as possible within the circle of publishing households; it was not the business of the larger lineage group or its head to settle disputes.[59]

The practice of *suiyi shua xin* was paired with another customary rule, *cangban suoyou* 藏版所有 (literally, "possession of stored blocks," meaning that a publisher had a proprietary claim to blocks in his possession), which stipulated that a Sibao *shufang* could not publish a text already published by another Sibao *shufang*—that is, a text the blocks for which were already cut and "stored" (*cang*) by another Sibao publisher. Informants insisted on identifying this customary arrangement, which allowed *shufang* to claim certain titles as their own, as a form of copyright (*banquan* 版權),[60] although clearly the principle's limited local application makes it very different from the contemporary meaning of the

---

58. Interviews 3, 10/28/93 (Wuge); 6, 12/2/93 (Liancheng); 24, 11/8/95 (Wuge). See also Chen Zhiping and Zheng Zhenman, "Qingdai Minxi Sibao zushang yanjiu," pp. 98–99; and Wu Shideng, "Qingdai Sibao keshuye diaocha baogao," p. 142.

59. Interview 25, 11/9/95 (Wuge). In an earlier article on Sibao, written before I had completed all the interviews, I overstated the role of the lineage heads (*zuzhang* 族長) in settling disputes (see "Commercial Publishing in Late Imperial China," p. 74 and n. 81). Most informants emphasized that the lineage heads did not generally oversee or interfere in the publishing industry in Sibao—the individual households were the largest units of operation, and conflicts between these units were mediated by other publishers or relatives of the publishers.

60. Wu Shideng, "Qingdai Sibao keshuye diaocha baogao," p. 142. Interview 26, 11/11/93 (Wuge). For all the claims made by the Sibao publishers, the concept of copyright was more closely approached in Japan; see Kornicki, *The Book in Japan*, pp. 179–83.

term. The rule was not, in any event, necessarily enforceable even in Sibao. As we shall see, one publisher dissatisfied with the result of informal negotiations over what he considered a violation of the *cangban suoyou* rule did take his case to the local magistrate—and lost.

One important exception to the *cangban suoyou* practice allowed for considerable flexibility in publishing: very popular texts were exempt from this regulation.[61] Thus *any* publishing house could publish works like the *Sanzi jing, Zengguang,* or the Four Books, since these, at least throughout the nineteenth century, enjoyed an apparently limitless demand. It was only the less common and/or longer and thus more expensive works that were protected by the *suiyi shua xin* and *cangban suoyou* regulations. This exception was apparently intended to ensure some profit for even the smallest shops; certainly, if observed, it would have prevented or at least inhibited large concerns from monopolizing these inexhaustibly popular educational texts.

Other rules governed the business conduct of publishers as well and protected ownership of certain titles. Shops might rent or purchase blocks from other shops; if rented, the original shop name had to be retained on the blocks. If the blocks were purchased, however, the new owner could replace the original shop name with his own.[62] It was fairly common for publishers to rent blocks or even to exchange sets of blocks of equal value, but quite rare for blocks to be sold, as only the most desperate *shufang* would part with a steady source of income, particularly since, as we saw in Chapter 3, block cutting represented the most substantial investment in book production.[63]

---

61. Interview 35, 11/14/95 (Wuge).

62. Interview 3, 10/28/93 A.M. (Wuge). Evidence for these practices can be found on surviving Sibao woodblocks; some of the title-page blocks have had the original shop name cut out and a new one inserted or placed on another part of the block.

63. Interview 44, 11/23/95 (Mawu). A shop manager might pawn or mortgage blocks. An agreement dated 1822 records the mortgage of the blocks for *Yingxiong pu* 英雄譜 (Register of heroes), a work of fiction, and *Sishu chuanzhu* 四書串珠 (Strung pearls of the Four Books) for 20 dollars (*yuan*); one dated 1849 records the mortgage of the blocks for the *Wanbei quanshu* 萬備全書 (perhaps an error for the *Wanbao quanshu* 萬寶全書, a popular encyclopedia) for six ounces of silver (*liang*), quite a substantial sum— although a few years later, in 1853, this title (though perhaps in a different edition) was mortgaged for only 3,000 copper cash (*wen*) or 3 ounces of silver. In 1863, the blocks for

According to two late Qing property-division documents, the cost of renting blocks ranged fairly widely, from four ounces of silver for a long and important text like the *Shiji* (Record of the Grand Historian) to a mere 3 *fen* (0.03 ounce) for a presumably very short collection of rhymed couplets (see Table 5.1). The *Xieji bianfang shu* 協紀辨方書 (Book for harmonizing the times and distinguishing the directions), a widely used treatise on cosmology, sold wholesale for 0.36 ounces of silver (3.6 *qian*) in the early twentieth century. If this is close to its late nineteenth-century wholesale price, then a publisher would had to have sold only eight or nine copies to have broken even on his investment (although this calculation does not include the cost of paper, printing, and binding for a work of thirty-six *juan*). Other rental prices also seem to have been reasonable. We can estimate that the blocks for the *Sishu jizhu* (see Table 5.2) rented for no more than 2.5 ounces of silver (*liang*);[64] since this work sold for one-tenth of an ounce of silver (that is, one *qian*) and was, thanks to the examination system, in high demand, sales of over twenty-five copies were probably almost guaranteed. Seven *qian* (0.7 ounce) for the blocks for the popular examination aid *Tangshi hexuan xiangjie* 唐詩合選詳解 (Combined selection of Tang poetry, with detailed explanations; see Table 5.1) also seems very reasonable, particularly since this text might sell wholesale for as much as one *qian* (0.1 ounce, though this price also dates from the early twentieth century, not 1894). And the rental price of 30 cents (3 *mao*) for a collection of rhymed couplets (Table 5.1) seems remarkably inexpensive, since such texts might sell (again, early in the next century) in great quantities for 35 copper cash (3.5 *fen*).[65] Unfortunately, these figures are

---

*Leifeng ta* 雷峰塔 and *Zuozhuan* 左傳 were pawned for 5,000 cash (*wen*) or roughly 5 ounces of silver.

64. The Sibu beiyao edition of the *Sishu jizhu* would have required about 350 blocks. I have used this figure to calculate the rental price, although it is unlikely that the Sibao publishers, who tried to cram as much text on a block as possible, printed a text that required this many blocks.

65. The wholesale prices for texts are drawn from the Wenhai lou account book. Otherwise variation in prices over space and over time (as well as a shortage of precise price data) makes it difficult to assess the relative value of the rental blocks. According to figures for foodstuff prices supplied by Tan Wenxi (*Zhongguo wujia shi*, pp. 252–87) for late Qing Sichuan, four ounces of silver (*liang*) would have purchased about 73 *jin* (44 kilograms) of soybeans in Hejiang 合江 county in 1895; 4 *dou* (about 42 liters) of rice

too incomplete to allow any generalizations about the practice of block rental in Sibao; presumably decisions to rent drew on calculations—of demand for specific titles, of the state of the blocks, of the shape of local markets, and of the finances of the publishing houses—which have not survived in the written record.

Some restrictions applied to the rental or sale of blocks. The general rule was that blocks could be rented only to brother shops after property division; as one informant explained, "Before property division, all blocks were shared; after they had to be rented."[66] Thus a man who had inherited too few sets of blocks to easily establish a new *shufang* might choose to rent these to a more active publishing brother. Some *shufang* dictated precise conditions for rental or sale. The Daoguang-era document dividing the property of the Yunshen chu, for example, forbids the sale of blocks for any of the Classics, although these blocks might be rented out among the brothers if they wished to "print cooperatively" (*tonghe shuayin* 通合刷印). The blocks for other "miscellaneous" texts (*zashu* 雜書), ones not as widely popular as the Classics, might also be rented out to a brother's shop, if the owner of the blocks were willing to rent. But the document emphasizes that the blocks of the original *shufang*, the Yunshen chu, were not to be rented to outsiders even after the property was divided: "Outsiders, even relatives and friends, cannot rent blocks. Each [heir] should respect the family rules." The point here is, as the document itself states, to "guard against impeding the livelihood of any member of the family" (*fang ai benren shengyi* 防碍本人生意).

---

in Dazhu 大竹 county in 1896; 5.44 *dou* (about 56.6 liters) of high-quality rice in Chongqing in 1898; 12 *jin* (about 7.3 kilograms) of salt in Changning 長寧 county in 1903. Four ounces would have purchased 59 *jin* (35.7 kilograms) of pork in Sibao in 1897 (this figure is from a ledger kept by the Lantern Festival Society [Huadeng hui 花燈會] of Mawu). These figures suggest that block rental, although expensive for longer works, might be very reasonable for shorter, cheaper texts (which would, of course, yield lower profits but might be easy to sell in Sibao's markets). The Daoguang-era Yunshen Chu property-division document suggests a rental rate of one-tenth the value of the whole set of blocks. But since this document does not record the number of blocks per title or the value of each set of blocks, this information is of limited use.

66. Interview 44, 11/23/95 (Mawu).

Table 5.1
Rental Prices for Woodblocks from the Wenhai lou, 1894

| Rental title* | Rental price (in *liang*) |
|---|---|
| *Chen Shiji* 陳史記 (Chen edition of *Records of the Grand Historian*) | 4 |
| *Xieji* [*bianfang shu*] 協紀 [辨防書] (Book for harmonizing the times and distinguishing the directions; an imperially sponsored cosmological treatise) | 3 |
| *Han Wei congshu* 漢魏叢書 (Collectanea of the Han and Wei) | 2 |
| *Daomen dingzhi* 道門定制 (Fixed regulations of the gate to the Way) | 2 |
| *Xiaoti zhenggu* 小題正鵠 (Hitting the target of the *xiaoti* essays; an examination-essay collection) | 1.3 |
| *Kanyu sanzhu* 堪輿三珠 (Three pearls of *fengshui*) | 1.3 |
| *Sanguo zhi* 三國志 (probably a reference to the *Sanguo yanyi* [Narrative of the Three Kingdoms]) | 1 |
| *Shanhu ji* 珊瑚集, both the old and new editions (Collection of coral; an examination-essay collection) | 1 |
| *Tangshi hexuan* 唐詩合選 [詳解] (Combined selection of Tang poetry[, with detailed explanations]) | 0.7 |
| *Tianxing xuanze* 天星選擇 (an astrological manual?) | 0.6 |
| *Tie? dao* 鐵? 刀 (?) | 0.3 |
| *Moxuan jingrui* 墨選精銳 (The pick of essay selections; an examination-essay collection) | 0.13 |
| *Yuejian* 月建 (an almanac?) | 0.1 |
| *Duilei* 對類 (a collection of rhymed couplets) | 0.03 |

*The titles in Table 5.1 are abbreviated in the property-division document. Since it is not always clear what the precise title is, I have in some cases listed a general description of the text rather than translate the abbreviated title.
SOURCE: Property-division document, dated 1894, of the Wenhai lou.

All these customary regulations protected the household *shufang*'s ownership of and "claim to print" (or, as local informants would have it, the "right" to print) certain blocks, and the claim of heirs to that publishing house to rent blocks even after family division. Clearly, they served to protect the economic security of the household and the joint family by encouraging some degree of cooperation among family members. Thus, if the system of property division stimulated the proliferation of new *shufang*, it also stimulated the formation of business alliances among related *shufang*. Although a single publishing house might never grow large and powerful enough to monopolize book production,

Table 5.2
Rental Prices for Woodblocks from the Yijing tang, Guangxu era

| Rental title* | Rental price per 100 blocks** (in *yuan* and *liang*) |
|---|---|
| *Sanming tonghui* 三命通會 (Compendium of the three fates, a guide to horoscope casting) | 3 *yuan* / 2.1 *liang* |
| *San Bai Qian Zengguang* 三百千增廣 (Combined edition of the *Sanzi jing, Baijia xing, Qianzi wen,* and *Zengguang xianwen*; a collection of primers) | 2 *yuan* / 1.4 *liang* |
| *Jin kou jue* 金口訣(?) | 2 *yuan* / 1.4 *liang* |
| *Sishu Zhu zhu* 四書朱註 (Four Books with the Zhu commentary; probably the *Sishu jizhu*) | 1 *yuan* / 0.7 *liang* |
| *Maijue* 脈訣 (Secrets of the pulse, attributed to Wang Shuhe 王叔和) | 1 *yuan* / 0.7 *liang* |

*The titles are abbreviated in the property-division document. Since it is not always clear what the precise title is, I have in some cases listed a general description of the text rather than translate the abbreviated title.

**The conversion from *yuan* to *liang* is based on Chang Chung-li's estimate that 1 *yuan* was approximately 0.7 *liang* (*The Income of the Chinese Gentry*, p. 17).

SOURCE: Guangxi-era property-division document of the Yijing tang.

a cluster of allied houses, all descended from a single "father" house, might well have operated as such a unit, formidable in the range of texts it could produce and in the sale networks it could command, yet flexible enough (through the participation of several multi-occupational households) to adjust to shifts in the market.

If strictly followed, the regulations summarized above would have had the effect of limiting competition by slowing the proliferation of *shufang* caused by the practice of partible inheritance. If all the publishing houses restricted block rental to family members as the Yunshen chu did, a bookseller who hoped to expand into publishing, for example, might have trouble renting blocks. The purchase of blocks was expensive, and in any case most publishing houses were unwilling to sell their blocks. An aspiring new publisher could not have blocks newly carved for any titles already "owned" by other shops.[67] Without

---

67. Wu Shideng ("Sibao shufang jingying qishi lu," p. 12) reports that a fine of up to 1,000 *qian* might be imposed on anyone who violated this local "copyright" rule.

inherited blocks or family connections, he might have to invest heavily in the carving of new blocks either for titles as yet unpublished in Sibao or for titles so popular (e.g., the Four Books) that the market could absorb another printing.

Thus most of the customary regulations that evolved within the Sibao publishing industry seem to have been designed to protect the household and the continuity of the industry—often in the form of clusters of "brother" publishing houses—within the descent lines of the household. Informal traditions of inter-house cooperation reinforced this protection and limited the proliferation of independent houses. We have already seen that block rental might be restricted to a circle of brother *shufang*. And, according to informants, publishing houses, particularly those managed by brothers or close relatives, might share business under certain circumstances: if one could not meet the demand for a particular title, its head would inform an allied house of the demand, in hopes of keeping business within the extended family. Shops might also cooperate to hire outside laborers, particularly for the skilled work of block cutting. During the last months of the year, the busiest printing season, the larger shops might farm certain steps in the publishing process out to the smaller shops, particularly those run by members of the extended family, providing them with supplementary income.[68] Although the evidence is too slight to be conclusive, it is worth mentioning that such arrangements might often function less as equal relationships of "cooperation" and more as unequal relationships of patronage—the manager of the larger shop implicitly promising business to the head of the smaller shop and receiving in return assurance of service on demand and the political capital to be gained from his position of dominance.[69] Both these arrangements—ad hoc, short-term cooperation between shops, and service on demand—served to strengthen ties between certain "related" *shufang*, even as they put those outside the network of relationships at a disadvantage.

Clearly, then, there were practices at work that limited the openness of the Sibao book trade by encouraging publishing houses to keep their

---

68. Interviews 4, 10/30/93 (Mawu); and 25, 11/9/95 (Wuge).

69. See Duara, *Culture, Power and the State in Rural North China*, p. 183. This point is cited in Faure, "The Lineage as Business Company," pp. 360–61.

business "in the family." Yet certain exchanges were not so restricted. In the wholesaling of Sibao imprints to Zou and Ma book merchants in Wuge and Mawu, apparently no limitations applied. Both independent Sibao merchants[70] and the far greater number attached to specific *shufang* could buy books wholesale from *any* Sibao *shufang*—although, of course, most booksellers would get their texts "in-house" (that is, from the *shufang* to which they were attached) if they could find what they needed there. Both the publishers and the booksellers benefited from this arrangement, the publishers getting business from other houses and the booksellers enjoying a wider range of texts to choose from. In addition, the arrangement offered a market niche to ambitious and knowledgeable but perhaps not very well connected publishers, for popular titles not yet "owned" by established local *shufang*.

So, too, the relation between the publishing and the bookselling aspects of the Sibao trade operated to diffuse the competitive pressures within the Sibao industry. Since most *shufang* both produced and sold books, ambitious younger sons and nephews of the manager often left Sibao to work for a period as sojourning merchants, returning only to take over their father's shop or to set up their own shop with inherited blocks. This common cycle—although it might engender internal tensions of its own, as we saw above—did serve to ease competition for positions within the publishing businesses in Wuge and Mawu while strengthening the distribution networks for Sibao texts, training young men in an important aspect of their profession, and providing a conduit for news of outside markets to reach the mountains of Minxi. And the Sibao publishers, just as they cooperated to some extent in determining what books to publish, also cooperated in dividing up the bookselling routes; as one informant put it, "they could sell the same texts in different places"[71] (see Chapter 6). All these principles and practices, reached by negotiation and cooperation, reduced the potential for competition that might undermine the stability and security of existing businesses.

---

70. Not all Sibao booksellers were linked to a *shufang*; some specialized in bookselling alone. Interviews 35, 11/14/95 (Wuge); and 25, 11/9/95 (Wuge).

71. Interview 1, 10/27/93 (Wuge).

## Managing Inter-Lineage Competition

Customary regulations and established business practices, as described above, reduced or at least enabled rational management of intra-lineage competition. How was *inter*-lineage competition managed? Relationships between the Zou and Ma publisher-booksellers must have been complex, given their geographical proximity and the history of marriage connections between the two lineages. Although woodblocks seem never to have formed part of a woman's dowry,[72] daughters of publishers might bring other resources to their marriages to publishers, such as experience, knowledge, and personal connections. When a daughter of the distinguished Wuge publisher Zou Shengmai married a member of the Ma lineage, this must have forged a bond between the households and significantly benefited the Ma business, particularly since Shengmai was said to have been especially fond of this daughter.[73]

Marriage arrangements undoubtedly served as a means of creating or consolidating business agreements between Zou and Ma publishing houses (although the sources are unfortunately silent about these agreements). Marriage between a Zou heir to a publishing house and a Ma daughter of a prosperous publisher-bookseller (or vice versa) might very well have reflected (and cemented) a long-term business agreement to divide up titles and/or bookselling routes. Minimizing competition in this way could secure and augment profits. Few *formal* business partnerships seem to have existed between the Zou and Ma. Informants mentioned only one, ultimately unsuccessful effort, in the late nineteenth century: the conversion of the Benli tang, originally a Ma operation, to a joint Ma-Zou *shufang* in the late nineteenth century (see Chapter 7). It is tempting to conclude, then, that the two groups relied primarily on marriage ties to negotiate informal—that is, not officially recorded—business agreements whereby *shufang* linked by marriage monopolized certain titles and bookselling routes.

---

72. See Chapter 3, p. 86, note 16.

73. *MSDZZP* (1945), 1.53a–54b. As noted above, Ma Dingbang did form a partnership with his brother-in-law, Zou Wenguang, but this was in the timber trade (ibid., *ji* 7, 1.75ab).

When conflicts did arise between Wuge and Mawu, it seems that the same regulations governing intra- and inter-*shufang* relations within the Zou and Ma lineages also governed relations between Zou and Ma *shufang*. Thus a *shufang* manager from one lineage who claimed wrongdoing by a *shufang* head from the other lineage would appeal for judgment to the other publishers and the local leaders of the alleged wrongdoer's village. Often a publisher would appeal to his maternal uncles (*jiugong* 舅公, *jiujiu* 舅舅), men perceived as disinterested enough to act as arbitrators, for help in settling disputes—another use of the marriage links between publishing families to regulate business relationships. Only as a last resort would a publisher take the case to court.[74]

The only explicit—albeit sketchy—written evidence we have of the functioning of the local "copyright" rule does in fact come from a Zou genealogy's account of a legal conflict between a Zou and a Ma publisher. The Ma publisher, not specifically identified, was accused of pirating the works of Zou Tingyou 廷猷 (1715–1803), a publisher-editor of many popular texts, in violation of the local customary regulation. Zou Tingbin 廷賓 (1728–98), a brother of Tingyou, took the case to court: "Many of our locality take the selling and printing of the Classics as their profession. Master [Tingbin] forbade his own shop (*benhang* 本行) from profiting by printing the same titles [as other shops]. A Ma violated the agreement (*pan yi* 叛議) and reprinted (*fanke* 翻刻) the blocks for Zou Tingyou's books, which were extremely popular. [The case] was taken to law." No details are forthcoming (and no other record of the case survives), although we do learn that the suit failed, causing Tingbin's family much financial hardship (indeed, the story is told primarily to highlight Tingbin's ideologically correct devotion to his brothers at the expense of his own nuclear family).[75]

In sum, then, the Sibao publisher-booksellers did collectively develop certain unwritten rules and customary practices, applying to interactions within and between the surname groups, to protect the special efforts of individual publishing houses (the local "copyright" regulations) while providing broad opportunities both to publishing

---

74. Interview 25, 11/9/95 (Wuge).

75. *MYLZXZSZP* (1911), 20.52a. See also Wu Shideng, "Qingdai Sibao keshuye diaocha baogao," pp. 142–43.

houses of different sizes (the exception that allowed any and all *shufang* to print widely popular texts) and to booksellers of different affiliations (the freedom to purchase wholesale any books from any Sibao shops). At the same time, the more parochial, family-centered nature of the business was confirmed in the restrictions imposed by publishing houses on the rental and sale of blocks to "outsiders" and in the advantages "brother" publishing houses enjoyed in the sharing of costs and in easy accessibility to a flexible pool of cheap labor. Combined with the practice of woodblock inheritance, these practices favorable to the family encouraged what we might call the intermittent continuity of publishing-bookselling lines like those of Ma Dafan and Zou Shuwen.

# SIX

## *Sibao Bookselling Routes*

THE PRECEDING three chapters have focused on the industrial aspect of the Sibao book business—that is, on the production of texts and the structure and management of the publishing houses in the Wuge and Mawu "headquarters." In this and the next chapter, the focus shifts to the commercial aspect of the business: the organization of Sibao bookselling activities, the strategies of the Zou and Ma book merchants, and the expansion of the trade outward, in almost all directions, from western Fujian. Although a book market was held annually in Sibao, without the determined efforts of *shufang* merchants to bring their texts to outside—and often quite distant—markets, the industry would never have evolved beyond a purely local concern.

This chapter deals specifically with the annual book market in Sibao, the original marketing site for Zou and Ma texts; and the development, beginning as early as the late seventeenth century, of markets outside Sibao through itinerant selling along established routes and/or the founding of branch bookstores devoted to the sale of Sibao texts. I consider the factors that shaped these outside markets: existing transport routes, the pattern of Hakka (and Zou and Ma) migration, and the new commercial opportunities that accompanied population and market growth in southern China.

## The Book Market in Sibao

As with the study of Sibao book production, the evidence for methods of sale becomes richer once the business reached its first peak of prosperity, in the eighteenth century. Only somewhat speculative generalizations are possible for earlier periods. The first publishers, as we saw in Chapter 2, began their careers as booksellers, working for publishers in Guangdong or Jiangxi before establishing their own *shufang* in Sibao. But an annual wholesale market or markets for books seems to have developed, rather rapidly, in Sibao itself. Located at Guandiba 官地壩, between the villages of Mawu and Wuge, it opened on the fifteenth day of the first month of the year, after the *shufang* had prepared for the new book year.[1] This market was apparently distinct from both the Laijia periodic market founded in Mawu in the Ming and the Gongping periodic market established in Wuge in 1778. These two markets sold a wide range of goods, often brought in from neighboring villages,[2] whereas the annual wholesale market at Guandiba, held after the New Year, was devoted entirely to books.[3]

Who came to buy these texts? Informants claim that, in addition to sojourning Sibao book merchants numbering in the hundreds, traders from the cities of Suzhou and Guilin and the provinces of Jiangxi, Guangdong, Guangxi, and Zhejiang[4]—in other words, from all directions and considerable distances—came to the market to purchase texts. Impressive sums are rumored to have changed hands. It is said that Ma Dingbang, routinely going early to this market, could count on returning home for breakfast with one thousand—some informants say two thousand—*liang* of pure silver (*baijin* 白金) in earnings. In one day, informants claimed, he earned the money to build his mansion of one

---

1. Ma Chuanyong, "Lianchengxian Sibaoxiang Mawucun minjian xisu," p. 311.

2. Interview 50, 11/25/95 (Mawu).

3. Informants claim that a book market was established at the Gongping market, in front of the temple to Tianhou, which was built at the market in 1792. Since Zou publishers were leaders in the establishment of the market, it seems likely that this was the case—but the silence of the sources makes it impossible to know. Interviews 11, 4/27/95 (Wuge); and 25, 11/9/95 (Wuge).

4. Interview 50, 11/25/95 (Mawu); and Ma Chuanyong, "Lianchengxian Sibaoxiang Mawucun minjian xisu," p. 311.

hundred rooms, nine courtyards, and nineteen skywells and to purchase 100 *mu* (7.7 hectares) of the finest farmland. Outside book merchants were so eager to buy his texts that on one occasion they even followed him into the privy, offering him a thousand *liang* of silver for his stock.[5] So popular was this market with book merchants from Xuwanzhen, Jiangxi, it is said, that the Mawu publishers considered building a hostel (*gongguan* 公館) for sojourning Xuwanzhen traders beside the market, in the public land between the villages of Wuge and Mawu. The land had been set aside and plans drawn up for the building, when the Xuwanzhen merchants demurred in favor of founding a publishing industry in their native place. According to contemporary informants, this decision, and the Xuwanzhen merchants' subsequent purchase of many sets of woodblocks from Sibao publishers, was the origin of the Xuwanzhen book industry,[6] which grew to be one of the largest in the Qing.

These accounts are probably apocryphal. Certainly the repetition of the magical sum of one thousand *liang* of silver is suspicious, and, not surprisingly, no verification of the Xuwanzhen story can be found in the sources on Xuwanzhen. Nor is it likely that book merchants traveled from Suzhou and Guilin, both publishing centers, to purchase books in remote Sibao. But these claims do reveal that by the end of the seventeenth century, early in the history of Sibao publishing, a specialized book market existed in Sibao and attracted some outside merchants.

At some point this annual book market ceased to be the only means— if, indeed, it had ever been the only or even the primary means—by which the Sibao publishers traded their texts. Zou and Ma booksellers began bringing Sibao imprints to markets outside Minxi either as itinerant merchants or as the managers of branch bookstores, and eventually most of the wholesale book trading occurred outside Sibao. The genealogies are silent about the timing of this shift, and local informants simply say, rather vaguely: "Earlier, there had been a market for books every year, but then most books were sold outside Sibao. Booksellers established bookstores [in 'outside' places]."[7]

---

5. Interviews 4, 10/30/93 (Mawu); and 50, 11/25/95 (Mawu).
6. Interviews 50, 11/25/95 (Mawu); and 51, 11/27/95 (Mawu).
7. Interview 25, 11/9/95 (Wuge).

The reason for the shift is not difficult to imagine. Given the isolation of Wuge and Mawu, it is probable that outside book merchants found it inconvenient and cost ineffective to travel to this distant mountain market and transport their bulky purchases back with them. The reported conclusion of the Xuwanzhen merchants, apocryphal or not, appears logical; given the portability of the carving and printing technology, it was economically advantageous to establish their own local industry rather than waste time and funds traveling to and from Sibao. If the Zou and Ma wanted to survive in the business, they would have to bring their products to a range of markets, even if that meant paying transport costs.[8] It is not surprising, then, that the Sibao publisher-booksellers worked to establish and multiply external trade routes and to develop or expand a network of branch stores. And the greater their success, the less important the central Sibao book market became, except in the purely local trade.

## *Bookselling Networks Outside Sibao*

Itinerant merchants and branch shops were the means by which the Zou and Ma sold their wares beyond Sibao. Some of the book merchants traveled considerable distances, not only to the neighboring provinces of Guangdong, Jiangxi, and Zhejiang but also to Guangxi, Yunnan, Guizhou, Hunan, Hubei, and Jiangsu. These men typically considered Wuge or Mawu their base, returning to their home village, if possible, at the end of each year to turn over profits to the *shufang* managers, compare accounts (see Chapter 5), advise the managers on the demand for texts—and, of course, celebrate the Spring Festival with their families. After the first of the year, they would stock up on new texts published by their own and other *shufang* and set out on another year's commercial peregrination. As indicated in Chapter 4, these booksellers usually traveled in groups, at least in pairs of fathers and sons, uncles and nephews, or brothers; the job of bookselling generally

---

8. Contemporary informants report that the markup might be as low as 10 percent for texts sold in the Sibao area, whereas texts sold outside the Sibao area might be priced from 20 to 60 percent above cost, to cover the expense of transportation. See Chapter 13, p. 514, note 2.

rotated among household males, so that all might participate in and learn the commercial aspect of the business. Unfortunately it is impossible to calculate how many book merchants were on the road at any given time.[9]

This particular pattern of commercial itinerancy was practiced throughout the history of Sibao publishing, although the scope of the trade routes fluctuated over time. Some of the routes were local, to be sure—Zou Weizong, son of the legendary originator of the Wuge publishing industry, is said to have traveled around to schools within the Sibao area, selling primers and the Four Books. Not surprisingly, the Zou and Ma appear to have begun with such local routes and then to have expanded their operations extensively over the course of the eighteenth and nineteenth centuries, shrinking them again in the early twentieth century as the business declined. The last known itinerant bookseller traveled, in the 1930s and 1940s, a route confined to Minxi and Minbei, through the market towns of Yongan, Shaxian 沙縣, Nanping 南平, and Shuikou 水口.

These booksellers paved the way for the establishment of branch bookstores, permanent shops along what had proved to be the most lucrative of the routes forged by the itinerant merchants. The first mention of such a shop (*shudian* 書店 or *shusi* 書肆), the bookshop run by

---

9. Some informants claimed that there were about six hundred booksellers working outside Sibao every year (Interview 14, 4/28/95 [Wuge]; see also Ma Yunzhang, "Sibao yinshuaye de xingshuai genggai"). Wu Shideng ("Qingdai Sibao keshuye diaocha baogao," p. 139) states that the genealogies of the Ma lower-shrine and Zou upper- and lower-shrine lineages together list 629 men who worked as sojourning book merchants, but his count seems to include men who are identified simply as traveling merchants. The 1996 edition of the *FYZSZP* records a register of 644 sojourning booksellers (*shang*, pp. 177–243), but this list includes all the upper-shrine Zou lineage members who moved away from Sibao, not only booksellers but also other merchants and migrants. Although many on these lists likely were in fact book merchants, the genealogies fail to identify them clearly. Since the Zou and Ma practiced other forms of sojourning commerce as well (and since many migrants were not involved in the book trade), the only men who can be accurately counted as booksellers are those so identified in the text. At the same time, the number of booksellers mentioned in the genealogies certainly grossly underrepresents the real figure, for only a small fraction of lineage members received biographies or special notices in these texts (the generational charts only rarely mention occupation). We must assume that many more lineage members were working in the book trade than are explicitly identified as booksellers.

Zou Shuwen in Zhangshuzhen, Jiangxi, suggests that its founding can be dated to the late seventeenth or early eighteenth century.[10] Presumably this more settled form of bookselling developed as the Zou and Ma operations prospered and the *shufang* managers and book merchants judged certain markets stable and lucrative enough to merit the investment required to establish permanent shops.

## THE SCOPE OF SIBAO BOOKSELLING

Networks of trade routes that would allow the Zou and Ma book merchants to sell outside isolated and relatively poor Sibao were essential to the survival and expansion of the Sibao book industry.[11] Nonetheless, the extent of these networks is striking. Although most booksellers kept to relatively familiar routes dominated by Hakka within the Min-Yue-Gan border region defined in Chapter 2, some traveled as far south as Leizhou 雷州 prefecture, at the southern tip of mainland Guangdong, as far west as Yunnan and Guizhou, as far north as Wuchang 武昌, Hubei, and as far east as Suzhou, through most of the southern provinces of China Proper and perhaps into Vietnam. The breadth of their sales networks made the Sibao booksellers participants in the increase in long-distance commerce in the late Ming and Qing.[12] Some booksellers may even have traded overseas, in Java and Siam, although the evidence for this is hard to verify.[13]

---

10. The genealogy explains that Zou Shuwen managed the bookstore in Zhangshuzhen after his father's death in 1710 and returned permanently to Sibao in 1755. It is possible, then, that the shop was established as early as the late seventeenth century by Zou Shuwen's father, Dianmo (1649–1710).

11. In the genealogies, the major sources for the definition of Sibao bookselling routes, the information provided is usually opaque and imprecise, making it difficult to establish all the routes exactly. Most biographies indicate only generally the direction of a bookseller's route: "he sold books in Min Yue 閩粤," that is, Fujian, Guangdong, and perhaps Guangxi. Thus this summary is necessarily uneven; it is possible to indicate destinations, but difficult to trace specific routes.

12. Wang Shixin, "Ming Qing shiqi shangye jingying fangshi de bianhua," pp. 14–15.

13. There is an oral tradition in Wuge today that at least one of the Sibao booksellers, Zou Bingjun, sold books in Malaysia, and that others might have exported Sibao imprints to Java (Baguo 巴國, 吧國, or Galabaguo 噶喇吧國) and Siam (Xianluoguo 暹羅國). Interview 32, 11/13/95 (Wuge). Zou Bingjun's biography does state that he traded in Java, but it is not clear precisely what he was trading, since he dealt in tea, silk,

This pattern was not necessarily atypical of book commerce. Thomas Cooper, traveling on the Yangzi in the late 1860s, met in Yichang 宜昌 (Hubei) a traveling bookseller from Jiangxi; the merchant was on his way to Chongqing and Chengdu to sell dictionaries and "collections of legends" and to bring back novels and historical works cheaply printed in Sichuan for sale in Hubei, Jiangxi, "and the neighboring provinces."[14] The Zou and Ma booksellers routinely covered similar distances, encompassing several provinces. Ma Cuida, to give just one of many examples, traveled in Fujian, Guangdong-Guangxi, and Hunan-Hubei (Min Yue Chu 閩粤楚).[15] A *shufang* might establish branch stores in two or more provinces, charging household members with the management of each. Thus, in the late nineteenth and early twentieth centuries, the enterprising Zou Jianchi oversaw a small empire of shops, in Fujian (Tingzhou), Guangdong (Chaozhou and Lingshan), and Guangxi (Nanning and Hengzhou 橫州 [modern Hengxian 橫縣]); he and his sons operated the Tingzhou, Chaozhou, and Lingshan shops, his brother the Nanning store, and his nephew the shop in Hengzhou. Stable networks of such size were rather unusual, however.

More commonly, extended long-distance sojourning seems to have been the temporary strategy of a relatively young *shufang* trying to discover good markets and choose stable routes. Zou Honghua 宏化 (1663–1727) and his descendants, of the lower-shrine Zou lineage, for example, established first a remarkably wide sales territory and then, over three generations, gradually reduced this territory to just two sites. Honghua, among the second generation of Zou booksellers, packed certain essentials—a *qin* 琴 (marker of literatus taste), a sword, a case of

---

and porcelain as well as books (*FYZSZP* [1947], 33.40a–41a). Both Zou genealogies report migration to Java and Siam but do not identify the migrants as book merchants (ibid., 33.22b–23b).

14. Cooper, *Travels of a Pioneer of Commerce*, p. 73.

15. *MSDZZP* (1945), 1.82b–83a, 21.54a–55a. "Yue" is often taken as a reference to Guangdong alone. The Zou and Ma genealogies, however, often make a distinction between "Dongyue" 東粤 (or "Yuedong" 粤東) and "Xiyue" 西粤 (or "Yuexi" 粤西); so I have, except in cases where it seems likely that only Guangdong is meant, taken "Yue" as a reference to Guangdong and Guangxi. "Liangyue" 兩粤, also a common reference, clearly refers to both provinces. Here and throughout this discussion I have included in parentheses the relevant place-names as they are listed in the genealogy biographies.

clothing—and a stock of books on two horses and traveled to the Ou valley in Zhejiang, Jiangsu, and Guangdong-Guangxi (Ou Wu Yue Ling 甌吳粵嶺) to sell books.[16] Later he worked out of Zhangzhou (Min Zhang 閩漳), in south coastal Fujian; it is likely that he established a bookstore there—at any rate, he died in the city of Zhangzhou. His son Yingqian 應乾 (1692–1764) took over the business, working only in Tingzhou and Zhangzhou (Ting Zhang 汀漳).[17] Two of Yingqian's six sons continued as book merchants: Shengquan 聖權 (1713–1804) and Shengpin 聖聘 (1719–57) took over their father's routes in Xiatan (in Fujian) and expanded them to Baisha (in either Jiangxi, Hunan, or Guangxi), Guangdong, and Guangxi (Xiatan Baisha Yue Ling 霞潭白沙粵嶺).[18] Finally, in the fourth generation from Honghua, the family narrowed its field of operation: Tingshi 廷師 (1737–1813) and Tingren 廷仁 (1750–?) traveled only to Zhangzhou and Chaozhou (Min Yue Zhang Chao 閩粵漳潮). Tingshi's biography states that he managed bookstores in both these "cities rich in culture," attracting local scholars with his virtuous behavior and "manners of a Yan Hui 顏回," Confucius's model disciple.[19] Here a once-extensive sales region, covering as many as four provinces, was eventually reduced to two cities, accessible to each other by river or sea. Presumably members of the Zou Honghua line went through a process of searching out book markets, identifying the most lucrative, and then centering their sales efforts—and even establishing sales outlets—where the returns were greatest. Routes might be apportioned among brothers or cousins, as publishing houses themselves divided or as bookstores were established in different sites, so that over time a more settled pattern of bookselling routes and sites evolved. Contemporary informants confirm that "related" *shufang* usually agreed to divide routes just as they divided woodblock titles,

---

16. *MTLZXZSZP* (1911), 20.5b.

17. Ibid., 20.9b.

18. *MTLZXZSZP* (1911), 19.13a–14a and 20.21b–22b. I am reading Xiazhang 霞漳 as an error for Xiatan 霞潭, near Zhangzhou; it may also mean Zhangzhou. There is a Baishazhen 白沙鎮 in Jiangxi (in the northeast), a Baisha xu 墟 in Guangxi (in the eastern part of the province), and a Baisha in Hunan (in the southeast, near Guiyang *zhou*, a site of Ma settlement and bookselling); the genealogy does not specify which is meant here.

19. *MTLZXZSZP* (1911), 20.21b–22b, 39b.

to reduce inter-familial competition.[20] Experimentation with a variety of often far-flung markets, as described here, made it possible for *shufang* to identify lucrative markets and ultimately to agree on a division of bookselling territory.

## BOOKSELLING SITES

*Fujian (and Zhejiang).*   What pattern of bookselling did the Zou and Ma merchants establish in southern China? Within Fujian, bookselling focused on three areas in the western half of the province. (See Map 6.1 and Appendix E1.) Some booksellers looked to Minbei, the northern portion of the province and easy of access from Wuge and Mawu; Chongan 崇安 and Wuyi 武夷, both in Jianning 建寧 prefecture, and Yongan 永安 and Shaxian 沙縣, in Yanping 延平 prefecture, were sites of Sibao bookselling. Minxi itself was also a ready market for Sibao texts throughout the history of the industry. Zou and Ma booksellers either traveled through or established branch bookstores in the county seats of Liancheng, Shanghang, Wuping, Yongding, Changting (also

---

20. Interview 2, 10/27/93 (Wuge). The line of Ma Dingbang, the enterprising publisher discussed in Chapter 5 (see Appendix C1), provides another good example of this pattern. Dingbang traveled widely as he struggled to establish the business of the Wencui lou on a firm foundation in the late seventeenth century: his father, Ma Quanheng, had first started selling books in Guangdong and Guangxi (Yue 粤); then Dingbang's two younger brothers, Ma Dingce and Ma Dinglüe, expanded this territory, selling books "in the area of Jiangsu and Guangdong and Guangxi" (Wu Yue *jian* 吳粤間). The youngest brother, Ma Dingtao, traveled to Zhejiang and Jiangxi as well (Wu Yue Jiang Guang *jian* 吳越江廣間), his goals being "the prefectural and county seats" (*junyi* 郡邑) of these provinces, where "all the local notables (*dafu* 大夫) welcomed and received him cordially." By the next generation, however, Dingbang's son Jiu—and perhaps Jiu's nephew Lüzhi as well—was selling books only in Guangdong and Guangxi, and eventually in Guangxi alone; and Dingtao's son Shu—and later Shu's son, Lügong—in Guangdong (Yuedong 粤東) alone. By Ma Shu's generation, the *shufang* had been divided into two separate shops (the Wencui lou and the Heshan tang 鶴山堂); and it seems that the two *shufang* descending from Ma Dingbang's shop agreed to split the Guangdong-Guangxi route between them. In any case, they had considerably shrunk their bookselling territory by this time from the three or five provinces covered by their immediate predecessors. Each had firmly established markets large enough to accommodate itself. See *MSDZZP* (1945), 1.5b, 1.7b; and *ji* 7, 1.43a, 1.59a, 1.61a, 1.64b, 1.95b, 1.99a.

Map 6.1  Zou and Ma bookselling sites in Fujian (post-1820 sites are underlined)

Tingzhou prefectural city), and in scattered settlements throughout Longyan 龍巖 department. And finally, the booksellers founded book-stores in the western Minnan area—Zhangzhou in particular was an important site for Zou merchants.

From Fujian, the booksellers traveled in three different directions: north to Zhejiang and Jiangsu; west to Jiangxi and from there either to Guangdong (and on to Guangxi and Yunnan) or to Hunan (and perhaps Guizhou) and Hubei; and south to Guangdong, Guangxi, and Yunnan. The northern route took the Zou and Ma merchants from their bases in Jianning prefecture either through Chuzhou 處州 prefecture and the Ou 歐 River valley and southern Zhejiang province to the port city of Wen-zhou; or via the Xianxia 仙霞 Pass into western Zhejiang to Hangzhou.[21] Wenzhou and Hangzhou were also stepping-stones to Suzhou. This northern route was not an important one, however; it seems to have been traveled only by booksellers of the Zou Dianmo publishing line.[22]

*Guangdong.* It was the provinces south of Fujian—Guangdong and Guangxi—that seemed to offer the Sibao merchants their richest op-portunities, however. (See Map 6.2 and Appendix E2.) The Lingnan area attracted, too, the greatest range of Sibao booksellers: whereas Si-bao bookselling in Jiangxi, Hunan, and Hubei seems to have been dominated by members of the lower-shrine branch of the Zou lineage, in Guangdong and Guangxi, both Zou branches and the Ma lineage were active, although often in different parts of the region. Accessible from both southern Jiangxi and southern Minxi, Guangdong in particu-lar remained, throughout the industry's history, a focal site. The Sibao booksellers generally avoided Guangzhou city (Yangcheng 羊城 or Wuyangcheng 五羊城) and the Pearl River Delta area, and of the

---

21. This latter route had been in use at least since the Northern Song. Although it was the most direct way from northern Fujian to Jiangnan, it was a difficult, mountain-ous route. See Chia, *Printing for Profit*, p. 20; and Su Jilang, *Tang Song shidai Minnan Quan-zhou shidi lungao*, pp. 136–39, 159–71.

22. See Chapter 5. Both Zou Hongxing and Zou Kongchun sold books (or, more likely, purchased texts for printing back in Sibao) in Hangzhou and Suzhou. Zou Xidao, two to three generations later, moved to Wenzhou to set up a bookstore (*FYZSZP* [1947], *j. shou*, 21b and 22.49b–50b).

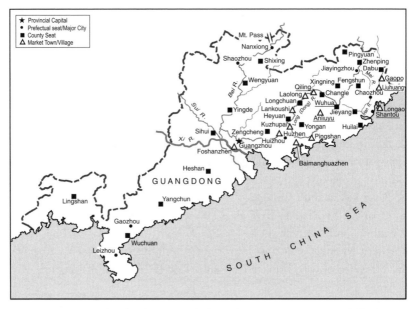

Map 6.2  Zou and Ma bookselling sites in Guangdong (post-1820 sites are underlined)

twelve merchants who worked in the area, only two established a book-store there (and that somewhat distant from Guangzhou, in the Zeng-cheng 增城 county seat, close to the border of Huizhou 惠州 prefec-ture). Rather, the eastern region of the province—Chaozhou 潮州 and Huizhou prefectures and Jiaying 嘉應 department—were the centers of Zou and Ma bookselling activity. Chaozhou alone attracted at least nineteen book merchants, eighteen from the lower branch of the Zou lineage and one from the Ma lineage;[23] Huizhou, eleven (ten from the Zou lower-shrine branch lineage and one from the Ma); and Jiaying, eight (seven from the Zou lower-shrine branch, and one from Zou

---

23. Business in this part of the province may in fact have become too competitive, at least by the late Qing. Zou Yiyou 宜祐 and his brother Yanchang 衍昌 started selling in Gaopo 高坡, in Chaozhou prefecture, on the Han River. But a lack of business soon drove the two men to abandon this site for Guangxi. When banditry and road blockages made Guangxi no longer profitable, they returned to Guangdong, to the much larger set-tlement of Chaozhou city, where they found business good enough that they could estab-lish two bookstores, both named Wenlan ge 文蘭閣, outlets for Cuiwen tang 萃文堂 texts. They sold both Chinese and "foreign" (that is, *yangban* 洋版) texts, the latter pur-chased from Shanghai (*MTLZXZSZP* [1911], 20.110b–111a).

upper-shrine branch lineages). Here, too, it was common for book-sellers to work in several different sites in this area. Although Zou Guoguang 國光 (1814–93) was content running just one bookstore, the Wenjing tang 文經堂, in Jiaying city (where he "visited with officials and conversed with brilliant Confucians"),[24] the Ma Dacheng lou 大成樓 *shufang* had by the early twentieth century established several shops, all named Dewen tang 德文堂, in a cluster of sites through Jiaying and Huizhou—in Jiaying city, Xingning 興寧 county seat, modern Anliuyu 安流圩 (in Wuhua 五華 county), Qiling 岐陵, Laolong 老龍 (between Xingning and Longchuan 龍川), and Pingshan 平山 market (modern Huidong 惠東).[25] Zou Guoliang 國良 (1822–96) established a little empire, selling texts in Chaozhou city and Jieyang 揭陽 and Huilai 惠來 county seats in Chaozhou prefecture; in Pingyuan 平遠, Xingning, and Changle 長樂 county seats in Jiaying department; and in Yongan 永安 county seat in Huizhou prefecture.[26]

Although eastern Guangdong probably contained the highest concentration of Sibao branch bookstores, the Zou and Ma established some sites in the other portions of the province: in county seats or market towns on the North River (Beijiang 北江) system, which gave merchants access to north-central Guangdong from Jiangxi; in Gaozhou 高州 and Leizhou prefectures; and in Lingshan county in the far western prefecture of Lianzhou 廉州. The mid-nineteenth-century threat to the stability of the book market in these hinterland areas from rebellion and banditry caused many booksellers to move farther west. Zou Bolong 伯龍 (1775–1844), for several decades a sojourning book merchant in Gaozhou and Leizhou, eventually accumulated enough profits to establish, with his brothers and his son Jiajun 家濬 (1799–1861), a bookstore named the Liuyiben tang 六宜本堂 in Gaozhou prefectural city. In 1861, bandits killed Jiajun, but his son, Zanlong 贊隆 (1834–79), was able to escape.[27] Deciding that Gaozhou was too

24. Ibid., 10.64a–65b, 20.89b–91a.

25. Interviews 5, 11/3/93 (Mawu); and 60, 12/3/95 (Mawu). Anliuyu, Qiling, and Wuhua are the current place-names.

26. *MTLZXZSZP* (1911), 20.93b–96ab.

27. The Gaozhou gazetteer records repeated bandit and rebel attacks in the area of the prefectural capital, as well as Xinyi 信宜, Huazhou 化州, and Wuchuan 吳川

dangerous, Zanlong moved to far western Guangdong, founding a bookstore in Lingshan county seat, on the Qin River 欽江 (in an area now part of Guangxi).[28]

*Guangxi (and Yunnan and Guizhou).*    Even quite early in the history of Sibao publishing, the Zou and Ma booksellers did business in Guangxi province. (See Map 6.3 and Appendix E3.) Here the upper-shrine branch of the Zou lineage supplied the pioneers: in the early eighteenth century, Zou Linshi 麟史 (1710–60) and his son, Minghui 明輝 (1735–?), sold books in the province, although the genealogy does not identify a specific site.[29] By mid-century, some Zou had established a branch bookstore in Nanning; Zou Kongshu and his cousin Kongqu 孔衢 (1756–98), among the most widely traveled of Sibao merchants, died in the Fujian Tianhou gong 福建天后宮 (that is, the Fujian *huiguan*) there, in 1793 and 1798, respectively.[30] The Sibao booksellers generally avoided the provincial capital of Guilin (perhaps because there was already an active commercial publishing industry there), traveling through and sometimes settling in port cities on the Gong River 龔江 (Wuzhou 梧州), its tributary the Yu River 郁江 (Pingnan 平南, Guixian, Hengzhou), and Nanning. A few of the hardier booksellers continued even farther west, along the You River 右江 to Pingma 平馬 (modern Tiandong 田東) and Bose 百色, some sixty kilometers from the Yunnan border. Zou Kongchang is said to have ventured across the border into Yunnan; and Ma Yulin 玉璘 (1820–Guangxu era), after ten years of bookselling in Guangdong and Guangxi, tested the markets in Yunnan and Guizhou for three years in the middle of the nineteenth

---

counties, over a series of years from the late 1850s through the 1860s (*Gaozhou fuzhi* [1889], *j.* 50–51 *passim*).

28. *MTLZXZSZP* (1911), 9b.10a–22b, 9b.51b, 20.76ab, 20.92a, 20.100a, 20.106a.

29. *FYZSZP* (1947), 9.49b–50b, 33.41a–42a. Mingzhen 明鎮 (1738–64), the second son, also sold books for a living, apparently in eastern Guangdong rather than Guangxi, for his biography records his death in Jiaying city. It is possible that the two sons divided their father's bookselling route between them.

30. Ibid., 10.24ab, 10.37a. Fujian *huiguan* were usually built around altars to Tianhou and thus were often called Tianhou gong. See Tan Qixiang, "Zhongguo neidi yiminshi— Hunan pian," p. 103; and Zhang Guilin and Luo Qingsi, "Fujian shangren yu Mazu xinyang," p. 110.

Map 6.3  Zou and Ma bookselling sites in Guangxi (post-1820 sites are underlined)

century.[31] But none of the Sibao merchants seems to have established a settled base or permanent network in these distant frontier provinces. Western Guangxi marked the western limit of sustained, effective—and clearly recorded—Sibao bookselling.

*Jiangxi.* Although the booksellers might also travel westward into northern Jiangxi from Shaowu or Jianning prefectures,[32] they more commonly crossed the provincial border near Tingzhou, traveling to

---

31. *MSDZZP* (1945), *ji* 8, 1.123a, 21.58ab. By 1871, Ma Yulin was back in Mawu sponsoring the construction of a branch ancestral temple and the publication of a genealogy; although his biography does not give the dates of his bookselling career, we might guess that he was active in the 1850s and 1860s.

32. From Guangze in Shaowu, merchants traveled through the Shan Pass 杉關 into Jiangxi, to Jianchang 建昌, Fuzhou, and finally to Nanchang. From the provincial capital, they had access both to the Gan River (and thus the rest of Jiangxi and Guangdong) and to the Yangzi River via Poyang Lake 鄱陽湖. From Chongan in Jianning prefecture, they entered Jiangxi through the Fenshui Pass 分水關 and journeyed on to Hekouzhen 河口鎮 and Poyang Lake. See Chia, *Printing for Profit*, pp. 20–21.

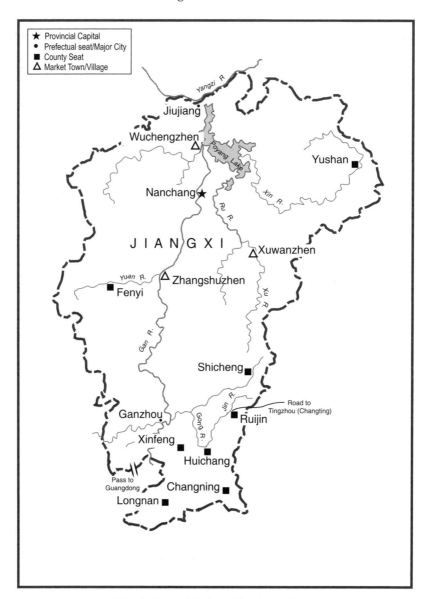

Map 6.4 Zou and Ma bookselling sites in Jiangxi

Ruijin 瑞金 on the Jin River 錦水 (and then the Gong River), in southeastern Jiangxi. (See Map 6.4 and Appendix E4.) Social ties between
Ruijin and Sibao were fairly close; several of the booksellers married
women from the Li lineage of Ruijin—either a result or a cause of connections made during the book trade. From Ruijin, the booksellers
traveled westward to the Gan River, the major north-south "highway"
of the province. The Zou and Ma booksellers took advantage of the
easy transport offered by the Gan to establish themselves in northern
as well as southern Jiangxi in a prefectural seat (Ganzhou 贛州), several
county seats (Longnan 龍南, Fenyi 分宜), and market towns (Zhang-
zhuzhen, Xuwanzhen, Wuchengzhen 吳城鎮) along the river and its
tributaries; some booksellers even made it to Jiujiang 九江, on the
Yangzi. Although they also sold books in Yushan 玉山 in the northeastern and Changning 長寧 (modern Xunwu 尋烏) in the southeastern
corner of the province, their primary bookselling sites were along the
north-south corridor of the Gan.

*Hubei and Hunan.*     Jiangxi provided one of the earliest and richest markets for Sibao sales. It also gave access, via Jiujiang and the Yangzi, to
Hubei (particularly Hanchuan 漢川 county seat and Wuchang) and
southward into Hunan, where the merchants targeted the prefectural
seats and some county seats along the Xiang 湘 River and its tributaries
(Changde 常德, Changsha 長沙, Hengzhou 衡州, Yuanzhou 沅州, Yiyang 益陽, and Guiyangzhou 桂陽州). (See Map 6.5 and Appendix E5.)
Although the Sibao book markets in Hunan were never as numerous or
as long-lived as those in Jiangxi or Guangdong, at least one major *shufang* made the province its primary distribution area: Zou Jun, descendant of Wuge's most famous publisher, Zou Shengmai, revived the
family business when he founded a lucrative outlet for its texts in
Changde. The profits from this shop funded the purchase of many new
sets of woodblocks, allowing for the expansion and stabilization of the
business; the shop was maintained for at least two more generations by
Jun's descendants.[33]

---

33. *MTLZXZSZP* (1911), 20.74b–75a.

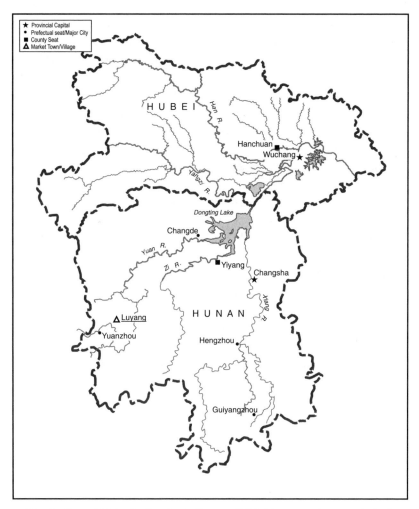

Map 6.5  Zou and Ma bookselling sites in Hunan and Hubei (post-1820 sites are underlined)

## The Pattern of Sibao Bookselling:
## Why They Went Where They Went

Why did the Zou and Ma booksellers choose these routes and these sites for the sale of their imprints?

Several, often overlapping factors seem to have determined or at least shaped the particular nature of the Sibao bookselling routes and branch sites. Accessibility—that is, the existence of trade routes that made travel to these sites possible (if not necessarily easy)—was crucial. The pattern of Hakka migration from the late Ming through the Qing,[34] more specifically, the pattern of migration by families within the Zou and Ma lineages during that period, was a second important factor. A third was the pattern of population growth and economic advance during the Qing; surely it is no accident that Zou and Ma distribution routes and branch shops were strategically located in areas experiencing both population increase and market growth from the late seventeenth to the early nineteenth centuries. Finally, within the wide region defined by these patterns, the Sibao book merchants apparently made market choices based on assessments of the demand for their particular products and the activities of their competitors.

## TRANSPORT NETWORKS

The Min-Gan-Yue region, the base of Sibao bookselling operations, forms, as we saw in Chapter 2, a coherent geographical, economic, and cultural unit in large part because of the land and river routes that knit western Fujian, western Jiangxi, and northern Guangdong together.[35] These routes both directed Sibao bookselling within the Hakka heartland and gave them access to river systems that took them beyond this base area. Late imperial merchant route books reveal that the Sibao booksellers gained access to almost all their markets through the Hakka homeland over the major roads and waterways of the south.

Land routes, although not the favored means of travel, nonetheless provided important links between waterways. By the early Qing a complex network of post roads (*guanma dalu* 管馬大陸) and postal stations (*yizhan* 驛站), reinforced by a subsidiary system of roadside or foot-courier stations (*pu* 鋪) that drew county seats into the post network, provided transportation to most of the markets targeted by the Sibao booksellers. Although these routes were intended primarily for official communication, and efforts were made in the early Qing to restrict their use to administrative and military purposes, once order had been

---

34. Chen Zhiping and Zheng Zhenman, "Qingdai Minxi Sibao zushang yanjiu," pp. 107–8.

35. For a description of these routes, see Appendix A.

restored to the empire—roughly the same time that the Sibao publishing industry got started—they came to serve as trade and nonofficial communication networks as well.[36]

The waterways were more important, however, for they provided the cheapest and most efficient means of transporting goods.[37] Perhaps most advantageous was the Gan River system in Jiangxi, which, as we have seen, allowed water travel both to the north through western Jiangxi to Hubei and to the south to Guangdong. Northward, merchants went from Ganzhou to Nanchang and Jiujiang, and then onto the major waterway in south China, the Yangzi, to the Wuchang area (and from there they could travel southward on the Yangzi, to the Zi 資江 and Xiang rivers and their tributaries in Hunan.[38] In the other direction, the increasingly popular route from Ganzhou through the Meiling Pass 梅嶺關 into Nanxiong 南雄 department in northern Guangdong gave access to Guangzhou[39] and, ultimately, via the West

---

36. Fan I-chun ("Long-Distance Trade and Market Integration in the Ming-Ch'ing Period," pp. 23–28) estimates that, in practice, most *pu* stations were at intervals of 10 to 30 *li* (5 to 15 kilometers). See also Ying-wan Cheng, *Postal Communication in China and Its Modernization*, pp. 8–29, for a brief description of the post and *pu* system; and Brook, *Geographical Sources of Ming-Qing History*, pp. 11–18, for a bibliography of guides to the postal stations.

37. Brook, "Communications and Commerce," p. 603; and Fan, "Long-Distance Trade and Market Integration in the Ming-Ch'ing Period," p. 44.

38. I rely here on two merchant route books from the late Ming, the *Tianxia shuilu lucheng* 天下水陸路程 (better known as *Yitong lucheng tuji*; 1570) of Huang Bian 黃汴 and the *Tianxia lucheng tuyin* (1626) by a "Danyizi" 憺漪子 (but included originally in the same author's *Shishang yaolan* and identical in parts with Cheng Chunyu's 程春宇 *Shishang leiyao* 士商類要, 1626), in a modern combined edition edited by Yang Zhengtai, *Tianxia shuilu lucheng, Tianxia lucheng tuyin, Keshang yilan xingmi*; see esp. *Tianxia lucheng tuyin*, p. 418–19; and Appendix A. Fan I-chun ("Long-Distance Trade and Market Integration in the Ming-Ch'ing Period," p. 33, esp. n. 26) argues that there are few additions or deletions in merchant route books of the Qing; what appear to be additions usually represent rather a division of older routes into smaller segments. See also Yang Zhengtai, *Tianxia shuilu lucheng*, pp. 10–12; and *Tianxia lucheng tuyin*, pp. 410–11. For more information on the range of route books available, see Brook, *Geographical Sources of Ming-Qing History*, pp. 13–27.

39. Yang Zhengtai, *Tianxia shuilu lucheng*, pp. 10–12, 47, 59–60; and *Tianxia shuilu tuyin*, pp. 410–11; see also Kingsmill, "Inland Communications in China," p. 115. This is the route that E. R. Huc and his companions traveled from Nanchang to Guangzhou; Meiling marks the halfway point. Huc noted that this route was "the sole passage for all

River 西江, to Guangxi.⁴⁰ Sibao itself was conveniently linked to this crucial transportation node, Ganzhou, by a combined water and overland route from Tingzhou through the eastern Jiangxi counties of Ruijin, Huichang 會昌, and Yudu 雩都.⁴¹

The eastern portion of Guangdong province could also easily be reached in one other way: via the Yin-Han River, from Tingzhou to Dabu 大埔 and Chaozhou (both in Guangdong).⁴² From Dabu, merchants could traverse much of Jiaying department. From Xingning county seat, they would have to carry their stock overland to Longchuan, but at that point they could pick up the East River (Dongjiang 東江 or the Long River 龍江) through Lankoushi 藍口市 and Kuzhupai 苦竹派 (both market towns and postal stations that were sites of Sibao bookstores), Huizhou, Dongguan 東莞, Zengcheng, and finally Guangzhou.⁴³ Once in Guangzhou, travelers and merchants had relatively easy access to Guangxi, on the West (or Gong 龔江) River to Wuzhou and from there to the major administrative and commercial centers of the province. At Wuzhou, most Sibao booksellers continued on the Gong River and its tributaries through the province to Bose and Guangnan 廣南 prefectural city over the Yunnan border.⁴⁴ Hengzhou,

---

the merchandise that the commerce of Canton is continually pouring into the interior provinces of the Empire," and thus includes a "multiplicity of paths" and was often crowded. It was also, as for the Sibao book merchants, a conduit to Guangdong for goods from the north; this was the route by which Jingdezhen porcelain was shipped to Guangzhou (see *The Chinese Empire*, 2: 383, 387, 400; and Nadler, *China to Order*, pp. 21–22).

40. Yang Zhengtai, *Tianxia shuilu lucheng*, pp. 59–60, 217, 219; and *Tianxia lucheng tuyin*, pp. 435–36.

41. Yang Zhengtai, *Tianxia shuilu lucheng*, pp. 243–44. Jiangxi also offered the booksellers an alternative route to Zhejiang, from Nanchang via a series of rivers to Hekouzhen (modern Yanshan 鉛山), Yushan, across the border to Jiangshan 江山, and from there on to Hangzhou (ibid., p. 203).

42. Yang Zhengtai, *Tianxia lucheng tuyin*, pp. 418–19. For detailed accounts of transport conditions on the Ting, see Zhang Hongxiang, "Tingjiang shangye hangyun de diaocha"; and Lan Hanmin, "Tingjiang Shanghang heduan hangyun yu shangsu"; both these essays focus on Republican-era transport.

43. Yang Zhengtai, *Tianxia lucheng tuyin*, pp. 418–19. For a discussion of riverine commercial networks in Guangdong and their increased use in the Qing, see Ye Xianen, "Qingdai Guangdong shuiyun yu shehui jingji," pp. 5–8.

44. Yang Zhengtai, *Tianxia shuilu lucheng*, p. 217; and Qi Yi, *Guangxi hangyun shi*, pp. 66–67.

on the Yu River 郁江, was also the starting point for an overland route south to Lingshan 靈山 (in Guangdong province throughout most of the Qing), a Sibao bookstore site.[45]

The Sibao booksellers thus enjoyed a complex network of trade routes, beginning with but not limited to those that bound the Min-Gan-Yue border region together. Zou and Ma merchants took advantage of several of the major long-distance transportation axes of their day, including three that extended beyond the Hakka heartland: the central axis, encompassing Hunan and Hubei; the east-central and central, including Jiangsu, Hunan, Hubei, Jiangxi, and Anhui; the east central and southeast, covering Jiangsu, Zhejiang, Fujian, and Guangdong; the southeastern, including Guangdong and Guangxi; and the central and southeast, linking Jiangxi, Fujian, and Guangdong.[46] They had a choice of routes to many of their markets—for example, two major routes into Guangdong, their primary market.

In offering multiple routes to Sibao markets, this network encouraged the development of trade circuits with "stations" along the way and helps to explain the often impressive combination of routes, spanning several provinces, traveled by the more ambitious booksellers. If a *shufang* could establish bookstores—or even simply storage depots—at a node in the transport network (a market town or county seat that was a *pu* station, for example), it became much easier to extend routes of sale. Thus, a bookstore strategically located in Zhangshuzhen or Ganzhou—on one of the important post and commercial roads of the

45. Yang Zhengtai, *Tianxia shuilu lucheng*, pp. 258–59; see also Kingsmill, "Inland Communications in China," pp. 114–15. There was also a major overland and river route through western Hunan into Guizhou and Yunnan, the most remote sites of Sibao bookselling: first on the Yuan River 沅江 (accessible from Dongting Lake) and its tributary, the Wu 潕水–Zhenyang 鎮揚江 River, into Guizhou and then, by combined land and water routes to Guiyang 貴陽; and then, on a largely overland route, through Anshun 案順 prefecture and Puan 普安 subprefecture to Yunnan (Yang Zhengtai, *Tianxia shuilu lucheng*, pp. 30–31, 54–55, and *Tianxia lucheng tuyin*, pp. 428–30).

46. Rozman, *Urban Networks in Ch'ing China and Tokugawa Japan*, p. 130. Rozman identifies fifteen major transportation routes; the Sibao merchants could employ five of these through three of the six major regions of China Proper (central China—Hubei, Hunan, and Jiangxi; southeast China—Fujian, Guangdong, and Guangxi; and southwest China—Guizhou, Yunnan, and Sichuan).

day—could serve as a way station for the advance of booksellers both northward to Hubei (and then from Hubei southwest into Hunan) and southward to Guangdong.

## HAKKA MIGRATION IN THE
## LATE MING AND QING

Accessibility to transport routes was the single most important determinant of the shape of the Sibao sales networks. But the booksellers also followed the flow of Hakka (and Zou and Ma) migration in choosing their markets within this transport system; the congruence between late imperial Hakka migration patterns and Sibao bookselling networks is striking. It made good business sense for the Zou and Ma merchants to operate in areas where they could communicate with local customers, where they fit into the social and linguistic landscape.

According to Sow-Theng Leong, the first series of Hakka migrations from their heartland into the "foothills surrounding the major commercial centers of the southeast coast and Lingnan" began in the mid-sixteenth century, when the silver trade with Manila and commercial expansion brought economic prosperity. Five groups of migrants, from different portions of the Hakka homeland, extended (or reinforced) Hakka settlement in roughly four directions: to the northeast, into eastern Fujian and southwestern Zhejiang, in the Ou basin area near Wenzhou, areas that already had Hakka communities; to the northwest, up the western edge of Jiangxi and the southern and eastern portions of Hunan; to the south, to eastern, northern, and southwestern Guangdong; and finally as far west as the Nanning area of Guangxi.[47] Thus well before the founding of the first *shufang* in Sibao there were already Hakka settlements in the sites later targeted by the Zou and Ma booksellers.

Economic depression during the 1630s and 1640s, intensified by the Manchus' scorched-earth policy and particularly by their forced evacuation of the Lingnan coast from 1662 to 1682, discouraged migration. Hard times persisted on the southeastern coast until the mid-nineteenth

---

47. For a more nuanced account of this series of migrations, see Leong, *Migration and Ethnicity in Chinese History*, pp. 41–53; the chart on pp. 48–50 is particularly helpful.

century, but Lingnan recovered much earlier, with the lifting of the ban on coastal settlement in 1682. The second series of Hakka migrations, dated by Leong from the late seventeenth century through the 1730s, therefore targeted that area. There was also some new settlement in the Ou River basin in Zhejiang and in southern Hunan, but the primary new settlements were close to the Lingnan regional core, in the Pearl River Delta area. In the 1720s and 1730s, Hakka flooded into "the immediate vicinity of Guangzhou." In Guangxi, Hakka settlement expanded in all directions. And it was during this second series of migrations that the Hakka also began moving to Taiwan. Hakka migration continued into western Guangdong and southwestern Guangxi through the rest of the eighteenth century and well into the nineteenth. The Hakka-Punti War of 1856 to 1868, which ended in the defeat and resettlement of the Hakka population of the Guangzhou area, stimulated migration to western Guangdong, including the Leizhou peninsula and Hainan 海南 island.[48] But the major areas of Hakka settlement had been established by the end of the Yongzheng era.[49]

The areas of Zou and Ma migration (see Appendix F) match fairly closely the general areas of Hakka settlement outlined above.[50] An initial period of migration in the late Ming corresponds to Leong's first phase, although the Zou and Ma migrants restricted their movements to a relatively small number of sites in Guangdong province: Shaozhou

---

48. Ho Ping-ti, *Studies on the Population of China*, p. 166.

49. Leong, *Migration and Ethnicity in Chinese History*, pp. 53–62.

50. The Sibao migrations differ in three ways from the Hakka pattern as Leong describes it. First, although Lingnan was probably the primary destination of these migrants (first Guangdong and eventually Guangxi as well), they continued, long after the late Ming migrations, to settle heavily in Jiangxi and to some extent in Hunan as well. Second, migration persisted, after a clear break in the mid-1800s, in the late nineteenth and into the early twentieth century. This last phase of Sibao migration, however, did not push into new areas but consisted largely of renewed migration to areas already settled by either Zou or Ma. Finally, the genealogies record steady movement within Fujian itself, the Ma beginning in the late Ming and both Zou lineages in the early Qing, and all continuing through the early nineteenth century. These intra-provincial shifts focused on Minbei and western Minnan; although some Zou and Ma moved eastward, to Xinghua 興化 and Fuzhou 福州 prefectures, in general the lineages seem wisely to have avoided pressing on the most heavily populated (and non-Hakka) areas of the province.

韶州 prefecture and Jiaying department, both already heavily settled by Hakkas; Heping 和平 county in Huizhou, at the edge of Hakka territory; and then, more adventurously in other provinces—Sichuan, Anhui, Hunan, and Hubei.

Not until the late seventeenth and early eighteenth century do the genealogies report extensive migration from Sibao, most heavily into Guangdong and Jiangxi. In Guangdong, the Zou and Ma followed the Hakka pattern, settling in the eastern, northern, and western portions of the province but bypassing the major urban core around Guangzhou and the Pearl River Delta area. So, too, in Jiangxi, migrants from Sibao chose to settle in sites in the Hakka heartland in the southeast or upland areas around, but not within the regional urban core encompassing Fuzhou 撫州, Nanchang 南昌, and Jiujiang.

Guangdong and Jiangxi, both of them neighboring Fujian, relatively easy of access, and already centers of Hakka settlement and migration, were obvious magnets for Sibao emigrants. But during this second period of migration, from the late seventeenth through the early eighteenth century, the lineages also began to settle in two new areas, Hunan and Guangxi. The Ma settled in southern Hunan and in scattered county seats along the Xiang River and its tributaries. The lower branch of the Zou lineage advanced into what at the time was a fairly wild frontier area, eastern Guangxi province. Once again, they avoided the major city, Guilin, settling in more isolated county seats or in market towns along the Gong River and its tributary the Yu. Some more venturesome family members went even farther, to Sichuan; to Wenzhou, Zhejiang (later a site of a Sibao branch bookstore); to Taiwan; and even to Java and Siam.

These settlements formed the jumping-off points for new waves of Zou and Ma migration, from the mid-eighteenth century through the first half of the nineteenth century. The primary destination remained Lingnan. And for the most part the Sibao migrants, in accord with the pattern described by Leong for this period, expanded existing settlements, particularly in Guangdong, but also in Zhejiang, Guangxi, Jiangxi, Hunan, Sichuan, and Taiwan. In the southwest several new settlements were founded, in far western Guangxi, Yunnan, and Guizhou.

The series of wars and rebellions that swept southeastern China between the 1840s and 1860s made migration difficult and unattractive, and there are few records of Zou and Ma migration during this period. But once order was restored, in the Tongzhi and Guangxu eras, families from Wuge and Mawu once again began emigrating from Sibao, in search of commercial opportunities or land to farm—often in hinterland mountain regions or areas laid waste in the middle decades of the century.[51] For the Zou and Ma, this last phase of migration was relatively limited—there were both fewer emigrants and a narrower range of destinations, with most of the migrants settling in or near communities already inhabited by relatives.

In these successive waves of migration, perhaps as intermarriage strengthened relationships between the Zou and the Ma lineages, the two families' migration patterns and destinations gradually became similar. During the first two waves, the Ma lineage was far more active, dominating most of the migration sites in Guangdong—at least in eastern and north-central Guangdong—all the sites in Hunan, and the major sites in Jiangxi. The upper-shrine branch of the Zou moved out, in considerably smaller numbers, to western Guangdong, and the lower branch pushed on to Guangxi, becoming the first of the lineage to settle that frontier province. By the last stage the pattern of settlement was more complex. Roughly speaking, the Zou continued to dominate in western Guangdong and Guangxi and the Ma in Hunan, but by the late eighteenth century, both lineages were migrating to areas first settled by the other.

As Map 6.6 reveals, the patterns described here, both generally for Hakka migration and, more specifically, for Zou and Ma migration, influenced the development of markets for Sibao books in areas accessible by established transport routes. By the early seventeenth century—before the Sibao publishing industry started—there were already considerable Hakka settlements in eastern, north-central, and western Guangdong; in central and southern Guangxi; and along the Jiangxi-Hunan border. The Zou and Ma, as Hakka, naturally followed these routes when they began to migrate in sizable numbers out of Fujian in the late seventeenth and early eighteenth centuries. It is hardly surprising that the Sibao booksellers sought markets in these areas, whose

---

51. Wang Tianjiang, "Qing Tong Guang shiqi kemin de yiken," pp. 225–26, 229–33.

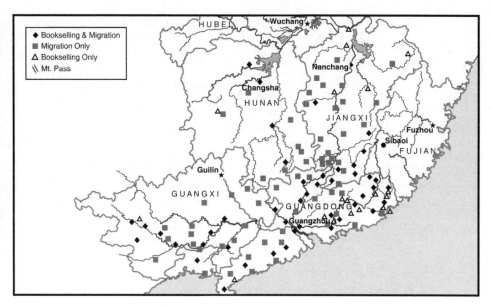

Map 6.6 Comparison of Zou and Ma migration and bookselling sites in Guangdong, Guangxi, Hunan, and Jiangxi (for migration sites in Anhui, Guizhou, Sichuan, Yunnan, and Zhejiang, see Appendix F)

inhabitants at least spoke the same (or roughly the same) language.[52] At best they would find, among the local populations, relatives who could provide them with important information about local markets, as well as shelter, storage, and perhaps some kind of banking and credit facilities. To gain such advantages, the booksellers sought markets in areas of Hakka and Zou and Ma settlement: in eastern, northern, and western Guangdong; in southern and western Jiangxi and in scattered sites in Hunan; and, increasingly over time, in central, southern, and western Guangxi.

---

52. Most of the areas settled by the Zou and Ma or targeted as sites for bookselling are listed in a modern encyclopedia of the Chinese language as areas where Hakka is spoken today. The exceptions are the important cities that were often included in their bookselling routes: Jiujiang, Nanchang, Zhangzhou, Fuzhou, Guangzhou, and Nanning (*Yuyan wenzi*, pp. 237–39). Sibao residents speak a Hakka subdialect ("Sibao hua") that differs somewhat from the dialect of the Jiaying department area—now, retroactively designated the home of "pure" Hakka—and the Hakka subdialects used in other areas of the homeland. But Hakka of different regions could apparently communicate despite the subdialectical differences.

## The Expanding Market for Books:
## Population Growth and the
## Proliferation of Markets

Webs of transport routes and networks of human contacts and business support, however efficient the one and strong the other, were only ancillary to demand. There had to be a market for books—the relatively inexpensive best-sellers of Sibao—for the Zou and Ma merchants to succeed. Here the timing of the Sibao expansion was crucial. The Zou and Ma publishers established *shufang* in Wuge and Mawu beginning in the 1660s (at the latest), while continuing to work as booksellers—work that had engaged them by that time perhaps for as much as half a century in a circuit of local schools and in some unidentified part of Guangdong province. The multiple crises of the mid- and late seventeenth century— the Kangxi depression, the devastation accompanying the Revolt of the Three Feudatories and its suppression, the hardship imposed by the government's coastal evacuation policy—had impoverished the peasantry of Guangdong and to some extent Jiangxi, disrupted the major trade routes of the Lingnan area, and reduced the population of the region by an estimated 22 percent.[53] Needless to say, this was not a good time to attempt an expansion of the book trade; in addition, low grain prices had undermined the spending power of the wealthy, leaving no one to purchase even such highly valued products as books. "The rich become poor, and the poor die" and "Merchants exchange only bitterness [not goods]" were popular contemporary sayings.[54]

The restoration of peace and the abolition of the evacuation policy in 1682–83, by helping to create conditions for economic and commercial revival, marked a clear change for the better. This revival was most striking in Guangdong, the focus of Sibao bookselling. The imperial decision in 1684 to grant Guangzhou the monopoly on foreign trade

---

53. Marks, *Tigers, Rice, Silk, & Silt*, p. 158; see pp. 134–62 for a general discussion of the crises. See also Kishimoto-Nakayama, "The Kangxi Depression and Early Qing Local Markets"; and Chen Zhiping, "Shilun Kangxi chunian dongnan zhusheng de 'shu huang.'"

54. Chen Zhiping, "Shilun Kangxi chunian dongnan zhusheng de 'shu huang,'" p. 45; cited in Marks, *Tigers, Rice, Silk, & Silt*, p. 155.

and the "sudden, substantial increase in foreign and domestic seaborne trade" that followed stimulated the development of commercial agriculture, as peasants in the area scrambled to supply the foreign demand for raw cotton and silk.[55] The increasing prosperity of the region attracted migrants, as we have seen, particularly those from the less fortunate southeastern coast area, which, without the boost provided by the trade monopoly, continued to suffer from economic depression. Government policies, particularly those of the Yongzheng emperor encouraging peasant migration and the opening of new land to cultivation, spurred the development of the hinterland areas and frontier provinces.[56] The population of Guangdong began to rise in the late seventeenth century and then increased rapidly throughout the eighteenth and early nineteenth centuries, to about sixteen million in 1787 and over twenty-eight million in 1850.[57]

Thus the Sibao booksellers found a steadily and rapidly growing market for their products in Guangdong. With the commercialization of the economy, the numbers of markets also increased. Hayashi Kazuo reports that the average number of markets per county increased steadily from 14.4 in 1731 to 28.7 in the nineteenth century and finally to 36.9 in the Xuantong era (1909–11). Of course, market density varied considerably within Guangdong. Not surprisingly, in the mid-Qing, the Foshan-

---

55. Marks, *Tigers, Rice, Silk, & Silt*, p. 163.

56. Cheng Chongde and Sun Zhe, "Lun Qingdai qianqi de xibu bianjiang kaifa," pp. 92, 95. Madeleine Zelin ("The Yung-cheng Reign," pp. 216–18) notes that, although the Qing government had begun encouraging land reclamation during the first two reign-periods, the land reclaimed "was in the economic heartland of China." Not until the Yongzheng era were reclaimed land and newly registered land "concentrated in the more distant provinces." Then Han settlers established themselves in Huguang, Guizhou, and Yunnan, and "cultivation was pushed into the mountains of Kwangtung [Guangdong] and Kwangsi [Guangxi]."

57. Ho Ping-ti, *Studies on the Population of China*, p. 283. Hayashi Kazuo ("Min Shin jidai, Kanton no kyo to shi," p. 85) provides roughly similar statistics: from 5,040,000 in 1578, the population rose to 12,370,000 in 1731 and then to 21,390,000 in 1819. James Lee and Wang Feng ("Population, Poverty, and Subsistence in China," pp. 85–87) calculate that the populations of Guangdong and Guangxi rose at an annual rate of 0.56 to 0.79 percent between 1776 and 1990. They link this population growth to "the sharp increase in geographical mobility that characterized late imperial China." Needless to say, in the absence of precise population statistics for the Qing, these figures and those offered throughout the rest of the chapter are rough estimates.

Guangzhou urban center and much of the Pearl River Delta consistently enjoyed the highest density; next in market density were the eastern coastal plain around Chaozhou—a target of Sibao bookselling—and northern Hainan island. But the hilly and mountainous topography and inadequate roads of northern Guangdong ensured that this part of the province lagged behind in commercial development. Thus, by the early nineteenth century, per 100 square kilometers there was an average of eight or more markets in the Guangzhou area, but only one in Huizhou prefecture.

Yet even in the poorer areas there was growth over the course of the eighteenth and early nineteenth centuries; market density doubled in Shaozhou, Huizhou, and Gaozhou prefectures and Jiaying department, and in Lianzhou prefecture (in the far western part of the province), density increased from 0.25–0.49 markets per 100 square kilometers to 0.50–0.99.[58] Thus the Sibao merchants, in selecting Guangdong as their primary commercial destination, were not simply following the path of Hakka or Zou and Ma migrations; they were also taking their goods to a region of rising population, growing prosperity, and increasing market density, where they could count on an increase in customers. And the revival of old trade networks severed during the crises of the mid- and late seventeenth century and the proliferation of financial institutions such as native banks (*qianzhuang* 錢莊) and currency-exchange shops (*qianpu* 錢舖) facilitated both the physical progress to these new markets and the business transactions of the Sibao merchants in them.[59]

How did the Sibao booksellers choose among these new markets? As noted above, for the most part they avoided the major urban core of the province. Although they made some effort to trade in Guangzhou and the Pearl River Delta (notably in Zengcheng, a largely Hakka settlement noted for its textile and mining industries),[60] this most densely populated, commercially active, and wealthiest part of the province was never a favored site. Throughout Sibao's publishing history, at most only twelve Zou and Ma booksellers worked in this area. Yet they did

---

58. Hayashi, "Min Shin jidai, Kanton no kyo to shi," p. 86.
59. Ye Xian'en, "Qingdai Guangdong shuiyun yu shehui jingji," pp. 5–10; Peng Xinwei, *A Monetary History of China*, 2: 814–15, 820–21, 830, 832.
60. Situ Shangji, *Lingnan shidi lunji*, pp. 359–67.

flock to urban centers of secondary and tertiary significance: twenty-three ran branch bookstores in Chaozhou city (the second most densely populated area in Guangdong), fifteen in Jiaying city, nine in Huizhou city, and seven each in Gaozhou city and Xingning county seat.[61] The remaining thirty Guangdong sites were, with a few exceptions, county seats or market towns in the hinterland, which attracted between one and five booksellers apiece.[62]

Thus, in Guangdong, the Sibao booksellers, while generally skirting the center of highest population and greatest market density, clustered in five urban centers—four prefectural or department seats and one county seat—of varying administrative, commercial, or educational importance. From these centers single or smaller groups of booksellers advanced into the hinterland, usually along the river systems, either as itinerant merchants or as founders of branch shops in less bustling county seats and market towns. Chaozhou city, the most prosperous and highly urbanized of the five major centers of Sibao bookselling, was a thriving commercial center in the Qing, having benefited from the gradual revival of trade in Zhangzhou, Quanzhou 泉州, and Fuzhou.[63] But the prefecture included relatively poor upland agricultural

---

61. The figures given here are intended to be suggestive, not conclusive. The Zou and Ma genealogies do not record all booksellers, and thus the numbers (derived from Appendix E2) underrepresent the number of booksellers. I am assessing the importance of an urban settlement according to the hierarchy of central places established by G. William Skinner: central places can be ordered in seven ranks, from number 1, the most highly urbanized and politically significant place, the capital, down to number 7, the "standard marketing settlement," a village with a periodic market. Gilbert Rozman (*Urban Networks in Ch'ing China and Tokugawa Japan*, pp. 14, 240–42), applying this hierarchy to Guangdong, identifies Guangzhou, a regional center, as a rank-2 city; Chaozhou, an "intermediate port city linking level 1 or 2 cities to distant areas," as rank 3, as is Jiaying; and Huizhou, Gaozhou, and Xingning, either prefectural capitals or major regional ports, as rank 4. This ranking does not reflect changes in the status of these places over the course of the Qing and thus offers only a rather crude measure of their relative importance.

62. The three exceptions are Huilai county seat, which is a rank-4 city, but it attracted only one bookseller; Leizhou prefectural city, also a rank-4 center, with two booksellers; and Shaozhou prefectural city, in one of the poorest parts of the province, with one bookseller. See Rozman, *Urban Networks in Ch'ing China and Tokugawa Japan*, p. 242.

63. Gardella, *Harvesting Mountains*, p. 33; Jiang Zuyuan and Fang Zhiqin, *Jianming Guangdong shi*, pp. 370–71.

areas as well as the prosperous lowland, and the Zou and Ma established shops in at least four county seats and two market towns in the prefecture.[64]

Jiaying city, in a landlocked upland agricultural area, benefited indirectly from Guangzhou's foreign trade and population increase, as the demand for foodstuffs stimulated the commercialization (and intensification) of agriculture, and the city became a market for agricultural exports. But Jiaying department as a whole, a popular site of both Hakka migration and Sibao bookselling, remained quite poor, particularly as the growing population began to exhaust the supply of land in the early nineteenth century. Jiaying, despite its poverty, did have a strong educational tradition; from the mid-seventeenth to the mid-nineteenth century, it produced more *jinshi* graduates than the more prosperous metropolitan areas of Nanhai 南海 and Panyu 番禺.[65] This tradition may have encouraged the Zou and Ma to target Jiaying as one of their major markets; they established branch stores throughout the department, in six county seats (most notably in Xingning) and one market town.

Huizhou and Gaozhou had mixed economies, including both poor upland, primarily agricultural, areas and more prosperous coastal regions. Huizhou prefectural city attracted a cluster of Sibao booksellers, and a scattering of others worked in the poorer upland region. Gaozhou in particular benefited from the province-wide economic upswing of the eighteenth century. More land came under cultivation, on which rice, sugarcane, peanuts, and flax were grown for export. The fishery and shipbuilding industries also grew. Commercial production required a more extensive transport system, which stimulated the growth of

---

64. Jieyang county seat, for example, although never as prosperous as nearby Chaozhou city, was a bookselling site for at least five Zou merchants (each of whom also worked in Chaozhou); on Jieyang, see *Jieyangxian zheng xuzhi, j.* 7, "Wuchan," 25a–26a.

65. Leong, *Migration and Ethnicity in Chinese History*, p. 76. Yet by the late nineteenth century, the department had only 14 academies and 32 local schools (compared to 42 academies and 46 schools in Chaozhou, and 152 academies and 317 schools in Guangzhou), making it educationally one of the weakest regions in the province. The decline may have been the result of the disorders of that century (Wakeman, *Strangers at the Gate*, pp. 184–85).

small market towns and ports within the prefecture; Wuchuan, a Sibao bookselling site, was one such port.[66]

How was Sibao bookselling in Guangdong affected by the economic contraction of the early nineteenth century? Already as early as the last quarter of the eighteenth century, contemporaries had begun to complain about the decline in living standards as population outstripped economic development,[67] and certainly by 1812 the rate of land reclamation could not keep pace with the population explosion in the south. By that time, Guangdong was among the most land-hungry provinces in the empire, with a rate of about 1.67 *mu* (approximately one-quarter of an acre) per person, well under the empire-wide average of 2.19 *mu* per person.[68] The Opium War (1839–41) and the Treaty of Nanjing exacerbated the problem. The opening of Shanghai "diverted trade away from its traditional routes northward" from Guangzhou, throwing thousands out of work.[69] Widespread impoverishment in the province, once the richest market for Sibao texts, might help to explain the reported decline in the business after the Jiaqing era.

The wars and rebellions that ravaged south China in mid-century, in part as a consequence of competition over increasingly scarce resources—the Taiping Rebellion, the Red Turban Rebellion (1854–56), the Hakka-Punti War (not to mention the sporadic uprisings of the Triads and other secret societies)—although centered in areas largely outside the Sibao booksellers' markets, nonetheless hurt business both by intensifying economic hardship (and reducing consumers' purchasing power) and by disrupting trade routes.[70] Crime, too, was on the rise in Guangdong, as mercenaries hired to fight in the Opium War were demobilized and turned to banditry for survival. Pirates, a scourge of the southern coast since the late eighteenth century, were forced inland by

---

66. Chen Zhonglie, "Ming Qing Gao Lei diqu shangpinxing jingjide fazhan ji qi pingjia," pp. 162–69. Chen also emphasizes the limits of economic development in Gaozhou; see pp. 170–72.

67. Ho, *Studies on the Population of China*, pp. 270–71. For a fuller discussion of the problem, see Kuhn, *Soulstealers*, chap. 2.

68. Woon, *Social Organization in South China*, p. 10; and Wakeman, *Strangers at the Gate*, pp. 179–80. Only Guizhou, Gansu, Fujian, and Anhui had less cultivatable land.

69. Kuhn, "The Taiping Rebellion," p. 264.

70. Fairbank, "The Creation of the Treaty System," p. 245.

British naval power and by the 1840s dominated the riverways of both Guangdong and Guangxi.[71] The disorders of mid-century and the general economic troubles caused a decline in education that was not seriously addressed until the 1860s, with the Tongzhi-era reforms. Since educational texts constituted the bulk of Sibao's stock, this decline surely hurt their business, particularly since they were, by this time, competing with other publishing industries in Guangdong, Guangxi, Jiangxi, Hunan, and Hubei. In short, it is not surprising that, throughout the Daoguang, Xianfeng, and part of the Tongzhi eras, publishing no longer yielded the profits it once had.

This is not to say that the Zou and Ma book merchants abandoned their Guangdong markets. They maintained their operations in Chaozhou, Jiaying (and Xingning), Huizhou, and Gaozhou cities throughout the nineteenth century. But it was in the early nineteenth century, just as the economic consequences of the population explosion were becoming acute, that they began establishing branches in the hinterland areas of these prefectures and in the most backward portions of the province—Leizhou prefectural city (with only seven academies and seventeen local schools by the late nineteenth century), Lingshan county in the westernmost prefecture of Lianzhou, and scattered communities in Nanxiong department and Zhaoqing 肇慶 prefecture. These advances into the hinterland may represent efforts to seek out new markets in areas with little competition at a time when established markets were drying up.

Perhaps it is no coincidence that it is around this time—the early nineteenth century—that the Zou and Ma book merchants started moving into Guangxi. By 1787 the population of the province was only about 6,376,000, well under that of its neighbor Guangdong. By the middle of the nineteenth century it had increased to about 7,827,000, while Guangdong's had risen to about 28 million. Yet by the middle of the next century, Guangxi's population had risen to 19,561,000.[72] The

---

71. Kuhn, "The Taiping Rebellion," p. 265.

72. Ho, *Studies on the Population of China*, p. 283. Cheng Chongde and Sun Zhe ("Lun Qingdai qianqi de xibu bianjiang kaifa," p. 95) provide somewhat more impressive figures for population growth in Guangxi: to 7.42 million in 1820, seven times the number in the early Qing.

province thus offered booksellers the market advantages of a frontier area during a time of rapid population growth and expansion: new markets developing in the wake of migration and the opening of new land to agriculture.

As in Guangdong, the booksellers seem to have avoided the major urban center of the province: Guilin, the capital and a city already well settled in the Ming and with an active publishing industry, attracted only two book merchants. There were in fact no major Sibao bookstores in the northern part of the province; rather, the Zou and Ma merchants generally chose prefectural and county seats along the major east-west river systems for their bookstores. Their starting point was Wuzhou prefectural city, on the Gong River; this major transport hub and commercial center, the gateway from Guangdong to the western provinces of Guangxi, Yunnan, and Guizhou, drew four booksellers.[73]

From there they moved southward and westward, establishing branches in the region along the Gong from Wuzhou to Nanning. This region, noted primarily for its silver and coal mines,[74] did offer a few pockets of agricultural fertility: most notably, the areas around Wuzhou, Guixian, and Nanning.[75] The Yongzheng emperor encouraged the opening of upland areas to agriculture in frontier areas; his policy had attracted immigrants in the eighteenth century, and Hakka migrants had continued to settle there through the nineteenth.[76] Xunzhou 潯州, Yulin 郁林, and Nanning prefectures had, by 1820, surpassed Guilin, the provincial capital, in population density, as they became exporters of rice to the Guangzhou area.[77] But much of the region was poor, its inhabitants forced to scrape a living from small upland farms, the mines, or itinerant labor. One resident (and Taiping rebel) described the desperate quality of life for the poor in the area: "My family was destitute

---

73. Tan Yanhuan and Liao Guoyi, *Guangxi shigao*, pp. 129–30.
74. Nanning was largely a mining town in the Ming and Qing, noted for the production of silver and lead (ibid., p. 128).
75. Oldfield, *Pioneering in Kwangsi*, p. 13.
76. Zelin, "The Yung-cheng Reign," p. 216; Tan Yanhuan and Liao Guoyi, *Guangxi shigao*, p. 119.
77. Marks, *Tigers, Rice, Silk, & Silt*, pp. 286–87.

and did not have enough to eat. We lived by tilling the land, cultivating mountain slopes, and hiring out as laborers. . . . At the age of eight, nine, and ten I studied with my uncle, but my family was poor and I could not study longer. But I worked as a laborer in many schools and knew them well. . . . [It] was difficult to make ends meet each day; to get enough a month was even more difficult."[78]

The Sibao merchants naturally chose to focus their efforts on the major centers in the most prosperous areas along the Gong and its tributary, the Yu River: after Wuzhou, Guixian, a regional port that attracted fourteen book merchants; Hengzhou, the site of operations for eight booksellers;[79] and Nanning, a mining center and port city linking the western and eastern sections of the province, which drew nine booksellers.[80] This city became the base for further expansion into the frontier. In the late nineteenth and early twentieth centuries, at least four booksellers of the upper-shrine Zou lineage pushed farther westward on the You River (the continuation of the Yu) to the seat of Bose subprefecture, about thirty kilometers from the border with Yunnan. Working out of Bose, they established branches in several nearby county seats and market towns. These booksellers were working as real pioneers (as they themselves claimed), genuinely bringing culture (in the form of textbooks, the Classics, how-to manuals, and popular novels) to the frontier.[81]

So, too, in the distant frontier of Yunnan and Guizhou—although only two booksellers ventured into these provinces. Yunnan, sparsely settled in the early Qing, experienced a dramatic increase in population over the course of the eighteenth century: its population in 1820 is

---

78. Curwen, *Taiping Rebel*, pp. 83, 88; cited in Spence, *God's Chinese Son*, pp. 80–81.

79. Hengzhou was also not far from one of their Guangdong bookselling sites and may have provided a link to that site: Lingshan, in northern Lianzhou prefecture.

80. There were also branches in Beiliu 北流, on the Rong River 容江; and Pingnan, on the Yu. Rozman identifies Wuzhou as a rank-3a city, "an intermediate port"; Guilin, the major city of the province, is also rank 3a. Nanning is rank 3b, and Guixian, rank 4. It is interesting that the booksellers avoided Xunzhou prefectural city (Guiping, rank 4), an important port at the confluence of the Gong, Yu, and Qian 黔江 rivers. Perhaps its location near the center of the activities of the God-Worshippers' Society made it too dangerous a site.

81. *FYZSZP* (1947), *j. shou*, "Jiaxun sitiao," 4b.

estimated to have been about 4.49 million, five times the total at the beginning of the dynasty.[82] This population increase was accompanied by a growth in educational institutions. William Rowe estimates that Chen Hongmou 陳宏謀 (1696–1771), in this "remote and still substantially aboriginal" province, had by 1738 revived or established nearly seven hundred elementary schools, a significant increase over the two hundred he found on his arrival as provincial financial commissioner in 1733.[83] These schools should have provided a ready market for Sibao's bestsellers—primers and editions of the Four Books and Five Classics. It is not clear why the Zou and Ma did not further exploit the markets in this province and Guizhou; perhaps the cost and physical difficulties of travel to these distant regions made them unattractive.

Although neither of the other important provinces for Sibao bookselling—Jiangxi and Hunan—could qualify as frontier areas, the disorders of the mid-seventeenth century did reduce their populations and lead to the abandonment of much of the arable land, opening them up for resettlement once order had been restored later in the century. Jiangxi suffered from the depredations of remnant rebel troops from Li Zicheng's 李自成 (1605?–45) forces, from the activities of the Qing army sent to pacify the province after the partial Manchu conquest of 1644, and from the efforts of scattered Ming-loyalist troops to hold the province against the Qing. The northern portion of Jiangxi was rather quickly subdued, and by 1646 the Manchus had succeeded in wiping out effective resistance in the Gannan or "southern Gan" region as well. Less than three decades later, however, Jiangxi once again became a battleground, this time in Wu Sangui's 吳三桂 (1612–78) rebellion against the Qing, headquartered in neighboring Hunan province.

---

82. Cheng Chongde and Sun Zhe, "Lun Qingdai qianqi de xibu bianqiang kaifa," p. 95. According to Lee and Wang ("Population, Poverty, and Subsistence in China," pp. 85–87), the population of Yunnan and Guizhou increased at an annual rate of 1–2 percent between 1776 and 1990; only the far northeast surpassed the population growth rate for Yunnan and Guizhou. Ho Ping-ti (*Studies on the Population of China*, p. 283) claims that Yunnan's population rose from 3,461,000 in 1787 to 7,376,000 in 1850 and 17,473,000 in 1953; and that Guizhou's population rose at a slower rate, from 5,158,000 in 1787 to 5,434,000 in 1850 to 15,037,000 in 1953).

83. Rowe, *Ordering the World*, p. 419; Ho Ping-ti, *The Ladder of Success in Imperial China*, p. 210.

Only with the defeat of this rebellion in 1681 did some stability return to the province, by then suffering from population decline and widespread abandonment of cultivated land (as were Hunan, western Fujian, and Lingnan). With the encouragement of favorable government policies, migrants—most particularly Hakka and "shed people" (*pengmin* 棚 民, thus named because they lived in flimsy shacks) from Fujian and Guangdong—began settling the areas most heavily devastated by war. The Qianlong-era Ganzhou gazetteer reported that "men from Min and Yue, who can farm mountain land, come with their families and support themselves through their labor."[84] Migration accelerated particularly in the Qianlong and Jiaqing eras; Ho Ping-ti estimates that the population of the province had reached 19,156,000 by 1787, increasing to 24,515,000 by the mid-nineteenth century.[85] Even as the new migrants reclaimed abandoned farmland—and, as the quotation above reveals—moved into less easily cultivated mountain land, Jiangxi also enjoyed some of the benefits of the renewed foreign and domestic trade. The imperial customs house at Jiujiang, a port on the Yangzi with easy access to the Gan River basin, had "the highest quota for domestic transit taxes in the empire." Porcelain from Jingdezhen 景德鎮 and timber and tea from Fujian were shipped from Jiujiang either for the domestic market or overland or on the Gan River system to Guangzhou for foreign export. Nanchang, the provincial capital, became with Changsha in Hunan and Wuhan in Hubei one of the largest urban centers in the middle Yangzi region.[86]

Following the pattern familiar from Guangdong and Guangxi, the Sibao merchants, although not entirely avoiding the major commercial centers of the province, established themselves more frequently in prefectural or county seats of some administrative significance or in market towns. The busy port city of Jiujiang, the conduit of goods to the Yangzi, attracted only one bookseller. Ganzhou prefectural city, located on both the central river system of Jiangxi and at the intersection of the two major north-south roads, was the most important commercial center in southern Jiangxi. As the last major city before the much-traveled

84. *Ganzhou fuzhi* (Qianlong era), *j.* 17; cited in Xu Huailin, *Jiangxi shigao*, p. 534.
85. Ho Ping-ti, *Studies on the Population of China*, p. 283.
86. Naquin and Rawski, *Chinese Society in the Eighteenth Century*, p. 162.

Meiling Pass, it commanded trade between Jiangxi and Guangdong. It was also a natural market for the abundant crops and handicraft products of the prefecture: tobacco, sugarcane, tea and *tong* oil, iron, cotton, ramie, and paper.[87] Yet only four booksellers (three of whom were of the same household) set up shops there.

The Sibao merchants seemed to prefer cities and towns that, although still administrative or trade centers, were not the dominant sites, politically or commercially, of the province. The settlement with the largest concentration of booksellers, Zhangshuzhen (modern Qingjiang 清江), with thirteen Sibao merchants, was a port at the confluence of the Yuan and Gan rivers and a noted market for medicines; it offered merchants—who "gathered like clouds" there—access to the major north-south transport route in western Jiangxi.[88] But, with a population of only about 10,000, it paled in significance in comparison to Jiujiang, Jingdezhen, or even nearby Linjiang 臨江 prefectural city. Of roughly the same size as Zhangshuzhen were Wuchengzhen (with one Sibao bookseller), at the point where the Gan river flows into Poyang Lake, a transport link to the Yangzi and a depot for the shipment of tea, timber, paper, salt, and ramie;[89] Xuwanzhen (also with one bookseller), just south of the more important city of Fuzhou on the Xu River, a regional port trading in rice, timber, and paper; and, in the northeast, Yushan county seat (one bookseller), on the Xin River 信河. After Ganzhou and Zhangshuzhen, the two settlements that had the highest concentration of Sibao booksellers were county seats in the poorer hinterland areas of the province: Ruijin (with three booksellers), on the Gong River, was usefully located on the major east–west road from Tingzhou to Ganzhou, but offered only a local market in products like tobacco, tea, tea oil, paper, and linen. Changning county seat, with six booksellers, was the most isolated and least commercially active of the Jiangxi bookselling sites—iron and lead seem to have been the only exports of the area, and the trade in these ores appears to have been limited.[90]

---

87. Xu Huailin, *Jiangxi shigao*, pp. 545–50.
88. *Qingjiang xianzhi*, 2b.11ab; and Xu Huailin, *Jiangxi shigao*, pp. 519–20, 561–62.
89. Xu Huailin, *Jiangxi shigao*, pp. 520–21.
90. The Changning gazetteer of 1876 provides a melancholy report on the local economy, stating that although both men and women worked hard, they earned very little. Many men went out as sojourning merchants. The two pairs of Zou merchants

Here, as in both Guangdong and Guangxi, the Sibao booksellers selected sites below—in some cases, well below—the ranks of the most administratively complex and commercially active centers of the province. Market towns and county seats (where they could expect to find a government school and at least a local market) were, with a few exceptions, their markets of choice.[91]

Like Jiangxi, Hunan suffered much from the series of rebellions—of Li Zicheng, Zhang Xianzhong, and Wu Sangui—that destroyed the economic center of the province, the area around Dongting Lake. The province was slow to recover; it was not until the late eighteenth century that production returned to the levels of the sixteenth century. In the early Qing, then, Hunan had regressed to the status of "a relatively underdeveloped region." With much abandoned agricultural land and a river system that offered a good communication network to at least certain portions of the province, it was ripe for resettlement.[92] Encouraged by policies of the Qing government promoting the reclamation of formerly cultivated land, peasants succeeded in doubling the amount of farmland between 1685 and 1724. Rice was a primary commercial crop, and Hunan a major player in the national rice market through the early nineteenth century. The population grew steadily, from 14.9 million in 1776 (the first year for which there are fairly reliable figures) to 20.9 in 1860, although a slowdown in the rate of increase from 1812 on suggests that at this time the province was reaching the limit of its "potential for rapid expansion . . . and could no longer absorb large numbers of immigrants."[93] Important markets on the Yuan and Xiang rivers shipped rice on the Yangzi to Hankou, Hubei, a city that had become, early in

---

who worked in Changning, however, were there earlier in the century, when the attraction of a migrant Hakka population and proximity to other Sibao bookselling sites in Fujian and Guangdong made the area more appealing. *Changning xianzhi*, *j.* 3, "Wuchan," 3ab; and *j.* 3, "Fengsu," 2b–3a.

91. Two booksellers also operated in the Fenyi county seat, on the Yuan River in western Jiangxi; one in Fuzhou prefectural city; one in Shicheng 石城 county seat; and one in Longnan county seat. Rozman (*Urban Networks in Ch'ing China and Tokugawa Japan*, pp. 232–36) ranks the Jiangxi cities as follows: Jiujiang, Jingdezhen (and the provincial capital, Nanchang) are 3a; Ganzhou and Fuzhou prefectural cities are 3b; and Linjiang prefectural city, 4. All the other settlements discussed here are rank 5 or below.

92. Rawski, *Agricultural Change and the Peasant Economy of South China*, pp. 101–2.

93. Perdue, *Exhausting the Earth*, pp. 55–57.

the Qing, "the single greatest port for the collection and sale of commodities in all of the empire."[94] Economic development in Hunan was uneven, however. Those prefectures on the major transport rivers, the Xiang, the Yuan, and the Zi—Changsha, Hengzhou, and Changde—flourished. Here, markets grew, often at a remarkable rate—Yiyang county in Changsha prefecture, for example, experienced a 500 percent growth in periodic markets between 1685 and 1747. But other areas of the province, those upland regions in the west and southwest not accessible to the major river systems, did not enjoy the same level of prosperity.[95]

The few Sibao booksellers who chose to trade in Hunan established shops in most of the major port cities—Changsha, the largest city, with a population between 200,000 and 300,000, Hengzhou prefectural city, and Yiyang county city drew one bookseller each, and Changde prefectural city three.[96] The least significant of the bookselling sites—Guiyang department seat (on a southern tributary of the Xiang River)—was still an administrative center and port of some local commercial importance.

The Sibao book merchants never developed a comprehensive and sustained interest in Hunan. To some extent the unevenness of the province's economic development might help explain this choice—certainly it helps to explain why the few bookselling sites were almost all on the major rivers. Competition from local industries might also have kept the Sibao merchants from expanding into the province; Baoqing prefectural city (modern Shaoyang 邵陽) developed a commercial publishing industry in the Qing, one that produced texts rather like Sibao's imprints. Although this industry seems to have been smaller than Sibao's, it may have been large enough to discourage Zou and Ma bookselling activity in central Hunan.[97] It is also possible that the Sibao merchants saw the province, with its relatively small urban centers

---

94. Naquin and Rawski, *Chinese Society in the Eighteenth Century*, p. 163. The citation is from an early Qing merchant manual.

95. Rawski, *Agricultural Change and the Peasant Economy of South China*, pp. 112, 125–26.

96. Changsha, the most populous city in the province, was a rank-3a central place, as was Hengzhou prefectural city; Changde was rank 3b (Rozman, *Urban Networks in Ch'ing China and Tokugawa Japan*, pp. 232, 237–38).

97. Hou Zhenping, "Hunan diaocha lu," in Brokaw, ed., "Mapping the Book Trade: The Expansion of Print Culture in Late Imperial China" (2004).

supportive of the much larger and more concentrated urban population of Hubei, primarily as a stepping-stone to Wuchang and Hankou, "the major locus of commercial exchange" in late Qing central China.[98] Although a few Sibao booksellers did work in eastern Hubei (two in the Wuchang-Hankou area and four in Hanchuan county seat, about fifty kilometers from Wuchang on the Han River 漢水), business there evidently was not brisk enough to merit a heavy investment in bookselling labor. Since Hankou had developed a sizable publishing industry of its own in the nineteenth century, the Zou and Ma probably found little business there.

Perhaps more important in limiting Sibao interest in Huguang was competition from immigrants from neighboring Jiangxi, who outnumbered those from Fujian.[99] Immigration to Hunan had slowed significantly by the early nineteenth century; a noticeable decline in the rate of population growth suggests that the province was already "filled up" with settlers.[100] Indeed, Zou and Ma migration to the province seems to have effectively stopped by the end of the eighteenth century. Bookselling activity in Hunan declined, too, over the course of the nineteenth century. Perhaps the absence of strong Sibao-migrant networks (and the presence of strong competing Jiangxi-migrant networks) encouraged the booksellers to turn elsewhere.

## Conclusion

The Zou and Ma migrants and booksellers were flocking, from the late seventeenth through the early nineteenth century, to regions economically on the rise. Of course, we must not exaggerate the newfound prosperity of the Lingnan and middle Yangzi regions, as population growth quickly outstripped the increase in arable land. The migrations by the Hakka and shed people that resettled much of the middle Yangzi and Lingnan in the early Qing created or exacerbated ethnic tensions in all these areas by the late eighteenth century, as increasing population

98. Rozman, Urban Networks in Ch'ing China and Tokugawa Japan, p. 233.

99. Tan Qixiang, "Zhongguo neidi yiminshi—Hunan pian," pp. 60–103; see also Perdue, *Exhausting the Earth*, p. 101.

100. Perdue, *Exhausting the Earth*, p. 57.

intensified competition over limited land and resources. These tensions finally exploded in wars and rebellions (of which the Taiping was only the most spectacular), which plagued nineteenth-century China and disrupted many of the areas of Zou and Ma settlement and bookselling.[101] But, given the continued economic woes of the Fujian area (which had even less arable land per capita than Guangdong),[102] from the perspective of Minxi residents, the Lingnan and middle Yangzi regions—even their hinterlands—offered attractive economic opportunities in the form of new land to cultivate and new commercial networks to work.

If the motives for Hakka migration, Zou and Ma migration, and Sibao bookselling in Guangdong, Guangxi, Hunan, Hubei, and Jiangxi are obvious enough, their specific choices for bookselling beg explanation—or at least speculation, since none of the sources explains their strategy. The major metropolitan and commercial centers of each area, the most heavily populated and wealthiest regional cores, never formed the backbone of Zou and Ma markets. As their primary market sites, the Sibao booksellers chose hinterland prefectural cities, county seats, and market towns near but not in the urban cores of the provinces of Guangdong, Guangxi, Jiangxi, and Hunan. Particularly attractive were administrative centers and trade nodes on river systems in relatively sparsely settled areas, where the population was growing but competition was scarce: Nanning and Bose, for example, were attractive because even in the nineteenth century they were still to some degree "frontier" areas, yet located on the trade and river routes linking Yunnan and Guizhou provinces to Guangdong.[103]

The pattern of Hakka settlement, more specifically of Zou and Ma migration and settlement, seems to have had a decisive influence on the formation of the Sibao trade routes. Presumably the security offered by linguistic, ethnic, and social connections outweighed the potentially richer commercial opportunities of centers such as Guangzhou and Nanchang. And since these larger cities had also developed their own

---

101. C. K. Yang, "Some Preliminary Statistical Patterns of Mass Actions in Nineteenth-Century China," pp. 209–10; Naquin and Rawski, *Chinese Society in the Eighteenth Century*, pp. 228–29.

102. Wakeman, *Strangers at the Gate*, p. 179.

103. Interview 94, 5/13/95 (Bose).

publishing industries by the late eighteenth century, it is unlikely that they were attractive markets for Sibao imprints. Foshanzhen, within the Guangdong urban core, was a major popular publishing site by the nineteenth century;[104] and Guangzhou had developed both important commercial and official publishing operations by the late eighteenth century. The most famous of the official publishers, the Xuehai tang 學海堂 founded by Ruan Yuan 阮元 (1764–1849), produced elite scholarly texts for a highly educated and discriminating readership very different from Sibao's target audience. Yet the city also supported commercial houses producing cheap popular texts that competed directly with Sibao's products.[105]

In Jiangxi, Xuwanzhen (in the early 1700s a market for Sibao imprints) had become a major commercial publishing center by the nineteenth century. The Xuwanzhen publishers, by distributing their texts to many of the major port cities of central China and the Jiangnan area (Nanchang, Jiujiang, Changsha, Wuhu [Anhui], and Nanjing), reduced opportunities in these areas for the Sibao merchants. Nanchang, too, as the provincial capital, was a center of government and commercial publishing.[106] And Hankou had become, with Xuwanzhen, one of the major publishing centers of the nineteenth century.[107] Given the advantageous position of that city as a major port connecting both east–west and north–south trade routes, the Sibao publisher-booksellers could not hope to compete with its distribution networks once a publishing industry developed there. Even Guilin had developed an active printing industry by the early nineteenth century; both the provincial government and a cluster of commercial houses produced examination guides and model essay collections, just the texts that formed the bulk of Sibao's offerings.[108] It may simply have not been worthwhile for the Zou and Ma booksellers to take their products to these urban centers. We may even wonder to what extent the few Zou and Ma merchants active in these

104. Zhang Xiumin, *Zhongguo yinshua shi*, pp. 556–57; *Guangdong shengzhi—chuban zhi*, pp. 71–72.

105. Li Xubo, "Qingdai Guangdong de shufang ji qi keshu"; *Guangdong shengzhi—chuban zhi*, pp. 59–60, 69–71.

106. *Jiangxisheng chuban zhi*, pp. 3–4, 175–79; for Xuwanzhen, see Chapter 1.

107. *Hubei shengzhi—Xinwen chuban*, 2: 11–28, 32–38, 49–51.

108. *Guangxi tongzhi—Chuban zhi*, pp. 18–24.

core areas were there to sell Sibao imprints. Guangzhou and Hankou, for example, may well have been visited primarily for news of the book trade or, toward the end of the industry, for the purchase of lithographic and other modern texts for sale in Sibao branch bookstores (see Chapter 7).

Given the rapid population increase and at least moderate economic improvement that characterized almost all the areas under discussion, these book merchants, in restricting themselves to smaller sites, were not necessarily making poor business choices. The texts that constituted the bulk of Sibao stock—reading primers, the Classics (especially the Four Books), how-to manuals, and popular novels—would have been welcome virtually anywhere in Chinese society, once enough of the population could afford to purchase them (and, as we shall see, Sibao texts were relatively inexpensive). By choosing prefectural and county seats as markets, the booksellers were concentrating, as they had in the early stages of their business (although at that point closer to home) on educational centers, the sites of county and prefectural schools, academies, and, in the case of the prefectural cities, examination compounds.

The yamen itself, in its official and suboffical staff, also provided something of a market. We shall see in Chapter 8 that the Zou and Ma publisher-booksellers met many of their customers (and important social contacts) either in local schools or government offices. Private academies and yamen, as well as supplying customers, might also provide the booksellers with information about changes in examination requirements and new educational texts. Zou Shengmai and his family learned very quickly, for example, about the publication of Li Guang-di's guide to the *Classic of Changes, Yuzuan Zhouyi zhezhong* 御纂周易折中, a text they eventually printed. This work was originally a government-sponsored publication distributed to official academies in 1715 (and again in 1736, 1750, 1779, and 1809),[109] and it is certainly possible that the Zou publishers learned of it through their contacts with academy teachers or officials.[110]

---

109. Ridley, "Educational Theory and Practice in Late Imperial China," pp. 167–84.

110. There are other "imperially sponsored" texts that might have come to the attention of the Sibao publishers through their official contacts: *Xieji bianfang shu* (1742), a work defining cosmological orthodoxy; and *Yizong jinjian* 醫宗金鑑 (Golden mirror of medical orthodoxy), a medical encyclopedia. See Chapter 11.

Commercial and transport centers, which attracted students and aspiring examination candidates, would also provide a more varied clientele, one interested in the whole range of texts—novels, medical handbooks, ritual manuals, *fengshui* guides, and so forth—that the Sibao publishers produced in addition to examination-oriented educational texts. Crucially, the location of most of their markets along major river systems—the Han, Long, East, West, and North rivers in Guangdong; the Gong, Rong, Yu, and You in Guangxi; the Gan and Xu in Jiangxi; and the Xiang, Zi, and Yuan in Hunan—made transportation even to remote areas on the frontier possible. Indeed, along the Gan in Jiangxi and the Yu in Guangxi, the Sibao booksellers seem to have been operating in a chain of river ports, often setting up branch shops in the next major transit point down- or upstream. Generally avoiding the greater competition, greater risks, and greater unfamiliarity of the richest and most crowded metropolitan markets, they chose, rather, the security and steady profits they could expect from middling and lower-level markets amid the rapidly expanding population of Lingnan and the middle Yangzi region.

# SEVEN

---

## Sojourning Bookselling
and the Operation of
the Branch Shops

AS WE SAW IN the preceding chapter, from the late seventeenth century through the late nineteenth, the Zou and Ma booksellers, following patterns of Hakka migration and moving into newly developing markets, were able to establish an impressive distribution network for Sibao imprints. This network encompassed two different modes: itinerant bookselling, in which merchants traveled from market to market with a supply of books, usually returning to Sibao once a year to replenish their stock and settle accounts; and branch bookstores, a more stable outlet for the distribution of Sibao imprints. In actuality, bookselling outside Sibao did not divide sharply into one or the other of these modes but often employed a range of marketing and transport practices, many of which combined itinerant selling and branch-shop management.

In this chapter I describe, as fully as the sources allow, first, how both types of booksellers conducted their business—that is, how the itinerant merchants managed the transport of texts, living on the road, fund transfers, and so forth—and second, how the managers of branch shops coordinated their business with the publishing activities of the parent house in Sibao and oversight by the house managers.

## *Life on the Road: Itinerant Bookselling*

In 1995 an informant from Wuge, now over eighty years of age, recounted for me his experiences as an itinerant bookseller in the early decades of the twentieth century. As a child, he helped in the *shufang* by inking the woodblocks for the printers, and at the age of seventeen *sui* he began traveling with his father in Fujian, or occasionally with his father and an uncle, selling books for the Suwei tang *shufang*. They traveled a variety of routes: from Wuge to Fuzhou, via Yongan, Shaxian, Yanping, and Shuikou, all on the Sha or Min rivers; from Wuge to Zhangzhou (where the Suwei tang had a branch store); and several circuits within Tingzhou prefecture, from Wuge to Liancheng and on to Shanghang, or from Wuge to portions of Ninghua, Qingliu, and Guihua counties. Each man typically carried two "loads" (*tiao* 挑) of books, each load weighing sixty *jin* 斤 (36.3 kilograms); they traveled to the market towns and county seats on each of these routes, trying to time their arrivals to coincide with the periodic market days in these towns. In major markets, they would stay from three to five days in a local hostel (*lüshe* 旅社 or *kejian* 客間), so that they could not only sell in that market town but also split up and visit surrounding villages on their different market days. So, for example, father and son would plan to arrive in Beituan, several kilometers from Wuge, just on or before its market day, on days 2 and 7, and then move on late that day or early the following morning to Liancheng, roughly fifteen kilometers away, whose markets took place on days 3 and 8. They might make as much as eight to ten silver dollars (*huabian* 花邊) or as little as one to two in these markets.[1] In a similar fashion, they scheduled stops in modern Pengkou 朋口 and Juxi 莒溪, Xinquan 新泉, and Shanghang, their ultimate destination. All three men were on the road most of the year—my informant reported that he spent only two, at most three, months of every year in Wuge.

---

1. *Huabian* or "flower border" coins, originally doubloons minted in Mexico City beginning in 1732, circulated widely in Fujian and Guangdong in the Qianlong and Jiaqing eras. The term later became a common name for silver dollars. Since these coins came in at least three different weights, it is not possible to guess how much these sums would be worth; see Peng Xinwei, *A Monetary History of China*, 2: 672.

These men were itinerant peddlers rather than merchants, spreading their wares out on bamboo mats in a series of local markets. In their time the Sibao industry was in its final decline—indeed, they could not support themselves through the sale of texts alone, certainly not through the sale of Sibao texts alone. They also purchased paper in the towns they visited—in Beituan, modern Gutian 古田, and Juxi, where it was relatively cheap—and transported it back to Sibao. And although demand for Sibao primers like *Sanzi jing* or *Renjia riyong* remained strong through the 1940s,[2] they also sold lithographic texts (*shiyinben* 石印本) published in Shanghai and shipped to Fuzhou. The son, once he reached adulthood, took Yongan to Shaxian as his regular route, selling Sibao woodblock texts along the way. In Shaxian he stored his unsold stock at the homes of relatives and friends, relying on the network of Sibao connections established over centuries of trading. From Shaxian he took a steamer to Fuzhou, and at the Xinhua shuju 新華書局 there purchased new-style lithographic texts, for the most part adventure stories like *Xue Rengui zheng dong* 薛仁貴征東 (Xue Rengui conquers the east), *Fan Tang yanyi zhuan* 反唐演義傳 (Narrative of the rebellion against the Tang), and *Xiyou ji* 西遊記 (Journey to the west), which had at one point been an important part of Sibao's stock. These "modern" (in the sense of production technology) volumes he then sold on the return route, in Shaxian, Yongan, and the Sibao area. In this case he was acting as the distributor of texts produced by rival, non-Sibao publishers who commanded the new print technologies that ultimately overpowered the old woodblock handicraft techniques. But this effort to supplement Sibao woodblock imprints with the better-produced and increasingly popular lithographic texts did little for this peddler and his family; bookselling was never for them the lucrative business it had been for the earlier Zou and Ma booksellers, who purchased land and built large houses with their profits. His meager earnings, supplemented by farm income, were just enough to keep his family alive.[3]

This particular example of itinerant book peddling is drawn from the declining years of the Sibao industry, and although it includes certain

---

2. See Chapter 13, pp. 529–32.
3. Interviews 36, 11/14/95 (Wuge); and 91, 4/25/95 (Wuge).

features—the steamship, the modern texts—unknown in earlier periods, it nonetheless illustrates a form of bookselling most likely practiced throughout Sibao's history. As we saw in Chapter 5, many of the more successful publishing houses were founded on just the kind of basic itinerancy described above. Ma Quanheng, for example, once he passed the family woodblocks to his younger brother, seems to have started again almost from scratch, appointing his son, Ma Dingbang, to oversee the family publishing venture in Mawu, while he worked as a traveling merchant in Guangdong. Zou Bolong turned to sojourning bookselling to support his growing family and, "after several decades of traveling back and forth" to sell books in Guangdong, "gradually accumulated profits" large enough to improve the family fortunes. He eventually established a bookstore in Gaozhou.[4] The genealogies are full of examples of impoverished young men who went out as itinerant booksellers, often working for other households' *shufang*, as a first step toward the establishment of their own publishing houses and bookstores. They would sell books wherever they could—on bamboo mats or from temporary stalls (*bai tanzi* 擺攤子) in market towns and the villages around them, or in county and prefectural seats.[5] They might also take their wares to the yamen and the homes of local gentry. Or they might travel a circuit of local schools and academies, displaying their own knowledge of the examination system (and thereby advertising their products) in exchanges with the teachers and students before offering their texts for sale.[6]

Such itinerant book peddlers—men who worked periodic markets within a relatively circumscribed area and carried their own wares— might, with luck and hard work, eventually establish themselves as sojourning book merchants—men who engaged in more sophisticated

---

4. *MTLZXZSZP* (1911), 20.76ab.

5. Hayashi Kazuo ("Min Shin jidai, Kanton no kyo to shi," pp. 82–84), while emphasizing the wide variety in size and complexity of markets in Guangdong in the Qing, identifies two basic types: the periodic market with no permanent buildings, which nonresident merchants visited on market day, displaying their goods in temporary stalls or on bamboo mats; and the daily market with permanent shops and resident merchants. Generally speaking, the first type, with local schools and county yamens, was the preserve of the itinerant booksellers; the second, that of sojourning merchants.

6. See Smith, *Village Life in China*, pp. 107–8; and Chapter 8, pp. 107–9.

methods of sale, traveling to and managing permanent branch bookstores at a considerable distance from Sibao. According to contemporary informants, the Sibao "empire" of shops was created following
roughly this progression: booksellers would go on the road, in essence
as petty merchants or peddlers, trying out different routes of sale, usually in areas where there existed some social and cultural support
networks. They started by working close to home in western Fujian
and then gradually expanded to Hakka settlements in surrounding
provinces, tracing circuits of market towns and county and/or prefectural seats. Finally, they would establish stable branch stores, requiring more systematic management and fuller and more varied stock,
in areas with the most promising markets.[7] Or, as one local scholar of
the Sibao industry explained, "First, the booksellers would go out to
different places to sell books on the road, to reconnoiter and find out
if there were good markets (*xiaolu* 銷路) for books in these places.
Then, once they had found a good market, they would set up a bookstore there."[8]

Although many founders of publishing houses seem to have started
out on the road, not all itinerant booksellers aimed to establish themselves as publishers. Many, particularly at the height of the business,
worked for prosperous *shufang* interested in extending their markets.
For example, the Hanbao lou 翰寶樓, established in the Qianlong or
Jiaqing era, had booksellers test the market in Shanghang (within easy
transport distance from Wuge on the Yin River); when Shanghang
proved lucrative, the Hanbao lou opened a shop there. As that shop
flourished, itinerant salesmen were sent from Sibao to scout the market
in Jiaying department, on a tributary of the Han (the Yin River in
Guangdong); eventually the Hanbao lou established a second bookstore
there.[9] Sometimes the hoped-for market did not materialize. One informant, for example, reported that his forebears worked for the Benzu
tang 本祖堂 *shufang*, selling books in Sichuan and Yunnan as itinerants.
Each year, these booksellers would leave Sibao after the Spring Festival
with about ten porters and make the two- to three-month journey to

---

7. Interviews 85, 86, and 88, 4/23/96 (Mawu); and 89, 4/24/96 (Wuge).
8. Interview 84, 4/21/96 (Wuge).
9. Interview 88, 4/23/96 (Wuge).

their destination, returning home before the next Spring Festival. But business never proved lucrative enough to justify founding a branch shop in either province.[10]

These itinerant booksellers relied heavily on the networks of Hakka and Sibao settlers to assist them in their business. Particularly on the longer routes through Guangdong and Guangxi, or through Jiangxi and Hunan, they needed way stations in which to store excess stock while they made the circuit of local market towns and county seats. They also, of course, needed places to stay. For both purposes, they relied on the homes and shops (not necessarily bookshops) of relatives and other former Sibao residents (*tongxiang* 同鄉). They also relied on other institutions for the commercial traveler. In the nineteenth century a special hostel for Sibao merchants was established in Pengkou (from which many merchants embarked for Guangdong via the Yin River).[11] Fujian *huiguan* also provided temporary residences and storage areas for sojourning book merchants (and we know that the Sibao booksellers took advantage of these, for two Zou booksellers died in the Fujian *huiguan* in Nanning). But *huiguan* were found largely in the bigger cities; in the county seats and smaller market towns that constituted the major nodes along most of the Sibao routes, booksellers relied either on trusted contacts or on cheap hostels.

## BANKING

How did itinerant booksellers and sojourning merchants handle their finances outside Sibao? How in particular did the traveling booksellers manage their money—safeguarding their profits yet ensuring a store of funds for travel expenses—while traveling from market to market?

By the time the Sibao booksellers began extending their routes beyond Fujian, they could rely on a range of formal institutions of deposit and remittance that eased somewhat the financial problems of life on the road. Currency-exchange shops (*qianpu* 錢舖) and local or native banks (*qianzhuang* and *yinhao* 銀號, "silver houses") offered a variety of services: exchange of currencies, issuance of paper notes, deposits,

---

10. Interview 30, 11/13/95 (Wuge).
11. Interview 14, 4/28/95 (Wuge).

loans, remittance of funds, and so forth.[12] Originating in the late Ming, these establishments proliferated in the late nineteenth and early twentieth century as a result of the increase in foreign trade and could be found at least in the more heavily settled areas of Sibao bookselling.[13] At least one Wuge native, the bookseller Zou Junlong 均龍 (1769–1832), founded two money shops (*qiandian* 錢店), one in Changde, Hunan, and one in an unspecified location in Jiangxi, presumably in response to a demand for exchange and deposit services in areas where Sibao merchants were active.[14] In the sites frequented by Sibao merchants in Guangdong province, as late as the late 1910s Guangzhou and Shantou offered a full range of exchange shops and local banks (and some modern banks). Foshan had roughly forty remittance and/or exchange shops; Chaozhou offered "some" *qianzhuang* and *qianpu*, Shaozhou had a few *qianzhuang*, and Huizhou seven.

In commercially less advanced areas, the booksellers might rely on firms that ran a remittance business on the side. Merchants in early twentieth-century Guangzhou, Shantou, Foshan, Chaozhou, Shaozhou, and Huizhou were able to choose among several sophisticated banking institutions; but in Nanxiong department seat, only two commercial firms remitted funds, and in the Longchuan county seat, cloth merchants handled remittances.[15] Pawnshops (*dianpu* 典鋪, *dangpu* 當鋪, *zhipu* 質鋪, *yadian* 押店), too, could serve as institutions of deposit; some issued "trader's road money" (*gulu qian* 賈路錢) in the form of receipts for funds deposited, freeing a merchant from the burden of transporting profits long distances while allowing him to draw funds for travel expenses at fixed points on his route.[16] The scale of

---

12. Interviews 15, 4/29/95 (Wuge); and 25, 11/9/95 (Wuge). Peng, *A Monetary History of China*, 2: 820. On the terms *qianpu* and *qianzhuang*, see Andrea McElderry, *Shanghai Old-Style Banks (Ch'ien-Chuang)*, pp. 10–11; and Shen, *Essai sur l'origine et l'evolution des banques en Chine*, pp. 30–51.

13. Chen Mingguang, *Qianzhuang shi*, pp. 29–30.

14. *MTLZXZSZP* (1911), 20.88ab. Zou Junlong had a partner in these ventures, a Chen Xiangshen 陳象山 of Liancheng; the genealogy supplies no details of the partnership.

15. McElderry, *Shanghai Old-Style Banks*, pp. 204–7.

16. Interview 19, 5/1/95 (Mawu); Peng, *A Monetary History of China*, 2: 815–20; Edkins, *Banking and Prices in China*, pp. 2–3.

pawnbroking expanded in the Qing; even the government funded the establishment of pawnshops in the frontier provinces of Guangxi and Yunnan in the late eighteenth century. Hence, these institutions would have been available even in Sibao's most isolated markets.[17] Presumably Sibao booksellers relied on pawnshops in Leizhou, Gaozhou, Huilai, and modern Heyuan 河源, all areas of Guangdong for which there is no record of any specialized financial institutions even in the early twentieth century.[18]

Informants suggest, however, that the Sibao booksellers relied most heavily not on pawnshops, *qianpu*, or *qianzhuang*, but on informal "banking" arrangements with personal contacts. They deposited profits with trusted relatives or friends as they progressed along their bookselling route and then picked up the funds on their return home. Merchants needing cash could also rely on this informal network for credit or cash advances.[19] One informant, who had worked as a young man in the Suwei shanfang in Zhangzhou, explained that his family had a special arrangement with a sojourning merchant based in Liancheng. When this merchant traveled to Zhangzhou on business, he never took funds with him but borrowed money from the Zou booksellers in Zhangzhou. Then, when the Zou booksellers returned home, they stopped in Liancheng for repayment, thus avoiding the dangers of transporting money to and from Sibao.[20] Of course, once branch bookstores were established, the itinerant booksellers could rely on these for assistance with both lodging and banking.

## TRANSPORTATION OF STOCK

How was the actual transport of books handled? Since texts were printed only in Sibao, how were the booksellers, either on the road or in the branch shops, kept supplied? Petty merchants and itinerant peddlers seem to have carried their stock themselves, balancing two book boxes (roughly 56 centimeters wide by 24 deep by 43 high; see Fig. 7.1)

---

17. Peng, *A Monetary History of China*, 2: 817.
18. McElderry, *Shanghai Old-Style Banks*, pp. 204–7.
19. Interview 26, 11/11/95 (Wuge).
20. Interview 34, 11/14/95(Wuge).

Fig. 7.1  Book boxes used to carry Sibao imprints. Photograph by the author.

on a shoulder pole and walking from market to market (or, when possible, taking a water route). The aged informant from Wuge mentioned above sold mostly short children's primers on the first leg of his route, out from Wuge, and he could fit several hundred such texts into his boxes. The much longer novels he carried from Fuzhou were compact lithographic editions, so he could carry a fair number on his return sales trip as well.

But clearly the larger and more prosperous Sibao operations, during the peaks of the trade in the Qianlong-Jiaqing and Guangxu eras, needed more efficient means of supplying often quite distant routes and sites. A variety of arrangements were made. Some publishing houses sent texts on a regular schedule devised to supply their branch stores in time for the peak selling season, when schools started after Spring Festival. In the early twentieth century, the publishing house that supplied the Huazhan shudian 華棧書店 in modern Anliuyu, Wuhua county, Guangdong, sent two or three shipments a year, usually in winter or early spring, to prepare for this season. The trip from Sibao to Wuhua, overseen by one or two of the publishing-house staff—usually a father-son, uncle-nephew, or brother-brother pair—took about ten days.[21] The Cuiyun tang sent imprints to its bookstores in Xingning, Nanning, and Bose only once a year but employed "several tens" of porters to carry the books on the long trip from Wuge to Bose, which took over one month; so this single venture required a very large shipment.[22] Other publishing houses might wait until they received orders for new stock from the branches, relying on informal networks of fellow-merchants and travelers—the miscellaneous collection of "friends, acquaintances, special messengers, travelers, chair-bearers, cart-drivers, or muleteers"[23]—who usually delivered letters. By the late nineteenth century, if the bookstores or booksellers were operating out of major market towns or cities, they might have used private letter agencies (*minxin ju* 民信局) to transmit mail.[24]

For the most part, however, little communication with Sibao was necessary. Publishers and booksellers understood the seasonal pattern of the trade. *Shufang* that had established branch shops simply followed a regular schedule, sending school texts and almanacs out so that they would reach their destination early in the New Year and shipping other texts—ritual manuals, correspondence models, medical and pharmaceutical handbooks, divination guides, and novels—"as soon as they

---

21. Interview 67, 12/5/95 (Wuge).

22. Interview 63, 12/5/95 (Wuge).

23. Ying-wan Cheng, *Postal Communication in China and Its Modernization*, p. 3.

24. Ibid., pp. 37–48. The system of couriers or private letter agencies developed only in the late nineteenth century and seems to have operated only between major cities and market towns (for example, such agencies did serve Nanchang, Wuchengzhen, Zhangshuzhen, and Ganzhou from Jiujiang in Jiangxi province in the 1890s) (ibid., p. 42). Constance Gordon Cumming (*Wanderings in China*, 2: 105) described how the system worked in a text published in 1886: "Letters are consigned to firms which have houses in all the large towns, whence letters are forwarded to distant posts, where they are distributed by special agents, who generally collect the postage from the receiver." The Sibao booksellers living in smaller and less important towns must have continued to rely on an informal network of merchants and travelers. Evariste Régis Huc (*The Chinese Empire*, 2: 281) noted, in the mid-nineteenth century, that "when you wish to send letters you must trust to the complaisance of some traveler, or send a messenger at your own expense, which is, of course, a very costly method." Given their patterns of bookstore establishment, in areas both settled and traveled by Hakka, the Zou and Ma booksellers could probably rely on traveling Hakka merchants from Tingzhou, perhaps even from Sibao, to carry their mail.

were printed."[25] Most of the time the books were carried by men from the poorer families within the Ma and Zou lineages.[26]

Some of these porters seem to have been attached to specific *shufang*—the Benli tang, for example, regularly employed the same six or seven porters to carry books to its branch store in Guangxi.[27] There was never any shortage of workers. Zou Bingjun, one of Sibao's most successful entrepreneurs, was apparently able to command the labor of roughly fifty porters (carrying 100 "loads," or *tiao*) whenever he felt he needed a supply of texts.[28] For the most part these porters were overseen by one or two members of the *shufang* household, although the Longfeng tang 龍豐堂, founded by Ma Yuanyong 源用 during the Qianlong era, relied on two lineage members unconnected to the publishing house to transport texts from Mawu to Wengyuan 翁源, Guangdong, the site of its branch store. Each month, they made two week-long trips, each carrying one *dan* (about 60 kilograms).[29] Another informant reported, too, that his maternal uncle, surnamed Yan, oversaw the ten-plus porters who regularly carried stock to the Yijing tang's 翼經堂 bookstore in Jiaying city.[30] *Shufang* also might cooperate in the transport of texts; booksellers from different publishing houses, with their porters, would travel together as long as possible, largely for safety, splitting off only to reach their different shops.[31]

Portage was hard work. In the nineteenth century, roads were generally in poor repair, since the local governments in charge of their maintenance lacked the funds to see to their upkeep. Even major roads were often deeply rutted. One Western observer complained, in 1846, that the imperial road from Hubei to Jiangxi was "in a detestable state, almost everywhere broken up, full of hillocks and hollows, and mud holes, and frightful ruts," making travel "extremely fatiguing."[32] Apart from major highways, most roads were merely "broad footpaths" only

---

25. Interviews 70, 12/6/95 (Wuge); and 92, 5/10/96 (Nanning).
26. Interview 25, 11/9/95 (Wuge).
27. Interview 28, 11/12/95 (Wuge).
28. Interview 32, 11/13/95 (Wuge).
29. Interview 50, 11/25/95 (Mawu).
30. Interview 55, 12/1/95 (Mawu).
31. Interview 25, 11/9/95 (Wuge).
32. Huc, *The Chinese Empire*, 2: 292–93.

eight–ten feet wide. The relatively minor *pu* routes sometimes disappeared altogether into farmland.[33] (It is easy to see why the repair of
roads and bridges was a favored charity of the Sibao book merchants.)
Over such roads each coolie carried up to 70 *jin* (about 42 kilograms) in
two 35-*jin* packs at the ends of a shoulder pole as far as 70 *li* (about 35
kilometers) a day.[34]

Booksellers did not rely exclusively on Sibao porters; when they
needed land transport, they could hire porters from the everywhere
abundant local population of coolies.[35] They might develop relationships with special groups of porters along their routes, men who would
be hired regularly for the segments of overland travel that would bring
the bookseller to the next navigable water route. Zou Xuhe 序和
(1808–81) seems to have developed just such a relationship with porters
in the Pingshan (modern Huidong) area—because he had treated them
fairly over the years, some time "in the later years of the Daoguang
era," they warned him secretly of an uprising planned in the area, enabling him to escape safely to Sibao.[36]

Porters did not usually travel the whole distance from *shufang* to destination. In Guangdong and Guangxi—and to some extent in Jiangxi
and Hunan—extensive river systems reduced the amount of rough
overland travel; water transport was, in addition, both quicker and
cheaper. Before the construction of the highway in 1937 made road

---

33. Fan I-chun, "Long-Distance Trade and Market Integration in the Ming-Ch'ing
Period," pp. 38–43; see pp. 42–44 on the difficulties of water transport as well; Kingsmill, "Inland Communications in China," p. 92. For complaints about roads in Fujian in
the late nineteenth century, see Dukes, *Along River and Road in Fuh-kien, China*, pp. 44–45;
Dukes, however, is quite enthusiastic about river travel in Fujian (see pp. 64–77).

34. Kingsmill, "Inland Communications in China," p. 108. Harry Franck (*Roving
Through Southern China*, p. 84), traveling in Jiangxi in the early twentieth century, estimated that his porter was carrying a load of about eighty pounds.

35. T. W. Kingsmill ("Inland Communications in China," pp. 91–92) notes that carts
and wheelbarrows, popular for overland transport in other parts of the country, were
not used in Fujian, Guangdong, and Guangxi: "No wheeled vehicle of any sort is to be
found in the three provinces, even the humble wheel-barrow being too great an
economizer of labour to find favour amongst a population where humanity is a drug on
the market." In Guangxi, however, oxcarts were occasionally used to transport goods
over level land.

36. *MTLZXZSZP* (1911), 20.*you*103b.

travel easier in western Fujian, booksellers used only one route that was entirely overland—from Sibao to Changting, then across the Jiangxi border over the Wuyi mountains on the main road to Ruijin and finally Ganzhou.[37] Even in the late nineteenth century, when river travel usually entailed higher *lijin* or customs charges (most of the stations were on rivers), the merchants preferred water travel.[38]

The water routes were, however, not always accessible; nor did they always make for easy traveling. Merchant route books frequently note that rapids or seasonal changes in water level made portions of important waterways dangerous or impassible at certain times of the year—the rapids on the Gan River below Ganzhou, for example, posed a particular challenge.[39] This was one of the major north–south routes, and one much frequented by Sibao booksellers traveling from Jiangxi to northern and western Guangdong. In addition to the dangerous rapids, it involved an arduous day of portage from Dayu over the Meiling Pass to Nanxiong. (The wear on the granite steps of the pass provides "mute evidence to [the] extraordinary toil" of the coolies hired to carry goods over the provincial border.)[40] The shortest route from Tingzhou to eastern Guangdong—down the Yin River—was problematic, too, not only because of the dangerous rapids but also because shallows between Fengshi 峰市 and Dabu (a distance of about 5.5 kilometers) were

---

37. There was, however, another route to Ganzhou that combined land and river travel: by foot to Changting and Ruijin and then by river to Ganzhou.

38. Kingsmill, "Inland Communications in China," pp. 91, 104–5, 132–33. If the booksellers wished to avoid the *lijin* stations on the West River, they could take a route from southwestern Guangdong, traveling from one of their established stores in Leizhou (and from there by sea to the Lianjiang 廉江 and northward to Yulin 郁林 department—very close to another branch store in Beiliu—and from there overland to Guixian and Nanning, etc.) or to Lingshan (and from there overland to Hengzhou and Nanning, etc.).

39. Yang Zhengtai, *Tianxia lucheng tuyin*, p. 411; see also Brook, "Communications and Commerce," pp. 606–7, for Huang Bian's warning about the dangers of travel on this stretch of the Gan. Huc (*The Chinese Empire*, 2: 383, 386–87, 400–401, 405–7) describes a pleasant trip (although he was not transporting goods) on the Gan River by junk, towed against the current when necessary, for fifteen days, then by foot or sedan chair over the Meiling Pass to Nanxiong, a trip of about one day. From Nanxiong, he traveled on to Guangzhou on a "little bark," a journey of roughly one week on the North River through Yingde 英德 and Qingyuan 清遠.

40. Nadler, *China to Order*, p. 21.

navigable only by small boats; cargo boats had to be unloaded and their freight transshipped overland, over a road almost twice the length of the river route.[41]

And even water travel could be slow. One informant reported that it took his grandfather, selling books for the Yijing tang 翼經堂 in Weng-yuan, half a month to travel from Sibao to his destination, a distance of roughly 400 kilometers (as the crow flies) and largely on rivers.[42] The trip from Sibao to the Gengxin tang 耕莘堂 in Guixian took over a month, even though the booksellers were able to avail themselves of sea transport from Chaozhou (and later Shantou) to Guangzhou and travel through western Guangdong and eastern Guangxi on the great West-Gong river system.[43] Both the difficulties of travel and the distance in time between Sibao and most of its branch bookstores—a

---

41. *Fujian gonglu shi*, p. 28; and Yang Jie, *Fujian hangyun shi*, pp. 216, 275, 366. Other portions of the river presented problems as well, although none as intractable. Above Changting, the river became too narrow for easy transport. And along a fifty-kilometer stretch of the river approaching Fengshi, steep banks, dangerous rocks, and frequent rapids challenged navigators and often slowed traffic. But from Changting to Fengshi sailing vessels of over 4,000 *jin* (2.4 metric tons) could use the river. Under good conditions, this stretch of the journey could be relatively short; in the spring and summer, when the water level rose, the trip from Changting to Shanghang might take only three days, and one would arrive in Fengshi the following day, a distance of about 175 kilometers. Throughout the Qing, the Yin remained a busy commercial waterway; a popular saying claimed, "Three thousand [boats] on the upper river [from Changting to Shanghang], eight hundred on the lower [Shanghang to Fengshi]." Failure to maintain the river, a fall in the water level, and the threat of banditry reduced traffic on the river in the early twentieth century.

42. Five or six times a year, he and the ten or more porters who carried his stock walked to Changting and then took the Yin River from Changting to Fengshi. At Fengshi, they had to leave the river and travel overland to Sanhezhen 三河鎮 (modern Sanhebei 三河埧). There they picked up the Mei 梅 River, which took them directly to Jiaying city, where the bookseller visited with other Sibao booksellers. From Jiaying city, he traveled on to Xingning (on a tributary of the Mei) and ultimately, combining overland and river routes, to Wengyuan. This trip took even longer than two weeks during the civil war, when fighting between the Communists and Nationalists disrupted travel. Interviews 55, 12/1/95 (Mawu); and 52, 11/27/95 (Mawu). Note, however, that another informant (see p. 323) claimed the trip from Sibao to Wengyuan took only one week.

43. Interview 51, 11/27/95 (Mawu). Booksellers with shops in Gaozhou and Leizhou could travel the same route to Shantou and then go by sea via Hong Kong to the modern port of Zhanjiang 湛江, conveniently located at the northeastern top of the Lei-zhou peninsula.

distance that did not seem to shrink significantly even as travel became more efficient in the late Qing and Republican periods—made the maintenance of firm central control difficult.

## THE DANGERS OF THE ROAD

In addition to the logistical difficulties of transporting large numbers of texts throughout southern China, the Zou and Ma booksellers had to face other threats to their security and success. Cautionary tales that survive even today warn against con men and tricksters. One such story illustrates the dangers of revealing too much of the family business to strangers on the road. A Sibao publisher was returning home, via the Yin River, with a newly purchased set of blocks for the *Kangxi zidian* 康熙字典 (Kangxi dictionary). He freely shared the details of his purchase—how many blocks made a complete set, where he had purchased them, and how much they had cost—with a stranger he met on the boat. When the boat docked in Changting and the publisher started unloading his blocks, the stranger, with a great show of indignation, demanded to know why he was taking "his" blocks. He accused the publisher of stealing and in court used the information the publisher had shared with him to defend his claim to the set. The case was decided in his favor, and the publisher lost an extremely valuable asset—the profits from the sale of the dictionary were said to have been sufficient to "support an entire household in comfort."[44]

The Sibao booksellers faced much more serious threats, however, particularly from the mid-nineteenth century on: theft and other forms of violence. Both the genealogies and local informants relate stories of booksellers' encounters with bandits, invariably on land. One of the more elaborate of these centers on two descendants of Zou Weizong, reputedly one of the earliest of the booksellers. The merchant and his nephew were returning to Sibao with a large load of silver, the earnings from a successful bookselling expedition. They were attacked by a band of thieves, and although the younger man escaped, his uncle was captured and all their silver seized. Just before the bandit chief was about to kill the bookseller, he asked where he was from. On hearing that he was a

---

44. Interview 26, 11/11/95 (Wuge).

descendant of Zou Weizong from Sibao in Changting, the bandit knelt before the startled but much relieved bookseller, explaining that Zou Weizong had once saved him from capture. The bandit chief kept the bookseller for one or two months, treating him to a banquet every night. He finally released his captive together with all his silver, plus lavish sums from the bandits' other victims, a white fan bearing a secret symbol to warn away other thieves, a sword, and a silver lion. With some variation in detail, this doubtless apocryphal story—which clearly owes much to novels like *Water Margin*—is told of several other booksellers as well.[45] These tales, fanciful though they may be, suggest by their very frequency that the threat of banditry was a major anxiety for the Sibao merchants.

Reports of other travelers and more sober entries in the genealogies suggest that this fear was not unfounded. After the mid-nineteenth century, banditry in southern and eastern Guangxi had increased significantly. As the British, in the wake of their victory in the Opium War, drove pirates out of the South China Sea, the bandits resettled along the West River, the major artery from Guangzhou into Guangxi.[46] Later in the century Westerners in China complained frequently of piracy on the rivers of both Guangdong and Guangxi, brigandry on routes outside the main government roads, random pilfering, and a kind of seasonal, pre–Spring Festival robbery practiced on travelers.[47]

-----

45. See, e.g., the account of Zou Kongjia's encounter with thieves as he was traveling with his nephew to Magang to purchase woodblocks. In this account Kongjia escaped death by producing, at the command of the bandit chief, a rhymed couplet praising the bandit gang as "heroes serving mankind." Impressed by Kongjia's status as an educated man—and doubtless also by his sycophantic rhymes—the chief released him and supplied him with travel money. The author of Kongjia's biography interprets this lucky outcome as a reward for his family's long-accumulated store of virtue; see *FYZSZP* (1947), 33.63b. See also *MTLZXZSZP* (1911), 20.1ab. It is possible that these stories recount brushes with protection societies like the Tiandihui.

46. For a vivid description of the problem of banditry and piracy in Guangxi, see Spence, *God's Chinese Son*, pp. 81–87.

47. Interestingly, nothing is made of the real dangers of water transport in the Zou and Ma genealogies. Yet Westerners frequently remarked on the problem. Harry A. Franck, in his *Roving Through Southern China* (see, e.g., pp. 151, 315), repeatedly mentions the threat of piracy, on both the South China Sea and the major river routes through Guangdong and Guangxi. See also Kingsmill, "Inland Communications in China," pp. 109–10, 139–45.

Throughout their history, the Sibao merchants had reason to worry about the problem. Ma Dafang, one of the most successful early merchants, a dealer in oil, paper, and whatever would sell, organized his sojourns so as to avoid bandit activity along the Fujian-Guangdong border during the Ming-Qing transition; on one occasion he was almost mistaken for a bandit himself. Zou Kongjia and his cousin Zou Pibin were attacked, and Kongjia wounded, in an encounter with thieves in the early nineteenth century.[48] Not so lucky, Zou Zhuohui 倬惠 was murdered by bandits (or Taiping rebels) while working as a sojourning merchant in Huichang county seat in Jiangxi in 1853.[49]

Contemporary informants described a variety of methods to ward off thieves. As indicated above, booksellers traveled as much as possible in groups, hoping for safety in numbers. Many of the other reported methods are suspiciously like those depicted in popular fiction. Booksellers wore worn and ragged clothing on the road, so as to appear poor; or merchants concealed their money in bags of salt,[50] or, more awkwardly, in coffins, the latter in the hope that fear of pollution from contact with the dead would discourage robbers.[51] Other informants proudly pointed to the Sibao tradition of martial arts, arguing that their ancestors' mastery of *wugong* 武功 kept them safe on the road.[52] It is also possible that booksellers routinely joined the secret societies—any one of the number of groups loosely identified as Tiandihui—that offered protection to travelers and sojourning merchants in Fujian, Guangdong, and Guangxi.[53] The book merchants may even have relied

---

48. *FYZSZP* (1947), 33.63ab, 77b–78a.

49. *MTLZXZSZP* (1911), 20.98ab.

50. Interview 54, 11/28/95 (Mawu).

51. Apparently this method was not always effective. Zou Bincai 斌才 (1778–1831?), son of the successful merchant Zou Bingjun, was traveling home from a business trip to Ningguo 寧國 city, Anhui, with his profits hidden in three coffins (a fourth coffin contained a real corpse). In Jiangxi his party was robbed—the thieves were not frightened off even by the genuine corpse. Bincai's life was spared, the story goes, because the bandit, also surnamed Zou, turned out to be a distant relative (he is said to have checked his genealogy). The bandit then had his men escort Bincai safely back to Changting. Interview 32, 11/13/95 (Wuge).

52. Interview 42, 11/19/95 (Wuge).

53. No records survive of Zou or Ma membership in the Tiandihui or any other kind of protection society, but the sojourning merchants may well have embraced the

on the local militias developed by both non-Hakka and Hakka in Guang-dong and Guangxi to combat the Tiandihui—although it is not clear how useful such forces were to highly mobile traders.

In any event, the Zou and Ma booksellers had to negotiate a path through a complex social and political landscape in their business trav-els, avoiding confrontations with a variety of potentially hostile forces: bandits, often linked to protection (or "mutual aid") societies like the Tiandihui; Punti antagonistic to Hakka; and the often deeply divided Hakka communities themselves.[54] In short, the strong need for local protection (and assistance in cases of robbery) is certainly one of the reasons that the networks of social and financial support offered by mi-grants from Sibao so profoundly shaped the market choices of the Zou and Ma merchants. They restricted their bookselling activities to re-gions where, given their social connections and identification with Hakka culture, they could hope for some degree of "banking" assis-tance (so that they did not have to carry all their money with them all the time), protection against theft, and, if worse came to worst, aid after being attacked and robbed.

## Branch Bookstores

The establishment of branch bookstores signified the growing prosper-ity of the Sibao publishing industry. As we have seen, these shops were usually set up only after itinerant booksellers had determined that the local market could support a branch shop. At the same time, the devel-opment of stable outlets for Sibao products helped the *shufang* and book merchants to deepen and regularize their access to markets, transportation of stock, and methods of accounting. In short, the net-

---

increased security such organizations offered. Dian Murray tells the story of a yeast peddler in Guangdong, just robbed of all his profits, who was told, "If you join the Tiandihui you can avoid being robbed on the road in the future." He joined the society and was taught a secret hand code that, when displayed to would-be robbers, averted attack (Murray and Qin Baoqi, *The Origins of the Tiandihui*, pp. 183–84; cited in Spence, *God's Chinese Son*, pp. 85–86; see also note 45 to this chapter).

54. For a vivid picture of the conflicts that might arise both between Hakka and Punti and within Hakka groups in Guangxi and Guangdong, see Spence, *God's Chinese Son*, pp. 87–88, 99–106.

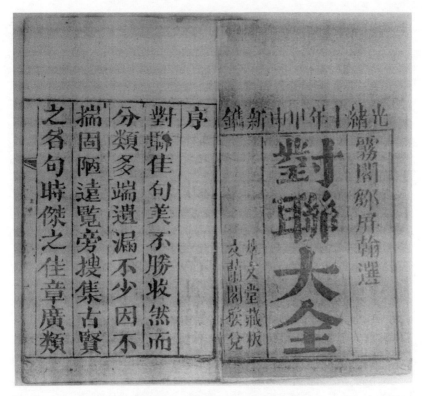

Fig. 7.2 Cover page of the *Duilian daquan* 對聯大全 (Compendium of rhymed couplets). Note that this text was published by the Cuiwen tang ("Cuiwen tang *cang ban*" 萃文堂藏版), but sold by the Wenlan ge ("Wenlan ge *fadui*" 文蘭閣發兌). Photograph by the author.

work of bookstores reflects not only the success but also the growing sophistication of the Sibao businesses.

Branch bookstores might be tied to a specific publishing house; the Wujing tang 五經堂 *shufang* in Wuge, for example, sold its texts through the Chongwen lou 崇文樓 *shudian* in Jiaying city.[55] The relationship might be formalized to the extent that it was announced within the texts themselves; one Sibao rhymed-couplet collection lists on its cover page the name of the bookstore that sold (*fadui* 發兌) the text as well as that of the house that published the text (*cang ban*) (see Fig. 7.2). Other *shufang* had no such outlet for their wares. One informant

---

55. Interviews 41, 11/15/95 (Wuge); and 59, 12/2/95 (Wuge).

remembers that his father and uncles, usually working in groups of three or four, traveled through Fujian (to Zhangzhou and Xiamen) and Guangdong (to Chaozhou, Shantou, and Jiaying city), selling their imprints wholesale to many different bookstores, all operated by "Sibao *ren*."[56]

Naturally a branch bookstore's most important market, tested previously by itinerant booksellers, was the local retail business. This cut across all status lines, attracting peasants visiting on market day who might purchase reading primers or basic medical manuals for use back in their villages, merchants of all ranks, students at all levels, educational officials, and local literati and gentry. Many of the biographies in the genealogies describe the Sibao bookstores as havens of culture, as centers of social and intellectual exchange with local scholars and literati. Although much of this is doubtless self-aggrandizing puffery, an effort to emphasize the elite connections and lofty cultural goals of the booksellers, there is probably some truth in the claim: in areas where there had previously been no bookstore, a Sibao branch represented a cultural center of sorts. When the Wenhai lou established its branch on Xingning lu 興寧路, one of Nanning's two major streets, in the late nineteenth century, it was apparently the only true bookstore in town.[57] As such, it might have formed something of a center for the local students and gentry.

The branch stores in administrative centers also did a more specialized business with local schools and academies. Bookstore managers worked to develop good relationships with local school officials, which perhaps explains the number of booksellers' biographies in the Zou and Ma genealogies written by county and prefectural academic officials and subofficials (see Chapter 8). Well before the beginning of the school year, store managers tried to ascertain what texts the schools needed, so that these texts could be produced at the Sibao *shufang* and transported to the branch in time for sale to the schools. One Ma informant reported that his great-uncle, whose mother was a Zou, acted as a kind of special agent for the sale of schoolbooks from the Zou-family Wenhai lou branch shop in Hengzhou, Guangxi. Several months before the beginning of the school year, he invited schools in the set-

---

56. Interviews 31, 11/13/95 (Wuge); and 89, 4/24/96 (Wuge).
57. Interview 92, 5/10/96 (Nanning).

tlements along the You River and its tributaries to send him their text-book orders; he promised to deliver the texts on time in return for each school's promise to purchase texts from him alone. The *shufang* in Wuge, on receiving the lists, printed up the titles in the requested num-bers and delivered them to the Hengzhou store. Ma's great-uncle, with the help of some of the other bookstore workers, then distributed the texts, collecting payment at the time of delivery. He was often away for two months, transporting books on a circuit extending to Wuyuan 武緣 county (modern Wuming 武鳴, north of Nanning on the Nanliu 南流 River) and even to Bose city in the far west, a distance of about 450 kilometers by water. In this way, the Hengzhou bookstore, in addi-tion to serving the residents of the county seat, also acted as a way sta-tion for the sale and distribution of Wenhai lou educational texts throughout central and western Guangxi.[58]

A tattered combination order-account book, probably dating from the late nineteenth century or the first decades of the twentieth cen-tury,[59] provides concrete evidence of this kind of arrangement. The unidentified bookseller-author traveled from one small village to the next, visiting lineage or village schools ("Zhang Family Academy" 張姓 書館, "Qingyun School" 青雲書室, and so forth) and a few village bookstores, taking orders. After each place and school or store name, he recorded the customer's name, the titles or products ordered (he also sold brushes, ink, small bowls, and medicines), and the price. Most of his customers were students, with the occasional teacher. He sold a range of texts, including not only the expected primers and textbooks such as the *Youxue gushi qionglin*, the Four Books, and the Five Classics, but also collections of couplets, medical and pharmaceutical guides (*Yizong jinjian*, *Yaoxing fu* 藥性賦 [Verses on the properties of medi-cines]), almanacs (*Yuxia ji* 玉匣記 [Record of the jade casket]), letter-writing manuals, *fengshui* handbooks, household encyclopedias, and

---

58. Interviews 54, 11/28/95 (Mawu); and 55, 12/1/95 (Mawu).

59. The names Zou Xinfeng, Zou Weinan, and Zou Xiyao, booksellers associated with the Wenhai lou complex of bookstores, appear at the end of the book. It thus might date from the late nineteenth century or early twentieth century. Since Zou Weinan became active in the establishment of a primary school in Wuge shortly after the founding of the Republic, it is unlikely that he was working at itinerant bookselling much after the 1920s. These booksellers were probably working in Guangxi.

some fiction. He took orders for over four hundred titles in less than a one-month period, suggesting that even as late as the early twentieth century there was a market for Sibao woodblock texts in the hinterland.

This bookseller's business took him to obscure villages and settlements, so obscure that it has proved impossible to identify precisely the area in which he worked. Other booksellers, too, were bringing texts deep into the countryside. Zou Hengpei 恒培, half-owner with Zou Hongxi 洪希 of the Datong shuju 大同書局 in Bose (one of two Zou-run bookstores in the city) in the early twentieth century, acted as delivery man (*youzi* 游子) for the store. He packed pre-ordered primary school textbooks (along with novels and picture-story books, or *lianhuanhua shu* 連環畫書—all lithographic texts ordered from Shanghai and Guangzhou) and stationery supplies into a bamboo shoulder basket (*matuo* or *maduo* 馬馱) and delivered them to the schools in the county seats and mountain villages of Tianzhou 田州 (modern Tianyang 田陽), Pingma (modern Tiandong), and Tianbao 天保 (modern Debao 德保).[60] Thus the branch stores might also act as headquarters for smaller circuits of itinerant peddlers or sojourning booksellers, sent out to sell texts in the surrounding villages.

The establishment of such stable outposts made it possible to regularize and formalize both the publication and the transportation and storage of Sibao stock. Coordination with branch store managers enabled *shufang* managers to plan their publishing lists, printing schedules, and employment of porters more rationally. An account book of the Wenhai lou from the early twentieth century reveals the degree of planning that the *shufang* could now perform: the account is organized as separate lots of titles, and for each lot the number of copies of each title is listed. Each store received a different lot, presumably configured according to its needs; for example, one store got 60 copies of the *Tangshi hexuan xiangjie* 唐詩合選詳解, an examination study guide to Tang poetry, another 44, and a third only 20; one store, 10 copies of *Choushi jinnang* 醜世錦囊, a popular household encyclopedia, and an-

---

60. Interviews 59, 12/2/95 (Wuge); and 93, 5/12/96 (Lingyun, Guangxi). Another informant reported that his father sold books in the mountain villages in the Xingning area, working out of the family's store in Anliuyu (in modern Wuhua county); Interview 67, 12/5/95 (Wuge).

other, 30, and so on. And bookstore managers could organize their business around pre-set delivery dates, although the endemic disorder of the 1920s, 1930s, and 1940s did much to disrupt transportation routes and throw delivery schedules into chaos. Once a publishing house had established a branch store, its itinerant booksellers no longer needed to rely on informal arrangements with Sibao migrants for temporary, stop-gap storage of texts. *Shufang* supplying a chain of stores could to some extent centralize distribution, sending everything to the largest, most centrally located branch, and then rely on that branch manager to send separate lots on to other branches.[61]

## THE COMPLICATION OF BUSINESS
## FORMS AND RELATIONSHIPS

Specialization seems to have increased and business relationships and networks to have become more complicated as the branch stores multiplied during the eighteenth and early nineteenth centuries and again in the late nineteenth century, although this trend is difficult to prove conclusively, given the spotty nature of the evidence. As we have seen, some publishing houses did not create their own outlets—they specialized in publishing and sold their texts wholesale to merchants working for other *shufang*. Certain families within the lineages specialized in transport, the men hiring themselves out as porters or as transport managers for specific *shufang*. Ties between *shufang* and unaffiliated bookstores, and cross-lineage ties between the managers and booksellers of the Zou and Ma lineages, intensified. *Shufang* often cooperated in the transport of texts, and bookstores might also help fill in gaps in the stock of other bookstores. The multiplication of bookstores, often in the same areas or even the same sites, required some degree of cooperation unless the local market was wide and deep enough to absorb all the books offered. In Lingshan, where the Wenhai lou established two bookstores, this seems to have been the case. But there is evidence that this was not always so; in Zhangzhou, bookstores operated by two branches of the Zou lineage agreed to specialize in different types of

---

61. Interview 92, 5/10/96 (Nanning).

texts so as not to encroach on each other's business. There, in the early twentieth century, the Suwei tang's outlet sold woodblock primers and school texts published in Sibao, and the Suwei shanfang's outlet sold, in addition to some Sibao woodblock literary collections and novels, new *yangban* versions of military romances and "mandarin and butterfly" fiction, and even some New Culture fiction.[62]

Members of different households also began to unite to form *shufang* and bookstores, each taking one or more shares (*gufen* 股份) in the business. A cluster of as many as five cousins within the Zou lineage united to form a bookstore in Bose in the late nineteenth century; each owned one share of the store.[63] The Licheng shuju 立成書局 was established in Guixian in 1927 by a partnership of two cousins not of the same household, Ma Rixuan 日宣 and Ma Riyao 日堯. Although an equal partnership, Ma Rixuan, the elder, was the primary manager of the store. There were even some joint Zou-Ma partnerships. The Gengxin tang, a *shufang* founded late in Sibao's history, was a five-share partnership between Zou Jianchi (who also managed the Wenhai lou *shufang* and a series of bookstores in Fujian, Guangdong, and Guangxi) and four members of the Ma lineage originally associated with the Benli tang. The blocks for the operation were purchased from a Zou family that had decided to stop publishing; and the main branch store of the publishing house was in Guixian, Guangxi.[64]

Anecdotal evidence suggests that these partnerships were fairly simple, at the opposite end of the spectrum from the complex and sophisticated variety of partnership agreements that supported the salt industry of Zigong, Sichuan. Zigong salt firms, often based in a lineage trust, might seek partnerships with non-kin investors and in certain cases with investors from outside Sichuan. The Zou and Ma *shufang*, based in the household, formed partnerships along kin lines—with other households either within the same lineage or with the lineage to which they had strong marriage ties. To some degree the relative technological

---

62. Interviews 61, 12/3/95 (Wuge); 68, 12/5/95 (Wuge); and 83, 4/1/96 (Zhangzhou).

63. Interview 63, 12/5/95 (Wuge).

64. Unfortunately the contracts defining the relationships within these partnerships have not survived. From the descriptions of informants, however, each partner contributed capital toward the establishment of the bookstore. See Xu Jianqing, "Qingdai shougongyezhong de hehuo zhi," pp. 126–30.

simplicity of woodblock printing made more complex arrangements unnecessary. At least as practiced in Sibao, publishing did not require the same level of capital investment or entail the same high risks that developing brine wells did—but nor did it yield the same profits.[65]

The Sibao publishing-bookselling partnerships—whether intra- or inter-lineage—simple or complex, do not seem to have been particularly successful. Family pressures undermined the Ma Rixuan–Ma Riyao venture. Ma Riyao, led astray by his older brother, tried to abscond with the bookstore profits. Ma Rixuan, by this time head of the Guixian merchants' association and a man of some local importance, had the police arrest the brother, whereupon Riyao withdrew his investment from the store, precipitating its collapse.[66] The Zou-Ma partnership in the Gengxin tang foundered on interfamilial tensions: some evidence points to one of the Ma partners as an incompetent manager, but the fatal conflict erupted when another Ma partner brought a lawsuit against Zou Jianchi, claiming that he was taking more than his fair share of the profits from the Guixian store. (My informant, needless to say a member of the Ma lineage, also claimed that Zou used to get his partners drunk when accounts were settled at the end of the year so that he could cheat them.)[67]

Sibao publishing houses and branch stores also developed relationships with non-Sibao *shufang* and, eventually, with non-Sibao bookstores and wholesale merchants, particularly in Guangdong. According to informants, in the late nineteenth century the Linlan tang *shufang* began purchasing books and purchasing or renting woodblocks from a Foshanzhen publishing house.[68] In the late Qing the Wenhai lou *shufang* sold texts wholesale to two retail shops in Foshanzhen, the Lianyuan ge 連元閣 and Chongbai tang 崇白堂. And a brief, unfortunately undated, notice tersely records a series of transactions between the Cuiyun lou and several different Foshan shops, suggesting that the connections between Sibao and Foshan were fairly extensive.[69] Many stores began,

---

65. Zelin, *The Merchants of Zigong*, chaps. 1–4.
66. Interview 54, 11/28/95 (Mawu).
67. Interview 51, 11/27/95 (Mawu).
68. Interview 44, 11/23/95 (Mawu).
69. The nature of the transactions is not clear; titles of texts or woodblocks are listed, but it is not clear whether these were purchased or sold by the Sibao shop.

early in the next century, to purchase lithographic texts from book-stores in Fuzhou, Xiamen, and Hong Kong and sell them alongside their Sibao woodblock imprints. A brief account book dating from the Republican period records the inventory of a store, the Qiongji (tang or lou) 瓊記 (堂 or 樓), linked to the old Yijing tang of Mawu. The inventory includes twenty-three titles of largely new textbooks (*Gao[deng] lishi* 高等歷史, a high-school history text; *Gonghe[guo] chudeng guowen* 共和國初等國文, an elementary Chinese-language text; *Gonghe[guo] jing* 共和國鏡, an account of the Chinese Republic; *Gonghe guomin duben* 共和國民讀本, a reader on Republican citizenship, and so forth),[70] all purchased from Fuzhou and sold at the Qiongji store; and five titles of clearly more old-fashioned works sold by the Yijing tang, including a lithographic edition of *Youxue gushi qionglin* and a woodblock version of a work of physiognomy, *Sanshi xiang* 三世相. The stock of this operation consisted almost entirely of lithographic works, largely textbooks for the modern school system. What this trend indicates, of course, is less a complication in business relationships than a sign that the Sibao publishing industry was in decline. These bookstore managers, in shifting to the sale of texts produced with the new technology, were in essence acknowledging that the market for the old-style woodblock texts was shrinking.

### THE INDEPENDENCE OF THE
### BRANCH SHOPS AND THE
### DECLINE OF SIBAO PUBLISHING

At the same time, many bookstores were beginning to assert their independence of Sibao oversight. The relationship between the home establishments and both the itinerant booksellers and the established branch stores had always been potentially uneasy. Although the founding of branch shops often made possible an expansion in book production

---

70. The titles are abbreviated in the account book, and I am guessing at the content of the books from these abbreviations. The location of the Qiongji tang/lou is not indicated, but it was probably in Jiaying city, Wengyuan county seat (both in Guangdong), or Guixian (Guangxi), the major sites of Yijing tang bookselling.

back home and marked the household business as a particularly successful one, these shops might also be a source of tension within the business as a whole, as the *shufang* managers in the Sibao "headquarters" struggled to maintain control over distant branch shops. As we saw in Chapter 4, from the beginning of Sibao printing history, measures were taken to ensure close ties between the more settled "outside" "guest households" (*kehu* 客户) in charge of the bookstores and publishers in Sibao—and, in particular, to ensure ultimate control of bookselling and branch stores by the *shufang* managers in Sibao.

Little evidence survives of the success of these measures in the first two centuries of Sibao history. The bookselling "empire" centered on the Wenhai lou provides some evidence for the late nineteenth century, however. The Wenhai lou traced its origins back to the early stages of the Sibao book trade. Its parent *shufang*, the Biqing tang 碧清堂, was founded in 1711 by Zou Shangzhong 尚忠 (1691–1761), a descendant of Zou Xuesheng (see Appendix C4). Two generations later, Shangzhong's heirs divided the *shufang* property, creating two new shops, the Yingwen tang 應文堂 and the Wenhai Lou. By the late nineteenth century, the Yingwen tang had closed, after the heir to the then-manager was killed during a bookselling expedition in Jiaying department, Guangdong.[71] After a rather bumpy course through the eighteenth and early nineteenth centuries, the Wenhai lou was one of the few Sibao *shufang* to enjoy a revival in the late nineteenth century.

This revival was largely the work of Zou Jianchi, under whose vigorous management the *shufang* had at least six different branch shops—in Tingzhou, Lingshan (the Wenhai lou and Biqing tang), Hengzhou (the Wenxiang Ge 文香閣), Nanning, and Bose—as well as a connection to the Foshan publishing house Lianyuan tang. Jianchi was a tireless supervisor, according to his genealogy biography:

> At that time there were *shufang* in Nanning, Lingshan, and Tingzhou, scattered all over, some at a distance of several thousand *li* from his native place, and in places one thousand or several hundred *li* distant from one another. But until the end of his life he traveled back and forth between them all, in order to grasp the overall picture and control the fruits of the business. By following

---

71. Interview 42 (11/19/95), Wuge.

his strategies, [the business] gradually conformed to his wishes. Those he employed were all happy to work tirelessly [for him], and there was none who would dare cheat him. As a result, the business flourished.[72]

One local informant presented a somewhat different view of Zou Jianchi's diligence; he recalled stories of a terrifying figure who, on his much-dreaded visits to the shop, minutely inspected the accounts and routinely harangued the manager (a younger brother, son, or nephew) about reporting all profits, accusing the man of holding back money for his own nuclear family unit.[73]

However one views his behavior, it is nonetheless clear that Jianchi did keep a close eye on his bookselling empire. But it is possible to interpret this strict oversight as evidence, not of a continuing traditional relationship between Sibao and its branch shops, but rather of Zou Jianchi's justified anxiety about the ability of the Sibao publishing houses to maintain centralized control. For by the late nineteenth century there were signs that the ties between center and branch were weakening and that the measures developed to tie the branch shops to the Sibao houses were failing. Marriage to a Sibao woman did not prevent branch store managers, particularly those living quite distant from "home," from settling near their shops and establishing a second family, whose support required at least some of the profits from the shop. Interestingly, Zou Jianchi himself eventually embraced this course; he made his headquarters at one of the two Wenhai lou shops in Lingshan, his birthplace: "Of all his places of business, the Lingshan *shufang* was the chief. In his middle years, he established a family there, with sons and a house in a site with excellent *fengshui*, propitious for the prosperity [of his line]."[74] The new emotional loyalties and financial responsibilities created in such a context—not to mention the power of daily routines in a new place, within a new family—formed incentives to renege on the obligations to the centralized household economy in Sibao.

Accounting methods in the branch stores (as well as in *shufang* households) encouraged managers to identify their shop's earnings with the needs of their new family. Although some managers kept the book-

---

72. *FYZSZP* (1947), 33.98b.
73. Interviews 70, 12/6/95 (Wuge); and 92, 5/10/95 (Nanning).
74. *FYZSZP* (1947), 33.98b–99a.

store accounts separate from their own daily accounts, most did not. They recorded *all* expenses for their family—the purchase of rice and clothing, for example, as well as the wages paid to the store workers— and the daily earnings from book sales together in a daybook (*liushui zhang*).[75] This system made it easier to conceal or muddle earnings and the calculation of profit, thus aiding just the kind of "individual family selfishness" the genealogies and the Sibao *shufang* managers feared.

Instead of returning to Sibao at each New Year's, many bookstore managers went only once every three to five years—or a group of managers might rotate the responsibility. Some bookstore managers established branch ancestral temples in their new homes, as descendants of the upper-shrine Zou branch did in Lingshan. Even as these monuments to their ancestors affirmed their link to Sibao, they also obviated the need to return there, loosening their real affective and ritual ties to—and lessening their obligation to heed—*shufang* managers or household heads. Remittances home seem to have declined. In the heyday of Sibao publishing, the profits from branch stores, submitted when the booksellers and branch store managers returned home, paid for great houses, land, and schooling. But by the early twentieth century, mostly much smaller sums, "just what one could afford," were sent back to support the base household sustenance.[76]

Perhaps the sharpest expression of both independence from Sibao and awareness of the changing nature of the book trade was the move by several branch bookstores to establish printing operations of their own. Violating the unwritten rule that branch shops were never to compete with the Sibao publishers by establishing *shufang*,[77] several

---

75. Interviews 25, 11/9/95 (Wuge); 32, 11/13/95 (Wuge); 44, 11/24/95 (Mawu); 59, 12/2/95 (Wuge); and 63, 12/5/95 (Wuge).

76. Local disorder also made it difficult to get remittances to Sibao. Ma Rixuan, manager of the Licheng shuju in Guixian, tried to send his family 500 silver dollars when his business was flourishing in the late 1920s. Fighting between the Red Army and Nationalist forces prevented the delivery of the money, however, and it was returned to Guixian. Interviews 54, 11/28/95 (Mawu); and 86, 4/23/96 (Mawu).

77. Interviews 13, 4/27/95 (Wuge); and 25, 11/9/95 (Wuge); see Chapter 4, p. 143. It is hard to tell how scrupulously this distinction between publishing and bookselling was maintained even in the earlier years of the Sibao industry. Given the portability of the printing technology and the difficulties of oversight from Sibao, it is likely that the rule was violated, but no evidence of this survives.

branch shops did begin publishing their own texts, possibly in the late nineteenth and certainly in the early twentieth century (see Fig. 10.12, the cover page of an examination essay collection published by the Wenhai lou in Nanning in 1890).[78] There is some evidence that the Sibao publishers, in response, attempted to extend the customary rules governing the publication of titles (*suiyi shua xin* and *cangban suoyou*; see Chapter 5) to the larger of these branch printing operations.[79] But close control over distant branch publishing businesses proved difficult over the long run.

To be sure, some of these shops were fairly close to hand: in Changting and Shanghang, printing operations could be fairly closely supervised. And these stores seem to have printed only from blocks sent the short distance from Sibao; arguably, they represent modest extensions of the Sibao business. But more distant branches also started printing—the Licheng shuju in Guixian, founded in 1927 and managed by Ma Rixuan, published woodblock and possibly lithographic and letterpress (*qianyin* 鉛印) texts as well.[80] The Wenhai lou in Lingshan, under the supervision of Zou Jianchi, began printing texts in the late nineteenth century. And the Nanning Wenhai lou began producing almanacs (*tongshu* 通書) on store premises, although these were, according to an informant, woodblock editions printed from blocks sent from Sibao.[81]

Other stores made more radical breaks with Sibao tradition. The Suwei shanfang store in Zhangzhou flourished during the Republican period because, as we have seen, modern lithographic texts of contemporary interest came to dominate its stock. In the late 1920s the shop manager began selling Sibao woodblock texts, largely editions of popular novels, to Shanghai publishers, to be reproduced in lithographic form and sold back to the Zhangzhou shop. In 1930, all the remaining woodblocks of the Suwei shanfang *shufang* were transported from Sibao to Zhangzhou, and the bookstore began printing those woodblock

---

78. An imprint of a manual for pulse-diagnosis (*Wang Shuhe tuzhu nan* 王叔和圖註難) published by the Yijing tang in Jiaying city also survives in Sibao.

79. Wu Shideng, "Qingdai Sibao keshuye diaocha baogao," p. 142.

80. Interview 54, 11/28/95 (Mawu).

81. Interview 92, 5/10/96 (Nanning). It seems, too, that the blocks belonging to the Sibao Longfeng tang *shufang* were, in the 1930s, transferred to its *shudian* in Wengyuan, the Qixin shuju 啓新書局; Interview 50, 11/25/95 (Mawu).

texts that remained popular (largely primers, almanacs, and fortune-telling manuals) on its own.[82] But by this time most of the bookstore's stock consisted of modern texts from Shanghai.

Of course, stores distant from Sibao quite easily drifted away from Sibao control. The Yinwu shuwu 印務書屋 in Bose, for example, was originally linked to the Wuge Wujing tang 五經堂, a *shufang* founded in the late eighteenth century by Zou Yueguan 岳官 (1768–1838), a nephew of Zou Shengmai. In the late nineteenth century Zou Yuanchang 遠昌, with four of his brothers, revived the by-then defunct publishing business and established a branch shop in western Guangxi. Yuanchang began by using the old blocks of the Wujing tang (apparently unused for three generations), but he rather quickly adopted modern print technologies as well. By the time his grandson, my informant, arrived in Bose, the shop included one lithographic printing master (*shiyin shifu* 石印師傅) and one apprentice; two letterpress printing masters (*qianyin shifu* 鉛印師傅), one lead-type casting craftsman, and one apprentice; and one scribe responsible for writing characters. The grandson became the second lead-type printing apprentice. Except for my informant, all the workers, including the shop manager and accountant, were from Guangxi. Limited woodblock printing was still being done: official forms (*gongwen zhi* 公文紙), composition paper for students (*zuowen zhi* 作文紙), envelopes (*xinfeng* 信封), stationery (*xinzhi* 信紙), diaries (*rijizhi* 日記紙), and so forth. But no longer were woodblock texts from Sibao—or anywhere else—sold in the Yinwu shuwu.[83]

The experience of the Yinwu shuwu reveals yet another problem facing the Sibao industry, although not one as serious as the changes in culture and technology. This was the new relationship between bookselling and the state. The Sibao publisher-booksellers, like all publishers, appear not to have paid commercial taxes under the Qing. The 1854 *Changting xianzhi* attributes the "not insignificant" profits of the Sibao booksellers to this freedom: "They print and sell books throughout half the empire, and customs duties never touch them."[84] Most informants emphasize that the Qing government was, at any rate, largely unaware

---

82. Interviews 68, 12/5/95 (Wuge); and 83, 4/1/96 (Zhangzhou).
83. Interview 59, 12/2/95 (Wuge).
84. *Changting xianzhi* (1854), 31.69b.

of the Sibao trade.[85] It is not even clear how heavily the imposition in the mid-nineteenth century of the *lijin*, a rigorously enforced transit tax on all goods, affected the Sibao publishers or booksellers. Contemporary Changting literati complained in poetry of the ubiquity of *lijin* bureaus: "The taxes are double what was extracted in previous years; customs barriers are scattered to the farthest corners of the seas." The local prefect lamented popular dissatisfaction with the new burden as well.[86] But there is no record, oral or written, of how this imposition affected either book production or sales.

But with the establishment of the Republic in 1911 and the reform of the tax structure, the booksellers were forced to participate in a new and more rigorous system of revenue collection. The manager of the Yinwu shuwu resisted, falsifying the total of his earnings. Convicted in 1944 of tax evasion, he was forced to sell the store property, including all his stock and lithographic machines, and he and his household members had to find work at other bookstores.[87]

---

85. Interviews 25, 11/9/95 (Wuge); and 26, 11/11/95 (Wuge).

86. Xie Shuishun and Li Ting, *Fujian gudai keshu*, p. 472. The Sibao booksellers *might* have had to pay the transit tax at customs stations on their routes—there were customs houses in the major cities along their routes, and also in county seats and market towns such as Ninghua, Tingzhou, Shanghang (Fujian); Ningdu, Ganzhou, Dayu, Zhangshuzhen (Jiangxi); Dabu, Chaozhou, Huilai, Changle, Heyuan (Guangdong); and Wuzhou, Tengxian, Guixian, Nanning, Bose (Guangxi)—in short, at most of the river ports they passed on their bookselling routes. See Xu Tan, "Dui Qingdai qianqi shangshui wenti de yidian kanfa," n.p. (pp. 1, 3–4); and Fan I-chun, "Long-Distance Trade and Market Integration in the Ming-Ch'ing Period," pp. 83–97.

87. In the end, Zou Yuanchang, the former bookstore manager, and his family were rescued by the Hakka warlord Zhang Fakui 張發奎, who hired him—apparently out of ethnic solidarity—to print official documents for his "government" in Guangdong and Guangxi. The family fortunes flourished once again; so much so that Yuanchang accumulated enough land in Sibao to be classified as a large landlord during land reform; Interview 59, 12/2/96 (Wuge). See Fu Jianmu, "Qingdai minjian kuaiji fushi jizhang gaishu," p. 77.

Informants report that it was quite common for the bookstore managers to keep two account books: one, the *waizhang* 外帳, or "outer account," was a record of the daily book sales and was kept openly on the store counter; the *neizhang* 內帳, or "inner account," recorded the true earnings of the store (that is, it was an accurate record of the difference between the wholesale and retail prices) and was kept hidden by the store manager; Interviews 33, 11/14/95 (Wuge); and 59, 12/2/95 (Wuge).

But by this time the Sibao publishing industry was dying. Several of its branch stores—in Changting, Shanghang, Zhangzhou, Hengzhou, and Nanning—were still in business, but the Wuge and Mawu publishing houses had stopped printing almost entirely. Very small operations were still producing a limited range of primers and texts of local interest (like the *Sanzi jing* and the glossary *Renjia riyong*, written in part in the Sibao subdialect) largely for sale by book peddlers. But by 1946 the last of these holdouts had ceased operations. Modern print technologies had by this time overtaken woodblock printing. The few "Sibao" bookstores that survived—the Nanning Wenhai lou did not close until 1952, the Changting Daguang shuju 大光書局 until 1954, and the Shanghang Zhongguo wenhua fuwushe 中國文化服務社 until 1957—sold (and often printed) primarily lithographic and letterpress texts.[88]

---

88. The Zhongguo wenhua fuwushe was an offshoot of the Ma-lineage Linlan tang; in 1957 it was forced to make way for the new Xinhua shudian. Interviews 33, 11/14/95 (Wuge); and 44, 11/23/95 (Mawu).

EIGHT

*Sibao's "Confucian Merchants"*
*in Minxi Society and the*
*Late Imperial Economy*

A DESCRIPTION OF the Sibao publishing-bookselling
concerns would not be complete without some consideration of the
ideology that the Zou and Ma entrepreneurs upheld—or claimed to
uphold—in the conduct of their business and of the image that they
constructed of themselves as "Confucian merchants" (*rushang* 儒商,
*rugu* 儒賈) or "scholar-merchants" (*shishang* 士商). Whether or not the
way they thought about their business and its moral, social, and cultural
meaning had a direct impact on their business behavior,[1] this way of
thinking was such a central part of their self-perception, and certainly
their self-presentation, that it deserves some discussion here.

Important, too, is a consideration of the place that the Sibao publisher-booksellers occupied in their local and regional society and in the
late imperial economy. What place did the profits from the book trade
and their claim to "Confucian merchant" status earn them not only
within Wuge, Mawu, and Sibao but also within Minxi and beyond?
And what place did the Zou and Ma businesses have in the larger late

1. See Chen Zhiping and Zheng Zhenman, "Qingdai Minxi Sibao zushang yanjiu,"
p. 102, for an effort to argue that the Confucian studies of the Zou and Ma merchants
restrained their pursuit of profit and ensured their honesty in business dealings.

imperial economy? How are we to evaluate their success and assess their limitations? These are the questions I deal with in this conclusion to the study of the business of Sibao publishing-bookselling.

## *"Confucian Merchants": The Image of the Sibao Publisher-Booksellers*

Behind the incessant emphasis in the Zou and Ma genealogies, echoed to some extent in the contemporary oral histories, on the essentially "Confucian" motives and conduct of the Sibao publisher-booksellers lies a consciousness of the low moral and social status ascribed to craftsmen and particularly to merchants. As we saw in Chapters 3 and 4, the choice of publishing and/or bookselling as a profession was almost always cast as a painful decision necessitated by financial circumstances and prompted by a very Confucian filial dedication to the family. Even the legendary account of the introduction of printing technology to Wuge described it as an act of filial piety: Zou Xuesheng returned to the village from the far-more-interesting Hangzhou in order to care for his aging parents, bringing with him woodblocks to provide for textbooks for the education of his sons. The first publisher in Mawu, Ma Weihan, reluctantly abandoned his "Confucian" studies (*ruxue* 儒學)—that is, study for the examinations—out of concern for his father's failing health; he took up bookselling to help his father support the family, eventually returning home, like Zou Xuesheng, to care for his parents in their old age. Ma Weihan's story in particular (see Chapter 3) furnished the rhetorical pattern that all later Sibao publishers followed: moved by filial piety and dedication to family welfare, they regretfully gave up their studies (although all were promising students) and their hopes of examination glory for the morally questionable, but more practical and more immediately lucrative, path of commerce. In short, they sacrificed a lower (and in itself potentially self-serving) Confucian value—study for the more rewarding path of official service—for a higher, purely selfless one—filial piety and devotion to the family. So, too, contemporary informants, when insisting on the lack of serious clashes among the Zou *shufang* or between the Zou and Ma *shufang*, adduce family feeling and Confucian ethics as the cause of this perfect harmony: "We were all brothers—and Confucian merchants—thus there were no conflicts."

Claims to the label "Confucian merchant" were by no means unique to the Sibao publisher-booksellers. The term (and the claim to have "abandoned Confucian study for commerce" out of economic necessity) was in common use well before the founding of the Zou and Ma book trade. Yü Ying-shih even goes so far as to identify "'abandoning Confucian studies for commercial pursuits'" as an "active social movement" that "swept China" in the sixteenth and seventeenth centuries.[2] And the label "Confucian merchant" appears frequently in the biographies of Huizhou merchants of the late Ming and Qing. The Zou and Ma could not boast of the success of the famous Huizhou families with either the "Confucian" or the "merchant" portion of the formula: they never rivaled these great lineages in either examination achievements or commercial wealth.[3] But they could point to one unassailable characteristic (one that, however great the other differences, they shared with some Huizhou merchants) that gave them a legitimate claim to the status of Confucian merchants: they dealt in books.

In the rhetoric of the genealogies, their choice of publishing-bookselling when they "abandoned Confucian studies" for commerce reveals the purity—the essentially Confucian nature, as it were—of their motives. While acknowledging the commercial nature of their activities with relative frankness (unlike, say, the Jianyang publishers), they insisted that they were engaged in a superior kind of business, one devoted not to the petty search for profit but to the spread of learning. The 1820 preface to the *Fanyang Zoushi zupu* talks of the family's publishing concerns as if their primary purpose were not securing a livelihood but enriching the cultural life of the country:

[In Sibao,] in addition to the eternal occupations of farming and studying, the residents collect ancient texts and cut blocks for printing them, binding them in yellow wrappers, to meet the extraordinarily high demand of the *shidafu*. This is indeed of great benefit to culture and education, which, as a result, are permeated with the spirit of the Classics.[4]

---

2. Yü Ying-shih, "Business Culture and Chinese Traditions," p. 45.

3. Ye Xian'en, *Ming Qing Huizhou nongcun shehui yu dianpu zhi*, pp. 125–26; and Zhang Haipeng and Tang Lixing, "Lun Huishang 'gu er haoru' de tese."

4. *FYZSZP* (1947), *j. shou*, 17b.

The family instructions in the same text argue that book production is a kind of public service:

Our region has many printing shops, which cut blocks for publishing, producing so many ancient texts that the oxen transporting them sweat with the labor. [Sibao book traders] rapidly disseminate these texts everywhere—certainly this work can be considered as assisting the empire's literati to be generals and ministers of state![5]

This theme recurs in the genealogy biographies as well as in the frequent laudatory descriptions of a publisher as one who "printed the Classics and histories in order to benefit posterity" or published books "in order to advance study and spread civilization."[6]

The choice the Zou and Ma publishers and booksellers made was in many ways a practically compelling one. Book printing and selling were natural refuges for the failed scholar or for the young man reluctant to undertake the rigors of examination study for what must have seemed, given the families' record and the intensifying competition in the eighteenth and nineteenth centuries, a slender chance of success. Publishing, after all, was far less laborious and more lucrative than farming, the occupation theoretically second to scholarship in the Confucian occupational hierarchy. And it had the added advantage of linking its merchant-practitioners to the world of learning, perfuming their morally questionable search for profit with the "scent of books" (*shuxiang* 書香).

According to the genealogies, publishing elevated not only the moral but also the social status of those engaged in otherwise ignoble business. Several genealogy biographies draw the distinction between other kinds of unambiguously "dirty" commerce and the relatively "pure" trade in books. Zou Xiyao, one of the many publishers who "abandoned study for commerce," defended the family profession thus:

My generation does business, every day in the company of sordid merchants—how hateful this is to our self-respect! I am disgusted; I despise it. But commerce enables us to earn a living and makes it easy for us to draw close to the speech and manner of the gentry and scholars. For those fragrant with learning

---

5. Ibid., *j. shou*, "Jiaxun sitiao," 4ab.
6. Ibid., 34.6a and 10b.

and perfect in virtue, selling books is the only occupation. Thus I make this my work.[7]

This association of the book trade with learning and high social status was frequently exploited by the authors of the Zou and Ma genealogies, although usually in more unequivocally flattering terms than those employed by Zou Xiyao. It performed the function of identifying the Zou and Ma publishers and book merchants as men of culture, well educated and fully conversant with not only the texts but also the ethical values that defined elite culture. Often this identification was cast, like the comment cited above, as a disdainful repudiation of all other types of commerce, designed to point up by contrast the non-mercantile and elevated qualities of the Sibao merchants. Even more extreme in this regard was Ma Jing'e 景峨 (fl. early eighteenth c.?), who, according to his biographer, heaped contempt on his own occupation in the presence of colleagues: "When friends and relatives gathered together at a banquet and their conversation turned to making profits and raising prices, he would sit without participating and then finally say, 'This is a vulgar subject—what is the use of discussing it?'"[8]

Occasionally the genealogies reveal, in painfully defensive passages, a tension between a desire to disavow the greed and selfishness associated, in the simplest Confucian view, with commerce and a need to justify the moral and social worth of the merchant's life. Consider the biography of Ma Cuida, a sojourning bookseller in Fujian, Guangdong and Guangxi, and Hubei:

[Ma Cuida] was energetic by nature. Already as a child he had the competence of an adult—his conversation always startled his elders with its maturity. When he saw that the household economy was failing, he thought of giving up his Confucian studies (*ruye* 儒業) to be a merchant, explaining, "That my generation labors one-tenth of every day dealing with marketplace brokers and traders—is this not a matter for disgrace? I despise low calculation [of profits], but it allows me to make a living and, at the same time, associate with the words and manners of the scholar-gentry (*jinshen xiansheng* 縉紳先生). Infused

---

7. Ibid., 33.95b.

8. *MSDZZP* (1945), *ji* 7, 1.72a; cited in Chen Zhiping and Zheng Zhenman, "Qingdai Minxi Sibao zushang yanjiu," pp. 103–4.

with their fragrance, I can achieve their virtue. The profession of bookselling alone is selfless; this is what I will do." Thereupon he traveled as a merchant through Fujian, Guangdong, and Hunan, almost half the empire. Wherever he went, he met the local *shidafu* 士大夫 and broadened his knowledge and experience. . . . During leisure moments in his shops, he would page through ancient texts so that he understood their general meaning; as a result the *shidafu* respected him. . . . [Ma Cuida] was a merchant, yet he acted like a scholar and gentleman (*shi junzi* 士君子)—how then can he be belittled as a merchant?

Up to this point, the argument seems to be that Ma Cuida, although a merchant, *acted* much more like a gentleman and thereby had avoided the stigma of trade. But then the biography ends with a statement that, far from repudiating merchant status, explicitly attributes moral value to merchants: "Merchants also practice the Way—this must be taken into account."[9] Here the argument comes close to the claims made in the merchant manuals of the late Ming and Qing studied by Richard Lufrano: that merchants can, by practicing the principles of Confucian self-cultivation, "conduct their commercial affairs successfully and . . . present themselves to their community as respectable and honorable gentlemen." [10]

Most biographies, however, were content to exonerate the trade in books while deploring commerce in general and, at the same time, to present their subjects as persons on whom moral purity and social respectability had "rubbed off." Thus Ma Mingqi 鳴岐 (fl. early nineteenth c.?) had "the nature of a Confucian scholar and nothing of the manner of a merchant." In his travels as a sojourning trader, he "preferred to associate with upright and proper men and to discuss issues of morality with them."[11] Zou Qicui 啓萃 (1634–93) "began his studies at an early age, learning extensively and reading widely. . . . He earned a name as a merchant in Jiangxi, Guangdong, Fujian, and Zhejiang, where he enjoyed meeting the local worthies and gentlemen. All these men revered him, saying he had the air of a Confucian scholar (*you*

---

9. *MSDZZP* (1945), 1.82b–84a.

10. Lufrano, *Honorable Merchants*, p. 177. Lufrano argues that these manuals were written for "mid-level" merchants, "those without political connections or immense wealth" (ibid.)—in short, merchants like the Zou and Ma.

11. *MSDZZP* (1945), 1.75a.

*ruzhe feng* 有儒者風)."[12] Zou Jiaying 家英 (1822–87) so loved his books that he could not bear to sell them;[13] and Zou Guanglong 光龍 (1765–1832) was interested more in discussing the Classics and other texts (*Shi Shu tushu* 詩書圖書) with his literati and scholar (*wenren xueshi* 文人學士) customers in the Pearl River Delta area than in selling books.[14] As a book merchant in Guangdong and Jiangxi, Zou Tingyu 鄒廷羽 (1755–1846) enjoyed friendships with the local *shidafu*; he "thought little of wealth and, a man of generous spirit, never fussed over petty sums, unlike normal merchants."[15] In short, the Zou and Ma publisher-booksellers, although making a living from the trade, did not *act* like the social stereotype of merchants. In presenting themselves in this fashion, they were taking a conservative stand in the late imperial debate over the value of merchants. Rather than aggressively asserting the value of commerce to society (as Yü Ying-shih argues many merchants and literati were doing),[16] the Sibao merchants were defensively arguing that the nature of their business exempted them from the traditional association of merchants with selfish profit-seeking and greed.

The genealogies also emphasize the book merchants' concern for their sons' education. As we have seen, founding a family school was one of the first acts of a successful book merchant. Ma Quanwen, even after he became very wealthy, "still regretted not having completed his studies" and set up a school for his sons and grandsons.[17] So, too, Zou Hongchun—ultimately ashamed of his own lack of learning, however eager he may have been to forgo examination study for bookselling as a teenager—was determined that his heirs would enjoy the education he lacked and so also established a family school.[18] Although, as explained

---

12. *FYZSZP* (1947), 33.9b; cited in Chen Zhiping and Zheng Zhenman, "Qingdai Minxi Sibao zushang yanjiu," p. 101.

13. *MTLZXZSZP* (1911), 20.101b.

14. Ibid., 20.78a.

15. Ibid., 20.50a. And Zou Xiyao, cited above, drew "all the *shidafu* of the area" to his shop in Changting, earning their respect because of his knowledge of the contents of the books he sold (*FYZSZP* [1947], 33.95b). See also the biographies of Ma Dingan 定庵 (*MSDZZP* [1945], *ji* 7, 1.85a); and Ma Jiakuan 佳寬 (*MSDZZP* [1945], *ji* 7, 1.93b).

16. Yü Ying-shih, "Business Culture and Chinese Traditions," pp. 59–65.

17. *MSDZZP* (1945), *ji* 7, 1.45b; cited in Chen Zhiping and Zheng Zhenman, "Qingdai Minxi Sibao zushang yanjiu," p. 104.

18. *FYZSZP* (1947), 33.28a.

in Chapter 4, such an education was as much training for the family business as it was preparation for the examinations,[19] the school founders are consistently presented as men concerned about the Confucian learning of their descendants. Like the other uses of publishing and bookselling profits—buying land and building houses—investment in schools and study helped both to reinforce (and perhaps expand) the economic foundations of the "family profession" and to advertise the family trade to a major target audience.

## The Zou and Ma Publishing Families as Local Gentry

The relentless emphasis in the Zou and Ma genealogies on the Confucian nature of the book trade, their studied expressions of contempt for the avarice and deceit traditionally associated with merchants, and their assertion of close relationships with local elites and the acquisition thereby of elite traits—these tropes performed a variety of functions, one of which was to claim elite status for the families themselves. What

---

19. This is not to suggest that all the Zou and Ma booksellers had given up aspirations to office or scholarship for its own sake. There were a few cases of booksellers who returned to examination study after a career in bookselling. Zou Bincai, for example, with the support of his merchant brothers, "abandoned commerce to return to study." He had earned a military *juren* degree in 1801, but selling books with his younger brother in Guangdong and Guangxi afforded a more lucrative means of making a living than a military post. But in 1824, upon rereading the *Hanshu* 漢書 (Dynastic history of the Han; the genealogy biography emphasizes that he was as knowledgeable of *wen* 文 as of *wu* 武), he began to reproach himself for not having entered officialdom; so he traveled to Beijing to request (or, more likely, purchase) a post. He was eventually appointed to a position in the transport command for Xingzhou, Hubei, and finally to the State Farms Commission in Xuanzhou, Jiangnan (*FYZSZP* [1947], 33.55ab and 56b). Others failed in their attempts to return to a life of study. See *FYZSZP* (1947), 33.56a–57b, for the story of Zou Bincai's brother, Bacai 拔才 (1793–1827), who worked with his brothers in the book trade, although he preferred study: "He was a merchant in name, but he was really a scholar. In the morning he would manage the shop, but in the evening he would dip into the wealth of the Classics." His brothers finally agreed to support him in his studies, and he left business to study with a teacher. But he never succeeded in the examinations. See also *MSDZZP* (1945), *ji* 7, 1.51a–52b, for the story of Ma Dingyi; and Ye Xian'en, *Ming Qing Huizhou nongcun shehui yu dianpu zhi*, pp. 126–27, for similar stories about Huizhou merchants.

can this rhetoric tell us about the real status achieved by the publishing families of Sibao in local society? What relationships did they in fact develop with Tingzhou officials and gentry families?

Within Wuge and Mawu and to some extent the larger entity of Sibao, successful publisher-booksellers, along with other successful merchants, formed the core of the local elite, at least through the eighteenth and most of the nineteenth century. Economically more powerful than the lineage heads, who seemed to have performed few if any regulatory functions within the publishing industry, these men dominate the genealogy biographies. The genealogies present a rosy picture of the leadership activities of these men, emphasizing their accumulation of "hidden virtue" through philanthropy. References to lawsuits and inter-lineage conflicts suggest, however, that not all Sibao residents were content with the authority that wealth allowed these men to wield. And modern informants more directly complain of their manipulation of lineage rental land—one man went so far as to identify the publishers of the late nineteenth century unflatteringly as the local *tuhao* 土豪, or strongmen.[20]

But unquestionably the more successful of the publishers did hold positions of local leadership, and the activities of publishers and book merchants helped to strengthen the Zou and Ma lineages. Liu Yonghua, in his study of Sibao society, identifies the publishers of Mawu and Wuge as leaders in "lineage building, community compacts, and the establishment of local temples." He attributes the high percentage of lineage corporate landholding in Sibao to the growth of handicraft industries and commerce—and particularly to the development of the printing-bookselling industry—for these activities supplied the capital necessary for the purchase of ancestral estates. We have seen, in Chapter 4, that rich publishers often took active roles in lineage activities. Many of them created or added to lineage estates, constructed or repaired ancestral halls, and established family schools.[21] Three of the twelve compilers of the 1764 *Zoushi zupu* 鄒氏族譜, the only Zou genealogy to include both the upper- and the lower-shrine branches, were publishers (and purchasers of *jiansheng*, or Imperial Academy student,

---

20. Interview 24, 11/8/95 (Wuge).
21. Liu Yonghua, "The World of Rituals," pp. 97–98, 261.

status).[22] As we have seen, successful publishers were also community philanthropists, constructing and repairing roads, bridges, tea pavilions, and fords, and providing famine relief and aid to the poor. Such activities, being common markers of gentry status, served also to identify their sponsors as gentry. The Sibao merchants were following a model already established by upwardly mobile merchants of the late Ming, most notably those of Huizhou.[23]

In their philanthropic activities or, more precisely, in the way in which these activities are presented in the Zou and Ma genealogies, the publisher-booksellers were also expressing what Richard von Glahn identifies as a new, "bourgeois" "ethic of moral temperance," an ethic that had a particular appeal for shopkeepers and petty merchants and that "stressed the practical piety of good deeds and magnanimity toward others as the wellsprings of fortune, for oneself and one's descendants." The belief that merchants earned commercial success through hard work and the performance of good deeds had replaced the older faith that one relied on the worship of gods for wealth.[24] Repeatedly the Zou and Ma genealogy biographies reveal this belief by attributing business success (and many sons) to the rich stores of virtue (*jishan* 積善, "accumulated goodness," or 陰德, "secret virtue") that the publisher-booksellers had built up through both dedication to their

---

22. Ibid., p. 228. Zou Kongai, one of the more prominent booksellers, contributed a preface to this genealogy; *FYZSZP* (1947), *j. shou*, 16b.

23. Chang, *The Chinese Gentry*, pp. 56–64. For a description of the extensive charitable activities of the Huizhou merchants in the Jiangnan area, see Fan Jinmin, "Qingdai Huizhou shangbang de cishan sheshi"; see also Ho Ping-ti, "The Salt Merchants of Yang-chou," pp. 158–61. Perhaps the clearest example of the association between certain types of charity and gentry status can be found in the biographies of virtuous merchants in Wang Daokun's 汪道昆 (1525–93) *Taihan ji* 太函集. Many of his merchant subjects devoted considerable portions of their fortunes to gentry-like activities: dispute mediation, establishment of famine-relief programs, aid to the poor, and so forth.

24. Von Glahn, *The Sinister Way*, pp. 244–45. Von Glahn argues that this attitude toward wealth as an expression of virtue is a new development in the late Ming and Qing, the "first stirrings of [a] bourgeois consciousness," which "promoted a synthetic ethic of moral integrity, wise investment of money, and philanthropy as superior to the straitlaced parsimony of both the sanctimonious Confucian and the abstemious miser" (p. 244). In earlier periods (and still to some extent through the late Ming and Qing), the accumulation of wealth, in contrast, was associated with the worship of demonic spirits like Wutong 五通.

profession and acts of charity. Even their business itself could be viewed as a means of accumulating merit, for the publication and dissemination of medical handbooks and morality books were commonly classified as merit-earning deeds.[25]

Publisher-booksellers and their family members also frequently played leading roles in the establishment of temples and religious associations. Ma Long, the son of the successful publisher Ma Dingbang and brother of Ma Jiu, who continued his father's trade and supported his brother's examination studies, sanctioned the introduction of a new spirit into the Sibao pantheon: Lord Ma, General Fubo 伏波, a deified Han figure, originally worshipped by Ma sojourning booksellers in Guangxi. Persuaded that Fubo had brought them high profits, these booksellers introduced his worship to Mawu on their return home, and Ma Long initiated the construction of a temple in his honor in the Laijia market. He also oversaw the building of a temple to Tianhou, a patron goddess of merchants, next to the Fubo temple, in the mid-eighteenth century.[26] Both temples, to spirits believed to aid commerce, were funded at least in part by profits from the publishing-bookselling trade.

The same pattern appears in Wuge. A temple to Tianhou was constructed at the Gongping market in 1792, under the supervision of a publishing-house manager, Zou Jin 進 (1755–1800).[27] The Longxiang hui, the association formed to manage the annual celebration of Tianhou's birthday, included at least several book merchants in its membership. Many other members belonged to households in the

---

25. The preface to a Sibao medical publication, the *Yuzuan Yizong jinjian waike* 御纂醫宗金鑑外科 (Imperially sponsored *Golden Mirror of Medical Orthodoxy: External Medicine*), announces: "The greatest service would be to print and distribute [this text] widely; the merit thus earned would be even greater than that from the dissemination of morality books or the Classics"—a plea found in many popular medical texts ("Xu," 1b). Of course, one was not supposed to profit from acts of merit—but the Sibao publishers might still hope to earn a little from what they presented as their dissemination of culturally, physically, and morally beneficial works.

26. Liu Yonghua, "The World of Rituals," pp. 420–26; *MSDZZP* (1993), *ji* 5, 59, 68–69, 80–81. For an appeal to Ma Fubo, see *FYZSZP* (1947), 33.30b–31a; here Zou Shuwen, one of the earlier Zou publisher-booksellers, takes Ma Fubo as a model in his efforts to instruct his nephews in the family business.

27. *MTLZXZSZP* (1911), 9b.36a–38a, 20.65ab.

book trade.[28] Indeed, it can be said that the book business significantly influenced the religious life of Sibao, for the success of the business certainly led to the introduction of one "outside" deity, Fubo, to the region and quite probably helped elevate Tianhou to prominence in both the Laijia and the Gongping markets. In close cooperation with other local notables (holders of government student status, largely purchased; managers of lineage estates; and provincial military graduates) the publisher-booksellers were important supporters of the institutions developed to support worship of these gods.

Publisher-booksellers were eager purchasers of examination degrees, another popular means for merchants to claim (perhaps somewhat dubious) gentry status.[29] As early as the eighteenth century, publisher-booksellers of some wealth bought *jiansheng* status. By the nineteenth century, it had become routine even for merchants of only moderate means to "contribute" the roughly one hundred *taels* required for the degree.[30] Liu Yonghua has calculated that 63.3 percent of the degree and official title holders listed in the genealogy of the lower-shrine Zou lineage were *jiansheng*,[31] which suggests that this was a popular strategy of upward mobility for those lineage members who could afford it. Although there is no way of knowing how many of these were publishers or book merchants, certainly many of them were. The profits from the book trade often purchased degrees for family members not themselves engaged in the book trade; we could argue that to a considerable extent

---

28. See Chapter 3, p. 106; Liu Yonghua, "The World of Rituals," pp. 432–34.

29. The sale of lower-level degrees by the Qing government peaked once in the late seventeenth century and again in the mid-nineteenth century, both times spurred by a need for military funding. Benjamin Elman (*A Cultural History of Civil Examinations in Late Imperial China,* pp. 687–88) has calculated that the percentage of local officials who achieved their posts through purchase increased steadily over most of the dynasty, from 22.4 percent in 1764 to 29.3 percent in 1840 to 51.2 percent in 1871; by 1895, there was a slight decline to 49.4 percent. In Fujian, over 20,000 *jiansheng* degrees were sold during the thirty years of the Daoguang era alone. Ho Ping-ti ("The Salt Merchants of Yangchou," p. 165) mentions the purchase of degrees as a strategy even among the wealthiest of the late imperial merchant groups: "Between 1644 and 1802, there were 140 members of salt merchant families who became officials by purchasing offices."

30. In Daoguang-era Fujian, the average cost of the *jiansheng* degree was 106 *taels*. See Elman, *A Cultural History of the Civil Examinations in Late Imperial China,* pp. 227, 233, 688.

31. Liu Yonghua, "The World of Rituals," pp. 96–98.

publishing funded the creation of a *jiansheng* elite in Wuge and Mawu in the late eighteenth and nineteenth centuries. All these men are listed in the genealogies as *guoxuesheng* 國學生 or *taixuesheng* 太學生—that is, Imperial Academy students—and some managed to achieve subofficial posts on the strength of this status. Given the swelling numbers of *jiansheng*—and, for that matter, licentiates—over the course of the nineteenth century and the notoriety of the practice of degree purchase,[32] it is not clear how much distinction this status bestowed, but the Zou and Ma publisher-booksellers doubtless felt that it helped overcome the stigma of commerce and constituted a credential that eased their contacts with scholar and literati customers. In this way, being a successful merchant could directly, if a bit crudely, provide entrée to gentry status.

There is evidence that the most successful Zou and Ma publishers were regarded as leaders and as men of county-level distinction by local officials, especially during the peak years of the industry in the late seventeenth and eighteenth centuries. Several of the larger publisher-booksellers—Zou Funan, Ma Quanwen, Ma Dingbang, and Ma Dingce—were awarded the status of "honored guest at the community wine ceremony" (*xiangyin bin* 鄉飲賓), in recognition of their local importance.[33] Changting county gazetteers occasionally include biographies of publishers and other Zou and Ma lineage members. Ma Quanwen, for example, was honored for his filial piety in carrying his mother to safety during the Revolt of the Three Feudatories; his nephew Dingbang was noted for his charitable activities.[34] Zou Shengmai, the most distinguished publisher of the Zou lineage, received a brief notice as a "lover of mountains and rivers" and "a member of the local gentry (*yishen* 邑紳) contemptuous of wealth and rank."[35] Based on number of biographies in the county gazetteers, the Ma lineage achieved greater local prominence than the Zou, garnering eight and ten biographies in the 1782 and the 1879 gazetteers, respectively, versus

---

32. Elman, *A Cultural History of Civil Examinations in Late Imperial China*, pp. 227–28.

33. *Changting xianzhi* (1879), *j.* 21, "Xiangyin bin fu" 鄉飲賓附, 3a–4b.

34. *Changting xianzhi* (1782), 18.24a, 31b.

35. Ibid., 18.40b; this notice is repeated verbatim in the 1879 edition of the gazetteer (24, "Renwu xiangxing," 9a).

one and two for the Zou.[36] Almost all of the Ma but neither of the Zou notables mentioned in the county texts were included in the higher-level *Tingzhou fuzhi* 汀州府志 (Tingzhou prefectural gazetteer) of 1867. In none of the gazetteers are men who were publishers or booksellers honored or even identified as such.

This evidence suggests that the Ma lineage at least was known beyond the society of Wuge, Mawu, and Sibao, albeit slightly, and only for filial piety, philanthropy, and local leadership—conventional virtues ascribed to minor social and political figures. Additional evidence from the lineage genealogies attests some social contacts between the Zou and Ma and members of the officeholding and scholarly elite during the first century and a half of Sibao publishing history, when the area enjoyed its greatest prosperity. Although family members wrote the majority of prefaces, biographies, commemorative essays (*shouwen* 壽文 or *jiwen* 祭文), and funerary dedications (*muzhi* 墓誌) in the Zou and Ma genealogies, some officials (including even a few from the central bureaucracy) and literati contributed to this literature as well. The Ma genealogy boasts commemorative essays by a district magistrate, four prefects, a Hanlin reader-in-waiting, a vice minister of the Board of War, and a minister of the Board of Rites.[37] Few of these authors referred to

36. Likely the Ma are more prominent by virtue of the reputation of the lineage's most famous member, the official Ma Xun. Other biographies note either an act of extraordinary filial piety, military leadership, charitable activities, or the practice of a special skill. For example, the second Zou to appear in the gazetteer, Zou Chengdong 成東, is honored for his skill as a physician (*Changting xianzhi* [1879], 24, "Renwu fangji" 人物方技, 3b). Other examples from various editions of the *Changting xianzhi* are: Ma Dingyi (*Changting xianzhi* [1782], 18.23b–24a); Ma Lüxu 履序 ([1782] 18.33a; [1879] 24, "Renwu yixing" 人物義行, 3ab); Ma Rubang 汝榜 ([1879] 24, "Renwu zhongjie" 人物忠節, 5a); Ma Tingxuan 廷萱 ([1879] 24, "Renwu wenyuan" 人物文苑, 10b–11b); and Ma Quanqi 權奇 ([1782] 18.30a; [1879] 24, "Renwu xiangxing," 2a).

37. In 1742, Tingzhou prefect Yu Dunren 俞敦仁 contributed a commemorative essay on Ma Quanwen, a publisher (*MSDZZP* [1945], *ji* 8, 1.71b–73a). The 1940 edition of the *Changting xianzhi* (12.34a) lists Yu as a Haining 海寧 *juren* who served in the position of prefect for eight years. Hu Xuecheng 胡學成, while serving as prefect of Hanyang 漢陽 (Hubei), composed a poem in honor of Quanwen's eighty-first birthday (*MSDZZP* [1945], *ji* 9, 1.25b–26a). Ma Jiu, a grand-nephew of Quanwen and a prominent book merchant, received accolades from a prefect of Fuzhou (Jiangxi), Qiu Xiande 邱先德 (a native of Qingliu) (*MSDZZP* [1945], *ji* 8, 1.105ab); a director of a bureau within the Board of Rites, Yuan Wenguan 葉文觀 (who had at one point taught in

the family publishing business. Exceptional here is the fulsome praise of Yu Guochen 余國琛, an official in the Board of War, who concludes his 1820 preface to the Fanyang Zou genealogy:

I have . . . heard that [residents of] this locality, in addition to the normal occupations of study and farming, accumulate woodblocks of ancient texts, [print them and] bind them in silk, in response to the demand from *shidafu*. Those who seek to buy their texts are countless. This truly benefits the teaching of culture, which will thereby be steeped in the spirit of the Classics (*Shi Shu*). This work can manifest and promote the beauty and splendor [of the Classics].[38]

Most of the other tributes are confined to celebrations of the virtues of individual members of the two lineages.

Such encomia, however, should not be overrated. Many writers were originally local contacts; one of the prefects was from Qingliu, and the director of a bureau under the Board of Rites had taught at the Longshan Academy in Changting. Clearly, too, many of these writers had minimal relationships with the lineages or men they were writing for: Yu Guochen was reporting what he has heard about Sibao publishing, not what he knew through personal observation. Their commendations cling tightly to well-worn conventions of allusion and style, often opening with a celebration of the sage-like virtue found within the "distinguished lineage" (*wangzu* 望族) hidden among "high mountains, thick forests, and deep valleys" and proceeding through rather vague and tired recitals of their subject's brilliance, filial piety, hard work, and well-deserved rewards.[39] The compilation of a genealogy, on the surface a

---

the Longshan Academy) (*Qingliu xianzhi* [Republican period], p. 494; *MSDZZP* [1945], *ji* 8, 1.93a–94b); and Vice Minister of the Board of War Shen Chu 沈初 (*MSDZZP* [1945], *ji* 8, 1.95a–96b). His brother Long was also honored with *shouwen* from Ye Guanguo 葉觀國, a Hanlin reader-in-waiting; and, more impressively, a commemoration from Cao Xiuxian 曹秀先, listed as a minister in the Board of Rites (*MSDZZP* [1945], *ji* 8, 1.88a–91a). The Ma genealogy also includes a letter by Li Shihong, Changting's most distinguished poet, replying to Ma Cijing's 次京 request for advice on study.

38. *FYZSZP* (1947), *j. shou*, "Zoushi zupu xu" 鄒氏族譜序, 17b; cited in Zou Risheng, "Zhongguo sida diaoban yinshua jidi zhi yi—Sibao," p. 113. Yu Dunren also refers in his essay in honor of Ma Quanwen to the family profession of publishing-bookselling.

39. See, e.g., *MSDZZP* (1945), *ji* 8, 1.71b.

very private act designed to define and thus limit membership in a kin group, was also a rather public event, in that the participation of outsiders, the more distinguished the better, enhanced the prestige of the branch lineage in question and provided the basis, perhaps, for future advantageous contacts.[40] Presumably the lineage leaders and genealogy editors took advantage of whatever personal contacts they had to persuade or hire men of some status to write commemorative essays and prefaces, but these reveal little of the real networks established by the Zou and Ma.

Curiously, no connection seems to have existed between the commercial publishing operations of Sibao and either government or private literati publishing in Minxi. As we saw in Chapter 2, little such publishing occurred in the late Ming or Qing: the Tingzhou prefect or county officials produced gazetteers and some texts for use in the local academies, the works of Minxi's few distinguished scholars were printed, and filial sons sponsored the publication of their fathers' poetry. If the Zou or Ma publisher-booksellers were ever commissioned to cut and print any of these works, we have no record of it; the Sibao publishers do not seem to have published the works of local scholars and writers for commercial sale either. Presumably the expansion of the Sibao businesses in the eighteenth century, by creating a pool of local block cutters and printers, made the technological process of publication easier for small-scale, often single-title, publishers. But there is no evidence—even though a few local officials obviously knew of the Sibao book trade—of any connection between the official and private publishing done in the county seats and the prefectural city of Tingzhou and the commercial publishing done in the villages of Wuge and Mawu.

There is considerable evidence, however, that lineage members forged connections with aspiring examination candidates and teachers within Minxi, particularly within the four counties (Changting, Liancheng, Ninghua, and Qingliu) that Sibao straddles. Essays by former teachers or fellow students (*tongsheng* 童生, *xiangsheng* 鄉生, or *yisheng* 邑生) from these areas are fairly common in the genealogies; indeed, all

---

40. Hymes, "Marriage, Descent Groups, and the Localist Strategy in Sung and Yuan Fu-chou," pp. 115–23.

the genealogy editors seem to have drawn on the same pool of contacts. Wu Lüduan 巫履段 (fl. late eighteenth century),[41] a Qingliu native who taught in a Sibao school, contributed several pieces to both Zou and Ma genealogies; he seems to have had first-hand knowledge of many of his subjects. A few members of the Tong 童 family, a Liancheng lineage of some note, were also frequent contributors—Tong Riding 日鼎 (d. 1728), noted for his filial piety and learning,[42] and Tong Ji 季 in particular.

Sojourning booksellers also established contacts with lower-level elite members—local educational officials and aspiring examination candidates—along their trade routes or in the towns in which they established branch stores. They cultivated local scholars like Zhou Zhaoyong 周肇鏞, who met the bookseller Zou Jiadong 鄒家棟 (1808–47) at Zou's bookstore in Gaozhou, where he was impressed with Jiadong's "extensive learning," not at all like that of "normal vulgar Confucians." The two, Zhou claims in his biography of Zou, often met at the Gaowen Academy 高文書院 to discuss scholarly matters.[43] Booksellers also developed collegial relationships with government-school and *shuyuan* instructors: Wu Heguang 吳河光, a teacher at the Wuchuan 吳川 Academy in Wuchuan, Gaozhou, became a friend of Ma Yuanbao 源寶 when Ma visited the academy to sell books to Wu's students.[44] Qiu Chunsan 邱春三, instructor of the Longxi 龍溪 county school in Zhangzhou, Fujian, frequently invited Zou Wenyuan 文元 (1794–1850), manager of the Wenlin tang in Zhangzhou (also the county seat of Longxi), to the yamen to discuss scholarly matters—or so he claims in his biography of Zou Wenyuan.[45] Successful officials from the Sibao area also proved useful contacts: Hu Yan 胡巖, a native of Changting, met bookseller Zou Bolong (and became his customer) while he was

---

41. In *Qingliu xianzhi* (Republican period), p. 462, Wu is briefly noted as a talented poet who failed consistently to earn an examination degree.

42. *Liancheng xianzhi* (1938), 22.13b. Members of the Tong family appear frequently as subjects of the biographies of this gazetteer; it is not clear, however, whether Tong Riding or Tong Ji was related to the most famous Tong of Liancheng, Tong Nengling, the Cheng-Zhu philosopher (see Chapter 2, p. 53).

43. *MTLZXZSZP* (1911), 20.100ab.

44. *MSDZZP* (1945), *ji* 8, 1.106ab.

45. *MTLZXZSZP* (1911), 20.92b.

serving as magistrate of Wuchuan, the native-place tie supporting the business relationship.[46]

Few of these Zou and Ma contacts appear to have enjoyed more than local distinction. They were at best county magistrates; more commonly they were lower-degree holders, teachers, or low-ranking educational officials. According to Miyazaki Ichisada, "Only the incompetent and inadequate were relegated to the schools, along with men who passed through the examination system at an advanced age or broke down in the middle of the examination sequence."[47] As business connections, of course, relationships with such men were ideal, for they constituted the target customers for the Zou and Ma book trade. But, by the mid- to late nineteenth century, these were also the relationships that the Zou and Ma seemed to be calling on in their efforts to present themselves as equals or near-equals of distinguished literati and gentry.

---

46. Ibid., 20.76b; *Changting xianzhi* (1879), *ji* 24, "Renwu huanji" 人物官績, 11b. Luo Guangwei 羅光偉, a *juren* from Yiyang, Hunan, notes in his *shouwen* to Ma Zhengqi 正箕 that he met Ma when Ma, "his uncles, cousins, and older and younger brothers were working as merchants in my native place," adding that "no fewer than several tens" of Zhengqi's family members might be there at any given time in the early eighteenth century (*MSDZZP* [1945], *ji* 8, 1.67a–68b). See also the biography of Ma Dingtao contributed by a Zhong Mengying 鍾夢瀛, identified only as a *juren*, which describes a similar situation: Dingtao traveled as a book merchant between Fujian and Guangdong and met Zhong at some point in the course of his work (*MSDZZP* [1945], *ji* 8, 1.68b–69b). Zou Yiguo 翊國, who sold books in Guangdong, formed an enduring friendship with a Lianzhou 連州 scholar, Wu Yuejing 麌岳静, whose highest academic achievement was inclusion on the Supplementary List of *juren* degree-holders; Wu wrote a poem on the occasion of his parting from Zou Yiguo and even sent a poem in honor of his friend's sixtieth birthday to Wuge—both are proudly included in Zou's biography (*FYZSZP* [1947], 33.20b–21a). See also *MSDZZP* (1945), *ji* 8, 1.115a–116b, for a *shouwen* in honor of the important Ma publisher-bookseller Cuizhong, by a minor educational official named Luo Liantang 羅聯棠, who apparently met Ma in the course of his travels to Fuzhou and Guangzhou in the early to mid-nineteenth century.

47. Miyazaki, *China's Examination Hell*, p. 34. The government school system at the county and prefectural levels did not function as a genuine educational institution; any ambitious *shengyuan* studied for the examinations on his own, not relying on instructors in these schools. Thus the frequent references, in both the Zou and Ma genealogy biographies, to the study of their subjects in the county or prefectural schools mean little in the way of academic achievement or advance toward an official post.

Even these lower-ranking scholars, in occasionally revealing some contempt for trade, suggest the difficulty that the Zou and Ma faced, as merchants, in securing an honored position in society. Qiu Chunsan, in his account of Zou Wenyuan, writes, "Even though he was calculating a livelihood, he did not forget the outlook of the Classics (*Shi Shu*); he saw commerce in texts as 'plowing the Classics and sowing the histories' (*geng jing jia shi* 耕經稼史), as earning one's food from the sages and worthies."[48] Lai Jin 賴晉, a Ruijin (Jiangxi) literatus, after describing the "rare books" (*shanben* 善本) to be found at Ma Minyu's 敏玉 (fl. mid–late eighteenth century) Ruijin bookstore, states even more damningly: "[At first] I privately avoided [Ma], considering him simply a wood cutter from a family well known as competent at its profession. I did not yet know that he was a man to be respected."[49] And Zhu Zipei 朱紫佩, a secretary in the Bureau of Construction of the Board of Public Works, in his commemoration of Ma Yulin, expressed amazement that a man who worked as a merchant could become a lineage leader: Ma, after working for fourteen years as a bookseller in Jiangxi, Guangdong, Guangxi, Guizhou, and Yunnan, returned to Sibao in 1871 and led his lineage in the publication of its genealogy and the construction of an ancestral temple.[50] These writers felt they had reason to be surprised by the knowledge and virtue of the Zou and Ma booksellers, whom they present as exceptional men in a somewhat tainted occupation. As individuals, they are credited with rising above their status, but the status itself remained a lowly one.

The Zou and Ma book entrepreneurs were thus able to achieve only relative, largely local social success. The more prosperous of them were leaders of the Sibao elite (certainly the Wuge and Mawu elite), and the Ma in particular seem to have enjoyed some connections, probably rather tenuous, to the elites of northern Minxi. Outside Tingzhou prefecture, the Zou and Ma associated at best with lower-level degree holders, educational officials (and the occasional district magistrate), schoolteachers, and local literati whom they met as customers on their bookselling routes or in their bookstores.

---

48. *MTLZXZSZP* (1911), 20.92b.
49. *MSDZZP* (1945), *ji* 8, 1.79b.
50. *MSDZZP*, *ji* 8, 1.124a–25a; 21.58ab.

## The Sibao Publisher-Booksellers
## in the Late Imperial Economy

If the Zou and Ma achieved only moderate social success, how should we assess their business efforts? How do we evaluate the effectiveness of the structure and operation of their publishing-bookselling enterprises? How do these enterprises compare, in organization and strategy, with other roughly contemporary Chinese enterprises? What place did the Sibao publishing-bookselling business have in the larger context of the late imperial economy?

### HOUSEHOLD BUSINESSES WITHIN
### CORPORATE LINEAGES

In evaluations of the Sibao publishing business, little is gained by abstracting the industry from its specific context and measuring it against a foreign model of capitalist enterprise.[51] Rather, it has to be considered first in terms of both the goals of the publisher-booksellers and the context in which they operated: the support and enrichment of the household in a lineage-based society set in an impoverished rural backwater. Many of the characteristics of the Zou and Ma household enterprises can be explained as an effort to achieve maximum flexibility to meet these goals in this setting.[52]

Occupational diversification within the household, in the context of the poverty, limited resources, and isolation of Minxi, provided each branch family with stable support for the development of the publish-

---

51. I try here to avoid as much as possible (and it is not entirely possible) the teleological search quite common in studies of Chinese businesses either for "capitalist" qualities and tendencies or for those factors that prevented a business from making the great leap forward to capitalism. The very different socioeconomic and political contexts of Qing Sibao and early modern Europe make either quest tendentious and ultimately irrelevant to an assessment of the success of a Chinese business. For a more extensive argument in favor of contextual assessment, see Hamilton, "Why No Capitalism in China?," pp. 70–71, 84–85.

52. Fu Yiling, in the posthumously published essay "Zhongguo chuantong shehui," argues a somewhat similar point: that the "pluralist structure" of "traditional Chinese society" lent the economy some necessary flexibility.

ing trade. If the book trade suffered a bad year, its members could be carried by the household farming "specialists," the merchants trading in some other commodity, or, optimally (although for the Zou and Ma, also very rarely), a successful scholar. The system of partible inheritance fostered the start-up of new shops, encouraging an expansion in markets (although this worked only when economic and demographic conditions were right, as they were from the late seventeenth through the early nineteenth centuries). If the inheritance were too small or the market could not support a new shop, then an heir could rent out or sell his blocks and supplement that income with the proceeds from inherited land. And, although family division and partible inheritance prevented the formation of publishing-bookselling monoliths, the customs encouraging cooperation among "brother" houses ensured some degree of coordination and rational expansion.

Keeping business "all in the family" ensured, too, that costs could be kept relatively low—sons or nephews were apprenticed to the business and received what amounted to on-the-job training, first in the household printshop and then, on the road, as itinerant booksellers. Once they had learned the trade, they might either establish a branch bookstore outside Sibao or return home to take over management of the family *shufang*. The greatest continuing production expense was block cutting, but ways were found to reduce this cost—either by having the work done in-house or by seeking out cutters like the Magang peasant women who worked for low wages. When the volume of production outstripped the labor resources of a household, it might have to hire extra printers or page-folders and binders. But since these tasks were essentially unskilled, women, even children, within the household could perform them—or women from other households could be hired very cheaply to perform them. Thus, the labor costs of production as well as distribution and sale could be kept down. And since cut blocks could be used for many print runs, the most significant investment cost could be minimized and controlled.

The diversion of some of the profits from publishing to the support of education in the examination curriculum was a good business practice. Indeed, it could be argued that it was essential to the success of the trade. Publishers had to know what texts best served students and examination candidates. And some publishers were able to use their education, as we shall see in Part II, either to compose or to compile their own books for publication or to produce expanded or newly edited versions of established texts, some of which became quite popular. As for the Zou and Ma booksellers, since a significant portion of their clients were students and literati, being able to understand their interests and requirements and to speak to them "in the manner of the scholars and gentry" made them more effective salesmen. The late-nineteenth-century observer Arthur Smith described stationery-and-book sellers ("Strolling Scholars") visiting schools with their wares; if a teacher saw that such a man was "a mere pretender, without real scholarship," he would see to the salesman's rapid departure.

If, however, the Strolling Scholar is a scholar in fact, as well as in name, so that his attainments become apparent, the teacher is obliged to treat him with much greater civility. Some of these roving pundits make a specialty of historical anecdotes, and miscellaneous knowledge, and in a general conversation with the teacher, the latter, who had not improbably confined himself to the beaten routine of classical study, is at a disadvantage. In this case, other scholars of the village are perhaps invited in to talk with the stranger, who may be requested to write a pair of scrolls, and asked to take a meal with the teacher, a small present in money being made to him on his departure.

Smith then recounted the story of a Strolling Scholar who shamed a teacher by besting his lecture on the Classics, producing such an elegant explication that "every sentence [was] like an examination essay."[53] Presumably the Zou and Ma were able to use their first-hand knowledge of the examination curriculum in the same way. The booksellers' education also helped them judge which new texts, discovered in their visits to schools and major publishing centers like Guangzhou, Suzhou, and Hankou, might be best to publish; and helped them, too, negotiate with authors from whom they might solicit manuscripts or prefaces for publication.

Similarly, the philanthropic activities and gentry-like behavior of the more prosperous publishers, although most immediately functioning to glorify the household and aid the descent group, also supported their business activities and reputations. By contributing to relief efforts and

---

53. Arthur H. Smith, *Village Life in China*, pp. 107–9.

cultural projects outside Sibao, these men advertised their willingness to assume (in the absence of firmer credentials like access to official positions) the social responsibilities of gentry. Their enhanced reputations as philanthropists and as gentry could only have helped them in their business dealings, allowing them to approach at least lower-level scholars and other book merchants as men of some status. And their local charitable efforts might on occasion have benefited their businesses directly: as we have seen, Ma Dingbang's two bridges facilitated traffic on the major trade routes out of Sibao to Jiangxi, Guangdong, and Guangxi; and Zou Zhaomin built a bridge that "opened up the road to Liancheng and Jiangxi."[54] Other activities imitative of the gentry lifestyle—the purchase of land, the construction of a fine home, the repair of the ancestral hall and local shrines, the purchase of degrees—certainly bolstered their standing within the villages of Sibao, providing visible incentives for ambitious Zou and Ma sons to enter the family businesses.

Inter-household and *shufang* cooperation also contributed significantly to the success of the Zou and Ma publishing industries. The rules that evolved to manage competition among the publishing shops within each descent group encouraged flexibility while reducing business risks. The ways in which the Zou and Ma each pooled information and resources—sharing news of the book trade, observing the informal "copyright" of *cangban suoyou* for titles already published, refraining from publishing competing editions of new titles through the *suiyi shua xin* rule, renting or exchanging woodblocks, passing excess business on to members of the extended family, and cooperating in the hire of block carvers from outside the descent group—made it easier for the smaller printing shops to sustain themselves and, at the same time, provided the larger and more prosperous shops with access to labor during busy times. Moreover, the interdependence of the Sibao shops made losses easier to absorb. We saw, in Chapters 6 and 7, how the network of branch bookstores and sojourning booksellers provided the publishing industry back in Sibao with access to the multiple and varied markets that supported the business for over 250 years.

---

54. *FYZSZP* (1947), 33.97a.

The Sibao household publishing operations were only rarely corporate enterprises.[55] The business of publishing-bookselling was centered in the household and managed by the household head or patriarch, with all profits ideally devoted to the social and economic advancement of the household unit as a whole. Household members did not own shares in the business; rather, they shared, communally, the earnings from the business, as they were budgeted by the household head and business manager. Only at family division was the business property split, but this division resulted in the creation of new, separate, household units, each the recipient of a portion of the parent household's assets and each functioning as a communal household business. In the system of accounting linked to this structure, there was commonly no distinction between household expenditures and business expenditures—all were calculated together in the *liushui* ("flowing water") style, as was usually the case for the Sibao *shufang* and bookstore households.

Crucial to understanding the structure of the Sibao industries is the fact that these household businesses each functioned under the umbrella of the lineage. The lineage apparently had no role in the running of the businesses or even in the adjudication of disputes between different households over business matters—that responsibility was the task of the group of business managers, not the lineage elders or heads. But, as David Faure has pointed out, the lineage nonetheless was usually the one true corporate entity in this system.[56] Lineages, composed of families whose male members claimed descent from a common ancestor, were often supported and perpetuated through the income from corporate property, usually land. We have already seen that rental of land from lineage estates was one means whereby publishing households in Sibao supplemented their income from the book trade. And successful publishers often included among their charitable activities the creation of a new branch lineage estate, contributions to an existing estate, repair of an ancestral hall, and/or editing of genealogies. Through the formation of branch lineages around new corporate estates, a single family might enjoy shares in more than one lineage

---

55. See Chapter 7, pp. 258–59, for the few known exceptions—that is, examples of bookstores established through multiple share-holding.

56. Faure, "The Lineage as Business Company," p. 353.

estate. (Thus, for example, a family might have a share in an estate formed at the death of a great-great-grandfather and, if property division had taken place, in an estate formed at the death of a grandfather as well.)

The major publishers' ties to lineage estates and their contributions to these estates and to "public" lineage causes played a major role in shaping the nature of the *shufang*-household finances and the social positions and obligations of their managers. Although the lineage leader and the managers of the lineage trusts had by virtue of these positions little or no role in the conduct of the publishing-bookselling business, lineage concerns nonetheless dominated the business: the profits of household *shufang* were often used to establish or expand lineage estates and trusts, but the resources of such estates and trusts do not seem to have been used to invest in publishing. Unlike the salt merchants of Zigong, Sichuan, the Sibao publishers did not found their concerns on the organizational foundation of lineage trusts; rather, lineage estates were founded on the prosperity of *shufang*.[57]

The lineage order helped shape the Sibao publishing and bookselling operations in at least one other important way as well, by encouraging the development of networks aiding the conduct of both publishing and selling. As mentioned in Chapter 4, networks of patronage within a lineage might be used by the publisher-booksellers to support their operations; the farming-out of printing from larger shops to smaller ones in the same lineage supplied the former with a flexible labor pool and the latter with extra income. More important, when the Sibao booksellers went on the road, they relied heavily on intralineage networks both to define and to support their bookselling routes, as we saw in Chapters 6 and 7.

Notwithstanding these structural strengths, derived in many cases from the household-centered nature of the business and the setting of the households within the larger lineage structure, the same characteristics could also present serious threats to the success of the Zou and Ma publisher-booksellers. Indeed, it can be argued that only the expanding market for books in the Qing enabled the organization of the Sibao trade to "work" for two and a half centuries. In this context, the recur-

---

57. Zelin, *The Merchants of Zigong*, p. 114.

ring division of household property and creation of new *shufang* drove and stimulated the growth of the Sibao trade. In a different economic and demographic climate, with a static or contracting market, however, the proliferation of *shufang* would probably have undercut or perhaps even destroyed the profitability of the business. Conflicts within household *shufang* over profit-reporting, profit-sharing, and property division were clearly perceived as a source of weakness by the Zou and Ma themselves—note their genealogies' relentless preaching of devotion to the common good and scrupulously equitable division of goods.

Tension between the demands of the household businesses for reinvestment of profits and the demands of the lineage organizations for investment in corporate property and other "public" charities might also pose a threat to the continuing prosperity and expansion of the business. The *shufang* managers in Sibao had to calculate two very complex, sometimes contradictory, relationships: first, how to attain and maintain some position of leadership within the lineage (helpful in political and economic relations with other *shufang* heads and in the maintenance of lineage connections that might help in the establishment of branch shops) without allowing lineage demands to drain profits; second, how to sustain and increase profits by extending sales networks ever farther and establishing more distant branch stores, while maintaining control over the family members sent out to manage these networks and stores. In order to remain in control of distant booksellers, as we have seen, the *shufang* managers stressed the importance of lineage ties, requiring booksellers to attend important lineage ritual events in Sibao and insisting on marriage arrangements that tied sojourning merchants to their home. Yet at the same time, within the lineage, they had to ensure, as much as possible, the business independence of their *shufang*.

COMPARISONS: SIBAO AND OTHER
LATE IMPERIAL ENTERPRISES

The structure of the Sibao publishing-bookselling industry as household enterprises set within a lineage (and the problems attendant on this structure) was neither unique nor unusual in late imperial China. It is, indeed, a cliché of Chinese business history that household, lineage, and ethnic (in the case of Hakka) networks played an important role in business enterprises.[58] David Faure has described and analyzed structures similar to Sibao's in his study of lineages in Guangdong province.[59] And, although the lack of detailed sources on the organization of the Jianyang publishing industry in the late Ming makes precise comparison difficult, the various publishing houses of the Yu, Liu, Xiong, Zheng, Chen, Ye, and Xiao were based in households within certain branches of these lineages (and, as in Sibao, intermarriage between the "publishing" branches of the various lineages served to buttress the household industries).[60]

But there is something different about the Sibao publishing-bookselling industry: the apparent determination of the Zou and Ma to maintain control over the publishing and the bookselling aspects of their business by keeping both firmly within the family. The Sibao publishing houses, from their beginnings until the late nineteenth and early twentieth centuries, asserted control over the distribution and wholesale and retail sales of their texts. In this the Zou and Ma businessmen seem to have taken a path quite different not only from the only other thoroughly studied rural publishing industry, that of Jianyang, but also from what economic historians have identified as the common late imperial pattern of industrial-commercial development. Jianyang, one of the great publishing centers of the Ming, operated a local book market, in Chonghua 崇化 district.[61] This monthly market attracted buyers from all over the empire and, although presumably most of the customers were book merchants who purchased texts wholesale for retail sale in

---

58. There is a large literature on this topic. See Brokaw, "Commercial Publishing in Late Imperial China," pp. 79–83, for references to some of the literature on the family; and Brown, "Introduction," pp. 2–9, for a summary of the roles that family networks and *guanxi* 關係 played in the development of Chinese business.

59. Faure, "The Lineage as Business Company," pp. 352–62.

60. Chia, *Printing for Profit*, pp. 78–80. In Jianyang, however, according to Chia, lineage branches seem to have specialized considerably, with all the lineage publishers coming from one branch or sub-branch, while other branches focused on study and examination success. In Wuge and Mawu, this kind of branch specialization was rare, as households in a variety of branches seem to have participated, at many different levels, in the publishing industry.

61. Chia, *Printing for Profit*, pp. 153, 189; and Zeng Ling, *Fujian shougongye fazhan shi*, p. 206. Chia suggests that books might also have been sold "by smaller printshops and by bookstores or book stalls set up during the periodic markets in Masha" (p. 189).

the major urban markets, it may have drawn retail customers as well.[62] There is evidence that in the late Ming some Jianyang publishers had also either established *shufang* in Nanjing or were cooperating with Nan-jing *shufang*, and these *shufang* may have doubled as bookstores, selling imprints produced in Jianyang by the manager's relatives.[63] But, in con-trast to the Sibao publishers, there is no evidence that the Jianyang *shu-fang* operated a complex and long-lived multi-province network; rather, an intervening body of merchants, unrelated to the Jianyang industry, handled the distribution and retail sale of Jianyang texts.

The other great publishing center of the late imperial period, Jiang-nan, operated through even more complex networks of middlemen, who handled certain parts of the production as well as the distribution process. Unlike Sibao—and Jianyang as well—the Jiangnan publishers relied on outside sources and outside merchants for the purchase of paper, the most important of the raw materials for printing; they shipped paper from Jiangxi, Fujian (from Minbei and Minxi), and southern Anhui. Such was the quantity they required that they often re-served production from certain sites for their exclusive purchase: in Jianyang, from the Kangxi era on, "each year *shufang* in Suzhou mo-nopolized the paper factories, forbidding them to sell to other custom-ers, so that Fujianese had no access to Jianyang paper (Jianyang *kou* 建陽扣)." And, although by the Qing the Jiangnan publishers had be-come increasingly reliant on just the sort of texts that Sibao produced (inexpensive primers, examination study guides, how-to manuals, and popular fiction), the market for their publications was much broader than that for Sibao's texts, encompassing not only all the provinces of China Proper but also Japan, Korea, Vietnam, and the Ryukyu Islands. To serve their extensive markets, the Jiangnan publishers, in contrast to the Zou and Ma of Sibao, worked through a complex network of mid-dlemen and "outside" merchants to sell their products. As Li Bozhong explains, the Jiangnan industry became increasingly commercialized

---

62. It is reported that, in 1429, the hereditary head of the Kong clan (the lineal de-scendants of Confucius), the Yansheng gong 衍聖公, sent an agent from Qufu to Masha to purchase texts for him (Liang Zhangju, *Guitian suoji*, "Masha banshu" 麻沙 板書, 3.8a; cited in Zeng Ling, *Fujian shougongye fazhan shi*, p. 206).

63. Chia, *Printing for Profit*, p. 209.

over the course of the late Ming and Qing, a process that involved "externalization" (*waishanghua* 外商化) or growing dependence on interaction with outside merchants.[64]

In this regard, rural Jianyang and urbanized Jiangnan were more typical of industrial-commercial organization in the late Ming and Qing than Sibao. Recent studies of Chinese business history have emphasized the growing complexity of financial and commercial forms and relationships in the late imperial period: the development of a range of partnership and contractual models and an increasing specialization of the functions of production, transport, and sale among separate groups of workers, brokers or middlemen, and merchants. Madeleine Zelin has shown how the Zigong salt merchants of the Qing created complex partnerships, drawing on the resources not only of lineage trusts but also of outside investors to support, often through a network of "fragmented" ownership arrangements, the capital-intensive, long-term development of brine wells and evaporation furnaces.[65] We know that the sojourning merchants of Shanxi and Shaanxi, trading in salt, silk, cotton, lumber, and metals, also relied heavily on partnerships to create extensive commercial networks that extended through much of China Proper.[66] Wang Shixin has described the variety of transport agents and

---

64. Li Bozhong, "Ming Qing Jiangnan de chuban yinshuaye," pp. 100–107, 146.

65. Zelin, *The Merchants of Zigong*, pp. 24–115. See also the essays in Zelin, Jonathan K. Ocko, and Robert Gardella, eds., *Contract and Property in Early Modern China.*

66. These were "share partnerships" (*hehuo* 合夥 or *hegu* 合股), in which the functions of capital contribution and capital management were separated. To establish a business, investors supplied capital and received corresponding shares and then selected a manager and agents to operate branch businesses under the manager, who was either paid a salary or given a capital share in the business. These partnerships, which might be formed between members of different families and even different lineage groups (and often on the basis of marriage ties between two lineages), were the vehicles by which these merchants expanded their operations throughout the empire. Myers, "Some Issues on Economic Organization During the Ming and Ch'ing Periods," p. 89. See also Wang Shixin, "Ming Qing shiqi shangye jingying fangshi de bianhua," pp. 26–28; and Gardella, "Contracting Business Partnerships in Late Qing and Republican China," pp. 329–30. The other notable lineage-based merchant network, that of the Huizhou merchants, relied on bondservants to manage branch shops and speed communication and financial transactions between shops. See Ye Xian'en, *Ming Qing Huizhou nongcun shehui yu dianpu zhi*, pp. 116–22.

firms that appeared in the late Ming to meet the demands of the rapidly growing long-distance trade.[67]

Several scholars of the Ming and Qing textile industry have described the complex series of intermediaries who handled the production, distribution, and sale of cotton and silk cloth: merchants, working through middlemen, might provide peasant households in the countryside (or weaving establishments in the cities) with spun silk or cotton purchased from other peasant households, again through an agent or broker. Once the woven cloth was ready, the middleman or a series of middlemen would arrange transport to the merchant, often employing licensed firms specializing in either water or overland transport and storage of goods.[68] The tea industry of Sibao's closest neighboring Fujian region, Minbei, operated through a similarly complex set of relationships in the eighteenth and nineteenth centuries. At the simplest level, peasant families rented land on which they grew and crudely processed tea for sale on the local market or to brokers for resale to merchants. At the most sophisticated level, merchant entrepreneurs rented or purchased plots of mountain land and, relying on middlemen to coordinate each step, hired outside cultivators and seasonal laborers to produce, process, and package the tea and transport firms to carry it to market. Tea production in Minbei was not organized as a large-scale plantation enterprise, but as a series of "operations of modest size, each employing no more than a few dozen male and female workers. . . . Production was dispersed and coordinated through rural markets and commercial middlemen."[69]

In sum, in the words of one scholar, the Chinese economy of the late imperial period was

---

67. Wang Shixin, "Ming Qing shiqi shangye jingying fangshi de bianhua," pp. 16–18.

68. See Myers, "Some Issues on Economic Organization During the Ming and Ch'ing Periods," pp. 80–85. For a fuller summary of the variety of different steps and relationships of production and sale in the textile industry, see Dietrich, "Cotton Culture and Manufacture in Early Ch'ing China," pp. 126–33; Xu Xinwu, *Jiangnan tubu shi*, pp. 27–113; and Lillian Li, *China's Silk Trade*, pp. 50–57. Similar points about the complex series of relationships that characterized business organization in the late Ming and Qing are made in Elvin, *The Pattern of the Chinese Past*, pp. 268–84; and Mazumdar, *Sugar and Society in China*.

69. Gardella, *Harvesting Mountains*, pp. 45–46.

articulated by a network of countless middlemen. . . . Merchants and middle-men controlled production and distribution by making contracts with agents to whom they advanced capital. Agents hired and managed the wage labor force needed by many enterprises. Brokers arranged contracts between the parties to business transactions, and both they and the agents bridged the frequent gap between the management of enterprises and their financing and actual ownership.[70]

In contrast to this pattern, Sibao *shufang* relied on in-house coordination of production, sales, and transportation, and, as a result, remained largely independent of the complex chain of middlemen and brokers (both individual brokers, *yaren* 牙人, and firms of brokers, *yahang* 牙行) that coordinated production and sale in other industries and even in other publishing industries.

All of the comparisons made above are problematic in different ways. We know too little about the distribution of Jianyang texts to draw a conclusive contrast to Sibao. It is difficult to measure publishing-bookselling in the two isolated, impoverished villages of Wuge and Mawu against publishing-bookselling in the much larger, much wealth-ier, and much more accessible Jiangnan region. And the very different capital demands and production processes in the salt, tea, and textile industries make precise comparison with publishing-bookselling impos-sible. Nonetheless, one general conclusion can be drawn: the Sibao enterprises are notable for their relative simplicity. The Zou and Ma, in contrast to most of the entrepreneurs mentioned above, based their market development and expansion almost exclusively on their own family labor. They relied on brothers, uncles, sons, nephews, and per-haps in-laws, not bondservants or hired managers, to manage their branch shops and take their books on the road. Although, as indicated above, there is evidence that at least one extra-lineage partnership was formed in the last decades of Sibao's publishing history, there is no ear-lier suggestion that this was a common method of managing and ex-panding the bookselling business—and in any event this partnership was a fairly simple one, between Zou and Ma households. The Sibao

---

70. Gardella, "Fukien's Tea Industry and Trade in Ch'ing and Republican China," p. 64; see also Myers, "Some Issues on Economic Organization During the Ming and Ch'ing Periods."

entrepreneurs relied primarily, almost exclusively, on household or extended-family relationships in both the production and the marketing of their texts.

What impact did this strategy have on the shape and scope of the Sibao trade? It allowed fairly tight control by Wuge and Mawu *shufang*, but it placed a heavy burden on the population resources of the Zou and Ma lineages. Since both production and sales were kept in the family, expansion required increasing numbers of commercially talented and trustworthy sons, men who could increase production at home and/or open new markets as sojourning merchants. The rotation of tasks (*shufang* manager, printer, bookseller, store manager), deemed necessary as a means of reducing "selfishness," undermined the greater expertise in each task that could develop with specialization. Dependence on family and lineage networks meant that Sibao bookselling had to be limited to areas where such networks existed—that is, largely to sites of Hakka migration in Guangdong, Guangxi, Jiangxi, and Hunan. Through the Qianlong and Jiaqing and into the Daoguang era, this strategy worked for Sibao, as the *shufang* and *shudian* households took advantage of the population boom and the increasing demand in the Guangdong, Jiangxi, and Hunan hinterlands and the Guangxi frontier. Indeed, during this period the Zou and Ma were surprisingly successful in expanding their routes of sale through three, four, and even five provinces, placing them among the cohort of long-distance merchants that developed in the late Ming and Qing, as we saw in Chapter 6. And, like such merchants, they were able to establish themselves in settled markets, even founding branch shops in many of them.[71]

But Sibao publisher-booksellers were not drawn, as they expanded their markets, into participation in the "triadic complex" of merchants, middlemen, and agents; the elaborate banking or remittance systems; or

---

71. Wang Shixin, "Ming Qing shiqi shangye jingying fangshi de bianhua," pp. 14–15. Wang argues that the development of long-distance trade encouraged the development of two new approaches—*ding hangye* 定行業 and *shuanzhu yitou* 拴住以頭 (the development of a single business or specialty and the monopoly on that business in a specific market)—that distinguished Ming-Qing long-distance merchants from the short-distance and intraregional merchants of that and previous periods. Long-distance trade and more stable, specialized markets enabled merchants to plan more carefully and further ahead, managing their businesses in more rational ways (see ibid., p. 15).

the relationships of partnership characteristic of the better-known and wealthier industries and long-distance merchants networks of the eighteenth and nineteenth centuries.[72] The considerable breadth and depth— the "long-distance"—of the Sibao markets grew, rather, out of a strategy that chose Hakka (and Zou and Ma) migration patterns and rapidly developing frontier areas as the basis for expansion and the establishment of new markets rather than access to sophisticated commercial institutions and heavily populated urban markets. This strategy limited, then, the types of markets they established, if not their distance from Sibao. As we have seen, the Zou and Ma booksellers only rarely sold texts in the major cities of the traditional cultural centers of the empire. Any effort to develop a circuit of such markets or to compete with existing bookstores in them might well have required engagement in the commercial institutions and relationships and the employment of "outsiders" practiced so successfully by Huizhou and Jiangnan (and to some extent the Shanxi and Shaanxi) merchants.

Other, more serious problems conjoined to undermine and ultimately destroy the Sibao industry: the disruptions of the mid-century rebellions and the civil conflicts of the early twentieth century, the rise of new print technologies not easily accessible to the Sibao publishers, and the abolition of the examination system (which depressed the value of much of Sibao's stock). But by taking the route of simplicity and control rather than utilization of the full range of complex economic relationships and institutions that supported the major commercial concerns of the day, the Zou and Ma limited the flexibility and potential for growth of their businesses.

Why did the Sibao publisher-booksellers take this route? We must assume from the genealogy pieties about family loyalty and the many measures taken to tie distant booksellers to the Wuge and Mawu *shufang* that the Zou and Ma were aware of the dangers this decision posed. How, then, can we account for their choice? Most likely it was made

---

72. Wang Shixin (ibid., pp. 15–28) lists a series of changes that came with the increase in long-distance commerce: the development of transport merchants, professional guilds of brokers, financial institutions, and forms of partnership. The Sibao publisher-booksellers seem to have made little use of these new agents and institutions, choosing rather to rely on lineage and ethnic ties and their own sojourning labor.

out of economic necessity. The reliance on household members both for labor in the Sibao *shufang* and for bookselling and on lineage members for support on the road was a means of cutting costs, since it obviated the need to pay *shufang* workers, brokers' commissions and fees, or heavy travel expenses. By the early twentieth century (and possibly well before that) profit margins were narrow enough to make the employment of middlemen unfeasible. By that time those *shufang* still printing texts operated on a shoestring, relying on cheap blocks from Magang, the hard labor of the printshop workers (and household members), and the frugality and the extensive travels of the booksellers to turn a profit. Even when the trade flourished in the eighteenth and early nineteenth centuries, the Sibao book merchants worked to keep costs as low as possible; the "mansions" they built and the "fertile fields" they purchased might not have been affordable had they had to employ agents and middlemen. In short, their reliance on personal networks of household and lineage members and Hakka migrants to contain the costs of production and marketing was necessary to make their hinterland book trade a profitable venture.

# PART II

*Sibao Imprints*

# NINE

## *The Nature and Sources of Sibao Imprints*

AS WE HAVE SEEN, the Sibao book trade, made possible by the availability of the necessary natural resources and the portability of print technology, owed much of its success to the organization of both the publishing and the bookselling sides of the business. The reliance on household labor, the system of inheritance, the customary rules developed to regulate the publishing houses made the production side flexible and sustainable in the particular socioeconomic context of Wuge and Mawu. On the distribution and sales side, the creation of distribution routes largely through Hakka territory, the relatively centralized control of these, and the establishment of branch shops in booming hinterland or frontier areas, ensured stability and security while allowing for expansion. Despite tensions within this structure (most notably between the Sibao *shufang* and the more distant bookstores), it was strong and flexible enough to support Sibao publishing-bookselling for over two and a half centuries.

Another component in Sibao's success was the judicious choice of texts to publish. The publishing-house managers in Wuge and Mawu, familiar with the examination curriculum and *au courant* with the book trade through sojourning booksellers returning to Sibao, selected works of well-attested popularity and usefulness. This was a necessary strategy; producing sophisticated and exceptional works of presumably limited appeal would have been an unaffordable gamble. The geographical, social, and economic constraints of the Sibao industry dictated a strategy of publishing only assured bestsellers.

From our perspective, this was also a useful strategy, for it allows us to draw from an examination of Sibao's output a fuller understanding of the market for its products and the larger social and cultural impact of the Zou and Ma publishers. Sibao publication lists provide an overview of what texts were popular in south China in the late Qing and, hence, suggest the textual foundations of Chinese popular culture. Part II describes and analyzes—as far as the evidence permits—the titles the Zou and Ma published. For reasons explained in Chapter 1, it is impossible to discover in detail the contents of the Sibao book trade before the nineteenth century. In the following chapters, relying on surviving imprints, property-division documents, two account books, two title inventories, and to a much lesser degree on the genealogies and oral histories, I attempt to reconstruct as much as possible the nature of Sibao's stock in trade in the second half of the nineteenth and twentieth centuries. I also draw on extant imprints to describe the physical appearance and production quality of Sibao texts.

## Overview of Sibao's Output

The genealogies and oral traditions, although they rarely mention specific titles, do provide some clues about the general configuration of Sibao publication strategies over time. In the late seventeenth century, at the beginning of publishing in Sibao, the demands of the educational system by and large determined what was published. We may discount the legend of Zou Xuesheng's founding of the publishing trade in Wuge, but the assumption on which the story rests—that he brought woodblocks from Hangzhou to Sibao to provide educational texts for his children—remains telling. Sibao's early customers were students and teachers in local schools, both "private" family schools and academies, who needed reading primers, the Classics and commentaries on them, and history texts. The self-glorifying claims of the genealogies hardly count as solid evidence, but in the context of other, more reliable, evidence it is significant that these claims consistently link Sibao publishing to the spread of the Classics and the demands of the examination system: the publishers were answering the "extraordinarily high demand of the *shidafu*," helping to "imbue" culture and education "with the spirit of the Classics," and "assisting the empire's literati to become generals and ministers of state."[1]

Some more solid evidence confirms that educational texts, particularly the Classics with commentaries, were the focus of the early Sibao publishers. Ma Dafan's sons hired workers to cut the *Sishu jicheng* 四書集成 (Collected commentaries on the Four Books) and the *Sishu beizhi* 四書備旨 (Full purport of the Four Books) for the family *shufang* in 1683 and 1684. In business on his own after the family divided, Ma Quanheng had blocks cut for, among others, the *Sishu* (Four Books), *Shijing zhu* 詩經註 (*Classic of Songs*, with commentary), *Youxue* (*gushi qionglin*) 幼學(故事瓊林) (Treasury of allusions for young students), and *Zengguang* (*xianwen*) 增廣(賢文) (Expanded words of wisdom). Repeated printings of these texts, supplemented (albeit meagerly) by the harvest from the three *mu* (0.21 hectare) of land that was the remaining portion of his inheritance, supported his family. Roughly two decades later, in 1707, when Quanheng's family could afford to cut the blocks for the "extremely popular" *Sishu zhu daquan* 四書注大全 (Compendium of the Four Books, with commentary), it finally achieved some degree of prosperity.[2] All the core texts that sustained the family were educational works: four editions of the Four Books, the major texts of the examination system; a comprehensive compilation of commentaries on the Four Books; one edition of the *Classic of Songs*, one of the most popular of the Five Classics among examination candidates; a children's textbook; and a reading primer.[3]

Of course, the genealogy editors, eager to portray the Zou and Ma publishers as scholars and contributors to the spread of culture, might well have emphasized the publishers' production of the Classics. But the titles listed are not sophisticated or learned enough to reflect literary or scholarly glory on the Zou and Ma. To men of learning and culture, those common primers and basic examination aids would have been trivial. Moreover, common sense suggests that a focus on standard educational works was a logical choice for beginning publishers,

---

1. *FYZSZP* (1947), *j. shou*, 4b.
2. *MSDZZP* (1945), *ji* 7, 1.74a–75b.
3. See Chapter 5, pp. 164–65 and nn. 12 and 22.

particularly those isolated from major book centers and thus from sophisticated and detailed knowledge of the nuances of the Qing book market. Given the importance of literacy and the overwhelming dominance of classical studies in the educational system, the Zou and Ma printers could count on a large and steady demand for reading primers and the Classics. And, if the decisions of Ma Quanheng were typical, beginning publishers also chose to print textbooks requiring limited capital outlay. With the possible exception of the *Sishu zhu daquan*, all of Ma's imprints were relatively *short* popular textbooks (and *Zengguang xianwen* was very short) which could be cut quickly and relatively cheaply—and then transported in large quantities. Investment in the production of such texts, particularly where labor costs were low and raw materials easy to hand, almost ensured safe and steady returns, if not enormous profit.

Such works remained the staples of the Sibao book trade for most of its history, certainly through the eighteenth and nineteenth centuries and until the abolition of the examination system in 1905. In the late 1870s Yang Lan attributed the success of the industry to its production of these ever-popular texts: "the texts required by students of the Classics and model examination essays" ( 經生應用典籍以及課藝應試 之文).[4] Oral tradition reinforces this reconstruction of Sibao production strategy: informants report that not only did the earliest printers focus primarily on primers and the Classics, but each new shop, whatever the date of its founding, began by accumulating a stock of such texts, whose assured popularity guaranteed at least a stable income.[5] Presumably this practice was not forbidden by the *cangban suoyou*, the local "copyright" regulation.

Very early on, however, as certain printing shops became more prosperous, they could afford to expand and to develop a somewhat more adventuresome publication list. Basic primers, textbooks, and

---

4. Yang Lan, *Linting huikao*, 4.8a.

5. Even after Sibao *publishing* declined in the Republican era, Sibao *booksellers* still specialized in educational texts—although these were now lithographic editions, from Fuzhou and Xiamen, of modern middle- and high-school textbooks, not the old primers. See the discussion of the inventory of the Qiongji (tang or lou) and Yijing tang in Chapter 7, pp. 259–60.

editions of the Four Books formed the bedrock of their business, but they also produced a range of supplemental educational works and somewhat more sophisticated aids to examination study, namely, encyclopedias of classical allusions, collections of examination essays, and dictionaries. They also published in a wide range of other genres—household encyclopedias, etiquette manuals, fortune-telling handbooks, medical and prescription guides, fiction, songbooks, and prose and poetry collections. None of the publishing houses seems to have specialized in any particular genre, although some might fail to move beyond production for the basic educational market.

Location also affected the range and types of works the Zou and Ma published. Distant from cultural centers, in a region never noted for famous writers or literary output, they were not in a position to publish the latest elite scholarly works or fashionable poetry collections (whereas they did have access to news of the examination curriculum in Tingzhou, the nearby prefectural city and site of an examination compound). To be sure, the itinerant booksellers and branch store operators, particularly those in important cities like Suzhou, Hangzhou, Wenzhou, Chaozhou, Guangzhou, and Wuchang, provided new titles from time to time—presumably that was one of the advantages of the Zou and Ma publishers' control over their booksellers. But they still could not compete with urban publishers in their access to new manuscripts and important living authors. Thus all their circumstances—social, economic, geographic—were conducive to a reliance on old classics (in whatever genre), replenished from time to time with relatively new but already well-received titles—permanent bestsellers, as it were.

## The Sources of Sibao Texts

Where did the Sibao publishers get their texts? Doubtless many were simply copied from editions published elsewhere purchased by booksellers in the course of their business sojourns, brought back to Sibao, recopied and the blocks cut anew (or cut from the purchased text, as a facsimile), with the name of a Zou or Ma shop replacing that of the original publisher. (Toward the end of Sibao publishing, publishers in Sibao often did not bother to replace the previous *shufang* name with their own.) Some shops exchanged blocks with other publishers by agreement, such as the arrangement between the Linlan tang and a Foshan publisher or that between the Wenhai lou and the Lianyuan ge of Foshan.[6] Such agreements, with publishing houses in a more active and centrally located publishing community, were one way for Sibao printers to acquire new texts. And publishing houses did, as custom allowed, sometimes purchase blocks from other shops.[7]

But in addition to appropriating texts and exchanging and purchasing blocks, the Zou and Ma also composed or compiled texts themselves and purchased or commissioned manuscripts from men who may have made a living writing and editing. Contemporary informants attribute many of the etiquette guides and household manuals to the Zou and Ma publishing house managers themselves. On sensing a demand for new titles in these categories, it was said, they would invite members of the local literati to tea, encourage them to converse on household management, family ritual, or the etiquette of daily life, assiduously take notes, and then write these notes up into full texts that would list the publisher as "author" or "compiler."[8] That occasionally members of the lineages actually authored, edited, or compiled texts, usually household manuals of some sort or editions of the Classics, is attested in the genealogies and in a few Sibao texts. Zou Qian 汧 (1627–99), for example, is said to have compiled a collection of letters of famous men, the *Gujin minggong chidu* 古今名公尺牘 (Model correspondence from notable men of ancient and modern times; 5 *juan*), although it is not clear whether this text was ever published.[9] The founder of one of the earliest Ma publishing houses, Ma Kuanyu, composed, compiled, or edited a considerable number of titles in various genres: an etiquette book entitled *Minggong yingchou* 名公應酬 (Models of etiquette from notable men), a correspondence guide (*Zhushu xingshi* 諸書行世 [Letters for all occasions]), a children's primer called *Xinzeng youxue* 新增幼學 (Newly expanded learning for children),[10] a children's history textbook,

---

6. See Chapter 3, p. 101, and Chapter 7, p. 259.

7. See Chapter 5, p. 179.

8. Interview 1, 10/27/93 (Wuge). The same informant claimed that the publishers might also eavesdrop on and record the conversations of scholars while they were smoking opium!

9. *MTLZXZSZP* (1911), 6.40a–41b; 20.3ab.

10. This text might also be an early edition of *Youxue gushi qionglin*.

a collection of classical allusions titled *Jingshi diangu* 經史典故 (Allusions from the Classics and histories), a collection of ancient-style prose writing, and what appear to be two almanacs with advice on how to accumulate good fortune, *Cui Fu tongshu* 崔福通書 (Cui Fu's almanac) and *Luchuan tongshu* 爐傳通書 (Almanac transmitted by the stove god).[11]

The one Sibao publisher/editor to achieve some renown was Zou Shengmai, a member of one of the most prolific of Sibao's publishing-bookselling families (see Appendix C3). He, with his son and grandsons,[12] is credited with compiling the *Wujing beizhi* 五經備旨 (Full purport of the Five Classics), a compendium of commentaries to the Five Classics that achieved considerable popularity, and an edition of the famous drama *Xixiang ji* 西廂記 (Record of the western chamber). He also "expanded and supplemented" (*zengbu* 增補) the very popular children's encyclopedia *Youxue gushi qionglin*, which was edited by his son Zou Tingyou and a relation by marriage, Xie Meilin 謝梅林. This text remained a staple of Sibao publishing throughout the history of the industry.[13] Shengmai also produced two rather fine works of calligraphy, reproducing a variety of moral texts and personal writings to display his skill in this premier literati art. His descendants continued editing, without, however, achieving even his limited degree of fame. His eldest son, Fei 斐 (1712–83),[14] as discussed below, seems to have focused on editing classical texts. His second son, Tingyou, worked in various genres, not only aiding his father with the *Wujing beishi* and the *Youxue gushi qionglin* but also compiling, with his son Jingyang 景揚 (1744–1809), a collection of *duilian* 對聯, or parallel rhymed couplets commonly written to celebrate holidays, special social occasions, and major rites of passage. Zou Jingyang went on to compile one of Sibao's bestselling household encyclopedias, *Choushi jinnang* 酬世錦囊 (Precious guide to social exchange).

The genealogies refer to many other lineage members who, having abandoned study of the examinations, turned to editing, revising,

---

11. *MSDZZP* (1945), 3.92b–93a. In translating *Jingshi diangu*, I am reading *Jingli* 經吏 as an error for *Jingshi*.
12. *MTLZXZSZP* (1911), 8.11b–12b.
13. Zou Chunsheng, "*Youxue qionglin* zengbuzhe Zou Shengmai," pp. 115–16, 119.
14. *MTLZXZSZP* (1911), 8.76a–77b.

"correcting," and proofreading texts for their own or other Sibao publishing houses. Ma Dayou "was fond of the Four Books and Five Classics and all such texts and corrected their errors so that he could publish them throughout the world" (手訂差額刊以行世).[15] Zou Fei "corrected the errors of the Four Books and Five Classics and published them for circulation throughout the world."[16] Zou Zheng'e 徵莪 (b. 1762?), too, is praised for his efforts in "collating and comparing" (*jiaokan* 校勘) to ensure accuracy in the works he published.[17] Zou Mo 謨 (1721–1805), the son of a bookseller in Guangdong, "had no rest during the day, collating the Classics and analyzing the histories (*jiao jing fen shi* 校經分史)," and was so busy that "his hands never stopped." He was also noted, according to his biography, for composing (*zhu* 著, but more likely editing) a series of works on poetry, *Shijing niti* 詩經擬題 (Model essays on the *Classic of Songs*), *Shixue hanying* 詩學含英 (Beauties of poetry study), *Shiyun hanying* 詩韻含英 (Beauties of poetry rhymes), and *Tangshi hexuan* 唐詩合選 (Combined selections of Tang poetry).[18] After failing at the examinations, Zou Tingzhong 廷忠 (1721–1807) also took to "writing his views and publishing texts in order to expand [the number of] texts of culture." He is said to have produced *Sishu beizhi tiqiao* 四書備旨題竅 (Full purport and explication of the subtleties of the Four Books), *Wujing pangxun tizhi* 五經旁訓題旨 (The Five Classics, with sideline explanations), *Tangshi heyun* 唐詩合韻 (Combined rhymes of Tang poetry), *Choushi hebi* 酬世合璧 (Combined treasures of etiquette), all texts that "circulated throughout the whole empire, nowhere failing to achieve popularity."[19] Zou Pinghan 屏翰 also compiled a rhymed-couplet collection, the *Duilian daquan* 對聯大全 (Compendium of rhymed couplets), which survives in a Sibao edition of 1884.

---

15. *MSDZZP* (1945), 3.100b–101a; *ji* 7, 1.27a–28b; and *ji* 8, 1.79b.
16. *MTLZXZSZP* (1911), 20.26b.
17. Ibid., 19.16b.
18. Ibid., 20.29b. This is probably the *Tangshi hexuan xiangjie* 唐詩合選詳解 (Combined selections of Tang poetry, with detailed explanations). Liu Wenwei 劉文蔚 (fl. mid- to late eighteenth century) is listed as the compiler of *Shixue hanying* (preface dated to 1772) and as a participant in the compilation of the *Tangshi hexuan xiangjie* in Wu Hongyi, ed., *Qingdai shihua zhijian lu*, p. 619. Zou Mo was probably merely an editor of these texts.
19. *MTLZXZSZP* (1911), 20.44b.

Thus publishers with the requisite learning might themselves edit and adapt—correct, expand, and/or supplement—certain established texts and even compose new texts to be published by the Zou and Ma shops. Since many of the titles attributed to Zou or Ma authors do not survive, we cannot judge their originality. But from the few works that do survive, we can surmise that authorship here meant, for the most part, editing, rearranging, selecting, and/or supplementing (with text or with notes and commentaries) rather than composing a wholly new work.

These efforts might genuinely enhance a useful but slightly outdated or inadequately developed text. Zou Shengmai's expansion of *Youxue gushi qionglin* is a good example; his additions do improve the text, and even modern versions note his contribution. And Ma Kuanyu's editing of an anthology of ancient-style prose adds useful historical and biographical data to the *Guwen xiyi* 古文析義 (Elucidation of ancient-style prose), with annotations by Lin Yunming 林雲銘 (*js* 1658) (see Chapter 10). But revisions could also be merely cosmetic—very lightly augmenting or re-editing an established title in hopes of increasing sales. Sometimes virtually the same text was issued under two different cover-page titles. For example, the *Xinding Sishu buzhu beizhi* 新訂四書補注備旨 (New revised *Full Purport of the Four Books*, supplemented with commentary) and the *Sishu buzhu beizhi tiqiao huican* 四書補註備旨題竅匯參 (Collation of the full purport and explication of the subtleties of the Four Books, supplemented with commentary), both attributed to the Hongwu-era (1368–98) official Deng Lin 鄧林 and sharing the same size and format, have virtually identical contents.

And many Sibao-authored texts were pastiches of other texts under new titles. On occasion the Sibao "authors" acknowledge the multiple sources of their texts. Zou Jingyang explains, in the preface to his collection of rhymed couplets, that it is composed of parallel couplets that he and his father gathered on their travels as sojourning booksellers;[20] and he describes compiling *Choushi jinnang* from excerpts from "a shelf-ful of books" and "miscellaneous jottings" made during his return from a trip to Beijing ("Xu," 1a).

---

20. "Xu," 1a, in *Caiji xinlian tuzhang jiaju* 採輯新聯圖章佳句 (Selected new beautiful phrases for couplets and seals). See Chapter 11, p. 424.

None of these men, then, were authors in the modern sense. They edited existing texts and/or compiled pastiches or, at most, contributed some essays on proper ritual or added notes and explanations to pre-existing collections. In this, of course, they were not unusual; a great number of Chinese texts were cut-and-paste productions, miscellanies of excerpts from other texts, usually unattributed. Often, too, texts were group efforts; the *Wujing beizhi*, for example, lists Zou Shengmai as responsible for *zuanji* 纂輯, "compiling," Zou Tingyou for *bianci* 編次, "arranging the order," and Zou Jingyang (and his brothers Jing-hong 景鴻 [1750–?] and Jingzhang 景章 [1759–?]) for *ding* 訂, "editing" or "correcting," the work. (In certain texts the precise function of each contributor is not clear.) The very different conception of authorship—or even of the book—makes it difficult at times to answer modern bibliographical questions about Sibao imprints.[21]

It is likely that the publishers drew on their immediate community not only for editorial skills but also for the expertise of lineage members in a range of specialties. Almost all the subjects of genealogy biographies are credited with skill in examination subjects—they were able to absorb the meaning of a text by just skimming the pages, they excelled in poetry recitation, and so forth. But some are credited with particular areas of talent and knowledge. Zou Chun 春 (1749–?), Fei's son, was noted for his knowledge of calligraphy, poetry, and the art of correspondence (*chidu* 尺牘).[22] Zou Tinglu's 廷爐 (1722–1808) notes on the Classics were treasured by his descendants;[23] and Ma Xianzuo 賢佐 (d. 1864?) was said to know everything about commentaries to the Classics—"there was no interlinear commentary, no note, no instruction to any of the Classics or any of the teachings of the Confucians with which he was unfamiliar."[24] Ma Yuanbi 源辟 (fl. nineteenth c.) was an authority on the rituals of social exchange (*yingchou* 應酬) and even produced a manuscript on this subject.[25] Others were expert in *fengshui*.

--------

21. See Brokaw, "On the History of the Book in China," pp. 19–20; for a brief discussion of a similar phenomenon in Europe, see Michel Foucault, "What Is an Author?" pp. 148–50.

22. *MTLZXZSZP* (1911), 8.103b–4a, 20.64a.

23. Ibid., 12.27a–28a, 20.28ab.

24. *MSDZZP* (1945), 1.77b.

25. Ibid., 1.69b–70a.

In the field of medicine in particular, the Zou and Ma had many experts to hand, as this seems to have been a popular alternative to examination study and publishing. Ma Longjin 隆晉 (fl. early nineteenth c.?) became a specialist in pulse analysis,[26] Zou Bingchun (also a bookseller and publisher) in acupuncture,[27] and Zou Xibao 希寶 (1847–96) in pediatrics.[28] Although none of these men seem to have compiled or edited any of the medical texts published in Sibao,[29] it is certainly possible that the physicians and medically knowledgeable family members acted as "acquisitions editors." Zou Bingchun, for example, would inevitably have brought his medical training to bear in selecting medical manuscripts for publication, and Zou Shengrui 聖瑞 (1694–1753), a physician, would likely have advised his brother, the publisher Zou Shengmai, in the selection of medical publications.[30] Indeed, many of the works that Sibao produced might well have been identical or similar to those used by the Zou and Ma physicians in training or practice. The genealogies record that Zou and Ma physicians studied such medical classics as the *Suwen*, *Lingshu*, Zhang Ji's 張機 (150–214) *Jingui yuhan yaoliie* 金匱玉函要略 (Summary of precious secrets), Wang Shuhe's 王叔和 (210–285) *Maijue* 脈訣 (Secrets of the pulse), the writings of the Jin physician Li Gao 李杲 (1180–1251) on drug therapy and digestion, and *Tangye* 湯液 (Prescriptions for decoctions)—all of which were published in Sibao editions.[31]

Finally, the Sibao publishers relied not only on knowledgeable family members but also on contacts with local and regional literati who might

26. Ibid., *ji* 7, 1.69a.

27. *FYZSZP* (1947), 33.39a–40a.

28. Ibid., 33.94a–95b.

29. Ma Heling 馬鶴齡 was said to have been the author of a medical text, the *Jiyan yian* 集驗醫案 (Collected experiences of medical cases), although there is no evidence that it was ever published by Sibao or any other printers. *MSDZZP* (1945), 1.69a.

30. *MTLZXZSZP* (1911), 20.17b–18a. There are a few other examples of close relationships between physicians and publishers: Zou Yuting 裕亭 was a physician whose sons were book merchants in Guangdong (ibid., 20.37ab); Zou Huiyue 徽躍 became a physician after working at the family profession of bookselling, also in Guangdong (ibid., 20.54ab); and Zou Huilong 惠龍 (1787–1877) appears to have been another publisher, like Zou Bingchun, with an interest in medicine (ibid., 9b.44a–46a, 20.85a).

31. See *MSDZZP* (1945), *ji* 7, 1.85ab; *MTLZXZSZP* (1911), 20.30b; and *FYZSZP* (1947), 33.46ab, 94a–95b.

act as editors, compilers, annotators, or authors. They employed (or, as the genealogies put it, "invited") local scholars to work in Sibao on specific projects. Wu Dajin 伍大縉 of Ninghua explains in the Zou genealogy that he worked "day and night" in Wuge in 1803, writing the commentary to be included in the *Sishu hejie* 四書合解 (Combined explanations of the Four Books).[32] Although Tingzhou produced few famous scholars or writers, with the proliferation of academies there in the eighteenth century, it could offer at least a steady supply of aspirants and lower-degree holders who might be employed by the Zou and Ma publishers to annotate and edit texts.

Other contributors seem to have been contacts made on the road: prefaces to some Sibao publications suggest that Zou and Ma traveling booksellers sought out unpublished texts for publication and commissioned prefaces for these texts among the literati and lower-level officials they met along their routes. The 1810 preface to *Huizuan Jiali tieshi jiyao* 彙纂家禮帖式集要 (Collected essentials of family rituals and model forms), by one Liao Tianjie 廖天杰, who identifies himself as a disciple of the author, Jiang Haoran 江浩然 of Zhangzhou, explains that Haoran's son, Jiang Jianzi 健資, had "followed his father's wishes and made [his teachings] into a book." This work—the *Huizuan Jiali tieshi jiyao*—originally circulated in manuscript and was frequently copied for broader circulation, becoming so popular that "the price of paper . . . rose."[33] Then it happened that a "guest from Tingzhou (*ke cong Ting lai* 客從汀來) came to pay his respects as a student and read the text"[34] and "wanted to purchase it [for publication], so as to earn heavy profits. He asked Jianzi to turn the text over to him so that printing blocks could be carved." Jianzi agreed, piously explaining that he wished his father's teachings to be widely disseminated. The "guest" asked Liao to write a preface ("Xu," 2a).

The Jiang family seems to have developed a special relationship with these "guests" from Tingzhou, almost certainly sojourning book mer-

---

32. *MTLZXZSZP* (1911), 20.48ab.

33. Literally, "nowhere did the price of paper not rise in Luoyang," the *chengyu* 紙貴 洛陽.

34. "Came to pay his respects as a student" is, literally, "paid a visit to the red curtain," *ye jiangzhang* 謁絳帳, a reference to the teaching of the famous Han-dynasty scholar Ma Rong 馬融.

chants from Sibao itself. Jiang Haoran is credited with editing a collection of Du Fu's poetry and, with his son, with the compilation of a collection of rhymed couplets, *Qiaozi xiulin* 橋梓繡林 (A father and son's embroidered forest), also published in Sibao. Its preface, dated 1811 and written by one Shen Baoshan 沈寶山 of Xinhui 新會 (Guangdong), reports that "a friend from Ting" (*Ting you* 汀友) had brought him the text and asked him to supply a preface. In this preface, Shen refers to *Huizuan Jiali tieshi jiyao*, adducing it as evidence of the Jiangs, command of family rituals and the rules of social interaction ("Xu," 1b–2a).

These comments, although too meager to be conclusive, indicate that it is possible that, as suggested in Chapter 7, the functions of Zou and Ma traveling merchants included not only the sale of Sibao publications but also the discovery and perhaps commissioning of new texts for publication in Sibao. The "guest" and "friend" from Tingzhou, whether they were Sibao publishers or their intermediaries, appear to have developed a small network of contacts—with the Jiang family, which seems to have specialized in the production of household manuals and rhymed-couplet collections, and with local scholars (Liao and Shen) willing to write prefaces to these productions. The polite language employed to describe the relationships between these men reveals the social dynamics at work: the merchants, lower in status than the literatus Jiang, came as "students" to learn from a teacher. At the same time it conceals the financial reality of the relationship: the merchant "guests" paid Jiang for the manuscript (and doubtless Liao and Shen for the prefaces as well). In acquiring texts as in selling them, the education of the merchants doubtless stood them in good stead, for it made their contacts with such literati (and would-be literati) along their routes much smoother, as long as they approached these men of higher status with suitable humility and respect. It was probably a relatively simple matter for a bookseller like Zou Qicui, who had earned the respect of the "worthies and gentlemen" along his routes with his "air of a Confucian scholar," to persuade his literati customers (or "hosts" and "friends," as the prefaces cited above would have it) to pass new manuscripts on to him.

Not surprisingly, Sibao publishers tended to publish works by southern Chinese authors. Many of the extant Sibao imprints were written, edited, or annotated by scholars from Fujian or neighboring Jiangxi and Guangdong. The popular medical writers Deng Liu 鄧旒 (1774–1842) and Chen Xiuyuan 陳修園 (1753–1823), both from Fujian (Shaowu and Changle, respectively), are each represented by at least two titles. One of the enduring editions of the Four Books, the *Sishu zhengwen* 四書正文 (Correct text of the Four Books), was in part the work of Yan Maoyou 顏茂猷, a late Ming scholar and *jinshi* degree holder (1634) from Fujian.[35] Sibao published ancient-style prose collections compiled in Jinxi 金谿 (Jiangxi) and several popular novels composed in Guangdong.

The Zou and Ma occasionally produced texts intended to have a limited local or regional appeal. Two texts in Hakka or the Sibao Hakka subdialect, both elementary glossaries, survive. *Renjia riyong* 人家日用 (Everyone, everyday) and *Yinian shiyong zaziwen* 一年使用雜字文 (Glossary for a year's activities) were by local men, the latter by a Wuping native. At least one popular novel published in Sibao, a fictionalized account of a Yongzheng-era *fengshui* lawsuit set in Guangdong, employs Cantonese dialect, and thus was probably of interest only to their customers in that region. And some of their songbooks seem to have been largely for local sale. But for the most part the publishers were interested in works that would appeal to the largest audience possible: standard primers and examination aids, how-to manuals, and popular fiction.

The three chapters that follow present a survey of Sibao's output for the most part from the 1840s through the early twentieth century. I have selected a few examples from the various genres of Sibao imprints to discuss in some detail (see Appendix G for a fuller list of Sibao imprints). I have tried to make the discussion proportional to the relative importance of each genre within the entirety of Sibao's repertory as we know it. Thus I devote far more space to primers than I do to editions of literary collectanea. In some respects, this effort is undercut by the uneven survival of Sibao texts: although the extant book lists suggest that the Zou and Ma published a considerable number of poetry manuals and collections, the rarity of such works among extant Sibao im-

---

35. Brokaw, *The Ledgers of Merit and Demerit*, p. 158.

prints makes it difficult to characterize them in any but the most general terms. When only titles of texts survive, I often speculate about what texts these are *likely* to have been, but the reader should be aware that, without the physical text in hand, it is impossible to do more than speculate about a work's contents.

As explained in Chapter 1, most extant imprints date from the period of Sibao's decline. The majority of the texts I describe are not finely produced (although there are certainly exceptions, that is, texts that are large, well cut, and clearly printed), but these may not be representative of Sibao's output in the industry's glory days. Although the booksellers' choice of markets suggests that they produced many inexpensive (and thus probably poorly produced) texts for a not very wealthy or discriminating hinterland readership even at the height of the trade, there is virtually no material evidence to support this supposition. Thus the conclusions that I draw about the physical qualities of Sibao's output are applicable only to the last several decades of Sibao's publishing history, from the mid-nineteenth through the early twentieth century.

This survey of Sibao texts is divided into three parts. Chapter 10 describes the types of texts that were the staples of the business, educational texts and reference aids for students of all levels. Chapter 11 is devoted to how-to manuals, the practical guides to family and community ritual, the cure of disease, and the manipulation of fate that form perhaps the next largest share of Sibao's stock. Finally, in Chapter 12, I turn to the popular fiction, songbooks, and belles-lettres texts published as the Sibao publishers expanded production. This division is by no means perfect.[36] Some texts might fit in either category; certain poetry collections, for example, although a necessary part of examination study, might also be read for entertainment and aesthetic pleasure. Conversely, historical fiction, which I have placed in the category of "entertainment literature," was often written as a vehicle of popular

---

36. I have chosen not to follow the traditional *siku* 四庫 ("four treasuries") classification, since that method sometimes groups together, for largely formal reasons, texts that show striking differences (*leishu* provide the best example). My classification roughly follows that employed in the Cuiyun tang inventory, suggesting that the Sibao publishers themselves had a somewhat similar view of the natural groupings of their products.

historical and moral instruction.[37] As we know almost nothing about how the texts were actually read, this essentially functional division relies on interpretations of producers' intentions rather than consumers' responses.

But this method of categorization has the advantage, first, of emphasizing the centrality of educational texts to the Sibao business and, second, of allowing a fairly consistent and coherent consideration of intended readership. By drawing on contemporary accounts of education and reading habits and informants' descriptions of local reading practices, I try to suggest, too, something of the context in which these various texts were most likely used and read. Finally, in Chapter 13, the conclusion to Part II, I use information about the prices of Sibao texts and their production quality to speculate about the consumers of these texts and draw on the characterization of Sibao's stock in Chapters 10 through 12 to devise a "Sibao model" of popular textual culture in the late Qing.

---

37. Idema, *Chinese Vernacular Fiction*, pp. xxiii–xxxii.

# TEN

## *Educational Works*

EDUCATIONAL IMPRINTS were the staples of the Sibao publishing-bookselling industry, arguably the texts that ensured its survival through two and a half centuries. Certainly it is no accident that the decline of the Sibao business coincided with the demise of the old educational system, the abolition of the civil-service examinations, and the reform of the curriculum. With the introduction of new textbooks under the Republic, the demand for the type of educational texts published in Sibao plummeted.

But before then, the relative stability of the basic educational curriculum favored small-scale operations such as those found in Sibao. In the Yuan and early Ming, the earlier stages of education were dominated by a limited set of core texts: a set of basic primers, usually the "San-Bai-Qian" 三百千 (that is, the *Sanzi jing* 三字經, or Three-character classic; *Baijia xing* 百家姓, or Myriad family names; and *Qianzi wen* 千字文, or Thousand-character essay), and the Four Books and Five Classics, with the appropriate commentaries.[1] By the early fourteenth century, the Four Books with the Cheng-Zhu commentaries had been designated the focus of classical study within the examination

---

1. Pei-yi Wu, "Education of Children in the Sung," pp. 309, 321–24. For a discussion of the range of texts available before the late Ming, see Limin Bai, *Shaping the Ideal Child*, pp. 21–45.

system.[2] And in the early fifteenth century, government-sanctioned compendia (*daquan* 大全) of the Four Books and the Five Classics and their standard Cheng-Zhu commentaries were produced as comprehensive guides to examination study.[3] More advanced students were also expected to master at least some of the histories and other major works of the tradition, but the Classics, and most particularly the Four Books, remained the core of the curriculum.

The Four Books and their standard commentaries remained the heart of education throughout the rest of the imperial period. In contrast with preceding eras, however, the late Ming and the Qing witnessed a marked increase in writings on educational theory and teaching methods, an interest in how children learn and how best to teach them, that suggests a growing professionalization among teachers. This interest spawned a flood of new primers and textbooks. A host of supplementary educational materials were created—"transitional" texts that guided the student from the basic literacy gained from reading the elementary primers to the Four Books, reference aids to the mastery of the Classics, and works that taught the rhetorical skills required for appropriate speech, good writing, or examination success.[4] Moreover, changes in examination policy, the most important of which was the reintroduction of the poetry requirement and a renewed emphasis on mastery of the Five Classics under the Qianlong emperor,[5] spurred publishers to print poetry collections, guides to writing poetry, and new aids to the Five Classics to meet the new demand from examination hopefuls.

Finally, the proliferation of schools—lineage or family schools, charitable or free elementary schools (*yixue* 義學), and academies—and the growth in the school population in the eighteenth and nineteenth

---

2. Gardner, "Principle and Pedagogy"; idem, "Transmitting the Way"; de Bary, *Neo-Confucian Orthodoxy and the Learning of the Heart-and-Mind*, pp. 1–66.

3. Wilson, *Genealogy of the Way*, pp. 54–55, 161–67; de Bary, *Neo-Confucian Orthodoxy and the Learning of the Heart-and-Mind*, pp. 164–66.

4. Ridley, "Educational Theory and Practice in Late Imperial China," p. 10. In labeling many of these texts "transitional," I am following a suggestion by Daniel Gardner.

5. Elman, *A Cultural History of Civil Examinations*, pp. 521–68.

centuries increased the demand for educational texts.[6] In 1625 Adriano de las Cortes (1580–1629) marveled at the number of schools he observed in Chaozhou and Guangzhou: "Schools are extremely numerous in China. There is not a small hamlet of twenty or forty houses that does not have its school, and no town whose streets do not have several. At almost every step, we fell upon one of them and could hear the children following the lesson by heart."[7] And once order and peace were restored to southern China in the 1680s after the turmoil of the Ming-Qing transition, the rising population and developing economy ensured the growth of schools. Sibao trade routes and branch shop sites were often located in just those areas where either new settlement or government policy had significantly increased the numbers of schools.

As we saw in Chapter 6, the Sibao booksellers were, in effect, following important routes of population migration into frontier areas in the early and mid-Qing. Many of these areas inspired imperial "civilizing" efforts, which often took the form of sponsoring the spread of educational institutions, particularly in rural areas. The first four emperors of the Qing supported the development of schools in the frontier areas of Guangxi, Yunnan, Guizhou, and Sichuan and the hinterland areas of eastern Guangdong and Hunan[8]—all, with the exception of Sichuan, sites of Sibao book sales.[9] Although Sibao publishers seem to have done relatively little business in the Pearl River Delta area around Guangzhou (where most schools in Guangdong were clustered),

---

6. Rawski, *Education and Popular Literacy*, pp. 89–92. See Leung, "Elementary Education in the Lower Yangtze Region," pp. 384–91, for a discussion of *yixue* and lineage schools.

7. De las Cortes, *Le Voyage en Chine*, p. 193.

8. Rawski, *Education and Popular Literacy*, pp. 33–34, 92–94.

9. Imperial educational policy and population increase over the course of the Qing had an obvious impact in three of these provinces. During the Qing, the number of *jinshi* per million mean population increased significantly in Guizhou, Yunnan, and Guangxi. During the Ming, Guangxi had ranked lowest of the eighteen provinces, but by the Qing it had risen to twelfth place; Guizhou rose from seventeenth to fifth; and Yunnan, from thirteenth to ninth place (see Ho Ping-ti, *The Ladder of Success in Imperial China*, p. 229). Of course, schools proliferated elsewhere as well; see Leung, "Elementary Education in the Lower Yangtze Region," pp. 386–87, 403–4, on the increase in numbers of schools (and in numbers of supplemental texts) in the Jiangnan area.

they were very active in eastern Guangdong and along the inland rivers, the former a focus of imperial efforts to establish schools from the 1720s through the 1750s, and the latter enjoying the highest concentration of schools within the province after Guangzhou prefecture.[10]

Thus Sibao's reliance on educational texts, a safe strategy in times or places of little or no growth, became a brilliant strategy—accidentally perhaps—during most of the Qing. The Zou and Ma publisher-booksellers were able to feed nicely off both the increasing demand for school texts and the proliferation of supplemental educational works. The Zou and Ma supplied the full range of educational texts, from the most elementary primers and glossaries through aids to the comprehension of the Four Books, Five Classics, and their commentaries to encyclopedias of classical allusions, collections of model examination essays, and even some of the more sophisticated texts of history, philosophy, and literature that formed the curriculum of advanced students and scholars who might already have earned licentiate or *juren* status.

Yet it is clear that they profited most from the lower-level texts. The bulk of their output was designed for use in elementary schools, the *mengguan* (either charitable schools or *yixue* 義學 or lower-level lineage or family schools), where pupils, starting around age five, learned basic reading and writing skills and, depending on their status, resources, talent, and ambition, began study of the Four Books, abridged histories, composition models, and perhaps the Five Classics.[11] Some Sibao editions of the Four Books and Five Classics and the more sophisticated works alluded to above might also be used at the next level, that of the *jingguan*, in the upper-level lineage schools or in academies devoted to the training of students who planned to sit for the examinations. At this level, students honed their writing skills, learning how to write eight-legged essays (the form required in the examinations), and engaged in deeper study of the Classics, while moving on to the standard histories and other texts. But elementary, transitional, and intermediate texts dominated Sibao's educational offerings, as we shall see.

---

10. Rawski, *Education and Popular Literacy*, pp. 93–94.

11. For summaries of the elementary curriculum, see Leung, "Elementary Education in the Lower Yangtze Region," pp. 393–98; and Wilkinson, *Chinese History: A Manual*, pp. 47–53.

In this chapter, I describe and analyze Sibao's educational offerings, while suggesting the contexts in which the various Sibao texts would have been used, in order to assess the Zou and Ma publishers' place in the world of education and examination study in the Qing. A variety of impediments confronts this effort: first, we know little about the actual use of Sibao textbooks. Thus any statements about contexts are based on what appear to have been the intended uses of the texts, deduced from their contents or prefaces. Second, there was no single standard curriculum (or even a set of standard curricula) or any standard sequence of textbooks, and the line between elementary and advanced study was fluid, drawn at different levels by different writers.[12] The proliferation of theories and methods in the Qing in particular stimulated this diversity.[13] Thus it has proved impossible to order the discussion according to a precise chronology of usage, and I have chosen a roughly topical organization: primers and glossaries; supplemental and transitional texts, which covered a range of topics; composition guides; poetry manuals and anthologies; the Four Books and Five Classics; reference works and study aids; and texts for advanced students.

Finally, the tyranny of the examination system over Chinese education as well as over studies of Chinese education often obscures the fact that not all students were studying for the examinations and not all texts were

---

12. For example, Chang Chung-li (*The Chinese Gentry*, pp. 165–66, n. 2) reports three different curricula: Yang Zhilian finished the Four Books by the age of thirteen; completed the Five Classics, the histories, and other works, and was practicing eight-legged essays by fifteen; and had earned the licentiate degree by twenty. Yang Enpei had completed the *Greater Learning, Doctrine of the Mean*, and the *Analects* by the age of nine. He then began the *Mencius, Classic of Songs, Classic of History, Classic of Changes, Record of Rites, Spring and Autumn Annals* with the *Zuo Commentary*, and a collection of ancient-prose essays. After fifteen, he learned to write examination essays and first took the *tongshi* 童試 ("youth examination" for licentiate status) at sixteen. Gu Zugao began to learn characters at five, completed the *Analects* at six, studied *Mencius* and the *Classic of Songs* at seven, the *Classic of History* and *Record of Rites* at eight, *Classic of Changes* and *Spring and Autumn Annals* at nine, a collection of ancient-prose essays at eleven, poetry-writing at twelve, and examination-essay composition at thirteen. He first attempted the *tongshi* at the age of fifteen but did not pass until he was twenty-one. For another example, see Durand, *Lettrés et pouvoirs*, p. 54.

13. See the collection of writings on teaching and education in Qing *yixue* and *jiashu*, *Lidai jiaoyu zhidu kao*, 2: 1467–536, for a sense of the range of different teaching materials and methods used.

geared to examination study. Elementary education taught many skills—reading, calligraphy, and, in some cases, arithmetic—of broad practical use for all students, even those who did not continue on to study for the examinations. For many teachers, the goal of elementary education was the inculcation of common cultural values and social rules and rituals rather than the mastery of skills and texts that might lead to examination study.[14] Many educational texts, particularly primers, "expressed the wisdom and experience of ordinary people rather than drawing only upon sources in the [Classics] and scholarly writings."[15] And some texts were intended for the specialized education of peasants or merchants. Although I have allowed the concerns of examination study to shape the organization of my analysis (just as it shaped, even dominated, education in the Qing), I also emphasize, first, that Sibao textbooks, even those explicitly directed to examination candidates, might well have been used by other students or adult readers interested in Chinese literature, culture, and history and, second, that Sibao published some textbooks designed for students outside the examination track.

## Primers and Glossaries for Beginning Students

Children's textbooks and primers for beginning learners were an important component of Sibao's book lists. All informants reported that their family publishing houses printed the *Sanzi jing*, *Baijia xing*, and *Qianzi wen*—the ubiquitous trinity of beginning readers. These texts were such guaranteed bestsellers that the rule restricting competitive printing of the same title did not apply. These texts were also perennial favorites—at the end of the Sibao trade, it was the "San-Bai-Qian," along with a few other primers, that were peddled in the villages of Fujian, Guangdong, and Guangxi.

*Sanzi jing*, *Baijia xing*, and *Qianzi wen* are so well known that they need little explanation here.[16] *Qianzi wen*, often the first text studied, consisted, as its title indicates, of 1,000 characters—all different. Organized

14. Leung, "Elementary Education in the Lower Yangtze Region," p. 396.
15. Limin Bai, *Shaping the Ideal Child*, p. 55.
16. Rawski, *Education and Popular Literacy*, pp. 47–52, 136–38; Zhang Zhigong, *Chuantong yuwen jiaoyu jiaocai lun*, pp. 16–30; and Limin Bai, *Shaping the Ideal Child*, pp. 26–29.

into four-character rhyming couplets, the text is in essence an introduction to a wide range of vocabulary words; it lists features of the natural world, important historical figures, emperors and dynasties, terms associated with self-cultivation and "taking one's place in the world," farming, study, food and drink, buildings, gardens, sacrifices, and so on, through all aspects of daily life. Although this text seems to have been popular from its creation by Zhou Xingsi 周興嗣 (?–520), its somewhat artificial construction—imposed by the constraint against repeating a character—made it valuable largely as a glossary of frequently used characters and literary allusions and as a model for calligraphy practice.

*Sanzi jing*, commonly although probably inaccurately attributed to the Song scholar Wang Yinglin 王應麟 (1223–96), is a somewhat more coherent text, approximately 1,140 characters long in the version that had become standard by the early Qing and employing about 500 different characters, which are organized into short, three-character rhyming couplets easy for children to memorize. This text, like *Qianzi wen*, provides the student with basic vocabulary, covering the topics of study, family relationships, numbers, the seasons, the six grains and types of livestock, the Classics, the periods of Chinese history, and brief biographies of famous men.[17] But unlike *Qianzi wen*, *Sanzi jing* reinforces knowledge of the basic characters most useful to a beginning learner— verbs (*you* 有, "have"; *xue* 學, "learn"; *yue* 曰, "say"), pronouns, conjunctions, and prepositions—because it repeats these essential words.[18] Even more than the *Qianzi wen*, this text emphasizes certain moral and intellectual values. The famous opening lines introduce the beginning reader to basic Neo-Confucian concepts:

17. James T. C. Liu, "The Classical Chinese Primer," p. 192. Liu cites the Japanese scholar Murakami Yoshihide's summary of the contents of the text as follows: two sentences on human nature; twenty-six on the importance of education; sixteen on filial piety; sixty-two on life in general; sixty-eight on important texts and methods of study; ninety-two on history throughout the dynasties; sixty-six encouraging study; and twenty-four explaining the goals of primary education. In sum, the student is being taught the primary values of his culture, is being given an outline of its history and great books, and—above all—is being urged to study.

18. See James T. C. Liu, "The Classical Chinese Primer," p. 192. Summarizing the work of Murakami, Liu notes that most of the characters in the text are relatively simple: characters written with from five to thirteen strokes are dominant; and only thirty-one characters in the text have more than eighteen strokes.

> Men at birth
> are naturally good.
> Their natures are much the same;
> their habits become widely different.
> If foolishly there is no teaching,
> the nature will deteriorate.[19]

—a neat capsule summary of the orthodox teaching about human nature.

*Baijia xing,* another Song product, is a list of four hundred of the most common Chinese family names in 472 characters, teaching the student new characters and providing socially useful information. Together these three books provided a "crash course" in roughly 2,000 characters, presented in an easy to memorize form; *Qianzi wen* and *Sanzi jing* also taught fundamental moral lessons and rules for proper behavior.[20] In addition, these two texts, in their emphasis on the vital importance of study—*Sanzi jing* even provides a simple overview of the standard curriculum—prepare the student for the course ahead of him.

By the early Qing, when the Sibao publishers started printing these primers, each existed in many different editions. The basic texts might be expanded or supplemented with notes; *Baijia xing* was current in many different arrangements.[21] The titles of surviving Sibao woodblocks and imprints suggest that the publishers were issuing a variety of editions—or perhaps the same text under several different titles: *Zengzhu Sanzi jing* 增註三字經 (*Three-Character Classic,* with expanded commentary; 1868), *Xinke zengbu Sanzi jing* 新刻增補三字經 (Newly published and expanded *Three-Character Classic*), *Sanzi jing zhujie beizhi* 三字經註解備旨 (Full purport of the *Three-Character Classic,* with commentary), and *Xinke zengbu Baijia xing* 新刻增補百家姓 (Newly published and expanded *Myriad Family Names*). Of these, only the *Zengzhu Sanzi jing* (see Fig. 10.1) exists in its entirety; it includes a third register of "notes" above the two registers of couplets. On the first page, this

---

19. Translation from Giles, *San Tzu Ching,* pp. 2–4.

20. Rawski, *Education and Popular Literacy,* p. 47.

21. See Zhang Zhigong, *Chuantong yuwen jiaoyu jiaocai lun,* pp. 16–29, for examples of some of these different editions.

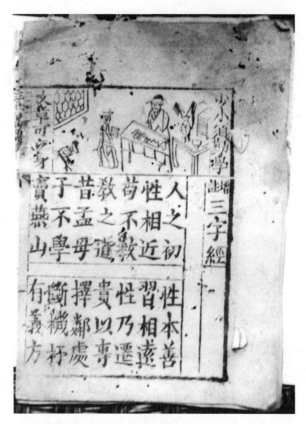

Fig. 10.1 *Zengzhu Sanzi jing* 增註三字經 (*Three-Character Classic,* with expanded commentary). The illustration and text were cut by different hands. Photograph by the author.

topmost register contains a crude picture of a schoolroom, with the teacher seated by a table stacked with books and writing materials, the student before him apparently reading an essay; on either side is a couplet from the text: "The young must diligently study" and "Writing essays is the way to establish oneself" (1a). The notes on the successive pages appear to exemplify the moral lessons of the text. Thus, a brief account of Mencius in the top register—"Mencius, given name Ke 珂, literary name Ziyu 子輿, was a man of the Warring States period. He wrote seven essays on morality, humaneness, and righteousness" (2a)— is provided presumably to demonstrate that writing essays is a good way to establish oneself; at the same time it introduces a few facts about Mencius's life.

The physical appearance of this text—its small size (14 cm h × 22 cm w),[22] its coarse and yellowed paper, and its single, crude illustration—suggests that by the late nineteenth century at least, Sibao publishers produced these texts in quantity, but at a very low quality. So, too, the only surviving Sibao edition of *Qianzi wen, Xinke zhengzihua Qianzi wen* 新刻正字畫千字文, belies its rather grand title, "*Thousand-Character Essay,* newly published with correct character strokes." This shabby booklet, probably intended as a calligraphy primer as well as a reader, lacks notes or even the single illustration that graces the opening page of the Sibao *Sanzi jing* and was part of the stock of Sibao's last book peddler in the 1930s (see Fig. 10.2).

Such texts were likely typical of primers used in most elementary schools. John Macgowan, a missionary who worked in south China in the late nineteenth and early twentieth centuries, reports that children's texts were in fact often quite shabby:

The books are printed upon the very poorest paper in order to lessen the cost. The words, too, are often blurred and indistinct, for the wooden blocks from which they are printed are generally so worn by years of use, that the delicate strokes and minute touches with the pen, and the involved and complicated interweaving of straight and waving lines that go to the making up of the [characters], get frayed and broken in the printing, so that it requires a practiced eye to distinguish some of them from others that have a natural likeness.[23]

Not surprisingly, these texts were not expensive. In the early twentieth century Sibao editions of the *Sanzi jing* and *Qianzi wen* sold wholesale for only 5 *li*, or 0.05 *qian*, each. In 1878 the retail price of a copy of the *Sanzi jing tukao* 三字經圖考 (*Three-Character Classic,* illustrated and investigated) published by the Nanjing printer of popular textbooks, Li Guangming 李光明, was 0.3 *qian*, six times that price—but Li's version

---

22. Here and elsewhere the measurements are of the block (and thus of a full folio page). The bound book would be slightly higher than the height measurement and a little more than half the width of the width measurement, since the page was always larger than the block, with a space at the top (the "heavenly head," *tiantou* 天頭) and bottom ("foot," *dijiao* 地腳). The extra paper at the sides was necessary for binding. See Chia, *Printing for Profit,* p. 43.

23. Macgowan, *Sidelights on Chinese Life,* p. 262. Macgowan, of the London Missionary Society, taught at the society's Tingzhou mission in 1899–1900.

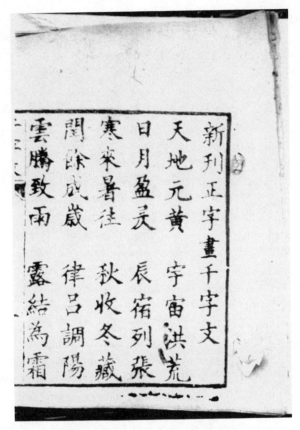

Fig. 10.2 *Xinke zhengzihua Qianzi wen* 新刊正字畫千字文 (*Thousand-Character Essay*, newly published with correct character strokes), a cheap version of *Qianzi wen* sold by Sibao book peddlers in the early twentieth century. Photograph by the author.

was much better produced, with relatively elegant illustrations.[24] The Sibao version seems to have been designed for a poorer and necessarily less demanding audience.

The "San-Bai-Qian" are by far the best known of Chinese elementary textbooks, widely used at least as late as the early twentieth century.[25] But in the Qing other beginning texts often supplemented this

---

24. Yuan Yi, "Qingdai de shuji jiaoyi ji shujia kao," p. 74.

25. These texts were commonly used in overseas Chinese communities as well; see Culin, "Popular Literature of the Chinese Laborers in the United States," pp. 57–58.

trinity. *Dizi gui* 弟子規 (Regulations for students), by the Kangxi-era scholar Li Yuxiu 李毓秀,[26] is, like *Sanzi jing*—perhaps even more than *Sanzi jing*—designed as a textbook for instruction in both reading and morality. The author, a native of Jiangzhou 絳州, Shanxi, devoted his life to teaching after failing to advance beyond licentiate status in the examinations. Very popular in the mid- and late Qing, his text is organized as an explication of a passage from the *Analects* containing Confucius's instructions to his disciples: 子曰, 弟子, 入則孝, 出則弟, 謹而信, 泛愛眾, 而親仁, 行有餘力, 則以學文 ("A youth, when at home, should be filial and, abroad, respectful to his elders. He should be earnest and truthful. He should overflow in love to all and cultivate the friendship of the good. When he has the time and opportunity, after the performance of these things, he should employ them in study").[27] This passage is explained in the primer as "*Dizi gui* is the instruction of the sage: first, you are filial to your parents and respect your elder brothers; then, you earnestly cultivate sincerity, overflow with love to the people, and befriend the benevolent; and then, if you have strength, you study texts" (弟子規, 聖人訓: 首孝弟, 次謹信, 泛愛眾, 而親仁, 有餘力, 則學文; 1a, unpaginated). The text is then divided into sections defined by phrases from the *Analects* passage, each of which explains, in simple characters and phrases (some of which are to be found in the *Analects* itself [in the following quotation, these characters are given in a different font]), the meaning of the phrase. Thus the section linked to 謹而信 ("earnest and truthful") includes the instruction 見人善, 即思齊, 總去遠, 以漸躋; 見人惡, 即內省, 有則改, 無則警 ("When you see a person who is virtuous, then think of equaling him [思齊]—even although you have far to go, gradually rise [to the task]. When you see a person who is evil, then examine yourself [內省], and if you find evil in yourself, change it, without requiring further warning"; 4b).[28] Two of the phrases here are from the *Analects* and clearly refer to Confucius's own explanation of how one should learn from the virtues and vices of others.[29] Li also draws on the *Record of*

---

26. Han Xiduo, *Zhonghua mengxue jicheng*, p. 1086.

27. Translation, slightly modified, from Legge, *The Chinese Classics*, 1: 140.

28. See Zhang Zhigong, *Chuantong yuwen jiaoyu jiacai lun*, pp. 51–52.

29. See *Analects*, 4.17; Legge, *The Chinese Classics*, 1: 170.

*Rites* to link proper behavior—standing, walking, and sitting correctly, and so forth—to the teachings of Confucius, so that students could learn how to express their mastery of Confucian ethics in appropriate ritual form.[30]

In this text, the beginning student was encountering at least four kinds of learning: characters (a total of 1,080, although this includes repeated characters);[31] basic moral precepts and ritual prescriptions to guide his behavior in the family and the community; some of the vocabulary and teachings of the *Analects*, a text that he would study intensively in the next stage of his education; and finally, through recitation of the easy-to-remember twelve-character lines (each in four rhymed three-character phrases), the parallelism and the rhythms of the language. Like the other primers described here, the surviving Sibao edition of this text is a shabby pamphlet—not badly cut, but unillustrated, small in size (13.5 cm h × 21.5 cm w), and printed in unlined columns on cheap paper. The only embellishments to the text are the occasional brief notes enclosed in boxes extending into the space above the top frame. These guide the pronunciation of new characters or identify alternative pronunciations of familiar ones—for example, "*fen* 分 [in the sense of "lot in life"] is [pronounced in the] fourth tone." (The Sibao edition contains deviations from standard pronunciations: *geng* 更, for example, is glossed as having the same pronunciation as *gen* 根, which it does in the south.)

Another of Sibao's best-selling primers, widely popular during the Qing, was *Zengguang xianwen* 增廣賢文 (Expanded words of wisdom; or *Zengguang zhengwen* 增廣正文 [Expanded correct words]), compiled in the mid-Ming and revised repeatedly thereafter. It was considered primarily a guide to proverbs and wise sayings useful in conversation: "Read *Zengguang* and learn how to speak" summarizes the traditional view of the role of the text.[32] Two copies survive in Sibao: an edition "newly cut" in 1892 entitled *Zengguang zhengwen* (*Da Zengguang* 大增廣 on the cover page: Figs. 10.3a and b), with no reference to a publisher;

<hr />

30. Limin Bai, *Shaping the Ideal Child*, p. 81.
31. Zhang, *Chuantong yuwen jiaoyu jiaocai lun*, pp. 51–52.
32. Mao Shuiqing and Liang Yang, *Zhongguo chuantong mengxue dadian*, p. 155.

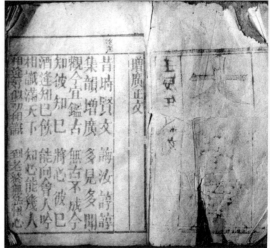

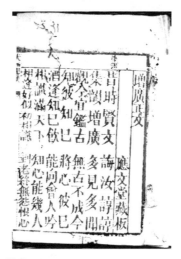

Fig. 10.3 *Zengguang zhengwen* 增廣正文 (Expanded correct words). (a, *upper left*) Cover page, which identifies the text as *Da Zengguang* 大增廣. (b, *upper right*) Title page. (c, *bottom*) Title page of edition published by the Yingwen tang 應文唐, from the same blocks as in 10.3b. Photographs by the author.

and a reprint of the same edition (that is, using the same blocks) that lacks a cover page and on the title page lists the Yingwen tang as publisher (Fig. 10.3c). In a narrow register above the two rows of text, the tones of certain characters are given. (These two copies nicely exemplify the decline of the Sibao industry: the first, with clear and well-cut characters, is a proper book, with a cover and cover page. The reprint, without cover or cover page, was peddled as a pamphlet in western Fujian in the Republican era.)

The opening lines of the text set forth its philosophy of education: "Use the great writings of the ancient sages and worthies to instruct your speech, and you will speak sincerely and precisely. Collect good phrases and rhymes, steadily increasing your store, and you will extend your experience and knowledge. To understand today, you must examine the past; without history, there is no present" (1ab). The remainder consists of a series of couplets transmitting the moral messages of the ancients; for example, "Life and death are fated; wealth and rank are decided by heaven," and "The good family teaches its sons and grandsons ritual and righteousness; the bad family teaches brutality and evil." Including sayings drawn from popular dramas and Buddhist and Daoist works, *Zengguang xianwen* has a broader scope than "Confucian" primers like *Sanzi jing* or *Dizi gui*. Limin Bai suggests that it was used primarily to teach literacy to adults or students in charitable schools (that is, those unlikely to move on to examination study).[33]

The student of this text, whatever his or her goals, was not only mastering new characters but also learning how to speak—that is, how to use set phrases and proverbs appropriately—along with conventional moral wisdom. He was beginning to learn, too, the building blocks of composition: the rhythm of phrases of equal length, rhyme, parallelism, and the association of certain characters or "tags" and sayings with specific situations, occupations, or states of mind. This inclusion of composition in elementary education is a distinctive feature of Chinese educational texts, as Benjamin Elman has pointed out. Skill in composition was a prerequisite for passage of the civil service examinations. Thus, in contrast to the primary curriculum in Europe, where the emphasis was on reading, even elementary Chinese educational texts inculcated approved writing styles.[34]

Before learning the art of composition, students had to learn to form the characters. Tracing characters from the beginning primers taught

---

33. Limin Bai, *Shaping the Ideal Child*, p. 55.
34. Elman, *A Cultural History of Civil Examinations*, pp. 276–77.

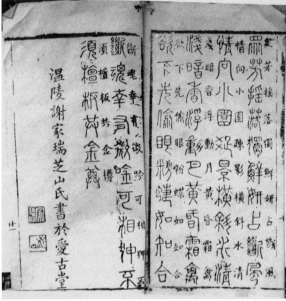

Fig. 10.4    *Longmen caofa* 龍門草法 (Gateway to successful grass script), a calligraphy manual published by the Suwei tang 素位堂. (a, *left*) Cover page. (b, *right*) Pages illustrating seal script. Photographs by the author.

students to write and simultaneously reinforced their memory of the text. Model books of calligraphy (*zitie* 字帖) might also be used, and these the Sibao publishers also produced. The *Longmen caofa* 龍門草法 (Gateway to successful grass script), for example, advertised on the cover page as a guide to "mastering the secrets of beginning study," provides (despite its title) models of both grass and seal script, with regular-script versions by the side of each character. This undated pamphlet (see Figs. 10.4a and b), a publication of the Suwei tang, is apparently a rare survivor of many ephemeral Sibao model calligraphy books.

Sibao also produced several glossaries (*zazi* 雜字), which usually present groupings of vocabulary words, but not necessarily in complete sentences or coherent rhymed phrases. Sibao seems to have specialized in a type that became popular rather late in Chinese educational history consisting of names and terms of everyday use embedded in four-, five-, or six-character rhymes. These texts often suggest a somewhat specialized occupational or regional use. Zhang Zhigong, in his study of educational texts, mentions as examples the *Shanxi zazi bidu* 山西雜字

必讀 (Essential Shanxi glossary), designed for the sons of Shanxi merchants and listing the names of products and handicrafts, and the *Shandong zhuangnong riyong zazi* 山東莊農日用雜字 (Glossary of everyday characters for Shandong farmers),[35] written for peasants and describing agricultural tools and activities.[36] This kind of glossary was usually not considered appropriate for elite students on the examination track; nor were they seen as suitable for use in charitable schools. "Generally what pertains to orthodox studies should be made primary; all *zazi* and vulgar books must not be studied," warned one such school's rules.[37] Usually cheaply printed on poor-quality paper, these pamphlet-like texts were for the use of peasants' and merchants' sons, who needed to learn only the basic vocabulary relevant to their future occupations.

Sibao, for obvious reasons, did not produce "northern" texts like the *Shanxi zazi bidu*, but published equally specialized—and equally "vulgar"—glossaries for its own particular audience.[38] For example, *Xinke Siyan zazi* 新刻四言雜字 (Newly published *Four-Word Glossary*; see Fig. 10.5),[39] surviving in Sibao in a cheaply printed and undated

---

35. Pu Songling 蒲松齡 (1640–1715) refers to a *Zhuangnong riyong zazi* 莊農日用雜字 (Glossary of everyday characters for farmers) used by peasant boys in Shandong in the early eighteenth century. See his preface to "Riyong suzi," *Pu Songling ji*, p. 733; cited in Rawski, *Education and Popular Literacy*, p. 128.

36. Zhang Zhigong (*Chuantong yuwen jiaoyu jiaocai lun*, pp. 33–36) divides glossaries into four types, the most popular of which, at least in the late imperial period, was the *zazi yunwen* 雜字韻文 (glossaries in rhyme) type. Most of the Sibao glossaries fit that category; they offer practical vocabulary, a popular (*tongsu* 通俗) writing style, and a distinctly local or regional tone.

37. *Shangrao xianzhi* (1873), 7.75ab, cited in Rawski, *Education and Popular Literacy*, p. 128; see also Limin Bai, *Shaping the Ideal Child*, pp. 167–68.

38. Sibao did produce at least one general-purpose glossary, *Xinshou Youxue qimeng tijing* 新授幼學啓蒙提徑 (*Shortcut to Children's Education*, newly published). In seven-character couplets this text introduces useful vocabulary words under twenty-four different categories. Unlike Sibao's other glossaries, the *Youxue qimeng tijing* had a moral message: study is the best of occupations, filial piety the highest of virtues, etc. The Sibao pamphlet *Xinke Jujia biyong zazi* 新刻居家必用雜字 (*Glossary Essential for Family Life*, newly cut) appears to be a cruder example of a similar general-purpose glossary.

39. This text is not the same as the better-known text of the same title, *Siyan zazi*, a longer glossary also organized into four-character clusters of characters. See Zhang Zhigong, *Chuantong yuwen jiaoyu jiaocai lun*, p. 32.

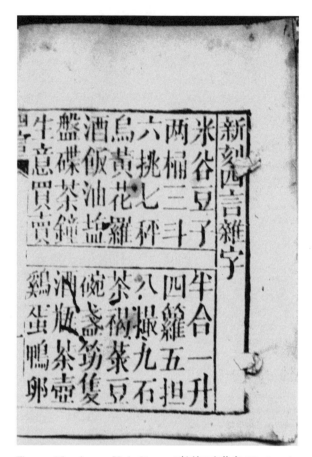

Fig. 10.5 The glossary *Xinke Siyan zazi* 新刻四言雜字 (Newly published *Four-Word Glossary*). Photograph by the author.

pamphlet, organizes vocabulary words more or less topically into four-character clusters. These clusters, whether composed of single words or two- or four-character phrases, introduce measures, foods and beverages, utensils, textiles, seasons, occupations, colors, parts of the body, family relationships, and so forth, in an almost random order. Some lines, for example, simply list items—"wine, rice, oil, salt" (*jiu fan you yan* 酒飯油鹽). Others present useful compounds or clusters of opposites—"wine bottle, tea pot" (*jiuping chahu* 酒瓶茶壺), "making a living, buying and selling" (*shengyi maimai* 生意買賣), or "thick, thin; distant, close" (*hou bo kuo xie* 厚薄濶挾). Yet others offer full phrases—"fair exchange" (*gongping jiaoyi* 公平交易) or "miscellaneous goods store" (*zahuo dianfang* 雜貨店房). Like most glossaries, this text does not bear the mark of the examination curriculum; unlike *Sanzi jing* and *Qianzi wen*, it contains no allusions to study or the Classics. It seems, in fact, an introduction to the vocabulary of the everyday life of ordinary people. If it has an orientation, it is toward merchants and commercial exchange, for many of the entries reproduce vocabulary about weights and measures, types of products, occupations, processes of exchange, and the tools of calculation basic to trade—even its rare moral references, such as to "fair exchange," are put in a commercial context.

Two other glossaries, *Renjia riyong* and *Yinian shiyong zaziwen*, in somewhat different ways also imply a specialized use. Presumably intended largely for sale within Tingzhou, the vocabulary they teach includes words from the Sibao or Tingzhou Hakka sub-dialects. The *Xinzeng zazi Renjia riyong* 新增雜字人家日用 (*Everyone, Everyday*, newly expanded glossary; 1922; see Figs. 10.6a and b), for example, is in many ways a conventional glossary, providing lists of plants, trees, famous products (Shaoxing wine, for example), animals, parts of the body, administrative units, measures, utensils, the provinces, family relations, and so forth, in four-character couplets. More comprehensive than the *Xinke Siyan zazi*, this text is advertised on the cover page as an "Expanded and illustrated easy-to-read glossary of all things" (*jiazeng huayang zhuwu zazi bianlan* 加增畫樣諸物雜字便覽). If the *Siyan zazi* contains a slight mercantile bent, the *Renjia riyong* is oriented toward agriculture, with lists of crops, livestock, and agricultural implements and activities predominating in the long catalogue of phrases. The local character of the text is revealed in the distinctive Sibao-*hua* terms used to name certain utensils and tools—a candleholder, bamboo basket, wooden pot, and the like (8b, 12b–13a). And after lists of the provinces of China and the prefectures of Fujian comes a list of the eight counties of "our prefecture," Tingzhou, revealing that this work was intended for use within Minxi (see Fig. 10.6b). A slightly more elaborate production than the *Zengbu Sanzi jing* described above, this small text (12.3 cm h × 21 cm w) is printed in four registers, two narrow bands above two registers of text. The top two registers supplement the well-cut glossary below with new characters illustrated with crude pictures; each narrow

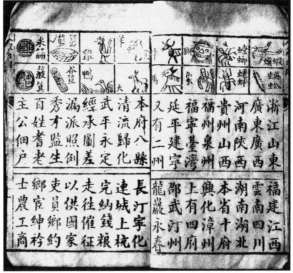

Fig. 10.6 *Xinzeng zazi Renjia riyong* 新增雜字人家日用 (*Everyone, Everyday*, newly expanded glossary), published by the Linlan yiji shuju 林蘭儀記書局 of Shanghang in 1922. (a, *top*) Cover page. (b, *bottom*) Pages from *Renjia riyong*, the second page lists the eight counties of "this prefecture" (*benfu* 本府), Tingzhou. The objects pictured and identified at the top supplement the text below. Photographs by the author.

band is divided into four picture boxes, for a total of eight pictures per half-folio page.[40] Published by the Linlan yiji shuju 林蘭儀記書局 of Shanghang,[41] one of the few Sibao shops to survive well into the twentieth century, the late publication date of this text suggests that there was still a market for such specialized glossaries in Minxi long after the establishment of the new schools and new textbooks.

The second distinctively Hakka glossary is the *Yinian shiyong zaziwen*, written by a Lin Liangfeng 林梁峰 (fl. late seventeenth–early eighteenth century) from Wuping county, Tingzhou. Although this text first circulated locally in Wuping in the Kangxi era, its value as a Hakka primer ensured its popularity—"Lose one thousand ounces of silver, but never lose *Zazi*" was a local saying—and it was eventually taken up by the Sibao publishers and sold more widely throughout Tingzhou.[42] Indeed, it was still being printed in the early twentieth century—an edition of the Ma family Linlan tang still survives from that period. As its title suggests, this work takes the student through one year, outlining, in simple vocabulary (with some distinctively Hakka phrases) and seven-character rhymes, the activities associated with each month or important event. Thus, in the first month, "On the third and fourth day, pay the New Year's calls / go to the home of one's son-in-law / or invite the new relatives to come to visit—/ father-in-law, brother-in-law, and nephew."

This text assumes rural readers familiar with the rhythms of peasant life, and much of it describes the agricultural schedule. Thus, for example, "In the fourth month, at the beginning of summer, as the days grow longer, / go out early to prepare the fields, / tracing the lines to plant the rice; / men and women, young and old, all get up early." But there are also references to crafts, in particular the craft of metalworking that was, indeed, common among the Hakka of Tingzhou. And unlike the two texts just discussed, the *Yinian shiyong zazi* devotes some attention to study and the progress of the scholar, beginning with

---

40. As with the *Zengzhu Sanzi jing* in Fig. 10.1, there is a sharp contrast between the clumsiness of the illustration and the clarity of the characters. See Chapter 3, p. 100.

41. Other versions survive as well, for example, a 1910 edition published by the Linlan tang; this text is not illustrated.

42. Xie Shuishun and Li Ting, *Fujian gudai keshu*, p. 468.

"backing the book" (reciting the *Sanzi jing* from memory), practicing writing, studying the Four Books and Five Classics, entering the *jingguan*, where "mornings one explicates texts, and afternoons thinks / and deep into the still of the night, reads essays," sitting for the county and pre-fectural examinations (with members of one's extended family eagerly awaiting the results), all the way through attaining first place in the pal-ace examination and admission into the Hanlin Academy. At that point Lin concisely remarks, "This is why study is of first importance—it is like climbing the steps to heaven."

This is a more difficult text than either the *Zengbu Siyan zazi* or the *Xinzeng zazi Renjia riyong*; at twenty-three-and-a-half folio pages, it is longer, and its use of six-to-seven-character phrases makes it grammati-cally more complex. It is not, in fact, a true glossary, because it does considerably more than simply list vocabulary in rhymed phrases—it presents, rather, a continuous narrative that requires a level of linguistic sophistication missing from the collection of disjointed clusters of characters that constitute the glossaries and some other primers (*Qianzi wen*, for example). And its longer phrases tax the memory more than does the *Sanzi jing*. Still, its rhymes—and its focus on the mundane ac-tivities of rural life presumably familiar to its readers—must have made it easy to remember.

The primers and even some of the glossaries in common use in ele-mentary education taught ethical and cultural values as well as character recognition. In the late Ming and Qing, the curriculum might also in-clude more direct moral instruction in the form of morality books, which taught that the gods rewarded good deeds (particularly those done in secret) and punished bad ones. *Yifang xunzi* 義方訓子 (In-structing sons in righteous behavior, 1901), for example, is a work de-signed first and foremost for moral instruction. Printed in Jiantou, a vil-lage bordering on Wuge, it includes songs celebrating industry and thrift, a series of three-character couplets on proper relations within the family and society, the text of the Yongzheng emperor's *Shengwu guang-xun* 聖諭廣訓 (Amplified instructions on the Sacred Edit), and two sets of seven-character phrases explaining "The ten marks of good for-tune of a successful family" and "The ten marks of poverty of a failed family." Sibao also produced a compact joint edition (14+ cm h × 20.5

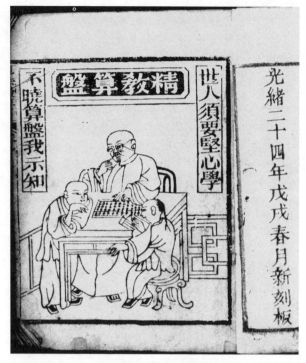

Fig. 10.7 Page from *Suanfa cuoyao* 算法撮要 (Essentials of calculation). Photograph by the author.

cm w) of two of the shortest and best-known morality books, the
*Yinzhi wen* 陰騭文 (Rewards for secret merit) and *Ganying pian* 感應篇
(Tract on action and response), that might well have been intended for
elementary students, as well as a few longer works that would have
provided teachers with numerous tales of supernatural retribution to
read to their students as a spur to good behavior.[43]

Sibao also published at least one primer for the abacus, the *Suanfa
cuoyao* 算法撮要 (Essentials of calculation; preface dated 1896). This
neatly cut little text, printed on coarse paper, is embellished with a well-
executed full-page illustration of a bespectacled teacher seated at a desk,
teaching two eager pupils (one of whom holds a copy of a text, presumably the *Suanfa cuoyao*) how to use an abacus (see Fig. 10.7). This

---

43. Leung, "Elementary Education in the Lower Yangtze Region," p. 397. See Chapter II.

picture is titled "Skillfully teaching the abacus" and is framed by the phrases: "All the world must set their minds on study" and "I inform those who do not know the abacus." The preface first establishes the antiquity of the study of calculation—it began in the Shang dynasty (ca. 1570–1045 BC)—and argues that anyone who wishes to master the Confucian six arts must study calculation, the art that will allow the student "to examine the beginning and end of heaven and earth." The *Suanfa cuoyao* claims to be the perfect guide to this study, for it incorporates all the details and subtle mysteries of the art of calculation yet presents its points so clearly that the beginning student need not fear it is too difficult. "Students of calculation who use this text harmonize with all within the four seas and five lakes; nothing surpasses this text for protecting oneself in the world." Here a primer that might be seen as a specialized textbook for aspiring merchants and craftsmen is advertised for its general utility: it teaches a skill that can prevent anyone, examination candidate or not, from being cheated.

One other entry in the Sibao primer category deserves some attention: a compendium of primers and other beginning instructional materials that could be used to teach a range of different subjects. *Zhushi San Bai Qian Zengguang heke* 註釋三百千增廣合刻 (Annotated combined edition of *Three-Character Classic, Myriad Family Names, Thousand-Character Essay,* and *Expanded Words of Wisdom;* see Fig. 10.8a), published by the Wenhai lou, offers a practical all-in-one compendium of texts apparently designed to meet all a child's early educational needs. In one cramped volume (15 cm h × 21.5 cm w), it not only combines annotated versions of the four most popular primers but also adds a top register comprising brief miscellaneous texts, including five basic calligraphy guides, a primer for the use of the abacus, two fortune-telling manuals, and three sets of moral exhortations.[44] The

---

44. The specific titles are: *Zhibi tushi,* a very basic set of instructions on how to hold a brush when writing; *Linchi kaifa* 臨池楷法 (Regular-script calligraphic models); *Caojue baiyun* 草訣百韻 (Secrets of grass script in one hundred rhymes); *Gushu zhuanwen* 古書篆文 (Seal script in ancient texts); and *Lishu fatie* 隸書法帖 (Clerical-script calligraphic models); *Suanfa yaojue* 算法要訣 (Essential secrets of calculation); *Zhan denghua jixiong* 占灯花吉凶 (Determining good and bad fortune through divination by candlewicks); *Liuren shike* 六壬時課 (Schedule of *liuren* divination); *Quanshi wen* 勸世文 (Exhortations to the world); *Jingshi chuanwen* 警世傳文 (Messages to awaken the world); and *Ershisi*

top register (4.3 cm h) presents its series of texts without commentary or annotation, but with frequent, albeit quite crude, illustrations. *Zhibi tushi* 執筆圖勢 (Illustrated instructions on holding a brush), for example, is aptly illustrated with a drawing of a hand grasping a writing brush in the proper way (see Fig. 10.8b); and the text of the *Ershisi xiao* 二十四孝 (Twenty-four exemplars of filial piety) is dotted with small, roughly executed pictures of its stories (see Fig. 10.8c). The small size of the upper register serves to subordinate the shorter and more peripheral texts—the calligraphy manuals, the fortune-telling guides, moral essays, and so forth—to the more important texts in the bottom register.

The preface, dated to 1809 and reproduced in clumsy semi-cursive calligraphy, promotes the text as one that "records the Way," explaining the "principles of the waxing and waning of *yin* and *yang*, the constant rules of the rise and fall of destiny in ancient and modern times, the classics of the unchanging teachings of famous [men]." Somewhat more practically, the unidentified author goes on to argue that the text offers something to everyone, although "everyone" is divided into two classes: the Confucian scholars who will appreciate its deep significance, and the "group of peasants, artisans, and merchants" (*nong gong shanggu zhi chou* 農工商賈之儔) who will find it useful (1b). The preface proclaims the text a work of philosophical and ethical import, a universal guide to the grand principles of the tradition. Even the semi-cursive calligraphy (Fig. 10.8d), although poorly executed, seems to be part of an effort to present the texts as an elevated work, the product of a sophisticated and knowledgeable gentleman's hand.

---

*xiao.* Shang Wei ("*Jin Ping Mei* and Late Ming Print Culture," pp. 204–5) analyzes the ways in which editors of drama and fiction miscellanies used the two- or three-register format to combine separate, usually unrelated narrative texts. Although the two-register format was developed as early as the Five Dynasties or Song, it became particularly popular in the Ming and Qing. Wei argues that, in fiction collections, the arrangement of disparate texts might be used to "[highlight] the ironic contrast between high and low, refined and vulgar, serious and comic" (p. 205). In the case of *Zhushi San Bai Qian Zengguang heke*, however, since the works are elementary textbooks of various types, the motive seems to have been to appeal to as broad an audience as possible. See pp. 382–87 in this chapter for other examples of how multiple-register texts functioned.

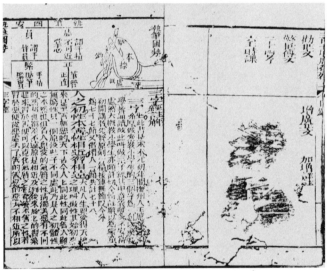

Fig. 10.8 *Zhushi San Bai Qian Zengguang heke* 註釋三百千增廣合刻 (Annotated combined edition of *Three-Character Classic, Myriad Family Names, Thousand-Character Essay,* and *Expanded Words of the Sages*), published by the Wenhai lou 文海樓. (a, *top*) Cover page. (b, *bottom*) The first text page, with *Zhibi tushi* 執筆 圖勢 (Illustrated instructions on holding a brush) in the top register and *Sanzi jing zhujie* 三字經註解 (*Three-Character Classic,* with commentary) in the bottom register. (c, *facing page top*) Illustrations and text of *Ershisi xiao* 二十四孝 (Twenty-four exemplars of filial piety), a text within the *Zhushi San Bai Qin Zengguang heke.* (d, *facing page bottom*) Preface to this edition. Photographs by the author.

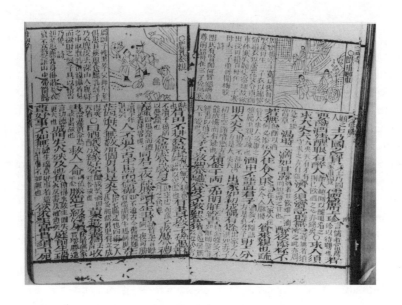

繁矣非有力之士不能致而父
詞深奧么性學古之儒門能通
雖以注於農工商賈之儔也矣
松此集有取為是集首列三字
經雖云無甚高論堪稱啟紫提
徑次列百家姓皆人右編成字
景呂以俾學者之涌讀幻列千

宇父令媄姐藥悉天道令事換
蓋盈豁之承理四列增廣雜懷
準渭背尨揩扞身波击有得之
格言若為加增注解係如指掌
矣而上屬又增以數錦背家者
家即朝夕危酹所不可少殆而
裁於百几頁之中名以至百千

What of the content? The four major texts in the larger bottom register (10.3 cm h) are heavily annotated with extensive commentary, written in unpunctuated but very simple classical Chinese, in interlinear double rows of smaller characters (see Fig. 10.8b). For example, the opening text, the *Sanzi jing zhujie* 三字經註解 (*Three-Character Classic, with commentary*), begins by explaining that it was written in the late Song or early Yuan by Wang Yinglin, who used it to teach elementary school students. The current editor (unidentified) has divided the text into sections and added comments to the text, "to be explained orally (*jiang* 講) to the young students starting the work." Then the opening passage of *Sanzi jing* is explicated, rather laboriously, in very simple Chinese. This explanation is then followed by an extended discussion of cosmology and of human nature as products of the interaction of *yin* and *yang* and the Five Agents. A circle marks off the next section of the commentary, a disquisition on the orthodox Cheng-Zhu understanding of human nature, complete with explanations of principle (*li* 理) and psycho-physical stuff (*qi* 氣). Zhu Xi's name is never mentioned; it is suggested, rather, that this whole theory developed out of Confucius's and Mencius's belief that human nature is good. The final little essay, again marked off by a circle, brings the student back to the *Sanzi jing*, explaining that the goal of study is to nurture the nature by transforming one's material substance (*qizhi* 氣質)—and that the *Sanzi jing* can aid in this task. Such extensive annotations, continued throughout the four main texts, confer on these four simple texts the status of Classics, a status already implied in the preface.

The density and relative complexity of the annotations suggests that this text was a compendium for teachers or parents; it is unlikely that a child of seven *sui* or younger could understand the references to principle and psycho-physical stuff, the Five Agents, and heaven's endowment of human nature that appear in the commentaries here. Since primary-school teachers, particularly those likely to be employed in the areas that Sibao was serving, were not necessarily well trained or even well educated, it is quite likely that these commentaries were designed to help the teacher himself understand the import of the text and how it should be taught.

What makes this text particularly interesting is the synergy of its parts, the way in which the selection of texts conditions the reader's perception of what constitutes an elementary education. The works included suggest a broad vision of the goals of elementary education. The *Zhushi San Bai Qian Zengguang heke* encompasses training in a wide range of basic, practical skills—reading, writing, calculating, and fortune-telling—as well as instruction in moral and ethical values. It also lends the two fortune-telling guides in the collection a legitimacy that they might not have on their own by printing them together on the same page as the "orthodox," respectable *Sanzi jing, Baijia xing, Qianzi wen,* and *Zengguang xianwen* (at the same time emphasizing the peripheral role of these practical texts by placing them in the much smaller upper register). The implicit promise of the compendium (like that of many of Sibao's household encyclopedias or medical compendia, as we shall see in the next chapter) was that this one text would supply all the needs, as a kind of encyclopedia on elementary education, of a peasant, merchant, or even literati household, or of a poorly trained teacher.

## *Beyond "Primer Literacy": Supplemental Texts for Elementary Education*

Once students had acquired "primer literacy,"[45] usually by mastering the "San-Bai-Qian," "the three classical primers that almost all children learned to recite during their first years in school," their teachers might choose from a range of introductory textbooks on Chinese history, geography, social relations, government, and so forth. Often these works were written in verse or song form to make them easier to memorize. At the same time, students would start memorizing the Four Books and the easier of the Five Classics.[46]

Sibao had close ties to one of the most popular of these supplemental texts, *Youxue xuzhi* 幼學須知 (Necessary knowledge for young students), better known under one of its alternative titles, *Youxue gushi qionglin* 幼學故事瓊林 (Treasury of allusions for young students). Attributed to the Ming scholar Cheng Dengji 程登吉 of Xichang 西昌,

45. Elman, *A Cultural History of Civil Examinations*, pp. 374, 376–77.

46. Leung, "Elementary Education in the Lower Yangtze Region," p. 394. See also "The Heart of the Curriculum" in this chapter, pp. 374–96.

Fig. 10.9 *Xinzeng Youxue gushi qionglin* 新增幼學故事瓊林 (*Treasury of Allusions for Young Students,* newly expanded), arranged (or edited?) by Zou Wugang 鄒梧岡 (Zou Shengmai 鄒聖脈) of Wuge and published by the Dawen tang 大文堂. (a, *left*) Cover page. (b, *right*) Title page, crediting Zou Shengmai with expanding and his son-in-law Xie Meilin 謝梅林 and his son Zou Tingyou 鄒廷猷 (Keting 可庭) with editing the text. Photographs by the author.

Sichuan,[47] the text was later expanded by Wuge's most distinguished scholar, Zou Shengmai, and was published regularly by the Sibao houses from the mid-eighteenth through the early twentieth century (Figs. 10.9a and b).[48]

---

47. This text, under one of its alternative titles, *Chengyu kao* 成語考 (Idioms investigated), is also attributed to Qiu Jun 邱濬 (1419–95) of Qiongshan 瓊山, a Jingtai-era (1450–56) *jinshi* and author of *Daxue yanyi bu* 大學衍義補 (Supplement to the *Extended Meaning of the Greater Learning*). A Lianyuan ge edition of the *Chengyu kao* was translated into English by J. H. Stewart Lockhart as *A Manual of Chinese Quotations;* see p. ii.

48. A modern photolithographic reproduction by Hainan chubanshe of the edition of *Youxue gushi qionglin* published by the prolific Nanjing publisher Li Guangming in the

*Youxue gushi qionglin* is a children's encyclopedia of literary quotations and famous allusions, a digest of information on a range of topics—the natural and supernatural worlds, social rituals, government, and more—presented through a series of idioms (*chengyu* 成語) and set phrases. An important aid in a culture that enjoyed both a long written tradition of and a fondness for allusion and euphuism, it incorporates many polite phrases and expressions frequently used in the exchanges of daily life. And, by identifying the sources of its allusions and quotations, it introduces the major works of Chinese literature and history. All this was necessary knowledge for anyone hoping to take his place among the educated elite. If, as the saying cited above claims, *Zengguang xianwen* taught children how to speak, then (as the saying continued), "After reading *Youxue qionglin*, they know how to study."[49]

The work was also a useful guide to beginning composition, providing models and allusions necessary to the kind of composition valued in letters, essays, and, most particularly, examination essays. John Nevius remarked in the late nineteenth century that the eight-legged essays "are a kind of literary mosaic, composed of ethical axioms, historical references, obscure allusions, and hints, poetical, biographical, and historical, with which [the students'] memories are stored; while they almost unconsciously fall into the style and forms of expression with which their minds have become familiar in the course of their *memoriter* studies."[50] Memorization of *Youxue gushi qionglin* added to the store of "mosaic tiles" out of which students composed essays. And recitation of the text

---

late nineteenth century lists Cheng Dengji as the author, "Wuge Zou Shengmai Wugang shi" 霧閣鄒聖脈梧鋼氏 as responsible for supplementing (*zengbu* 增補) the text, and "Qingxi Xie Meilin Yanyong shi" 清溪謝梅林硯傭氏 and Zou's son, "Zou Keting Sheyuan shi" 鄒可庭涉園氏, as joint collators (*he canding* 合參訂). Other scholars also revised and expanded the text; see Zhang Zhigong, *Chuantong yuwen jiaoyu jiaocai lun*, pp. 64–66, for some examples. But the Zou revision seems to have remained the most popular. For the variety of different editions (and different versions) of this popular work, see Appendix G; and *Zhongguo dashudian*, pp. 505–6.

49. Wang Maohe, *Baihua mengxue jingxuan*, p. 399.

50. Nevius, *China and the Chinese*, p. 65. See also S. Wells Williams's brief comment on this text in *The Middle Kingdom* (1882 ed.), vol. 1, pt. 2, p. 720. Culin ("Popular Literature of the Chinese Laborers in the United States," p. 58) also mentions the (*Youxue*) *gushi qionglin* as another popular text among overseas Chinese.

helped implant the rhythms of parallel prose in the student's mind at the same time that the topically arranged citations provided an invaluable index to allusions for essay writers.[51] Thus the text reflects, at a more advanced level, the same complex of concerns with reading and writing found in the classical primers.

*Youxue qionglin* covers a wide range of material in four *juan*: astronomy; geography; the seasons; the court; civil officials; military officials; parents and children; brothers; husbands and wives; uncles and nephews; teachers and pupils; friends, guests, and hosts; marriage; women; relations by marriage; age and youth; the body; buildings; tools; flowers and trees; birds and beasts; clothing; food and drink; precious things; inventions; literary matters; the civil examinations; Buddhism, Daoism, ghosts and spirits; the arts; criminal proceedings; poverty and wealth; human affairs; and diseases and death. The choice and arrangement of topics present the student with the important cultural categories through which the world was apprehended, reinforcing and perpetuating existing assumptions about the organization of knowledge.

Under each topic, Cheng Dengji listed a string of allusions, with brief indications of their sources and explanations of their meaning, occasionally followed by a historical reference. For example, the section on the examinations opens with the statement, in large characters: "A scholar's entering the government school [for the licentiate degree] is called 'wandering to the pool' (*you pan* 遊泮); it is also called 'picking the watercress' (*cai qin* 采芹)." Then in two columns of interlinear characters, he gives first the *locus classicus* of the expressions: "*Classic of Songs* (*Shi* 詩): 'Pleasant is the semicircular pool / and we will gather the cress about it.'" Next comes an explanation (*shi* 釋): "The school of the feudal lords was called *pangong* 泮宮 [palace of the semicircular pool]. Watercress is a water plant." Thus, the student learns two allusions, their source, and the sparest bit of historical context: *pan*, "pool," alludes to the school of the Zhou aristocracy, *cai qin*, "gathering the watercress," to plucking the watercress that grows on the pool (and, by extrapolation, earning licentiate status). Zou Shengmai's additions, similar in organization, are appended to each section, following the character *zeng* 增, "expansion." This text also introduced students to the sources of

----

51. See Zhang Zhigong, *Chuantong yuwen jiaoyu jiaocai lun*, pp. 64–66.

these allusions and idioms in the major texts of the tradition: the Classics, the *Shuowen jiezi* 說文解字 (Explanation of single graphs and analyses of compound characters), the *Huainanzi* 淮南子, the dynastic histories, the *Tongdian* 通典 (Encyclopedic history of institutions), and so forth.

Like most popular textbooks, however, this work was subject to much manipulation, presented in different formats and different types of commentaries. It is safe to say, however, that the text, even in its various manifestations, provided the student with an overview of a wide range of knowledge, presenting a summary of the assumptions, beliefs, and principles of Chinese culture through popular idioms and allusions.

The *Wenliao dacheng* 文料大成 (Collection of literary materials) appears to be a more detailed encyclopedia, perhaps for somewhat more advanced students. Only a portion of a compact Sibao edition (10.8 cm h × 15.2 cm w) survives, but enough to suggest something of the range of this reference work. The four *juan* (of at least twenty-five) that survive treat ritual and music, official positions, kings and feudal lords, and human relationships. Each section (*bu* 部) or *juan* is divided into subcategories. Thus the section on human beings ("Renbu" 人部) has sections on ritual and music, official service, feudal relations, human relationships, and so on. The "Category of human relationships" ("Lunji lei" 倫紀類) opens with a "Summary of human relationships" ("Lunji zong" 倫紀總): "The hidden nature of men originally derives from Shangdi. The norms of social relationships, sent down to the people, enabled them to live in order together" (25.1ab). This summary treats human relationships as the self-conscious creations of the sage-kings. The appointment of the official *situ* 司徒 to oversee human relationships, the spread of ritual, the teaching of the virtues of reverence, filial piety, and harmony—these mark the stages in the development of the crucial five relationships: emperor-subject, father-son, elder brother–younger brother, husband-wife, teacher-pupil. What follows is a topically organized series of word and phrase lists describing the qualities associated with the given topic. Thus "Human beings" ("Ren" 人) opens: "good and evil," "intelligent and stupid," "fulfilling their nature," "unequal in fortune," "rooted in their ancestors," and so forth. "Human relationships" ("Renlun" 人倫) includes the phrases "sons are filial," "the three submissions," "wives follow," "teachers instruct," and so on; toward the end of each section, the descriptive phrases become longer and more detailed. A final category entitled simply "Violations" ("Fan" 反) lists phrases describing behavior that violates the five relationships: "the mean defeating the noble," "distancing oneself from one's relatives," "the new interfering with the old," "licentiousness destroying righteousness," and so on (25.2a–4a).

What is the purpose of this text? Like *Youxue gushi qionglin*, it organizes knowledge in culturally acceptable categories. It reinforces ethical values, defining, as the examples above show, what qualities and behavior are expected in human relationships. But it most pointedly supplies the beginning essay writer with conventional phrases that can be used in letters, examination essays, and other writings (and, for that matter, in speech).

Young students at this stage might also begin to learn more about the outline of Chinese history. Ma Kuanyu, one of the earliest of the Ma publishers, is credited with editing an elementary history textbook, the *Xinzeng Mingji jianlüe wuyan duben* 新增明紀鑑略五言讀本 (Newly expanded *Annals of the Ming*, abridged in five-character phrases), a brief annalistic history of China up through the Ming, presented in rhymes for easy memorization.[52] Surviving only in a tattered and partial volume, this work was once a handsome text—large, clearly cut, punctuated, and with extensive interlinear commentary that provided pronunciation and explained the text in considerable detail. More advanced students could turn to historical digests or outlines of annalistic history like the *Dafang gangjian* 大方綱鑑 (Scholarly outlines of the annalistic histories). This work, attributed to Yuan Huang 袁黃 (1533–1606, *js* 1586) and surviving in a partial volume with *Xinkan Liaofan Yuan xiansheng bianzuan guben lishi Dafang gangjian bu* 新刊了凡袁先生編纂古本歷史大方綱鑑補

---

52. This is probably the same work described in Leung, "Elementary Education in the Lower Yangtze Region," p. 394, as the *Jianlüe* 鑑略, "which summarized the history of China from the mythical age to the late Ming in three short chapters of quinmetrical verses." The text was attributed to Li Tingji 李廷機 (d. 1616), a *zhuangyuan* 狀元 of 1583, Hanlin academician, and grand secretary—and thus a man whose name was often gratuitously added to educational texts by commercial publishers. Zou Shengmai contributed notes to another edition of this work, *Jianlüe tuozhu* 鑑略妥註.

(Supplemented old versions of the *Scholarly Outlines of the Annalistic Histories*, edited by Master Yuan Liaofan, and newly published) on the cover page,[53] provides a narrative summary of each dynasty and more detailed information, arranged chronologically, about each reign within it. The characters are large and clear, with double rows of interlinear commentary, which explain place-names or present points of controversy. A narrow top register provides additional brief notes. Following the text and interlinear notes come the views of various commentators; in the surviving fragment are analyses attributed to Hu Hong 胡宏 (1105–55), the Song historian and Confucian thinker, and Yuan Huang himself. In sum, this nicely produced text promised, at least by its size and format, a full and comprehensively annotated chronicle of Chinese history.

Although these supplemental textbooks might be useful for students continuing on the examination track, they taught a general knowledge of Chinese language, history, and culture appropriate for any student or reader. Some of the supplemental textbooks had a narrower focus, however. For example, the *Xinzha/Zibian* 信札／字辨 (Writing letters/Distinguishing characters; preface dated 1876), by Tan Yuanbiao 譚元標 of Nanhai 南海 and Li Chunshan 李春山 of Hecheng 鶴山, Guangdong, seems to have been designed for aspiring merchants (see Fig. 10.10). At first glance, this textbook looks like a useful aid in distinguishing similar characters and a guide to certain rules of behavior and etiquette. The top register of this small, two-*juan* work, entitled *Chuxue zibian* 初學字辨 (Distinguishing characters for beginning students), contains a double row of paired similar characters, with their pronunciation and an example of their use in a compound as a means of explaining the differences in meaning. The larger bottom register contains first a brief set of instructions, "Ten rules for embarking on a profession" (1.1a–2b), and then, a second text, *Chuxue yingchou shuxin quanji* 初學應酬書信全集 (Complete collection of letters for beginning students of social exchange). This is a guide to addressing and composing

---

53. At the end of the only surviving *ce*, at *juan* 2b, the title is given as *Xinkan Tongjian jiyao*. See Chia, *Printing for Profit*, p. 227, for an alternative attribution to Li Tingji (although, as Chia explains, "More examination literature was attributed to him by Fujian's commercial publishers than he could possibly have written").

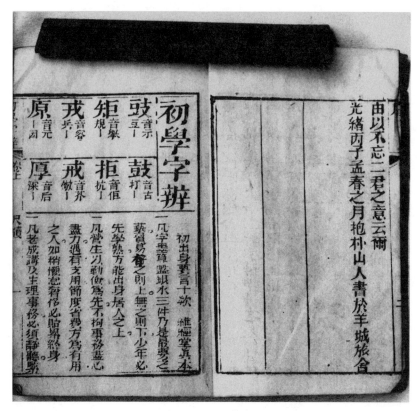

Fig. 10.10 *Xinzha/Zibian* 信札／字辨 (Writing letters / Distinguishing characters). The top register contains *Chuxue zibian* 初學字辨 (Distinguishing characters for beginning students); the bottom, *Chuxue yingchou shuxin quanji* 初學應酬書信全集 (Complete collection of letters for beginning students of social exchange). Photograph by the author.

letters and other forms of social correspondence (invitations, funeral announcements, etc.; 1.3a–60b, 2.1a–41b), organized around two principles: the relationship between the sender and recipient and the purpose of the letter.

Presumably anyone would find this text useful, but it is explicitly presented as a work for the sons of traveling merchants, men very much in the situation of the Zou and Ma booksellers themselves. The preface-writer, identified only as "Baopu shanren" 抱朴山人, explains that his father had ordered him to abandon his studies at the age of eighteen *sui* in order to "travel to distant places as a merchant." Now he regrets the resulting deficiencies in his education: "Whenever I have to write anything, I cannot distinguish clearly the forms of the different characters. I scratch my head, bitterly wasting much time and energy [trying to think of the right character], and regretting that my earlier study was not [more] careful and focused." He worries about his sons' education: "I am old now, and when I am traveling away from home, I often think of my sons back home, wondering how their studies progress." On returning home from business in Shaoxing the previous year, he was shocked to find that his eldest son, who had been studying for five years, had the same problem; he could not distinguish *bu* 簿 from *bo* 薄 or *wei* 微 from *zheng* 徵. The son, shamed by his father's anger and disappointment, procured a copy of *Xinzha/Zibian* and, after a mere month of study, passed an extensive reading test, including several tens of similar characters. "That only one month of work would be enough to supplement five years of study—this is indeed extraordinary!" marvels the proud father, and he then goes on to praise the clarity of the textbook ("Xu," 1ab).

The commercial context of the preface is directly reinforced at the beginning of the text; in the lower register, the first of the "Ten rules for embarking on a profession" explains, "Knowing how to read, to use the abacus, and to distinguish grades of silver are the most important skills. If, as a merchant, you have these skills, you will do well; if you don't, you will do poorly. When young you should study these skills thoroughly first, and then you will be able to take your place among men once you embark on a profession" (1a). At the end of the text is a list of terms for different types of silver and other metals, foods, "miscellaneous products," clothing, colors, bamboo implements, placenames, and so on—all of particular use to merchants (2.42a–52b). Although *Xinzha/Zibian*, like the other texts cited above, could be used by any student who needed help in distinguishing similar characters or wanted to learn how to write letters, it was marketed particularly to aspiring merchants. It is difficult to imagine an examination-bound student from an elite family turning to a text so clearly designed for the use of merchants and merchants' sons, particularly since Sibao produced other beginning letter-writing guides probably more attractive to readers outside the mercantile classes (see Chapter 11).

## Textbooks for Composition

After completing the basic primers and acquiring the core cultural fundamentals, the student, in addition to continuing his memorization of the Classics and expanding his reading skills and knowledge of Chinese culture and history through the supplementary texts discussed above, would begin to study composition. To be sure, just about all the textbooks in the elementary curriculum offered partial guides to composition. Other texts, however, more directly addressed compositional skills by providing model essays for study and emulation.

Although the eight-legged essay was required for the examinations, intensive study of this specialized form of composition began only after the student had mastered the principles of good essay writing in ancient-style prose (*guwen* 古文).[54] The large store of model ancient-style prose essay collections[55] were of two types—relatively brief collections of essays by the great Tang and Song writers (like Shen Deqian's 沈德潛 [1673–1769] *Tang Song badajia wenchao* 唐宋八大家文鈔 [Writings of eight great Tang and Song authors]) and surveys of great prose writing from the Eastern Zhou to the Qing (like Lin Yunming's *Guwen xiyi* 古文析義 [Elucidation of ancient-style

---

54. Ridley, "Educational Theory and Practice in Late Imperial China," pp. 415–27, 440–75.

55. Another Sibao publication, *Pubian tang xunmeng cao* 浦編堂訓蒙草 (Draft instruction for young students from the Pubian tang; preface dated 1837), seems to have been an even more elementary text for beginning composition students, published by the Wenhai lou in the late nineteenth century and compiled, according to the preface, for the use of the compiler's son, aged twelve or thirteen *sui*. At this age, when "the flower of his mind/heart had not yet blossomed" (that is, before he had reached the age of understanding, believed to be fourteen *sui*), he could nonetheless "begin to grasp how to write essays of simple sentences (*danju tiwen* 單句題文)." The text's twelve essays are of substantial length, roughly 700 to 900 characters, with clear and conventional moral lessons—"Hold goods cheap," "Frugality and restraint," "Yu identified liquor as an evil," are typical. Above the main text is a narrow register of notes, most of which aid in analyzing the argument, pointing up the crucial characters and the contrasts and comparisons, so that the reader will not "swallow the argument whole," without reflection. On occasion the compiler also adds smaller characters to the right of the main text, usually explaining referents or providing the implied subject of a phrase.

prose]).⁵⁶ Both types of collections presented famous essays by China's greatest stylists, with annotation (*zhu* 註), commentary (*ping* 評 or *pi* 批), and often punctuation.

Although Sibao published many collections of both types, the few titles that survive are for the most part variations of the *Guwen xiyi*. This text appears in a 1776 edition entitled *Zengding Guwen xiyi hebian* 增訂 古文析義合編 (Combined *Elucidation of Ancient-Style Prose*, expanded), with Lin Yunming identified as the commentator and annotator (*ping zhu* 評註) and his son and sons-in-law as collators. In sixteen *juan* and eight *ce*, this is a sizable text (19.5 h × 30 cm w); it includes essays dating from the *Zuozhuan* through Wang Shizhen 王世貞 (1526–90) and Wang Daokun 汪道昆 (1525–93) of the Ming. In a preface dated 1682 (an earlier version of the text is said to have been lost in the course of the "Fujian troubles" of 1662–63), Lin explains that he compiled the text to combat, first, the focus on the eight-legged essay that often led students to neglect the great essays of the tradition and, second, the corrupt editions of ancient-style prose essays produced by commercial publishing houses. In his notes to the reader ("Fanli" 凡例) Lin provides detailed instructions on how to read the essays: read the text through several times to get the general sense, reread the portions that you did not fully understand, and then memorize the piece, reciting it several tens of times; finally, write out an explanation of each sentence. He continues to warn against commercial editions of ancient-style prose essays, which he portrays as full of errors and distracting and often irrelevant notes. Yet he provides a dazzling array of flanking editorial notes: concentric circles mark the leading idea of an essay, solid circles mark difficulties and weak points, slugs mark writing of particular brilliance or vividness, and open circles mark clever transitions or changes in style (see Fig. 10.11). To distinguish different types of explanation within the interlinear commentary, a small open circle is used to separate the explanations of sentences from the explanations of sections and the criticism; pronunciation of difficult characters is explained in smaller

56. Ridley, "Educational Theory and Practice in Late Imperial China," pp. 416–25; Zhang Zhigong, *Chuantong yuwen jiaoyu jiaocai lun*, pp. 112–14; and Zhang Longhua and Zeng Zhongshan, *Zhongguo gudai yuwen jiaoyu shi*, pp. 367–68.

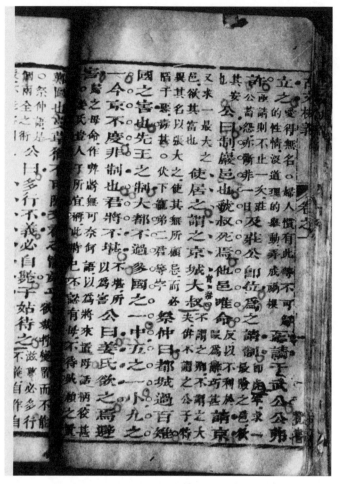

Fig. 10.11 Editorial marks in *Zengding Guwen xiyi hebian* 增訂古文析義合編 (Combined *Elucidation of Ancient Prose,* expanded). Photograph by the author.

characters to the right. Following each essay is Lin's analysis. Produced during the golden age of Sibao publishing, *Zengding Guwen xiyi hebian* is a rather nicely cut text, with eight rows of twenty-three characters each on a half-folio page. Even given the profusion of double-column interlinear commentary, sideline notes, and punctuation on each page, it is relatively easy to read.

The Mawu publisher Ma Kuanyu edited a version of this work, *Zengding Guwen jingyan xiangzhu pangxun hebian* 增訂古文精言詳註旁訓

合編 (*The Finest Ancient-style Prose Writings*, with both detailed commentary and sideline guides, newly revised; 16 *juan*), which survives in an 1884 edition.[57] Ma's preface explains the need for this text: each sentence of the essays "contains several sentences; each character contains several characters," and only by explaining the allusions, taken from the Classics, the traditions of the worthies, the histories, and the philosophers, can the compiler make the complex meanings of these works clear ("Xu," 1b–2a). The notes to the reader, also written by Ma, assure the reader of the very high quality of his edition, as usual contrasting it to most other commercial productions:

This collection is named *jingyan* 精言 ["the finest words"] because it selects the original text of ancient-style prose essays and examines them meticulously and in detail, so that there are no missing characters and no errors. It should be considered a rare book, not comparable to recent commercial publications of ancient-style prose, which are full of mistakes and thus perpetuate an uncalculable number of errors. My publishing house carefully collated and revised [the text]; the punctuation is error-free. The reader will do best to discriminate carefully.

In this edition, a top register of explanations and some sideline notes, as well as punctuation, were used to instruct the student in the structure and deep meaning of the selections. In line with the assertions of the preface, Ma states that all the allusions in the essays—not necessarily known to later readers—are explained, so that the reader will fully grasp the beauty and meaning of the texts. He then goes on to advise readers on studying the text, presenting, like Lin above, a brief "Method of reading" ("Dushu fa" 讀書法) for ancient-style prose collections:

To memorize ancient-style prose, it is necessary to start with exacting reflection [on the text], carefully investigating its theme and how [the author] first sets it forth and begins to develop it [literally, how he sets brush to paper and how he begins]. Once you have read one section, go on to finish the next sec-

---

57. See Chapter 9, pp. 310–11. This version reproduces Lin's original selections, but with notes attributed to a Zhou Dazhang 周大章 of Tongcheng 桐城 (Anhui). Edited by Ma Kuanyu in the late seventeenth or early eighteenth century, this version must have been one of Sibao's earliest attempts at this text. The 1884 edition is one of Sibao's more attractive instructional offerings—a rather finely cut text of reasonable proportions (block: 19.2 h × 30 cm w), with clear, well-spaced characters.

tion, [considering] how he reinforces it and orders [his point]. Once the end of the line of a thought is reached, you will then know that there are no heights the ancients could not reach. After you have finished reading, you can simply memorize their successes.

In studying ancient-style prose, you must first understand precisely the overall point. Then, in the midst of the essay, repeatedly trace the "veins and arteries" back to their sources, so that you understand clearly the line of a thought and it can be said that you well and broadly grasp the ancients—or, if the essay expresses magnanimous emotions, so that they arise vividly [in your heart]. This is what examination candidates (*juyejia* 舉業家) must learn through careful practice.

This last sentence makes clear the context for and goal of studying this text: success in the examinations.

Wang Tao 王韜 (1828–?) is said to have characterized such texts (and in particular Lin Yunming's *Guwen xiyi*) rather contemptuously to his student James Legge (1815–97) as "a series of Lessons for [teaching elementary students in] a village school" (*xiangshu kemeng zhi ben* 鄉塾課蒙之本).[58] And indeed, these are clearly textbooks of composition. But they were also, like any anthology of great writing, presenting the major literary and moral works of the tradition.

These works, however, did not teach the more specialized skill required of examination candidates: the composition of eight-legged essays. For this, students on the examination track turned to specialized handbooks on "contemporary essays," or *shiwen* 時文, a genre produced in great abundance by commercial publishers since the late Ming and usually consisting of a collection of model essays.[59] Although these works, unlike the more respectable collections of model ancient-style prose essays, were not normally approved of for school use,[60] they were nonetheless extremely popular, for obvious reasons. As explained in the

---

58. Legge, *The Chinese Classics*, vol. 5, "The Prolegomena," p. 146. Legge lists several works similar to the *Guwen xiyi*, suggesting again just how popular such texts were.

59. Durand, *Lettrés et pouvoirs*, pp. 83–86.

60. This point is somewhat undermined by the evidence presented below, that at least one published collection of eight-legged essays originated in a manuscript copy used in a family school. See Ridley, "Educational Theory and Practice in Late Imperial China," pp. 472–74.

Fig. 10.12 *Tiegang shanhu sanji xinbian* 鐵綱珊瑚三集新編
(Newly compiled three collections for examination success;
identified as 鐵綱珊瑚全集, Complete collection for examination success, on the cover page), a collection of examination essays published by the Wenhai lou 文海樓 in
Nanning, Guangxi, in 1890. Photograph by the author.

1844 preface to the Sibao eight-legged essay collection *Tiegang shanhu
sanji xinbian* 鐵綱珊瑚三集新編 (Newly compiled three collections for
examination success;[61] see Fig. 10.12), published by the Nanning Wenhai lou in 1890, "The state has used the examination institution to select
scholars. Even one possessing overwhelming talent must study [the art
of essay writing] in order to make a name in the examinations" (*ji* 1,
"Xu," 1ab).

_____

61. *Tiegang shanhu* is literally "fishing for coral"—it refers to the use of an iron tool to
draw coral from the sea.

Sibao appears to have published considerable numbers of these texts; from the titles that have survived, most focused on the particularly difficult *xiaoti* 小題 essays, whose topic was a fragment of a classical text (sometimes only two to three characters), rather than a whole sentence or even a phrase (*dati* 大題).[62] Sibao also produced a collection of model "policy" essays, or *celun* 策論, entitled *Xin celun* 新策論 (New policy essays). This work, large but poorly printed, reproduces essays on policy questions, which constituted the third portion of the provincial and metropolitan examinations in the Qing through the nineteenth century. It may be a text of local authorship; the portion that remains includes essays by students from the Longshan Academy 龍山書院, including one by a Zou Lianhui 聯輝 of Wuge.

Many of these texts appear simply to have reproduced the eight-legged essays of successful examination candidates, with little annotation or explication. But some compilers attempted to teach from the model essays, providing notations and even commentary to guide the student.[63] For example, *Tongzi wenlu* 童子問路 (A youth asks the way), compiled by Zheng Zhicong 鄭之琮 in the Kangxi era and surviving in Sibao in two undated editions, appears to be an introductory text, containing model essays on phrases from the Four Books—forty phrases from the *Analects*, three from the *Greater Learning* and *Doctrine of the Mean*, and seventeen from *Mencius*. Zheng's preface associates learning to compose eight-legged essays with the "opening of intelligence," which most Chinese educators considered to occur at about fourteen *sui*. Zheng explains certain features of the structure of eight-legged essays, including, for example, a brief discussion of *poti* 破題, "breaking open the topic," the name given to the opening section of eight-legged

---

62. Some essay collections were organized by the length of the classical citation required for different essays, so that, for example, *juan* 1 might contain two- and three-character citations, and *juan* 2, single-sentence (*danju*) citations.

63. The most famous of these is Fang Bao's 方苞 (1688–1749) 41-*juan Qinding Sishu wen* 欽訂四書文 (Imperially sponsored *Essays on the Four Books*; 1739), perhaps the most comprehensive and popular handbook to the eight-legged essay, which in its original form both explains the terminology and structure of the essay and provides hundreds of sample essays from the Ming and Qing. This title appears on the Cuiyun tang inventory, but in the absence of the text itself, it is impossible to know what the Sibao edition contained.

essays.[64] He provides both *xiaoti* and *dati* model essays, with sideline pointers to the use of antithesis and parallelism, essential features of the essays.

A more advanced guide is *Zhupi Xiaoti zhenggu chuji, erji, sanji* 硃批小題正鵠初集, 二集, 三集 (First, second, and third collections of *Hitting the* Xiaoti *Target*, with vermilion notes; preface dated 1847), compiled by Li Fumin 李傅敏 of Pingjiang 平江, Hunan, with the assistance of no fewer than eleven relatives and other scholars. A three-volume set originating as a handcopied textbook used in a family school, *Xiaoti zhenggu* consists of eight-legged essays of the Ming period (when *baguwen* became the dominant examination form), in order of increasing difficulty. Each essay is punctuated, with slugs marking phrase breaks, and open circles indicating points of emphasis (although the utility of these latter marks is undermined by their overuse). Comments flanking the text explain grammar or signification. For example, an essay on the opening line of the *Analects*—"To learn and rehearse it constantly, is this indeed not a pleasure?"[65]—argues that learning is, rather, bitter and painful; the sideline comment reads "[it] opposes [the meaning of] the character *yue* 説, 'pleasure.'" A final discursive commentary by the editor, the compiler's son, outlines the different stages (*ceng* 層, "layers") of the essay, explaining how these are ordered and manipulated. The more difficult essays receive extra "eyebrow notes" (*meipi* 眉批, added above the top border of the main text), largely highlighting the parallelism in the use of characters and phrases. Published by the Wenhai Lou, this text is not well produced—small (12.1 h × 17.4 w), inelegantly cut, and crowded, it is not very easy to read (see Fig. 10.13). The reader is rescued from confusion, however, by a touch unusual in Sibao texts: the punctuation markers and sideline comments are printed in red ink, as the title indicates.

Sibao publishers thus provided a range of educational texts for the student who had graduated from primers and glossaries. These offered general knowledge of his culture and the natural world (*Youxue gushi*

---

64. Ching-i Tu, "The Chinese Examination Essay," p. 398; Durand, *Lettrés et pouvoir*, pp. 79–81.

65. Translation from Gardner, *Zhu Xi's Reading of the* Analects, p. 31.

Fig. 10.13 *Zhupi Xiaoti zhenggu* 硃批小題正鵠 (*Hitting the* Xiaoti *Target,* with vermilion notes), a collection of examination essays. The punctuation markers and sideline comments are printed in red ink. Photograph by the author.

*qionglin*), set phrases and allusions used in polite speech[66] and writing (*Youxue gushi qionglin* and the ancient-style prose collections), the principles of good writing (the ancient-style prose collections), and finally, the technical compositional skills required for the examination essays (the eight-legged essay collections).

---

66. Sibao produced at least one guide to "correct"—i.e., northern—pronunciation: *Guanhua yin* 官話音 (Pronunciation of officials' language). By the Qing, "officials' language" (*guanhua* 官話) was based on the dialect of the capital area. *Guanhua* presented a particular challenge to residents of the southern provinces, especially Fujian and Guangdong; the Yongzheng emperor complained specifically of the incomprehensible accents of officials from these two provinces and intensified his predecessor's efforts to found "correct pronunciation academies" (*zhengyin shuyuan* 正音書院) there (see Hanan, *The Chinese Vernacular Story,* pp. 1, 13–16; and Naquin and Rawski, *Chinese Society in the Eighteenth Century,* p. 173). The Sibao publishers, like most commercial publishers of the Ming and Qing, also found other ways of providing guides to pronunciation. As indicated above—and as will be clear in the discussion of the Four Books and Five Classics—the inclusion of notes on sound and tone were standard features of many of their textbooks and textbook editions of the Classics.

## Poetry Anthologies and Manuals

After the mid-eighteenth century, mastery of the eight-legged essay form was not sufficient for success in the examinations. From the mid-1750s on, a candidate also needed some acquaintance with the poetic canon and some skill in composing antithetical couplets, the basic constituents of Chinese verse. In 1756 poetic composition, specifically of eight-rhyme regulated verse (*bayun lüshi* 八韻律詩), was reinstituted as a requirement on the examinations.[67] In the following year, a poetry assignment appeared on the metropolitan examination, and in 1759 on the provincial examinations as well. In the local qualifying examinations for licentiate status (the *tongshi*), the requirement was imposed in 1758 and extended to include the renewal and licensing examinations (*suikao* 歲考) in 1760.[68] More than a polite accomplishment, the mark of a cultivated man, poetic (at least regulated verse) composition was now a necessity for the examinations at every level.

Naturally this change in the examination requirements touched off a proliferation of poetry primers, Tang-Song poetry anthologies, and poetry criticism (*shihua* 詩話), which provided advanced instruction in poetry writing. This is not to say that such texts were not published commercially before 1758; given the status of poetry in Chinese literature and its importance in social exchange, poetry primers and collections had always enjoyed popularity. But the change in the examination requirements stimulated a boom in the genre.

Sibao produced some of the most common poetry primers and anthologies. *Qianjia shi* 千家詩 (Myriad poems), the beginning text for learning poetry and "one of the key collections students and candidates

---

67. Rules of prosody, both phonic and tonal, for this kind of verse were inordinately complex; for an explanation, see James J. Y. Liu, *The Art of Chinese Poetry*, pp. 26–29; or Nienhauser, *The Indiana Companion to Traditional Chinese Literature*, pp. 682–86.

68. Elman, *A Cultural History of Civil Examinations*, pp. 548–49. During the Qing, even before 1757, poetic composition had been required on some special examinations, including, in 1723, the examination used to rank *jinshi* for entry into the Hanlin Academy (ibid., pp. 546–49). For a summary of the stages of the examinations in the Qing, see Chang, *The Chinese Gentry*, pp. 4–32; and Parker, "The Educational Curriculum of the Chinese."

referred to to learn regulated verse,"[69] was an ever-popular Sibao product, lumped with *Sanzi jing, Baijia xing, Qianzi wen, Zengguang xianwen,* and the Four Books as one of the texts that contemporary informants claim the Zou and Ma "always" printed. This work, generally attributed either to the Song scholar Liu Kezhuang 劉克莊 (1187–1269) or to a later contemporary, Xie Fangde 謝枋得 (1226–89), circulated in several editions by the Qing. As Zhang Zhigong remarks, there was a flood of widely circulating texts, all with *Qianjia shi* in their title, but containing different collections of seven- and five-character poems. At the same time, editors and publishers often took one of the earlier editions, very slightly edited or supplemented it, and presented it as a new text, as an "expanded and supplemented" or "newly revised" version.[70] In sum, the history of this work mimics the history of most popular educational volumes in two ways: many differing texts were titled *Qianjia shi,* presumably to profit from its enormous popularity; and many compilers, editors, and publishers reproduced the same text under a series of differing titles (although all containing *Qianjia shi*) in order to profit by suggesting that they had created an expanded, corrected, or improved edition.

Nor were the Sibao publishers behind in this effort. *Qianjia shi tuzhu* 千家詩圖註 (*Myriad Poems,* with illustrations and commentary) was advertised on the cover page as "revised by Master Zhong Bojing" (*Zhong Bojing xiansheng dingbu* 鍾伯敬先生訂補; see Fig. 10.14)—that is, as a version of the text falsely ascribed to Zhong Xing 鍾惺 (*zi* Bojing 伯敬, 1574–1624; *js* 1610), a noted poet and poetry anthologist of the late Ming.[71] This version has one or two simple illustrations in the narrower

---

69. Elman, *A Cultural History of Civil Examinations,* p. 551; see also Zhang Zhigong, *Chuantong yuwen jiaoyu jiaocai lun,* pp. 90–92.

70. See Zhang Zhigong, *Chuantong yuwen jiaoyu jiaocai lun,* p. 91.

71. Goodrich and Fang, *Dictionary of Ming Biography,* 1: 408. Zhong Xing's name, like that of Chen Jiru 陳繼儒 (1558–1646) and Li Tingji, was often affixed to works not his own. L. Carrington Goodrich and C. N. Tay, in their biography of Zhong, state, "It seems that from 1616 to 1621 Chung edited a few collections of 'eight-legged' essays for the examination hall trade and his popularity in that respect and in the field of poetry writing induced some unscrupulous publishers to capitalize on his name" (p. 409). This text is an example of either a pirated text or a text published from purchased blocks. The cover page of the text lists a Cuiying ju 萃英居 of Xiazhang 霞漳 as publisher, but the title page (1.1a) provides the full title of the text and identifies the

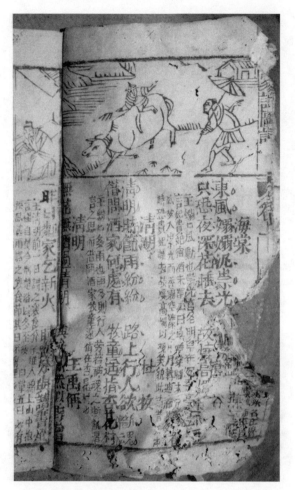

Fig. 10.14 *Zhong Bojing xiansheng dingbu Qianjia shi tuzhu* 鍾伯敬先
生訂補千家詩圖註 (*Myriad Poems*, with illustrations and commentary, revised by Master Zhong Bojing), an illustrated edition of
the poetry primer *Qianjia shi*. Photograph by the author.

upper register and the poems, followed by "Zhong's" commentary, in
the broad lower register. The commentaries are straightforward explanations of the poem's contents, with little in the way of metrical analysis.

---

publishing house that "reprinted" (*chongzi* 重梓) the text as the Wanxian tang 萬賢堂
of Minting (Tingzhou).

Fig. 10.15 *Xinke Qianjia shi* 新刻千家詩 (*Myriad Poems,* newly published), published by the Linlan tang 林蘭堂. The top register contains a guide to the composition of paired antithetical couplets, *Xinke Shenglü qimeng duilei* 新刻聲律啓蒙對類 (*Primer of the Rules of Sound,* newly published); *Qianjia shi* is in the bottom register. Photograph by the author.

Other Sibao versions were designed more explicitly as poetry textbooks. *Xinke Qianjia shi* 新刻千家詩 (*Myriad Poems,* newly published; Fig. 10.15), published by the Linlan tang in Tingzhou, places *Qianjia shi* in the bottom register and *Xinke Shenglü qimeng duilei* 新刻聲律啓蒙對類 (*Primer of the Rules of Sound,* newly published), a popular elementary primer of poetry writing, in the top register. The *Shenglü qimeng* introduced students to the construction of the paired antithetical couplets essential not only in regulated verse but also in the eight-legged essay.[72] This text, often appended to *Qianjia shi*, provided series of matched-character pairs, from matched single characters up to matched ten-character phrases, organized by rhyme; since the paired characters had the same grammatical as well as general semantic function, the student was learning something of classical grammar as well. Thus, the student began with simple pairs like "cloud/rain" (1.1a) or "poverty/wealth" (1.1b) and moved on to more complex pairs like "In the pool, water that washes one's feet / Outside the door, wind that beats against one's head" or "Liangdi lectures on the Classics at Tongqin Temple / Hanhuang lays out wine at the Weiyang Palace" (1.1b). This text was to be memorized, and the student "would in time acquire a stock of ready-made pairs for use in constructing his own verse."[73] Here, then, the Linlan tang produced a text that handily included both basic instruction in poetry writing and the collection of poetry that most commonly provided exemplars to beginning students.

*Qianjia shi*, in the version most commonly used in the Sibao editions, collects, as Zhang Zhigong has explained, "some very bad [poems], as well as some rather profound ones," but "the majority of them are simple and easy to understand, good for children, or at least not harmful; and among them there are many often quoted and widely loved pieces."[74] Used as the beginning poetry primer in elementary education, this text introduced students not simply to a form of writing extremely popular within the culture but also to a form of recitation, a source of common oral references, that in a sense helped to socialize them.[75] For

---

72. *Shenglü qimeng* was composed by Che Wanyu 車萬育 ( *js* 1664) of Baoqing, Hunan (Han Xiduo, *Zhonghua mengxue jicheng*, p. 801).

73. Ridley, "Educational Theory and Practice in Late Imperial China," p. 401; Elman, *A Cultural History of Civil Examinations*, p. 549.

74. Zhang Zhigong, *Chuantong yuwen jiaoyu jiaocai lun*, p. 91.

75. Another Sibao edition of the *Qianjia shi* includes, in a top register, the *Zhumingjia baishou shi* 諸名家百壽詩 (One hundred poems honoring long life by famous writers), a series of model poems for celebrating longevity—"On an eighty-*sui*-old magistrate's arriving at his post," "On an eighty-*sui*-old military official," and so forth. Presumably this work performed a social service by providing models for poetic birthday commemorations. On the different editions of this text, see Wang Maohe, *Baihua mengxue jingxuan*, p. 225.

some, it also introduced the structure and rhythm of a verse form they would be required to learn to pass any examination offered after 1760.

Having absorbed the elementary *Qianjia shi*, the student would mostly likely progress to the well-known *Tangshi sanbaishou* 唐詩三百首 (Three hundred poems of the Tang), compiled in its original edition by Sun Zhu 孫洙 (1711–78) in 1763 or 1764, shortly after the poetry requirement was reintroduced into the civil-service examinations. Explicitly designed for young children, this text presents, like *Qianjia shi*, easy-to-understand-and-memorize poems. It represents an advance on its predecessor, however, in its wider variety of poetic forms and its more discriminating selections.[76] Sun's claim in his preface that he hoped to prove the common saying, "By mastering three hundred Tang poems, one learns how to compose poetry,"[77] suggests the educational usefulness of his compilation.

This anthology, like all the other works treated thus far, was many times republished, with additional commentary and poems added by later scholars. The partial extant Sibao edition, *Tangshi sanbaishou zhushu* 唐詩三百首註疏 (*Three Hundred Poems of the Tang*, with annotations and commentary), credits Sun Zhu as editor, a Zhang Xie 章燮 of Jianning as annotator, and a Sun Xiaogen 孫孝根 of Renhe 仁和, Zhejiang, as collator.[78] The small text (12.2 cm h × 20.6 cm w), clearly if not elegantly cut, includes up to three types of commentary: after the title, a brief explanation of the context in which the poem was composed; within the poem, double rows of interlinear commentary explaining the references and the connections between characters; and at the end an evaluation of the poet and the poem. Thus Du Fu's 杜甫 (712–70) "Chun wang" 春望 (Looking toward spring) begins with an account of the An Lushan 安祿山 rebellion, during which it was composed; the commentator explains that "A letter from home is worth ten thousand pieces of gold" refers to rebels blocking the road between Du and his

---

76. Zhang Longhua and Zeng Zhongshan, *Zhongguo gudai yuwen jiaoyu shi*, pp. 364–65.

77. Nienhauser, *The Indiana Companion to Traditional Chinese Literature*, p. 755. In this work, Shuen-fu Lin claims that this text would have been "the Chinese child's first introduction to his poetry tradition," but it seems likely that the shorter and simpler *Qianjia shi* held that honor.

78. Nienhauser, *The Indiana Companion to Traditional Chinese Literature*, p. 756.

distant family and home. Within the poem itself the characters *henbie* 恨別 (enmity) are explained as expanding on the two characters that open the poem, *guo po* 國破 (the country destroyed; 4.12a). The final statement cites phrases from the poem in which meaning and feeling are poignantly fused and extols Du Fu's greatness (4.12b).

In sum, the notes and comments are aimed at beginning readers of poetry: they present a straightforward, nontechnical account of the poem, explaining its context—information that an advanced reader would not have needed—pointing up some of the more obvious poetic techniques and emphasizing Du Fu's high standing in the poetic canon. If this is the same text as the *Tangshi sanbaishou zhushu* listed in the Wenhai lou account book, it was also, as befitted a widely popular beginning poetry reader, relatively inexpensive: 0.3 *qian* wholesale.

A somewhat larger and more advanced collection, the *Tangshi hexuan xiangjie* 唐詩合選詳解 (Combined selection of Tang poetry, with detailed explanations) by Liu Wenwei 劉文蔚 (*js* 1822) of Shanyin 山陰, Zhejiang, advertised as "worthy to be the poetry student's jade statutes and golden rules" (*yulü jinke* 玉律金科),[79] was priced at either 0.8 or 1.0 *qian*. Despite its considerably higher price, it seems to have sold well, for the account book lists 242 copies, and it appears to have been one of those texts that any Sibao publishing house could produce.[80]

Sibao publishers produced a host of similar poetry anthologies— many, like the *Jiyueyun zhai shiti shifu shizhu* 寄嶽雲齋試體詩賦詩註 (Annotated poems in the examination style from the Jiyueyun Studio), explicitly advertised for examination study—and also other aids to poetry writing. They published rhyming dictionaries, ranging in sophistication from the most famous, the *Peiwen yunfu* 佩文韻府 (Rhyming treasury of the Honoring Literature Library), compiled at imperial command in 1711, to cheap and conveniently small "sleeve" editions

---

79. See the modern edition with notes by Yang Yerong, *Tangshi hexuan*, p. 7.

80. Second in popularity only to *Tangshi sanbaishou*, *Tangshi hexuan xiangjie* collects 368 poems, over 270 of which, many by great poets like Du Fu and Li Bai 李白 (701–62), are not in the more famous collection. Unfortunately only a few blocks of this text survive, from which we know that it was a sizable text, roughly 14.3 cm high and 21.3 cm wide (each full folio page), and that it included, as the title promises, double-column commentary in reduced size between the columns of the poems.

(*xiuzhen* 袖珍, like Western pocket editions)[81] of works like the *Shiyun jicheng* 詩韻集成 (Collected poetic rhymes). In addition to a rhyming dictionary, this text presented in a top register a thesaurus of poetic synonyms—for example, jujubes might be called "vermilion hearts," "ram's horns," "red kernels," or any of at least twenty-four different phrases). Textbooks of poetry composition appear to have been popular, and the Zou and Ma published some poetry criticism as well. Although some of these texts might be quite expensive—the *Shixue xinlun* 詩學新論 (New treatise on the study of poetry) sold wholesale for 2.4 *qian*, Yuan Mei's (1716–98) path-breaking *Suiyuan shihua* 隨園詩話 (Poetry discussions from Sui garden)[82] for 1.2 *qian*, and the *Shixue jicheng* (Collected poetry studies) for 0.9 *qian*—most seem to have been small and inexpensive editions intended for students scrambling to master the examination poetry requirement. Some of these works may well have been compiled or edited by Zou and Ma lineage members; Zou Mo, as we saw, was credited in a genealogy biography with compiling the *Tangshi hexuan*, *Shixue hanying*, and *Shiyun hanying*, all of which appear on the Cuiyun tang inventory.

## The Heart of the Curriculum:
## The Classics

At the heart of the educational curriculum were the Classics, first and foremost the Four Books (*Greater Learning, Analects, Mencius, Doctrine of the Mean*), and then, increasingly important throughout the Qing, the Five Classics (*Classic of Songs, Classic of History, Classic of Changes, Spring and Autumn Annals* with the *Zuo Commentary, Record of Rites*). These texts, or at least the Four Books and the *Classic of Songs*, might be introduced quite early, once the student had mastered the basic "San-Bai-Qian" and the *Qianjia shi*. Following rote memorization came comprehension,

---

81. So called because they could be kept in the loose sleeves worn by Chinese scholars.

82. Originally published by the author himself in 1790, *Suiyuan shihua* was an influential work of poetry criticism that repudiated the contemporary emphasis on imitation of the great poets of the past and advocated, in its place, that poets practice technique as a vehicle for the expression of their own emotions; see Waley, *Yuan Mei*, pp. 167–74.

to be achieved through lectures by a teacher and study of the standard commentaries on the Classics. While continuing increasingly sophisticated study of the Four Books and their commentaries, students would move on, perhaps as early as age twelve or thirteen *sui*, to the more challenging Five Classics. (Composition practice, of course, was ongoing, in both poetry and prose, and particularly in the eight-legged essay form for those "junior students" [*tongsheng* 童生] preparing to take the examination for licentiate status.)

Not surprisingly, given their centrality in the examination system, demand for editions of the Classics was constant and heavy. Different (and sometimes not-so-different) editions of these texts were staples of Zou and Ma publishing. Certainly they led Sibao's output of educational texts beyond the primer level. The account book of the Wenhai lou suggests that, over the course of one year, roughly 22 percent of that *shufang*'s trade (about 1,850 out of a total of 8,440 copies) was in classical texts. At least 117 titles of the 860 on the Cuiyun tang inventory are editions of the Classics. Within the Classics category, the Four Books, usually published as a set, dominated; 52 percent of the Wenhai lou and 42 percent of the Cuiyun tang Classics titles were editions of the Four Books or one of the Four Books. In the category of the Five Classics, certain texts were clearly more popular than others. In the Wenhai lou account book, the *Classic of Songs*, with 319 copies, the *Classic of History*, with 316, and the *Classic of Changes*, with 121, far exceeded the *Record of Rites* (42) and *Spring and Autumn Annals* with the *Zuo Commentary* (25) in popularity. The Cuiyun tang inventory conforms roughly to this order, which corresponds with what we know of the popularity of these texts among examination candidates.[83]

---

83. Of the seventy-five titles in the Five Classics category in the Cuiyun tang inventory, fifteen are collections of all five; then twelve are editions of the *Classic of Songs*, eleven of the *Spring and Autumn Annals* (including editions of the *Zuo Commentary*), ten of the *Classic of Changes*, ten of the *Classic of History*, nine of the *Record of the Rites*, six of the *Rites of Zhou*, and two of the *Three Rites*. (These numbers are approximate, as they are based on readings of often abbreviated titles.) The ranking of the Five Classics by popularity among examination candidates in the Qing was: *Classic of Songs*, *Classic of Changes*, *Classic of History*, *Spring and Autumn Annals*, and *Record of Rites* (Elman, *A Cultural History of Civil Examinations*, pp. 702–3).

## THE FOUR BOOKS

Since the Four Books remained the central texts of early study and examination preparation throughout the Qing—even despite efforts to shift the focus of the examinations to the Five Classics in the late Qianlong era—neither their popularity nor their dominance of the Sibao publication lists is surprising.[84] Generally the Zou and Ma publishers found it convenient and profitable to bundle the four works and whatever commentary was deemed necessary under one title.[85] In the nineteenth century, Sibao produced at least fifteen different versions of such collections.[86] But since many of these are known only as titles, we cannot tell how these texts differed in content or how strictly they fulfilled the claims made by their titles.

The significant variations in annotation, commentary, and format of the extant versions of the Four Books suggest that the Sibao publishers were marketing these texts to readers of different abilities and goals. A detailed look at a few Sibao editions reveals the range in intended readership. Perhaps the simplest explanation strategy is deployed in *Sishu yizhu* 四書繹註 (Unraveling the Four Books), a late nineteenth-century

---

84. Barr, "Four Schoolmasters," pp. 55–57. Elman (*A Cultural History of Civil Examinations*, p. 567) points out that, although the Han learning advocates succeeded by the late eighteenth century in establishing knowledge of all of the Five Classics as a requirement for the provincial and metropolitan examinations (instead of a specialization in just one), the Four Books retained their primacy: "Except for the beginning period in 1794, the best essays on the Five Classics were usually less important than those on the Four Books in determining a candidate's final rank. The Han Learning challenge to the Four Books had been successful in authorizing the Five Classics for all candidates, but the Four Books monopoly on the highest ranks in the local, provincial, and metropolitan civil examinations had been maintained. Indeed, the examiners' tendency to grade each candidate's essays on the Five Classics uniformly undermined their significance individually in the rankings."

85. A few editions of a single Classic were produced, most notably of *Mencius* and the *Doctrine of the Mean*. There was also an edition of the ritual expert Jiang Yong's 江永 (1681–1762) *Xiangdang tukao* 鄉黨圖考 (Investigation of "Xiangdang," with illustrations; 1761), a text that reproduces, with extensive commentary by the author, just the tenth book of the *Analects*, analyzing it as a guide to proper ritual (see Legge, *The Chinese Classics*, vols. 1 and 2, "Prolegomena," p. 131).

86. See Appendix G for a list of Sibao editions of the Four Books.

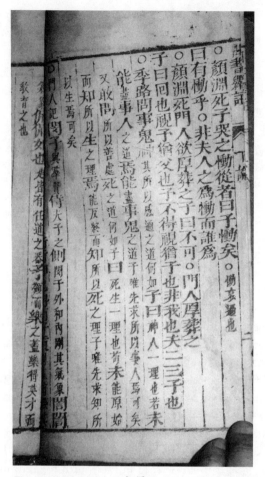

Fig. 10.16 *Sishu yizhu* 四書繹註 (Unraveling the Four Books). The smaller interlinear characters flesh out the meaning of the *Analects*. Photograph by the author.

Sibao publication (Fig. 10.16). Here the explanation or, to cite the title, the "unraveling," is accomplished by expanding the terse text of each Classic into fuller, more intelligible passages. For example, the famous passage in which Confucius's disciple Ji Lu asks about serving ghosts and spirits is treated thus (the passage from the *Analects* is in a different typeface): 季路問事鬼神其所以感通之道何如子曰神人一理也若未能盡事人之道焉能盡事鬼之道予唯先求所以事人焉可矣 ("Ji Lu asked, 'In serving ghosts and spirits, how does one go about contacting them?' The master replied, 'Spirits and people are of one principle. If you are not yet able to realize fully the way of serving people, then how can you realize fully the way of serving ghosts? You should simply first seek the way to serve people'"). The meaning is made clear by amplifying the text of the Classic, rather than by adding notes or commentary.

The 1868 Wenhai lou version of the *Sishu zhengwen* (full title: *Wenhai lou jiaozheng jianyun fenzhang fenjie Sishu zhengwen* 文海樓校正監韻分章分節四書正文, Wenhai lou *Orthodox Text of the Four Books*, standardized, with corrected pronunciations, and divided into sections), collated by Wu Jupo 巫鞠坡, edited by Lai Fengqian 賴鳳謙, and corrected by Yan Maoyou (fl. 1620s–30s), represents a very conservative, even parsimonious, approach to semantic annotation; as its full title indicates, its purpose seems to be the standardization of passage divisions and of pronunciation in the Four Books (Fig. 10.17). The text is divided into two registers, the lower one (12.8 cm) containing the text of the Classic in large, clear characters (nineteen to a column, with ten columns per half-folio page), with very sparse notes, and the narrow upper register (2.3 cm) devoted entirely to notes. The Classic portion is unpunctuated, with each chapter marked off by an initial circle. Each conventional division within the chapter begins at the top of a new column; additional lines in the division, if any, are indented one character space. The terse notes in the lower register are guides to pronunciation and thus to meaning: in *Mencius* 4.1, for example, the first few lines of the Classic are glossed with the single point (in a different typeface here) that the *wen* of *renwen* 仁聞 should be read in the fourth tone, to indicate that it means "reputation":

孟子曰離婁之明公輸子之巧不以規矩不能成方員師曠之聰不以六律不能正五音堯舜之道不以仁政不能平治天下

今有仁心仁聞而民不被其澤不可法於後世者不行先王之道也　聞去聲

(*ce* 2, 1a).

Mencius said, "Even if you had the keen eyes of Li Lou and the skill of Kung-shu Tzu, you could not draw squares or circles without a carpenter's square or a pair of compasses; even if you had the acute ears of Shih K'uang, you could not adjust the pitch of the five notes correctly without the six pipes; even if you knew the way of Yao and Shun, you could not rule the Empire equitably except through benevolent government. Now there are some who, despite

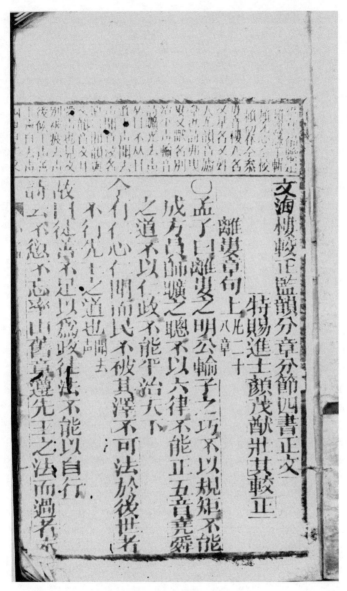

Fig. 10.17 Page from the *Mencius,* in *Wenhai lou jiaozheng jianyun fenzhang fenjie Sishu zhengwen* 文海樓校正監韻分章分節四書正文 (Wenhai lou *Orthodox Text of the Four Books,* standardized, with corrected pronunciations, and divided into sections), published by the Wenhai lou. The text in the top register provides a guide to pronunciation and alternative meanings of some of the characters in the Classic. Photograph by the author.

their benevolent hearts and reputations, succeed neither in benefiting the people by their benevolence nor in setting an example for posterity. This is because they do not practice the way of the Former Kings."[87]

More extensive notes, crowded into the top register (twenty columns per page, with five characters per column), provide more information on pronunciation than is strictly necessary, but less information than one might like on identification and meaning. Thus, a variety of different pronunciations and meanings is given for the character 婁 (it can be pronounced as 樓 or as 盧, as in the passage from the *Classic of Odes*, 弗曳弗婁, "you will not wear them"; it can be a person's given name, the name of a constellation, a surname, or the name of an animal). But Li Lou himself, the legendary figure of exceptional vision cited by Mencius, is never explained. Yet the extended gloss of the note reproduced above (聞去聲) lists two different possible pronunciations and meanings for 聞, only one of which is relevant to its usage in the *Mencius* passage: "聞 is fourth tone. 聞 is pronounced 汶. It means 'reputation' [literally, 'name extending over a distance']. When 聞 rhymes with 文, it is pronounced 文 and it means 'to hear' [literally, 'the ear receiving sound']" (*ce* 2, 1a). There is no discussion of the passage as a whole or of its philosophical significance. Throughout this text, an interest in phonology, rhyme, and vocabulary dominates the notes; the reader learns many possible readings of a character, of varying relevance to the larger meaning of the text. What was the purpose of this text? Given the emphasis on proper pronunciation, rhyme, and standard section divisions, it is likely that it was intended to serve as a guide to accurate recitation and memorization of the Classic and, with its lists of variant meanings, as a means of increasing lexical knowledge.

Other Sibao versions of these Classics provide fuller annotation and commentary and were obviously designed to explicate the texts. For example, the 1883 edition of *Yuanben Erlun qiyou yinduan* 原本二論啟幼印端 (Original edition of *Two Treatises for the Education of Children and the*

87. The translation is from D. C. Lau, *Mencius*, p. 149. Li Lou, a contemporary of Huangdi, was said to have such sharp vision that he could see a hair at one hundred paces. Gongshu is better known as Lu Ban, who became the patron god of carpenters. Kuang was a musician and counselor in the state of Jin.

*Stimulation of Virtue*, 1776),[88] compiled by Liu Zhong 劉忠 of Tongbo 桐柏, Henan, is explicitly designed for teaching beginning students of eight to nine *sui*. The preface presents this work as a protest against the conventional method of early education in the Classics, "backing the book"—that is, rote memorization of dictated passages without instruction in their meaning. (Progress was tested by having the student stand with his back to the book and recite the passage in question.) On the one hand, beginning students were too young and ignorant to read the texts of the Classics and understand their "extensive and profound" meaning. On the other, the dictation of the texts, as "unfounded speech," left them without references to the solid support of the written word. Moreover, they often got lost if the dictated passages grew too long. Existing textual efforts to explain the Classics either distorted the meaning, threatening to "poison the vital parts" of the young, or broke them up into fragments, "at times following the text, at others cutting it off," so that the student was confused.

A teacher himself, Liu Zhong set about to remedy this by providing students at a critical age with a moral guide, a means of "nurturing rectitude," through simple explanations of the *Greater Learning* and the *Analects* (according to Zhu Xi, the two of the Four Books that should be read first, as the foundational texts of the Confucian curriculum). The result, according to the admiring preface, is perfection: "Just the right degree of simplicity and sophistication, easiness and accuracy, correctness and solidity, distance and closeness to the text" ("Jiangshu erlun xu," 1ab).

How did Liu achieve this? First, he explained the text in very simple colloquial Chinese, presenting the basic sense of the orthodox interpretation (that is, the Zhu Xi interpretation), stripped of potentially confusing ontological elaborations. Second, he provided multiple (often repetitious) annotations of characters and phrases in a format that encouraged the student to progress slowly through the text. Liu divided the page into two complementary registers, each of which reproduced the text of the Classic in large characters, but with different interlinear

---

88. This text was also published as *Erlun chuanwen beizhi* 二論串文備旨 (Two treatises with linked explanations). It was completed for publication by Liu Zhong's followers, Liu Mao 劉懋 and Liu Duozhen 劉鐸振.

commentaries. The commentary in the bottom register includes opening summaries of each chapter, explanations of the meaning of the text,
and colloquial "translations" of each phrase. The commentary in the
top register breaks the text into smaller units (sometimes just a single
character) and explains the meaning of characters and identifies the
people mentioned in the text. Circles separate each unit of text-and-
commentary. As is usually the case in such books, the reader was supposed to start with the bottom register, stopping to consult the detailed
notes at the top as necessary (or going back to read them once a section
of the lower register had been completed).

Figure 10.18 shows, for example, the way in which the opening passage of the *Analects*, 子曰學而時習之不亦說乎 ("The Master said, 'To
learn and rehearse it constantly, is this indeed not a pleasure?'") is handled. The rather labored explanation reproduces, in simplified form and
colloquial language, what we might call the practically useful portion of
Zhu Xi's orthodox gloss in classical Chinese.[89] It emphasizes the course
of action the student is to take as well as the attitude he is to adopt:
emulating the behavior of those more advanced in virtue, constantly
practicing or reviewing this behavior, and finding the whole process enjoyable. It strips away Zhu Xi's citations of other commentators (such
as Cheng Yi 程頤 and Xie Liangzuo 謝良佐), his fuller and more ar-
cane definitions ("*Xi* 習 is the frequent, rapid motion of a bird's wings
in flight"), and, most important, his effort to connect the passage to his
ontological explanation of why one derives pleasure from study (the
claim that human nature is innately good, and that by emulating the
good, one comes to understand the good and return, happily, to one's
original nature).[90]

Liu succeeds in making the text linguistically and semantically intelligible to young students (and to unskilled teachers in need of a lesson
plan) without baffling them with its profounder meanings. In the bottom register the moral message of the passage is emphasized first in the

---

89. That is, it adopts Zhu's understanding of 學 as 效, "to emulate" (rather than He
Yan's rendering, "to learn," as in "book learning"; see Gardner, *Zhu Xi's Reading of the
Analects*, pp. 30–31).

90. *Sishu jizhu, Lunyu*, 1a. The translation is from Gardner, *Zhu Xi's Reading of the
Analects*, p. 31.

子 This means "the master." His surname is Kong, his name is Qiu, and his *zi* is Chongni. He was a sage of the state of Lu. 曰 This means "to speak." 子曰 refers to the master's speech. 學 This is to copy the manner of those before you. What I don't understand, I learn from those who do. What I'm not able to do, I learn from those who are able to do. Both explicating books and managing affairs are learning. Now, the ancients were humane, righteous, loyal, and trustworthy, tirelessly taking pleasure in virtue. 時 This means "time." 習 This means "review." 時習之 This means "to take what one has learned and constantly review it." 説 This has the meaning of "enjoy." 不亦説乎 How can the mind not be pleased? O This section explains the benefits to oneself of learning.

O This chapter shows the master citing the benefits of learning to urge people to study and to encourage them to take pleasure in learning. Naturally, if one takes pleasure in learning, one will become a gentleman. 子曰 The master said O Everyone can become good simply by learning. 學而時習之 What I don't understand, I learn from those who do. What I'm not able to do, I learn from those who are able to do. When I finish learning, I constantly review what I have studied. O Then what I have studied is familiar. 不亦説乎 The mind is naturally satisfied. Does this not make learning even more pleasurable? O I take pleasure in learning (1a).

Fig. 10.18  Page layout of the *Yuanben Erlun qiyou yinduan* 原本二論啓幼印端 (Original edition of *Two Treatises for the Education of Children and the Stimulation of Virtue*).

simple colloquial summary of each phrase from the Classic and second in the equally simple colloquial translation that follows. Here Liu uses the text to "draw out the beginnings of virtue" (*yin duan* 引端) in his young students, the purpose announced in the title. In the top register, he defines each character separately and then places it firmly back into the larger message of the passage, providing the student with the vocabulary he needs to understand the Classic. In this redaction, a simple and partial but clear understanding of the orthodox interpretation of the *Analects* is impeded only by poor production—the cramped and very faint characters make it difficult to decipher the easy colloquial explanations.

Sibao also produced more sophisticated commentaries on the Four Books, designed for more advanced students clearly on the examination "track." The *Sishu buzhu beizhi tiqiao huican* 四書補註備旨題竅匯參 (Collation of the full purport and explication of the subtleties of the Four Books, supplemented with commentary; Fig. 10.19), for example, packs three crowded registers of explanation on each page. As usual,

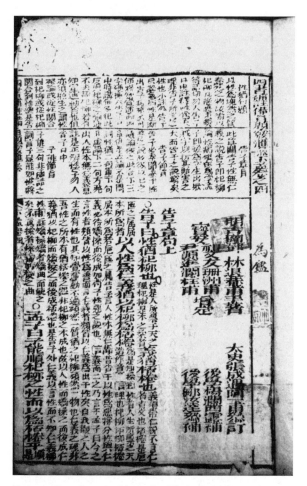

Fig. 10.19 Page from the *Mencius,* in *Sishu buzhu beizhi tiqiao huican* 四
書補註備旨題竅匯參 (Collation of the full purport and explication
of the subtleties of the Four Books, supplemented with commentary).
The text of the Classic, with the standard commentary, occupies the
lowest register; the top two registers contain explanations of the Classic. Photograph by the author.

the text of the Classic is printed in the largest characters in the lowest and
most commodious register (15.3 cm). In that level, units of text, consisting of a sentence or two from the Classic and a series of four different
types of annotations, are marked off by circles. Each sentence of the
Classic is divided into phrases, and after each phrase a series of definitions or simple translations (in classical Chinese) are provided in smaller

interlinear characters. Once the whole sentence has been glossed, a section headed with the boxed-in character *zhu* 註 in larger type transcribes the orthodox Zhu Xi commentary found in Zhu's *Sishu jizhu*, mastery of which was essential to success in the examinations. Then a section marked *jiang* 講 (interpretation, lecture) elaborates on the passage's meaning. Thus, the opening line of Mencius's debate with Gaozi—告子曰性猶杞柳也義猶桮棬也以人性爲仁義猶以杞柳爲桮棬 ("Gaozi said, 'Human nature is like the *qi* willow. Righteousness is like cups and bowls. To make righteousness out of human nature is like making cups and bowls out of the willow'")[91]—is first glossed, then annotated with Zhu Xi's commentary, and then "interpreted" as follows:

In former times, Gaozi took human nature to be evil, dividing human nature and humaneness-and-righteousness into two. And he said to Mencius, "Today all those who speak of human nature alike take human nature to be good; and all those who speak of humaneness and righteousness alike take humaneness and righteousness to be derived from human nature. From my point of view, man has human nature at birth. His perceptions and movements are insensately one substance, just as the *qi* willow is insensately one thing. The principle of humaneness and righteousness is not something that my nature originally has, just as the utensils, cups, and bowls are not formed originally in the *qi* willow. Therefore, human nature will become humane and righteous only after it has been forced and bent, just as the *qi* willow becomes cups and bowls only after it has been forced and bent." This is Gaozi seeing humaneness and righteousness as external to human nature; he does not understand that humaneness and righteousness are the willow's nature. (*Mengzi*, *xia*, 4.1a)

This "interpretation" adds little, simply expanding on the explanation of the text given by Zhu Xi. Finally, a short section marked *bu* 補 (supplement) contains additional glosses, often defining or clarifying characters mentioned in the annotations—in this case, defining the characters Zhu Xi had used to describe the action required to make cups and bowls from willow wood: *jiao* 矯, "to force," and *rou* 揉, "to bend." In this bottom register the text is continuous, although the notes, as usual, are set in double columns and in much smaller characters than is the text of the Classic itself.

---

91. The translation, with slight modification, is from Lau, *Mencius, A Bilingual Edition*, p. 241.

The middle register (4.7 cm h), presumably to be read after the lowest, comments on whole chapters (*zhangzhi* 章旨) and sections (*jiezhi* 節旨). On the page shown in Fig. 10.19, the middle register above the "Gaozi" chapter of *Mencius* opens with a section entitled "Meaning of the Gaozi chapter," which explains the major point of the passage—Mencius's attack on Gaozi's view that human nature lacks humaneness and righteousness. It also points up the source of Gaozi's error, in his use of the character *wei* 為 to imply that human nature has to "be made" or forced to be humane and righteous. Mencius challenges his use of *wei* by reinterpreting it to mean, in effect, "to do violence to" human nature, and argues that because humaneness and righteousness are in fact original to human nature, no force is needed to acquire them. This analysis disposes of Gaozi's "calamitous theory."

Next comes a very sketchy rhetorical analysis of the passage: "Gaozi had certainly often heard of Mencius's theory that human nature was good, and he therefore wished to use his own theory to destroy it. These three phrases are essentially all establishing his theory, rather than posing questions." The phrases are broken down into semantic groups for easy understanding, and the commentary is interpreted, rather colloquially, as "explaining correctly that the character 性 does not enter Gaozi's mouth"—that is, that Gaozi does not really understand what human nature is (*Mengzi, xia*, 4.1a).

The top register (2.6 cm h) deals, often at considerable length, with specific themes, identified by sentence ("Xing you *juti*" 性猶句題, "theme of the sentence [beginning] 'Xing you'"). Here again we see the influence of Zhu Xi's state-sanctioned teaching: Gaozi is wrong about human nature because he "only acknowledges *qi* [psycho-physical stuff] as human nature" (*Mengzi, xia*, 4.1a–3a). This point refers for the first time to the ontological underpinnings of the orthodox view of human nature, introducing the reader to the larger ideas behind Zhu Xi's interpretation. The top register also provides notes about people and place-names mentioned in the Classic. These various sets of notes are not well coordinated physically, and no punctuation is provided to make the cramped text easier to read.

This text was obviously designed for students on the examination track, but still by no means sophisticated or knowledgeable. Interestingly, James Legge characterized this text—or a version close to it—as "perhaps the best of all editions of the Four Books for a learner" because of its profusion of aids to interpretation.[92] He might have added that this panoply of comments and notes serves to drive home the standard understanding of the text. The "Gaozi" chapter of the *Sishu buzhu beizhi tiqiao huican* provides the orthodox interpretation, taken character for character from the *Sishu jizhu*. Zhu Xi is not named as the commentator; the interpretation is a given, *the* way of reading the text. Contending views are not even hinted at. Brief glosses on two crucial characters in Zhu's commentary (*jiao* and *rou*) clarify Mencius's critique of Gaozi's use of *wei* to mean "force" or "bend." The compiler then devotes a great deal of space to driving home the point that Gaozi is wrong and Mencius right—presumably a more experienced reader of these texts would not need this point repeated so frequently. In short, the whole elaborate apparatus of commentary, interpretation, supplements, "meanings of chapters," "meanings of sections," and "themes of sentences" is devoted to explicating the orthodox Cheng-Zhu interpretation of the passage for a student, new to the text, who wants to understand beyond all doubt "what will be on the test."

## THE FIVE CLASSICS

As the classical texts that were easiest to learn and most susceptible to the Cheng-Zhu Confucian interpretations favored by the state, the Four Books remained throughout the Qing the basic texts of the examination system. But reforms of the system in the eighteenth century required candidates to master the Five Classics—or at least one of these texts—as well. During the early decades of the Qing, candidates for licentiate status might get by without writing on any of the Five Classics. But the Yongzheng emperor decreed at least one essay on one of these more difficult texts at all levels of the examinations, with more stringent grading of the provincial and metropolitan examinations.[93] Candidates were permitted to choose which of the five to write on. Naturally most students chose the easiest and shortest of the five, either the *Classic of*

---

92. Legge, *The Chinese Classics*, vol. I, "Prolegomena," p. 130.

93. Ridley, "Educational Theory and Practice in Late Imperial China," p. 214; and Elman, *A Cultural History of the Civil Examinations*, pp. 283–84.

*Songs*, which was relatively easy to memorize; the *Classic of Changes*, the briefest, with 24,107 characters; or the *Classic of History*, the next briefest, with 25,700.[94] Doubtless this helps to explain the popularity of these three texts among Sibao editions of the Five Classics.

In 1787, responding in part to a consensus among leading literati that mastery of only one of the Five Classics did not provide prospective officials with the comprehensive classical knowledge they needed, the Qianlong emperor decided to require candidates to master all five. Recognizing the weight of this extra burden—candidates now had to memorize roughly 470,000 characters, rather than (at most) 99,010 (the length of the *Record of Rites*, the longest of the five)—the emperor phased the new curriculum in over the course of four years. By 1793 all candidates for the *juren* and *jinshi* degrees had to have memorized the Four Books *and* all of the Five Classics—a fourfold increase—as well as mastering the art of regulated verse composition.[95]

Not surprisingly, then, the Five Classics, either as single titles or collections, formed a considerable portion of Sibao's output: half to three-fifths of the total output of Classics titles on the Wenhai lou account book and the Cuiyun Tang inventory. The greater length of the Five Classics (roughly eight times the character count of the Four Books) and the fact that they were not equally popular encouraged publication of individual texts, particularly the *Classic of Songs*, *Classic of Changes*, and *Classic of History*.[96]

One of Wuge's few joint editions of the Five Classics deserves attention: *Wujing beizhi* 五經備旨 (Full purport of the Five Classics), com-

---

94. During the Ming and Qing, the *Shijing* remained, with the *Yijing*, the most popular specialization within the category of the Five Classics. Elman remarks on the "remarkable consistency in the popularity of the *Poetry Classic*" in the Ming, reporting that "about 30% to 35% of young literati consistently chose it for their specialization" (*A Cultural History of the Civil Examinations*, pp. 267, 282–83, 563–66).

95. Ibid., p. 285.

96. Unfortunately, few single-title volumes have survived. The *Shijing*, which according to property-division documents, account books, and inventories was the most popular, exists now only in several sets of fragments. For example, the *Jianben Shijing quanwen* 監本詩經全文 (Directorate of Education edition of the complete text of the *Classic of Songs*; although the cover page names it *Shijing duben* 詩經讀本, *Classic of Songs* reader), originally handsome, but now virtually illegible, appears to present the Zhu Xi commentary.

piled by Zou Shengmai from 1715 to his death in 1762, then arranged by his son Zou Tingyou and revised by his grandsons Zou Jingyang, Jinghong, and Jingzhang. Zou's undated preface to the *Chunqiu beizhi* 春秋備旨 (Full purport of the *Spring and Autumn Annals*) explains that he developed the text for his family school, the Ji'ao shanfang 寄傲山房, and then repeats a conventional authorial disclaimer: "without my knowledge, a commercial publisher secretly took [the text] and expended the labor in having it cut" ("Xu," 1b). The 1764 preface to the *Liji beizhi* 禮記備旨 (Full purport of the *Record of Rites*), by Wang Zishen 王紫紳 of Sibao, further explains that it was Shengmai's son Tingyou who decided that the text should be disseminated outside the Ji'ao Shanfang school ("Xu," 1b). Indeed, this publication seems to have been a family project; the title pages of each Classic identify the text as the "lessons of the Ji'ao Shanfang school" (Ji'ao Shanfang *shuke* 寄傲山房塾課). (See Fig. 10.20.)

The *Wujing beizhi* was clearly designed for use in the examination curriculum. The author's preface to the *Shijing beizhi* 詩經備旨 (Full purport of the *Classic of Songs*), posthumously dated 1763, links the text directly to Deng Lin's *Sishu beizhi*, one of Sibao's most popular guides to the orthodox reading of the Four Books ("Xu," 1b).[97] Zou's 1715 preface to the *Yijing beizhi* 易經備旨 (Full purport of the *Classic of Changes*), after declaring Zhu Xi the premier explicator of the text, praises Zhu's most ardent early Qing follower and editor, Li Guangdi, and, in particular, Li's annotated version of the *Classic of Changes*, the *Zhouyi zhezhong*.[98] The second preface (dated 1798), by Ma Lüfeng 呂豐, a Ma-family publisher and relative of Zou Shengmai, praises Zou's classical learning and places Zou's edition of the text firmly in the line of Cheng-Zhu Confucianism, adducing Shao Yong 邵雍 (1011–77), Zhou Dunyi 周敦頤 (1017–73), Cheng Yi, and of course the master himself, as inspirations for this particular edition.

The appended prefaces and notes to the reader suggest the degree to which the publishers were aware of useful new examination aids and of imperial examination policies. Zou Shengmai's fulsome reference to Li

---

97. See also Legge, *The Chinese Classics*, vol. 4, "Prolegomena," p. 176.
98. This work was also printed by a Mawu shop, the Zaizi tang.

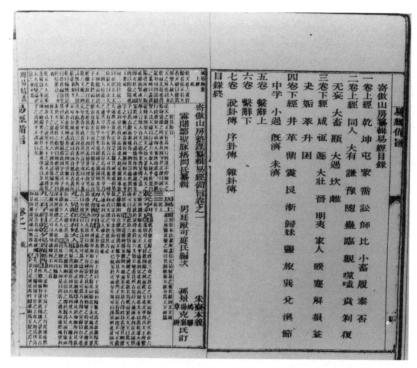

Fig. 10.20 Title page of a late Qing edition of *Wujing beizhi* 五經備旨 (Full purpose of the Five Classics), a text edited by Zou Shengmai 鄒聖脈, with the opening of the *Classic of Changes* (this is not a Sibao edition). The full title identifies the text as a school text. Courtesy of the Shanghai Library.

Guangdi's *Zhouyi zhezhong* is dated to the year of that text's publication—1715—suggesting that Zou was able to update his guides to the examinations quickly. In his preface and notes to the reader in *Chunqiu beizhi*, Zou praises in particular Hu Anguo's 胡安國 (1074–1138) then-standard commentary, as well as three Han commentaries, on the *Spring and Autumn Annals*; all, he claims, explain the text "as the stars beautify the heavens." He was modeling his guide to the text on the imperially sponsored *Qinding Chunqiu zhuanshuo huizuan* 欽定春秋傳説彙纂 (Imperially sponsored compilation and digest of commentaries and explanations of the *Spring and Autumn Annals*), first published in 1721, which reproduces the Hu and these same Han commentaries.[99]

---

99. Legge, *The Chinese Classics*, vol. 5, "The Prolegomena," pp. 136–37. A later preface (1758), written by an official in the Board of Punishments, specifically cites this imperi-

The *Wujing beizhi* was apparently quite popular; the Shanghai Library holds no fewer than three different editions, all dating from the late nineteenth and early twentieth centuries—1879, 1886, and 1904. Unfortunately since none of these is a Sibao edition, it is impossible to tell how much of the commentary and notes formed part of Zou's original editions.

Some single-title editions of the Five Classics survive in Sibao, however, and these suggest the level of assistance readers could expect from Zou or Ma versions of these texts. Elsewhere I have analyzed the student aids—the punctuation, the interlinear, sideline, and discursive commentaries—that make Sibao editions of the *Zuo Commentary* and the *Classic of History* accessible to first-time readers.[100] The same general approach, with an emphasis on simple explanations of meaning and historical allusions, characterizes almost all Sibao editions of the Five Classics. Many of these texts were advertised, with reasonable accuracy, as presenting "the essence" (*jinghua* 精華) of a Classic.

For example, an undated Mawu edition of the *Record of Rites*, titled *Liji jinghua* 禮記精華 (Essence of the *Record of Rites*), lists as compilers two noted Qing scholars of the ritual Classics, Wang Ji 汪基 and Jiang Yong; it is likely that this was a ploy to make the text seem authoritative. Like most of Sibao's classical texts, this work reproduces the Classic in large characters in a lower register, interspersed with interlinear commentary; a narrow upper register provides additional notes on the text (see Figs. 10.21a and b). The commentary is fairly straightforward, for the most part restating the meaning of the Classic in easier-to-understand classical Chinese. Thus the opening lines of the chapter on study ("Xue ji" 學記) reads (the commentary is bracketed):

When a ruler is concerned that his measures should accord with law, and seeks for the assistance of the good and upright, this is sufficient to secure him a considerable reputation, but not to move the multitudes (*fa lü xian, qiu shan*

---

ally sponsored version as a model ("*Yuzuan Chunqiu zhizhuan* xu," 1b). Hu's commentary remained the standard interpretation of the *Spring and Autumn Annals* until 1793, when the Qianlong emperor debarred it (Elman, *A Cultural History of Civil Examinations*, p. 567).

100. See Brokaw, "The Best-sellers of the Nineteenth Century," pp. 203–5.

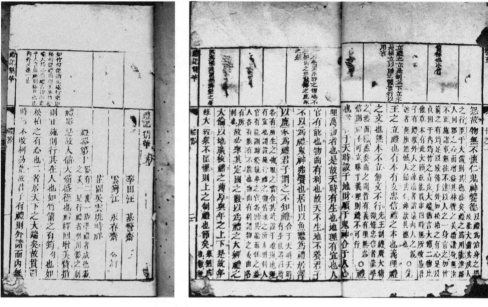

Fig. 10.21 *Liji jinghua* 禮記精華 (Essence of the *Record of Rites*). (a, *left*) Title page. (b, *right*) Sample pages; the top register contains additional notes on the text below. Photographs by the author.

*liang, zuyi xiaowen, bu zuyi dong zhong* 發慮憲, 求善良, 足以謏聞, 不足以動眾). [*Fa lü xian* means "to arrive at his measures by seeking to accord with the law." Then he "seeks the virtuous and good" (*qiu shan liang*) and draws close to the worthy. From these two courses of action, he can achieve a little reputation, but he cannot move the masses.] When he cultivates the society of the worthy and tries to embody the views of subjects who are remote from the court, this is sufficient to move the multitudes, but not to transform the people (*jiu xian ti yuan zuyi dong zhong wei xuyi hua min* 就賢體遠足以動眾未足以化民). [*Jiu xian* is to draw close to worthy and virtuous scholars. *Yuan* is those who are distant.] If the ruler wishes to transform the people and to perfect their manners and customs, must he not start from the lessons of the school (*junzi ru yu hua min cheng su qi bi you xue hu* 君子如欲化民成俗其必由學乎)? [*Hua min cheng su* is a little like Yao and Shun's "transforming the people and achieving universal concord."[101] This is nothing less than the way of greater learning.][102]

---

101. A citation from the "Yaodian," Book of Tang, *Classic of History;* see Legge, *The Chinese Classics*, 3: 17.

102. I have relied on James Legge's translation of the Classic, with only minor alterations; see Legge, trans., *Li chi, Book of Rites*, 2: 82.

The comments in the top register gloss the last sentence of the Classic: "*Junzi* 君子 refers to the ruler of all under heaven. This correctly shows the great source of study. Study must come from the ruler's own implementation of his own inborn virtue (*mingde* 明德) and his establishment of schools to teach [virtue to] the people. Only then will the fundamentals be inculcated" (18.24a).

The commentary here "translates" the Classic's terse Han-dynasty classical Chinese into the fuller and more discursive classical Chinese of the later imperial period—in many cases simply substituting a compound for a single character. The upper-register commentary adds some explanation not found in the interlinear comments (the definition, for example, of *junzi*, "the superior man") and, more important, summarizes and to some extent extrapolates the point of the passage: that the ruler has to cultivate himself before he can hope to teach the people. Both commentaries include references to other Classics: the interlinear commentary cites the *Classic of History*'s description of Yu's transformation of the people (*yu bianshi yong* 於變時雍), and the upper-register comments note another portion of the *Record of Rites*, the famous phrase *mingde* from the "Greater Learning." Interestingly, this edition does not follow the commentaries of either Zheng Xuan 鄭玄 (127–200) and Kong Yingda 孔穎達 (574–648) or Chen Hao 陳澔 (1261–1341), both of which were considered standard for the examinations,[103] perhaps because it was intended as an introductory text to a Classic that seems to have been little emphasized in the examinations. If this were the case, students would really need to know only the *jinghua* or essence of the text.[104]

How do the Sibao editions of the Five Classics compare with those of the Four Books? Generally speaking, the editions of the Five Classics are consistently better produced than those of the Four Books. Although none is beautifully cut, the Five Classics are at least clearly cut, with large characters and unambiguous demarcation of commentary and Classic. Almost all volumes of the Five Classics are also larger than those of the Four Books (see, for example, the Sibao edition of the

---

103. Elman, *A Cultural History of Civil Examinations*, p. 410.

104. At least one Sibao version did provide the Chen Hao commentary: the *Liji zeng-ding jujie* 禮記增訂句解 (Expanded and revised sentence-by-sentence explanation of the *Record of Rites*).

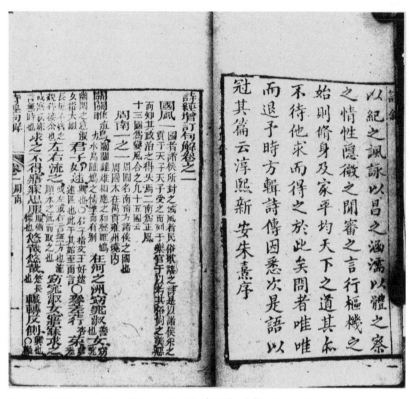

Fig. 10.22 Title page of the *Shijing zengding jujie* 詩經增訂句解 (*Classic of Songs,* expanded, revised, with phrase-by-phrase explanations). Photograph by the author.

*Classic of Songs* in Fig. 10.22). Only the *Sishu buzhu beizhi tiqiao huican,* discussed above, rivals the editions of the Five Classics in size—and that is owing to the amount of commentary that had to be crammed, at great sacrifice of legibility, on each page. Presumably quality was partially determined by demand and by differences in audience: the Four Books were for young students still in the elementary stage of education and for poor and perhaps inadequately educated village schoolteachers. And if a considerable portion of the market for these texts consisted of families who could afford only the first few years of schooling, more beautiful and hence more expensive versions would have sold poorly. By the time a student embarked on the Five Classics, however, he (and his family and perhaps lineage and village) had made a serious commitment to examination study and might be able and willing to pay

more for clearer and more helpful texts. Textbook versions of the Five
Classics likely had a wealthier readership.

It is clear that Sibao editions of the Five Classics, like those of the
Four Books, were intended for students. They present for the most
part not only the approved commentaries but also the sort of basic information that would be necessary for a student new to the texts. Following the Qing trend toward increased use of punctuation, most of
the Sibao editions of the Five Classics are also punctuated, with markers that indicate phrase breaks and emphasize important passages—just
the sort of guidance a student would need.[105] A fully literate scholar
would not require—indeed, might feel affronted by—a punctuated text.
(Surprisingly, all Sibao versions of the Four Books mentioned above
are unpunctuated, perhaps because the Four Books, as the first Classics
to be learned, were memorized by rote from a teacher's oral recitation,
with no regard, at least initially, to their meaning. By the time a student
encountered a written text of the Four Books, he probably did not need
punctuation, since he had by then internalized the appropriate pauses in
the course of memorization. Or perhaps he would learn to punctuate,
with the guidance of a teacher, using these texts.)

Sibao's classical output appears to have been untouched by the controversies that preoccupied scholars of Han and Song learning and the
empirical studies (*kaozheng* 考證) movement in the eighteenth and nineteenth centuries. This intellectual orientation may be explained as a
function of the intellectual conservatism of western Fujian, long a bas-
tion of Cheng-Zhu orthodoxy,[106] but more likely it reflects the Sibao
publishers' awareness that examination candidates composed their largest audience. Thus they were careful to publish texts for examination
studies (like the *Zhouyi zhezhong* of Li Guangdi) and to adjust to changes
in the examination curriculum, but probably saw no advantage in producing works like Yan Ruoju's 閻若璩 (1636–1704) pioneering work
challenging the authenticity of the Old Text version of the *Classic of*

---

105. Guan Xihua, *Zhongguo gudai biaodian fuhao fazhan shi*, pp. 260–69. Zhang Xiumin
(*Zhongguo yinshua shi*, pp. 510–12), also provides a useful chart of commonly used symbols but emphasizes that there is considerable variation in usage.

106. See Chapter 2, pp. 52–53.

*History.*[107] Generic editions of the Classics, provided with either the orthodox commentaries or simplified versions of these commentaries, were accessible and presumably desirable to a broad audience. More original, complex, or idiosyncratic interpretations might have attracted a small number of devoted scholars, but as commercial publishers operating at a small profit margin, the Zou and Ma pragmatically chose to appeal to the larger readership.

## Beyond the Four Books and Five Classics

### OTHER "CLASSICS"

The Four Books and Five Classics were not, however, the sole items on the examination reading list. Cheng Duanli 程端禮 (1271–1345), in his influential model curriculum, originally designed for his lineage school, recommended the *Zizhi tongjian* 資治通鑑 (Comprehensive mirror for aid in government) of Sima Guang 司馬光 (1019–86) and authors like the famous Tang essayist Han Yu 韓愈 (768–824) once the students had mastered the Four Books and Five Classics. Many Qing educational theorists recommended the addition of other "classic" texts to the curriculum.[108] Lu Shiyi 陸世儀 (1611–72), for example, recommended following the Four Books and Five Classics with the *Zizhi tongjian gangmu* 資治通鑑綱目 (Summary of the *Comprehensive Mirror for Aid in Government*), a moralistic redaction of Sima Guang's history by Zhu Xi and his students; *Guoce* 國策 (Stratagems of the Warring States); *Shiji* (Records of the Grand Historian); and *Hanshu* (Dynastic history of the Han). Wang Yun 王筠 (1784–1854) expected students to have learned, by the age of fifteen *sui*, not only all the Thirteen Classics, but also *Guoyu* 國語 (Deliberations of the Warring States), *Guoce*, and *Wenxuan* 文選 (Anthology of literature), the great literary anthology of the sixth century that served as the model for later collections. Zhang Jian 張謇 (b. 1853), who earned first place in the palace examination at forty-one *sui*, included in his reading, between the time he earned licentiate status

---

107. The Cuiyun tang book list includes, however, Yan Ruoju's *Sishu shidi* 四書釋地, a study of place-names in the Four Books; see Appendix G.

108. Elman, *A Cultural History of Civil Examinations*, pp. 272–63; and Ridley, "Educational Theory and Practice in Late Imperial China," pp. 371–79.

in 1868 and *juren* status in 1885, the simplified version of the *Tongjian gangmu, Gangjian yizhi lu* 鋼鑑易知錄 (Easy to know *Mirror [of History]*) by Wu Chengquan 吳乘權 (fl. 1695–1711), the *Tongjian gangmu* itself, and eventually the *Shiji* and *Qian Hanshu* 前漢書 (Dynastic history of the Former Han), and the Daoist classics *Laozi* 老子 and *Zhuangzi* 莊子.[109] Most of these readings were, with the exception of the *Wenxuan*, works of history or philosophy.

Of these sorts of texts, the Zou and Ma produced a smattering, although less commonly toward the end of their history. Some were directly relevant to examination study. The Biqing tang published a text titled *Xingli daquan* 性理大全 (Compendium on nature and principle), an abbreviated version of the large work of the same title, the standard guide to the orthodox readings of the Classics. Sibao book lists also include collections of Song Confucian writings like the *Zhuzi huowen* 朱子或問 (presumably a collection of Zhu Xi's comments on the Classics), *Zhuzi jingyan* 朱子精言, the "highlights" of Zhu's writings; and the *Jinsi lu* 近思錄 (Reflections on things at hand), the great anthology of Northern Song Confucian writings edited by Zhu Xi and Lü Zuqian 呂祖謙 (1137–81). Perhaps the most interesting and unusual offering was an edition of the *Kunxue jiwen* 困學紀聞, a collection of "essential things to be learned" about the Classics and other writings made by the Song scholar Wang Yinglin.[110]

Other non-Confucian philosophers and some literary collections appeared intermittently on Sibao book lists. The *Wenxuan* is listed in at least five editions on different book lists. In the Guangxu era, the Yijing tang published *Baizi quance* 百子全冊 (Complete collection of the hundred masters), the writings of pre-Han thinkers, and the Wenhai lou's 1894 title list included a collection of works from the Han and Wei-Jin period, the *Han Wei congshu* 漢魏叢書 (Collectanea of the Han and Wei). The *Daode jing* 道德經 (The Way and its power, or the *Laozi*) and *Zhuangzi* appear once each on three publishing house lists. Also rather sparsely represented are works of history beyond the textbook level;

---

109. Ridley, "Educational Theory and Practice in Late Imperial China," pp. 154, 371–78. Of course, students would have read portions of many of these texts earlier, excerpted in works like *Guwen xiyi* and *Guwen jingyan*.

110. Hervouet, *A Sung Bibliography*, p. 231.

*Guoyu, Shiji, Zizhi tongjian,* and the *Mingshi jishi benmo* 明史紀事本末 (Topically arranged history of the Ming) of Gu Yingtai 谷應泰 (1620–90), an account of the major events and controversies of the Ming, are the only titles listed. Sibao's neglect of the dynastic histories and other historical works can be explained to some extent by the length and high cost of (and limited audience for) these texts: the *Guoyu* sold wholesale for 3.6 *qian,* making it among the more expensive texts recorded in the Wenhai lou account book.

The Zou and Ma published a few texts that might be considered practical aids to officials. The *Da Qing huidian* 大清會典 (Collected statutes of the Great Qing) is listed on the Cuiyun tang inventory, along with several other works of instruction and advice to officials: the *Xuezheng quanshu* 學政全書 (Complete book for the study of government), the important magistrate's handbook *Fuhui quanshu* 福惠全書 (Complete book concerning happiness and benevolence; 1694) by Huang Liuhong 黃六鴻, *Zizhi xinshu* 資治新書 (New book for aid in government), *Zhijun shu* 致君書 (Book for rulers), and so forth. There seems to have been some effort to keep up with legal changes: *Qianlong xinlü* 乾隆新律 (New codes of the Qianlong era) appears on a late eighteenth-century property division document; the *Da Qing xinlü* 大清新律 (New codes of the Qing) on the early nineteenth-century book list of the Zaizi tang; and *Da Qing lü* 大清律 (Codes of the Great Qing) on the Cuiyun tang inventory.

Given the importance of military education and the relative success of military examination candidates in Wuge and Mawu, it is perhaps surprising that only four military titles appear in Sibao records—and all on the same book list, dating from the late eighteenth century: the *Wujing gaotou* 武經高頭 (Top military classics), *Wujing qishu* 武經七書 (Seven military classics), *Wujing sanshu* 武經三書 (Three military classics), and *Wujing duanpian* 武經短篇 (Abridged military classics).[111]

---

111. I have not been able to identify the *Wujing gaotou* or *Wujing duanpian.* It is possible that the *Wujing qishu* was a collection of ancient military texts first published together in 1080 by order of Song Shenzong 宋神宗 (r. 1068–85): *Sunzi bingfa* 孫子兵法 (Sunzi's art of war; sixth–fourth centuries BC), *Sima fa* 司馬法 (Minister of War's methods; fourth–third centuries BC), *Wuzi* 吳子 (attributed to Wu Qi 吳起, a general of the fifth century BC; the text in its final form dates to the Han), *Wei Liaozi* 尉繚子 (attributed to Wei Liao, a strategist of the late fourth and third centuries BC), *Taigong liutao*

The scant information we have about these titles suggests that they were printed by large publishing houses at the height of their prosperity, in the late eighteenth or early nineteenth centuries—that is, that only the most successful houses could afford to publish these texts, which would necessarily have a much smaller market than the primers, supplementary texts, poetry and essay collections, and the Classics.

## DICTIONARIES AND
## REFERENCE WORKS

Sibao produced a range of reference works that served as aids to students, including character dictionaries (and the rhyming dictionaries mentioned earlier), encyclopedias of literary allusions, and guides to allusions and personages in the Classics. Except for the dictionaries, these reference works appear to have been designed largely for study of the Classics.

Although Sibao did produce editions of the Classic dictionary *Erya* 爾雅 (Examples of refined usage; third century BC),[112] its most popular dictionaries were works compiled in the late Ming and Qing to meet the demand from a growing reading population for more usable and accessible dictionaries.[113] The *Xuanjin Zihui* 懸金字彙 (Gold award *Lexicon*) was a version of Mei Yingzuo's 梅膺祚 (fl. 1570–1615) pioneering *Zihui* 字彙 (Lexicon; 1615), which simplified dictionary use considerably by

---

六韜 (Taigong's six secret teachings; third century BC; Taigong was the general who helped the Zhou defeat the Shang), *Huangshi gong sanlüe* 黃石公三略 (Three strategies of the Duke of Yellow Rock; first century BC), and *Tang Taizong Li Weigong wendui* 唐太宗李衛公問對 (Questions and replies between Tang Taizong and Duke Li of Wei; late Tang or early Northern Song). The *Wujing sanshu* is probably a collection of three of these texts—perhaps *Sunzi bingfa*, *Sima fa*, and *Wuzi*. But since there were many different editions of military texts with these titles, it is impossible, without the Sibao volumes, to know what these titles include. See Sawyer, "Military Writings," pp. 98–108; and, for translations, idem, *The Seven Military Classics of China*; and Xu Baolin, *Zhongguo bingshu tonglan*, pp. 496–500, 566–69.

112. The *Erya zhu* 爾雅注 (*Examples of Refined Usage*, annotated), an edition of the dictionary-Classic *Erya*, figures unimportantly in the Wenhai lou account book—only five copies at 0.5 *qian* each, perhaps reflecting the relatively minor status of Classic.

113. Lin Yushan, *Zhongguo cishu bianzuan shilüe*, pp. 73, 82–85; Cao Xianzhuo and Chen Bingcai, *Baqianzhong Zhongwen cishu leibian tiyao*, p. 17.

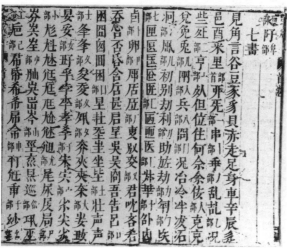

Fig. 10.23 *Xuanjin Zihui* 懸金字彙 (Gold award *Lexicon*), published by the Yijing tang 翼經堂. (a, *top*) Cover page. (b, *bottom*) Sample pages. Photographs by the author.

reducing the number of radicals from 517 to 214, revising the format of definitions, and including popular as well as "correct" usages. The Yijing tang edition (see Figs. 10.23a and b) includes the 1681 preface of Liu Yongmao 劉永懋, who, after a brief survey of the development of language and the major categories of texts, praises the scholarly quality of the text: "Now all under heaven who read the Classics, histories, and philosophers will have a proven [aid]." Liu claims to have found the text so valuable that he hid it in his pillow to protect it during military turmoil, presumably of the Ming-Qing transition ("Xu," 5b–6a). Several Sibao publishing houses also produced the *Zhengzi tong* 正字通 (Encyclopedia of correct characters) of the late Ming scholar Zhang Zilie 張自烈, who claimed to have corrected the errors in the *Zihui*.[114]

*Zihui* and *Zhengzi tong* are significant as the prototypes for the best known of Qing dictionaries—and certainly the most popular Sibao offering in this category—the ubiquitous *Kangxi zidian* 康熙字典 (Kangxi character dictionary), which combined the convenience of its two predecessors with a higher degree of accuracy.[115] This dictionary was a staple of almost all Wuge and Mawu publishing houses, but only a few small volumes (16.4 cm h × 21.6 cm w) survive. It was one of Sibao's more valuable products: the Wenhai lou account book cites a wholesale price of 8.3 *qian* per copy. And a set of blocks of the text was said to be enough to "support an entire household in comfort" (see Chapter 7).

The Sibao publishers issued a few encyclopedias designed largely to aid examination students in mastering the Classics. For example, the *Sishu renwu leidian chuanzhu* 四書人物類典串珠 (Historical figures in the Four Books, arranged as strung pearls; Fig. 10.24), compiled by Zang Zhiren 臧志仁 for his students in a lineage school in Nanjing, is an encyclopedia of information about not only the historical figures but also the institutions and concepts mentioned in the Four Books. A student wishing to understand the historical development of the system of official selection and review, *kaoke* 考課, for example, would find under that entry a description of the evolution of institutions of selection and evaluation, with special attention to relevant terms used in the Classics (not just the Four Books); "demoting the inefficient" (*chuzhi* 黜陟) from the *Classic of History*, for example, is explained in a lengthy paragraph. The *Sishu renwu leidian chuanzhu* functions primarily as an

---

114. One Sibao edition advertises itself as the "original edition of 'Liao Baizi' 廖百子," a reference to Liao Wenying 廖文英, a Qing writer who unscrupulously disseminated Zhang's text under his own name.

115. Lin Yushan, *Zhongguo cishu bianzuan shilüe*, pp. 95–99.

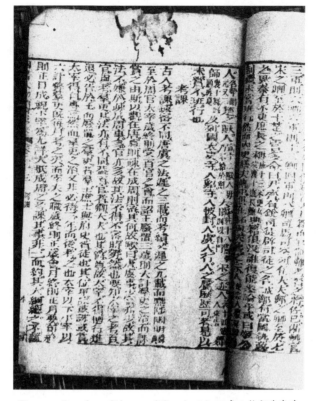

Fig. 10.24 Page from *Sishu renwu leidian chuanzhu* 四書人物類典串珠 (Historical figures in the Four Books, arranged as strung pearls). Photograph by the author.

encyclopedia of people, concepts, and institutions in the Four Books, but by drawing together allusions to these from a variety of texts, it suggests the interrelatedness of the philosophical and historical canon. In this way it helped the student to see how the teachings of the disparate texts cohered.

## Conclusion

What can we conclude from this overview of the educational and scholarly texts produced in Sibao?

First, with the exception of the Hakka primers published for local sale, Sibao's educational and scholarly titles were in no way unusual—

they were similar, in many cases identical, to those produced in Xuwan, Jiangxi, and even to those published in larger centers like Nanjing in the nineteenth century. Sensibly, given its situation and its markets, Sibao appears to have chosen to publish texts widely in demand—the Four Books and Five Classics, the "San-Bai-Qian," *Youxue gushi qionglin, Tangshi sanbaishou, Guwen xiyi, Sishu buzhu beizhi, Wujing beizhi, Kangxi zidian*, and so on. New modes of elite scholarship, such as the texts of the empirical studies movement, do not figure in Sibao's output—and only the very greatest of new scholarly works, such as Gu Yanwu's 顧炎武 (1613–82) *Rizhi lu* 日知錄 (Record of knowledge gained day by day), appear on the Zou and Ma book lists. On the other hand, Sibao publishers certainly tried to keep abreast of changes in the examination requirements: adding texts on the composition of regulated verse or the Five Classics and keeping *au courant* of changes in or new aids to the approved interpretations of the Classics. In sum, their interests were, for very sound business reasons, both rigorously conventional and conventionally up-to-date.

Second, Sibao texts were very practical. They seem to include few writings on teaching methods or theories of learning. Even those texts that can be read as handbooks for teachers convey only very specific information about interpretation, line by line or passage by passage. They offer little analysis of the process or stages of learning. Nor are the individual texts tailored to constitute a fully worked out curriculum.

Third, Sibao texts seem to have been intended for the lower and perhaps middle stretches of the education and examination continuum—that is, Sibao produced many more texts for aspirants to basic literacy, junior student, and licentiate status than for aspiring *juren, jinshi*, or established scholars. The educational output of Sibao resembles this description by James Hayes of "educational texts and aids to literacy" found in Hong Kong peasant villages in the late nineteenth and early twentieth century:

It seems that the Four Books and Five Classics were readily available in cheap red paper-backed editions, without annotation. These were obviously intended to be learned by rote under the teacher's instructions and bawled out by memory in the famed "backing the book" procedure. There were also annotated printed editions for the benefit of higher students. There was a similar range of editions of such other important educational texts as the [Three-character] Classic, the

Thousand-character Classic, and the Hundred Names. There were also more practical primers and word lists prepared at different times. . . . [C]heap editions of [Tang] poetry were commonly available in nineteenth century Canton, locally printed and seemingly widely distributed. . . . In Tsuen Wan and elsewhere in the New Territories of Hong Kong old men say they were among the remembered books of their boyhood, whilst verses are still to be seen on the wall of many of the surviving old ancestral halls, houses and schools.[116]

The Zou and Ma publisher-booksellers supported most fully the schedule of elementary study, which, with its focus on the "San-Bai-Qian," the Four Books, the Five Classics, and Tang poetry, came closest to being the standard in late imperial China. Most students lacked the leisure or the resources to master this curriculum, but those who did might hope to earn licentiate status and its attendant social standing and legal and economic privileges.[117] For many, these privileges alone made licentiate status worth studying for, and further achievement not worth the burdensome investment of time and intellectual effort. The acquisition of *juren* and certainly *jinshi* status demanded, from the high Qing on, an extraordinary degree of dedication and a sober calculation of opportunity costs, given the mid-Qing reforms that made the examinations more difficult and the demographic growth that made the system even more competitive.

A look at the educational texts Sibao did *not* publish throws in sharp relief the focus on the lower end of the market. The dynastic histories, literary collectanea, scholarly encyclopedias, philosophical writings—texts useful to *jinshi* candidates (and, indeed, any aspirant to a high level of cultural literacy)—appear only rarely on early Zou and Ma book lists and not at all on those from the late nineteenth and early twentieth centuries. These were long texts, expensive to cut; the publishers doubtless knew that, given their markets, they were unlikely to profit from their sale. Even at the primer level the Sibao publishers avoided texts like Zhu Xi's *Xiaoxue* 小學 (Elementary learning)—once a common elementary

---

116. Hayes, "Popular Culture in Late Ch'ing China," pp. 61 and 64.

117. Holders of licentiate status were exempt from the head tax and labor conscription (in the early Qing, their family members were exempt from the head tax as well). They were also protected, to some degree, against physical punishment by local officials and against insult or injury by commoners. For a full explanation of the privileges and exemptions due *shengyuan*, see Chang Chung-li, *The Chinese Gentry*, pp. 32–43.

textbook but often dismissed in the Qing as too difficult—and the "daunting collection" of texts that Chen Hongmou mandated for the charitable schools he founded in Yunnan.[118] They targeted primarily the largest textbook market: the students at the base of the educational pyramid, from those eager to acquire some literacy up through the smaller, but still significant group of aspiring licentiate-degree holders, a population of about five million in the Qing.[119] These were boys and young men very much like those of the Wuge and Mawu *shufang* households.

Is there, in turn, anything to be learned about elementary education in the Qing from the range of textbooks that Sibao produced? If the assessment in Chapters 6 and 7 of the markets the Zou and Ma supplied and the business contacts they formed is correct, then the contents of these works reflect the kind of education to be had in family schools, *yixue*, *shexue*, and perhaps some academies located in prefectural and county seats, market towns, and villages in the hinterland and frontier regions of south China.

Almost all the primers and elementary textbooks that Sibao produced confirm the importance of recitation and "learning aloud" in late imperial schools. This is hardly a new point—indeed, it has become perhaps the best-known cliché about Chinese education. The sounds of recitation at the village school were, for Chinese authors, "schoolboys' chants" that bespoke an ordered and prosperous society; and, for late nineteenth-century Western observers and many early twentieth-century Chinese reformers, a dreadful din, a "bellowing," a "bedlam," a "babel of sound," a "squawking" that revealed the weaknesses of the Chinese educational system.[120] Contemporary scholarly opinion gener-

---

118. On *Xiaoxue*, see Kelleher, "Back to Basics." On Chen Hongmou's curriculum, see Rowe, "Education and Empire in Southwest China," pp. 440–41. Some of these texts were: *Guwen yuanjian* 古文淵鑑 (Reader in classical prose), *Gangjian zhengshi yue* 鋼鑑正史約 (Abridged mirror of the dynastic histories), *Daxue yanyi bu jiyao* 大學衍義補輯要 (Abridgment of the *Extended Meaning of the Greater Learning* and its supplement), *Xingli jingyi* 性理精義 (Essence of writings on nature and principle), and *Xiaoxue zuanzhu* 小學纂註 (Elementary learning, revised and annotated).

119. Johnson, "Communication, Class, and Consciousness in Late Imperial China," p. 59.

120. Arthur Smith, *Village Life in China*, p. 80. Ma Xulun 馬敘倫 (1884–1970), a noted philologist, complained in his memoirs of classes with "ten-odd students in a small room, all squawking nonstop. . . . I got away with just opening my mouth and

ally supports the latter evaluation—"rote memorization" is dismissed as a mechanical and painful process, useless as a genuine means of learning.

It might be useful, however, to reconsider this judgment, or at least to consider more carefully the function of memorization and recitation, given the particular goals of the Chinese educational system. The primers, glossaries, and transitional texts (like *Youxue gushi qionglin*) were carefully designed for easy memorization and recitation, to implant the vocabulary, rhythms, grammar, and stock allusions of the written and spoken language and the basic moral and ethical values of the culture in the child's mind. They trained him in the proper patterns of speech and rhetoric and, after a certain point, in the particular styles of writing most highly valued (and rewarded) in the culture. In a society in which the proof of learning and culture was close adherence to a long-established, supposedly universal standard of ritualized behavior and expression (both oral and written), such a method of education was ideally suitable.

As Zhu Xi indicated in his well-known treatise on studying, recitation was proof that one "owned" a text, that one had fully absorbed or internalized its teachings.[121] As late as 1899, a Western observer in western Fujian commented, in language not too far from Zhu's, on the assumptions underlying the process: "Everything must be read aloud, in a high tone and with great emphasis, and with all the fervour of spirit a man possesses, so that he may enter into the very passion of the thing he is learning, so as to make it part of himself."[122] The process may not have been as painful and tiresome as most modern scholars have assumed;[123] simple texts could be taught as games or songs to young chil-

---

making noises with the best of them. All Mr. Zhang required of his students was recitation. . . . I was already ten *sui*, but only on the third book of *Mencius*; moreover, I didn't understand what it was about" (*Wo zai liushisui yiqian*, pp. 3–4, cited in Borthwick, *Education and Social Change in China*, p. 32). Such complaints were standard among the reformers of the May Fourth era.

121. Chu Hsi, *Learning To Be a Sage*, pp. 130–39.

122. London Missionary Society, Report no. 105 (1900), p. 46.

123. Chang Wejen of the Institute of History and Philology, Academia Sinica, explained that, as a child taught by his father to chant texts like the *Daxue*, he had found the process "rather fun." Kwangju Park of the University of Oregon also described his experience learning *Sanzi jing* in Korea—his father drew the characters in sand while teaching him the sounds—as a pleasantly remembered game. Neither example repli-

dren.[124] Western teachers often found it difficult to persuade Chinese students to learn through silent reading; the missionary John Macgowan reported from Tingzhou on his efforts to convert students to Western reading practice: "It would seem to the minds of the students as although the shades of Confucius and Mencius were rising up from the misty path to upbraid them for turning traitor to their teachings, and to the traditions of the ages after them. They say, 'We cannot study unless we read aloud.'"[125]

Enjoyable or not, memorization and recitation were inextricable parts of the process of learning not only to read and write but also to participate in a common culture. Even poor students who could not afford to advance beyond mastery of the "San-Bai-Qian," *Zengguang xianwen*, *Dizi gui*, and *Youxue gushi qionglin* would be learning many of the common idioms, historical allusions, and classical tags that formed the basis of a shared culture, and that were "taught" to the illiterate and reinforced for the semi-literate in plays and oral literature. Arthur Smith, a vociferous critic of early Chinese schooling, nonetheless noted one of the culturally unifying consequences of this kind of early education: "The classical wisdom of the Ancients is the common heritage of all the sons and daughters of Han, from Emperors to old women, and one stratum of society can quote them as well as another."[126]

A few of Sibao's educational texts presented alternatives to this kind of cultural unity or integration. A single title like the *Zhushi San Bai Qian Zengguang heke*, which combined instruction in reading, speaking, and writing with moral teachings—and with methods of fortune-telling—suggests an oddly assorted multivalence of functions and of topics for

---

cates the memorization process as it was performed in Chinese schools, before bored and poorly paid teachers rather than fond fathers, but each does suggest that memorization might not have been the cruel and meaningless technique it is so often designated in Western writings.

124. See Ridley, "Educational Theory and Practice in Late Imperial China," pp. 315–17, for examples of such songs. Jiantou, a Sibao village not otherwise noted as a publishing center, did produce one work, *Yifang xunzi* (1909), which includes songs on the virtues of industry and thrift. See p. 433.

125. London Missionary Society, Report no. 105 (1900), p. 46.

126. Arthur Smith, *Pearls of Wisdom from China*, p. 7, cited in McLaren, *Chinese Popular Culture and Ming Chantefables*, p. 5.

elementary instruction. Some students might end their schooling with primers in their local dialect (like the Hakka *Renjia riyong*), which would provide an education of only limited use outside Minxi or the Hakka heartland. As we have seen, in addition to the "standard" primers, the Zou and Ma published specialized texts that taught the vocabulary (*Siyan zazi*) and to some extent the ritual behavior (in the maxims for merchant conduct in the lower register of *Xinzha/Zibian*) of commerce. But, with the possible exception of *Xinzha/Zibian*, there seem to have been no intermediate or advanced textbooks for merchants or Hakka-speakers in Sibao's stock. It was difficult for students to receive a full education in anything but the examination curriculum. And the ubiquity of the "San-Bai-Qian" and similar elementary textbooks meant that even that majority of students who never advanced far beyond these works had been taught the basic values of "the common heritage of the sons and daughters of Han." (In Chapter 14 we will consider the concrete social, political, and economic significance of this cultural integration.)

Within the examination-centered curriculum, Sibao's educational output does suggest a considerable variety in approaches to teaching, belying the common assumption that texts were always "learned by rote" and "bawled out by memory" without comprehension. As Angela Leung has pointed out, at least some teachers believed it important to teach the sense as well as the words of the texts to their beginning students. We have seen that Liu Zhong, in his *Yuanben Erlun qiyou yinduan*, provided simple commentary, in the grammar and vocabulary of the spoken language, to explain the meaning of the *Analects* to students of eight or nine *sui*. Centuries earlier, Liu Zongzhou 劉宗周 (1578–1645) had also advocated explaining a text in detail to elementary students, first by introducing the main point and then breaking the text down to character, phrase, and sentence units, all of which had to be analyzed before the meaning of the text could be clear.[127] Annotations in Sibao

---

127. Liu Zongzhou, "Xiaoxue yue" 小學約 in *Liuzi quanshu*, 25.9b–10a (4: 2072–73); cited in Angela Leung, "Elementary Education in the Lower Yangtze Region," p. 394. Leung also cites other authors, Tang Biao 唐彪 (eighteenth century) and Wang Yun, who seemed to share Liu's views. Dun Li (*The Ageless Chinese*, p. 365), in his very general outline of the examination track, also suggests that at about nine or ten years a student would begin to be taught the meaning of the Four Books (after memorizing the basic

editions of the *Sanzi jing* and *Qianjia shi*, not to mention the Four Books and Five Classics, also suggest efforts to explain what the students were memorizing. In this way Sibao's educational products reflect, if not a profound understanding of the new theories of education that proliferated in the Ming and Qing, at least a shrewd commercial awareness of the gains to be made from suiting school texts to a range of teaching strategies and capabilities.

---

primers and these classical texts from the age of five or six). See also Ridley, "Educational Theory and Practice in Late Imperial China," pp. 342–91; *Lidai jiaoyu zhidu kao*, 2: 1459–543; *Lidai jiaoyu lunzhu xuanping*, 2: 1578–80; and Gardner, "'To Be a Teacher Is Hard.'"

# ELEVEN

## Guides to Good Manners, Good Health, and Good Fortune

ALTHOUGH EDUCATIONAL texts, particularly aids to examination study, dominate surviving Sibao book lists, the Zou and Ma publishers also did a brisk business in texts useful and appealing outside the worlds of the schoolroom and examination compound. From the sparse surviving evidence, it appears that in the early years of Sibao publishing, most new publishing houses began with the Four Books and educational texts, relying on these sure sellers to generate the capital needed to expand their list. Yet at least some *shufang* branched out quite early into the publication of other types of popular texts. Ma Quanheng and his son Ma Dingbang may have built their fortune on the basis of editions of primers and the Four Books, but at roughly the same time Ma Kuanyu was producing etiquette manuals and almanacs, which included instructions on acquiring good fortune, as well as a children's textbook and an anthology of ancient-prose essays.

This chapter presents as representative a sampling as the evidence allows of the texts that, after examination education texts, contributed significantly to the profits of the Sibao publishers in the nineteenth and early twentieth centuries: works of practical advice on optimizing human relationships, health, and relations with the gods and cosmic forces. Among them were handbooks on the rituals of daily life (ritual or etiquette books, household encyclopedias, letter-writing manuals, guides to the writing of rhymed couplets); on medicine (medical compendia, *materia medica*, prescription collections, specialized texts for women, children, and specific types of diseases, and medical casebooks); and on ways to attract good fortune and ward off bad (almanacs, *feng-shui* manuals, guides to various methods of divination, morality books).

These categories are far from watertight. Just as many of the texts discussed in the preceding chapter might well have been read by persons uninterested in sitting the examinations, so, too, many of the texts listed here could be considered educational. Most of the medical manuals teach medical techniques and were probably used by physicians in training. The ritual or etiquette handbooks teach proper forms of social interaction; indeed, we know from a partially extant bookseller's account book that collections of rhymed couplets, etiquette handbooks, and correspondence manuals were often sold to students in village schools along with primers and editions of the Four Books (see Chapter 7). Even many of the guides to good fortune appear to have been used to educate fortune-telling professionals in their art. And some morality books served as textbooks in elementary schools during the Qing, instilling good behavior along with the ability to read. In grouping these disparate works together, I have chosen to emphasize their practical qualities as "how-to" guides to matters of everyday life generally outside the purview of the examination curriculum in the schools.

## Household Encyclopedias and Guides
## to the Rituals of Daily Life

Sibao produced a number of texts best described as compendia of information necessary to the proper conduct of daily life. Scholars have commented on the proliferation of such texts in the late Ming; Sakai Tadao in particular has demonstrated that "encyclopedias for daily use" (*riyong leishu* 日用類書) then began to include more material designed for the use of commoners, people who could not claim scholar-official status.[1] These "daily life" encyclopedias differed sharply from reference

---

1. See Sakai Tadao, "Mindai no nichiyō ruisho to shomin kyōiku," pp. 27–28, 148–51; idem, "Confucianism and Popular Educational Works," pp. 331–38; and Chia, *Printing for Profit*, pp. 237–38.

encyclopedias designed for scholar and official use in their inclusion of mundane information—travel guidance, jokes, medical advice, correspondence models, and so forth—of interest to a broad readership. Instead of following the strict ordering principle of the elite texts, which created a hierarchy of knowledge emphasizing the cultural centrality of literati and officials and marginalizing lower social statuses, the *riyong leishu* made "ordinary practices . . . not only subjects important enough to warrant definition, classification, and explanation but also the guiding ethos for organizing the entire body of knowledge and one's frame of social reference."[2]

By the Qing, generic texts designed for the everyday use of "all people" were quite common. These are the texts the Sibao publishers produced: wide-ranging compendia, providing bits of information on a variety of useful topics: terms of address, wedding and funeral rituals, letter and announcement models, sample rhymed couplets, descriptions of merchant travel routes, and lists of phrases covering food and drink, clothing, plants and animals, the five relationships, basic cosmological terms, and so forth. More narrowly focused texts taught the proper way of writing letters or offered models of rhymed couplets for all occasions and contexts.

Household encyclopedias, if genuinely comprehensive, were rather lengthy (for popular works) and required frequent revision to reflect changing times—or at least new prefaces promising revised contents. They demanded considerable investment on the part of the publishers. On the other hand, since these texts were not "classics," sales did not depend on an author-editor possessed of a famous name or an examination degree. Indeed, the Sibao publishers were able to compile some of these popular and profitable works on their own. The most famous of Sibao's offerings in this category was the very popular encyclopedia compiled by Zou Jingyang and/or his father, Zou Tingyou: the *Yunlin*

---

2. Shang Wei, "The Making of the Everyday World," pp. 67–69. Sakai Tadao links these changes to the effort among the elite of the late Ming to popularize Confucian, Buddhist, and Daoist standards and beliefs for a broader, less literate, readership—to translate the fundamental ethical principles of elite culture into practical prescriptions for non-elite use. Shang Wei interprets them rather as reflections of the popularization of commercial publishing in the late Ming.

*bieshu xinji Choushi jinnang quanji* 雲林別墅新輯酬世錦囊全集 (Complete collection of the *Precious Guide to Social Exchange* from the Yunlin Retreat, newly edited; preface dated 1771), which was reproduced many times by different publishers as the *Choushi jinnang*. In his preface Zou Jingyang took pains to defend the legitimacy of the genre of household manuals. As a young man studying for the examinations, he was told that "scattered writings on social exchange" were irrelevant. Later in life, having abandoned his studies, he selected the best of such writings, edited them, and anthologized them for convenience of reference and portability. He acknowledged that this kind of work was not comparable to the broad learning advocated by Confucius or to the extensive scholarship of "Guo Tai 郭泰, with his five thousand *juan*, and Zhang Hua 張華, with his three thousand carts [of books],"[3] which have the power to transform the world. And yet, he argued, his humble contribution did not differ in principle from their great ones, implying that the teaching of proper ritual also, in a sense, transforms the world. He was publishing the work, he modestly explained, at the urging of many friends who, having seen the manuscript, exclaimed over its value: "*Choushi jinnang* can act as private secretary and 'friend of the inkblock' [*mishu yanyou* 秘書硯友; that is, as a writing aid]."

What does this treasure contain? It consists of four "collections": "Letters" ("Shuqi" 書啓); "Collected Family Rituals" ("Jiali jicheng" 家禮集成); an untitled miscellany of information on terms of address and proper forms of etiquette; and "Select New Rhymed Couplets" ("Caiji xinlian" 採輯新聯). Each collection contains two registers of texts. For example, the smaller upper register of "Letters" contains "brocade fragments" and "beautiful phrases" to be used in letters—these are couplets of four characters per line that can be used to adorn one's correspondence, with helpful hints about use ("to a teacher or elder," "to a Buddhist," "to a Daoist," etc.)—and suggestions on "how to behave as an official." The larger and more discursive lower register of

---

3. These are references to ancient scholars noted for their broad learning. Guo Tai (127–69) was a famous teacher; when he returned home from official service in Luoyang, it is said that he transported 5,000 *juan* back with him. Zhang Hua (232–300), a man who rose from poverty to high office, was said to have been so learned that, when he moved house, his books filled thirty (not three thousand) carts.

text covers an equally wide range of topics in considerably greater detail. It provides model correspondence (*chidu* 尺牘), including forms for petitions, invitations, notes of congratulation, recommendation letters, and so forth. The models subsume a host of different situations, from how to write admonishing a friend to study harder to how to write asking the loan of a sedan chair or article of clothing. "Collected Family Rituals" describes the important rituals of family life—cappings, weddings, funerals, and ancestral sacrifices; it then provides models or forms for the range of documents and announcements that might accompany these rituals (notices of examination success, essays accompanying sacrifices to the ancestors, funeral odes, genealogy prefaces, essays honoring longevity, biographies, portrait tributes, tablet inscriptions, and congratulatory messages). The third collection, untitled, deals largely with the etiquette and written forms of social interaction outside the family; it includes forms for "each type [of occasion]," a chart explaining proper seating order, the appropriate ceremony for welcoming a guest, the standard rituals to be observed in the classroom, terms of address used in entertaining, standard forms of social chat and ornamental phrases, a model announcement of a teacher's employment, and essential terms for legal cases. Lastly, the fourth collection, "Select New Couplets," presents rhymed couplets suitable for commemorating a variety of social occasions.

*Choushi jinnang* in its entirety was published repeatedly throughout the nineteenth and even early twentieth centuries. James Hayes reports that this work "seems to have served its purpose so well that it was still being reprinted by Shanghai book publishers at the end of the nineteenth century."[4] The Zou publishers certainly made thorough use of this text, for they also published portions of it as separate, distinct works. "Collected Family Rituals" traveled as a separate text, *Jiali jicheng* 家禮集成 (with a preface by Zou Jingyang deploring commercial publishers' unscrupulous recycling of household manuals!), slightly expanded by a section on surnames and a collection of rhymed couplets

---

4. He says that he acquired late nineteenth-century editions of the text from three different publishing houses, "adding substance to contemporary complaints about book pirating" (Hayes, "Specialists and Written Materials in the Village World," pp. 87–88).

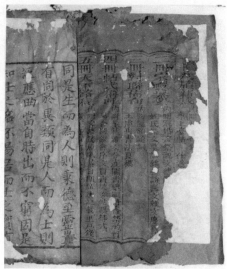

Fig. 11.1 *Xinjian Choushi jinnang* 新鐫酬世錦囊 (*Precious Guide to Social Exchange*, newly cut; identified as *Choushi jinghua* 酬世精華, Essence of social exchange, on the title page), compiled by Zou Tingyou 鄒廷猷 and Zou Tingzhong 鄒廷忠. (a, *left*) Cover page. (b, *right*) List of contents. Photographs by the author.

"to cover all human affairs." "Select New Couplets" was also published separately as *Caiji xinlian* 採輯新聯 (see below).

Finally, the Sibao (and other) commercial publishers, as they did with many successful titles, recycled the words *Choushi jinnang* into the titles of other and often rather different texts. For example, the cover page of *Choushi jinghua* 酬世精華 (Essence of social exchange) proclaims it as a "newly cut" version of the *Choushi jinnang* (*Xinjian Choushi jinnang* 新鐫酬世錦囊, *Precious Guide to Social Exchange*, newly cut; Figs. 11.1a and b), yet it is actually a significantly different work. Attributed to Zou Tingyou, Jingyang's father, and Zou Tingzhong, with a preface dated 1802, and surviving in a heavily damaged partial edition, it is advertised, like the "real" *Choushi jinnang*, as a guide to proper social interaction. The first preface argues for the value of the work despite its irrelevance to the examination system and the achievement of official degrees—it can teach readers to practice "the reality of living as a *shi* 士 [scholar, member of the educated elite]," even if it cannot assist them to become "a *shi* in name."

What distinguishes *Choushi jinghua* is the way in which it has been fashioned to appeal to merchants and their families. It provides guidelines for family rituals and general correspondence but abridges this information in order to add two new sections. The first, "Document Forms and Modes of Address" ("Tieshi chenghu" 帖世稱呼), is advertised as a collection of model forms for petitions, family property–division documents, instructions to heirs, commercial partnership agreements, regulations for loan associations, contracts of purchase and sale, posted notices, and so forth. The second, with the title of a well-known merchant route book, "Routes of the Empire" ("Tianxia lucheng" 天下路程), promises "admonitions to travelers, descriptions of scenery, travel times, geography, local populations, currency and provisions, local products, poetry about scenic spots, and information about new customs charges" (verso of cover page). The contents suggest that the "*shi* in behavior if not in name" designated as the target readership would most likely have been merchants or aspiring merchants, men who would need a reference that provided sample business forms, rhymed couplets, correspondence models for all occasions, and a route book, in addition to guidelines for the proper *shi*-like observance of family rituals.

Sibao also produced household encyclopedias that focused almost exclusively on social relations within the family and community. *Huizuan Jiali tieshi jiyao*, published by the Wanjuan lou, was first compiled in the early nineteenth century by Jiang Jianzi from the writings of his father, Jiang Haoran. The preface (dated 1810), written by a student of Haoran's, explains the work's context:

My teacher Jiang [Haoran] was superior in conduct and broad in knowledge, an outstanding resident of Zhangzhou. His skill at eight-legged essays was so great that he could have sold his essays—there is no point in elaborating on these known facts. He was also learned in ritual and excelled at calligraphy. Thus, in addition to soliciting him for rhymed couplets, eulogies, commemorative essays, and prefaces, the local people would consult him about weddings, announcements of funerals, sacrifices, and all ceremonies for the attraction of good fortune and the expulsion of bad. When asked, he would immediately go to help. . . .

This compendium of models (*xuanji tieshi* 纂集帖式) passes unchanging principles on to the world. My teacher wanted to sum up family ritual and transmit his family learning, but because he was overwhelmed with teaching, he entrusted the project to his son. Jiang [Jianzi] used the *Jiali zuanyao* 家禮纂要 [Essentials of family ritual], which had been transmitted through the family, together with his father's notations, as the foundation for this text. After consulting *Zhengsu jiali* 正俗家禮 [Correct customs and family rituals], *Jiali zhuo* 家禮酌 [Family rituals and social occasions], *Jiali dacheng* 家禮大成 [Great collection of family rituals], *Jiali daquan* 家禮大全 [Compendium of family rituals], *Jiali chidu* 家禮尺牘 [Family rituals and model correspondence], and so on, he combined thirteen texts into one. . . .

But times change and contexts differ [literally, "there are times of loss and gain, circumstances of poverty and wealth"]—how could changes not be made to accord with popular practice? This text draws on all these other texts, cutting out the repetitions, correcting the errors, and filling in the information that was missing—thus my teacher has also done a great service to the present. ("Xu," 1ab)

Backed, then, by the learning and practice of a noted local scholar, the text provides, in six *juan*, detailed information about naming and terms of address, correct performance of family rituals, and models for correspondence.

In the world of the *Jiali tieshi jiyao*, the proper naming of both things and people was essential to family order and proper social interaction. The text opens with lists of names of things and events—months, seasons, festivals, teas and wines, grains and food, delicacies, stationery, military equipment, utensils, clothing, jewels and ornaments, musical instruments, flowers and trees, and so on. This section functions rather like a thesaurus organized by theme. "Terms for the category of grains," for example, reads simply: "'Uncooked rice' (*mi* 米) is called 'white feast' (*baican* 白粲) when cooked; it is called 'the king's kernel' (*wang li* 王粒), measured in piculs (*shi* 石)." Occasionally there is an effort to provide somewhat fuller information and to display a little classical learning; "Terms for the stems and branches of the year" opens with a reference to the *Erya* definition of "year," and the following "Names for the ordering of divisions of time" provides brief definitions; "spring," for example, is explained as "the sending forth of life" (*fasheng* 發生). Presumably such sections helped the upwardly mobile learn how to speak and write—what euphemisms or ornamented phrases to use, even about subjects as homey as rice or as conventional as the changing seasons—in conversation or correspondence with their better-educated acquaintances. Polite phrases are introduced; "Conventional phrases for special circumstances," for example, offers "the little son [will make a] famous name" as the appropriate compliment to a man whose son has just celebrated his first month. "Conventional phrases in common use" lists two- and four-character phrases useful in polite conversation (e.g., "pleased to receive" [*xiyan* 喜延]).

Proper terms of address and self-reference were a matter of even greater importance. Some information is provided on how one should address outsiders and refer to oneself in their presence, but most space (roughly one-third of the entire text) is devoted to terms of address and self-reference within the family and lineage as these were determined by relationship, gender, and status of the speaker and the person addressed. Assuming a male reader, Jiang first explains how to address and refer to oneself in speaking to different members of one's own lineage, of one's lineage of adoption (if relevant), of the lineages of one's mother, grandmother, wife, daughter-in-law, and so forth. Parallel lists follow for women, for men addressing women, for women addressing men, and finally for men and women addressing members of other lineages. The sheer number of terms—158 terms of address and self-reference are listed for forty-two relationships with one's mother's lineage, for example—reflects the Confucian assumption that "rectifying names" (*zheng ming* 正名) was a prerequisite for moral order and social harmony.

*Jiali tieshi jiyao* also explains family ritual practice, with particular attention to the intricacies of funeral rituals. Jiang takes pains to explain the rationale of the major rituals. The discussion of the rules of mourning, entitled, in emulation of scholarly works,[5] "Investigation of the rules of mourning" ("Fuzhi kao" 服制考), defines the function of mourning as the disciplined expression of grief and emphasizes that the relationship between the mourner and the deceased is the determinant of the degree of mourning. Thus, for example, the highest degree, "zhengfu" 正服 ("principal mourning"), is that of the closest relatives, such as sons mourning their parents, who feel naturally the deepest grief; "yifu" 義服 ("dutiful mourning") is the degree for mourners unrelated to the deceased who grieve out of duty, such as wives grieving for their hus-

---

5. Following another scholarly convention, the *Jiali tieshi jiyao* is annotated. Allusions in polite phrases are explained and their source often listed. In a model wedding announcement, for example, Jiang explains the term "Zhu Chen" 朱陳: drawn from a folk song (*yuefu* 樂府), it is a reference to a village named Zhuchen because two families surnamed Zhu and Chen had intermarried there for generations (2.38a).

bands' parents. A series of charts then conveniently outlines what ritual clothing and behavior are required of each mourner according to his/her place in the five degrees of mourning and in the nine generations through which mourning was to be observed, and to his/her age (see Fig. 11.2a).

Proper ritual conduct requires mastery of the forms of ritual correspondence, and this text proves its worth by including extensive models for just about every imaginable occasion: funeral and wedding announcements, notices of congratulation (to be sent when a family completes a house or moves to a new house, when a teacher finds employment, when a man retires from office, when a relative has a birthday, and so forth), invitations (to celebrate a birthday, the birth of a son, the taking of a disciple, the beginning of study, or to attend a feast given by a Buddhist monk or Daoist master to thank a patron), thank-you notes, spirit tablets, funerary odes, prayers to gods and spirits, and on and on (Fig. 11.2b). Many of these models are preceded by precise instructions on how to present the document—what kind of paper to write it on, in what sort of characters, and where to display it. Different models are provided for different social statuses—in wedding announcements, for example, if one of the new in-laws is a licentiate, the form is different from that used for a mere student. (The lack of a model for a *juren* or *jinshi* may reflect the assumption that no family needing this compendium was likely to acquire in-laws of such distinction.) Jiang seems to have covered almost every possible social contingency, every modification in language required by differences in status, gender, and circumstance, and every potentially difficult social exchange—how, for example, to announce the birth of a son simultaneous with the death of a grandmother. A ritual model was defined for virtually all social interactions.

Throughout the *Jiali tieshi jiyao* Jiang assumed the role of arbiter of ritual controversies, substantiating the claim in the preface that he was both knowledgeable about ritual prescriptions and sensitive to changes in custom. In a discussion of the proper form for funeral placards, for example, he confronted a thorny problem: if the deceased had two wives, which son or sons of these wives were to be listed as mourner(s) on the placard? Jiang criticized some contemporary practices that he had seen and suggested sensible solutions: if the first wife had already died and the second wife had raised the first wife's orphan son(s) as

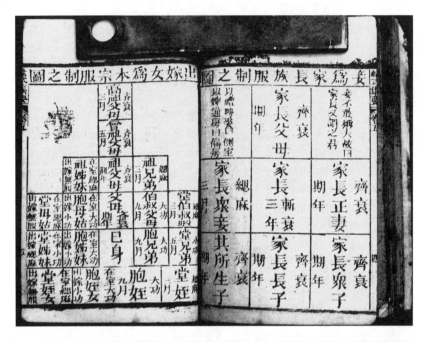

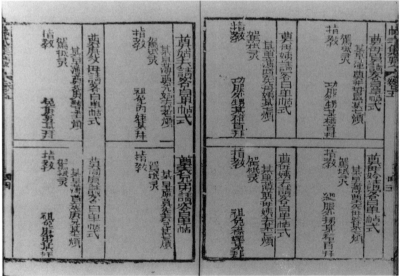

Fig. 11.2 *Huizuan Jiali tieshi jiyao* 彙纂家禮帖式集要 (Collected essentials of family rituals and model forms). (a, *top*) Mourning chart. (b, *bottom*) Proper forms for invitations. Photographs by the author.

well as her own, then her own sons should be listed as mourners as well, but with the *ai* 哀 (mourning) character slightly to the side; but if the first wife had died young before having children and the sons of the second wife were the father's heirs, then these sons could be listed as mourners in the conventional fashion without the slight displacement of *ai*.

Unlike the *Choushi jinghua* and even, to some extent, *Yunlin bieshu xinji Choushi jinnang quanji*, this text is preoccupied with the world of family and lineage. It does not contain the business forms or merchant route information of the *Choushi jinghua* or the plethora of rules for extra-familial social relationships and legal actions found in the *Quanji*. Its advice for the family and lineage is strictly orthodox, and, unlike some other popular ritual manuals, it is in the humanistic Confucian tradition in that it focuses almost exclusively on rituals governing human relationships. The *Zengding Yingshi bianshu* 增訂應世便書 (*Convenient Guide to Social Interaction*, expanded and revised; in at least four *juan*), another popular text published by several Sibao publishing houses, is very similar in its contents to *Jiali tieshi jiyao*, except that it devotes far more attention to worship of gods and spirits. One whole *juan* of this text (compared with just a portion of a *juan* in *Jiali tieshi jiyao*) provides a series of "memorials" (*biaowen* 表文) to various gods—"Form for praying to Guanyin for a child," "Form for thanking Guanyin for good fortune," "Form for calling on the gods for rain," "Form for an appeal for security and peace," "Form for an appeal for a safe and united family," and so on.

For whom was the *Jiali tieshi jiyao* written? The easy-to-understand language, generally bereft of classical allusions; the careful explanation of practices and annotation of allusions unnecessary to an elite reader; the fancy names for mundane items—all suggest a work intended for insufficiently educated readers who wanted to learn how to do rituals "right," presumably to fulfill social aspirations, to join the community of the elite, within either their lineage or their local society. The painstakingly detailed descriptions of funeral rituals and inclusion of sacrificial texts suggests that it was intended as well for the use of "masters of ritual" (*lisheng* 禮生), local specialists who would be hired by families to manage the rituals of death and mourning.[6] The poor production

---

6. See Liu Yonghua, "The World of Rituals," pp. 101–74, for a discussion of these *lisheng* and the ritual manuals they used.

quality of the three surviving versions of this text[7]—it is small (14.5 cm
h × 20.6 cm w) and poorly cut, with difficult-to-read and frequently erroneous characters—likewise suggests such an intended audience. It is
hard to imagine a well-educated man or woman of assured social standing needing much of the information in this text or—if they did need
it—purchasing such a shabby volume.

Other types of encyclopedias published in Sibao promise instruction
on more than family or community etiquette. The Cuiyun tang inventory,
for example, lists two versions of the well-known Qing work *Chuanjia bao*
傳家寶 (Treasure to be transmitted to the family), compiled by Shi
Chengjin 石成金 (1659?–1736?). This heavily moralistic work consists of
essays on proper behavior, with many brief didactic texts, including a series of songs, among them, the "Good Boy," "Good Girl," "Correct
Study," and "Rituals for Youth" songs. It also contains family instructions (*jiaxun* 家訓), essays on proper study methods, "pledges to study"
(*dushu yue* 讀書約), and guides to the achievement of happiness through
good conduct. The text's intellectual assumptions would best be described as eclectic; it includes a version of the Diamond Sutra annotated
by Shi.

Distinctive in a different way is the *Wanbao quanshu* 萬寶全書 (Complete book of myriad treasures), which appeared in a variety of editions
of different lengths in the Ming and Qing,[8] and was produced by both
the Zaizi tang and the Wanjuan lou in the mid- to late nineteenth century. This work is a true miscellany, purporting to offer general information that the reader "cannot not know" but might be embarrassed to
ask. (Hence the text's nickname, *Wan buqiu ren* 萬不求人, Myriad
things one need not ask.) It attempts to cover a little of everything—
geography, history, and the difference between Chinese and Manchu
customs; rules for calligraphy; instruction in using the abacus; oneiromancy and fortune-telling; basic medicine and a variety of other skills;
guides to games and entertainment; and much more.

The Zou and Ma publishers also produced quite specialized works
providing instruction or ritual guidance either in a profession or in one

---

7. A very similar, if not identical, text may have circulated under the title *Jiali guanglei*
家禮廣類 (Expanded categories of family ritual).

8. Wu Huifang, *Wanbao quanshu*, pp. 67–114.

aspect of community life. *Lu Ban jing* 魯班經 (Classic of Lu Ban, named after the fifth-century BC craftsman who later became the patron deity of carpenters) is an example of an instruction manual. Compiled originally in the fifteenth century and incorporating materials dating from the Song and Yuan, *Lu Ban jing* explains the techniques of house and furniture construction. Much of the work, however, is devoted to the ceremonies that should mark each step in the construction of a house and to the charms and incantations that builders might use to bring either good or bad fortune to their customers.[9] This work was, of course, most popular among professional carpenters; we can assume that it was well known in Minxi, where many men worked as sojourning construction laborers.[10]

Among the most popular of the more specialized Sibao handbooks to daily life were guides to letter writing and the composition of rhymed couplets. Only one letter-writing guide, the *Xinke chidu* 新刻尺牘 (*Model Correspondence*, newly cut; identified on the cover page as *Zhinan chidu shengli yaojue* 指南尺牘生理要訣 [Guide to model correspondence essential to livelihood]; see Fig. 11.3a), survives. Compiled by a Li Aiting 黎靄亭 of Shunde (Guangdong), and published in 1876 by the Wanjuan lou in four *juan*, this is a relatively compact text devoted largely to model correspondence. The preface (1860) opens with an elaborate advertisement for the importance of letter-writing, complete with a classical allusion:

The *Classic of Changes* begins, "The same sounds resonate"; then it says, "The same *qi* seek each other out." The mutual resonance of sounds and *qi* means

---

9. See Ruitenbeek, *Carpentry & Building in Late Imperial China*, pp. 1–2, 4–7. Ruitenbeek emphasizes the magical potency the text was believed to possess; certain sources claim that one had to perform certain rituals of purification before attempting to read the book, others that the work required the reader to commit an evil deed (see p. 1). For an account of the potential uses of the text, see Kuhn, *Soulstealers*, pp. 104–6.

10. It might also be used by do-it-yourself home builders, although it was also possible to find information, both technical and ritual, about house construction in the more comprehensive of the household encyclopedias—the *Jiabao quanji* 家寶全集 (Complete collection of family treasures) and a Sibao publication, the *Tongtian xiao* 通天曉 (Understanding everything under heaven), for example, both had such sections on building—and in some *fengshui* manuals and even almanacs (Ruitenbeek, *Carpentry & Building in Late Imperial China*, pp. 34–45).

each responds to its own. Now, within the five relationships, if people live apart and long separated from their families, how can they not at times feel distant? If people travel afar and are often away from home, how can they not feel out of place? Thus letter writing is something that must be done every day.

Thus the *Xinke chidu* is "essential for merchants and dealers and even more for scholars"; it promises that if its models are followed, "even although you are one thousand *li* distant from your correspondent, it will be like chatting with him face to face" ("Xu," 1ab). This text seems to be intended for beginning letter writers, for it also provides very basic instruction in format (where to leave blank spaces, where to elevate characters, etc.). And, in addition to the basic punctuation, the editor has included brief sideline definitions of difficult characters. Thus, next to the character *jin* 盡, "to exhaust" or "to finish," is printed the easier synonym *wan* 完; *xiaxi* 暇隙, "leisure time," is glossed as *xianshi* 閒時, and so forth (1.6b; see Fig. 11.3b). Moral guidance is offered to the young, in sections such as "Words of Warning to the Beginning Student," which explains the twenty principles that should guide the student's efforts to "become a man." These principles emphasize industry and study but focus most pointedly on relations with people outside one's family: learn to judge other men astutely, be cautious in affairs involving joint expenditures of money, avoid social disgrace by knowing characters and how to write (1.1a–10a). The text concludes on a very different note, with a series of cures for common ailments. In its jumble of epistolary instruction, advice on economic and social relations, and list of home remedies, this work could serve as a basic guide for aspiring merchants and traders, rather like the *Xinzha/Zibian* discussed in Chapter 10.

Sibao also produced handbooks of rhymed couplets for household use. Zou Tingyou and Xie Meilin—the most prolific team of Sibao editor-publishers—produced, with the assistance of Zou's son Jingyang, the *Caiji xinlian tuzhang jiaju* 採輯新聯圖章佳句 (Selected new beautiful phrases for couplets and seals).[11] Zou Jingyang, in the preface,

---

11. This appears to be the last "collection" in the *Yunlin bieshu xinji Choushi jinnang quanji* (see p. 507), providing another example of the publishers' readiness to recycle texts. The stand-alone text has a top register of seal inscriptions in cursive script.

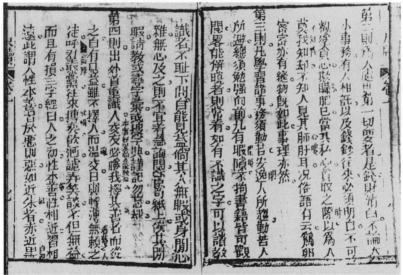

Fig. 11.3 *Zhinan chidu shengli yaojue* 指南尺牘生理要訣 (Guide to model correspondence essential to livelihood; identified as *Xinke chidu* 新刻尺牘, *Model Correspondence,* newly cut, on the title page), published by the Wanjuan lou 萬卷樓 in 1876. (a, *top*) Cover page. (b, *bottom*) "Admonitions to beginning students" (*Chuxue zhengui* 初學箴規). Note the sideline explanations of the meanings of "difficult" characters. Photographs by the author.

explains that he and his father had collected "not fewer than several thousand" fine examples of the rhymed-couplet genre in the course of their extensive travels (to cities as distant as Beijing), so that, despite the ubiquity of commercial couplet collections, they still felt they had something new to offer (1a). Another Sibao product, the *Duilian daquan* 對聯大全 (Compendium of rhymed couplets), compiled by Zou Ping-han 鄒屏翰 and published by the Cuiwen tang in 1884 (see Fig. 7.2, p. 253), aimed at comprehensiveness, providing couplets for just about every occasion. It organized couplets by subject: weddings and other family activities, divided by month; offices and occupational sites, from the Hanlin Academy down to tea pavilions and incinerators for the ritual burning of paper; spirits and temples; and finally shops, from high-status purveyors of books, brushes, inkstones, ink, fans, paper, paintings, and seals to humbler establishments offering fortune-telling services, bean curd, or shoes. The most elegant of the Sibao couplet collections, however, was the *Qiaozi xiulin* (Fig. 11.4), compiled by the same father-and-son team, Jiang Haoran and Jiang Jianzi, who produced the *Jiali tieshi jiyao*, and who had a working relationship with the Sibao publishers. In addition to couplets, this book offers model letter and contract forms. The preface, dated 1811, emphasizes not the popularity or usefulness of the text, but its link to the more glorious literati task of classical study, suggesting, too, that it would be a useful manual for scholars seeking a livelihood as professional writers:

In the examinations, the eight-legged essay is venerated. Both poetry and policy statements are tested in order to decide who passes. The study of the Classics glorifies the country; this, indeed, is the rationale for the examinations. But, in addition to this study, literati have other means of supporting themselves and benefiting the world with models for writing—correspondence, rhymed couplets, rules, and contracts. Even although this work cannot compare with passing the examinations, it must be placed alongside the study of the Classics. ("Xu," 1ab)

To further enhance the high-culture tone, this text includes notes at the end of each *juan*, so that the serious student can understand the classical and literary allusions contained in the couplets.

    The prefaces to almost all the Sibao household encyclopedias and guides to ritual forms (with the obvious exception of *Lu Ban jing*)

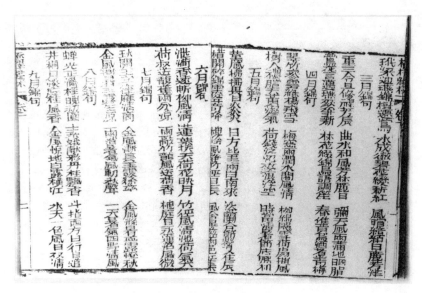

Fig. 11.4 Couplets for different months from *Qiaozi xiulin* 橋梓繡林 (A father and son's embroidered forest). Photograph by the author.

advertise the works as comprehensive and universally useful guides, designed for "all four classes of people"—scholars, peasants, craftsmen, or merchants—for anyone, in short, interested in learning the proper forms of Chinese society. In their range of epistolary and couplet models, they do, indeed, seem to be attempting to cover every social contingency. So, too, those that provide model prayers and sacrificial rites present samples for all varieties of belief, with something for Buddhist and Daoist divinities and spirits as well as "Confucian" ancestors.

Yet, as we have seen, texts like the *Huizuan Jiali tieshi jiyao*, simply written, containing elementary information, and cheaply printed, appear to have been produced to inform marginally educated readers of the proper forms of speech and behavior. Similarly, the *Xinke chidu*, with its sideline definitions of simple words and its rules for "beginning students," was intended for a readership of limited education, possibly with mercantile ambitions. And *Choushi jinghua* makes the social limits of its readership clear in the preface that promises to teach the reader to act like a *shi*, although he is not one. There is a range in sophistication: *Yunlin bieshu xinji Choushi jinnang quanji*, for example, provides more ornate phrases for letter writers and includes forms for legal documents and community associations that imply readers operating at a fairly high level within large lineages and complex social institutions. For its part, the pretentious preface of the *Qiaozi xiulin* may reflect an attempt to appeal to a literati readership. More likely, however, it was an attempt to persuade a gullible buyer of the text's literary value. Indeed, it is difficult to imagine that *any* of these texts, even the most sophisticated, would have been of great interest to the elite, to people who not only acted like but actually were *shi*. Established scholar-official (and wealthy merchant) families would certainly not have purchased a text explicitly directed to "all the classes of people," since such a purchase would have undermined the assertion of distinction that lay at the heart of elite self-definition. Finally, one "to the manner born" would not have needed the instructions—the rules for proper seating, classroom etiquette, the proper way to greet a guest, and so forth—being offered in these Sibao productions.

## Medical and Pharmaceutical Manuals

A considerable number of Sibao imprints surviving from late in the industry's history are medical and pharmaceutical guides. Property-division documents and account books suggest that these were among the most popular of Sibao products, rivaling the Classics, primers, household manuals, and fiction in selling power. These sources list roughly eighty titles, including manuals of acupuncture and pulse diagnosis, pharmaceutical guides, and basic medical handbooks, as well as titles on specialized subjects such as gynecology, pediatrics, smallpox, and eye diseases.

Most of the medical texts published in Sibao were well-known works; the book lists contain few surprises. The Wenhai lou produced the famous late Ming pharmacopeia *Bencao gangmu* 本草綱目 (Outline of *materia medica*) of Li Shizhen 李時珍 (1518–93) in a very expensive edition (for Sibao) costing 8 *qian* wholesale, almost as much as the *Kangxi zidian*. Several publishers printed the important Qing medical encyclopedia *Yuzuan Yizong jinjian* 御纂醫宗金鑒 (Imperially sponsored *Golden Mirror of Medical Orthodoxy*; with 15 titles in 90 *juan*), first published in 1742 at the command of the Qianlong emperor (and still an important reference work). This text, edited by Wu Qian 吳謙, the supervisor of the

Imperial Medical Bureau, claimed to "rectify medical learning" by establishing a medical orthodoxy based on the "Way of medicine of the ancients"—that is, on the Han-dynasty medical classics *Huangdi neijing: Suwen Lingshu* 黃帝內經: 素問靈樞 (Inner canon of the Yellow Emperor: Plain questions, Efficacious pivot) and Zhang Ji's *Shanghan lun* 傷寒論 (Treatise on cold damage disorders) and *Jingui yuhan yaoliie* 金匱 玉函要略 (Summary of precious secrets).[12]

These texts (particularly the last two, which were published as the first section of the *Yuzuan Yizong jinjian*) had dominated Chinese medical theory from the Han through the Ming, but in the early Qing they were challenged by the revived *wenbing* 瘟病 (warm factors disorders) tradition. This sought to modify or replace the universal, monolithic model of disease and diagnosis in the *shanghan* (cold damage) tradition with a regional model that acknowledged the role played by local conditions in the nature, diagnosis, and treatment of diseases. In the face of this challenge—which came largely from Jiangnan physicians—*Yuzuan Yizong jinjian* asserted the orthodoxy of the "cold damage" tradition by identifying Zhang Ji's writings as the foundational texts of Chinese medicine.[13] *Yuzuan Yizong jinjian* balances this theoretical orientation with a practical clinical approach typical of Qing medical writing. It not only includes texts that explain the diagnosis of diseases (that is, how to analyze the imbalance of cosmic forces in the organs of the body) but also lists approved versions of prescriptions developed to restore the cosmic balance in the diseased organs, instruct in pulse reading, explain the circulation of air in the body, and teach how to set bones.[14] Much information is presented in rhyme or verse form for easy memorization. The *Yizong jinjian* "combined, somewhat unusually, the functions of . . . an introductory textbook and a reference book to general medicine."[15]

---

12. Ma Jixing, *Zhongyi wenxian xue*, p. 384; Hoizey and Hoizey, *A History of Chinese Medicine*, p. 134; and Liao Yujun et al., *Yixue juan*, pp. 392–93 (this reference includes a list of the titles in the *Yuzuan Yizong jinjian*). For a discussion of the intellectual background to Qing medicine, see Unschuld, *Medicine in China: A History of Ideas*, pp. 194–97; and Leung, "Medical Instruction and Popularization in Ming-Qing China," pp. 138–39.

13. Hanson, "Inventing a Tradition in Chinese Medicine," pp. 204–12.

14. Wylie, *Notes on Chinese Literature*, pp. 101–2.

15. Leung, "Medical Instruction and Popularization in Ming-Qing China," p. 139.

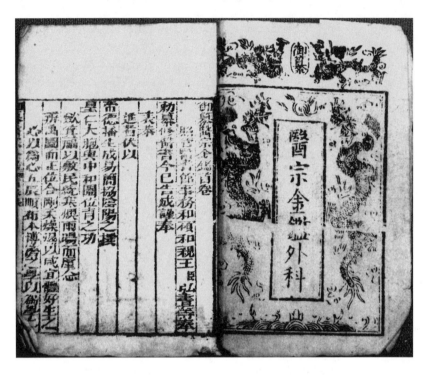

Fig. 11.5 *Yuzuan Yizong jinjian waike* 御纂醫宗金鑑外科 (Imperially sponsored *Golden Mirror of Medical Orthodoxy: External Medicine*). (a, *above*) Cover page of a Sibao edition. (b, *facing page top*) Comparison of the same page in two different Sibao editions. (c, *facing page bottom*) Page from the Siku quanshu edition of the *Yuzuan Yizong jinjian*. (a, b) Photographs by the author; (c) from the facsimile edition published by the Shanghai guji chubanshe, 1991, 3: 782–83.

Thus in publishing the *Yuzuan Yizong jinjian*, the Zou and Ma were reproducing a work important not for its pathbreaking new theories or cures but for its definition of "correct" medical thinking and its usefulness as a broadly accessible and comprehensive guide to standard medical practice and professional medical instruction in the eighteenth century. They continued producing this work, in whole and in part (see Figs. 11.5a and b),[16] throughout the nineteenth century, long after *wenbing* advocates had gained a considerable following and established a "lineage" of their own. In this, as in their publication of the Classics

---

16. Wylie, *Notes on Chinese Literature*, p. 102.

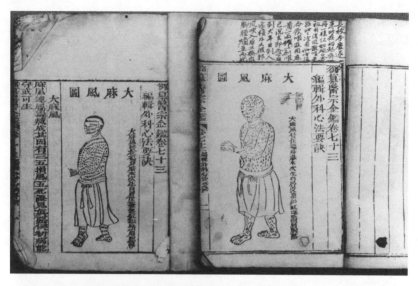

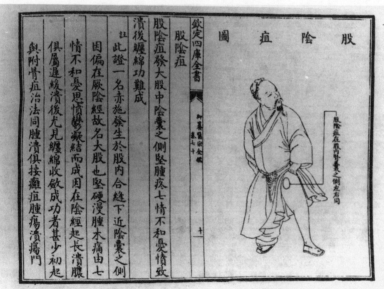

and primers, Sibao stuck to conventional, "safe" texts, eschewing interpretations that might clash with the declared orthodoxy, even after
these new interpretations had earned some acceptance. And the Zou
and Ma could be confident that the *Yuzuan Yizong jinjian* would sell, for

it was an authoritative medical guide that attracted both a professional and a popular audience. As the preface to one of their editions of the work proclaimed, "This work contains many proven prescriptions that are both economical and labor-saving. Both poor and rich families should have a copy" ("Xu," 1b). An American author observed, in the late 1880s or early 1890s, that Chinese laborers in the United States were often "well acquainted" with an abridged version of this work.[17] The crudely printed and illustrated extant Sibao editions (see Figs. 11.5b and c for a comparison with the more elegant Siku edition) may have been designed for a popular audience; it was doubtless the low production quality that allowed the Wenhai lou to sell this text wholesale for 2.5 *qian*[18]—expensive by Sibao standards, but a relatively low price for such a long text.

Most Sibao medical publications appear to have been less expensive popular texts, which might serve as basic textbooks for village physicians or local specialists or as practical guides to home treatment for literate merchants or peasants. Such works, written in a simplified medical language (and sometimes in rhymed verses), began to appear in sizable numbers in the late fourteenth century and proliferated during the rest of the Ming and the Qing. The medical primers of the Qing were distinctive for "a greater simplification of language and content but also for an increasingly pragmatic and clinical approach," with less emphasis on medical theory than the Ming texts.[19] The popularity of these texts owes something to changes taking place within the medical profession, as it came to be viewed more as a trade than an elite intellectual pursuit. Angela Leung notes that the Ming and Qing witness "the gradual transfiguration of the ideal, moralistic model of the 'Confucian doctor,' emerging in the Song and maturing in the Yuan, into the more pragmatic, realistic, and 'professional' medical practitioner."

---

17. The other medical work they were familiar with was the *Bencao gangmu* (Culin, "Popular Literature of the Chinese Laborers in the United States," pp. 56–57).

18. Other relatively expensive medical titles from the Wenhai lou account book were the *Yanfang huipian* 驗方彙編 (Collated efficacious prescriptions) at 1.2 *qian* and the *Yixue heke* 醫學合刻 (Combined medical studies) at 0.8–1.0 *qian*; cheaper texts, apparently simple acupuncture guides, sold wholesale for roughly 0.5 *qian*.

19. Leung, "Medical Instruction and Popularization in Ming-Qing China," pp. 130–31, 136, 139.

Commercial publishers like the Zou and Ma provided the textbooks for this "occupational medical training." But the proliferation of simple medical guides also meant that medical knowledge was more accessible to nonprofessionals; any reader could turn to these texts for do-it-yourself home remedies.[20]

Although several of the better-known medical textbooks appear on the Sibao book lists,[21] the publishers seem to have found the works of the physician Chen Nianzu 陳念祖 (*zi* Xiuyuan 修園; 1753–1823, *jr* 1792), a native of Changle county, Fujian, particularly profitable. Chen was a noted teacher of medicine and popularizer of medical information—and apparently also an astute judge of the commercial demand for elementary medical texts.[22] As a magistrate in Weixian 威縣, Nan Zhili, he was credited with organizing medical relief efforts during a devastating epidemic. Horrified by the primitive and wrongheaded techniques used by local physicians to cure the ill, he resolved to publicize more widely simple explanations of effective cures. In particular, he hoped, as he explains repeatedly, to warn amateur practitioners against the dangerous innovations of "modern" physicians.[23]

The first product of this resolve was the *Shifang gekuo* 時方歌括[24] (Reliable prescriptions brought together in song, in two *juan*; first published in 1801; see Fig. 11.6), a collection of 108 prescriptions dating from as early as the Tang, presented in easy-to-memorize verse form,

---

20. Ibid., pp. 146–49.

21. The Wenhai lou account book lists *Yixue xinwu* 醫學心悟 (Mental comprehension of medical learning), the title of a work by Cheng Guopeng 程國彭 (1679?–1735?); Angela Leung ("Medical Instruction and Popularization in Ming-Qing China," p. 134) identifies this work as the "ultimate representative of Qing medical primers." The Xiangshan tang property-division document also lists an *Yixue rumen* 醫學入門 (Introduction to medicine), the title of an influential introductory textbook by Li Chan 李梴 (late sixteenth–early seventeenth century) (ibid., p. 137).

22. Leung, "Medical Instruction and Popularization in Ming-Qing China," p. 144; Hoizey and Hoizey, *A History of Chinese Medicine*, p. 135.

23. Liao Yuqun et al., *Yixue juan*, p. 409; Sun Wenqi, *Zhongguo lidai mingyi jilu*, pp. 213–14; and Ren'an, *Zhongguo gudai yixuejia*, pp. 127–30.

24. *Shifang* 時方 refers to prescriptions not found in the Han-dynasty classics of medicine, but developed later by physicians following the principles established in these texts.

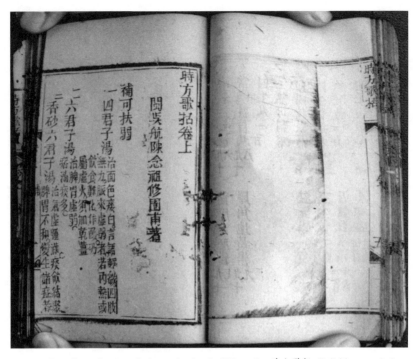

Fig. 11.6 Page from the prescription-recipe book *Shifang gekuo* 時方歌括 (Reliable prescriptions brought together in song), compiled by Chen Nianzu 陳念祖. Photograph by the author.

arranged according to the types of illness they cured ("tonics for debility," "heavy medicines for calming," "light medicines for attacks of wind-evil," etc.). The preface alludes to Chen's sobering experience in Weixian: "Now medicine is the art of keeping people alive, but one needs to make only one mistake to kill someone." Fearful that people saw medicine as too abstruse a subject to master and thus remained unnecessarily ignorant of even those simple medical practices that anyone could use to ease suffering or cure illness, the preface continues, the author decided to make public a compendium of simple prescriptions ("Xu," 1ab).

Along with *Shifang miaoyong* 時方妙用 (Reliable prescriptions with marvelous effects) in four *juan*, first published in 1803, a companion volume, which also provides cures for a wide variety of external and internal medical problems, this work became very popular. Written in simple language and in verse form, with clear instructions and practical prescriptions, both texts circulated widely throughout the nineteenth and early twentieth centuries and, indeed, have been reprinted in the 1950s, 1960s, and 1980s. Useful to any literate person looking for a home remedy, they would also have appealed to students of medicine, many of whom might have begun learning their trade as adults and much appreciated the easy-to-memorize rhymes. Dai Baoyuan 戴葆元 (1828–88?), for example, a failed examination candidate who started studying medicine when he was over thirty, found that because he "had lost the sharpness of his youthful mind," he quickly forgot whatever he learned and thus relied on verses to make his lessons easier to remember.[25] *Shifang gekuo* and *Shifang miaoyong*, as well as many other of Sibao's medical and pharmaceutical guides, supplied just the kind of lessons Dai needed. The Sibao editions of these texts are appropriately practical in format: punctuated, small (12.5 cm h × 21 cm w), easily portable, and clearly although crudely printed.

Chen's *Yixue sanzi jing* 醫學三字經 (Three-character classic of medical studies) was explicitly designed, as its title indicates, as an educational text for beginning physicians. Chen explains,

When boys enter school, the teacher first teaches them the *Three-Character Classic*, wanting them to memorize it. This is the path to knowledge. A first text for beginning students of medicine has not yet been established, so that they are navigating a roiling sea, with a compass that leads them to mistake half the characters, until they end up in the land of ox-headed demons and snake-bodied spirits [i.e., in confusion]. Thus I have published the *Three-Character Classic* [for medicine]. ("Xiaoyin," 1a)

The first two *juan*, after a brief history of medicine and its major texts, describe symptoms of illnesses in different categories (apoplexy, consumptive diseases, coughs, etc.); two *juan* list over 180 prescriptions; finally, an appendix consists of essays on five important theoretical discussions (on *yinyang*, the viscera, the meridians, the four methods of examination, and the movement of *qi*). Written, like the *Sanzi jing*, in three-character rhyming couplets, this text provides a comprehensive introduction to the study of medicine in simple, easy-to-memorize language. It opens, for example, with the statement "The beginning of

---

25. Leung, "Medical Instruction and Popularization in Ming-Qing China," p. 145.

medicine / lies originally in Qi Huang 歧黃 / *Lingshu* was written / and *Suwen* elaborated on it." Notes in simple language follow each couplet. The first two couplets are explained as follows:

**Yi zhi shi, ben Qi Huang** 醫之始, 本歧黃. "Huang" is Huangdi 黃帝. "Qi" is Qi Bo 歧伯. The emperor [Huangdi] and his minister [Qi Bo], in questions and answers, illuminated the origins of the meridians, the viscera, the circulation of *qi* 氣, and methods of cure. Thus they are considered the founding ancestors of medicine. Even although the *Shennong benjing* 神農本經 existed before Huangdi, the principles of enlightened use of medicine began with the *Neijing*. **Lingshu zuo Suwen xiang** 靈樞作, 素問詳. The *Lingshu* in nine *juan* and the *Suwen* in nine *juan* are together called the *Neijing*. This is what the "Yiwen zhi" 藝文志 [Dynastic bibliography] of the *Hanshu* records as the *Huangdi neijing* 黃帝內經 in eighteen essays. For students of medicine, this work is like the Five Classics for students of Confucianism.

In this fashion the student was introduced to the major texts and thinkers of the medical tradition, much as the *Sanzi jing* listed the classical texts the aspiring examination candidate would have to learn. Since, in the couplets introducing the categories of diseases, Chen cited many of these medical texts, the student was repeatedly made aware of their importance—and of the medical views associated with each. In these notes Chen passed judgment, strongly favoring the ancient classics and contemptuously dismissing the newfangled theories of contemporary physicians. The medical prescriptions often include precise measurements of ingredients, as well as Cheng's empirically based assurance that these formulas actually work. The Sibao edition of the *Yixue sanzi jing* is a small (11.5 cm h × 17.6 cm w), poorly cut work, with occasional markers for phrase breaks or emphasis—in short, in production quality rather like Sibao editions of *Sanzi jing* (see Fig. 11.7).

Chen also wrote commentaries on medical classics, including *Shennong bencao jingdu* 神農本草經讀 (Reading the *Materia medica* classic of Shennong; published by the Suwei tang in an undated edition), one of his more scholarly works. Here as elsewhere, Chen is firmly on the side of Qing medical orthodoxy. Like the other works discussed here, this text is designed to explain the principles underlying the famous early pharmacopoeia *Shennong bencao jing*, usually dated to the Eastern Han and considered the founding classic of the Chinese pharmacological

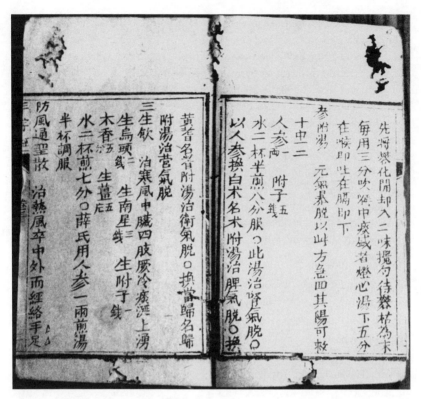

Fig. 11.7 Page from *Yixue sanzi jing* 醫學三字經 (Three-character classic of medical studies) of Chen Nianzu 陳念祖. Photograph by the author.

tradition.[26] The preface (by a Jiang Qingling 蔣慶齡, dated to 1803) suggests something of Chen's common touch:

Chen Xiuyuan is an old friend skilled in the techniques of medicine. He prides himself on being the heir to Changsha 長沙 [i.e., Zhang Ji, founder of the

---

26. The origins of the *Shennong bencao jing* are unclear. The scholarly consensus seems to be that it was compiled by many hands and that it records pharmacological information from the Shang, Zhou, and Warring States periods. Tao Hongjing 陶弘景 (452–536) wrote a text titled *Shennong bencao jing*, but was working from an earlier text with that title. The text that is now identified as the *Shennong bencao jing* is based on the versions presented in Tao's *Shennong bencao jing* and *Shennong bencao jing jizhu* 神農本草經集注 (Collected commentaries on the *Materia medica* classic of Shennong). See Ma Jixing, *Zhongyi wenxian xue*, p. 246; Unschuld, *Medicine in China: A History of Pharmaceuticals*, pp. 17, 30; and Liao Yuqun et al., *Yixue juan*, pp. 146–48.

"cold damage" tradition]. As a result, other physicians of his generation laugh at him. But when an illness becomes serious, these men are useless, just wringing their hands. Xiuyuan [Chen Nianzu] comes, removes his hat and puts it on the bench, raising his eyes as he takes the patient's arm to feel the pulse; and after a while he laughs dryly, saying, "The symptoms originally were not serious, but whoever has tried to cure the disease has made it worse." The host says, "But he is a famous physician." Xiuyuan replies, "He was mistaken." The host protests, "But his method followed that of Zhu 朱 [Zhenheng 震亨?], Zhang 張 [Jiebin 介賓?], Wang [Haogu 好古?], and Li 李 [Zhongzi 中梓?]." Xiuyuan replies, "All the more mistaken. How can one cure illness by following Zhu, Zhang, Wang, or Li?" Muttering and cursing, he confidently writes out the prescription, adds his own analysis, praising and explaining his diagnosis. He prepares the medicine himself and quickly hands it to the patient, urging, "Swallow this, swallow this!"

This passage, while describing Chen's practical, hands-on skill, reiterates his allegiance to the orthodox "cold damage" school and his scorn for contemporary medical practice—presumably the physicians Chen disparages here are noted late imperial medical theorists, men who modified or challenged traditional practices.[27] Chen apparently also dismissed the work of Li Shizhen, author of the pathbreaking pharmacopeia *Bencao gangmu*. Indeed, Chen's *Shennong bencao jingdu* was in part an attack on Li's famous text, which Chen belittled as "vulgar and simplistic": "Only after scholars get rid of this and other similar texts will they be able to discuss the Way of medicine" ("Xu," 1b–2a). Throughout, Chen's text advocates discarding medical innovations of the

---

27. "Zhu" may refer to Zhu Zhenheng (1281–1358), one of many Song and Yuan thinkers who tried to reconcile the contradictions between traditional pharmaceutical classifications and theory and contemporary practice; "Zhang" to Zhang Jiebin (*hao* Jingyue 景岳, 1563–1640), who may have aroused Chen's ire by his advocacy of exorcistic healing in *Leijing* 類經 (Classic arranged by categories, 1624); and "Li" to Li Zhongzi (1588–1655), who attempted to reconcile conflicting theories in the promotion of eclectic practice. "Wang" may refer to Wang Haogu (fl. 1246–48), the author of *Tangye bencao* 湯液本草 (*Materia medica* of decoctions), who, like Zhu Zhenheng, tried to develop a rational system of pharmaceutical classification. To Chen Nianzu, these men represented, it seems, wrongheaded departures from the medical teachings of the ancients. See Unschuld, *Medicine in China, A History of Ideas*, pp. 177–204; and Liao Yuqun et al., *Yixue juan*, pp. 348–410, for a fuller explanation of the medical context and the development of the controversies over pharmaceutics.

preceding fifteen centuries and relying solely on the medical classics of the Han.[28]

Despite these references to ongoing medical controversies, it would be a mistake to identify Chen's work as an effort at sophisticated medical scholarship or synthesis. Its ultimate purpose was, rather, to provide a useful pharmaceutical guide to people not conversant with medical debates or the technical aspects of pharmacology. As Jiang noted:

Its language is simple and its points comprehensive. . . . [Chen's] work penetrates mysteries, but is very clear and easy to understand. As with Bai Juyi's 白居易 poetry, even the old woman in the kitchen can understand it. He explains what cannot be explained and people understand. . . . His ideas are brilliant and he knows how to express them [literally, "he has golden thoughts and silver hands"]. ("Xu," 1b–2a)

The Sibao edition of this text, edited by one of Chen's sons and collated by two of his grandsons, is, like that of *Shifang gekuo*, *Shifang miaoyong*, and *Yixue sanzi jing*, small (11 cm h × 17 cm w) and poorly produced. It may have been published as part of a set of Chen's popular medical works, which were commonly published together.[29]

Most of Sibao's remaining medical titles, like those by Chen Nianzu, focus on practical applications, on remedies. Particularly popular were collections of prescriptions. Sibao shops printed apparently at least two

---

28. Chen draws in his own notes on the commentary of Zhang Zhicong 張志聰 (fl. 1650), a noted early Qing physician (who claimed descent from Zhang Ji himself) and advocate of "absolute observance of the rules and regulations of all [the] old classics." Chen relies in particular on Zhang's *Bencao chongyuan* 本草崇原 (Exalted origin of the *materia medica*), a commentary on the *Shennong bencao jing* (Unschuld, *Medicine in China: A History of Pharmaceutics*, pp. 185–86). But Chen also claims to draw on the commentary of Ye Gui 葉桂 (1667–1746) ("Fanli," 1b), the Suzhou physician famous for challenging the dominance of the "cold damage" tradition.

The preface to *Shennong bencao jingdu* is printed at the end of *Yixue sanzi jing*. This might be a sign of the sloppiness of some Sibao publishing, or an effort to advertise another medical textbook to the readers of *Yixue sanzi jing*.

29. Publishers in Xuwan, Jiangxi, rivals of the Sibao publishers, produced several collections of Chen's works. A collection of his works (supposedly seventy-two) was published as recently as 1982 by the Wenhua tushu gongci in Hong Kong; the text is advertised on the cover page as "necessary preparation for examinations in Chinese medicine."

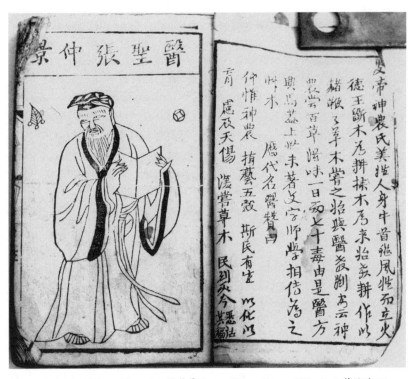

Fig. 11.8 Portrait of Zhang Zhongjing 張仲景 from a Sibao edition of *Yaoxing fu* 藥性賦 (Verses on the properties of medicines). Photograph by the author.

editions of the popular and comprehensive *Yifang jijie* 醫方集解 (Medical prescriptions collected and explained; 1682), by Wang Ang 汪昂 (fl. late seventeenth–early eighteenth centuries). Wang, "probably . . . the most successful medical writer" of the Qing, owed his popularity—his work is still used today—to his simple language and his focus on practical cures.[30] Several publishing houses also produced works in verse on the properties of drugs; the well-known *Lei Gong paozhi yaoxing fu* 雷公爆制藥性賦 (Lei Gong's song of drug preparation and drug properties), for example, appears on several book lists.[31] (See Fig. 11.8.)

---

30. Unschuld, *Medicine in China: A History of Pharmaceutics*, p. 170.

31. Sibao editions of *Lei Gong baozhi yaoxing fu* and *Yifang jijie* do not survive (although several partial versions of a text identified simply as *Yaoxing fu* do). The former seems to have been a popularized version, in verse, of two collections of prescriptions: the late Ming *Zhenzhu nang zhizhang buyi Yaoxing fu* 珍珠囊指掌補遺藥性賦 (*The Pearl*

*Yanfang xinbian* 驗方新編 (New collection of proven prescriptions; published in 1883) is perhaps the most comprehensive of Sibao prescription collections. First produced in 1846 by the official and physician Bao Xiang'ao 鮑相璈 while serving in a suboffical position in Wuxuan 武宣, Guangxi, and collated by his brothers, it categorizes prescriptions according to parts of the body in *juan* 1 through 3, and according to medical specialty in the remaining five *juan:* gynecology, pediatrics, wounds, and miscellaneous diseases. An exhaustive table of contents lists all the prescriptions included in the work, providing the user with a quick means of reference. As one admirer exclaimed: "It is refined and comprehensive, yet simply written and handy; the ill can look up their sickness under the appropriate category and then find the recipe for the medicine under the appropriate sickness—as easy as using a lodestone to find iron."[32]

Anyone and everyone might find this text useful, Bao declared in his preface, but it will be particularly helpful to the poor:

There is no one who does not get sick. When one is sick, it is necessary to call for a physician to administer medicine. But physicians at times are hard to get; medicine at times is too expensive. The wealthy certainly need not worry about these problems, but the poor will often be wringing their hands in anxiety over them. In order to ensure the greatest convenience, every household should have a copy of this text. Since the prescriptions are both numerous and of high quality, it is possible to match each illness with a prescription that will cure it, without the aid of a physician.

He goes on to relate how he collected the prescriptions for his text:

---

*Bag*, expanded and made easily understood [combined with the] *Song of Drug Properties*) and the seventeenth-century *Lei Gong paozhi yaoxing jie* 雷公炮制藥性解 (Lei Gong's explanation of drug preparation and drug properties). *Yaoxing fu* (Song of drug properties), an entry on several Sibao book lists, was attributed to no less a figure than Li Gao, the important Jin-dynasty physician and medical theoretician. Presumably the Sibao publishers found it expedient to claim famous physicians as authors of these popular texts. Wang Ang's *Yifang jijie* was a more comprehensive work, which synthesized earlier pharmaceutical traditions. See Unschuld, *Medicine in China: A History of Pharmaceutics*, pp. 106–8, 170–73, 251; and Leung, "Medical Instruction and Popularization in Ming-Qing China," pp. 139–40.

32. Bao Xiang'ao, ed., *Yanfang xinbian*, p. i. (This modern edition of the *Yanfang xinbian* reproduces the expanded version of the text edited by Mei Qizhao 梅啓照 in 1878.)

When I was young, I knew a man who kept one excellent prescription secret, refusing to transmit it to the world. I thought this behavior was base and therefore set my will on tirelessly seeking for prescriptions, either through ancient and modern texts or through the reports of relatives and friends. After a while I had an abundant collection, with each school included. I dropped those prescriptions that did not work, weeded out repetitions, and omitted those that required medicine too expensive to buy. What now remains supplies a prescription for every sickness and a medicine for every prescription. Moreover, these prescriptions need not cost even one *qian*, and yet are miraculously efficacious. Even although you live in an isolated, rural area, one that rarely sees a boat or horse, you will still be able to find the necessary medicines. ("Xu," 1b)

Bao specifically directs his work, then, to the poor and isolated, perhaps thinking of much of the population of his site of service, Wuxuan.

Sibao also produced specialized medical texts—that is, guides to certain types of diagnosis[33] or to the treatment of certain diseases or populations. Several of the property-division documents and account books list works on external medicine, pediatrics, smallpox and other epidemic diseases, the interpretation of pulses, and gynecology. Those that have been preserved in Sibao seem, in keeping with the general orientation of the publishers' medical output, to have been designed either for basic instruction or for home use. Several texts were devoted jointly to the problems of pregnancy and children's diseases.[34] For example, *Baochi zhinan che* 保赤指南車 (Guide to infant care), compiled by Deng Liu 鄧旒 (*zi* Letian 樂天, 1774–1842) of Shaowu, Fujian, was published by

---

33. The Cuiyun tang inventory lists *Wanbing huichun* 萬病回春 (Return to spring from a myriad illnesses), which probably refers to the well-known diagnostic manual of Gong Tingxian 龔廷賢 (seventeenth century), an official in the Ming Imperial Medical Academy. But there is another work with this title, a guide to preserving good health or extending life (*yang sheng* 養生) by a Fang Kaiyuan 方開原 (fl. Kangxi–Yongzheng eras), published first in 1880. Unschuld, *Medicine in China: A History of Pharmaceutics*, p. 252; *Zhongguo yiji dacidian*, 2: 1265.

34. See, e.g., *Yingtong baiwen* 嬰童百問 (One hundred questions about the care of infants), *You[ke] zhinan* 幼[科]指南 (Guide to pediatrics), and *You[ke] jicheng* 幼[科]集成 (Collected works on pediatrics), listed in Appendix G. The first title here might be the *Yingtong baiwen* of Lu Bosi 魯伯嗣 (Ming), first published in 1539, and a source cited in many later works on children's diseases (see *Zhongguo yiji dacidian*, 2: 903).

the Sibao Zushu tang in 1880, at the behest of the author's great-grandson Deng Bifei 避非 (1842–1908).[35] Although the book in fact includes much general information about and prescriptions for internal and external medicine, it is promoted in a preface as well as the title as a work on children's diseases. It is also advertised as a work of great merit; Deng and his great-grandson have repudiated the greed and jealousy that lead many to hide their prescriptions from the world and benevolently chosen to disseminate them as widely as possible in the *Baochi zhinan che*:

The benefit of doctoring to the world is great! But carrying medical techniques to many is even more meritorious, and disseminating these techniques throughout the whole world is yet greater in merit. . . . Gentleman Deng Bifei of Beixiang 北鄉, Qiaochuan 樵川 [Shaowu], through Confucian study became learned in medicine. He received the *Jingui mishu* 金匱秘書 [Secret book of the golden cupboard], on external and internal medicine, from his forebear Deng Letian. The principles of this text are brilliant and its language clear; for all illnesses it produces effective cures. The gentleman is particularly brilliant on the subject of children's measles—many times children suffering from this illness have been cured by his methods, even those who had reached the crisis stage. Did not Han Feizi say that universal love is benevolence? Certainly this gentleman is a practitioner of universal love. Since his techniques are respected by his contemporaries, [his great-grandson] wanted to disseminate them widely, to benefit later generations of the empire. Therefore, he collected his methods, recorded them in ten *juan*, titled the text *Baochi zhinan che*, and handed it over to be cut and printed. ("Xu" 3, 1b)

A second preface suggests that, with this text, "anyone can learn how to treat children" (1a). Like most of the other Sibao medical texts, this is a small, unpunctuated text, and sparsely illustrated (see Figs. 11.9a and b).[36]

------

35. Deng Liu, *Baochi zhinan che*, p. 1. The text was published first in 1834, but not disseminated widely; apparently no copies of this first edition survive. It was not until the Zushu tang (and the Wuben tang) published it that it circulated fairly widely.

36. This text exists in another edition, undated, published by the Wuben tang, but with a completely different title on the cover page: *Neiwaike jizheng* 內外科集症 (Collected internal and external diseases). It seems that the Wuben tang simply used a new cover page as a means of pirating a popular text; prominent on the cover page of this edition is the phrase "reprinting forbidden" (*fanke bijiu* 番刻必究)!

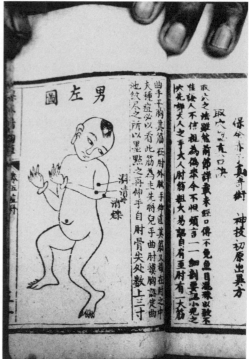

Fig. 11.9 *Baochi zhinan che yishu* 保赤指南車醫書 (Guide to infant care), published by the Zushu tang 祖述堂 in 1880. (a, *left*) Cover page. (b, *right*) Sample illustration. Photographs by the author.

Finally, the Zou and Ma produced a variety of manuals for the use of what we might call popular specialists or practitioners. As Angela Leung has demonstrated, after the Song, certain types of medicine, "notably those considered technical, 'manual,' or superstitious," including ophthalmology, midwifery, acupuncture, moxabustion, and massage, came to be assigned to a popular, often oral, tradition distinct from the elite academic study of medical theory and the practice of fully trained (and fully literate) physicians.[37] Scholars have assumed that the popular practitioners, whose ranks included women and "'vulgar' and 'lowly' country people," were taught what was perceived as a craft through oral instruction and hands-on practice.[38] Sibao, however, did produce a few texts

37. Leung, "Medical Learning from the Song to the Ming," p. 383.
38. Ibid., pp. 396–97.

that might have been useful in such training, either as a source of teaching methods for a literate master or as a textbook for a literate or semi-literate disciple. The *Yanke jingyi* 眼科精義 (Essential principles of ophthalmology), *Shen yanke* 審眼科 (Ophthalmology), *Yanke zuanyao* 眼科纂要 (Collected essentials of ophthalmology), and *Yinhai jingwei* 銀海精微 (Subtleties of the eye)[39] dealt with eye diseases, although since none has survived, it is impossible to judge their contents. The *Antai baochan liangfang* 安胎保產良方 (Excellent prescriptions for easy delivery; published by the Chongde tang 崇德堂 in 1886), which describes prescriptions and treatments for women in pregnancy and childbirth ("the immortals' method for difficult childbirths," "what to avoid when close to childbirth," "medicines to take when close to childbirth," "guaranteed—effective every time—method for difficult childbirth"), could easily have been a guide for midwives as well as local practitioners. By including a method of childbirth attributed to immortals, this text announces itself as a popular work, for the claim of mythical transmission was often adduced to enhance the prestige of popular practitioners among the common people; no self-respecting scholar-physician would have countenanced such a claim.[40]

Acupuncture, moxibustion, and massage were also often the domains of popular specialists. The titles that appear on Sibao book lists suggest that the Zou and Ma published a few of the "classics" as well as many cheaper manuals of these techniques. The Cuiyun tang inventory lists *Zhenjiu dacheng* 針灸大成 (Great collection of acupuncture and moxibustion), the title of one of the longest and most authoritative works on acupuncture and moxibustion, attributed to the Ming physician Yang Jishi

---

39. This last work may be the text described by Wylie (*Notes on Chinese Literature*, p. 97) as a "small treatise on eye complaints, which professes to be written by Sun Simiao [孫思邈, 581–682?] of the Tang dynasty; but the evidence seems to indicate that it is a production subsequent to the Song. It is esteemed, however, for the method in which it treats the subject." It could also be a later Qing work, the *Yinhai jingwei bu* 銀海精微補 (Supplement to the *Subtleties of the Eye*), compiled by Zhao Shuangbi 趙雙璧, and published first in 1673; this work concludes with an appendix on acupuncture and moxibustion, which would suggest it was a text used by the medical technicians discussed above (*Zhongguo yiji dacidian*, 2: 1076–78).

40. Leung, "Medical Learning from the Song to the Ming," p. 386.

楊濟時 and published in 1601.[41] It also includes *Caiai bian* 采艾編 (Selecting moxa plants), the title of a compilation by Ye Guangzuo 葉廣祚 (fl. late seventeenth century), which, drawing on previous writings on moxabustion, categorizes the various uses of moxa plants.[42] But the Wenhai lou account book also lists inexpensive acupuncture manuals—for example, *Fazhen du* 發針度 at 7 *fen* wholesale—that were likely purchased by the lowest-status popular specialists. Sibao published at least one handbook of massage, *Xiao'er tuina* 小兒推拿 (Massage for children), but this title might refer to a variety of different works.[43]

In this category of popular specialized texts belongs Sibao's lone surviving veterinary tract—*Yuan Heng liao niu ji* 元亨療牛集 (Collection of cures for water buffalo by Yuan and Heng; see Figs. 11.10a and b), by Yu Ren 喻仁 (Benyuan 本元) and Jie 傑 (Benheng 本亨) of Liuanzhou 六安州 (Anhui) and published by the Chongde tang.[44] This small (12.7

---

41. Weikang Fu, *The Story of Chinese Acupuncture and Moxibustion*, pp. 25–26; *Zhongguo yiji dacidian*, 2: 1145. Since the text does not survive, it is impossible to verify that it was Yang's work. There is also an entry for *Tongren zhenjiu* 銅人針灸 (Acupuncture and moxibustion on the bronze men), which may refer to one of the best-known texts on acupuncture, *Tongren yuxue zhenjiu tujing* 銅人腧穴針灸圖經 (3 *juan*), attributed to Wang Weiyi 王惟一 (the "bronze men" of the title refers to anatomical figures made by Wang in 1026, at the command of the emperor, as a means of illustrating acupuncture meridians). But it may also be a briefer and much less sophisticated manual titled *Tongren zhenjiu* to attract gullible customers. See *Zhongguo yiji dacidian*, 2: 1139; and Wylie, *Notes on Chinese Literature*, p. 101.

42. *Zhongguo yiji dacidian*, 2: 1146–47. The inventory also lists *Zhenjiu daquan* 針灸大全 (Compendium of acupuncture and moxibustion), the title of a work compiled by Xu Feng 徐鳳 (Ming); it largely repeats *Zhenjiu dacheng* (*Zhongguo yiji dacidian*, 2: 1142–43).

43. See *Zhongguo yiji dacidian*, 2: 1216–20; *Xiao'er tuina quanshu* 小兒推拿全書 (Complete book of massage for children), *Xiao'er tuina fa* 小兒推拿法 (Method of massage for children), *Xiao'er tuina xianshu* 小兒推拿仙書 (Immortals' book of massage for children) are just a few of the possibilities.

44. The cover page promises that the *Tuojing* 駝經 (Camel classic) is appended to the text, although it is difficult to see what use this work would have been in any of Sibao's market areas. The Cuiyun tang lists another text, on horses. This may refer to a second work of Yu Ren and Yu Jie, listed in Wylie's *Notes on Chinese Literature* (p. 106) as the *Liaoma ji* 療馬集 (Collection of cures for horses); he lists their work on water buffalo as *Niujing daquan* 牛經大全 (Compendium of the water buffalo classic), and suggests that they were published first in the late sixteenth century (in 1598 for the *Liao ma ji*).

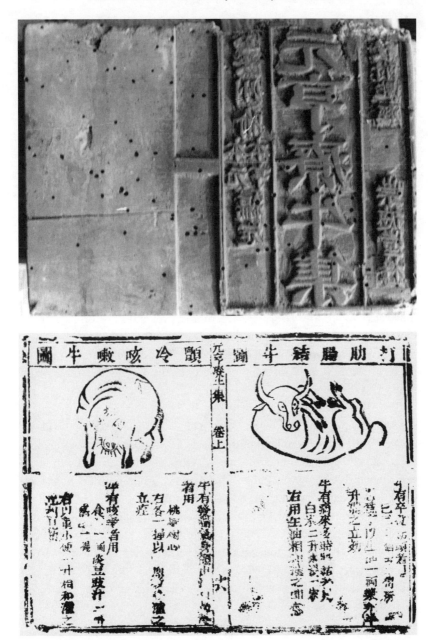

Fig. 11.10 *Yuan Heng liao niu ji* 元亨療牛集 (Collection of cures for water buffalo by Yuan and Heng), published by the Chongde tang 崇德堂. (a, *top*) Block for cover page. (b, *bottom*) Sample illustrations. Photographs by the author.

cm h × 17.7 cm w) illustrated text was presumably in demand in Sibao's many rural markets.

This discussion of Sibao's medical output has emphasized the popular nature of that output. Titles from publishing house property-division documents suggest that the Zou and Ma also produced more sophisticated works suitable for highly educated physicians desirous of keeping up with medical controversies or advanced medical students interested in mastering the landmark texts of their profession: the writings of the famous physicians and theorists Li Gao (*Dongyuan shishu* 東垣十書 [Ten works of Li Gao]) and Zhang Jiebin (fl. ca. 1624) (*Jingyue quanshu* 景岳全書 [The complete works of Zhang Jiebin]), the casebook of the prolific Ming physician Xue Ji 薛己 (1488–1558)[45] (*Xueshi yian* 薛氏醫案 [Casebook of Master Xue]), and the *Shishi milu* 石室秘錄 (Secret records from the mountain cave) of Chen Shiduo 陳士鐸 (ca. 1687), an influential analysis and categorization of therapeutic techniques,[46] to name just a few. Li, Xue, and Zhang could be grouped into a trend in early Qing medical thinking toward the treatment and prevention of disease by replenishing the body with *yang* influences, but it would probably be wisest to see Sibao's more sophisticated medical publications not as partisan choices but as reflections of the heterogeneity of medical theory and practice in the Qing.[47]

Sibao's medical offerings were for the most part directed to beginning (and non-elite) students of medicine; partially trained "country doctors"; literate or semiliterate therapists of acupuncture, moxibustion, massage, and the like; and households for whom a trained physician was unavailable or unaffordable. The Zou and Ma publishers kept their stock up to date in that they published mostly contemporary medical works, either early medical classics with later commentaries or encyclopedias and prescription collections by late Ming or Qing physicians. But highly trained and knowledgeable physicians eager for the latest controversial theories or practices—for example, within the "warm factor" school of analysis, increasingly popular through the nineteenth

---

45. See Furth, *A Flourishing Yin*, pp. 280–81.

46. Unschuld, *Medicine in China: A History of Ideas*, pp. 206–8, 220; and *Zhongguo yiji dacidian*, 1: 613.

47. Unschuld, *Medicine in China: A History of Ideas*, pp. 196–200, 223.

century—had to look elsewhere. Sibao supplied a less sophisticated, although much larger, audience with easy-to-understand modern texts that promised, above all else, effective remedies for a range of diseases.

## *Guides to Good Fortune: Almanacs, Fengshui and Divination Manuals, and Morality Books*

Sibao's guides to good fortune shared the intent, although not the methods, of the ritual handbooks and the medical manuals: to provide practical instructions to well-being. Just as the household encyclopedias precisely describe rituals and forms that promise to establish individuals and families as virtuous, civilized, and even cultivated members of a lineage and community, so, too, these guides to good fortune describe the calculations and rituals that individuals and families had to perform in order to manipulate cosmic forces on their behalf or to establish themselves as worthy of supernatural favor. And, just as the medical manuals instruct in diagnosing and treating diseases, so, too, these works "diagnose" the fate allotted to the individual at birth and "prescribe" the techniques, rituals, and behaviors that can be used to "treat"—that is, either change or reinforce—this allotment.[48] In the traditional "four treasuries" (*siku* 四庫) bibliographic classification system, these texts were placed together in the "philosophy" treasury (*zibu* 子部), and it is easy to see why: the medical and fortune-telling manuals interpret the balance of cosmic forces, in one case within the body and in the other within an individual's or family's allotted future, and identify how to manipulate or correct that balance.[49]

The overlap among these works can be considerable—some household encyclopedias instruct readers in making appeals to the gods; works like *Wanbao quanshu* and *Chuanjia bao* include sections on divination and

---

48. A common popular belief held that an individual's fate (*ming* 命), allotted at birth, was changeable. Thus a man allotted thirty years of life at birth could, through the accumulation of good deeds, extend his lifespan or through evil deeds, shorten it. If he accepted his fate, without making an effort to change it, he would die at thirty (see Brokaw, *The Ledgers of Merit and Demerit*, p. 34).

49. See Leung, "Medical Learning from the Song to the Ming," pp. 383–86; and Chia, *Printing for Profit*, p. 231, on the connection between medicine, spirit mediums, and fortune-telling.

the accumulation of merit alongside information on household rituals and the proper forms of instruction and social interaction. And medical manuals are based on the same cosmological assumptions about *yin* and *yang* that underlie many works of divination, particularly *fengshui* interpretation.[50] Handbooks developed for the use of popular specialists often adduce supernatural inspiration for their prescriptions and techniques.[51] All are designed to place the individual and the family in harmony, at social, bodily, or cosmic levels, with the universe.

The Chinese developed a multitude of techniques for calculating and shaping one's or one's family's fate, and thus this section includes works that describe a wide range of approaches: *fengshui*, the siting of cities and human dwellings (and especially graves) so as to harmonize with natural energies and thereby bring good fortune; the reading of body features or physiognomy; the casting of eight-character horoscopes; the use of the diagrams of the *Classic of Changes* (and, in certain texts, the disposition of the Five Agents, *wuxing* 五行, as well); charms to ward off evil spirits and attract good; the scheduling of activities— even those as mundane as washing one's hair—on designated lucky days; oneiromancy, or the interpretation of dreams; the different forms and times of worship appropriate to different spirits; and the practice of good deeds as a means of accumulating merit and rewards from the spirits or cosmos. These texts, among the most popular of Sibao publications, are analyzed below, with some effort to define their relative importance within the sprawling category of guides to good fortune.

First, it appears—from several inventory titles and a one-page fragment—that several Sibao shops published (or pirated) editions of the *Qinding Xieji bianfang shu* 欽定協紀辨方書 (Imperially sponsored book for harmonizing the times and distinguishing the directions), the most "accurate" and comprehensive statement of cosmological orthodoxy, produced by the Qing government in 1741. Commissioned by the Qianlong emperor to combat popular confusion over false divinations and "machinations of the conjurers and fortune-tellers" (as well as to correct errors in a previous state publication, the *Qinding Xingli kaoyuan*

---

50. The connection is implicit in the biography of Zou Qianguang 謙光 of Wuge, skilled in both medicine and *fengshui*; see *FYZSZP* (1947), 33. 46ab.

51. Leung, "Medical Learning from the Song to the Ming," pp. 385–86.

欽定星曆考原, Imperially sponsored *Investigation into Astrological Calendrics*), *Xieji bianfang shu* explains the principles that guided the calculation of the imperial calendar and that were supposed to guide private astrological calculations or prognostications—"the principal object being to show how to select lucky, and avoid unlucky times and places, for all the affairs, great and small, of public and private life."[52] It first explicates the complex system set forth in the *Classic of Changes* and the various methods of numerological calculation that could be deduced from it, and then moves, in a total of thirty *juan*, through a discussion of the celestial bodies and the correlations between heavenly and human affairs. Richard Smith describes this work as aimed at "an exclusively elite audience," grouping it with other reference works on divination that provided readers with "concrete information on how to use cosmic variables . . . to 'control' (*zhi* 制) and 'cultivate' (*xiu* 修) certain situations or spirits."[53] In sum, it can be seen as a kind of comprehensive guide to the cosmological principles that support the great variety of fortune-telling (and fortune-manipulating) techniques practiced in late imperial China. It stands at the high end of Sibao's guides to good fortune.

But the *Xieji bianfang shu* could also be put to humble uses: the production of almanacs, among the most broadly popular of guides to good fortune. Western observers in nineteenth- and early twentieth-century China repeatedly commented on the ubiquity of these works. One late nineteenth-century Western observer described these texts as "perhaps the most universally circulated book[s] in China."[54] And both Daniel Kulp and James Hayes, visiting south China in the early and

---

52. See A. P. Parker, "Review of the Imperial Guide to Astrology," pp. 495–97, for a translation of the preface to this work. Parker explains that the title is an allusion to the "Hongfan" 洪範 (The great plan) chapter of the *Classic of History*; *xie ji* means harmonizing the five dividers (the year, month, day, stars, and calendrical calculations), *bian fang* means distinguishing the positions or directions (cited in Richard J. Smith, *Fortune-Tellers and Philosophers*, p. 51).

53. See Richard J. Smith, *Fortune-tellers and Philosophers*, pp. 51ff, for a description of the contents of the *Xieji bianfang shu*, and 83; see also Wylie, *Notes on Chinese Literature*, pp. 133–34.

54. A. P. Parker, "The Chinese Almanac," p. 61; see also Richard J. Smith, *Fortune-tellers and Philosophers*, pp. 89–90.

middle decades of the twentieth century, observed that these works were everywhere in "small towns and villages."[55] Drawing on the cosmological calculations in works like the *Xieji bianfang shu*, as well as in official and unofficial versions of the state calendars, these texts, often sold very cheaply, provided the lay reader with a wealth of practical information about means of attaining good fortune, especially the selection of auspicious days for particular activities.[56] The Sibao *Xingping yaojue Bainian jing heke* 星平要訣百年經合刻 (*Essential Secrets of the Xingping Method*[57] and *Hundred-Year Classic*, combined), published in 1879 by the Linlan tang, and attributed to the mythical Guiguzi 鬼谷子 and a Yang Tianjue 楊天爵, crams just such a "farrago of odds and ends"[58]—methods of divination, advice about lucky days, techniques of casting horoscopes, charms, descriptions of gods and spirits—into its 19.5 cm h × 26 cm w format. The 100-year calendar advertised in the title is almost an afterthought.

Sibao also published an edition of one of the most popular almanacs, the *Yuxia ji* 玉匣記 (Record of the jade casket), a composite work dating from the mid-fifteenth century, popularly attributed to the third-century immortal Xu Zhenjun 許眞君.[59] A Sibao version of this text, *Zengbu zhujia xuanze guang Yuxia ji* 增補諸家選擇廣玉匣記 (Expanded *Record of the Jade Casket*, with supplements from a host of experts), with a preface dated 1684, includes comprehensive advice on how to avert bad and attract good fortune, largely through the choice of auspicious days and the worship of selected deities. Intended, according to its

---

55. Hayes, "Specialists and Written Materials in the Village World," p. 83. Richard J. Smith (*Fortune Tellers and Philosophers*, p. 82) suggests that such works were "quite possibly the best-selling books in all of China—not only because they were extremely cheap, but also because they were extremely useful."

56. Smith, "A Note on Qing Dynasty Calendars," pp. 127–28. For a description of the contents of most almanacs, see A. P. Parker, "The Chinese Almanac," pp. 71–72; and Palmer, *T'ung Shu*.

57. The phrase "*xingping*" 星平 in the title refers to the eight-character method of casting horoscopes; see Richard J. Smith, *Fortune-tellers and Philosophers*, pp. 43, 177–80, and n. 90.

58. Lister, "Chinese Almanacs," p. 239.

59. It was reprinted as part of the *Zhengtong Daozang* 正通道藏 (Orthodox Daoist canon; 1436–49) and included in the *Xu Daozang* 續道藏 (Continuation of the Daoist canon; 1607). See Roy, *The Plum in the Golden Vase*, 2: 565, n. 9.

preface, for use by all the four classes—scholars, peasants, craftsmen, and merchants—it provides a series of schedules of optimal days for appeals to the spirits. If, for example, on an *yiwei* 乙未 day, one seeks good fortune, one will gain "a little benefit"; but on *bingjia* 丙甲, *dingyou* 丁酉, and *wuxu* 戊戌 days, "since all the spirits are in heaven, serving in the court of the Jade Emperor, balancing the registers of life and death, noting the good and evil deeds of all people, to seek wealth on these days brings great misfortune" (11b). The text also includes lists of the birthdays of various spirits (so that the reader can learn when to worship them most effectively) and pictures and verse descriptions of a variety of star spirits (Fig. 11.11a), including brief charts of the constellations they reside in and the charms with which to solicit them. The text ends with a potpourri of tips, including charms for warding off sickness, descriptions of various fortune-telling methods (using snow, insects, clouds, etc.), and specific advice for different sectors of the population (women, men, the rich, the poor).

*Yuxia ji* attracted a wide and varied readership. It appears in the late Ming novel *Plum in a Golden Vase* as a reference work consulted by a Daoist acolyte to determine a good day for the *jiao* 醮 rites of cosmic renewal.[60] And Wang Xifeng, the household manager of the wealthy Jia family in the *Dream of the Red Chamber*, consults it to determine the reason for her daughter's illness.[61] As Miura Kunio has pointed out, it includes specialized information that would be of use only to scholars (on lucky days for beginning study or taking office, etc.), as well as advice applicable to a general popular readership. He suggests, therefore, that it was aimed at professional fortune-tellers (as the example from *Plum in a Golden Vase* suggests), who could derive from it responses for a wide range of clients.[62] It might well also have been used by lay persons in their homes (as the example from *Dream of the Red Chamber* suggests), just as some of the medical manuals described above might have been used by laymen as well as popular specialists or physicians. The almanac has appeared in dozens of different versions,[63] and these different

60. Roy, *The Plum in the Golden Vase*, 2: 407.
61. Cao Xueqin, *The Story of the Stone*, 2: 325.
62. Miura Kunio, "Kaisetsu," pp. 142–143.
63. Miura surveys nine editions in "'Ōkō ki' no Okinawa ruiden."

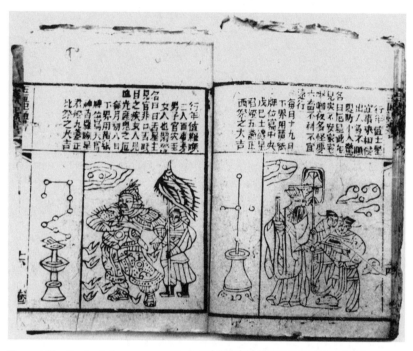

Fig. 11.11 The *Zengbu zhujia xuanze guang Yuxia ji* 增補諸家選擇廣玉匣記 (Expanded *Record of the Jade Casket,* with supplements from a host of experts), an almanac. Illustrations of (a, *above*) star spirits and (b, *facing page left*) the ox spirit from the Sibao edition. (c, *facing page right*) Illustration of the ox spirit from *Xinjuan Xu Zhenjun Yuxia ji zengbu zhujia xuanze riyong tongshu* 新鐫許眞君玉匣記增補諸家選擇日用通書 (Xu Zhenjun's *Record of the Jade Casket,* a daily-use almanac with supplements from a host of experts, newly published; 1797). (a, b) Photographs by the author; (c) courtesy of the Morrison Collection of Chinese Books.

editions might have been shaped to meet the needs of different readers. The surviving Sibao edition (11.5 cm h × 24 cm w) is cramped and poorly printed on coarse paper, now browned with age, its illustrations of the spirits crudely drawn and cut (although still rather lively and appealing)—presumably this was not the sort of edition that Cao Xueqin envisioned Wang Xifeng consulting (see Figs. 11.11b and c).[64]

---

64. Another Sibao almanac title is *Xiangji [beiyao] tongshu* 象吉[備要]通書 (Almanac explaining symbols of good fortune). Wylie (*Notes on Chinese Literature,* p. 134) mentions this work, by a Wei Jian 魏鑑, as "a most elaborate code of rules for the discrimination of lucky and unlucky days, by means of the usual conventional system of cycles and symbols"; it was first published in 1721.

Almanacs offered a range of techniques for divination and attracting
good fortune. But there were many more specialized texts, ones that
focused on a single approach or a cluster of related techniques. For example, charms or magical characters and appeals to the gods were one
means of manipulating fate frequently promoted by Daoist practitioners. Sibao published a collection of such charms (*fu* 符) and invocations (*zhou* 咒) that promised to expel evil spirits and attract the favor
of the gods.[65] The *Wanfa guizong* 萬法歸宗 (Orthodox guide to a myriad methods), which survives only as a set of woodblocks, is a little encyclopedia of charms, invocations, and miscellaneous other methods. It
explains as well the cosmological basis for the efficacy of its different
methods, so that the user would understand why they worked.

---

65. See de Groot, *The Religious System of China*, 6: 1024–61, on the uses of charms and
incantations. These methods of exorcising evil spirits and invoking the gods are usually
performed by Daoist practitioners, although the methods listed in the *Wanfa guizong* appear to be eclectic.

By far the most popular of Sibao works on fate manipulation, how-ever, were *fengshui* manuals. These form the largest subgroup within the category of guides to good fortune; the Cuiyun tang inventory records at least twenty-nine titles, of which roughly eight have survived in Sibao. The Zou and Ma emphasis on *fengshui* manuals reproduced contempo-rary empirewide trends; many foreign observers commented on the ubiquity of *fengshui* writings and practices in the nineteenth century.[66] "Popular expositions of the theory and its practical application are on sale in every bookshop, mostly of considerable bulk, and illustrated with woodcuts," according to J. J. M. de Groot.[67] *Fengshui* was of keen interest to Sibao residents themselves, as the art was taken very seri-ously in those areas of the province, like Sibao, where reburial was practiced.[68] Indeed, grave sitings were the cause of major disputes be-tween the Zou and Ma; *fengshui* is still cited as a major determinant in the history of Wuge and Mawu;[69] and surviving *fengshui* texts in Sibao are still much in use by contemporary geomancers.

Fujian was also the center of one of the two great schools of *fengshui*, the more theoretical and esoteric school, which emphasized the cosmol-ogy of *fengshui*, the links between heavenly bodies and the hexagrams and numerological charts of the *Classic of Changes*, and real earthly sites. Known as the "method of Min," this school relied heavily on the geo-mantic compass, or *luopan* 羅盤, as an aid in calculation. Incorporating some of the metaphysical concerns of Song Confucianism, it developed in opposition to the Jiangxi or Ganzhou school of Yang Yunsong 楊筠松 (fl. late ninth century), which emphasized the importance of ob-servation and analysis of the shapes and orientations of the earth's physical forms over cosmological influences. By the Ming the Jiangxi school had become dominant south of the Yangzi;[70] in the late nine-teenth century, J. J. M. De Groot notes that this "school of forms" (or

---

66. Richard J. Smith, *Fortune-Tellers and Philosophers*, pp. 170–71. See also Hayes, "Spe-cialists and Written Materials in the Village World," pp. 93–96.

67. De Groot, *The Religious System of China*, 3: 1009.

68. Richard J. Smith, *Fortune-Tellers and Philosophers*, p. 151.

69. Informants claim that the poor examination showing of the Zou lineages re-sulted from Wuge's position relative to the mountain behind it. Interview 32, 11/13/95 (Wuge); see also Chapter 2, p. 68, note 107, and p. 67.

70. See March, "An Appreciation of Chinese Geomancy," p. 261.

"shapes") or the "Ganzhou method" predominated in "the mountainous southern provinces," even in Fujian. And by the Qing the two schools had been considerably synthesized, so that *fengshui* experts could both "assert that there still exists a distinct line of demarcation between the two schools" and, at the same time, claim that they are "so far fused together that no good expert in either ever neglects to practice the methods of the other school as well as his own."[71]

This synthetic approach is mirrored in Sibao's *fengshui* texts, which include works that could be used by practitioners of either school. The *Luojing jie* 羅經解 (Explanation of the geomantic compass), a Ming dynasty work by Wu Tianhong 吳天洪, describes the use of the *luopan*, which is at the heart of Fujian-school *fengshui* practice[72] but also is used as an important "secondary aid" by the Ganzhou school.[73] This basic guide survives in a rather nicely produced late nineteenth-century version edited by a Xiong Ruyu 熊汝獄 (Figs. 11.12a and b). The preface announces its allegiance to the Fujian school and the analysis of the relationship between earthly forms and the heavens, principle (*li*), and *qi*, but insists that it can instruct Jiangxi-school adherents as well. The work itself consists of a description of a prototypical geomantic compass, identifying the cosmological associations of each section of the instrument. Thus, the inner circle, the "heavenly pool," represents the Taiji 太極, the Supreme Ultimate, the progenitor of *yin* and *yang*; the next ring contains the "eight trigrams that precede heaven," and so on, each ring introducing ever more complex cosmological associations, each of which had to be related to those of previous rings.[74] Some of these explanations are presented in verse form, presumably to help the student of *fengshui* memorize the dazzling array of information packed onto the geomantic compass. Somewhat larger than most Sibao

---

71. De Groot, *The Religious System of China*, 3: 1008; Richard J. Smith, *Fortune-Tellers and Philosophers*, pp. 132–36.

72. Richard J. Smith, *Fortune-Tellers and Philosophers*, p. 134.

73. De Groot, *The Religious System of China*, 3: 1008. The compass in the Ganzhou school is used to "sound the influences of the country after its forms and contours have been pronounced to be favorable."

74. For a fuller explanation of the compass according to the *Luojing jie*, see Feuchtwang, *An Anthropological Analysis of Chinese Geomancy*, pp. 18–30 and *passim*.

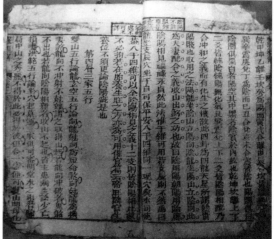

Fig. 11.12 *Luojing jie* 羅經解 (Explanation of the geomantic compass), published by the Juxian tang 聚賢堂. (a, *left*) Cover page. (b, *right*) Sample pages, with "eyebrow notes." Photographs by the author.

imprints at 13.8 cm h × 24 cm w, this undated edition from the Juxian tang is clearly cut, with large, easy-to-read, evenly spaced characters in the standard, blocky, "craftsman's" style typical of Sibao imprints. The text is not punctuated, but occasional sideline circles point up particularly important passages. Brief notes were added (presumably by Xiong) at the top of the single register in small boxes placed over the relevant passages. Like at least one other edition of this work, it is not illustrated, although one might think that illustrations would aid significantly in the explication of *luopan* use.[75]

Many of Sibao's geomantic texts were designed to be accessible to a broader readership; although they might explain the principles of the art, they also provided specific guidelines for its practice.[76] Often these

---

75. Richard J. Smith, *Fortune-Tellers and Philosophers*, p. 137.

76. Sibao may, however, have published a version of the difficult geomantic text that has been described as "the single most influential book on *fengshui* produced in the Qing period": the *Dili bianzheng* 地理辨正 (Distinguishing geomantic orthodoxy) of Jiang Pingjie 蔣平階. This title is listed on the Cuiyun tang inventory, although no text survives. Jiang, the grandson of a late Ming *fengshui* expert, was a well-known practitioner of the Jiangxi school and also learned in the *fengshui* canon. He established a kind of *feng-*

works contained testimonials to their efficacy. The *Dili wujue* 地理五訣 (Five secrets of geomancy), for example, one of the most popular manuals, was attributed to a Zhao Tingdong 趙廷棟, an official active during the later Qianlong era, well known for his ability to read *fengshui*. Typical of the accounts of his prowess was the report that he had transformed the fortunes of Pengxian 彭縣, Sichuan, by suggesting certain modifications to the gates of the county seat. Before these changes, Pengxian students had consistently failed the examinations; afterwards, the county enjoyed several stunning successes.[77]

The Sibao edition of *Dili He Luo jingyi* 地理河洛精義 (Essence of geomancy, the Yellow River Chart, and the Luo River Writing; Figs. 11.13a and b), written by a Meng Danqi 孟澹其 and expanded and edited by a Tingzhou native, Liu Buqing 劉步青, exemplifies this more popular sort of geomantic manual. Although the "He Luo" of the title refers to the Yellow River Chart and Luo River Writing of the *Classic of Changes*, both props of the more abstract Fujian school, the contents of the work reveal an eclectic interest in presenting, in simplified form, a range of *fengshui* theories and practices. *Dili He Luo jingyi* claims to recover methods defined originally in the *fengshui* classics of the Song and Ming, many of which are now lost, scattered, or simply misunderstood. It also promises to transmit recondite secrets absent from other commercial publications. Above all else, it offers clarity: "Because profound words are difficult to understand and thus may end in delusion, detailed commentary has been added to the text" ("Fanli," 2a).

After general essays on *fengshui*, *Dili He Luo jingyi*, in ten short *juan*, deals in turn with the forms central to *fengshui*. Thus "Rules of the Dragon," for example, treats the configuration of mountains and direction of rivers and streams. The work focuses on methods of identifying favorable grave sites (*xue* 穴), dividing these into sand (*shafa* 沙法) and water (*shuifa* 水法) methods—that is, ways of adjusting a site to land forms or to bodies of water. The reader is assured of these methods' proven efficacy: "This book has already been tried and tested. The placement of ancestral mounds and graves, whether in the mountains

---

*shui* orthodoxy with the *Dili bianzheng*, but the text was difficult and seems not to have been particularly popular (Richard J. Smith, *Fortune-Tellers and Philosophers*, pp. 152–53).

77. Ibid., p. 157.

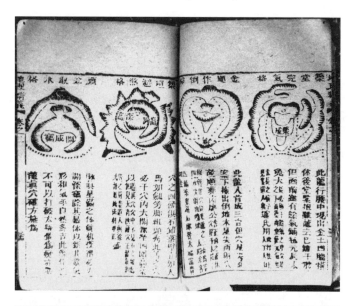

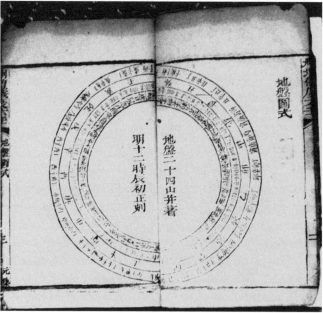

Fig. 11.13 *Dili He Luo jingyi* 地理河洛精義 (Essence of geomancy, the Yellow River Chart, and the Luo River Writing). (a, *top*) Configurations of graves. (b, *bottom*) The "earthly compass." Photographs by the author.

or on the plains, in every case created a wealthy and noble lineage. . . . Examine the application of principle and *qi* outlined here, and you will understand that the efficacy of this text is heaven-endowed" ("Fanli," 2a). Some care has been taken with format: the text is punctuated with phrase markers and occasionally annotated with double rows of interlinear commentary. It also includes illustrations—cosmological diagrams, charts of land formations, and, of course, examples of different kinds of grave sites (see Fig. 11.13a). But it is small (12.7 cm h × 21 cm w), crudely cut, and poorly printed, a useful text, perhaps, but not a pleasure to use.

Who purchased these texts? De Groot, no admirer of *fengshui*, dismisses the educational level of most practitioners as nugatory:

A geomancer has, as a rule, learnt to read and to write at school; but, for the rest, he has picked up almost all his wisdom by strolling about in the open country for a few years at the heels of some professor who had adopted him as his disciple, catching from his lips a large supply of empty phrases about dragons, tigers, branches and other mysteries of the compass. . . . At best he may have consulted one or two handbooks badly printed. . . . Clever Fung-shui professors are accustomed to resort to other devices, in order to keep up the reputation of their calling and that of their own persons. The names of the ancient sages and sovereigns, revered by the whole nation as the holiest and most perfect of creatures the Universe ever produced, are constantly on their lips. . . . Thus they ably contrive to get themselves associated by the people with great and famous names in history.[78]

A few of the extant Sibao editions of *fengshui* manuals resemble the "one or two handbooks badly printed" that de Groot mentions here; certainly the *Dili He Luo jingyi* might fit this description. *Dili wujue* seems also to have been an introductory text, designed for beginners or *fengshui* "amateurs." Indeed, village *fengshui* specialists today use these and similar texts; presumably they are sufficient to instruct practitioners in the fundaments of the art—or at least in the terminology and references that make them appear knowledgeable. And the jumble of historical and mythological figures, adduced in the prefaces of these works as authorities on *fengshui*, supplied would-be practitioners with the store of "great and famous names in history" they needed to impress their customers.

---

78. De Groot, *The Religious System of China*, 3: 1011.

Whatever de Groot may have thought of *fengshui*, its practitioners and their customers saw it as a serious practice. Widely popular, *fengshui* was considered as essential to family prosperity as knowledge of the proper rituals (as explained in Sibao publications like *Jiali tieshi jiyao*). Most of Sibao's *fengshui* manuals were efforts to explicate clearly the major techniques of what had become, by the Qing, a highly complex and challenging art. In their production of *fengshui* texts, the Sibao publishers were responding to multiple levels of interest and expertise: lay practitioners hoping to advance their families, local experts servicing their communities, and more knowledgeable and sophisticated specialists teaching as well as practicing their profession. The range in prices of these texts supports this conclusion; a very popular work like the *Dili wujue* might sell wholesale for as little as 9 *fen*, but more complete and sophisticated texts—presumably for specialists who would purchase such a text as a professional investment—might cost as much as 1.3 or 2.5 *qian* wholesale.

*Fengshui* seeks to ensure a prosperous future; divining, to understand what the future holds. Effective divination, no less than *fengshui* analysis, relied on mastery of a long and complex textual tradition. Henri Doré noted that "the divining art, as practiced in China, requires skilful training, necessitates recurring to various guide-books filled with intricate formulas, and supposes in the votary of the art a prompt and powerful memory, in order to have at one's fingers' ends the countless combinations and deductions which are characteristic of this so-called science."[79] And Chinese diviners, even more than geomancers, had a dazzling array of different techniques—tossing coins, interpreting the *Classic of Changes*, reading cyclical characters, physiognomy, horoscope extrapolation, to name just a few—to choose from. Although divination manuals never rivaled *fengshui* guides in the numbers that appear on Sibao book lists, the Zou and Ma publishers did produce a fair variety of divination textbooks or handbooks.

Unfortunately most of them, as rather ephemeral texts wholesaling at low prices (1.5 to 9 *fen* per copy), do not survive today. Several titles appear to be based on the prognostications of the *Classic of Changes*. One of these, the *Bushi zhengzong* 卜筮正宗 (Orthodox divination) was

---

79. Dore, *Researches into Chinese Superstitions*, 4: 347–48.

a well-known diviner's manual by a Wang Weide 王維德, first published around 1709. This work was, according to the reports of Western observers, often consulted by professional fortune-tellers in interpreting the trigrams formed by a series of coin-tossing procedures.[80] Its preface asserts the orthodoxy of the techniques it teaches for calculating the fluctuations of *yin* and *yang* and the cycle of the Five Agents. Then, like many prefaces to *fengshui* manuals, it claims as its lofty goal the understanding of moral principle: "This book is taken to be a book about fate-calculation (*shu* 數), but it is really a book about principle (*li*)" ("Xu," 1b). As is typical of popular fortune-telling manuals of the late imperial era, *Bushi zhengzong* instructs in calculating fate not just from the diagrams of the *Classic of Changes* but from *yinyang*, Five Agents, stem and branch correlations, and character analysis as well.[81]

It also provides an interesting insight into the breadth of the readership for such texts and of the audience for the divinatory methods it teaches. The preface warns that sincerity is essential to the success of divination. It scolds in particular "the wealthy or honorable, [who,] affecting a contempt for the art of divination, either look to a friend or send a servant to ask a response in their stead, without showing their zeal and earnestness by presenting themselves in person"; for these people, divination will not work.[82] This confirms Richard Smith's claim that, although the practice of divination had its critics, it was nonetheless "deeply woven into the fabric of Qing society at all levels."[83] The elites may have tried to conceal their interest in predicting and control-

---

80. Nevius, *China and the Chinese*, pp. 182–84; cited in Richard J. Smith, *Fortune-tellers and Philosophers*, p. 118.

81. Another well-known title in this category is *Zhouyi meihua shu* 周易梅花數 (Plum blossom calculations from the *Classic of Changes*), popularly attributed to the Song cosmologist and numerologist Shao Yong. Its first two *juan* teach prognostication with visualized hexagrams (*tui gua* 推挂)—that is, hexagrams formed without the aid of coins or milfoil stalks), but the remaining two treat fortune-telling through the analysis of written characters (*ce zi* 測字). In this method the diviner is given a character (or his customers choose from a set of characters), which he then dissects or rearranges to create one or more new characters, which form the prognostication. See Richard J. Smith, *Fortune-tellers and Philosophers*, pp. 111–12; and Dore, *Researches into Chinese Superstitions*, 4: 356–62.

82. Translation, with minor changes, is from Nevius, *China and the Chinese*, p. 181.

83. Richard J. Smith, *Fortune-tellers and Philosophers*, p. 74.

ling fate, but they, too, sought the advice of fortune-tellers and texts like *Bushi zhengzong*. Divination, like *fengshui*, attracted all social classes.

One of the few Sibao divination manuals to survive is the *Shanzeng Yidu liuren ke xuanri yaojue* 删增儀度六壬課選日要訣 (Essentials of correctly divining auspicious days by the Yidu method of the six cyclic characters, revised and expanded), attributed to Zhang Jiuyi 張九儀 of Yanling 嚴陵 (Zhejiang). Published in 1822, this work explains how to select proper days for given activities through the *liuren ke* 六壬課 method—that is, the reading of paired earthly branches and heavenly stems, the cosmological symbols used in dating.[84] Ultimately derived from the correlative thinking of the *Classic of Changes*, this numerological art could demand, at its most sophisticated, quite complex calculations (often requiring the use of special heavenly and earthly compasses, or *tianpan* 天盤 and *dipan* 地盤) of the interaction of numerous cosmological variables. But it might also be practiced as a fairly straightforward and mechanical method of fortune-telling: a customer would select a heavenly stem, that character would be paired with an earthly branch by the fortune-teller, who would then consult a *liuren ke* manual, reading out the prognostication that was associated with that particular combination.[85] The Sibao text belongs to the more sophisticated tradition of *liuren* calculation: this is a discursive work in four *juan*, explaining in a series of essays the relationships among the cyclical characters, the stars, the Five Agents, *yin* and *yang*, and so forth, and illustrated with diagrams of the heavenly and earthly compasses. Plainly cut and only

---

84. The Cuiyun tang lists several other titles that seemed to explicate the *liuren* method of calculation, as well as that of a similar system, called *qimen dunjia* 奇門遁甲, "the skillful arrangement of cyclic characters." See Dore, *Researches into Chinese Superstitions*, 4: 345–47; and Richard J. Smith, *Fortune-Tellers and Philosophers*, p. 185.

85. See Dore, *Researches into Chinese Superstitions*, 4: 344–45, for a description of a fortune-teller's use of the *liuren* system. Dore also explains the name of this method of calculation: "This method of Chinese divination is practiced by combining each of the 'ten heavenly stems' . . . with the 'twelve earthly branches' . . . , taking care, however, to select but one out of every two of the latter. Thus six of the 'stems' joined with six of the 'branches' form six combinations. Hence comes the name 'divining by means of the six [*liu*].'" The cyclic character *ren* is chosen to name this method because "Heaven formed at first 'Water,' denoted by the character *Jen* 壬. For this reason, it represents the primordial foundation of all mundane matter, the very origin of things, that is water."

lightly punctuated, this work (12.4 cm h × 18 cm w) was written for a reader interested in the cosmological beliefs underlying the calculation of auspicious days.

Other works teach the techniques of fortune-telling through observation (*xiang* 相).[86] Some of these are clearly physiognomy manuals—that is, handbooks that read a person's fate as it is manifested in his/her appearance—like the well-known *Mayi xiangfa* 麻衣相法 (Physiognomy of Mayi), a practical illustrated guide to the art.[87] Sibao published "the single most important Chinese reference work for 'body divination,'"[88] the *Shenxiang quanbian* 神相全編 (Complete guide to spirit physiognomy), a comprehensive and eclectic compilation of methods of physiognomic analysis, attributed to an early Ming practitioner of the art, Yuan Zhongche 袁忠徹 (1367–1458). Drawing on numerology and Five Agents cosmological correlations, this text classifies several dozen different body types and categories of body parts (almost forty kinds of eyes, thirty kinds of eyebrows, twenty-four kinds of noses, etc.). It has remained, since its first known appearance in a late Ming edition, a standard textbook of "the Chinese traditional way of reading a person's health, character, and—most of all—fate, in his physical appearance." (Like the *Mayi xiangfa*, it is still in use today.)[89] In addition to this encyclopedia of physiognomy (selling wholesale for a relatively high 0.9 *qian*), Sibao produced at least three other guides to *xiang* prognostication, all relatively cheap works costing 0.4 to 0.6 *qian* wholesale.

Sibao also published the primary resource for perhaps the most popular form of fate extrapolation (*tui ming* 推命), the casting of horoscopes to determine the astrological forces that shaped a person's life. This was the *Sanming tonghui* 三命通會 (Compendium of the three fates), usually attributed to the Ming astrologer Wan Minying 萬民英,

---

86. Richard J. Smith, *Fortune-Tellers and Philosophers*, p. 173.

87. Dore, *Researches into Chinese Superstitions*, 4: 338–39. This text is attributed to an obscure Daoist practitioner of the tenth century named Mayi (who is purported to have prognosticated using *qi* analysis and physiognomy, and to have authored a text entitled *Xinfa* 新法); supposedly a product of the Song, it remained a popular physiognomy guide through the next several dynasties. See Kohn, "A Textbook of Physiognomy," p. 232.

88. Richard J. Smith, *Fortune-Tellers and Philosophers*, p. 188.

89. Kohn, "A Textbook of Physiognomy," pp. 228–30.

and not only the "primary textual authority for fate extrapolators in Qing times," but also a work still very much in use today.[90] Like the *Shenxiang quanbian* a comprehensive and widely eclectic work, this text draws on *yinyang*, Five Agents, stems and branches, solar periods, celestial palaces, and star spirits to explain both the cosmological foundations for horoscopes and the method for extrapolating them. It addresses social and historical aspects as well, explaining the relationship between different kinds of divination and different classes of people and outlining a brief history of horoscope extrapolation. It even explains the two major competing methods of casting horoscopes—the "Xuzhong" 虛中 method (using the two-character units for the year, month, and day of a person's birth) and the "Ziping" 子平 or "eight-character" (*bazi* 八字) method (which adds a two-character unit for the hour of birth to the Xuzhong calculations); it judges the latter method superior.[91] This is a work that would clearly appeal to a professional as well as a serious amateur.

In addition to this substantial and discursive work, Sibao also published practical handbooks for the deployment of a single method, the much more popular Ziping "eight-character" extrapolation technique. The *Baizhong jing* 百中經 (Classic for hitting the mark every time), for example, was a cheap (0.25 *qian*) manual sold in considerable quantities in the early twentieth century (200 copies are listed in the Wenhai lou account book) to customers who did not need to understand the underlying cosmological principles of divinatory techniques: itinerant or street fortune-tellers, go-betweens, and lay amateurs. In the early twentieth century, Sibao book peddlers included a similar manual, *Xinke Guigu xiansheng mingli sizi jing* 新刻鬼谷先生命理四字經 (Four-

---

90. Richard J. Smith, *Fortune-Tellers and Philosophers*, p. 177.

91. Ibid.; Chao, "The Chinese Science of Fate Calculation"; see also Chen Shuizheng, *Zhongguo xingming cidian*, p. 43. The Xuzhong method was named after Li 李 Xuzhong (fl. 790–835), a famous horoscope calculator of the Tang, who argued in his influential *Mingshu* 命書 (Book of fate) that the date of birth was the most important factor in the determination of fate. Xu 徐 Ziping, a recluse of the tenth century, developed the second method, which took the hour of birth into account in fate extrapolation; this method, known in the late imperial and modern periods more commonly as the "eight characters" (*bazi*), became dominant. On the practical operation of this method, see Nevius, *China and the Chinese*, pp. 185–86.

character classic of the principles of fate by Master Guigu, newly cut), in the store of cheap pamphlets that they hawked in market towns and peasant villages in Fujian.

The last set of guides to good fortune—the morality books— urge ethical action as the means to attain merit and material blessings. Nineteenth- and twentieth-century Western observers mention these among the most commonly circulating texts. James Hayes remarks that they were "probably in greater supply than the various guides to daily life or even cheaply printed novels."[92] Yet Sibao seems to have published very few of these texts, perhaps because they were normally printed by religious establishments, benevolent societies (*shantang* 善堂), or individuals hoping to earn merit through the free distribution of such works.[93] Indeed, one Sibao publisher, a devout Buddhist, on his retirement from business in the early twentieth century, devoted himself to publishing morality books and Buddhist tracts (none extant) for free distribution at a nearby Buddhist temple.[94] Religious texts and morality books may also have been produced by specialized publishers working for religious establishments. Informants reporting on the book scene in early twentieth-century Tingzhou city remember two entrepreneurs, Jiang Buyun 蔣步雲 and Jin Shizai 金實在, who established *keyin dian* 刻印店 (cutting and printing shops) devoted to the production of limited copies of Buddhist sutras and popular religious texts.[95] And certainly the message of the morality books could be found in many encyclopedias—the *Jiabao quanji* and certain editions of the *Wanbao quanshu*, for example—and works of fiction. Under the circumstances, it might be surprising that the Sibao publishers produced any morality books at all.

In fact, the few titles they did produce were of texts so well known as to be viable commercial products. The *Taishang ganying pian* 太上感

---

92. Hayes, "Popular Culture in Late Ch'ing China," p. 65.

93. These works were also distributed through separate channels; although some might be passed on by itinerant peddlers, many were given away at bookstores, temples, and even examination compounds (ibid.; see also Nevius, *China and the Chinese*, p. 230).

94. Interview 58, 12/2/95 (Wuge). The biography of Ma Kekuan mentions that he disseminated morality books as a work of charity, but no publisher or titles are mentioned; see *MSDZZP* (1945), *ji* 7, 1.*you*4ab.

95. Interview 74, 12/14/95 (Changting).

應篇 (Tract of Taishang on action and response), perhaps the most famous of all morality books and reportedly the most commonly printed book in nineteenth-century China,[96] is recorded in the Wenhai lou account book. (It may have been sold as a primer along with Sibao's other primers, since it was commonly taught in elementary schools during the Qing.)[97] This work was published countless times in a wide variety of different editions, from lavish imperially sponsored versions, finely cut and illustrated, to cheap, crude pamphlets available free at temples throughout China. Sibao's version was probably more like the pamphlet than the imperially sponsored "art" editions.[98]

Only one other Sibao morality book survives, and only in fragmentary form. This is the *Yuli zhibao bian* 玉歷[曆]至寶編 (Most precious jade chronicle). Like the popular text *Yuli* 玉歷[曆] (Jade chronicle) (of which this is perhaps one of many variants),[99] this work is a guide to the courts of hell, stating their locations, rulers, the particular misdeeds each punishes, and the punishments (including the forms of reincarnation) meted out. Interspersed throughout the text are cautionary tales of the good deeds that deliver one from and the bad deeds that doom one to each of the ten courts. The range of beliefs is eclectic: frequent appeals are made to Daoist and Buddhist deities, and the text begins by listing the most important gods and their birthdays, which implies that

---

96. Carus and Suzuki, *T'ai Shang Kan-Ying P'ien*, p. 3.

97. Leung, "Elementary Education in the Lower Yangtze Region," pp. 397, 401; see Chapter 10, p. 343.

98. The one woodblock that survives from a collection of morality books published in Sibao suggests that the text was quite small and crudely cut. *Jingxin lu* 敬信錄 (Record of reverence and trust) is also listed on one Guangxu-era property-division document; this refers, perhaps, to the popular work of Zhou Dingchen 周鼎臣, first published in the mid-eighteenth century (Brokaw, *The Ledgers of Merit and Demerit*, p. 224).

99. George W. Clarke translated a work entitled *Yuli*, stating only that "there are several editions of this book. I have seen six different ones, but none were like the copy of which the following is a translation." Indeed, the *Yuli zhibao bian*, although its arrangement and categories appear to be the same as those of the *Yuli* that Clark translates, does include different exemplary stories. It nonetheless refers, in these stories, repeatedly to the *Yuli*, as if this were the same text. Clarke, "The Yü-li or Precious Records," p. 233. The Sibao *Yuli zhibao bian* dates no earlier than the early nineteenth century, for one of its stories refers to events supposed to have taken place in 1809 (65a).

worshiping these spirits is also a means of earning merit and escaping the tortures of hell. Like most morality books, the text includes Confucian references as well, in this case citations of the famous Song Confucian thinkers Zhou Dunyi and Zhu Xi in a brief essay entitled "*Yuli* proven to be a Confucian text" (49ab and 53a–55a).

The numbers from the Cuiyun tang inventory suggest that the Sibao publishers found "guides to good fortune" to be among their most lucrative texts. And the compilation by Ma Kuanyu, one of the first of the Mawu publishers, of two almanacs suggests that such works, or at least the most popular of them, were produced in Sibao at the very earliest stages of its publishing history. Over time, however, Sibao published a great many other more specialized titles in this category as well, impressive not only for the range of fortune-telling methods they attest but also for the levels of sophistication they encompass. Sibao published elite, government-sponsored texts expounding a cosmological orthodoxy (*Xieji bianfang shu*), discursive and complex discussions of various approaches to cosmological manipulations (*Shanzeng Yidu liuren ke xuanri yaojue*), simple but comprehensive introductions to particular forms of fate extrapolation (*Mayi xiangfa*), and cheap manuals that matched cyclical dates or the eight characters with standard prognostications (*Baizhong jing*). The more sophisticated works were presumably for the use of professionals or aspiring professionals and for well-educated amateurs interested in cosmology or the principles of *fengshui* and divination. The cheaply produced pamphlets on cyclical character or eight-character calculation could serve marriage go-betweens or humble marketplace fortune-tellers—or nonprofessionals wishing to calculate their own fate—as simple handbooks.

For all their variety, however, works in this category expressed cosmological beliefs and ethical values common to all statuses and educational levels in the society. As Richard Smith has emphasized, the fact that these beliefs and values were interpreted in different methods of fate manipulation and expressed at different levels of linguistic complexity "did not diminish their significance as cultural common denominators in the Middle Kingdom across time and space."[100]

---

100. Richard J. Smith, *Fortune-tellers and Philosophers*, p. 91.

## Conclusion

In choosing which "how-to" manuals for daily life to publish, the Zou and Ma seem to have tried to appeal to as wide-ranging a readership as possible, targeting in particular readers in the middle and lower ranges. At the top end, they produced one or two comprehensive and lengthy imperially sponsored medical and cosmological encyclopedias (*Yizong jinjian* and *Xieji bianfang shu*) and a few sophisticated medical collections. Most of their practical handbooks were ritual guides, correspondence and document models, rhymed-couplet collections, prescription recipes, medical textbooks, *fengshui* and divination manuals, and almanacs that might appeal to two broad audiences: the literate layman interested in do-it-yourself guides to family ritual, medical care, and good fortune; and the professionals (or, to use James Hayes's term, the "specialists") who interpreted and applied the knowledge in these guides for illiterate or less well-educated customers. Failed examination candidates desperately searching for employment might turn to such works as "textbooks" for a new livelihood. "Thousands of them get employment as school-teachers, pettifogging notaries, and clerks in the public offices," explained S. Wells Williams in the late nineteenth century: "Some are reduced by degrees to beggary, and resort to medicine, fortune-telling, letter-writing, and other such shifts to eke out a living. Many turn their attention to learning the modes of drawing up deeds and forms used in dealings regarding property; others look to aiding military men in their duties, and a few turn authors, and thus in one way or another contrive to turn their learning to account."[101] A man with no hope of advancing beyond junior student or licentiate status might well use Sibao's practical guides as training manuals in ritual propriety, medicine, or fortune-telling—and, as Williams suggests, might even use the knowledge thus learned to write new, "revised" editions of such manuals. It is tempting to see two of Sibao's favorite author-editors, the Jiangs, father and son, as men who became ritual specialists and authors in the absence of scholarly or official success.

---

101. Williams, *The Middle Kingdom* (1882 ed.), 1.2: 571; and Hayes, "Specialists and Written Materials in the Village World," pp. 75–76, 92–105. Hayes identifies two types of specialists: those dealing with human fate and those dealing with "social rites and protocol."

A comparison of Sibao's output with some useful surveys of works found in villages in late nineteenth- and early twentieth-century south China and some reports on the reading habits of overseas Chinese workers from south China during roughly the same period suggest that the types of how-to texts Sibao produced were commonly found in use among the middle and lower levels of the literate population. In his surveys of popular written culture in rural Hong Kong from roughly 1870 to 1937, Hayes catalogues a range of texts similar in most respects to those on Sibao's book lists. In addition to "educational texts and aids to literacy" (see Chapter 10), he mentions a great many texts that fit into the first category discussed in this chapter: "handbooks of family and social rites and procedures," general encyclopedias for daily use, guides to letter writing, guides to contract forms, and "collections of couplets for every occasion."[102] Indeed, Hayes refers to an encyclopedia of daily life edited by a Sibao publishing family, *Choushi jinnang*. He also found almanacs, morality books, and fortune-telling and divination texts, although he suggests that this last category was likely to be in the possession of "village specialists."[103] His findings, then, are not inconsistent with the evidence from Sibao imprints: that practical manuals of daily life enjoyed widespread distribution.[104]

Other direct observers of Chinese reading habits confirm, more generally, this picture. Stewart Culin, reporting on the reading material of Chinese laborers in late nineteenth-century America, claimed that after fiction, drama, and songbooks, "'folk literature,' including books on divination and other means of fortune-telling, . . . the use of the abacus,

---

102. One type of text that Hayes found to be common—collections of contract forms—are not found on Sibao lists. In Sibao publications, such forms were included in the family ritual manuals, encyclopedias for daily use, and letter-writing manuals (Hayes, "Popular Culture in Late Ch'ing China," pp. 62–63; and idem, "Popular Culture of Late Ch'ing and Early Twentieth Century China," pp. 171, 180).

103. Hayes, "Popular Culture in Late Ch'ing China," pp. 63, 66–67. Hayes notes that he did not pay much attention to titles in the fortune-telling genre, since he felt inadequate to interpret them.

104. Hayes did not, however, find many medical texts. But Angela Leung ("Medical Instruction and Popularization in Ming-Qing China," *passim*) provides evidence from novels and accounts of medical education that demonstrate these works were widely used; in some cases, the number of editions issued (see Appendix G) indicates their popularity.

medicine, school texts, history, and dictionaries and letter-writing guides" were the most popular.[105] A. W. Loomis, in an article published in 1868 on the reading habits of Chinese laborers in San Francisco, noted that these men always had medical books in their lodgings. He provided a good illustration of both the "do-it-yourself" and the "village specialist" usage of such texts:

> There are few old students that have not read the medical books; and wherever they go they take these books with them, in order that, in case of necessity, they may be their own physicians. The sick sometimes seem inclined to trust such men rather than the regular practitioners. When applied to for 'advice,' they examine the patient, consult the books, and write the prescription as fearlessly and perhaps as successfully as most of the Chinese doctors.[106]

It is probably no accident that these practical how-to manuals are just the texts that survive in greatest abundance in Sibao today. Hidden during the Cultural Revolution, they are now back in use: the local *fengshui* experts were my sources for Sibao's extant *fengshui* manuals; the ritual manual *Jiali tieshi jiyao* was to be found in many homes and was used in the planning of funerals; and prescription collections were hoarded as valuable family property as well as sources for home remedies.[107] These two pieces of evidence are not conclusive—overseas Chinese communities were not necessarily representative of populations back home, and contemporary practices cannot be read back into the past. But in the absence of fuller evidence of reading practices in south China in the late Qing and early Republic, these reports hint at the place these texts had in earlier village society.

There are hints, too, in some of the texts themselves that they assumed a broad audience—that they transmitted orthodox ritual and social practices, orthodox medical remedies, and orthodox cosmological knowledge to the population at large. *Yizong jinjian* and *Xieji bianfang shu*

105. Hayes ("Popular Culture in Late Ch'ing China," pp. 72–73, n. 25) summarizing Culin, "Popular Literature of the Chinese Laborers in the United States," pp. 52–62.

106. Loomis, "What Our Chinamen Read," pp. 525–26; cited in Cohen, "Notes on a Chinese Workingclass Bookshelf," p. 428, no. 30.

107. Residents of Wuge and Mawu still rely on these texts and on local practitioners. Informants in Sibao and elsewhere were often reluctant to show me their medical texts, fearing that I might reproduce and circulate them, thereby undermining the profit their owners could earn by selling their precious secret prescriptions.

promise to provide all the correct medical and cosmological principles necessary for the development of effective cures and effective divination, respectively. Chen Nianzu, in his series of popular medical textbooks and prescription collections, claims to be disseminating correct and orthodox cures in simplified form, making them accessible to all people, particularly the rural poor. (We might see a rough parallel in the proliferation of "home medical encyclopedias" and manuals of "domestic medicine" designed to aid the rural poor in Europe and the hinterland and frontier populations of America in the late eighteenth and nineteen centuries.)[108] And Jiang Haoran's *Jiali tieshi jiyao* is presented as a compendium of the "unchanging principles" of ritual conduct appropriate for all families. To put their common goal in anachronistically modern terms, these works were vehicles of social, medical, and technological integration, means of spreading elite, orthodox values, practices, and knowledge—often in highly simplified form—to a rapidly growing population.

If Sibao's popular medical manuals and divination guides offered prescription remedies and good fortune, Sibao's guides to ritual practice and correspondence and encyclopedias of essential information for daily life carried a more complex message. In offering guidelines for proper behavior and a body of essential common knowledge, they were popularizing orthodox ritual patterns and socially useful information. But they were also presenting themselves as tools of social advancement. As the *Choushi jinghua* claimed, they were to teach non-elites to act like elites. They can be seen as companions to many of Sibao's educational texts, discussed in Chapter 10: while these latter texts offered access to elite knowledge and examination success, the ritual handbooks and encyclopedias of common knowledge offered lessons in the social practices and "cultural literacy" of the elite. Like etiquette texts and guides to *civilité* in early modern Europe, they claimed to teach a set of standards derived from the practices of the elite.[109]

---

108. These medical guides, although quite various in style and motive, seem to have been written for the growing middle class so that they might aid the illiterate poor to better health. See Rosenberg, "Medical Text and Social Context"; Risse, "Introduction," pp. 1–3; Blake, "From Buchan to Fishbein"; and Cassedy, "Why Self-Help?," pp. 33–36.

109. Chartier, *The Cultural Uses of Print in Early Modern France*, pp. 71–109; Revel, "The Uses of Civility"; and Chartier et al., *Correspondence*, pp. 1–23, 59–157.

Yet, at the same time, certainly no one born to these standards would ever need the wealth of information and explanation provided in works like *Jiali tieshi jiyao*. If the evidence from the late Ming or contemporary Europe is any indicator, real elites scorned these guides as vulgarizations of elite rituals and knowledge and anyone who used them as upstarts.[110] These texts may have spread and standardized ritual forms, but it is hard to see how they could have ensured their practitioners acceptance into an elite society jealous of its privileges and suspicious of those who had to learn proper behavior from a book. And their use at a time when upward mobility was becoming increasingly difficult more likely had the effect of confirming rather than challenging elite hegemony.

Presumably all these how-to texts—to good manners, good health, and good fortune—were of interest to the swelling population of people between elite and peasant status (although including literate peasants) in the Qing: artisans, middlemen, transport workers, brokers, bankers, sojourning merchants, shopkeepers, petty traders, pawnbrokers, schoolteachers, tutors, private secretaries, estate managers, tax farmers, pettifoggers, publishers, professional writers, physicians, popular medical practitioners, *fengshui* experts, fortune-tellers, and so forth. Several scholars have argued for the growth, in the wake of the commercialization of the economy in the late Ming and Qing, of an "urban middle class of self-made shopkeepers, petty merchants, and artisans."[111] The prefectural capitals and even the hinterland country seats and market towns that formed the backbone of Sibao's market network would have seen an increase in this "middle class" by the nineteenth century. Sibao's popular how-to manuals could appeal to those in this population eager for do-it-yourself guides, providing standards for family order, effective home remedies, and techniques for improving fate. The population explosion and the increasing competitiveness of the

---

110. Craig Clunas, in his study of manuals of taste in the late Ming, makes this point; he also emphasizes that such manuals of taste, by spreading guidelines to a non-elite population, commodified and thus subverted the idea of elite taste; see *Superfluous Things*, pp. 140–65. For the elite reaction to the popularization of standards of taste and material life in the late Ming, see Brook, *The Confusions of Pleasure*, pp. 222–28.

111. Von Glahn, *The Sinister Way*, pp. 244–45; see also Rowe, *Hankow: Commerce and Society in a Chinese City*, esp. p. 345.

examinations also created, by the same time, a large group of men educated (or partially educated; this group would include both junior students, or *tongsheng,* and licentiates) in the classical tradition who, with no
hope of earning official status, turned to a variety of other occupations
(many of which are listed above) to support themselves.[112] Sibao's texts
might provide such men with training in new professions—as ritual
masters, physicians, acupuncturists, geomancers, or fortune-tellers. And
to these men and their families, the ritual manuals and household encyclopedias in particular promised an inexpensive means of learning the
outer forms—the rituals, polite expressions, and common cultural
knowledge—that, it was claimed, marked one as a member of an elite
group they had little practical chance of joining.

---

112. Wakeman, *The Fall of Imperial China,* pp. 27–35.

# TWELVE

## *Fiction and Belles-Lettres*

THE MAJORITY OF Sibao's imprints were texts of assured practical usefulness, either educational works or guides to ritual and etiquette, to treatment and prevention of physical ailments, and to prediction and manipulation of fate. But the Zou and Ma publishers also published works of fiction designed to entertain (although some doubtless also aimed to instruct), songbooks, and some art and elite literary productions intended to provide uplifting aesthetic pleasure. In general these appear to have been published only after the "useful" book list had been built up, perhaps because they were often the most expensive to produce. Some works of fiction were quite long, necessitating a considerable investment in woodblocks, and high-quality calligraphy albums, although usually short, required skilled cutters. As luxury items—and even a cheap, crudely printed Sibao novel might be a luxury to a poor family—they probably represented some risk to the publishers, at least more of a risk than the Four Books. And the poetry and essay collections did not necessarily enjoy an assured and broad readership among Sibao's markets; they might express the highest literary values, the finest emblems of *wen* 文 (Culture), but, although they might endow readers with some cultural capital, they did not for the most part have the directly practical usefulness of the texts of the examination curriculum. Thus only a fairly well established publishing house would have been likely to invest in such texts.

Nonetheless, the Sibao publishers were able to profit in particular from the growing demand for fiction, which stimulated publication of novels and story collections from the late Ming through the Qing, and to a lesser degree from a steady demand for the most highly respected products of the elite literary tradition.[1] Never the staples of Sibao publishing, these works represented between 15 and 20 percent of the titles in the Cuiyun tang inventory. Most of these were popular novels and story collections.

Unfortunately, almost none of these fictional texts survives. This low survival rate tells us much about contemporary opinion of these works: they were entertainments to be passed about, shared (and often lost), in contrast to practical works such as the household and medical manuals; to the socially sanctioned, ethically and philosophically weighty Classics; and to the "true" and therefore respectable and instructional histories.[2] But, however widely these works may have circulated, the rarity of surviving texts affords us little to discuss besides titles, or even—given the instability of titles in Chinese book culture—types of texts. Thus the following analysis of Sibao's fiction output is somewhat speculative, extrapolated from titles, oral histories, and the few surviving texts.

---

1. On the increased demand for fiction in the nineteenth century, see Widmer, "Modernization Without Mechanization." In grouping fiction with poetry and literary collections in one chapter, I am violating traditional Chinese bibliographic categorization. Fiction was part of the *xiaoshuo* 小説 (insignificant talk) category; it labeled writings that, because they describe events that never happened and the feelings of people who never existed, were seen as trivial and not really appropriate for inclusion in the category of true literature (*xiaoshuo* also included works like joke books, recorded gossip, and collections of popular sayings). In contrast, poetry and essay collections (*shiji* 詩集 and *wenji* 文集) were considered among the finest products of Chinese literature. See Idema and Haft, *Guide to Chinese Literature*, pp. 56–57; and Nienhauser, *The Indiana Companion to Traditional Chinese Literature*, pp. 423–26.

2. In describing and dating the fiction titles Sibao published, I have relied on the following sources: *Zhongguo tongsu xiaoshuo zongmu tiyao*; Sun Kaidi, *Zhongguo tongsu xiaoshuo shumu*; Ōtsuka, *Zōho Chūgoku tsūzoku shōsetsu shomoku*; Liu Ts'un-yan, *Chinese Popular Fiction in Two London Libraries*; *Zhongguo gudai xiaoshuo baike quanshu*; Yuan Xingpei and Hou Zhongyi, *Zhongguo wenyan xiaoshuo shumu*; Ning Jiayu, *Zhongguo wenyan xiaoshuo zongmu tiyao*; and Idema and Haft, *Guide to Chinese Literature*.

## Fiction

The Zou and Ma shops seem, by the nineteenth century at the latest, to have printed all the best-selling titles of vernacular fiction:[3] *Honglou meng* 紅樓夢 (Dream of the red chamber; first published 1792), three sequels, and a prequel were products of either the Zaizi tang or the Wenhai lou.[4] Four popular novels of the Ming—*Shuihu zhuan* 水滸傳 (Water margin), *Xiyou ji* 西遊記 (Journey to the west), *Sanguo yanyi* 三國演義 (Narrative of the Three Kingdoms; entitled *Diyi caizi shu* 第一才子書, First book of genius),[5] *Fengshen bang* 封神榜 (Investiture of the gods; better known as *Fengshen yanyi* 封神演義)—and one of the Qing—*Jinghua yuan* 鏡花緣 (Flowers in the mirror; early nineteenth century)—appear in the Wenhai lou account book. A combined edition of *Narrative of the Three Kingdoms* and *Water Margin* with the title *Yingxiong pu* 英雄譜 (Register of heroes) was also a Sibao publication. The Cuiyun tang inventory, in addition to all these texts, also lists a text entitled *Sida qishu* 四大奇書 (Four masterworks), presumably a set containing *Narrative of the Three Kingdoms*, *Water Margin*, *Journey to the West*, and *Jin Ping Mei* 金瓶梅 (Plum in a golden vase), the "four masterworks" of Ming fiction, as well as independent editions of *Plum in the Golden Vase*, *Narrative of the Three Kingdoms*, and *Journey to the West*.

The Zou and Ma also produced a few of the best-known Ming and Qing novellas (*huaben* 話本). The Cuiyun tang inventory lists two collections of stories by Ling Mengchu 凌蒙初 (1580–1644), known together as *Liangpai* 兩拍 (Two poundings) and comprising *Chuke Paian*

---

3. The dates provided for all the works mentioned in this chapter are approximate dates of composition or first publication. Unless explicitly stated, they do *not* indicate the dates of the Sibao editions, for in most cases these editions do not survive.

4. These are: *Hou Honglou meng* 後紅樓夢 (After *Dream of the Red Chamber*), the first sequel, written by a Xiao Yaozi 逍遙子 (he completed it in 1796); *Xu Honglou meng* 續紅樓夢 (*Dream of the Red Chamber*, continued), by Qin Zichen 秦子忱; *Fu Honglou meng* 復紅樓夢 (Return to *Dream of the Red Chamber*); and *Qian Honglou meng* 前紅樓夢 (Before *Dream of the Red Chamber*); see Zhang Jun, *Qingdai xiaoshuo shi*, p. 396. I have been unable to find information on the last two (probably abbreviated) titles.

5. The Sibao book lists mention a series of "works of genius" (*caizi shu* 才子書). But since the designations of these numbers were not stable, it is not always clear which particular texts these titles name; see Rolston, *Traditional Chinese Fiction and Fiction Commentary*, pp. 46–47.

*jingqi* 初刻拍案驚奇 (Pounding the table in amazement, volume one; first published 1628) and *Erke Paian jingqi* 二刻拍案驚奇 (Pounding the table in amazement, volume two; first published 1632). Most of the stories concern the workings of supernatural retribution (and frequently the dangers of adultery and sexual excess). Also on the inventory is an edition of Li Yu's 李漁 (1611–ca. 1679) *Shier lou* 十二樓 (Twelve towers), stories mocking conventional moral assumptions, the operation of supernatural retribution in particular. It also produced what was to become the most popular of story collections in the Qing, the *Jingu qiguan* 今古奇觀 (Strange scenes from past and present; first published about 1640), a selection of stories from Feng Menglong's 馮夢龍 (1574–1646) famous *Sanyan* 三言 (Three "words") collection and Ling's *Liangpai*.

Sibao produced some thematic collections as well. In the late nineteenth century, the Wenhai lou published an edition of *Qingshi* 情史 (History of feeling), a late Ming collection of love stories in classical Chinese commonly attributed to Feng Menglong, combining accounts from earlier *biji* with stories purportedly drawn from the author's own experience. Several decades earlier the Zaizi tang listed in its property-division document the blocks for *Fengliu wu* 風流悟 (Enlightened by romance), a late Ming or early Qing collection of love stories emphasizing the role of cosmic justice in determining the separation or union of lovers. Both the Wanjuan lou and the Cuiyun tang book lists include the early Qing classical-language collection of fictional biographies of beautiful and talented women, the *Nücaizi shu* 女才子書 (Book of talented women; completed 1658). Finally, Sibao published *Xihu jiahua* 西湖佳話 (Memorable stories of West Lake), a collection of stories connected by their setting at West Lake in Hangzhou (the oldest editions date from the Qing).[6]

No imprints of these texts survive, except for a few volumes of the *Narrative of the Three Kingdoms*, titled *Diyi caizi shu* (Fig. 12.1). This text is a small (13.2 cm h × 21 cm w), unpunctuated and unillustrated edition, printed from worn blocks and including a commentary spuriously attributed to Jin Shengtan 金聖歎 (1608–61), the famous seventeenth-century commentator on vernacular literature and thus frequently a

---

6. Idema and Haft, *Guide to Chinese Literature*, p. 218.

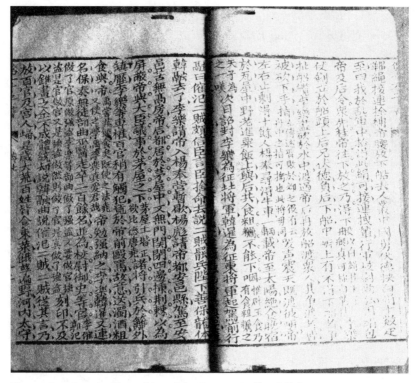

Fig. 12.1 Page from the Sibao edition of the *Diyi caizi shu* 第一才子書 (First work of genius or *Narrative of the Three Kingdoms*). Photograph by the author.

victim of publishers eager to promote their products by attaching a prominent critic's name.[7] These works were usually printed with some sort of commentary, in either *dapi* 大批 or *xiaopi* 小批 format. *Dapi* editions added commentary at the end of each chapter (*hui* 回), thus providing a general discussion of the story; *xiaopi* editions included interlinear commentary, offering a more detailed, line-by-line explanation of the text (possibly for less advanced readers).[8] The Cuiyun tang inventory also indicates different varieties of annotation: *Jinpi* 金批 (with commentary by Jin Shengtan), *pidian* 批点 (with commentary and punctuation), and *jiazhu* 加註 (with added notes). If the shabby surviving Sibao version of *Narrative of the Three Kingdoms* typifies the production

---

7. Rolston, *Traditional Chinese Fiction and Fiction Commentary*, p. 48.
8. Interview 44, 11/23/95 (Mawu).

qualities of novels published by the Zou and Ma, then they specialized in poorly printed, unillustrated editions. The extant volume is a clear step down even from the much-scorned *Mashaben* 麻沙本 (books from Masha) published in Jianyang in the late Ming; *Mashaben*, although dismissed as cheap and vulgar by contemporaries, were at least enlivened with top-register illustrations.[9]

Whatever the production quality, the Zou and Ma published works in all the major fictional genres of the late imperial period. Historical fiction dating from the sixteenth through the eighteenth centuries was one of the most popular genres. Works of historical fiction (or historical "romance" when they strayed far from the historical record) were also the novels most nearly educational in purpose. They were often explicitly advertised as history lessons for readers unequal to the archaic language and complicated narratives of the standard histories. Yuan Hongdao 袁宏道 (1568–1610), one of the pre-eminent literati of his day, after admitting that the standard histories put him to sleep, argued that historical romances, by using contemporary language and entertaining stories to present historical events, could deliver the messages of the Classics and histories to all, literate and illiterate, "garbed [officials] and women."[10] And since these works often highlighted the operation of

---

9. Chia, *Printing for Profit*, p. 242.

10. See Yuan's preface to the *Dong Xi Han tongsu yanyi* 東西漢通俗演義 (Narrative of the Eastern and Western Han), in Huang Lin and Han Tongwen, *Zhongguo lidai xiaoshuo lunzhu xuan*, p. 176; cited in McLaren, "Constructing New Reading Publics," pp. 156–58. The phrase *yanyi* 演義, "elaboration of meaning," in the titles of many of these works suggests this educational goal: these texts were explaining and fleshing out the meaning of the histories for readers unlikely to work through true works of history. Idema, McLaren, and Y. W. Ma all emphasize the heuristic goals of many late Ming historical novels. Ma ("The Chinese Historical Novel," pp. 287–88) observes a correlation between the degree of historical accuracy in a novel and its specific educational function; the authors of fiction mined the standard histories for source material that could be reworked into "either a popularized version of conventional history education, precise and restricted, or a didactic lesson in the name of history, imaginative and unconstrained." McLaren ("Ming Audiences and Vernacular Hermeneutics") has also shown that special editions of novels might be crafted to instruct interested readers in specialized topics; thus, for example, the *Xinke an jian quanxiang piping Sanguo zhizhuan* 新刻按鑑全像批評三國志傳 (Newly cut and fully illustrated *Chronicle of the Three Kingdoms*, with commentary), an edition of *Narrative of the Three Kingdoms* published by the Jianyang

cosmic retribution in history, they taught moral lessons as well; Wilt Idema has suggested that they might be similar in purpose and function to the popular morality books published in the late Ming to educate the people in virtuous behavior.[11]

Many works of historical fiction published in Sibao seem to have evolved out of this late Ming popularizing trend. Two works on the Song dynasty, both attributed to Xiong Damu 熊大木 (fl. mid-sixteenth century), a relative of the Xiong publishers of Jianyang, are listed in the Cuiyun tang inventory: *Nan Bei liang Song zhizhuan* 南北兩宋志傳 (Chronicle of the Northern and Southern Song), on the founding of the dynasty by Zhao Kuangyin 趙匡胤 (r. 960–75), and *Da Song zhongxing tongsu yanyi* 大宋中興通俗演義 (Popular narrative of the return of the great Song), on the reconstitution of the Song state in the south after 1126. The first reworked an earlier late thirteenth- or fourteenth-century popular "simple story" (*pinghua* 平話)[12] version of the same events, the *Wudai pinghua* 五代評話 (Simple story of the Five Dynasties), simplifying some of the narrative even further while intensifying the suspense.[13] The second, according to the author's preface of 1552, was an effort "to rework the official histories' accounts of the Northern–Southern Song transition to render it more accessible to 'ignorant men and women.'" Publishers often further "modified" such works in order to broaden their appeal.[14]

---

publisher Yu Xiangdou 余象斗 in 1592, was edited as a manual of military strategy. For other examples, see Idema, *Chinese Vernacular Fiction*, pp. xxv–xxxii.

11. Idema, *Chinese Vernacular Fiction*, p. xxx; see also Ma, "The Chinese Historical Novel," p. 288.

12. *Pinghua*, dating from the second half of the thirteenth and the fourteenth centuries, "present familiar legends or stories in a very simple style clearly influenced by the contemporary spoken language" (Idema and Haft, *Guide to Chinese Literature*, p. 163).

13. Idema ("Novels About the Founding of the Sung Dynasty," p. 4) explains that Xiong "divided the continuous text of the *p'ing-hua* into chapters, if possible at moments of suspense. If necessary, however, he would provide the suspense himself by adding a scene. Battle scenes were inflated by stock phrases and poetical embellishment was provided, although sparsely. The intricacies of fighting in the original were markedly simplified, and those passages dealing with the civilian aspects of government, urging frugality on the part of the ruler and condemning excessive spending on Buddhist temples, were sometimes copied literally but more often omitted."

14. Chia, *Printing for Profit*, pp. 167 and 368, n. 64. It is possible that these two texts, despite their different titles, were more or less the same. Liu Ts'un-yan (*Chinese Popular Fiction in Two London Libraries*, pp. 17–18) identifies three different works, all bearing

Since no Sibao editions of these late Ming historical fictions have survived, we can only guess that they drew on the historical record but considerably simplified and dramatized that record for broader public consumption.[15]

The Zou and Ma kept up with contemporary writing in this genre, publishing several eighteenth-century historical romances, although many of these were revised and annotated versions of earlier works.[16] Perhaps the most famous of these was the *Dong Zhou lieguo zhi* 東周列國志 (History of the various states under the Eastern Zhou), an eighteenth-century revision by Cai Yuanfeng 蔡元放 (fl. Qianlong era) of Feng Menglong's *Xin lieguo zhi* 新列國志 (New chronicle of the various states). This title appears in both the Cuiyun tang and the Wenhai lou book lists and to this day remains one of the most popular (and reasonably orthodox) accounts of the Spring and Autumn and Warring States periods.[17] Far more fantastic was *Sun Pang yanyi qiguo zhi quanzhuan* 孫龐演義七國志全傳 (preface dated 1795), by Yang Jingchang 楊景淐, another elaboration of an earlier narrative of this period of history, focusing on the marvelous stories surrounding the legendary

---

Xiong Damu's name—*Nan Bei Song zhizhuan, Da Song yanyi zhongxing yinglie zhuan*, and *Nan Song zhizhuan*—and concludes that "there is not much discrepancy in the story and texts. These slightly varying versions are probably derived from one manuscript." He also notes that the titles of the texts, in particular the references to the Southern Song in the first and third titles, bear little relation to the real historical periods covered in the texts, which predate the establishment of the Southern Song. The most that can be concluded from the Sibao titles, then, is that these were either historical or military romances about the Song dynasty.

15. In addition to Xiong's novels, Sibao published several other late Ming historical romances; see Appendix G. Sibao also produced one rather unusual historical novel on early Chinese history, *Kaipi yanyi tongsu zhizhuan* 開闢衍繹通俗志傳 (Popular chronicle of the opening of heaven and the enlargement of the empire), of uncertain authorship. This drew closely on early histories such as the *Records of the Grand Historian* and *Lu shi* 路史 (Grand history from high antiquity to the Eastern Han; by Luo Bi 羅泌 [?–after 1176]) to reconstruct the ancient history of China, from Pan Gu's separation of heaven and earth, through the Three Sovereigns and Five Emperors to the time of King Wu of the Zhou.

16. Zhang Jun, *Qingdai xiaoshuo shi*, p. 228.

17. Feng's own version was based on Yu Shaoyu's 余邵魚 *Lieguo zhizhuan* 列國志傳 (Chronicle of the various states), first published in the Wanli era by the Jianyang publisher Yu Xiangdou (Chia, *Printing for Profit*, p. 365, n. 29).

political philosopher of that era, Guiguzi 鬼谷子 (fourth century BC) or Wang Xu 王栩, and his disciples Sun Bin 孫臏 (reputed author of the *Sunzi bingfa*), Pang Juan 龐涓, Su Qin 蘇秦, and Zhang Yi 張儀.[18] More recent history was treated in Wu Xuan's 吳璿 *Feilong zhuan* 飛龍傳 (Story of the flying dragons; preface dated 1768), a retelling of the story of the origins of the Song dynasty found in a sixteenth-century work by the Jianyang writer Xiong Damu, *Nan Song zhuan* 南宋傳 (Story of [the prince] of the Southern Song). Wu tells the story as two parallel but contrasting moral narratives, the rise of the worthy and virtuous Zhao Kuangyin and the fall of the cowardly and base Chai Rong 柴榮, the last ruler of the previous dynasty.[19]

The number of new titles of historical fiction declined in the high Qing, and most historical romances produced during this period were revisions, abridgments, or elaborations of earlier works. Beginning around the middle of the seventeenth century, however, a related form had evolved to become one of the most popular types of the later imperial period: the military romance. Often centered around a single hero or a band of heroes (and heroines), very loosely based on real historical personages, these military romances presented highly fictionalized, often fantastic, accounts of their subjects' lives, inflating their powers and their achievements for dramatic effect.[20] Like the historical romances,

---

18. This work is listed on the Cuiyun tang inventory, and under its alternative title, *Guiguzi siyou zhi* 鬼谷子四友志 (Chronicle of Guiguzi and his four friends), was mentioned frequently by informants as a popular work. Like its even more popular rival, *Dong Zhou lieguo zhi*, it draws on Yu Shaoyu's *Lieguo zhizhuan* as well as earlier versions of the Guiguzi story (Zhang Jun, *Qingdai xiaoshuo shi*, p. 229; and Hsia, "The Military Romance," p. 347). Guiguzi is said to have boasted that he was such a skilled debater that he could persuade men to embrace opposing political strategies, either federalism (that is, a system of alliances) or conquest. The views of his disciples seem to support this claim: Su Qin championed the policy of alliances, and Zhang Yi, more successfully, that of conquest. Guiguzi was entered into the pantheon of gods and is most commonly known as the patron god of fortune-tellers.

19. Idema, "Novels About the Founding of the Sung Dynasty," p. 6.

20. Idema and Haft, *Guide to Chinese Literature*, pp. 229–30. For more detailed analyses of the characteristics and development of this genre, see Hsia, "The Military Romance"; and Wan, "*Green Peony* as New Popular Fiction," pp. 1–84. Scholars often categorize the works discussed here in different ways. Some of the works I am treating as "military romances" have been identified also as court-case fiction or romances; see Wan, pp. 3–5.

they were clearly designed for a popular audience, but for the most part they show no educational intent. Written in "a most stereotyped language, better characterized as simplified *wen-yen* [classical Chinese] than as real *pai-hua* [vernacular Chinese], a dreary, repetitive and monotonous 'novelese,'" and lacking any but the most obvious historical and literary allusions, these romances, whatever their aesthetic failings, were accessible to a broad, not necessarily well-educated audience interested in action-packed, easy-to-read stories.[21] On the evidence that survives, they constituted by far the most popular of the fiction genres that Sibao published, with at least twenty titles listed in the Cuiyun tang inventory. Military romances were also, along with primers, the Four Books, and the Five Classics, the works most commonly mentioned by informants as part of Sibao's regular stock.

The Zou and Ma seem to have published the major works of this genre. *Shuo Yue quanzhuan* 説岳全傳 (Complete story of Yue Fei), written by Qian Cai 錢彩 and with a preface dated 1744, is among the earliest and most familiar.[22] This is a highly fictionalized account of the life of Yue Fei 岳飛 (1103–41), the great Song general who tried, vainly, to rescue north China from the Jurchen. *Shuo Yue* embodies, as one scholar has put it, a refusal to "accept the limits of historical narrative"[23]—or, as another would have it, the addition to Yue's life of "countless legendary episodes" and a conclusion that depicts "a preposterously implausible campaign undertaken by his (mainly fictitious) sons" to avenge their father's death.[24] In short, in *Shuo Yue*, Qian Cai crossed the boundary of historical fiction into the realm of historical fantasy. The focus here on the military campaigns of a specific hero or lineage of heroes is typical of this genre: although *Shuo Tang yanyi quanzhuan* 説唐演義全傳 (Complete romance of the Tang; preface dated 1736), another popular example of this genre, relates the military exploits of the many heroes who extinguished the Sui and established

---

21. Idema, *Chinese Vernacular Fiction*, p. xi.

22. This work might date to before 1744, perhaps as early as 1684, as the preface provides no reign name. The primary source for this hero-centered military romance genre is the late Ming novel *Fengshen yanyi*.

23. Zhang Jun, *Qingdai xiaoshuo shi*, p. 123.

24. Idema and Haft, *Guide to Chinese Literature*, p. 229.

the Tang, its multiple sequels center around one lineage of heroes, Xue Rengui 薛仁貴 (fl. late seventh century) and his relatives.[25]

During the late Qianlong and Jiaqing eras, there was a boom in the production of these military romances. Their popularity endured well beyond the early nineteenth century, for many appear on Sibao's book lists in the early twentieth century. Extremely popular were a series of texts about the Northern Song general Di Qing 狄青 (1008–57). *Wanhua lou* 萬花樓 (Tower of myriad flowers; preface dated 1808), by a Li Yutang 李雨堂, focuses on the early adventures of Di Qing (although it also celebrates General Yang Zongbao 楊宗包 and the official Judge Bao 包). *Wuhu ping xi* 五虎平西 (Five tigers pacify the West) and *Wuhu ping nan* 五虎平南 (Five tigers pacify the South), both appearing in the early Jiaqing era (with prefaces dated 1801 and 1807, respectively), treated Di Qing's conquest of the Tangut and Vietnam, respectively. Other generals enjoyed their story cycles as well; *Shuo Hu quanzhuan* 說呼全傳 (Complete story of Hu), recounted the exploits of General Huyan Bixian 呼延必顯 and his sons during the reign of Emperor Renzong 仁宗 (r. 1023–63);[26] this work was criticized by the early twentieth-century scholar Zheng Zhenduo for its "clumsy and weak" vernacular, which "had apparently never been edited by a literary man."[27]

Many works of fiction from this period—certainly those favored by the Sibao publishers—are best characterized as episodic novels of adventure. Like the military romances, they usually center around a hero or group of heroes (although not necessarily historical heroes) but include elements from a variety of fictional genres: magic and supernatural events, court cases, and love stories, as well as martial feats.[28] *Zheng-*

---

25. It is possible that *Shuo Tang yanyi quanzhuan* refers not to *Shuo Tang* alone, but to this text as well as its sequels: *Xue Rengui zheng dong* 薛仁貴征東 (Xue Rengui subjugates the East [Korea]), *Xue Dingshan zheng xi* 薛丁山征西 (Xue Dingshan subjugates the West [Central Asia]), and *Fan Tang yanyi zhuan* 反唐演義傳 (Narrative of the overturning of the Tang), about the restoration of the true Tang line after the interregnum of Wu Zetian 武則天 (r. 690–705). These texts, according to informants, were also published as separate titles in Sibao. See Hsia, "The Military Romance," p. 340.

26. Liu Ts'un-yan, *Chinese Popular Fiction in Two London Libraries*, pp. 17, 272; Zhang Jun, *Qingdai xiaoshuo shi*, pp. 240–43.

27. Zheng Zhenduo, *Sidi huashu*; cited in Zhang Jun, *Qingdai xiaoshuo shi*, p. 241.

28. Scholars of Chinese literature would divide these "episodic novels of adventure" into a variety of categories: historical or military romance, tales of heroes and heroines,

*chun yuan* 爭春園 (Vying for spring; preface dated 1819) describes the struggle of the hero, Ma Jun 馬俊, with the aid of his band of eight sworn brothers, to right injustices and avert rebellion during the reign of Han Pingti 漢平帝 (r. AD 1–5), but it is also a tale of "heroic lovers."[29] This "hugely popular" work became the basis for a later Sibao title, *Da Han sanhe mingzhu baojian zhuan* 大漢三合明珠寶劍全傳 (Complete story of the precious sword reunited three times in the Han; first published in 1848).[30] And Sibao apparently published, under the title *Zhonglie xiayi zhuan* 忠烈俠義傳 (Righteous story of loyal and chaste knights-errant), the very popular *Sanxia wuyi* 三俠五義 (The three valiant and five righteous men; 1879). Recounting the often fantastic adventures of the martial-arts experts working as assistants to Judge Bao, the perennial hero of court-case (*gongan* 公案) fiction, this work is closely derived from the mid-nineteenth-century oral tradition; it is based on "more or less stenographic transcriptions" of the performances of the famous storyteller Shi Yukun 石玉昆 (ca. 1805–71). This "classic" "novel of knights-errant" (*wuxia xiaoshuo* 武俠小說) attracted a broad readership—the distinguished classical scholar Yu Yue 俞樾 (1821–1906, *js* 1850) was such an admirer of the work that he wrote an expanded version of the novel.[31]

Many of these adventure stories, like *Sanxia wuyi*, had tenuous links to court-case fiction—that is, works that center on the wisdom and

---

love stories, court cases, and tales of the supernatural. Much has been written about the development of these different fiction genres; see Zhang Jun, *Qingdai xiaoshuo shi*; Wan, "*Green Peony* as New Popular Fiction"; and Sun Kaidi, *Zhongguo tongsu xiaoshuo shumu*. Since my goal is to describe the types of texts Sibao produced and to explain their appeal, I have at times ignored the finer distinctions among genres. In assessing the readership for these texts, language and frequency and sophistication of allusion are better indicators.

29. Sun Kaidi, *Zhongguo tongsu xiaoshuo shumu*, p. 152; cited in Wan, "*Green Peony* as New Popular Fiction," p. 3.

30. Wan, "*Green Peony* as New Popular Fiction," pp. 69–70. An interesting variation on these adventure stories occurs in late nineteenth-century Sibao editions of works like *Wannian qing* 萬年青 (Forever green), a vernacular work of uncertain date that works a familiar theme: the Qianlong emperor leaves his palace in disguise and travels to Jiangnan to spy on the activities of his officials—and eventually to right the wrongs that they had perpetrated on the population; see Idema and Haft, *Guide to Chinese Literature*, p. 230.

31. Ibid., p. 242.

integrity of a district magistrate solving a series of difficult legal cases. Sibao may have published at least one such work, *Longtu gongan* 龍圖 公案 (Cases of Judge Bao), a sixteenth-century work of 100 chapters, each of which recounts Judge Bao's successful resolution of a case. (This title is listed in both the Wenhai lou account book and the Cuiyun tang inventory.) But it is quite likely that, by the time the Sibao publishers were printing it, the title referred to a significantly reduced, heavily revised, and more popular version, in which Bao is as much a skilled Daoist magician as a wise judge[32]—the Confucian model official transformed into a more eclectic and more powerful hero. In these works, Judge Bao has become a supporting character; the "court cases" of *Sanxia wuyi*, for example, are usually solved through the martial efforts of his assistants, some of them former bandits.[33] Two other Sibao productions, *Shi gongan* 施公案 (Court cases of Shi; first published by 1798) and *Peng gongan* 彭公案 (Court cases of Peng; first known edition 1891), supposedly relating cases solved by the virtuous and just magistrates Shi Shilun 施世綸 (d. 1722) and Peng Peng 彭鵬 (1637–1704), fit well into this adventure-story or martial arts category, despite titles identifying them as court-case fiction. Crudely written—one scholar suggests that the author of *Shi gongan* was "a poorly-educated person from the lower fringe of the official class," and another describes the language of *Peng gongan* as "atrocious, barely grammatical Chinese"[34]—these works were nonetheless enormously popular, rivaling *Sanxia wuyi* in audience appeal and, like that work, spawning a series of sequels.

Thus the Zou and Ma publishers capitalized on the growing popularity, over the course of the late eighteenth and early nineteenth centuries, of works of martial adventure, particularly those set, however loosely, against a historical background. Another profitable genre was the "talent and beauty" (*caizi jiaren* 才子佳人) love stories, appearing

---

32. Ibid., p. 218. *Longtu gongan* may also have been an alternative title for *Sanxia wuyi* (Y. W. Ma, "Kung-an Fiction," p. 245). See Hanan, "Judge Bao's Hundred Cases Reconstructed," for a discussion of some of the different works traveling under this title.

33. Y. W. Ma, "Kung-an Fiction," p. 240; see ibid., pp. 240–55, for the development in the Qing of two types of court-case fiction, one concerning genuine court cases and the other the martial activities of knights-errant.

34. Anneberg, "The Chinese Novel of the Nineteenth Century and Late Ch'ing Period," p. 22; and Lu Xun, *A Brief History of Chinese Fiction*, p. 368.

first in the late Ming and continuing to be written in some numbers well into the nineteenth century. These usually rather short works concerned talented scholars and beautiful (and often even more talented) women who, after lengthy and sometimes ludicrous impediments, marry and live happily ever after. They vary widely in quality: "At their best these novels . . . are reminiscent of eighteenth-century French comedies. At their worst, however, they are pedantic and soporific Chinese equivalents of the dime novel."[35] With convoluted plot lines, most were written in a "beautiful and refined" style appropriate to their subject matter; they seem to have been intended for a fairly literate readership.[36]

Sibao produced a sprinkling of such works, including the famous *Haoqiu zhuan* 好逑傳 (The fortunate union), the Shunzhi (1644–61)–era text that is often taken to be the template for the genre, and the roughly contemporaneous *Liangjiaohun xiaozhuan* 兩交婚小傳 (Brief story of two marriages). The Cuiyun tang lists some of the better-known *caizi jiaren* novels, particularly those produced in the mid- to late eighteenth century, when the genre peaked in quality and popularity: *Ying Yun meng* 英雲夢 (Dream of Ying Yun) and *Wufeng yin* 五鳳吟 (Cries of five phoenixes), both works of the Yongzheng era that followed the tradition of *Haoqiu zhuan*; and three other works that pushed the genre in slightly new directions. *Erdu mei quanzhuan* 二度梅全傳 (The plum tree flowers twice, the complete story; completed in the early Qing?), a love story set in the Tang, is a more serious and moralistic effort, in which official corruption is condemned and loyalty to the ruler, filial piety, chastity, and fidelity are rewarded. This quite popular work was made into a ballad as well. Both *Jinxiang ting* 錦香亭 (Pavilion of brocade and perfume; completed by the mid-eighteenth century?) and *Tiehua xianshi* 鐵花仙史 (History of the iron-flower immortals; Qing) introduced martial, and in the latter, supernatural, elements into their convoluted love stories.[37] By the late eighteenth and early nineteenth centuries, the genre was beginning to decline. But Sibao's book lists include, in addition to the earlier works mentioned here, several works from this

---

35. Idema and Haft, *Guide to Chinese Literature*, p. 227.

36. Zhang Jun, *Qingdai xiaoshuo shi*, p. 55.

37. Lu Xun (*A Brief History of Chinese Fiction*, p. 255) is critical of *Tiehua xianshi* for its "rough" style and "confused" plot.

period: the elegant *Zhuchun yuan* 駐春園 (Dwelling-in-spring garden; first published 1783) and *Xihu xiaoshi* 西湖小史 (Brief history of West Lake; preface dated 1817), which, like *Erdu mei*, expands the concerns of the tradition somewhat by introducing elements of political criticism.[38]

Stories of the strange also had some appeal, to judge from their presence on Sibao book lists. One of the earliest collections of supernatural tales, *Soushen ji* 搜神記 (Record of investigations of the supernatural), by the early fourth-century Gan Bao 干寶, was included in the Cuiyun tang inventory. But Sibao published roughly contemporary additions to the genre as well: for example, *Siyou ji* 四游記 (Record of four journeys), a collection of four short works describing quests by gods and mythological figures in search of cosmological orientation. Written in simple language, this "chapbook" (that is, a brief work in simple language, not intended primarily for a literati audience) of somewhat mysterious origins seems to have been published first by the prolific Jianyang publisher Yu Xiangdou, who is also credited with revising what was originally a record of spirit-medium séances into a popular work of spiritual adventure.[39] The more sophisticated *Pingyao zhuan* 平妖傳 (Subduing of the monsters), Feng Menglong's popular fiction about a family of foxes and their formative influence on the Wang Ze 王澤 uprising of 1047–48, was also on the Cuiyun tang's list. So, too, was the somewhat more esoteric early Qing work, *Caomu chunqiu yanyi* 草木春秋演義 (Annals of herbs and trees), a work describing a Han-period military encounter between Chinese and "barbarians," made "strange" by the fact that all the characters are named after herbal medicines.[40]

---

38. I have relied in the description of these works on Zhang Jun, *Qingdai xiaoshuo shi*, pp. 55–66, 157–66, 296–301.

39. For a discussion of this text, see Seaman, *Journey to the North*, pp. 12–16, 38–39. Drawing on the work of Liu Ts'un-yan and Anthony Yu, Seaman suggests that at least one of the "journeys," the *Beiyou ji* 北游記 (Journey to the north), was originally a planchette writing or record of spirit-medium séances held at the Jiajing court; Yu Xiangdou then popularized the text, removing references to the court and adding verse and passages that would make it more appealing to a general readership. See also Idema and Haft, *Guide to Chinese Literature*, p. 211; and, on chapbooks, Idema, *Chinese Vernacular Fiction*, pp. liii–liv.

40. Zhang Jun, *Qingdai xiaoshuo shi*, p. 131; Idema and Haft (*Guide to Chinese Literature*, p. 228) identify this work as a "reductionist" novel—that is, one in which "the author

Sibao produced perhaps the best known collection of "strange" stories, Pu Songling's 蒲松齡 (1640–1715) *Liaozhai zhiyi* 聊齋誌異 (Notes on the strange from the Studio of Idleness)—it was, on the evidence we have to date, the most expensive of their publications, listed at 1.1 *liang* wholesale on the Wenhai lou account book. Four different listings of this and related titles appear on the Cuiyun tang inventory: in addition to *Liaozhai zhiyi*, a *Jiazhu Liaozhai zhiyi* 加註聊齋誌異 (*Notes on the Strange from the Studio of Idleness*, with notes added), a *Pidian Liaozhai zhiyi* 批点聊齋誌異 (*Notes on the Strange from the Studio of Idleness*, with commentary and punctuation), and a *Xu Liaozhai zhiyi* 續聊齋誌異 (*Notes on the Strange from the Studio of Idleness*, continued). Yuan Mei's 袁枚 (1716–97) *Zi buyu* 子不語 (What the Master did not discuss)[41] appears on the early nineteenth-century property-division document of the Zaizi tang and the later Cuiyun tang inventory. This collection of anecdotes about ghosts and spirits and strange happenings, was, according to the author's preface, written in simple classical Chinese in an effort to make the text accessible to a wide audience.[42] *Yetan suilu* 夜譚隨錄 (Random notes after night-time chat; preface dated 1779), by the Manchu writer He Bang'e 何邦額 (b. 1736?), was also a collection of stories of the strange in classical Chinese. Although dismissed by Lu Xun as unoriginal and "often coarse" in language,[43] this work, with *Liaozhai zhiyi* and *Zi buyu*, was one of the more popular collections of tales of the supernatural.[44]

Three works of fiction on Sibao's book lists may have attracted a regional readership. *Jingfu xinshu* 警富新書 (New book of warnings against wealth; first known publication date 1809) claims to recount a real case of arson and murder that grew out of a *fengshui* dispute between two families of Panyu 番禺, Guangdong, in the Yongzheng era. This "rather crude

---

limits himself to describing a single aspect of reality, or to using a single register of the language."

41. The "Master" of the title is Confucius, and the phrase refers to the line in the *Analects*, "The Master never spoke of the strange, feats of strength, disorder, and spirits" (Legge, *The Chinese Classics*, 1: 201).

42. Waley, *Yuan Mei*, pp. 20–124. See the translation of this text in Louie and Edwards, *Censored by Confucius*.

43. Lu Xun, *A Brief History of Chinese Fiction*, p. 276.

44. Zhang Jun, *Qingdai xiaoshuo shi*, pp. 331–33.

fictional work" follows the conventions of the court-case genre: corrupt officials mishandle the case until a single virtuous official steps forward to render the correct judgment and distribute appropriate punishments. But it is remarkable for the unusual prominence it gives the evil officials who delay and complicate the solution of the case: "these 'bad' officials form an almost indestructible force directly against the duties they are supposed to perform, not having so much to do with their inefficiency as with their own vicious intentions."[45] Presumably it was of considerable interest to many Sibao customers at least in part because it elaborates on a famous case set in the heart of Guangdong province, one of Sibao's best markets. *Yinshi* 蟫史 (History of the bookworm), an adventure story by Tu Shen 屠紳 (1744–1801) centering on the Qing suppression of a Miao uprising in 1795, has as its hero a Fujianese who, shipwrecked in Guangdong, fights with Chinese troops (with some supernatural assistance) against rebels in Guangzhou and Annam and against Miao tribes in Hunan and Guizhou. Tu claims in his preface that he collected material for his story while serving as an official in Guangzhou. Written in an "archaic and bizarre" style and "full of purple passages"—and many pornographic episodes as well[46]—*Yinshi*'s greatest appeal for the Sibao publishers may have been its setting in just those areas where the Zou and Ma merchants sold their books.

More interesting is *Lingnan yishi* 嶺南逸史 (Unofficial history of Lingnan; originally published in 1809, but probably completed by 1793), by a Guangdong literatus, Huang Naian 黃耐庵 from Jiaying department (and thus possibly a Hakka). Huang narrates the adventures of a late Ming scholar Huang Fengyu 黃逢玉, also from Jiaying department, specifically his role in suppressing a rebellion of the Yao and his encounters with and eventual marriages to women (three of them queens) of the Zhuang and Yao minorities. In notes to the reader, the author emphasizes the factual basis of much of his story, listing the gazetteers he used for research. He seems to have written for a regional audience, for *Lingnan yishi* includes Lingnan dialect words and songs.[47]

---

45. Y. W. Ma, "Kung-an Fiction," pp. 252–54; *Zhongguo tongsu xiaoshuo zongmu tiyao*, pp. 614–15. This was also known as *Yipeng xue jingfu xinshu* 一捧雪警富新書.

46. Lu Xun, *A Brief History of Chinese Fiction*, pp. 321–26.

47. Zhang Jun, *Qingdai xiaoshuo shi*, pp. 303–5.

What is perhaps most interesting about this work (and to some extent about *Yinshi* as well) is the fascination with ethnic difference. Both were written at a time of ethnic tensions; the Miao rose against Qing rule several times in the eighteenth century, and relations with the Zhuang and Yao were not easy. (This is also the time when Hakka difference was first articulated, in an 1808 lecture by Xu Xuzeng 徐旭曾 [*js* 1799], a Hakka literatus.)[48] Both works seem to confirm Han authority and dominance. Although Huang Naian expresses admiration and sympathy for his Yao rebels, and although his hero's wives are depicted as highly competent women capable of repeatedly rescuing the hero from danger,[49] in the end it is the Han scholar-warrior Huang Fengyu who triumphs, defeating the Yao and marrying all the heroines. Order is restored not only through the military suppression of the rebels but also through the absorption of the different ethnicities into a Han patriarchal family. It is tempting to assume that such stories would have been particularly appealing to Han settlers in the ethnically diverse Lingnan region. Perhaps they would be even more attractive to Hakka settlers, increasingly aware of their own difference, yet eager to assert their essential "Han-ness" and thus happy to contemplate the even greater difference of the Miao, Zhuang, and Yao.

As we have seen, Sibao published a notable variety of fiction. The Zou publishers in particular seem to have offered a considerable range of genres and levels of difficulty: historical chronicles and romances, happy-ending love stories (and a few tragedies) in the classical language, martial-hero adventures, moral tales of retribution, domestic novels of manners, some works of detection and the righting of legal injustices, tales of the strange, and a little pornography. They covered a range of linguistic levels: "literati novels" like the four Ming masterworks and *Dream of the Red Chamber*, "employing both abstruse *wen-yen* [classical Chinese] and racy local dialect" and presuming highly literate readers, if only because these works are "rich in puns and parodies";[50] elegant classical fiction, like that of Pu Songling; "chapbooks" such as *Longtu gongan*, *Shuo Yue quanzhuan*, and the *Wuhu* series, written in "a very

---

48. Sow-Theng Leung, *Migration and Ethnicity in Chinese History*, p. 76.
49. Zhang Jun, *Qingdai xiaoshuo shi*, p. 304.
50. Idema, *Chinese Vernacular Fiction*, p. liv.

simple *wen-yen* with the occasional use of some *pai-hua* [vernacular] particles," and thus accessible to those with only a smattering of classical education; and the worst of "trash" fiction, like *Peng gongan*, written in "atrocious" Chinese. These categories are by no means exclusive, either in degree of linguistic complexity or in audience. A considerable linguistic distance separates the complex classical Chinese of *Liaozhai zhiyi* from the simpler, more accessible classical language of Yuan Mei's *Zi buyu*, yet both are categorized as works on the strange in classical Chinese.[51] And the highly educated might enjoy the simply or even badly written martial romances as much as did the poorly educated (and there is abundant evidence that many of them did). In sum, Sibao's fiction offered something for almost every reader.

By the late Qing, however, this was no longer true. Up until that time the Sibao publishers kept their fiction offerings up to date, producing newly written works in popular categories, such as the adventure stories *Lü mudan* 綠牡丹 (Green peony), *Sanxia wuyi*, *Shi gongan*, and *Peng gongan*. But they did not, apparently, publish any of the new genres that flourished at the end of the dynasty: works about the demimonde (*Haishanghua liezhuan* 海上花列傳 [Exemplary biographies of the flowers of Shanghai; 1894], for example) or works of social and political criticism like Wu Woyao's 吳沃堯 (1866–1910) *Ershinian mudu zhi guai xianzhuang* 二十年目睹之怪現狀 (Strange phenomena of the past twenty years, seen with my own eyes; 1902) or Li Baojia's 李寶嘉 (1867–1906) *Guanchang xianxing ji* 官場現形記 (Record of the bureaucratic world today; 1903).[52] By this time Sibao's publishing industry was no longer keeping up with the latest trends; those publishing houses still in operation were apt more to replicate old favorites than to produce new, untested works. Shanghai had begun to monopolize publishing and to exploit new printing technologies and was now the primary producer of new works, many of which were about life in Shanghai—and thus far removed from the world of most Sibao markets.

Through the early twentieth century, the martial-hero adventure and *caizi jiaren* stories dominated Sibao fiction output. Adventure stories

---

51. Nienhauser, *The Indiana Companion to Traditional Chinese Literature*, p. 957.

52. On these works and others representative of the trends of late Qing fiction, see Ouyang Jian, *Wan Qing xiaoshuo shi, passim.*

generated the greatest number of different titles. These works, usually shorter than the literati novels, were cheaper to produce and thus could be sold at quite low prices. *Xue Rengui zheng dong*, a popular military romance set in the Tang, sold for as little as 3.5 *fen* wholesale. The "five tiger" novels were a little more expensive: 0.4 to 0.5 *qian* (for the six-*juan Wuhu ping nan*) to 1.5 *qian* (for the fourteen-*juan Wuhu ping xi*). The Wenhai lou editions of *Longtu gongan*, *Hongwu zhuan* 洪武傳 (Story of the Hongwu emperor), and *Nücaizi shu* were all priced at 7 *fen* wholesale. In the romance category, *Erdu mei* sold wholesale for 5 *fen*, and *Shuangfeng qiyuan* 雙鳳奇緣 (Destiny of the paired phoenixes; first published 1809, recounting the tragic love story of Han Yuandi 元帝, r. 48–31 BC, and his favorite consort, Wang Zhaojun 王昭君) wholesale for 6 to 9 *fen*. Eight of the twenty-three fiction titles listed were under one *qian* in wholesale price.

The longer and more finely produced works of fiction were, in contrast, among the most expensive Sibao products. Most cost between 1 and 2 *qian* wholesale (ten titles), but copies of *Sanguo yanyi* and *Qingshi* each cost 2.4 *qian*, and *Yingxiong pu* (two titles in one) cost 3.8 *qian* wholesale. Although the Wenhai lou sold a 2-*qian* version of *Liaozhai zhiyi*, this publishing house also offered what must have been a deluxe edition for 1.1 *liang* wholesale, its most expensive text and exorbitant by Sibao standards. This admittedly scanty price information mirrors the evidence of the Sibao inventories: the largest output in the fiction category consisted of popular "chapbook" adventure stories of martial heroes and a smaller number of *caizi jiaren* stories written in a style that suggests an audience ranging from the minimally to the fully literate. These texts, probably crudely produced and often without illustrations, were generally priced low enough for those of limited means. Sibao's customers might include highly literate and wealthy readers, but the publishers targeted men and women who had received enough education to make their way through a chapbook in simple classical Chinese and had enough disposable income to expend on "luxuries" such as these cheap editions.

The dominant themes of Sibao's fictional works—the elevation of a hero or band of heroes and heroines possessed of extraordinary martial skills, the celebration of brotherhood, loyalty, and justice outside (and at times in opposition to) a corrupt political and social order, the racy excitement of unconventional but successful courtships—may well have had a particular appeal, both as accurate visions of reality and as fantasies of rescue, revenge, and escape, to readers largely excluded from access to political, social, and economic power. Sibao in fact produced a few works that could be read as political critiques. *Hou Shuihu zhuan* 後水滸傳 (*Water Margin*, continued; probably a work of the late seventeenth century), one of many sequels to *Water Margin* (a novel that could itself be considered subversive), is the story of a group of bandit-heroes, some from the original novel, who devote themselves to righting social wrongs by robbing from the rich and aiding the poor. Lacking even the ambivalent loyalty of the Liangshan bandits of *Water Margin*, these heroes directly blame the emperor, not evil ministers, for misgovernment, and rebel against him. This work, "powerfully critical of the imperial system," is not particularly well-written, and does not appear to have been directed to a literati audience—it does not, for example, cite classical literature and lacks commentary.[53]

Less radical in its critique was *Da hongpao* 大紅袍 ([Hai Rui's] Scarlet robe), a highly fictionalized account of the "virtuous official" Hai Rui 海瑞 (1513–87) and his struggles with the "evil minister" Yan Song 嚴嵩 (1480–1565) and one of the few original productions of the historical-romance genre in the eighteenth century.[54] *Hou Shuihu zhuan* seems to suggest that there was no hope for good government under the imperial system, but *Da hongpao* offers some hope in the form of a single courageous and pure official willing to do battle against a corrupt grand secretary.

The imperial government was certainly sensitive to the potentially subversive or morally transgressive elements of many works of fiction, including some of those published in Sibao. *Water Margin*, *Plum in a Golden Vase*, and *Rou putuan* 肉蒲團 (Prayer mat of flesh; 1657) were repeatedly banned, the first for its criticism of officials and glorification of its bandit-heroes, the last two for their pornographic passages. During the Qianlong literary inquisition, *Shuo Yue quanzhuan* was prohibited, presumably because of its celebration of a patriotic Han general who

53. Widmer, *The Margins of Utopia*, pp. 197, 290, n. 4.
54. Zhang Jun, *Qingdai xiaoshuo shi*, pp. 232–33.

died fighting "barbarian" invaders.[55] In 1868, during the efforts of the Tongzhi bureaucracy to restore Confucian education and values in the wake of the Taiping rebellion, Ding Richang 丁日昌 (1823–82), governor of Jiangsu, prohibited an impressive array of fictional works, on the grounds that they were "licentious" (*yin* 淫). Many of these works were included in Sibao's stock: the historical romance *Shuangfeng qiyuan*; several adventure stories (*Yinshi*, *Longtu gongan*, *Shuo Yue quanzhuan*, *Wanhua lou*, *Lü mudan*); many works in the *caizi jiaren* category (*Wufeng yin*, *Jinxiang ting*, and *Wumei yuan* 五美緣 [Destinies of five beauties]); and two joke books (*Xiaolin guangji* 笑林廣記 [Wide-ranging notes from the forest of laughs] and *Jie renyi* 解人頤 [Telling jokes]).[56]

Thus from a certain official perspective much of Sibao's stock of popular fiction was seen as threatening to proper moral and ethical values, specifically to the standards regulating relationships between ruler and ruled and among family members (most particularly between men and women). Although it is difficult to read many of the chapbook adventure novels and *caizi jiaren* stories as works of social criticism, they do often overturn orthodox models of morality and ritual: officials are corrupt; parents often push their children into bad marriages; husbands often betray their wives, and vice versa. Often, too, they present appealing, sometimes comic, alternatives to the rather stuffy models of Confucian orthodoxy strictly defined: the uncouth and violent bandit hero, ready to fight at any moment, but loyal, brave, strong, and sincere; or the far-from-submissive young lady, clever at intrigue, but beautiful, determined, talented, and passionate. There is a love of violence and extreme action, far removed from the formal Confucian emphasis on peaceful means and the doctrine of the middle way. The frequent appearance of gods and spirits, not to mention the supernatural powers of many of the heroes, reflects the influence of popular religious beliefs. But the core values—loyalty, sincerity, paternalistic compassion for the

---

55. Ma Tai-loi, "Novels Prohibited in the Literary Inquisition of Emperor Ch'ien-lung," p. 211.

56. *Xiaolin guangji* was a very popular work based on Feng Menglong's *Xiaofu* 笑府 (Storehouse of laughs) and first published in 1781. *Jie renyi* has a preface dated 1761. On the prohibition of the texts listed here, see Wang Bin, *Qingdai jinshu congshu*, pp. 204–5, 231, 236, 281–82, 286–87, 345–46, 380, 392, 396, 456–58, 478, 518.

poor—are nonetheless Confucian. When these works are critical of the established order (as in *Water Margin* or *Plum in the Golden Vase*), their criticism is morally conservative, a critique of elite failure to embody these core values as they were supposed to rather than an attack on the values themselves. Although they may imply a vision different from that of the imperial ideology and critical of political and social reality, it was one nonetheless compatible with Confucian values and ideals.

In spite of (or perhaps because of) this vision, these works remained perennially popular—and not just among the politically powerless and poorer sectors of the population. Throughout the Qing, fiction of this sort was reproduced by many commercial publishers, not just the Zou and Ma, and, however much these works may have been disdained as "insignificant talk," they seem to have been read avidly at all social levels. There is little evidence that the imperial government succeeded in preventing or limiting either the publication or the consumption of these texts in Sibao or anywhere else. All remained on Sibao book lists during the late nineteenth and early twentieth centuries.[57]

---

57. There is no evidence that Sibao publishing ever came under the scrutiny of government officials charged with censoring inappropriate texts. The Qing government practiced two types of censorship: pre-publication and post-publication. The Qing, like the Song, Yuan, and Ming, proscribed the private (or commercial) printing of government publications such as almanacs, astronomical charts, prognostication texts, imperial pronouncements, legal works, examination literature, "and the like." In 1778 the Qianlong emperor also proclaimed that all private writings were to be reviewed and approved by educational officials before they could be published (see Chan, *Control of Publishing in China*, pp. 22–24). But these regulations do not seem to have been systematically enforced—there is, at any rate, no evidence that they were ever enforced in Sibao.

The notorious literary inquisitions of the Kangxi, Yongzheng, and Qianlong eras, epitomizing post-publication censorship, also appear to have had no impact on Sibao. Given the Zou and Ma publishers' avoidance of politically sensitive elite scholarship, this is not surprising. In any event, it is not clear how effectively the Qing court was able to enforce prohibitions against certain publications even at the height of the Qianlong inquisition; see Brook, "Censorship in Eighteenth-Century China," pp. 195–96; and Ma Tai-loi, "Novels Prohibited in the Literary Inquisitions of Emperor Ch'ienlung," p. 212. And Ding Richang's later prohibitions applied only to Jiangsu.

## Drama and Songbooks

Somewhat surprising, given Sibao's publication of the major literati novels of the late imperial period, is the very poor representation on the Zou and Ma book lists of major works of drama, another genre that enjoyed a surge in popularity in the late Ming and Qing. All informants assured me that Sibao published the famous dramas *Xixiang ji* 西廂記 (Record of the western chamber; written in the late thirteenth century), *Pipa ji* 琵琶記 (Record of the lute; written in the late fourteenth century), and *Mudan ting* 牡丹亭 (Peony pavilion; late sixteenth or early seventeenth century). But the only dramas that were assuredly on the Sibao book list were *Peony Pavilion* and *Record of the Western Chamber*. *Peony Pavilion* exists only as a title on a Sibao book list; *Record of the Western Chamber*, "probably the most famous and most widely read traditional Chinese play,"[58] was edited by Zou Shengmai in a version entitled *Yunlin bieshu huixiang tuozhu diliu caizi shu* 雲林別墅繪像妥註第六才子書 (The sixth work of genius, with illustrations and correct annotations, from the Yunlin Retreat; preface dated to 1785). It does not survive as a Sibao imprint, but the 1817 edition by the Qiyuan tang 啓元堂 in the Shanghai Municipal Library provides some evidence of the nature of this work. It opens with a poorly cut preface, instructions on how to read the play, and a series of simple illustrations of the story. The table of contents lists Zou Shengmai as the author of the "prepared notes" (*tuozhu* 妥註) on the text; these notes are quite elementary, indicating the pronunciation of characters and explaining the allusions of the text. This is not a work for the elite but a version of a famous drama for beginners—that is, for readers who, although they might know the story, needed guidance to work their way through the text.

The Zou and Ma publishers did not, it seems, invest heavily in the production of drama, preferring to expand their publication of assuredly popular martial romances and *caizi jiaren* stories. Flourishing local drama and oral performance traditions might also have undermined the

---

58. Idema and Haft, *Guide to Chinese Literature*, p. 175. *Record of the Western Chamber* is listed on Sibao book lists either as *Jin pi Xixiang ji tuozhu* 金批西廂記妥註 (*Record of the Western Chamber*, with commentary by Jin Shengtan and appended notes) or as *Diliu caizi shu*.

popularity of the universally famous mainstream dramas. By the mid-Qing, a drama form imported from Hunan had been domesticated in Minxi. This "drama from beyond the river" (*waijiang xi* 外江戲), in the standard, official dialect (*guanhua* 官話), became popular first in the counties of Ninghua, Changting, and Liancheng—that is, in the Sibao area. From Minxi it spread to Guangdong, probably along the same routes taken by Sibao booksellers. In addition, there was in Minxi a strong oral tradition of ballads and mountain songs (*shan'ge* 山歌) in local dialects.[59]

The relationship between Sibao publishing and these local traditions is uncertain. But the Zou and Ma did publish a variety of songbooks, presumably to be used as promptbooks for performers and textbooks for those interested in learning to perform. And of course these works, like *Record of the Western Chamber*, could be read as entertainment. Most significant, however, were the link they created between book culture and oral culture and, through that link, the impact that they might have on illiterates. Books of lyrics to popular narrative songs, like the chapbooks discussed above, were strong sellers among readers ranging widely in literacy and income, but these works, through performance, reached those who could not read as well. By present-day accounts, these texts may have been the most popular of Sibao imprints in the fiction category—older informants could still recall with pleasure the titles of many of these texts, and I was repeatedly assured that "hundreds" were churned out even as recently as the early twentieth century. Unfortunately, it is difficult to substantiate these claims for, although the songbooks may have been among the most popular of Sibao productions, they are also among the most ephemeral. The few extant songbooks are for the most part pamphlets, each containing a single narrative song.

The Zou and Ma apparently published a range of texts in this category, from books of lyrics that recounted universally known legends and stories to songs of regional or local popularity, including works specifically intended for the Sibao community. In the first group was *Xinke Liang Shanbo Zhu Yingtai* 新刻梁山伯祝英台 (Liang Shanbo and

---

59. Chen Lei et al., *Fujian difang xiju*, pp. 80–83.

Fig. 12.2 Block for *Xinke Liang Shanbo Zhu Yingtai* 新刻梁山伯祝英台 (*Liang Shanbo and Zhu Ying-tai,* newly published). Photograph by the author.

Zhu Yingtai, newly cut), a ballad version of the famous story of tragic love and transformation. A few woodblocks of this work survive in Wuge; 14 cm high by 20 cm wide, they are divided into three registers, a narrow top panel (3.5 cm) of roughly cut illustrations, and two panels (5 cm each) of text (Fig. 12.2). The Wenhai lou also produced a songbook version of the even more famous lament of the widowed Meng Jiangnü (*Meng Jiangnü ku changcheng* 孟姜女哭長城 [Meng Jiangnü weeps at the Great Wall]), both a celebration of wifely devotion and a protest against government oppression.

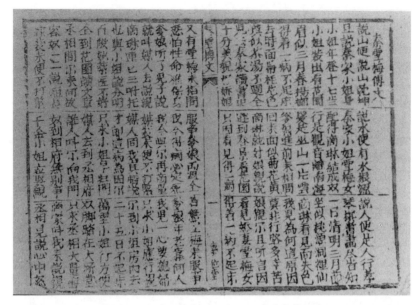

Fig. 12.3 Page from a Sibao songbook, *Qin Xuemei zhuanwen* 秦雪梅傳文 (Story of Qin Xuemei), published by the Suwei tang 素位堂. Photograph by the author.

Presumably both of these works, drawing on long-known tales, would find a market almost anywhere within China Proper. But the Sibao publishers also produced works whose appeal was only regional or even local. Many of these seem to have been slightly racy songs of a sort likely to have been condemned as "licentious" by sanctimonious officials. Certainly *Shisha ting* 十杉亭 (Pavilion of the ten firs), *Shili ting* 十里亭 (Pavilion of ten *li*), and *Qin Xuemei zhuanwen* 秦雪梅傳文 (Story of Qin Xuemei), titles mentioned by almost all informants (sometimes as the titles of mountain songs), appear from contemporary reports to have been works of this sort.[60] To judge from the extant fragments of these songbooks, they are short works in rhyming seven-character strophes, of no more than nine to fifteen folio pages, crudely and sloppily printed in pamphlet form (14.8 cm h × 21 cm w; see Fig. 12.3).

---

60. Interviews 44, 11/23/95 (Mawu); 89, 4/24/06 (Wuge); 91, 4/25/96 (Wuge). On *shan'ge*, see Chen Lei et al., *Fujian difang xiju*, pp. 80–82, and on the popularity of mountain songs among Hakka populations in Guangdong, see Ye Chunsheng, *Lingnan suwenxue jianshi*, pp. 84–111. These studies of *shan'ge* explain them as brief responsive or dialogue songs; the Sibao texts are longer narrative songs.

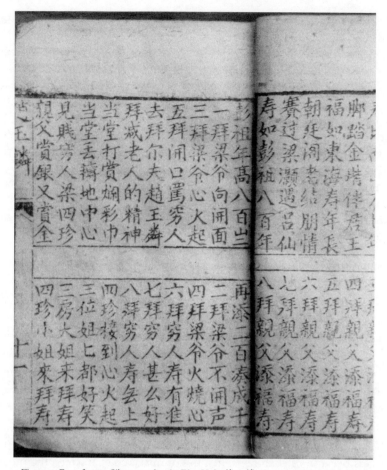

Fig. 12.4 Page from a Sibao songbook, *Zhao Yulin* 趙玉麟. Photograph by the author.

*Zhao Yulin* 趙玉麟 (Zhao Yulin; Fig. 12.4), a story of a struggling scholar abused by his in-laws until he triumphs in the examinations, survives almost entire in a more carefully produced edition, small (12.1 cm h ×21.6 cm w), unpunctuated, and unillustrated but clearly cut in simplified characters. Set in Wuzhou prefecture, Guangxi, this story, according to informants, was particularly popular along Sibao market routes in Guangdong and Guangxi as well as in Minxi itself. It is written in extremely simple and repetitive language, as befits a sung narrative. The introduction of Zhao's in-laws, the Liang family, reads (1a):

| | |
|---|---|
| Father Liang had no sons, his family was greatly rich; | 梁爺無男家豪福 |
| Early he had four daughters, each worth one thousand pieces of silver. | 早生四女值千金 |
| The eldest was named Liang Guishen, | 長女安名梁桂深 |
| the next Liang Guiying, | 次女安名梁桂英 |
| the third Liang Sangui, | 三女安名梁三桂 |
| the fourth Liang Sizhen. | 四女安名四珍 |
| Each of these thousand pieces of silver had mates; | 四個千金來匹配 |
| they were married to four gentleman of *xiucai* status. | 配得四位秀才朗 |
| The eldest was married to the Huang family's son, | 長女配給黃家子 |
| the next was married to a man named Liu, | 次女配給姓劉人 |
| the third was married to the Lin family's son, | 三女配給林家子 |
| Sizhen was married to Zhao Yulin. | 四珍配給趙玉麟 |

The formulas for introducing the daughters and their husbands, the repetition of numbers, and, of course, the choice of simple characters made this an easy text to learn.

This work, or at least the song it records, has remained popular. At least one handwritten and stenciled version of this story (entitled *Zhao Yulin changci* 唱詞) still circulates in Wuge (and reportedly also in Changting). A brief comparison of the contemporary text and the woodblock edition suggests how fluid this form of largely oral literature could be. First, the owner-performer of the contemporary text has written in or altered certain characters, suggesting that this, as a text for oral performance, might have been subject to frequent editorial revision at the hands of performers. Second, the contemporary text is, despite or perhaps because of such revisions, full of mistaken characters, the most common being simpler characters substituted for more complex homophones. For example, in the contemporary version *Zhao Yulin* is written as 趙玉林, whereas the original *lin* was written as 麟. Such substitutions appear throughout the text, suggesting that the songbooks, at least in their contemporary form, are used more as phonetic guides to the singing of the text (the story of which is widely known) than as real representations of meaning.

Other works survive only as fragments or as references in inventories. A few pages of the *Che Long huadeng ji* 車龍花燈記 (Record of Che Long's lantern festival) reveal that this work—whose contents cannot be determined from the fragment at hand—opens with the same formula as does *Zhao Yulin* ("Ever since Pan Gu separated heaven and earth, each dynasty has had its emperors and each its ministers"), suggesting another technique common in this genre: the repetition across titles of certain phrases and formulas, particularly those used to frame the story, as an aid to oral performance. And this work appears, like *Zhao Yulin*, to be composed in very simple language, with easy characters and short phrases frequently repeated to aid memorization and performance.

Some evidence suggests that this might be a tale of a "fated love match," a *caizi jiaren* story in ballad form. A longer "wooden-fish book" (*muyushu* 木魚書) telling just such a story has a similar title: *Che Long gongzi huadeng ji* 車龍公子花燈記 (Record of Master Che Long's lantern festival).[61] Wooden-fish songs were Cantonese ballads in seven-character rhymed strophes, named for the pair of fish-shaped wooden blocks struck together to mark time as the ballad was sung. Produced in Foshanzhen and environs and popular in the Pearl River delta and West river areas, they were based on fictional stories, tales from history, or local events; they might also be radical abridgments of famous stories like *Dream of the Red Chamber*.[62] It is possible that this story was brought back to Sibao (or alternatively, introduced to Guangdong from Sibao) through the business ties between certain Sibao houses and

---

61. Leung Pui-chee, *Xianggang daxue suocang muyushu shulu yu yanjiu*, pp. 52, 213. The Sibao songbook is a much briefer text than the wooden-fish book, so that (if there is any relationship at all between the two), it may be an abridgment or partial rendition of the longer work.

62. Ibid., pp. 205–20, 245–56. Certain titles on the Cuiyun tang inventory are similar to those of wooden-fish stories: *Jiu caizi* [*shu*] 九才子[書] (Ninth book of genius), for example, which appears as *Jiu caizi Erhehua shi* 九才子二荷花史 (The ninth work of genius: history of two lotus flowers), a *caizi jiaren* story, in the University of Hong Kong catalogue (p. 3); or *Xiuzhen Ba caizi* [*shu*] 袖珍八才子[書] (Eighth book of genius, sleeve edition), or *Diba caizi Huajian ji* 第八才子花箋記 (Eighth work of genius: Record of the *billet-doux*) in the Hong Kong catalogue (pp. 81–6). *Erdu mei* and *Honglou meng* also appear as *muyushu* titles. There were many other song forms popular in Sibao market areas in Guangdong: Chaozhou dialect songbooks (*gece* 歌冊), "southern-pronunciation" songbooks (*nanyin* 南音), "bamboo-branch stories" (*zhuzhi ci* 竹枝詞), etc. It is possible that some Sibao titles refer to such works as well. See Ye Chunsheng, *Lingnan suwenxue jianshi*, pp. 1125–48, 207–43; and Leung Pui-chee, *Nanyin yu Yueou zhi yanjiu, passim*.

Foshanzhen publishers (see Chapter 7) or by Zou or Ma booksellers looking for new texts to publish for sale in Guangdong. These contacts might well have served to transmit stories from one area to another, where they might be turned into lyrics in the appropriate dialect or used as the basis for new stories.

In sum, Sibao's songbooks, whether well printed or crudely reproduced in pamphlets, offered works with two different arenas of appeal. The few universally known works such as *Liang Shanbo* and *Meng Jiangnü* (and, at a more advanced level of performance or readership, Zou Shengmai's edition of *Record of the Western Chamber*) would have been welcome almost anywhere. By publishing and distributing these works throughout south China, the Zou and Ma were disseminating the "classic" songs and ballads of Chinese culture and advancing cultural integration. But cheap songbooks like *Shisha ting* (selling wholesale for only 0.3 *qian*) probably enjoyed largely local Sibao sales. More neatly published ballads like *Zhao Yulin*, although sold and used in Sibao and Minxi, were also popular throughout Lingnan (and *Zhao Yulin* may in fact have originated in Guangxi, given its setting in Wuzhou). In the marketing of songbooks, Sibao publisher-booksellers acted as vehicles not only for the spread of common cultural references but also for the extension of local or regional cultures to new areas of settlement—and thus for the strengthening of separate regional and/or ethnic consciousness. And, given the nature of these texts and their link to oral culture, these were influences that operated at all educational levels, embracing the illiterate as well as the educated.

### The Elite Arts: Poetry Collections and Calligraphy and Painting Albums

Although Sibao publishers concentrated on texts they knew would sell steadily to as many customers as possible, they did produce some scholarly texts and literary collections that, if not rare and sophisticated, at least seemed intended for a highly educated readership. In this vein, Sibao also produced a fair number of poetry collections and works of poetry criticism, perhaps in part for examination study (after the poetry requirement was reintroduced in the mid-eighteenth century) but certainly also for aesthetic pleasure.[63] The Cuiyun tang inventory lists the famous Qing poet, anthologist, and literary theorist Shen Deqian 沈 德潛 (1673–1769) as the compiler of "sleeve editions" (*xiuzhen* 袖珍) of *Tangshi biecai ji* 唐詩別裁集 (Anthology of Tang poetry; 1717), *Mingshi biecai ji* 明詩別裁集 (Anthology of Ming poetry; 1739), and *Guochao biecai ji* 國朝別裁集 (Anthology of Qing poetry; 1759)—and a *Songshi biecai ji* 宋詩別裁集 (Anthology of Song poetry) and *Yuan biecai ji* 元別 裁集 (Anthology of Yuan poetry),[64] as well, although none of these texts survives. Several other well-known works appear: a collection of Du Fu's poetry and an edition of the Yuan collection *Yongwu shi* 詠物詩 (Poems in praise of objects), for example. Some of Sibao's many poetry collections, particularly the cheaper ones, may have been the work of lesser-known local poets.[65]

More interesting for this study—and more substantial in that there are extant texts to analyze—are two collections of calligraphy and drawing issued by a Wuge publisher. These are the *Shuhua tongzhen* 書畫 同珍 (Calligraphy and painting, treasures together), first cut in 1742, and then newly cut in 1874, and the *Ji'ao shanfang xinji shilian zaojing* 寄傲 山房新集詩聯藻鏡 (Elegant mirror of poetic couplets, newly collected from the Ji'ao shanfang), of somewhat uncertain date. *Shuhua tongzhen* (Fig. 12.5a), as its title indicates, displays calligraphy, specifically the calligraphy of Zou Shengmai, one of Sibao's most prolific

---

63. Most of these texts are discussed in Chapter 10, for they seem to have been designed for examination study.

64. Although these last two works are attributed to Shen in the Sibao book lists, I can find no independent confirmation of this attribution. He is known to have compiled works with the first three titles.

65. These collections survive as titles only (most of which I have not yet been able to identify): *Yangyun shi* 養雲詩, *Qingyun shi* 青雲詩, *Lingtong shi* 靈通詩, *Guan'ge shicai* 館閣詩裁, etc. They were presumably rather brief collections, for they ranged in price from 0.35 *qian* to 0.7 *qian* in the Wenhai lou account book.

Both the Cuiyun tang and the Wenhai lou list a surprisingly large number of *fu* 賦 (rhapsody) collections and manuals—the Cuiyun tang inventory alone lists twenty-three titles—at a time when the form is said to have languished. See Appendix G. On the decline of interest in the *fu* form during the Qing, see Nienhauser, *The Indiana Companion to Traditional Chinese Literature*, p. 390.

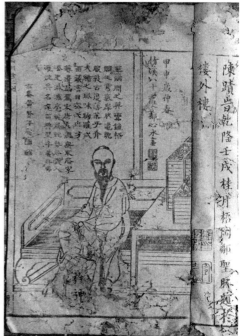

Fig. 12.5 *Shuhua tongzhen* 書畫同珍 (Calligraphy and painting, treasures together), published by Ji'ao shanfang 寄傲山房 in 1874. (a, *above left*) Cover page. (b, *above right*) Portrait of Zou Sheng-mai 鄒聖脈. (c, d, *facing page*) Calligraphy by Zou Shengmai. Photographs by the author.

publisher-editors. Although Zou failed to earn an examination degree, he achieved some distinction as a local literatus and talented calligrapher.[66] Once, when bookselling in Guangdong, he came upon a crowd standing outside a newly built academy, all staring up at the inscription over the gate, which was missing the character *yi* 一 (one), the most difficult character to write well. None of the local literati had the assurance or the artistry to attempt this tricky character. Zou boldly picked up the calligrapher's brush and wrote in the character, earning praise not only for his skill but also for his courage and confidence.[67]

---

66. *Changting xianzhi* (1782), 16.40b; *MTLZXZSZP* (1911), 20.16b–17b.

67. Zou Chunsheng, "*Youxue qionglin* zengbuzhe Zou Shengmai," p. 116. I learned of the existence of Zou's poetry collection, *Ji'ao shanfang shiji* 寄傲山房詩集, too late to included a discussion of it here.

The *Shuhua tongzhen* is, in essence, a sampler of Zou's calligraphy. Although the preface expresses the author's pious wish that the texts he has chosen to copy (morality books like the *Wenchang dijun yinzhi wen* 文昌帝君隱隲文 [Lord Wenchang's rewards for secret merit]) may instruct people in proper behavior ("Xu," 1b), it is clear that the book's primary purpose is to demonstrate Zou's artistry. The work opens with a portrait of the artist, seated in his study and surrounded by books (see Fig. 12.5b). The largest of any Sibao editions I have seen (the carved portion of the block is 21.5 cm × at least 15.5 cm), this is also the most beautifully cut—the characters are large, clearly defined, and widely spaced, so that the reader can easily appreciate the beauty of the calligraphy (Figs. 12.5c and d). In some editions the calligraphic texts are followed by a series of illustrations of famous historical and mythological personages, a kind of abridged catalogue of renditions of archetypal figures. Although the Sibao publishing houses produced many cheap calligraphy manuals,[68] largely for the use of beginning students, the *Shuhua tongzhen* and *Ji'ao shanfang xinji shilian zaojing* are genuinely elegant models for those interested in this most elevated of all the Chinese arts.[69]

## Conclusion

From their literature book lists, it appears that once again the Sibao publishers were targeting as broad a "popular" audience as possible—that is, they chose to publish texts with a wide appeal, in relatively inexpensive and poorly produced editions. Those who thought of themselves as members of the literate elite would readily have spent a small sum on a "trashy" martial romance or *caizi jiaren* novel, and humbler and poorer readers might just have been able to afford the cheap editions Sibao turned out.

---

68. See Chapter 10, pp. 335–36.

69. In addition to these two well-produced imprints, the Cuiyun tang inventory includes two famous painting manuals of the late Ming and early Qing: the *Shizhu zhai shuhuapu* 十竹齋書畫譜 (Manual of calligraphy and painting from the Ten Bamboo Studio; first published 1619–33) and *Jiezi yuan huazhuan* 芥子園畫傳 (Manual of painting of the Mustard Seed Garden; first published 1679–1701). No imprints survive, but it seems likely that these were relatively simple, monochrome versions of these manuals.

Late nineteenth-century reports of Chinese book culture support the judgment of the Zou and Ma publisher-booksellers. S. Wells Williams, commenting on the popularity of cheap novels in the mid-nineteenth century, claims that the "books on the stalls along the sides of the streets are chiefly of this class of writings. . . . They form the common mental aliment of the lower classes, being read by those who are able, and talked about by all, and consequently exert a great influence."[70] James Hayes, writing about a century later, emphasized the popularity of fiction—or at least the widespread knowledge of the stories of popular fiction—among the rural New Territories population he studied. Although skeptical about how broadly novels and longer short stories circulated, he noted the popularity of ballads or songbooks as promptbooks for entertainment, particularly among village women.[71] These appear to have been texts rather like Sibao's songbooks: "printed on low quality paper in wood-cut print, which is often smeared and hard to read. The size of such ballad books is often quite small, consisting of two or three pages only."[72] And Stewart Culin, observing yet another reading audience, claimed that "romances, dramas and song books constituted the greater part of the Chinese literature current among the Chinese laborers in the United States" in the late nineteenth century.[73] A. W. Loomis, in an article published in 1868, noted:

There are many of the Chinese people who have had some opportunities of learning, but whose education is not equal to an easy and intelligible reading of the classic books, for the style of most of these is very "deep"; but they can make their way through the novels, and the song books, and the legendary history of the Three States, for these are written in what is termed the "shallow" style; therefore, this sort of light literature is met with in almost every lodging room in the city [San Francisco], and in many of the laborers' camps in the country.[74]

---

70. Williams, *The Middle Kingdom* (1848 ed.), 1: 561.

71. Hayes, "Popular Culture in Late Ch'ing China," pp. 63–65.

72. Ibid., citing Eberhard, *Cantonese Ballads*, p. 1.

73. Culin, "Popular Literature of the Chinese Laborers in the United States"; summarized in Hayes, "Popular Culture in Late Ch'ing China," pp. 71–72, n. 25.

74. Loomis, "What Our Chinamen Read," pp. 525–26; cited in Cohen, "Notes on a Chinese Workingclass Bookshelf," p. 428, n. 30. Cohen also reports on a store of texts collected by Chinese workers in a Sacramento Chinese restaurant, buried in the late

In conjunction with reports from observers in China, this suggests the broad and far-reaching appeal of inexpensive, easy-to-read "light" fiction of the sort that the Sibao publisher-booksellers embraced.

As Hayes and David Johnson have emphasized, the illiterate, too, had some access to the contents of these works through oral performance. The stories in these chapbooks often reproduced stories known through the popular theater, the written texts recounting stories already well known in the oral tradition (just as *Sanxia wuyi* recorded the oral performances of Shi Yukun).[75] But stories that originally appeared in written form might also be adapted for oral performance; witness the existence of songbooks and wooden-fish books retelling portions of *Dream of the Red Chamber* and *Erdu mei*. Thus, the dissemination of printed fiction might also serve eventually to spread popular stories to illiterates as well as readers.

In addition to fiction, the Zou and Ma publishers produced some highly respectable literary works as well: poetry collections that transmitted what was considered the noblest form of literature and some "literati novels." Like many of Sibao's educational texts (the Four Books, Five Classics, ancient-prose essay collections), these would be appealing to any reader desirous of learning the cultural tradition. But the overwhelming majority of Sibao publications in the broadly defined literature category suggest an effort to attract as large a market as possible, including the only moderately or partially literate population as well as the many highly literate and sophisticated readers who might also enjoy "lighter" adventure and *caizi jiaren* stories.

---

1950s and recovered in 1970. Of 66 titles, 38 percent were of the "novels of knight-errants" (*wuxia xiaoshuo*) variety, just the sort of text that formed the bulk of Sibao's fiction output; 23 percent were pornographic; 22 percent were other novels, largely of the adventure-story or *caizi jiaren* variety, including *Yanshan waishi* 燕山外史 (A tale of Yanshan; ca. 1810, a novel written in parallel prose), *Water Margin*, *Sui Tang yanyi* 隋唐演義 (Narrative of the Sui and Tang), *Beiyou jizhuan* 北游紀傳 (Record of a journey to the north, one of the volumes of *Siyou ji*), and *Lü mudan*, all part of Sibao's stock. A miscellaneous category included, among others, a poetry collection by the Song poetess Li Qingzhao 李清照 (1084–ca. 1151), a book of poetry criticism, a letter-writing handbook, a rhyming dictionary, two *fengshui* and divination manuals, and a pharmacopoeia based on the *Bencao gangmu*.

75. Hayes, "Specialists and Written Materials in the Village World," p. 107; and Johnson, "Communication, Class, and Consciousness in Late Imperial China," pp. 65–69.

# THIRTEEN

## Sibao's Customers and Popular Textual Culture in the Qing

THE ZOU AND MA publisher-booksellers were, for the most part, offering texts of assured popularity largely to readers who hoped to achieve or had achieved literacy sufficient to obtain *shengyuan* (licentiate) status.[1] Of course, their readers might also include highly literate scholars, officials, and merchants. But accounts of their customers in the Zou and Ma genealogies, present-day informants, the logic of the markets for their books, the nature of their output, and, as we shall see, the prices of their books, allow us to infer their primary intended audience: at the top, low-ranking officials and local literati; then in the middle a large and miscellaneous group of students, merchants, artisans, and village specialists; and, at the bottom, literate (or even semi-literate) peasants and traders of moderate means eager for education or recreation for themselves and their families.

### Audience and the Prices of Sibao Imprints

Could consumers at the lower socioeconomic end of this hierarchy afford Sibao imprints? The little we know about the prices of these texts suggests that even peasants and petty merchants living in hinterland areas would have found at least some of them affordable. The Wenhai

---

1. For a discussion of a related concept, *shengyuan* book culture, see McDermott, "The Ascendance of the Imprint in China," pp. 86–87.

lou account book (dating from the very late Qing or early Republic) lists wholesale prices as low as 0.05 *qian* (or 5 *li*) for versions of *Qianjia shi* and *Sanzijing zhu* 三字經注 (*Three-Character Classic*, with commentary); 0.3 *qian* (or 3 *fen*) for an edition of *Tangshi sanbaishou* and for simply annotated editions of the *Yijing* (*Yijing pangxun* 易經旁訓 [*Classic of Changes* with sideline instructions]) and *Shujing* (*Shujing pangxun* 書經旁訓 [*Classic of History* with sideline instructions]). Informants claim that retail prices were usually 20 to 30 percent higher than wholesale prices for Sibao's staple texts; new "bestsellers" might be marked up as much as 50 to 60 percent.[2] These long-established titles, then, would cost a retail buyer as little as 6 to 8 *li* and from 3.6 to 4.8 *fen*, respectively. Slightly more elaborate editions of the Classics (*Shujing liju* 書經離句, *Classic of History*, sentence by sentence), collections of eight-legged essays, *fengshui* manuals (*Qiandanzi yuanzhu jing* 鉛彈子元珠經 [*Classic of the lead pellet and original pearl*]), novels (*Wuhu ping nan*), and brief acupuncture guides wholesaled for 0.4 to 0.8 *qian* (retail 0.48–0.64 to 0.96–1.28 *qian*, respectively). The collection of the Four Books with the standard Zhu Xi commentaries (the *Sishu jizhu*) was 1 *qian* wholesale (1.2–1.63 *qian* retail); an edition with a full set of annotations and explanations (like *Sishu buzhu beizhi tiqiao huican*; see Chapter 10) ran as high as 2 *qian* (2.4–3.2 *qian* retail). The most expensive text listed is an edition of *Liaozhai zhiyi*, wholesale 1.1 *liang* (retail 1.32–1.76 *liang*). Other longer works also cost more: for example, the wholesale price of the imperially sponsored cosmological encyclopedia *Qinding Xieji bianfang shu* was 4.5 *qian* (retail 5.4–7.2 *qian*), of the imperially sponsored medical reference *Yuzuan Yizong jinjian* 6.5 *qian* (retail 7.8–10.4 *qian*), and of the *Kangxi zidian* 8.3 *qian* (retail 9.96–13.28 *qian*). But of the 379 titles with legible wholesale prices listed in the Wenhai lou account book, almost exactly half (191 titles, or 50.4 percent) wholesaled for less than 1.0 *qian*. The retail prices listed in the account book kept by three members of a Zou

---

2. Interviews 45, 11/23/95 (Mawu); 25, 11/9/95 (Wuge); 71, 12/9/95 (Wuge); and 44, 11/23/95 (Mawu). One informant mentioned a markup on staple titles as low as 10 percent. Twenty percent seemed to be the markup most commonly cited by informants. In estimating retail prices here, I provide the full range, from 20 percent to 60 percent. As mentioned in Chapter 6, books seem to have retailed for less in Sibao than outside the basin. This might explain the different markups cited by informants. Interviews 63, 12/5/95 (Wuge); and 85, 4/23/96 (Mawu).

publishing house in the late Qing are higher: an edition of the Four Books with commentary cost 3.6 *qian*, over one *qian* more than the Wenhai lou Four Books. Generally speaking, the price of works from this document are roughly one *qian* higher than those of similar texts in the Wenhai lou account book, although the Zou account book does not list any text as expensive as the Wenhai lou's edition of *Liaozhai zhiyi*.[3]

How much, then, might a customer purchasing over the course of several years the standard group of beginning educational texts spend at a Sibao outlet? Since the prices listed on the account books are not legible for all texts, we have to construct a less-than-ideal group from a limited number of educational works (see Table 13.1). It seems that a modest collection of basic texts for the examination curriculum would cost between 17.28 and 25.80 *qian*.

What would these prices have meant to a family in the context of their total income? Given the considerable regional and temporal variation in wages, prices, and currency exchange rates in the late Qing and the paucity of consistent information about wages and prices, this crucial question is difficult to answer. Evelyn Rawski's analysis of the salaries of schoolteachers in the late nineteenth century supplies some evidence for at least one sector of the Sibao market. A book costing 1 *qian* would have represented less than a full day's pay for a schoolteacher working at the median annual salary of 44 *liang* (during the period 1875–1900); either one of the "collections" from Table 13.1 would have cost between 4 and 6 percent of such a teacher's annual income (although it would not have been an annual expense, but rather one spread over a series of years). Of course, salaries varied greatly. In 1884 a schoolteacher in Wuchang, Hubei, might earn as little as 18 *liang* per year; in 1881, one in Huolu 獲鹿, Zhili, as much as 48 *liang*.[4] Clearly the Wuchang teacher would have found it difficult to purchase any but the cheapest of Sibao's texts, the ones costing only about 7.5 *li* a title. Yet

---

3. See Appendix G for a comparison of prices from these account books.

4. Rawski, *Education and Popular Literacy*, pp. 56–61. This information, drawn from provinces on the fringes of Sibao's distribution routes, can provide only a rough idea of the value of Sibao's imprints.

Table 13.1
Estimated Retail Prices of Some Sibao Imprints
(in *qian*), ca. early twentieth century

| Title | WHL | ZWN |
|---|---|---|
| *Sanzi jing* 三字經 (Three-character classic) | 0.075 | |
| *Qianzi wen* 千字文 (Thousand-character essay) | 0.075 | 0.2 |
| *Baijia xing* 百家姓 (Myriad family names) | 0.075 | |
| "San-Bai-Qian" 三百千 | | 1.6 |
| *Qianjia shi* 千家詩 (Myriad poems) | 0.075 | |
| *Youxue gushi qionglin* 幼學故事瓊林 (Treasury of allusions for young students) | | 2.2 |
| Four Books | 2.25 | |
| *Sishu buzhu* 四書補註 (Four Books, supplemented with commentary) | | 3.6 |
| *Shujing liju* 書經離句 (*Classic of History*, sentence by sentence) | 0.7 | 1.3 |
| *Shangshu [li]ju* 尚書[離]句 (*Classic of History* [*Book of Documents*], sentence by sentence | | 1.1 |
| *Shijing beizhi* 詩經備旨 (Full purport of the *Classic of Songs*) | 2.1 | |
| *Shijing jinghua* 詩經精華 (Essence of the *Classic of Songs*) | | 2.9 |
| *Yijing pangxun* 易經旁訓 (*Classic of Changes* with sideline instructions) | 0.45 | |
| *Yijing liju* 易經離句 (*Classic of Changes*, sentence by sentence) | | 1.0 |
| *Chunqiu pangxun* 春秋旁訓 (*Spring and Autumn Annals* with sideline instructions) | 0.53 | |
| *Liji pangxun* 禮記旁訓 (*Record of Rites* with sideline instructions) | 2.1 | |
| *Liji jinghua* 禮記精華 (Essence of the *Record of Rites*) | | 2.7 |
| *Tangshi hexuan* 唐詩合選 (Combined selection of Tang poetry) | 1.5 | 3.6 |
| *Guwen xiyi* 古文析義 (Elucidation of ancient-style prose) | 6.0 | |
| *Guwen shiyi* 古文釋義 (Explaining the meaning of ancient-style prose) | | 2.8 |
| *Shiyun jicheng* 詩韻集成 (Collected poetic rhymes) | 1.35 | 1.4 |
| *Shixue hanying* 詩學含英 (Beauties of poetry study) | | 1.4 |
| TOTAL | 17.28 | 25.80 |

NOTES: WHL = Wenhai lou account book (ca. early twentieth century); ZWN = Account book of Zou Weinan (1860–1933), Zou Xiyao (1866–1926), and Zou Xinfeng (fl. late nineteenth c.) In calculating the retail prices from the Wenhai lou account book's wholesale prices, I have assumed a markup of 50 percent.

the teacher earning 48 *liang* could afford not only these titles but also several of Sibao's more expensive offerings.

For students, too, purchasing power varied widely; their stipends might be as little as just over 20 percent or as much as 75 percent of their teacher's salary.[5] Rural student customers of some itinerant Sibao booksellers were able to pay as much as 1.5 *qian* for a copy of a popular household encyclopedia (*Yingshi bianshu*), 2 *qian* for *Youxue gushi qionglin*, 2.8 *qian* for a guide to allusions in the Four Books (*Sishu dianlin* 四書典林), 4.5 *qian* for *Sanguo tongsu yanyi*, and an impressive 9.2 *qian* for the medical encyclopedia *Yizong jinjian* (as well as sums as small as 1.6 *fen* for rhymed couplet collections), suggesting that in some areas at least students were able to purchase not only the standard textbooks, but fiction, medical handbooks, and socially useful ritual guides as well.[6]

Sibao texts seem to have been relatively cheap in the context of the Qing book market as well. In a study of the cost of books during that dynasty, Yuan Yi concludes that prices of woodblock texts declined significantly from the Jiaqing era on. He estimates that the average per-*ce* retail cost of texts in the Qianlong era was 6 *qian*; this declined to 4.3 *qian* in the Jiaqing era; and finally to 1.5 *qian* by the Guangxu era, an overall decrease of 75 percent.[7] But this low price of 1.5 *qian* per *ce* is still high by Sibao standards: the Sibao edition of the *Kangxi zidian*, in 15 *ce*, probably sold for about 12.45 *qian* (assuming a markup of 50 percent

---

5. Rawski, *Education and Popular Literacy*, pp. 64–65.

6. Wage information for other sectors of the population below the official elite is difficult to find. Chang Chung-li (*The Income of the Chinese Gentry*, p. 12) states that a laborer earned only 5 to 10 *liang* (taels) a year, although his employer would supply him with food. This would obviously leave little for book buying; at the most, such a man could purchase only one of Sibao's cheapest pamphlets selling for a few *fen*. Jing Su and Luo Lun (*Land and Labor in Late Imperial China*, pp. 41, 171–73), in their study of agricultural labor in Shandong in the late nineteenth and early twentieth centuries, report annual wages for long-term workers (again, these men were fed by their employers) that varied from 8 taels to 50 taels during the period from 1891 to 1908; the average wage was 21.3 taels. The average and the high wages would have allowed for greater purchasing power; the best-paid laborer would have been roughly in the position of the best-paid teacher in the example above; and the worker paid the average wage would have had the spending power of many students. But these figures are from Shandong, and it is not clear how relevant they are for Sibao's market areas, in Fujian, Jiangxi, Guangdong, and Guangxi.

7. Yuan Yi, "Qingdai de shuji jiaoyi ji shujia kao," pp. 73–74. The exceptions were movable-type texts, which were usually more expensive. In the late nineteenth century, when woodblock text prices were still declining, prices of goods in general were apparently on the rise; see Wang Yeh-chien, "The Secular Trend of Prices During the Ch'ing Period," pp. 357–62, 366. Depending on the trend in wages, this might have made books more affordable.

from the retail price of 8.3 *qian*), compared with 22.5 *qian* by Yuan's calculation—and that was one of Sibao's most expensive items. Equally
persuasive is the evidence from Sibao booksellers active in the early
twentieth century: they repeatedly commented on the cheapness and affordability of their imprints.[8]

Although poverty might prevent a person from purchasing even the
cheapest of Sibao texts, there were other ways of getting access to
books and the information in them. Book rental shops provided temporary access at lower prices (although inadequate information on these
shops makes it impossible to say how common they were).[9] Literates
could be hired to read to the unschooled. As Hayes has pointed out, literate "village specialists" in geomancy, fortune-telling, letter-writing,
and ritual could be employed to pass on expert advice from their own
store of texts, as it were, reading for illiterates. As mentioned in Chapter 11, "masters of rituals," one type of village specialist, were probably
customers for Sibao texts like *Jiali tieshi jiyao* and could use that text to
instruct villagers how to conduct weddings and funerals.

---

8. Interviews 37, 11/14/95 (Wuge); 44, 11/23/95 (Mawu); and 46, 11/24/95 (Mawu).
One informant claimed that the Sibao outlet in Changting in the early Republic was
noted for its small "sleeve" (*xiuzhen*) editions, "much cheaper than any other texts" (interview 75, 12/15/95 [Changting]). And an itinerant book peddler active in the 1930s
claimed that the primer *Zengguang* cost only 2 to 3 *mao* in his markets (interview 37,
11/14/95 [Wuge]). Some scattered price information from Sibao itself suggests something of the relative value of these imprints. An ancestral hall account book (Yesheng
Gong *fang*) from the late nineteenth century lists prices for items used in lineage rituals:
1 *fen* for an ounce of fruit, 4 *fen* for two ounces of sandalwood incense, 2.4 *fen* for four
pairs of candles, 7 *fen* for 7 pieces of *doufu*, 1.575 *qian* for nine bottles of wine, and so
forth. The costliest expenditure—the 1.575 *qian* for the wine—would have purchased
any title among the cheapest 50 percent of the entries in the Wenhai lou account book.
Of course, local residents were not the primary audience for Sibao texts in the late nineteenth century, but these prices from a relatively poor region give some idea of the relative value of the texts, suggesting that at least the cheapest of them would have been
affordable to moderately well-off peasant families. And even if such families were too
cautious to spend a few *fen* on Sibao's lower-end texts and pamphlets, village experts in
education, medicine, and fortune-telling, who depended for their livelihood (or a portion of their livelihood) on the knowledge contained in these texts, had a much stronger
motive for investing in them.
9. Murakami Kimikazu, "Chūgoku no shoseki ryūtsū to taishi hon'ya—kinsho
shiryō kara—"; and idem, "Chūgoku no shoseki ryūtsū to taishi hon'ya" (2).

## The Production Quality
## of Sibao Imprints

Sibao publishers of the late nineteenth and early twentieth centuries were able to sell their texts cheaply primarily because they kept production costs low. As indicated in the descriptions of surviving Sibao texts in the preceding chapters, most imprints were small volumes printed on cheap *maobian* paper, at times from worn blocks. A comparison of contemporaneous texts from Sibao's wealthier rival, Xuwan, reveals a clear difference. The Xuwan editions of *Yixue sanzi jing* and *Shennong bencao jingdu*, for example, although by no means extraordinarily fine, are larger and clearer, much easier to read, than the Sibao versions (see Figs. 13.1a, b, and c).[10] The blocks for Sibao texts (and, for that matter, for most Xuwan texts) were usually cut in the *jiangti* 匠體, or "craftsman's style," standard in the Qing, which produced blocky, uniform characters that were easier and cheaper to cut as well as easier to read.[11] But many Sibao imprints do not offer even this last advantage: in some texts characters (in *bianti* 扁體, or "flattened style") are so crammed together on the page that it is difficult to figure out where one ends and the next begins (see Fig. 10.19). And attempted touches of refinement, notably prefaces in a more cursive calligraphic style, usually only emphasized the awkwardness of the calligraphy (see Fig. 10.8d).

The widespread use of simplified characters (particularly in popular songbooks; see Fig. 11.4) and the frequency of erroneous characters also diminished the pleasure or instruction to be gained from many Sibao imprints—and contributed to their low cost. One Fujian literatus, Huang Junyuan 黃俊苑 of Nanping 南平 (fl. 1870s), in a statement that is the closest we have to a contemporary reaction to Sibao texts, dismissed these works as useless to students: "Today, commercial shops sell only cheap and disposable texts, like the editions of Tingjun [i.e., Tingzhou], so full of errors that it is impossible to point them all

---

10. Note, too, that the Sibao versions are more heavily punctuated than the Xuwan editions.

11. Heijdra, "A Tale of Two Aesthetics"; Heijdra's *Mingchaoti* 明朝體 is the same as *jiangti*. See also Hegel, *Reading Illustrated Fiction in Late Imperial China*, pp. 110–13.

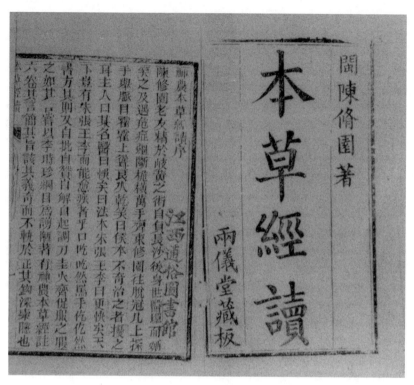

Fig. 13.1 (a, *above*) Xuwan edition of *Shennong bencao jingdu* [神農]本草經讀 (Reading the *Materia medica* class [of Shennong]), published by the Liangyi tang 兩儀堂. (b, c, *facing page*) Sibao edition of the same text, published by the Suwei tang 素位堂. Note that the Sibao editions are more heavily punctuated as well as more crudely cut. (a) Courtesy of the Jiangxi Provincial Library; (b, c) photographs by the author.

out. If tutors do not pay special attention [to correcting these], then the harm will not be inconsiderable."[12] (Here Sibao imprints were typical, as Huang suggests, of many commercial productions; educational manuals routinely explain that the teacher's first task was to help students correct the printing errors in their textbooks.)[13]

---

12. Huang Junyuan, *Zhizhai yishu* 止齋遺書 (1875), 13.9a; cited in Xie Shuishun and Li Ting, *Fujian gudai keshu*, p. 471. Since Sibao was the only publishing site of any size in Tingzhou, I think it is reasonable to assume that "the editions of Tingjun" refers to Sibao imprints.

13. See, e.g., Shen Li, "Yixue yue," p. 1232; cited in Gardner, "'To Be a Teacher Is Hard.'"

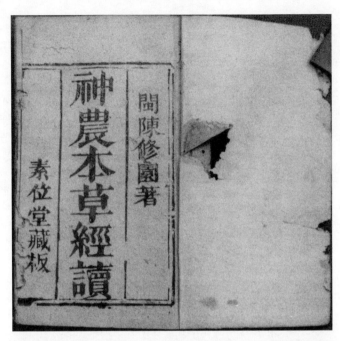

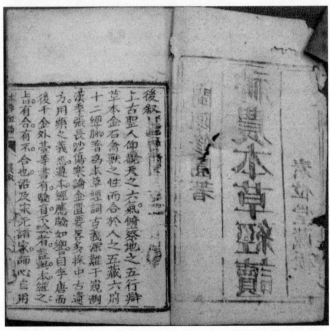

Of course, not *all* Sibao texts were cheap and shabby. As noted in Chapters 10 and 12, some editions were clearly if not elegantly cut. And the Zou and Ma appear to have done some color printing as well—two editions with color printing (*taoban* 套版) of the *Liji* are listed (*Taoban Liji huican* 套版禮記匯參, *Taoban Liji shengdu* 套版禮記省度) on the Cuiyun tang inventory, along with other more pedestrian and probably less expensive editions.[14] Scattered evidence suggests that some publishing houses printed the same title in editions of differing size and quality, presumably for different audiences. Thus the Cuiyun tang inventory lists three different editions of *Liaozhai zhiyi* (one plain, one with "added commentary," and one with "punctuation and comments");[15] also a "large" edition of *Wu caizi shu* with commentary by Jin Shengtan (*Jinpi*) and a regular edition, apparently unannotated. The notation on this inventory of the page size of each title—large (*daban* 大板), medium (*zhongban* 中板), small (*xiaoban* 小板), or sleeve (*xiuzhen*)—indicates that the publishers produced editions for different markets. The variety of reading aids and commentaries attached to many editions of the Classics and novels also suggests they attempted to meet the needs of readers of widely ranging educations, expectations, and reading habits.

For the most part, however, the Sibao publisher-booksellers seemed to target an audience of relatively undiscriminating readers of at best modest means. Isolated in the mountains of western Fujian, with little capital, they could afford to produce only texts with a guaranteed readership. Serving largely rural and hinterland markets, they were in no position to specialize in finely produced texts or rarefied scholarly and literary works for a tiny elite. The steady sale of inexpensive "bestsellers" appealing to the broadest possible literate population was their key to success.

------------

14. See also the description of one examination-essay collection, with annotations in red; Chapter 10, p. 365.

15. The Wenhai lou account book also lists a very expensive colored edition of *Liaozhai zhiyi* (1.1 *liang* wholesale), along with monochrome editions at a fraction of that price (2 *qian* wholesale). And two property-division documents list sets of "large" and "small" blocks for the same titles. The Xiangshan tang, for example, lists a "large" and a "small" *Nan Bei Song* (see p. 482), presumably the historical romance authored by Xiong Damu; the Zaizi tang also lists a "small" *Shijing jianben* 詩經監本 (Directorate of Education edition of *Classic of Songs*), but without a reference to a corresponding "large" version.

## Sibao and Popular Textual Culture

If Sibao's imprints were widely popular, the sure sellers of their day, they can tell us something about the nature of popular textual culture in late Qing south China. (I mean "popular" here in the sense of "commonly known"; "popular textual culture" is the text-based culture shared by all status groups in the population.) By thinking of Sibao's imprints as constituents of a popular textual culture, we can characterize their function and place in late imperial society more broadly, beyond the convenient but somewhat artificial categories used in Chapters 10 through 12: educational texts centered around the examination curriculum; how-to manuals teaching ritual propriety, medicine and home remedies, and techniques for divination and earning good fortune; and fiction and belles-lettres.[16]

For example, the Sibao model of popular textual culture includes the classical primers, the Four Books, a few of the Five Classics (the *Classic of Songs, Classic of Changes,* and perhaps the *Classic of History*), collections of Tang poetry, and essay collections of the great ancient-style prose masters, as well as some supporting works—all of which I have treated as textbooks for examination preparation. But, by virtue of their status as vehicles for the cosmology, core ethical standards, aesthetic values, and historiography of the Chinese people, these works also had a larger significance. First, knowledge of these works defined what it meant to

---

16. Strikingly lacking from this Sibao model of popular textual culture are religious texts—the precious scrolls (*baojuan* 寶卷) of popular religious societies, morality books, sutras and scriptures, and Buddhist and Daoist tracts. These were undoubtedly popular; even in the United States, Chinese in the late 1860s were "often found reading their books of mythology—the legends relating to their many gods and goddesses; many of which books are crowded with rude wood cuts"—and moral tracts (see Loomis, "What Our Chinamen Read," p. 526; cited in Cohen, "Notes on a Chinese Workingclass Bookshelf," p. 428). The relative absence of such texts in Sibao's stock can be explained easily by the existence of parallel systems of production and dissemination: precious scrolls, as works deemed heterodox by the state, were usually manuscripts kept secretly by religious leaders; and morality books, sutras and scriptures, and Buddhist and Daoist tracts were most likely printed by religious institutions—"benevolence halls" and Buddhist and Daoist temples and monasteries—rather than commercial publishers. Of course, many Sibao almanacs, divination manuals, ritual handbooks, novels, and songbooks transmitted the beliefs and practices of popular religion. See Chapter 11, pp. 537–55.

be cultivated in Chinese society. Ambitious men with no thought of attempting the examinations in the highly competitive nineteenth century might still turn to these works as sources of the knowledge and language necessary to the appearance of education and culture.

This is, perhaps, to emphasize too heavily expediency and ambition as reasons for the popularity of these "classics": they must also have had a broad appeal simply as carriers of the tradition, for they defined, too, what it meant to be Chinese. Describing the reading habits of Chinese immigrants living in San Francisco in the 1860s, A. W. Loomis provides a moving example of how these texts might be valued in a context that denied them any utility as tools of examination success or status advancement:

The educated men, wherever they go, carry with them some of their favorite volumes which they often review, chanting them aloud as when they first studied them in the schools. It is a common thing also to hear these men at night, while lying awake in bed, repeating chapter after chapter of Confucius and Mencius, and of the Book of History, and the Book of Poetry. . . . The chanting of the sentiments of the sages, arranged in a style which is music to the ear of a Chinese scholar, is as agreeable to him as it is for some of other nations to sing the old songs, or to repeat aloud passages from their favorite authors. We fancy, also, that the Chinese gentleman, self-exiled to a country seven or eight thousand miles from his home, from wife and children, and from neighbors, is sometimes affected with home sickness, and is ready to do anything that will in imagination transport him back to his own flowery kingdom.[17]

We might well imagine that there were at home, too, many Chinese eager to educate themselves in the most honored texts of the cultural tradition. Sibao editions of these texts, annotated for use in schools, would have been particularly helpful to readers unable to complete more than a few years of schooling.

We could argue, too, that the educational texts, in particular the Four Books and Five Classics, form the slender thread that links many of the disparate works of this textual popular culture together—or at least that supports claims for the coherence of this culture. Over and over the reader is told, in prefaces and in commentaries, that the texts of this culture are popularizing or extrapolating the principles of the Classics

---

17. Loomis, "What Our Chinamen Read," p. 525.

(and histories) for the edification of and/or practical use by "the people." The ritual handbooks, correspondence models, and household encyclopedias teach the rituals of speech, dress, gesture, and composition that allowed the individual and family to take their proper place in a harmonious social order; they were, in essence, updated popularizations of the *Record of Rites*. If the ritual manuals derived ultimately from the *Record of Rites*, the medical texts and fate-manipulation guides might be said to have descended ultimately from the *Classic of Changes*: the medical texts promise to explain, simply and clearly, how to restore the balance of *yin* and *yang* within the body; the fate-manipulation guides, the techniques for understanding and manipulating cosmic forces to the benefit of the family and individual. Morality books, too, were touted as texts that revealed the subtle and complex meanings of the Classics to those of limited education. And historical fiction was a way of teaching history and the lessons of cosmic retribution to readers either not competent (or too bored) to read the *Record of the Grand Historian* and the standard histories.

But these claims for the coherence of much of popular textual culture (and its derivation from the Classics and histories) are only superficially persuasive. They cannot disguise one striking characteristic of this culture: its rich variety of ideas, values, and models. Nowhere is this clearer than in the category of Sibao's fate-manipulation guides, which ranged from an imperially sponsored encyclopedia of orthodox calendrical calculation and a *fengshui* classic to cheap fortune-telling pamphlets and almanacs. These works might share fundamental cosmological assumptions, but they derived an impressive array of specific techniques of fate manipulation from these shared assumptions, including some that were considered heterodox.[18] And, as we saw in Chapter

---

18. The *Xieji bianfang shu*, by laying out the state-approved basis for calendrical calculation, was designed in part to serve as a measure of what calculations were correct and what not. But here the government, or at least the Qianlong emperor, tacitly allowed a variety of popular practices even though they might not be consistent with the orthodox cosmology—as long as these practices were not seen as threatening to state security. Thus, although the cheap almanacs and divination pamphlets churned out by Sibao and other commercial publishers doubtless violated some of the principles set forth in the *Xieji bianfang shu*, they were never proscribed. See Richard J. Smith, *Fortune-tellers and Philosophers*, p. 51.

12, Sibao's popular novels frequently celebrated heroes and heroines who presented at least an implicit challenge to the models of behavior set forth in the Classics and ritual manuals.

The range in linguistic sophistication makes clear, too, that we have to think of popular textual culture not as a mass of texts equally accessible to all literates but as texts on a continuum shaped by both language and, to some extent, genre. As Stephen Owen has suggested, written Chinese consisted of a number of registers "loosely located on a gradation between the 'popular,' *su* 俗, and a variety of 'elevated' registers suggesting erudition."[19] Sibao's chapbook novels, written in simple classical Chinese, would rank rather low on the continuum, presumably, and would be accessible to readers of limited literacy as long as they had been trained in classical primers and textbooks such as *Sanzi jing* and *Qianzi wen*.[20] Sibao's literati novels, written in a rich and complex vernacular language (with sophisticated classical allusions and often some dialect), would certainly rank higher in difficulty, although their status as "insignificant talk" would keep them in the "popular" range. Complicating any effort to define these stages or registers and to correlate them to educational or literacy levels is the fact that by the late Ming and Qing many works were written in a mixed, "heavily vernacularized literary style."[21] Moreover, a text written in an "elevated" register was not necessarily inaccessible to those less than fully literate: schoolboys learned the archaic Chinese of the Four Books (with the aid of simple classical or mixed classical and vernacular commentaries) well before they could grasp the rich language and literary allusions of *Dream of the Red Chamber*, a "popular" novel.

---

19. See Owen, "The End of the Past," pp. 171–72.

20. It is likely that most literates had been taught the classical language first, when children. Li Yu describes using vernacular texts to teach his concubines, relying on the similarity to speech to speed their progress (Hanan, *The Chinese Vernacular Story*, p. 10). But this kind of teaching seems to have been unusual and was perhaps used primarily for adult learners; most schools taught the classical primers.

21. Mair, "Buddhism and the Rise of the Written Vernacular in East Asia," p. 738. Mair (pp. 707–8) argues that classical Chinese ("Literary Sinitic") and vernacular Chinese ("Vernacular Sinitic") "belong to wholly different categories of language," but that this difference is often difficult to discern, since most writers use a mixed form, combining the two.

This popular textual culture—including even its linguistically most difficult texts—may have had an influence well beyond the population of book readers in late imperial China. The interaction between textual and oral culture is most obvious in the arena of fiction, as mentioned in Chapter 12, where writers and editors often borrowed their stories from oral performance (and vice versa). But other kinds of texts were transmitted orally as well. Primers like *Sanzi jing* and *Dizi gui*, not to mention the Four Books, were first memorized and recited; a man who had never learned to read but had attended a year or two of school would have some experience of these texts through a kind of oral performance. Phrases from *Sanzi jing* became popular proverbs (e.g., *yu buzhuo bucheng qi* 玉不琢不成器, "If jade is not polished, it cannot become a thing of use"). As one scholar has explained, the enormous popularity of this text derives not just from its use as a primer but also from its function as "a book of initiation into the culture for everyone."[22] Tang poetry was meant to be chanted and was first taught, like the Four Books, to be recited. The "Song Urging Hard Work," "Song Urging Frugality," "Good Boy Song," and "Good Girl Song," printed both in cheap morality books like *Yifang xunzi* and in household encyclopedias like *Chuanjia bao*, were presumably to be taught to children before they had learned to read (and to many children who would never learn to read). Even certain prescription collections and medical textbooks might have served both literates and illiterates: works like *Shifang gekuo*, explicitly identified in its title as a collection of prescriptions in song form, assumed a literate teacher who could teach illiterates the prescription-songs (as well as an aged student with a poor memory).

The links between textual culture and oral performance of all sorts gave females, whose literacy rate, even by the most generous estimates,[23] was significantly lower than that of males, broader access to texts and textual knowledge. The memorization and recitation of songs

---

22. Yang Dan, "Le *Classique en trois caractères* ou le passé au service du présent," p. 179.

23. The work of Dorothy Ko, Susan Mann, and Ellen Widmer has demonstrated that literacy was relatively common among elite women of the Jiangnan area in the late Ming and Qing. Indeed, these women were often participants in elite literary culture. But the overall literacy rate for women remained low; by Rawski's (*Education and Popular Literacy in Ch'ing China*, p. 140) estimate, between 2 and 10 percent in the nineteenth century.

and poetry might lead to literacy for girls with the leisure and resources to pursue it. In the autobiographical *Six Records of a Floating Life*, Chen Yun, the wife of Shen Fu, begins to learn to read by linking written characters to her oral knowledge of Bai Juyi's famous "Pipa xing" 琵琶行 (Ballad of the lute).[24] But girls and women without Chen Yun's advantages could absorb values and cultural references from didactic songs, performances of songbook narratives, storytelling, and local opera productions. The contents of the orally transmitted culture, like that of the texts from which it derived, were not necessarily homogeneous or internally consistent. For poor girls and women, moral songs like Shi Chengjin's "Song of Instruction for Girls" transmitted orthodox gender values, at the same time that ballads, the recitations of storytellers, and opera performances disseminated tales that might present a different set of values and models.

In sum, the Sibao model of popular textual culture encompasses works presenting a variety of interpretations of Confucian values and religious beliefs in a range of linguistic styles and levels of difficulty. By disseminating this body of texts through the hinterlands and frontiers of south China, the Zou and Ma were bringing not only the Classics and handbooks of ritual propriety but also stories of bandit-heroes and women warriors, "licentious" love, and popular almanacs to the literate population (and through recitation and oral performance, to illiterates). The publisher-booksellers were acting as agents of cultural integration, an integration that included, on one hand, the orthodox values and classical language of the major primers, the Four Books, and Five Classics and, on the other, the somewhat different (but at points overlapping) values and mixed language of popular fiction, songbooks, almanacs, and some "heterodox" divination manuals. Arthur Smith, remarking on what he saw as a high degree of cultural integration in the 1880s, observed that "the classical wisdom of the Ancients is the common heritage of all the sons and daughters of Han, from Emperors to old women, and one stratum of society can quote them as well as another."[25] At the same time, "all the sons and daughters of Han" would

---

24. Shen Fu, *Six Records of a Floating Life*, pp. 25–26.

25. Arthur H. Smith, *Pearls of Wisdom from China*, p. 7; cited in McLaren, *Chinese Popular Culture*, p. 5.

also presumably be familiar with the rough-and-ready martial heroes found in *Wuhu ping nan* and *Sanxia wuyi* and the gods and spirits itemized in *Yuxia ji*. Thus, the kind of text-based cultural integration encouraged by the labor of the Sibao publisher-booksellers, although creating a common store of cultural referents, did not necessarily forge a common outlook or interpretation. The referents, drawn not only from the Classics and state-sanctioned teachings but also from folk stories about bandit-rebels and forward women, were too various and too contradictory for that to happen.

## The Stability of Sibao's Popular Canon

This text-based popular culture had a remarkably long and stable life. The works of the Sibao model of popular culture, in general type if not in precise title, had developed fully by the mid- to late Ming and maintained their dominant (that is, popular) status through the early twentieth century. Many titles predate the late Ming, most notably the Classics, the Tang poetry collections, and the primers. But the publication of popular versions of the Classics and poetry collections, not to mention ritual handbooks, household encyclopedias, medical guides, and fiction, was largely a phenomenon of the late Ming and Qing.[26] New titles were added from time to time, and certain genres (such as historical fiction or *caizi jiaren* stories) blossomed at different points within those three and a half centuries. But the overall shape of what we might call the popular canon remained the same.[27]

This canon endured in some form even beyond the abolition of the examination system, the fall of the Qing, the rise of a new literature—and the decline of the Sibao book trade. Although the demand for the

---

26. Many of the genres published in the late Ming had Song and Yuan precedents: simple explanations of the Classics, abridged histories, collections of examination essays, handbooks of composition, and prescription recipe collections and *materia medica*. But there is a lull in the publication of these (and other) texts in the early Ming, and it was only in the mid-sixteenth century that such works began to appear again, in much greater numbers (see Chia, *Printing for Profit*, pp. 126–41; and *idem*, "*Mashaben*," pp. 302–7).

27. Tsuen-hsuin Tsien (Qian Cunxun), "Yinshuashu zai Zhongguo chuantong wenhuazhong de gongneng," pp. 245–47.

classical primers, the Four Books and Five Classics, and study aids for these texts decreased once the examination system was abolished in 1905, it by no means disappeared. In many areas, Sibao included, a dual structure of education developed in the late Qing and continued throughout much of the Republican period: the old elementary schools, *mengguan* and *jiashu*, continued to teach *Sanzi jing*, *Qianzi wen*, and the Four Books, whereas the new primary schools used the modern textbooks approved by the state.[28] Many informants from Wuge and Mawu report that they attended both types of schools.[29] This was not the practice only in Minxi. As late as 1938, an observer in rural Ding 定 county, Hebei, commented: "Not only do private, family schools use [the classical primers and the Four Books] but foreign-style, modern schools also use them as supplementary reading material. Many uneducated peasants, in town to trade in their spare time, often buy a copy of the *Three Character Classic* to take home with them. I hardly ever see them buy a modern, vernacular book put out by the Commercial Press in Shanghai." This same writer noted two rundown bookstores that "completely relied on the wholesale trade of those outdated old books that still (somehow) survive: the *Hundred Family Names*, the *Thousand Character Classic*, and the *Three Character Classic*."[30]

Nor was the use of the traditional textbooks the practice just in out-of-the-way rural communities. In 1924 Guangzhou—after Shanghai the most active center of modern publishing—had 636 private elementary

28. In 1918, the first modern primary school was established in Wuge by Zou Lian-chan 聯蟬, noted for his "attack on the old culture and support of the new studies." He later also established a second primary school in the village, the Jingchu xiaoxue 景初小學, in 1928 (*FYZSZP* [1947], 33.89b–90a). In Mawu, Ma Bozhi 伯智 founded the Fufeng xiaoxue 扶風小學 in 1919 (*MSDZZP* [1945], *ji* 7, j.1.*you*29b; and *Changting xianzhi* [1940], 13.53b).

29. At least three family schools survived in Wuge, two of which had been founded by publishing households: the Zhiyuan shuwu 致遠書屋, established by Zou Bingjun and his son, and the Wugang shuwu, established by Zou Funan. Open to all members of the appropriate lineage who could help support the teacher (with cash from the better-off families and unhusked rice or other food from the poorer families), these schools usually had enrollments of ten to twenty students each. Interviews 25, 11/9/95 (Wuge); 85, 4/23/96 (Mawu); 88, 4/23/96 (Wuge); and 89 and 90, 4/24/96 (Wuge).

30. Lao Xiang 老向, "Guanyu kang Ri *Sanzijing*" 关于抗日三字经, p. 292; cited in Borthwick, *Education and Social Change in China*, p. 123.

schools (*sishu*) with about 30,000 students (roughly the same number of students attended the modern primary schools). These schools still taught the "San-Bai-Qian" and the Four Books. The number of private schools dropped precipitously, to only 74 by 1937, only to increase again during the Sino-Japanese War (1937–45), when the city government could not afford to support the modern school system. It was not until after 1949 that the *sishu* finally disappeared.[31]

And it was not only in the sphere of educational texts that Sibao's major titles continued in demand. The early twentieth-century experience of the Sibao Suwei shanfang branch store in Zhangzhou is illuminating. This shop continued to sell Sibao woodblock texts until the store closed in 1942 (from 1930 to 1942, these texts were printed in Zhangzhou, from blocks shipped from Wuge). Some of these were books specifically cut for the local market: a Zhangzhou dialect dictionary (*Shiwu yin* 十五音) and a collection of Zhangzhou anecdotes (*Zhangzhou minjian gushi* 漳州民間故事). But most were among Sibao's universal bestsellers: *Sanzi jing, Zengguang xianwen*, the Four Books and other educational texts; a morality book (*Wugong jing* 五公經); and *fengshui*, physiognomy, and divination manuals. Most striking, though, was the preponderance of novels of all sorts: *Narrative of the Three Kingdoms*; *Dream of the Red Chamber*; *Erdu mei*; *Sanguo yin* 三國因 (a "prequel" to *Narrative of the Three Kingdoms*); *Xue Rengui zheng dong*; *Wanhua lou*; *Bao gongan*; *Peng gongan*; *Qian wuhu* 前五虎 and *Hou wuhu* 後五虎, both on the conquest of Taiwan by heroes from Zhangzhou; and *Qixia wuyi* 七俠五義 (The seven valiant and five righteous men), the "improvement" of *Sanxia wuyi* by Yu Yue—to name just a few.[32]

The shop also sold more up-to-date publications—both the "mandarin duck and butterfly" classical-style love stories of Zou Taofen 鄒韜番 and Feng Yushui 馮玉水[33] and the radically new fiction of writers like Lu Xun 魯迅 (1881–1936), Mao Dun 矛盾 (1896–1981), and Ba Jin 巴金 (1904–2005). But these modern works had no link at all to Sibao: they

31. Cao Sibin et al., *Guangzhou jinbainian jiaoyu shiliao*, pp. 263–64. For a fuller discussion of the persistence of the *jiashu* or *sishu* through the Republican period, see Brokaw, "Commercial Woodblock Publishing in the Qing."

32. *Zhongguo tongsu xiaoshuo zongmu tiyao*, pp. 826–28, 1257–58.

33. See Link, *Mandarin Ducks and Butterflies*, p. 7.

were lithographic editions purchased wholesale from the Kaiming shudian 開明書店 in Xiamen (which imported them from Shanghai). The
older adventure novels and *caizi jiaren* stories still had a large audience,
as is attested by the eagerness of Shanghai publishers in the late 1920s
to purchase woodblock versions of all the "traditional" fiction titles
listed above, for reproduction in lithographic or letterpress editions.
Woodblock copies of at least ten titles were shipped to Shanghai in
1928 and 1929, and there reprinted by lithography "on very low-quality
paper, like newspaper." The new "foreign editions" of these old texts
were then returned to Zhangzhou for sale in the Suwei shanfang.[34]

The role of the Sibao publisher-booksellers in the formation, dissemination, stabilization, and perpetuation of this text-based popular
culture was complex. They had least to do with its formation or creation, contributing only a few educational texts, ritual manuals, and
medical texts, all works that for the most part merely swelled the numbers of other similar texts. They were, in fact, often simply re-edited or
expanded versions of earlier texts. But, as argued in Chapter 6, they had
a great deal to do with this culture's dissemination, carrying these works
throughout the hinterlands and frontiers of most of south China during
the Qing and early Republic; in this regard, the Zou and Ma booksellers
were vigorous agents of textual cultural integration.

Finally, the socioeconomic context and structure of their business
led them to play an important role in the stabilization and perpetuation
of this culture as well. In his study of English book culture in the
Romantic period, William St Clair shows that publishers in the seventeenth and eighteenth centuries had a vested interest in limiting the circulation of new texts among their largest "popular" reading constitu-
ency, choosing to make new works available only in small numbers and
only to elite readers.[35] The forces at work in Sibao were quite different,
yet they had a roughly similar effect: the isolation of Sibao, the limited
capital resources of the Zou and Ma, and the constraints of the household and lineage order encouraged conservative publishing choices. Jus-
tifiably fearful of business risks, they chose to publish and sell only
"safe" works of proven popularity or works that were sure to be popu-

---

34. Interviews 68, 12/5/95 (Wuge); and 83, 4/1/96 (Zhangzhou).
35. St Clair, *The Reading Nation in the Romantic Period*.

lar, given changes in the examination system. By publishing and disseminating these texts, particularly in areas without easy access to other
bookstores or booksellers, they ensured that these were the works that
would *remain* popular. They were, in short, from the late seventeenth
through the early twentieth century, purveying a stable and conservative
popular culture of texts.

# FOURTEEN

## *The Diffusion of Print Culture in Qing China*

THE SIBAO PUBLISHERS illustrate the general historical trend noted in Chapter 1: the spread of woodblock publishing and book culture geographically outward, into the hinterlands of south China, and socially downward, to the minimally educated levels of the population. Over the course of their history, they sold their texts throughout most of the provinces of south China, not only in some of the major commercial and administrative centers of Jiangxi, Hunan, and Guangdong but also in the backwaters of these provinces, extending their reach into the frontier regions of Guangxi, Yunnan, and Guizhou. They sold to academy instructors, educational officials, magistrates, local literati, and family and charitable schools. By the late nineteenth century at the latest, their publications reached populations far distant, physically, socially, and culturally, from the major seats of education and political authority.

They sold a wide variety of texts, largely excluding works of elite literature, philosophy, history, and controversial contemporary scholarship, but including most of the major educational texts of the examination system, a considerable number of ritual and etiquette guides, household encyclopedias, medical manuals, and fortune-telling handbooks, and a representative sampling of the most popular works of fiction of the eighteenth and nineteenth centuries. Within each of these categories, the Zou and Ma produced a range of titles.

What place did Sibao occupy in the book industry of southern China in the Qing? Was it unique in its operation and scope? Or does it present simply one variation on a common pattern of production and distribution? And what was the social and cultural impact of the growth and spread of commercial publishing? Did it, as the Zou and Ma publisher-booksellers claimed, bring elite culture to the hinterlands and assist in the training of future "generals and ministers of state"? Although much more research must be done on publishing and bookselling in the Qing before these questions can be answered conclusively, I offer here some preliminary observations and a few speculations about the scope of commercial woodblock publishing and its impact on book culture, cultural integration, and literacy in the Qing.

## Sibao in Context: Other Commercial Publishing Sites of the Qing

The greater accessibility of texts in south China in the nineteenth century was not the work of the Sibao publishers alone. Many other sites of commercial publishing were active at the time. What do these other sites tell us about the distribution of texts and the nature of late imperial book culture?

Below I briefly consider three other sites, each, like Sibao, a site of commercial enterprise, and each distant from major metropolitan centers: Xuwanzhen, a market town in eastern Jiangxi, which became one of the major centers of book publication in the Qing; Yuechi county, an impoverished rural backwater in eastern Sichuan, whose block cutters served both urban publishing houses in Chengdu and Chongqing and a local publishing industry; and Magang, a cluster of villages in the Pearl River Delta area, where peasant women worked as cutters supplying publishers as far away as Zhejiang with woodblocks. I have asserted, in Part I, the distinctiveness of the Sibao publishing-bookselling operation, and the material presented below does reveal glimpses of other forms of organization and marketing within the publishing industry. At the same time, these three examples reinforce the broad conclusions presented in Chapter 1 about the extent and depth of book distribution in southern China in the Qing.

## XUWANZHEN, JIANGXI

In the Qing dynasty, Xuwanzhen was a prosperous market town in Jinxi county, Jiangxi, one of four important market towns in the northern and eastern section of the province (the others were Zhangshuzhen, Jingdezhen, and Hekouzhen). Strategically located on the upper reaches of the Xu river, Xuwanzhen had easy access by water to the provincial capital, Nanchang, the prefectural capital Fuzhou, and other regional market towns such as Nancheng 南城, Nanfeng 南峰, Guangchang 廣昌, and Jiujiang. It was also on the post road through Jinxi and Linchuan 臨川 counties. Throughout the Qing it was an entrepôt for the shipment of rice, paper, and wood products for distribution throughout Jiangxi and beyond. Paper was also an important product of Xuwanzhen; it was noted in particular for the production of colored paper and *maobian* paper, the bamboo paper commonly used in commercial printing.[1]

It is difficult to say when Xuwanzhen became a publishing center. Local scholars date it to the early seventeenth century, but the industry really flourished only during the mid- and late Qing—that is, the Qianlong, Jiaqing, and Daoguang eras, from the early eighteenth through the mid-nineteenth century. During the Tongzhi era, when Xuwanzhen publishing began to decline, as many as sixty publishing houses were still in business, however. During its peak years, the industry dominated the town physically: the two main parallel streets, Qian shupu jie 前書鋪街 (Front bookshop street) and Hou shupu jie 後書鋪街 (Back bookshop street), consisted of rows of publishing houses, bookshops, and book storehouses. At the mouth of each street was an engraved gate: the inscription at the entrance to Qian shupu jie read "The empire illuminated by the canon"; that at the head of Hou shupu jie, "Heaven's resplendent book treasury." In front of these gates was a large pool of water named Ximo chi 洗墨池, or "Washing Ink Pond," where the printers washed their blocks. The water in the pool is still black—it is said that even the mud at the bottom is black—because of the thousands of woodblocks that were washed there.[2]

---

1. Zhao Shuiquan, "Jinxi de 'xiao Shanghai'—Xuwanzhen"; idem, "Xuwan yu muke yinshu," pp. 51–52.
2. Xu Zhengfu, "Jinxi shu," pp. 36–37.

Most of the Xuwanzhen publishing houses seem to have been established and managed by failed scholars or lower-degree holders. The local scholar Xie Ganpan 謝甘盤 is said to have established the Jiuxue shanfang 舊學山房 publishing house in the Daoguang era with the purpose of reprinting ancient texts of his choice. Yu Zhongxiang 余鍾祥, who earned tribute student status in the Jiaqing era, established the Yu Dawen tang 余大文堂 in 1815 largely to publish the Classics and educational texts.[3] Whatever their scholarly credentials, most of the publishing-house managers did not limit their production to scholarly reprints or literary collections. The larger publishing houses, like the Liangyi tang 兩儀堂, turned out a wide range of publications, including not only the writings of Jiangxi literati but also reading primers, editions of the Classics, household encyclopedias, fiction, drama, medical manuals, rhymed-couplet collections, letter-writing guides, and almanacs.[4] As a group, the Xuwanzhen publishers seem to have aimed a little higher than the Zou and Ma of Sibao; their lists include texts of higher production quality and intellectual content.[5]

Labor for the industry was drawn from the surrounding countryside. A Republican-era geography states that "both men and women from Xuwanzhen were good at cutting woodblocks."[6] Many publishers employed permanent cutters, men (and occasionally women) who worked in the shops on Qian shupu jie and Hou shupu jie. Certain publishers might also farm out cutting and printing tasks to peasants in the surrounding countryside. The Wang family, owner of the Zhongxin tang 忠心堂, for example, had their tenant farmers in the nearby village of Zhongzhou 中洲 cut texts in the winter, when farmwork was minimal, and then keep the blocks in their homes, to be printed on demand, usually by the women and children of the household, throughout the

---

3. Ibid.; *Jinxi xianzhi* (1992), pp. 387–88.

4. Some of the more popular titles in these categories were *Qianzi wen, Youxue gushi qionglin, Baijia xing, Sanzi jing, Yuxia ji, Guwen guanzhi* 古文觀止, *Yizong jinjian, Honglou meng, Liang Shanbo yu Zhu Yingtai* (Xu Zhengfu, "Jinxi shu," pp. 37–38; Interviews 2, 12/23/95 [Xuwan]; 3, 6/25/96 [Xuwan]; and 4, 6/25/96 [Xuwan]).

5. See Du Xinfu and Qi Shenqi, *Jiangxi lidai keshu.*

6. *Jiangxi sheng* (Republican era); cited in Zhao Shuiquan, "Xuwan yu muke yinshu," p. 54.

year.[7] Local *maobian* paper might be used to print the cheaper books, but for finer editions, *lianshi* paper was purchased from Fujian.[8]

The publishers operated retail shops in Xuwanzhen (the shops were in the front, the publishing operations in the back of buildings, each of which stretched the width of a city block). From these shops they sold texts to local customers and to agents for local schools and academies. The largest portion of their sales was wholesale, to sojourning merchants who traveled to Xuwanzhen (far easier of access than Sibao) and then transported the texts by river back home.[9] It is said that Xuwanzhen thus supplied the book markets of Nanchang, Jiujiang, Changsha, Wuhu, Anqing, Nanjing, and even Beijing.

The Xuwanzhen publishers, given their more accessible location, could expect book merchants to come to them to purchase texts wholesale. There is little evidence that they developed an extensive, centrally controlled network of distribution routes like that of the Sibao publisher-booksellers. But they did, like their Sibao counterparts, establish branch shops, selling their imprints in crucial cities on the middle and lower reaches of the Yangzi. Although they had an outlet in Changsha, to the west, their primary orientation was northeastward to Jiangnan; they founded outlets in Nanchang (the provincial capital), Jiujiang, an important market town on the Yangzi; and then northeast along the Yangzi in Anqing and Wuhu (both in Anhui province) to Nanjing.[10] This chain of shops gave them access to the richest book markets of Jiangnan, and the shop in Changsha (accessible via the Yangzi and the Xiang) provided them with a western market. Xuwanzhen seems also to have been integrated to some extent into a north-south publishing network; the Shancheng tang, a publishing house with stores in Chongqing and Beijing, apparently had a shop in Xuwanzhen.[11]

---

7. Interviews 2, 12/23/95 (Xuwan); and 7, 7/6/96 (Jinxi).

8. Zhao Shuiquan, "Xuwan yu muke yinshu," p. 53. One informant still in the printing trade claimed that the Xuwanzhen publishers also purchased *maobian* paper from Fujian (Interview 2, 12/23/95 [Xuwan]).

9. Interview 2, 12/23/95 (Xuwan); Zhao Shuiquan, "Xuwan yu muke yinshu," p. 52.

10. Zhao Shuiquan, "Xuwan yu muke yinshu," p. 52.

11. *Jinxi xianzhi* (1992), p. 388.

Given the lack of precise statistics about production quantities, it is difficult to assess Xuwanzhen's significance in the Qing book trade. But some evidence suggests that it was almost as important as larger and more prominent economic and political centers. In the late nineteenth century, Jin Wuxiang 金武祥, a Jiangsu native, claimed that Xuwanzhen, along with Magang in Guangdong, produced more texts than any other woodblock publishing site of the day—although he was not very complimentary about the quality of the texts:

For the production of text blocks, the provinces of Jiangxi and Guangdong are first; the cutters of Jiangxi are in Xuwanzhen, Jinxi county, those of Guangdong in Magang, Shunde county. In both places the accumulation of many blocks is a sign of wealth. When daughters are given in marriage, blocks are often part of their dowries. But the blocks are full of errors, for each character is carelessly cut, because half the work of cutting the blocks is done by female workers.[12]

More recently, in the mid-twentieth century, Zheng Zhenduo also identified Xuwanzhen, with Beijing, Hankou, and Sibao, as one of the four great publishing centers of the Qing.[13]

Xuwanzhen, then, was a regional market town and publishing center, which, through its strategic location on a provincial river and postal route, was able to supply eastern Jiangxi and, more broadly, northern Jiangxi, eastern Hunan, southern Anhui, and eastern Jiangsu with texts ranging from simple primers to quite sophisticated and relatively elegant literary collections.

## YUECHI, SICHUAN

The block-cutting and printing industry centered in the seat of Yuechi county, in eastern Sichuan province, provides a sharp contrast to that of Xuwanzhen. Yuechi is by no means a regional center of any importance: it does not lie on any important river or land transport routes, and it is distant from the major centers of Sichuan, over 100 kilometers

---

12. Jin Wuxiang, *Suxiang sanbi* (preface dated 1884), 4.10b; cited in Nagasawa Kikuya, *Wa Kan sho no insatsu to sono rekishi*, p. 85.

13. Zou Risheng, "Zhongguo sida diaoban yinshua jidi zhi yi—Sibao," p. 102.

from Chongqing and over 200 from Chengdu. Situated in a poor agricultural area, it does not produce any commercial goods or offer any transport advantages such as lent Xuwanzhen its regional importance.

What Yuechi did have to offer was labor. Because it was such a poor area, Yuechi's peasants needed to supplement their seasonal agricultural work with some other craft or by hiring out their labor. We do not know how block cutting became a specialty of the area, but we do know that by the mid-eighteenth century Yuechi had become the most important source of printing blocks for the major publishers in Chengdu and Chongqing. Like Xuwanzhen, Yuechi became famous as a place where "everyone, male and female, old and young, knew how to cut."[14]

The arrangements between Yuechi block cutters and Chengdu-Chongqing publishers varied quite widely. Several villages, including Qiaojia 喬家, Tumen 土門, Hongmiao 紅廟, Wanshou 萬壽, Dashi 大石, and Yixing 義興, became known for the skill of their cutters, apparently (despite the comment cited above) all male; most of them seem to have learned their craft in their villages. As early as age nine, they would begin to study block cutting with local teachers. After a two-to-three-year training period, the teacher could choose to keep a student in his employ, without wages, for one year, before releasing him to contract his services out to local cutting shops or to operate as a seasonal freelance cutter.[15] The local block-cutting shops managed arrangements with the publishers and booksellers in Chengdu and Chongqing, saw to the preparation of the blocks, hired scribes to write out the manuscripts, and then farmed the blocks out to their own employees and, if necessary, to freelance cutters—that is, trained workers who combined cutting with their regular agricultural labor. Once completed, the blocks were transported by water to Chongqing or overland, through the mountains, to Chengdu.[16]

The wages paid the Yuechi cutters were apparently low enough to justify the expense and trouble of transporting the woodblocks. Many

---

14. Interview 1, 7/29/96 (Yuechi).

15. Interviews 8, 7/15/97 (Baimiao); 11, 7/17/97 (Yuechi); 19 and 20, 7/24/97 (Zhenlongxiang [Yixing]); 25, 7/26/97 (Yuechi); 26, 7/27/97 (Yuechi); and 17, 7/23/97 (Dashi).

16. Interview 4, 7/31/96 (Yuechi); Wang Gang, "Qingdai Sichuan de yinshuye," p. 63.

Chengdu and Chongqing publishing houses, however, hired the more skilled Yuechi cutters as permanent on-site workers. These men lived as sojourning craftsmen—that is, they spent most of the year in the city, living and working in the shops of the major publishers, traveling home every New Year's to visit their families. Others labored as itinerant cutters, seeking work not only in the cities of Sichuan but also in the neighboring frontier provinces of Gansu, Guizhou, and Yunnan.[17] Indeed, this was one of the ways in which woodblock publishing was disseminated in the late Ming and Qing—skilled but poor craftsmen, seeking employment, would travel to newly settled frontier regions in search of work, introducing block-cutting and printing technologies to their new, often temporary, homes. One informant related that his grandfather, who had learned to cut at a temple in Yuechi, traveled to Chengdu, Chongqing, and Kunming (Yunnan) for work, supporting himself by cutting for temples or individuals and by teaching his skill to others. He might be gone from home for as long as two years, but commonly was away for about half a year at a time.[18]

Thus the Yuechi block-cutters worked largely for publishers outside Yuechi, mostly in Chengdu and Chongqing, either on-site in those cities or through the Yuechi character-cutting shops. But the presence of a pool of cutters in Yuechi also stimulated the development of a small local publishing industry. It made a great deal of sense for the owners of the block-cutting shops to set up printing businesses, since they already commanded the most expensive, difficult, and labor-intensive step in the publishing process, the cutting of the blocks. Centered largely in the county seat and in the village of Qiaojia, these businesses remained small in scope, printing and distributing texts for a local readership. Most of their texts were reading primers like the *Sanzi jing* or *Dizi gui*; editions of the Classics, particularly the Four Books, for students; and popular fiction and drama.[19] Figures 14.1 and 14.2 show two examples of these texts, one a page from a simple edition of the Four

---

17. Interviews 4, 7/31/96 (Yuechi); 19, 7/24/97 (Zhenlongxiang [Yixing]); 21, 7/24/97 (Zhenlongxiang [Yixing]); 25, 7/26/97 (Yuechi); and 27, 7/28/97 (Yuechi).

18. Interview 7, 7/14/97 (Shiyazhen).

19. Interviews 11, 7/17/97 (Yuechi); 13, 7/18/97 (Qiaojia); and 19, 7/24/97 (Zhenlongxiang [Yixing]).

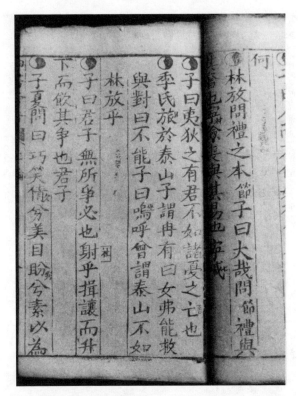

Fig. 14.1 Page from the *Analects* from a Yuechi edition of *Sishu pangyin* 四書旁音 (The Four Books, with sideline pronunciations). Note the guides to pronunciation to the right of each column of characters. Photograph by the author.

Books with sideline pronunciation guides (*Sishu pangyin* 四書旁音); and one from a song instructing girls in proper behavior, Shi Chengjin's *Xun younü ge* 訓幼女歌.

Particularly popular were songbooks, cheaply printed editions of local narrative songs that could be used as promptbooks in village entertainments. Booksellers and peddlers from the surrounding villages, and even from as far away as Nanchong 南充 and Guang'an 廣安, the two closest cities of any note, would travel to Yuechi and Qiaojia to purchase songbooks and primers wholesale, carrying them home for resale to an urban readership. Or peddlers would purchase texts in Yuechi and make a circuit through the larger peasant villages, passing through each on its market day if possible. They would carry a large portable

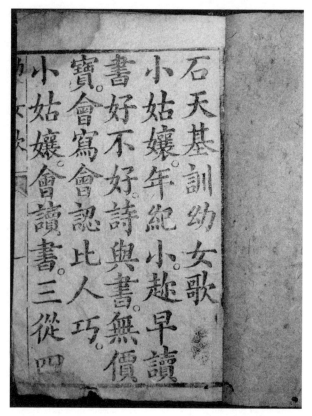

Fig. 14.2  Yuechi edition of *Xun younü ge* 訓幼女歌 (Song for the instruction of young girls) by Shi Chengjin 石成金. Photograph by the author.

bookrack, a bamboo pole crossed with several horizontal bamboo bars, on which the books for sale were displayed.[20]

In this way the printed word penetrated fairly deeply into Chinese society, into remote peasant villages of little interest to booksellers in the major printing centers, the capital and Jiangnan. To be sure, the literature on offer was shaped very much by aspirations to basic literacy and the need for familiar entertainment, but it does represent a fairly thorough dissemination of the fruits of print technology not only outward, to isolated hinterland areas like Yuechi, but also downward, to peasant communities socially well outside the elite book market.

---

20. Interview 11, 7/17/97 (Yuechi).

### MAGANG, GUANGDONG

Magang never developed a publishing industry; rather, it was an important site of block cutting. As such, it seems to have played a significant role in the Qing publishing world; Jin Wuxiang ranked it with Xu-wanzhen as one of the most prolific block-cutting areas of his day. Located in Shunde county, in the Pearl River delta area, Magang also provides a striking illustration of the portability of woodblock print technology—and the portability of woodblocks themselves. The block cutters of Magang, mostly female, supplied blocks to commercial publishers not only in nearby Guangzhou and Foshanzhen (another booming publishing site of the Qing) but also in distant Sibao and Suzhou. Throughout the nineteenth century, six or seven Magang block-cutting shops, managed by men, recruited peasant girls from the poorest neighboring villages, usually Mabei 馬北 and Mazhong 馬中, to the craft. Girls of about ten or eleven years of age, after passing tests of manual dexterity and general intelligence, would be assigned an older female teacher by the shop manager. Following one to two years of study with their "aunt," they would be ready to start working.[21] The blocks were prepared either by the publisher who was commissioning the work or by the shop manager, who would see not only to the preparation of the blocks but also to the writing out of the manuscript template to be used in the cutting. The shop manager distributed the prepared blocks and the relevant portions of the template to the home of each worker, where the cutting was done.[22]

Some women specialized in this work alone; one informant explained that a woman could support herself by cutting blocks, "if she lived very carefully."[23] But for many, this was subsidiary work, done in addition to household tasks or the raising of silkworms as a means of supplementing a family's income.[24] Since the workers were female, there was no chance of any of them moving to a publishing center and

---

21. Interview 1, 10/28/96 (Guangzhou); Huang Guosheng, "Guangdong Magang nüzi keshu kaosuo."
22. Interviews 3, 10/31/96 (Mabei); 4 and 5, 11/5/96 (Mabei).
23. Interview 5, 11/5/96 (Mabei).
24. Ibid.

finding permanent employment with a publisher, as many of the male
Yuechi cutters did; the managers of the Magang character-cutting shops
could count on a fairly stable pool of workers.

To the publishers, the great advantage of this arrangement was the
cheapness of the labor costs for block cutting, usually the most expensive part of book production. Yuechi cutters were relatively inexpensive
because they came from a poor area and were willing to work for little
in order to survive. Magang cutters were even cheaper simply because
they were female as well as poor—Jin's disparagement of blocks cut by
female workers reveals the general attitude toward the value of female
labor. This explains the benefit of the arrangement to the distant
Suzhou publishers: the labor costs were low enough to make up for the
expense of transporting the bulky blocks to Jiangnan.[25]

What do these cases tell us about Sibao and about the configuration of
late imperial print culture? First, it is clear that Sibao was neither unique
nor typical. If Zheng Zhenduo was correct, it may have been one of the
larger publishing centers of the Qing, but it appears to have been outstripped by Xuwanzhen, Hankou, and the cities of Jiangnan. Second,
there was clearly no established structural form for the business. Sibao
operated household-based publishing houses within a strong lineage
system. Family members provided the primary labor for production. In
Xuwanzhen, the shops were family owned but not entirely family operated; both cutters and printers were usually hired from outside the family, or cutters might be drawn from among the *shufang* owner's tenants
and dependents, living in villages in the surrounding area.

The Xuwanzhen publishers seemed to have practiced, at least in part,
a kind of putting-out system, commissioning families in the surrounding villages to cut blocks. Yuechi and Magang provide a somewhat different model: peasant laborers, employed by local block-cutting shops,
cut blocks that were then transported, often quite considerable distances, to various publishers. Yuechi produced some variations on this

---

25. Interview 1, 10/28/96 (Guangzhou). For more on Magang, see Huang Guosheng,
"Guangdong Magang nüzi keshu kaosuo"; and *Guangdong shengzhi—chuban zhi*, pp. 72–73.

model: some of its cutters became sojourning craftsmen in printing-publishing sites in Chengdu and Chongqing or neighboring provinces, and a small local publishing industry developed in response to the presence of the cutters.

Methods of distribution seem to have varied as well. Sibao appears unusual in two respects: throughout most of its history, its publishers maintained close control over the distribution and sale of the texts they produced (see Chapter 8); and its routes of distribution were shaped heavily by the ethnic identity of the publishers and the migration patterns of the Hakka. The Xuwanzhen publishers were not, for the most part, sojourners; they distributed their products largely by selling them wholesale to book merchants who came to Xuwanzhen to purchase texts. They did, however, like the Sibao booksellers, establish some branch shops—although far fewer and in cities of greater commercial and administrative importance. For Yuechi and Magang, the issue of distribution did not arise (except for the short distribution links, worked by both book peddlers and wholesale merchants, that characterized the small local Yuechi industry), although the distances publishers were willing to transport blocks from these sites reveals both the utility of cheap labor and the high degree of mobility that characterized the business. Scholars have imagined that the expense and difficulty of transporting woodblocks inhibited the exchange and spread of texts; the evidence from Yuechi, Magang, and Sibao (in its relations with Guangdong publishers) suggests that this was not the case.

In sum, these examples reveal something of the variety in commercial publishing operations in the Qing. They indicate that, in addition to the portability and relative simplicity of woodblock printing technology, the flexibility of labor relations and marketing systems developed within these operations facilitated the decentralization of Chinese printing and the diffusion of printing and publishing into the hinterlands and through the lower-status ranks of society. In the face of an increasing and regionally scattered demand for texts in the Qing, the technology allowed for the spread of publishing industries not only to provincial capitals and major market towns but also to county seats (Yuechi), market towns (Xuwanzhen), and even isolated peasant villages (the villages around Yuechi, Magang, and Sibao). Enterprising publishers developed a variety of employment strategies and methods of distribution to use this technology in the various geographical, economic, and social contexts in which they were operating—and the result was the creation of a certain type of book culture fairly broadly available throughout south China.

## The Circulation of Texts in the Qing

Observers' reports suggest, too, that Sibao was by no means the first or the only publishing industry in Qing China to provide wider access to texts and make them affordable to a large sector of the population. In the late sixteenth century, Matteo Ricci remarked on the widespread circulation of inexpensive texts in south China, a phenomenon that he explained as resulting from the facility of the print technology: "The simplicity of Chinese printing is what accounts for the exceedingly large numbers of books in circulation here and the ridiculously low prices at which they are sold."[26] Over two centuries later, in the 1830s, W. H. Medhurst echoed this observation: "Books are multiplied, at a cheap rate, to an almost indefinite extent; and every peasant and pedlar has the common depositories of knowledge within his reach. It would not be hazarding too much to say, that, in China, there are more books, and more people to read them, than in any other country of the world."[27] Like Ricci, Medhurst attributed the ubiquity of books to the ease of production. S. Wells Williams, in the middle of the century, also suggests that books were fairly widely available, relatively cheaply, either for sale or rent:

The *San Kwoh Chi* [*Sanguo zhi*], or History of the Three States [*Narrative of the Three Kingdoms*], may be cited as a cheap book; it is bound in twenty-one volumes 12 mo. [i.e., duodecimo], printed on white paper, and is usually sold for seventy-five cents or a dollar. Kanghi's [Kangxi's] Dictionary in twenty-one volumes 8vo. [i.e., octavo] on yellow paper sells for four dollars; and all the

---

26. Gallagher, *China in the Sixteenth Century*, pp. 20–21; cited in Rawski, "Economic and Social Foundations of Late Imperial Culture," p. 17. Adriano de las Cortes (*Le Voyage en Chine*, p. 194), writing just a few decades after Ricci, makes a similar point about the "good number of texts" available, at least in the Chaozhou area, on all topics.

27. Medhurst, *China*, p. 106.

nine classics can be purchased for less than two. Books are hawked about the streets, circulating libraries are carried from house to house upon movable stands, and booksellers' shops are frequent in large towns.[28]

The unequaled decline in book prices between the Jiaqing and Guangxu eras, discussed in Chapter 13, also suggests how fully developed the book industry was in the nineteenth century. This decline in prices did not affect just the elite book market: popular texts (*pujiben* 普及本) fell even more dramatically in price over this period, a phenomenon that suggests that Sibao was not alone in offering widely affordable texts.[29]

But scholars are not unanimous in accepting the low price of books in the late imperial period. Contrary reports argue that books were in fact quite expensive. Chun Shum (Shen Jin), in his study of late Ming book prices, for example, finds that books, even from Jianyang, a notable production center for inexpensive texts, were quite expensive; the *Da Ming yitong zhi* 大明一統志 (Comprehensive gazetteer of the great Ming), in 90 *juan*, for example, cost about one-quarter of the monthly salary of a county magistrate in 1588, at about the same time that Ricci was commenting on the cheapness of Chinese texts. If Chun's data are representative of late Ming prices, as Chia has said, then "surely book collecting was the privilege of the wealthy few."[30]

Later authors present similar evidence that books were too expensive for most people to own. Arthur Smith, writing in Shandong in the late nineteenth century, emphasized the high price of books, noting that a new, good edition of the *Kangxi zidian* would cost a village schoolmaster a year's pay. Thus, "within a circle of eight or ten villages, there may be only a single copy." In one unnamed county, he wrote, it was a "well-known fact" that only one wealthy family possessed a copy of a dynastic history. Smith claims that "ordinary" Chinese scholars owned few books, "for in the country where printing was invented, books are the luxury of the rich."[31] James Hayes, describing life in the

---

28. Williams, *The Middle Kingdom* (1848 ed.), 1: 479.

29. Yuan Yi, "Qingdai de shuji jiaoyi ji shujia kao," pp. 73–74.

30. Chun Shum, "Mingdai fangke tushu zhi liutong yu jiage," pp. 110–11, 116–17; idem, "Guanyu Mingdai Wanli zhi Chongzhen qijian de shujia," p. 2; and Chia, *Printing for Profit*, p. 191.

31. Arthur Smith, *Village Life in China*, pp. 97, 99.

rural villages in Hong Kong from the 1870s to 1937, also emphasized the paucity of texts: "From my own observations in Hong Kong villages before their modernization, I am fairly pessimistic about the presence of books in many village houses and town dwellings at that time." His explanation for the "lack of books that may have characterized many, even most, rural settlements" in Hong Kong was not poverty, but rather the presence of village specialists who could be consulted on a wide range of topics (and who were probably the primary book owners in the villages) and thus made widespread possession of printed handbooks unnecessary.[32] Wilt Idema, drawing on the writings of many of these men, also expresses skepticism both about the availability of books in the countryside and about the interest of the peasantry in purchasing what was available: "Admittedly, some books were very cheap, but even so buying books must have been a useless dissipation of hard-won money to the perennially poor peasantry."[33]

How can we explain these quite contradictory views, all from reliable observers and/or scholars? One possible clue to this puzzle is that these men are looking at different types of texts, commenting on conditions in different regions of China, or using different methods to evaluate access to texts. Ricci and Chun are considering two very different levels of publishing, Chun the top level, composed in the late Ming of (largely Jiangnan and Jianyang) publishers producing texts for a fairly select audience, and Ricci, the bottom of the industry, which produced cheap texts for a broader and poorer market.[34] All the texts that Chun found to be extraordinarily expensive in the late Ming are for the most part lengthy and sophisticated works of scholarship. Tellingly, the cheapest text he discusses, a collection of arias from plays, sold for 1.2 *qian*, considerably less than the gazetteer mentioned above.[35] The paucity of evidence from the Ming makes it very difficult to correlate

---

32. Hayes, "Specialists and Written Materials in the Village World," pp. 107–8.

33. Idema, Review of Rawski, *Education and Popular Literacy*, p. 322.

34. Ricci might also have been impressed by the *relative* cheapness of Chinese texts generally, for in sixteenth-century Europe books were still expensive luxuries.

35. Chun Shum, "Mingdai fangke tushu zhi liutong yu jiage," p. 113; the title is *Xindiao Wanqu changchun* 新調萬曲長春. Kai-wing Chow (*Publishing, Culture, and Power in Early Modern China*, chap. 1) argues that many books were quite inexpensive by the late Ming.

prices and types of texts, but it seems reasonable to hypothesize that, alongside expensive texts costing 1 to 3 *liang*, the number of texts costing as little as 1 *qian* or less might explain Ricci's observation of "the exceedingly large numbers of books in circulation here and the ridiculously low prices at which they are sold."

Arthur Smith's comments raise this issue as well. The texts Smith mentions—the *Kangxi zidian* and the dynastic histories—are long and thus expensive works.[36] The Sibao edition of the dictionary, at 8.3 *qian* wholesale, was among the industry's more expensive titles; and the Zou and Ma houses apparently did not publish the standard histories (with the exception of an early edition of *Records of the Grand Historian*), perhaps in part because they realized that they could not sell such texts in their markets. Smith's observations also raise the matter of region. Quite possibly books of whatever type were scarcer in the north, where more limited access to cheap paper made them more expensive to produce. In fact, the diffusion of commercial publishing sites in the Qing seems to have been predominantly a phenomenon of the south.[37] Nor, according to two nineteenth-century observers, were schools as common in the north. Williams remarked, "It appears that as one goes north, the extent and thoroughness of education diminishes"; Evariste Huc, too, noted that schools were "rather less numerous in the northern provinces."[38] Perhaps the difference both these men noticed was related to lower levels of book production in the north (or perhaps the lower frequency of schools reduced the demand for books).

Hayes, of course, was discussing an area not far outside Sibao's distribution circuits (there is no evidence that Sibao publishers sold texts in Hong Kong) during roughly the period of Sibao activity. Thus, his testimony is particularly useful. His impression of the paucity of texts in

---

36. As Evelyn Rawski (*Education and Popular Literacy*, p. 122) explains, the edition of the *Kangxi zidian* that Smith mentions was a high quality one, with "'clear type and no false characters.'" Lower quality versions of this dictionary and certainly short "sleeve" dictionaries would sell for considerably less.

37. This is not to say that commercial publishing failed to expand in the north. Beijing, as we saw in Chapter 1, experienced a significant publishing boom, and commercial operations spread to smaller towns—Ji'nan and Liaocheng—as well.

38. Williams, *The Middle Kingdom* (1882 ed.), vol. 1, part 2, p. 544; Huc, *The Chinese Empire*, 1: 111.

the hands of individual peasants, however, was made in the context of reports that described at some length the range of different titles in New Territories villages,[39] titles that correspond in type to many published in Sibao. And his tentative conclusion that most of these texts were in the possession not of all or even most peasants but of village specialists does not necessarily undermine the argument for greater access to texts, or more precisely, to the information conveyed in texts. Rather, it simply indicates that this access may have been indirect, mediated through local experts. Coupled with his rich evidence about the titles present in New Territories villages, Hayes's conclusion suggests that even peasants living in hinterland areas of south China had access to textual culture by the nineteenth century, if only through the medium of a local specialist. This same argument applies to Idema's view that "the perennially poor peasantry" could not afford to buy even the cheapest texts: they might nonetheless, through a village scribe, ritual master, or fortune-teller, absorb something of the contents of book culture. And of course not all peasants were too poor to buy books; the better-off among them might find the low investment required by the cheapest of Sibao's texts worth the access to literacy or the cultural capital that book ownership offered.

I am arguing here, then, for a broader and deeper circulation of texts and the information in them throughout south China in the Qing, certainly by the nineteenth century, although most likely by the late eighteenth century. Because of the proliferation of lower- and middle-level commercial publishing operations and the development of new networks of text distribution in hinterland and even frontier areas, books were accessible to a geographically and socially broader swath of the population. Gentry and well-to-do merchants, by virtue of spending power and access to cultural centers, had enjoyed increasing access to texts as early as the late Ming. By the mid-Qing, access to books had increased as well for peasants and petty traders living in the hinterlands or in frontier areas as far distant from the major cultural centers of Jiangnan or the southeast coast as western Guangxi. These peasants

---

39. In addition to Hayes, "Specialists and Written Materials in the Village World," see idem, "Popular Culture of Late Ch'ing and Early Twentieth Century China"; and idem, "Popular Culture in Late Ch'ing China."

and petty traders might not themselves have been regular purchasers of texts, although it seems likely that the more prosperous of them would have been able to afford at least the cheapest of Sibao's texts. But even if they did not buy books themselves, they (and their poorer fellows) could have gained access to the culture of books through the agency of a literate village specialist in education, ritual, medicine, fortune-telling, or story-telling, through oral recitation or performance, through the mediation of a paid reader, or perhaps through the rental of books.

## *The Book Cultures of the Qing*

What does this broader circulation of texts and textual knowledge mean for our understanding of Chinese book culture and the thorny problem of literacy? Did the fact that more people had access to texts create a fully integrated book culture and stimulate a significant increase in literacy?

Research on the output of publishers in such regionally and demographically disparate areas as Chengdu (a considerable urban center), Xuwanzhen (a flourishing market town), Yuechi (a county seat in a poor rural area), and Sibao (an isolated cluster of peasant villages) in the high and late Qing reveals a surprising homogeneity in types and often in titles of texts printed. Basic primers, examination guides, Classics, histories, medical manuals, divination guides, and novels and stories— the striking similarity of titles among all these genres suggests that by the eighteenth century a kind of common book culture had developed in much of southern China. From a publisher's point of view, such works were sure sellers; from a buyer's, they were a good investment, in part because of their timelessness—a single volume could be used by several generations of a family. They also had an appeal that transcended regional boundaries. Many of these texts were part of what Glen Dudbridge has named the "metropolitan language culture."[40] Often written in the common language of officialdom, *guanhua* 官話, they were accessible to any literate, anywhere in the empire. Texts might, to be sure, be read in different ways by readers at different literacy and

---

40. Dudbridge, *China's Vernacular Cultures*, p 6.

status levels (not to mention the variations imposed by the fertility of individual imaginations)—and, indeed, certain texts, in their format and organization, *invited* different readings[41]—but there does appear to have been a fairly large pool of texts that overlapped all markets. These core texts, roughly homogeneous in type and stable over time, were produced at all levels of the publishing hierarchy, from the most sophisticated of Beijing publishing houses to the cruder printing rooms of Sibao or Yuechi—although, to be sure, at different levels of quality, from fine to shoddy.

This core conforms closely to the Sibao model of textual popular culture outlined in Chapter 13; it consisted of (1) educational works (primers, the Four Books and Five Classics, and some supplemental educational material); (2) how-to guides (ritual and etiquette manuals, household encyclopedias, medical manuals, prescription-recipe collections, fortune-telling handbooks, and almanacs); and (3) fiction, songbooks, and some popular poetry collections. Presumably this core of apparently shared titles or types of texts accounts for a larger and larger share of the output of publishers as we descend the hierarchy of publishing sites. That is, larger, more centrally located publishing industries (such as those in Beijing or the cities of Jiangnan) might print a great many other titles in addition or expand one part of the core, specializing, say, in the production of dramas (as many Nanjing houses did in the late Ming).[42] As one moves down the publishing hierarchy, good business sense would seem to dictate an increasingly tight focus on the common core—on proven popular titles for a broad market. In the eighteenth and nineteenth centuries, the rise of more rural, lower-level publishing sites like Sibao, dependent on this core of texts for their survival, would in turn reinforce the homogeneity of imprints offered for sale. This kind of dialectic between supply and demand would have had particular force in the markets Sibao served, where limitations on supply shaped demand.

The existence of a fairly stable common core of texts has been seen as evidence for "the uniformity of the Chinese cultural heritage and for

---

41. See Brokaw, "Reading the Best-sellers of the Nineteenth Century."

42. See Hegel, "Niche Marketing for Late Imperial Fiction," pp. 248–53; and Chia, "Of Three Mountains Street: The Commercial Publishers of Ming Nanjing," pp. 137–40.

how highly its written basis was valued, how widely it was spread, and how deeply it penetrated."[43] In taking this common core of texts to the hinterlands of south China, the Sibao publisher-booksellers were, as they repeatedly remind us, spreading culture. And, in transmitting the technology of block cutting to Yunnan and Guizhou, the Yuechi block cutters were introducing the means by which this common core of texts could be reproduced on the frontiers of China Proper and, in their own way, spreading Chinese culture.

Thus, the extension of commercial publishing and the technology of woodblock printing (and the increase in schools) operated throughout the Qing both to deepen and to extend cultural integration. Even those peasant boys who had studied the basic primers of elementary education only briefly and inadequately would retain some scraps of knowledge in common with members of the elite who had thoroughly mastered works like the *Sanzi jing, Youxue gushi qionglin*, and the Four Books, enough perhaps to explain Smith's observation that "the classical wisdom of the Ancients is the common heritage of all the sons and daughters of Han." And the songbooks and much of the chapbook fiction widely distributed by publishers like the Zou and Ma, as David Johnson has pointed out, by virtue of the link they formed between the written and the oral, "played a crucial role in the complex process by which elements of elite literary culture were translated into terms that the illiterate could understand."[44]

Integration was by no means a simple trickle-down process. While orthodox and elite values were incorporated into popular educational texts and ritual handbooks, for example, beliefs and attitudes not fully compatible with these values—and in some cases overtly critical of elites and the sociopolitical status quo—were transmitted in fortune-telling guides, fiction, and songbooks. Fiction, drama, and songbooks in particular functioned as pivotal texts in this two-way integration: they might reinforce orthodox morality at the same time that they satirized the existing power structure and celebrated heroes and heroines who regularly violated orthodox norms.

---

43. Hayes, "Specialists and Written Materials in the Village World," p. 110.

44. Johnson, "Communication, Class, and Consciousness in Late Imperial China," p. 65.

The increased publication of the "common-core" texts defined above also served to broaden the scope of cultural integration as booksellers like the sojourning Zou and Ma carried them to hinterland and frontier areas in the eighteenth and nineteenth centuries. These booksellers were bringing the universal textual culture—and thus, to some degree, Chinese civilization—to villagers in the poorer areas of Jiangxi, Guangdong, and eastern Guangxi and to new settlers in western Guangxi, Yunnan, and Guizhou. Their work supported the spread of schools (such as the hundreds of *yixue* founded by Chen Hongmou in Yunnan) and helped knit regions distant from the major seats of culture and learning into the web of an integrated culture.

We might at this point question, however, if not the fact of deeper and broader integration, then the uniformity of beliefs, values, and references this integration is said to have supported. As explained in Chapter 13, the common core of texts was itself heterogeneous. Titles ranged widely in linguistic sophistication and differed in the values they expressed and models they presented to readers. The potential range of meanings over different editions of the same title also implies widely different reading choices and practices. This obtained even within the Sibao industry: differences in types of prefaces, commentaries, punctuation, page layout, illustration, paper quality, binding, and so forth affected the reading experience and, presumably, the degree to which individual readers accepted or participated in a common culture. Between Sibao and luxury editions, the contrast in reading experience was likely to be significantly sharper. And the status of a book or books within a household— whether collector's item, luxury, commonplace resource for education and entertainment, or rare and highly valued (no matter how cheap the purchase price) link to a distant elite culture—might also condition the experience of reading. More obviously, the way in which a text was absorbed—through private reading, instruction in school, oral performance, or transmission by a literate specialist to an illiterate audience— might influence its impact it on different "readers." In sum, the existence of a common core of texts and the persistence of the body of shared references this core doubtless created in the Qing probably disguises a range of different experiences and interpretations.[45]

---

45. See Brokaw, "Reading the Best-sellers of the Nineteenth Century."

Other powerful reasons militate against an easy assumption of a simple cultural uniformity achieved through dissemination of a common core of texts. There were at least two other categories of imprints—two other book cultures—that served to undermine the unifying impact of the common core. First, there was a category of texts produced largely (although not exclusively) in major urban centers, or at least major publishing sites, for a highly educated, elite readership. This "select" category included, distinctively, esoteric works of scholarship and facsimile reproductions of rare texts; new works valued for their contemporaneity, their relevance to ongoing scholarly or literary debates or current fashions (in the Qing, for example, the development of empirical research scholarship); and finely edited and produced editions of standard belles-lettres, history, and philosophy texts. Certain publishers, like some of the Huizhou merchants or the drama-and-fiction publishers of late Ming Nanjing, might produce only such rarefied texts and market them to a wealthy, elite audience. Publishers like the Zou and Ma of western Fujian did not, generally speaking, produce this type of text. Although the Sibao publishers were careful to keep up with changes in the examination literature that constituted a significant proportion of their business, they did not produce works of empirical research or facsimile reproductions of Song editions.

Second, there existed a category of specialized local imprints, either texts produced by local residents largely for local consumption, such as the poetry collections of obscure local authors, or texts written in a local dialect. The audience for such texts, like that for the common core of universally popular texts, would be socially diverse, encompassing all status levels, but unlike the common core audience, it would be geographically limited. The type of text that I have encountered most frequently in this category are songbooks written in local dialects—in the Pearl River Delta region, for example, the wooden-fish books in Cantonese; or, in western Fujian, *Zhao Yulin* in Hakka; or in Chaozhou in Guangdong, a large store of songbooks recounting local legends and fictionalized accounts of local scandals in Chaozhouhua.[46] These

---

46. On the Chaozhou songbooks, see Chen Jingxi, "Qingmo Minguo ban Chaozhou quce shulu"; and the *Chuban zhi* volume of *Guangdong shengzhi*, p. 71.

distinctive regional songbooks allowed the literate in a community to enjoy a special and exclusive type of literature, an enjoyment that might be shared by the semi-literate or even illiterate members of the same community, who could "read" such works through oral performances.

There might be other texts in this category as well—Sibao's two elementary textbooks in the local Hakka subdialect, *Renjia riyong* and *Yinian shiyong zaziwen*, for example.[47] The Suwei shanfang bookstore in Zhangzhou also published a dictionary in the local dialect, *Shiwu yin*, as well as a collection of popular stories about Zhangzhou.[48] Possibly, too, stories set in particular regions and employing some regional dialect—like *Jingfu xinshu* or *Lingnan yishi*, both set in Guangdong—might be restricted in popularity. These "local interest" texts might be published by regional publishing concerns, like the Sibao publishing houses, whose sales orbit included the locales of the stories, or by local shops that specialized exclusively in their publication (for example, a cluster of small publishing houses in late nineteenth- and early twentieth-century Chaozhou were "niche" publishers of local songbooks).[49]

It was this type of text that helped perpetuate distinctive local cultural traditions parallel to—although not entirely unrelated to—the "universal" core textual culture described above. Thus, at the same time that the Sibao booksellers were carrying the core texts of the common culture to frontier areas, "civilizing" (as the Zou and Ma themselves claimed) local populations of mixed ethnicity, they were also distributing Hakka texts to the immigrant Hakka populations along their bookselling routes, strengthening awareness of ethnic differences in new areas of settlement. In this way, Chinese book culture offered a flexibility of association rather similar to that found in the ritual system. We might, in fact, describe its operation in terms borrowed from James

---

47. For examples from the Ming, see van der Loon, *The Classical Theatre and Art Song of Southern Fukien.*

48. Interview 68, 12/5/95 (Wuge).

49. Such texts could also be published by shops quite distant from their points of origin or sale, however. Anne McLaren (*Chinese Popular Culture and Ming* Chantefables, pp. 44–45) suggests that in the fifteenth-century chantefables based on stories of southern origin and often using the rhyming patterns of the Wu dialect may have been published in Beijing and then distributed by traveling merchants in the Suzhou area.

Watson's analysis of the function of ritual: "[It] was so flexible that those who called themselves Chinese could have their cake and eat it too: They participated in a unified centrally organized culture and at the same time celebrated their local or regional [and, I would add here, status] differences."[50]

The existence of different book cultures in the Qing complicates, then, claims made for the uniformity of Chinese culture and the deep integrative function of the expanding book trade. Although the broader distribution of the common core of texts by publishers like the Zou and Ma promoted cultural integration, the variety within that common core (in contents, linguistic levels, and production qualities) and the operation of two other book cultures—an exclusive elite book culture and a multiplicity of distinctive regional book cultures—tempered the homogenizing impact of that core.

## *Literacy, Social Status, and Political Power*

Relevant to this question, too, is the social, cultural, and political function of text-based integration. Did the broader and deeper circulation of texts in the Qing and the cultural integration associated with the common core texts increase literacy, encourage social integration, and make for easier access to elite status?

### LITERACY AND EDUCATION
### IN LATE IMPERIAL CHINA

At first glance it might seem obvious that a broader and deeper circulation of texts would naturally increase literacy and thus opportunities for upward mobility, particularly in a society where literacy was a prerequisite for social and political advance. But consideration of the nature of literacy (and of education) in late imperial China suggests that the relationship was not necessarily so clearly direct.[51]

---

50. Watson, "The Structure of Chinese Funerary Rites," p. 17.

51. In thinking through the problems of literacy, I have relied on the work of Harvey Graff, in particular *The Literacy Myth*.

It is hard to find a topic for which the sources are more irritatingly contradictory.[52] Adriano de las Cortes claimed, as early as the 1620s, "It is rare that a boy, even if he is the son of a miserably poor Chinese of low status, does not know how to read and write."[53] Roughly two centuries later, Medhurst, writing in the 1830s, made a similar observation: "The number of individuals acquainted with letters in China, is amazingly great. One half of the male population are able to read."[54] Mid-century, Huc presented an even rosier picture: "With few exceptions, every Chinese knows how to read and write, at least sufficiently for the ordinary occasions of life. Thus the workmen, the peasants even, are capable of taking notes concerning their daily affairs, of carrying on their own correspondence, of reading the proclamations of the Mandarins, and often also the productions of the current literature."[55] And in 1888, Ernst Eitel vigorously asserted that most Chinese could read, adducing as evidence the ease with which the common people were able to carry out "important and complicated commercial transactions" in written Chinese and understand "the placards and advertisements posted up at every street corner" in Hong Kong, although these were "couched in the written characters used by Confucius."[56] Nor were Western observers the only ones to make such claims. Ye Mingchen 葉名琛 (1807–59), while serving as governor-general of Guangdong and Guangxi in the 1850s, asserted that "there is not a

---

52. Erling von Mende ("Literacy in Traditional China"), who favors a rather generous estimate of literacy in late Qing China, has collected examples of the range of views to be found in nineteenth- and early twentieth-century, largely Western, sources.

53. De las Cortes, *Le Voyage en Chine*, p. 191.

54. Medhurst, *China*, p. 106.

55. Huc, *The Chinese Empire*, 1: 111; cited in Rawski, *Education and Popular Literacy*, p. 2.

56. Eitel attacked "the assumption that the written Chinese character is a foreign tongue to the ordinary Chinaman, the exclusive monopoly and sacred mystery of a literary caste, and therefore useless as a medium for reaching the heart and life of the common people." For example, "when Chiarini wishes to inform the two-hundred thousand Chinese of Hongkong that he will open his circus to-morrow evening at 9 p.m., he has not the slightest difficulty in making every possible detail of his exhibition known, in a few hours, to every Chinaman or Chinawoman in Hongkong, but he does it by using the classical written language of China" (Eitel, Review of *Learning to Read in South China*, p. 119; cited in part in von Mende, "Literacy in Traditional China," p. 53).

single household in China which has not at least one member able to read."[57]

Yet there is also considerable testimony to the contrary. Williams, writing at about the same time as Huc, gave a much more pessimistic (or nuanced) view of literacy in China. After briefly pointing out the considerable demographic variation in reading abilities (urban males are likely to be able to read, whereas in "less thickly settled districts, not more than four or five tenths, and even less, can read"), he wrote:

Owing to the manner in which education is commenced,—learning the form and names [pronunciations] of characters before their meaning and connexion are understood, it comes to pass that many persons can run over the names of the characters on a page while they do not comprehend the meaning of what they read. They can pick out a word here and there which they know, it may be a phrase or a sentence, but they derive no clearer meaning from what they read than a lad who has just learned to scan, and had proceeded half through the Latin Reader, does from reading Virgil; while in both cases an intelligent audience, unacquainted with the circumstances, might justly infer that the reader understood what he was reading as well as his hearers did. Moreover, among the Chinese, different subjects demand the use of different characters; and although a man may be well versed in the classics or in legal writings, he may be easily posed by being asked to explain a simple treatise in medicine or mathematics, in consequence of the many new or unfamiliar words on every page. This is a serious obstacle in the way of obtaining a general acquaintance with books.[58]

Some thirty years later, in 1880, an anonymous reviewer of W. A. P. Martin's *Hanlin Papers* cited an unnamed "native scholar" as "admit[ing] that one in twenty was about the average of those who might reasonably try for degrees, but . . . that ten in twenty might be able to keep accounts and write business and family letters."[59]

In a work published in 1886, the American missionary Edwin Dukes provides perhaps the clearest analysis of the question, expanding on

---

57. Ye is quoted in a report by C. Alabaster in 1859; "Memorandum on Education in China Drawn Up from Information Afforded by the Ex-Imperial Commissioner Yeh," p. 49. On Ye, see Hummel, *Eminent Chinese of the Ch'ing Period*, pp. 904–5.

58. Williams, *The Middle Kingdom* (1882 ed.), vol. 1, part 2, pp. 544–45.

59. "*Hanlin Papers*. Essays on the Intellectual Life of the Chinese," p. 110; cited in von Mende, "Literacy in Traditional China," p. 53.

points made by both Williams and the anonymous Chinese scholar. Remarking that "one of the commonest delusions in regard to China is that all the people can read," he goes on to emphasize that this perception of widespread literacy is based on a faulty assessment of what it takes to be literate in Chinese:

> There is scarcely an adult male but can pick out a few characters here and there in a proclamation posted on the wall, but, in the Chinese language, to know a few characters does not assist one in the least to understand the meaning of others. Multitudes can read the characters so as to know the names of hundreds of them without being able to read a book so as to make out the sense of it. There is also an exceedingly numerous class of men who can read one book, but not another.[60]

As Dukes suggests here, the calculation, or even estimation, of literacy in China is extraordinarily complicated, not susceptible to neat summation in a single percentage rate (which we do not, in any event, have sufficient evidence to develop).

Certainly access to—or even possession of—texts is no necessary indicator of literacy. As Idema has argued, in the absence of direct sources of information, what is crucial to our estimates of literacy is the customary nature of education: the fact that, although many males received at least some schooling, few were able to continue their schooling to the achievement of basic general literacy (the ability to read and comprehend a simple prose text in a nontechnical vocabulary). Moreover, since standard teaching methods might delay instruction in the meaning of words for several years, a poor boy could leave elementary school (the *mengguan*) with only the barest grasp of the skills required for literacy. J. Macgowan, writing in the early twentieth century, argued, in essence, that early education in China was often a waste of time:

> All these boys [that is, those who have had only four or five years of schooling] have acquired a certain smattering of knowledge, which, however, is absolutely

---

60. Dukes, *Along River and Road in Fuh-kien*, pp. 244–45; cited in Rawski, *Education and Popular Literacy*, pp. 2–3. For other samples of views on this question, see W. A. P. Martin, *The Lore of Cathay*, pp. 300–301; Woodside and Elman, "Afterword: The Expansion of Education in Ch'ing China," pp. 530–32; von Mende, "Literacy in Traditional China," *passim*; Idema, *Chinese Vernacular Fiction*, xliv–lxiv; and idem, Review of Rawski, *Education and Popular Literacy*, pp. 317–22.

useless to them for the purpose of enabling them to read. One constantly meets with men that can read a page of a book who have not the remotest idea of what the meaning of the passage is. This is because they left school before the second stage in their education was reached [that is, before entering the *jingguan*], and therefore for all practical purposes they are no better off than those who have never received any instruction when they were lads.[61]

Lack of opportunity to practice reading skills also limited the benefits of schooling. Poor schoolboys in rural family schools might pick up a few phrases from primers like *Sanzi jing* or perhaps even from the Four Books—they might, in fact, even memorize whole texts and learn something of their meaning—but without the reinforcement of continual use, the characters they had learned would quickly be wholly or partially forgotten. Dukes, again, makes this point:

There is an immense class of men who knew a good deal of the character in their younger days, but who, in a country without newspapers and magazines and the ordinary kinds of mental stimulus that obtain among ourselves, have grown very rusty in it. It is, let us say, extremely easy to forget the arbitrary and unalphabetical hieroglyphics that form the written medium of the language. Another considerable class consists of those who through pressure of business, infirmity, and, above all, short-sightedness, have for many years lost the art of reading.[62]

In consequence, then, of the nature of the Chinese language and of methods of education, many men who, when young, had "enjoyed" several years of education, retained only a partial, perhaps fragmentary, grasp of the written language.

Not surprisingly, then, estimates of literacy in nineteenth-century China have varied widely. Different definitions of literacy explain some of this variation. Frederick Mote concluded that "a literacy rate of ten per cent, or very possibly more, is virtually inescapable," including among the literate both those who had achieved "full" or "high" literacy (and thus were qualified to take the examination for licentiate status) and those who had attained "basic" or "functional" literacy (including "sub-officials, clerks, merchants and traders, military men other than

---

61. Macgowan, *Sidelights on Chinese Life*, p. 258.
62. Dukes, *Along River and Road in Fuh-kien*, pp. 246–47.

holders of military degrees, Buddhist and Taoist clergy, and even some women").[63] Roughly the same statistics are offered, in a rather offhand manner, by the anonymous Chinese scholar cited above; for him, 5 percent of the adult male population (perhaps 1.25 percent of the total population) was literate enough to sit for the examinations,[64] and apparently 50 percent of that same population (and thus about 12.5 percent of the total population) had achieved what Mote identifies as functional literacy.

Evelyn Rawski has developed probably the most generous estimate of literacy rates for the nineteenth century—quadrupling Mote's figure—using a definition of literacy that ranges from knowledge of a few hundred characters to "full" literacy. She concludes that "basic" or "functional" literacy was "unevenly distributed between males and females, with perhaps 30 to 45 percent of males and only 2 to 10 percent of females possessing some ability to read and write."[65] But scholars have questioned the low end of a definition such as Rawski's, on the grounds that knowledge of a few hundred characters was in effect useless.[66]

More conservatively, Idema has proposed that, given the uneven distribution and high dropout rate of schooling and the frequent failure of those only "basically" literate to retain what they had learned, a male literacy rate of about 20 to 25 percent is reasonable.[67] Here he seems to employ a three-tiered definition of literacy: "moderate literacy," the ability to understand simple books "more or less, if written in an easy style" and to use a limited number of characters (estimated at about 2,000)[68] "in largely practical ways, as in book-keeping or letter-writing."

---

63. Mote, "China's Past in the Study of China Today," pp. 109–10.

64. "*Hanlin Papers*. Essays on the Intellectual Life of the Chinese," p. 110. This is the figure that David Johnson ("Communication, Class, and Consciousness in Late Imperial China," p. 59) proposes for "classically educated male commoners" (that is, *tongsheng* and former *tongsheng*) at the beginning of the nineteenth century: 5 percent of the adult male population. See also Idema, *Chinese Vernacular Fiction*, p. xlvii.

65. Rawski, *Education and Popular Literacy*, pp. 22–23.

66. Idema, Review of Rawski, *Education and Popular Literacy*, pp. 321–22.

67. Ibid.

68. The most frequently cited measure of basic literacy is the figure of 2,000 characters. Alexander Woodside ("Real and Imagined Continuities in the Chinese Struggle for Literacy," pp. 23–24, 29–30) has pointed out, however, that there is no firm consen-

The next rung is "full literacy," the ability to "read the Classics and to write a composition according to a set pattern," corresponding roughly to Mote's pool of licentiate candidates. Idema argues that such men might not necessarily be well read or broadly knowledgeable in vocabularies and writings other than the texts of the examination curriculum; therefore he posits a third level of literacy, "high literacy," achieved by those who "engaged in a relatively broad reading program" and who were prepared to take or had taken, examinations for the *juren* degree. [69] (Applying Idema's definition to Sibao's output, I would say that the Zou and Ma were overwhelmingly publishing for readers of moderate and full literacy—and also for those aspiring to literacy.)

The efforts to calculate a literacy rate for Qing China are, in the end, most interesting and helpful for the ways in which they force us to rethink how literacy should be defined in China and how it should be interpreted in the Chinese social and cultural context. They reveal, too, why it is difficult to think of literacy and impossible to calculate a literacy rate for China in quite the same way as for Western societies—the Chinese linguistic, educational, and social context simply demands a different approach. For, in addition to the levels of literacy that Idema and others have defined—levels that certainly exist in Western societies as well—there existed in China highly specialized (and thus quite limited) basic "literacies." The clearest and apparently most realistic example is the specialized literacy that a merchant or petty trader might develop, a narrowly specialized knowledge of the characters for commercial products, the terms used in keeping simple accounts, and the phrases of business letters. Dukes describes just this kind of partial literacy at the conclusion of his tirade on the limits of Chinese literacy:

---

sus on this point; he cites studies that claim a variety of other figures, ranging from 1,500 to 4,261.

69. Here I am conflating arguments made by Idema in two different texts. For the three different levels of literacy, see *Chinese Vernacular Fiction*, pp. li–lii. In his review of Rawski, *Education and Popular Literacy in Ch'ing China* (pp. 321–22), he appears to associate "moderate literacy" with a knowledge of 2,000 characters: "For reading elementary books, one has to be able to recognize (pronounce and understand) roughly 2,000 characters." Contra Rawski's criterion, he argues that knowledge of only a few hundred characters made one "scarcely literate": a rate of 30 percent (not 45 percent) literacy for males is plausible only "if one would adopt Evelyn Rawski's minimal definition of literacy."

"They know the characters they require in their business; it may be a hundred or a thousand. They can often read and write business letters, but they cannot read even a simple book at sight."[70]

Some of the primers and glossaries sold by Sibao and other publishers were apparently designed to teach just such specialized literacy. The *Siyan zazi* glossary, for example, although it includes many terms in general daily use, emphasizes terms and names used in trade. *Shandong zhuangnong riyong zazi*, a glossary popular in the north, taught peasants' sons the basic vocabulary they would need in their rural communities.[71] The Hakka *Renjia riyong* would have performed a similar function for Sibao's peasant readers. The nonalphabetic nature of the Chinese language made this kind of highly specialized "literacy" relatively easy,[72] at least achievable even for a poor trader's or peasant's son with little time for schooling.

The nature of education in vocations other than officialdom did not either require or encourage students to gain general literacy. There are few intermediate or advanced texts for instruction in business or agriculture within the common core of texts widely distributed by commercial publishers. The merchant manuals that Richard Lufrano has studied are not textbooks of commerce—that is, there is no evidence that they were conceived as texts in any kind of business education.[73] Agricultural manuals, which were specialized technical works, were in a sense advanced texts for instruction in farming. But they appear to have been intended not as instructional texts to be distributed to peasants but, rather, as handbooks for elite managers or district magistrates to consult and use as guides in demonstrating farming techniques to their tenants and bondservants or local peasants. For the most part farmers, merchants, and craftsmen had to learn their jobs on the job; even phy-

---

70. Dukes, *Along River and Road in Fuh-kien*, p. 247. For more on this type of literacy, see Rawski, *Education and Popular Literacy*, pp. 1–4 and chap. 6.

71. Evelyn Rawski discusses these works in *Education and Popular Literacy*, pp. 128–29, 137–38.

72. Rawski, *Education and Popular Literacy*, p. 2. Rawski here notes, "With a nonalphabetic language, individuals with knowledge of a limited number of characters possessed narrowly specialized vocabularies."

73. As Richard Lufrano (*Honorable Merchants*, pp. 51–67, 182–86) points out, they are concerned more with asserting Confucian values and goals of self-cultivation for merchants than with any specialized and technical instruction in commerce.

sicians learned their trade through an apprentice system (although, thanks to publishers like the Zou and Ma, they did have a store of textbooks to draw on).[74] As Williams explains, in describing the training of merchants and craftsmen:

The number of years spent at school depends upon the position and prospects of the parents. Tradesmen, mechanics, and country gentlemen endeavor to give their sons a competent knowledge of the usual series of books, so that they can creditably manage the common affairs of life. No other branches of study are pursued than the classics and histories, and practice in composing; no arithmetic or any department of mathematics, nothing of the geography of their own or other countries. . . . Consequently, persons in these classes of society are obliged to put their sons into shops or counting-houses to obtain the routine of business with a knowledge of figures and the style of letter writing; they are not kept at school more than three or four years, nor as long as that if the family be poor.[75]

Thus a future merchant might begin his education with a specialized primer and then, in the absence of any more advanced texts (or in the absence of the leisure or funds to continue study), shift to hands-on learning in business. Or he might begin with the "classic" (and classical) primers *Sanzi jing* and *Qianzi wen*, and move on, if his family's resources allowed, to the Four Books, but then be diverted into the completely different educational track of apprenticeship in a merchant house.[76] In the latter case, his later training had almost nothing to do with his early education, and notwithstanding that education, he might well end up, as Dukes suggests, able to write business letters but incapable of reading "even a simple book at sight."

---

74. Leung, "Medical Instruction and Popularization in Ming-Qing China," pp. 145–49.

75. Williams, *The Middle Kingdom* (1882 ed.), vol. 1, part 2, p. 542. Alabaster, paraphrasing information provided by Ye Mingchen, confirms Williams's point: "They [the Chinese] have no industrial, agricultural or Art-Schools, sons, generally following in the footsteps of their fathers, thus rendering these unnecessary, for although, says the Ex-Commissioner[,] their establishment might lead to improvement, they are not required, things going on very well as they are, and no improvement being wanted" ("Memorandum on Education in China Drawn Up from Information Afforded by the Ex-Imperial-Commissioner Yeh," p. 52).

76. For the education of apprentices and the texts used in that education, see Lufrano, *Honorable Merchants*, pp. 68–85.

Well below men with this kind of specialized partial literacy was the mass of peasants and laborers possessed of fragmentary literacy—that is, knowledge of perhaps a few hundred random characters comprising some place-names or terms but insufficient as a foundation for advancement either to general basic literacy or to the specialized literacy of a craft or business. A study of rickshaw coolies in Chengdu in the 1930s concluded that "57 percent of such coolies could read at least some written characters"—and presumably this knowledge was useful in their work.[77] But it was far from a meaningful ability to read.

In this context, then, the greater access to texts, particularly primers and elementary educational works, unaccompanied by any changes in the structure of education, might well have done little to stimulate a significant increase in full literacy, although it may have promoted moderate literacy and almost certainly would have advanced the spread of specialized or limited—we might even say stunted—basic "literacies."

## THE SOCIAL AND POLITICAL IMPACT
## OF POPULAR TEXTUAL CULTURE

Given the limits of education and the nature of literacy, what impact would the widespread distribution of texts—in particular, the common core of texts that dominated the output of Sibao and other commercial publishing enterprises—have had on late imperial Chinese society and social mobility? Most likely, it would have stimulated an increase in the numbers of men and women who achieved some degree of literacy. What is less certain is the degree to which this increase in literacy opened up opportunities for upward mobility through the primary path of advancement, the civil-service examination system, and access to effective social and political power. The distance between peasants and merchants who, after a few years of schooling, might dimly remember tags from the *Sanzi jing* and the Four Books and students who had mastered that literature thoroughly enough to pass the civil-service examinations and become *jinshi, juren,* or even simply licentiates, remained vast.

---

77. Woodside and Elman, "Afterword," p. 530; the study cited is Yong Ming, "Chengdushi de renli chefu."

In maintaining that distance, the quality of the texts produced by some of the commercial publishers of the Qing played a role. The first task commonly set a teacher in Qing teaching manuals—going through the textbook with his students to correct all the mistakes—suggests the prevalence of error-riddled editions.[78] How could such textbooks offer students suffering under an inadequate teacher or readers struggling through the texts on their own any hope of genuine comprehension and mastery? Furthermore, the texts that offered specialized and limited literacy (such as *Shanxi zazi bidu* or *Renjia riyong*) generally diverted students from the examination path, without at the same time providing them a very sophisticated education in an alternative profession. The existing method of training men outside the examination track—through specialized primers followed by early apprenticeships—served to confirm and perpetuate existing occupational and socioeconomic distinctions.

Alexander Woodside has made the point that the widely prevailing ceiling on classical education for the lower classes, which was limited to such classical-language primers as *Sanzi jing* and *Qianzi wen*, and the specialized literacies taught in a set of nonclassical elementary texts helped to preserve a small elite founded to a large degree on exclusive control over education/literacy—and thus on limited access to the kind of literacy that mattered, full literacy in classical texts.[79] The penetration of a common core of texts down to small market towns and even to peasant villages in the high and late Qing—unaccompanied by any change in schooling—was thus unlikely to advance the achievement of politically meaningful literacy or the access to elite status in most of the population. Particularly in the late eighteenth and nineteenth centuries, when the examination system had become intensely competitive, poorly printed, error-ridden editions of the Four Books and other examination materials provided a mostly false hope of advancement to political power and elite status. In this context, the more thoroughgoing dissemination of such texts throughout the south China hinterlands likely did considerably more to perpetuate the values and status distinctions

---

78. Gardner, "'To Be a Teacher Is Hard.'"

79. Woodside, "Real and Imagined Continuities in the Chinese Struggle for Literacy," pp. 35–36. See also Johnson, "Communication, Class, and Consciousness in Late Imperial China"; Limin Bai, *Shaping the Ideal Child*, pp. 167–68; and Elman, *A Cultural History of the Civil Examinations*, pp. 374–76.

promulgated by the dominant elite than to offer genuine opportunity for sociopolitical advancement.

This is not to say that the spread of texts had little or no impact on Chinese society. It augmented the opportunities for education, and even minimal literacy might lead to economic and social betterment— presumably merchants who could keep accounts and write letters and peasants who could read land contracts and write tenancy agreements were better off than those who could not. Increased publication of correspondence models, ritual handbooks, medical and pharmaceutical textbooks, *fengshui* manuals, and fortune-telling guides provided the growing population of literates, including many failed examination candidates, with means of mastering occupations outside official service, thereby supporting the development of a new "middle class" of professionals in the Qing.

And, as explained earlier, the proliferation and broader dissemination of texts, by spreading a common store of referents geographically throughout the southern portion of the empire and socially to all statuses, promoted cultural integration and encouraged the development of a more widely and deeply shared cultural identity. This identity, encompassing a rich variety of different beliefs, values, and models, should not be confused with uniformity of thought or practice. Nor should it necessarily be seen as a simple instrument of elite dominance and exclusion. The educational system and the nature of the educational texts in Sibao's "common core" may have limited the development of politically meaningful literacy (that is, literacy leading to examination success and official service), but there were many other texts in the core that could serve to undermine elite authority: stories that challenged the Confucian legitimacy of the status quo might fan awareness of social injustice and political corruption just as easily as the Four Books with Cheng-Zhu commentary might inspire allegiance to the political order. Surely it is no accident that the young revolutionary Mao Zedong, however much he was influenced by Marxist ideals borrowed from the West, modeled himself on the rough-and-ready rebel heroes of *Water Margin*, a text he read (concealed under a copy of the Four Books) as a peasant student in the rural elementary school of Shaoshan 韶山 village, Hunan.[80]

---

80. Snow, *Red Star over China*, pp. 139–40. Mao's favorite reading included other novels published by the Zou and Ma: *Fan Tang yanyi*, *Yue Fei zhuan*, *Xiyou ji*, and *Sanguo yanyi*.

# Appendixes

# APPENDIX A

## *Transport Routes Within the Min-Gan-Yue Region*

A NETWORK OF RIVER and land routes supported the formation of the Min-Gan-Yue 閩贛粵 area as a distinct economic and cultural region.

The Yin River 鄞江 provided a natural transport route from western Fujian to Guangdong province, taking travelers either all the way to the eastern Guangdong coast at Chaozhou 潮州 (as the Han River 韓江 in Guangdong) or toward western Guangdong via the connecting Mei River 梅溪. Minxi 閩西 is also connected, by water routes, to southeastern Jiangxi province. Indeed, the seat of Tingzhou 汀州 prefecture (also Changting 長汀 county seat) was settled in 736 by colonists from Jiangxi who entered Fujian near the mouth of the Sha River 沙溪 (also known as the Qing 清溪) and traveled the short distance from there, along the Ji River 吉溪 (now known as the Wen river 文川), to the upper reaches of the Yin.[1]

Travelers between southeastern Jiangxi and southwestern Fujian could also take advantage of the Gan River 贛江 system and its network of tributaries to travel throughout southern Jiangxi (and through the Meiling 梅嶺 Pass to the North River [Beijiang 北江] in Guangdong). For example, via the Gong River 貢水 and its branches, traders

---

1. Bielenstein, "The Chinese Colonization of Fukien Until the End of the T'ang," pp. 109, 112.

could reach Ruijin 瑞金, Huichang 會昌, Yudu 雩都, Ganzhou 贛州 and, via the Mei River 梅江 and the Qin River 琴水, Ningduzhou 寧都州 and Shicheng 石城 in Jiangxi and Tingzhou and other cities on the Yin in western Fujian. As early as the Tang and Song, the route from Tingzhou to Ganzhou provided Minxi with its most important trade connection. In addition, there was also a poorly maintained road from Tingzhou to the port of Zhangzhou 漳州.[2]

There were also land routes linking Minxi directly to Jiangxi: (1) from Tingzhou to Ruijin and westward through Yudu to Ganzhou; (2) from Tingzhou to Ninghua 寧化 and then to Guangchang 廣昌 and Jianchang 建昌 in eastern central Jiangxi; and (3) from Tingzhou to Pengkou 朋口 in Liancheng 連成 county, then to Xinquan 新泉 and Baisha 白砂 in Shanghang 上杭 county to the county seat and Wuping 武平, and from there westward to Huichang, in southeastern Jiangxi.[3] Residents of western Fujian also had access to Jiangxi through Minbei 閩北: they could pass into northeastern Jiangxi from either Chongan 崇安 county in Jianning 建寧 prefecture (to the Yanshan 鉛山 area in Guangxin 廣信 prefecture) or Guangze 光澤 county in Shaowu 邵武 prefecture (to Jianchang prefecture); or, for that matter, to Zhejiang (and on to the provincial capital, Hangzhou) at Pucheng 浦城.

There were also several overland postal and trade routes from Minxi to Guangdong, often used in combination with the waterways: (1) from Tingzhou through Liancheng to Pengkou, Xinquan, Baisha, Shanghang, and Wuping and on to Pingyuan 平遠 in Guangdong; (2) from Tingzhou to Shanghang, Fengshi 峰市 in Yongding 永定 county, and from there on to Dabu 大埔, Changle 長樂, and Chaozhou, Guangdong; and (3) from Tingzhou to Pengkou, Xinquan, Gutian 古田, and Long-

---

2. Su Jilang, *Tang Song shidai Minnan Quanzhou shidi lungao*, pp. 159, 171–76.

3. *Fujiansheng Longyan diqu gonglu shi*, p. 14. Miki Satoshi ("Qingdai qianqi Fujian nongcun shehui yu diannong kangzu douzheng," p. 54) has also drawn these routes from a study of seven major route books: Huang Bian's 黃汴 *Yitong lucheng tuji* 一統路程圖記 (1570), Tao Chengqing's 陶承慶 *Shangcheng yilan* 商程一覽 (Wanli edition), "Danyizi's" 澹漪子 *Shishang yaolan* 士商要覽 (Qing?), Dai Shiqi's 戴士奇 *Lucheng yaolan* 路程要覽 (Yongzheng era?), Chen Qiji's 陳其楫 *Tianxia lucheng* 天下路程 (1741), Lai Shengyuan's 賴盛遠 *Shiwo zhouxing* 示我周行 (1774), and Wu Zhongfu's 吳中孚 *Shanggu bianlan* 商賈便覽 (1792). See also Brook, *Geographical Sources of Ming-Qing History*, pp. 24–27.

yan 龍巖, from there by the Xiao River 小溪 to Zhangzhou and then southward to Chaozhou.[4]

According to the route books of the day, the most heavily traveled route within this Min-Gan-Yue network was the land-and-water route from Ruijin in southeastern Jiangxi, due east through the Tingzhou prefectural seat, and down the Yin River (the Han River in Guangdong) to Chaozhou. Wang Yeh-chien identifies this circuit ("the Western Area"), with Tingzhou as its pivot, as essential to the import of rice to western Fujian and eastern Guangdong, of salt to Jiangxi, and of timber, tobacco, and paper to Chaozhou in the eighteenth century. He claims, too, that the orientation of this route to areas outside Fujian province suggests that, at least in economic terms, the southwestern prefecture of the province formed a unit distinct from coastal Fujian: "The Western Area with Ting-chou Prefecture as its exclusive domain . . . depended almost entirely on shipments from Kiangsi, and, in so far as grain trade is concerned, had little business to do with the rest of the province."[5]

In terms of trade and transport routes, then, western Fujian more naturally formed a unit with eastern Jiangxi and eastern Guangdong than it did with the rest of Fujian province. Hans Bielenstein suggests that this was the case from the earliest Han settlement of Fujian: settlers of the inland area of the province came from eastern Jiangxi (and southern Zhejiang), whereas migrants to the coastal area formed a separate group of colonists, arriving at the mouth of the Min River 閩江 by sea from Zhejiang.[6] The close ties between western Fujian and eastern Jiangxi persisted through the twentieth century. Medical missionaries working in Tingzhou in 1913 observed that they were treating many Jiangxi natives as well as local Fujianese: patients from "the neighboring Province of Kiang-si" [Jiangxi] were beginning to visit the mission

---

4. *Fujiansheng Longyan diqu gonglu shi*, p. 14; Price and Wiant, "Transportation and Public Works," p. 73; and *Fujian gonglu shi*, pp. 28–29. This last source lists one other route to Guangdong: a combined land and water route from Wuping to Zhenping 鎮平 (p. 29). See also Rawski, *Agricultural Change and the Peasant Economy of South China*, p. 59.

5. Wang Yeh-chien, "Food Supply in Eighteenth-Century Fukien," p. 102.

6. Bielenstein, "The Chinese Colonization of Fukien Until the End of the T'ang," pp. 103–6.

hospital—"It is only two days' journey to the place."[7] It is telling, too, that this region, roughly the area of the Central Soviet, was identified as a distinct unit of revolutionary activity from the late 1920s until the Long March.

Western Fujian was not, however, completely isolated from other parts of the province. The northern portion of Tingzhou prefecture, notably the counties of Ninghua and Qingliu 清流, was also included in a provincial rice-distribution network linking Fuzhou, via the Min River, to northern Fujian (Yanping 延平, Jianning, and Shaowu prefectures).[8] Land routes also connected the west to Shaowu, Shunchang 順昌, Yanping, and Yongan 永安 and gave traders and migrants from Minxi access to southern Zhejiang. And the southern portion of Tingzhou had access to Longyan 龍巖 and, via the Jiulong 九龍江 River, the port of Zhangzhou.

7. London Missionary Society, Report no. 119 (1914), pp. 206c–d.
8. Miki, "Kōzo to sobei," pp. 40–41.

# APPENDIX B

*Value of Woodblocks
from the Juxian tang
and Dawen tang, 1897*

| Title* | Value per 100 blocks (in *yuan*) |
|---|---|
| *Sanjing jinghua* 三經精華 (Essence of the Three Classics) | 6 |
| *Shijing* 詩經 (Classic of songs) | 2.6 |
| *Shujing* 書經 (Classic of history) | 1.7 |
| *Yijing* 經 (Classic of changes) | 1.7 |
| *Wujing jujie* 五經句解 (The Five Classics, explained phrase by phrase) | 3 |
| *Kesun cao* 課孫草 (a calligraphy manual?) | 15** |
| *Yangzheng cao* 養正草 (a calligraphy manual?) | 15** |
| *Yiguan kanyu* 一貫堪輿 (a *fengshui* manual) | 2 |
| *Lizhi xuanjing* 吏治懸鏡 (Mirror of administration) | 2 |
| *Zhengyin cuoyao* 正音撮要 (Resumé of correct pronunciation) | 6 |
| *Yundui xieyu* 韻對屑玉 (a collection of rhymed couplets) | 6 |
| *Cixue quanshu* 詞學全書 (Complete book of *ci* poetry study) | 3 |

*The titles listed in this table are abbreviated in the property-division document. Since it is not always clear what the precise title is, I have in some cases listed a general description of the text rather than translate the abbreviated title.

**A value of 15 *yuan* seems disproportionately high for these texts. Since these entries are the only two that do not include the character for *yuan*, it is possible that the amount meant is 1.5 *yuan* or 0.15 *yuan*.

SOURCE: Document dividing the property of the Juxian tang of Zou Yiting in 1897.

# APPENDIX C

*Genealogical Charts*

C.1  Simplified genealogy of publisher-booksellers in the line of Ma Yipiao
(names of known publisher-booksellers are underlined)

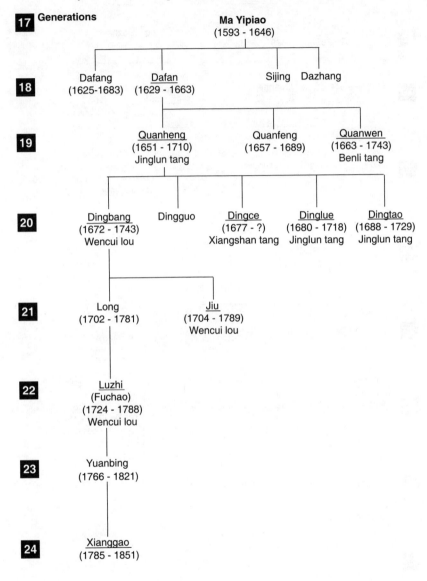

580    *Appendix C*

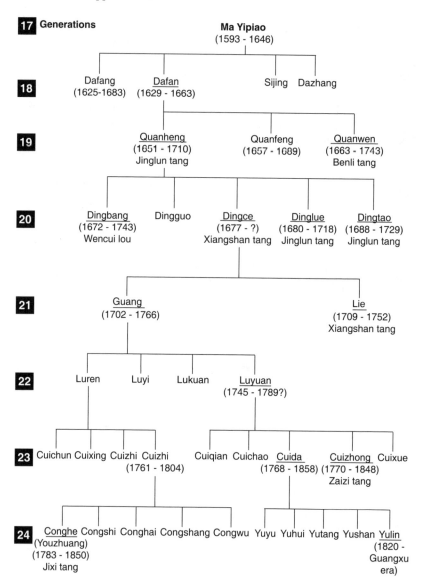

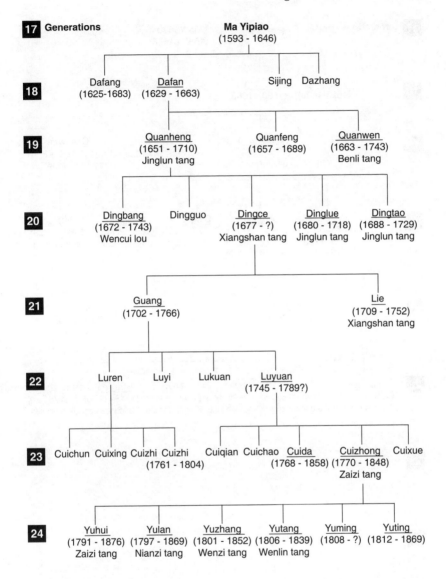

**17** Generations

Ma Yipiao
(1593 - 1646)

**18**
Dafang
(1625-1683)
Dafan
(1629 - 1663)
Sijing   Dazhang

**19**
Quanheng
(1651 - 1710)
Jinglun tang
Quanfeng
(1657 - 1689)
Quanwen
(1663 - 1743)
Benli tang

**20**
Dingbang
(1672 - 1743)
Wencui lou
Dingguo
Dingce
(1677 - ?)
Xiangshan tang
Dinglue
(1680 - 1718)
Jinglun tang
Dingtao
(1688 - 1729)
Jinglun tang

**21**
Guang
(1702 - 1766)
Lie
(1709 - 1752)
Xiangshan tang

**22**
Luren   Luyi   Lukuan   Luyuan
(1745 - 1789?)

**23**
Cuichun  Cuixing  Cuizhi  Cuizhi
(1761 - 1804)
Cuiqian  Cuichao  Cuida
(1768 - 1858)
Cuizhong
(1770 - 1848)
Zaizi tang
Cuixue

**24**
Yuhui
(1791 - 1876)
Zaizi tang
Yulan
(1797 - 1869)
Nianzi tang
Yuzhang
(1801 - 1852)
Wenzi tang
Yutang
(1806 - 1839)
Wenlin tang
Yuming
(1808 - ?)
Yuting
(1812 - 1869)

**25**

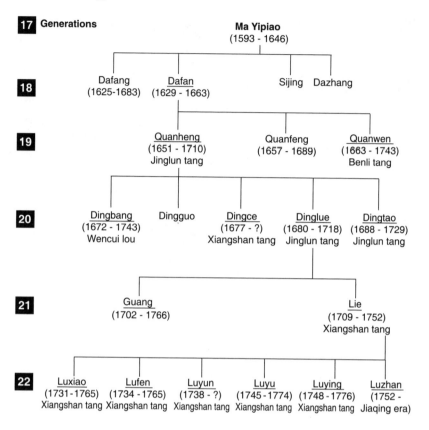

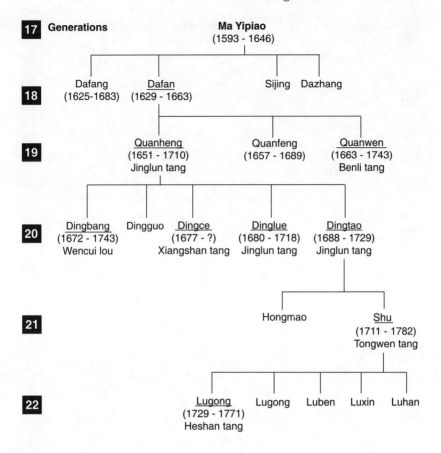

584      *Appendix C*

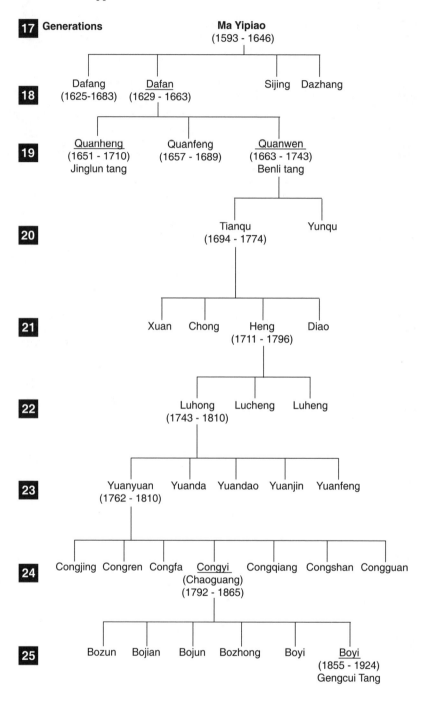

C.2 Simplified genealogy of publisher-booksellers in the line of Zou Dianmo
(names of known publisher-booksellers are underlined)

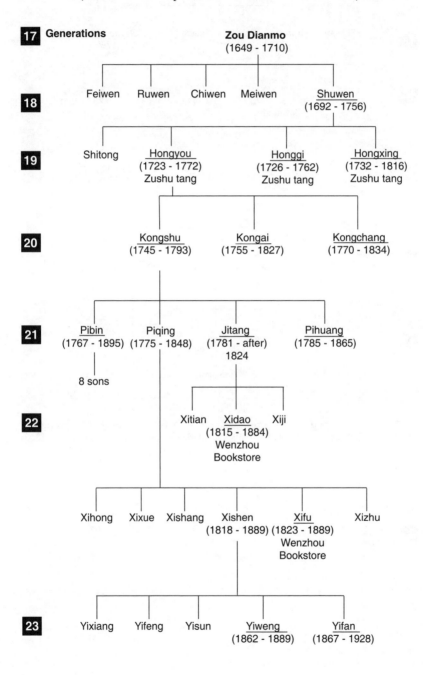

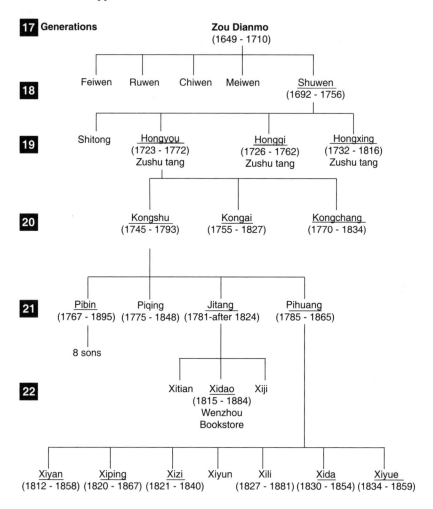

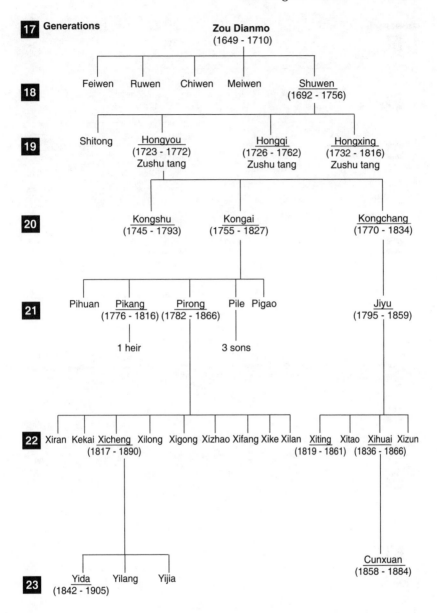

**Generations**

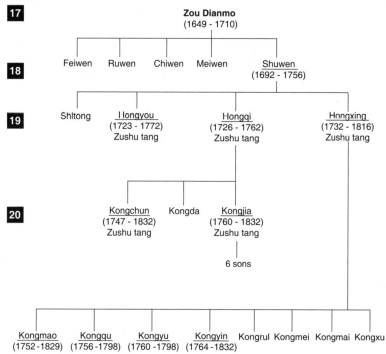

C.3  Simplified genealogy of publisher-booksellers in the line of Zou Zhaoxiong (names of  known publisher-booksellers are underlined)

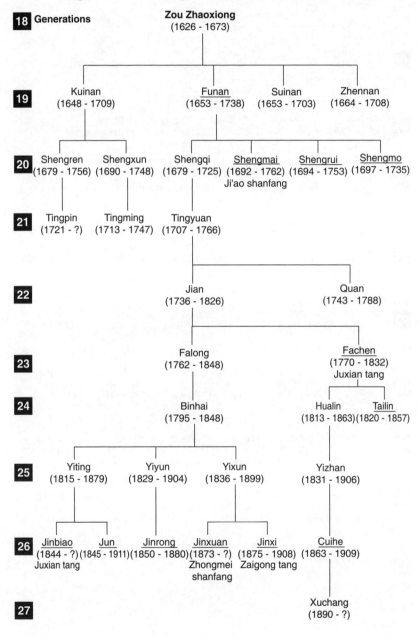

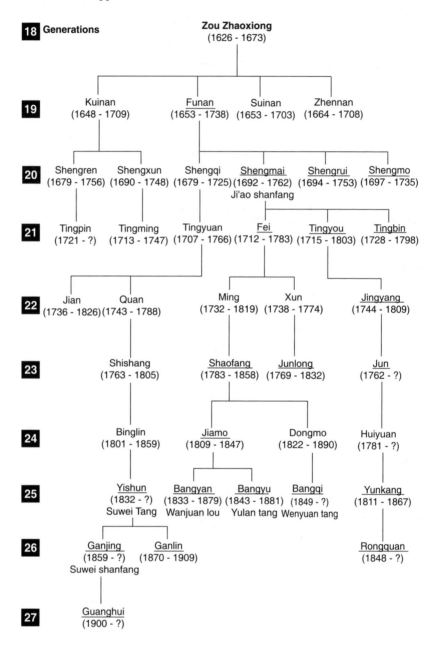

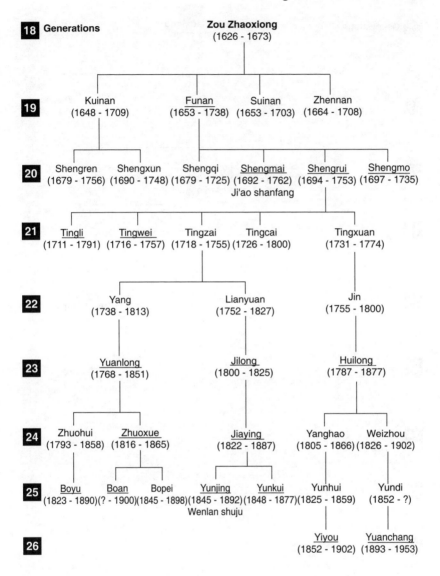

18 Generations

**Zou Zhaoxiong**
(1626 - 1673)

19
Kuinan
(1648 - 1709)

Funan
(1653 - 1738)

Suinan
(1653 - 1703)

Zhennan
(1664 - 1708)

20
Shengren
(1679 - 1756)

Shengxun
(1690 - 1748)

Shengqi
(1679 - 1725)

Shengmai
(1692 - 1762)
Ji'ao shanfang

Shengrui
(1694 - 1753)

Shengmo
(1697 - 1735)

21
Tingli
(1711 - 1791)

Tingwei
(1716 - 1757)

Tingzai
(1718 - 1755)

Tingcai
(1726 - 1800)

Tingxuan
(1731 - 1774)

22
Yang
(1738 - 1813)

Lianyuan
(1752 - 1827)

Jin
(1755 - 1800)

23
Yuanlong
(1768 - 1851)

Jilong
(1800 - 1825)

Huilong
(1787 - 1877)

24
Zhuohui
(1793 - 1858)

Zhuoxue
(1816 - 1865)

Jiaying
(1822 - 1887)

Yanghao
(1805 - 1866)

Weizhou
(1826 - 1902)

25
Boyu
(1823 - 1890)

Boan
(? - 1900)

Bopei
(1845 - 1898)

Yunjing
(1845 - 1892)
Wenlan shuju

Yunkui
(1848 - 1877)

Yunhui
(1825 - 1859)

Yundi
(1852 - ?)

26
Yiyou
(1852 - 1902)

Yuanchang
(1893 - 1953)

27

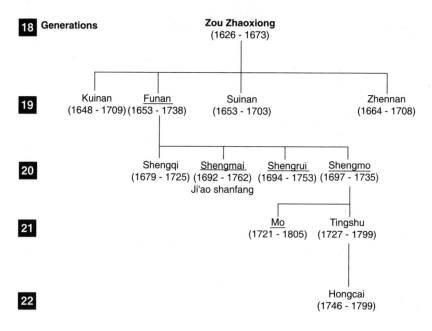

18 Generations

**Zou Zhaoxiong**
(1626 - 1673)

19

Kuinan
(1648 - 1709)

Funan
(1653 - 1738)

Suinan
(1653 - 1703)

Zhennan
(1664 - 1708)

20

Shengqi
(1679 - 1725)
Ji'ao shanfang

Shengmai
(1692 - 1762)

Shengrui
(1694 - 1753)

Shengmo
(1697 - 1735)

21

Mo
(1721 - 1805)

Tingshu
(1727 - 1799)

22

Hongcai
(1746 - 1799)

23

24

25

26

27

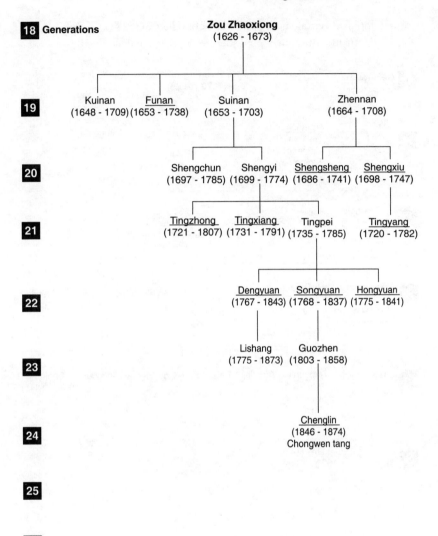

**18** Generations

**Zou Zhaoxiong**
(1626 - 1673)

**19**

Kuinan
(1648 - 1709)

<u>Funan</u>
(1653 - 1738)

Suinan
(1653 - 1703)

Zhennan
(1664 - 1708)

**20**

Shengchun
(1697 - 1785)

Shengyi
(1699 - 1774)

<u>Shengsheng</u>
(1686 - 1741)

<u>Shengxiu</u>
(1698 - 1747)

**21**

<u>Tingzhong</u>
(1721 - 1807)

<u>Tingxiang</u>
(1731 - 1791)

Tingpei
(1735 - 1785)

<u>Tingyang</u>
(1720 - 1782)

**22**

<u>Dengyuan</u>
(1767 - 1843)

<u>Songyuan</u>
(1768 - 1837)

<u>Hongyuan</u>
(1775 - 1841)

**23**

Lishang
(1775 - 1873)

Guozhen
(1803 - 1858)

**24**

<u>Chenglin</u>
(1846 - 1874)
Chongwen tang

**25**

**26**

**27**

C.4 Simplified genealogy of publisher-booksellers in the line of Zou Fuguo (names of known publisher-booksellers are underlined)

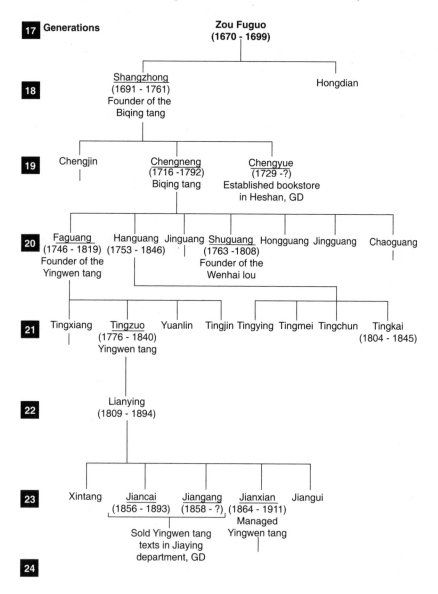

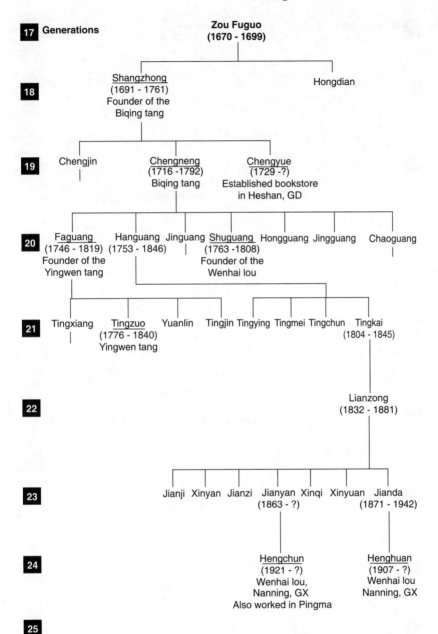

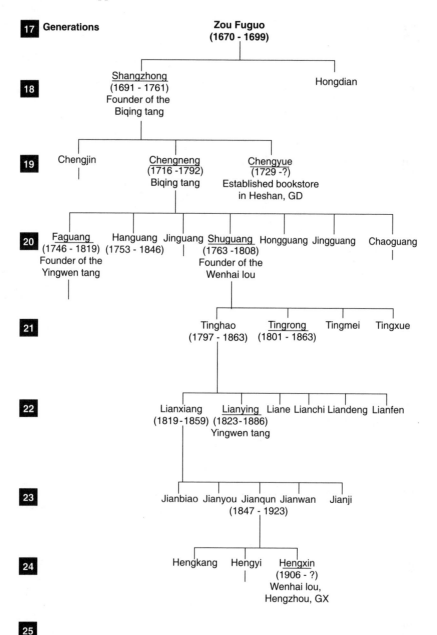

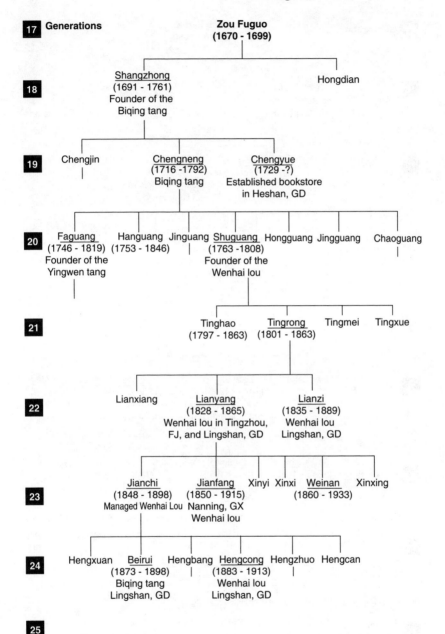

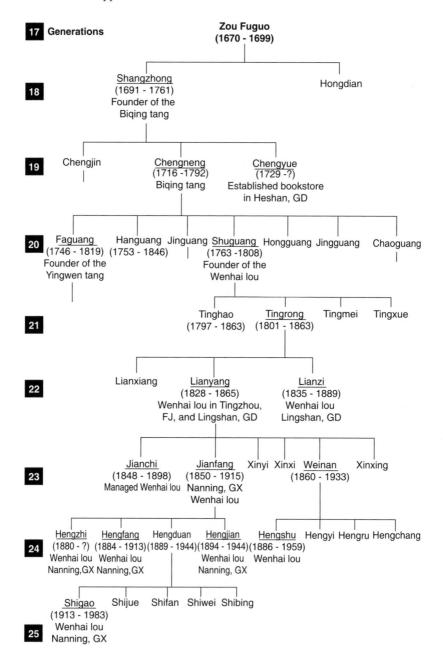

**17** Generations

**Zou Fuguo**
**(1670 - 1699)**

**18**

Shangzhong
(1691 - 1761)
Founder of the
Biqing tang

Hongdian

**19**

Chengjin

Chengneng
(1716 -1792)
Biqing tang

Chengyue
(1729 -?)
Established bookstore
in Heshan, GD

**20**

Faguang
(1746 - 1819)
Founder of the
Yingwen tang

Hanguang
(1753 - 1846)

Jinguang

Shuguang
(1763 -1808)
Founder of the
Wenhai lou

Hongguang

Jingguang

Chaoguang

**21**

Tinghao
(1797 - 1863)

Tingrong
(1801 - 1863)

Tingmei

Tingxue

**22**

Lianxiang

Lianyang
(1828 - 1865)
Wenhai lou in Tingzhou,
FJ, and Lingshan, GD

Lianzi
(1835 - 1889)
Wenhai lou
Lingshan, GD

**23**

Jianchi
(1848 - 1898)
Managed Wenhai lou

Jianfang
(1850 - 1915)
Nanning, GX
Wenhai lou

Xinyi

Xinxi

Weinan
(1860 - 1933)

Xinxing

**24**

Hengzhi
(1880 - ?)
Wenhai lou
Nanning,GX

Hengfang
(1884 - 1913)
Wenhai lou
Nanning,GX

Hengduan
(1889 - 1944)

Hengjian
(1894 - 1944)
Wenhai lou
Nanning, GX

Hengshu
(1886 - 1959)
Wenhai lou

Hengyi

Hengru

Hengchang

**25**

Shigao
(1913 - 1983)
Wenhai lou
Nanning, GX

Shijue

Shifan

Shiwei

Shibing

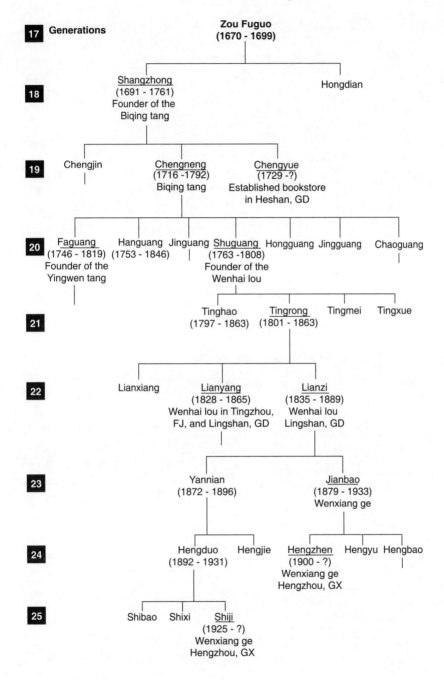

# REFERENCE MATTER

# Works Cited

## Unpublished Sources

### ACCOUNT BOOKS

Account book of Huadeng hui 花燈會 of Mawu, 1897.
Account book of Wenhai lou 文海樓, n.d.
Account book of the Yesheng gong *fang* 葉勝公房, late 19th century.
Account book of Zou Weinan 鄒位南 (1860–1933), Zou Xiyao 鄒希堯 (1866–1926), and Zou Xinfeng 鄒新豐 (fl. late 19th c.).

### PROPERTY-DIVISION DOCUMENTS

Juxian tang, 聚賢堂 of Zou Yiting 鄒翼廷, 1897.
Untitled document, 1853.
Wanjuan lou 萬卷樓, 1897.
Wenhai lou 文海樓, 1894.
Xiangshan tang 湘山堂 of Ma Lie 馬烈, 1773.
Yijing tang 翼經堂 of Ma Yibao 馬益保, Guangxu era.
Yunshen chu 雲深處 of Zou Buchan 鄒步蟬, Daoguang era (1937 copy).
Zaizi tang 在茲堂 of Ma Cuizhong 馬萃仲, 1839.

### PAWN CONTRACTS

Dated 1822 (2), 1849, 1853, and 1863.

BOOK LISTS

Anonymous *shufang* book list, n.d.
Cuiyun tang 萃雲堂 paper inventory, n.d.

DOCUMENTS OF SALE/PURCHASE
OF TEXTS OR WOODBLOCKS

Anonymous, n.d.
Cuiyun tang 萃雲堂, n.d.

GENEALOGIES

*Changting Sibaoli Mashi zupu* 長汀四堡里馬氏族譜. 13 vols. (*juan shou*, 12 *juan*). 1913.
*Fanyang Zoushi zupu* 范陽鄒氏族譜. 34 vols. (*juan shou*, 36 *juan*, *juan mo*). 1947.
*Fanyang Zoushi zupu* 范陽鄒氏族譜. 13 vols. (*juan shou*, 29 *juan*). 1996.
*Mashi dazong zupu* 馬氏大宗族譜. 35 vols. (*juan shou*, 35 *juan*). 1945.
*Mashi dazong zupu* 馬氏大宗族譜. 34 vols. (*juan shou*, 33 *juan*). 1993.
*Minting Longzuxiang Zoushi zupu* 閩汀龍足鄉鄒氏族譜. 22 vols (*juan shou*, 21 *juan*). 1911.
*Minting Longzuxiang Zoushi zupu* 閩汀龍足鄉鄒氏族譜. 23 *juan*. 1994.

*Other Primary and Secondary Works*

Adams, Thomas R., and Nicolas Barker. "A New Model for the Study of the Book." In *A Potencie of Life: Books in Society*, ed. Nicolas Barker, 5–43. London: British Library; New Castle, Del.: Oak Knoll Press, 2001.
Alabaster, C. "Memorandum on Education in China Drawn Up from Information Afforded by the Ex-Imperial Commissioner Yeh." *Journal of the Asiatic Society of Bengal* 28, no. 1 (1859): 48–53.
Alger, Grant. "Skill, Silence and Speed: Boat Workers on the Rapids in Early Qing Fujian." Paper presented at the annual meeting of the Association for Asian Studies, Chicago, Mar. 23, 2001.
Anneberg, Margery C. "The Chinese Novel of the Nineteenth Century and Late Ch'ing Period: A Short Literary and Social History with Special Reference to the *Kuan-ch'ang hsien-hsing chi*." Master's thesis, University of Washington, 1952.

*Ba Min tongzhi* 八閩通志. Comp. Huang Zhongzhao 黃仲昭 et al. 1490. 87 *juan.* Reprinted in 2 vols., Fuzhou: Fujian renmin chubanshe, 1989.

Bai, Limin. *Shaping the Ideal Child: Children and Their Primers in Late Imperial China.* Hong Kong: Chinese University Press, 2005.

Bao Fasheng 包发生. "Sibao diaoban yinshuaye de qingkuang diaocha" 四堡 雕版印刷业的情况调查. *Liancheng wenshi ziliao* 连城文史资料 18 (1993): 70–82.

Bao Xiang'ao 鲍相璈. *Yanfang xinbian* 验方新编. 1878. 16 *juan.* Reprinted—in 2 vols., Beijing: Renmin weisheng chubanshe, 1990.

Barker, David. *Traditional Techniques in Contemporary Chinese Printmaking.* Honolulu, Hawai'i: University of Hawai'i Press, 2005.

Barr, Allan. "Four Schoolmasters: Educational Issues in Li Hai-kuan's *Lamp at the Crossroads.*" In *Education and Society in Late Imperial China,* ed. Benjamin A. Elman and Alexander Woodside, 50–75. Berkeley: University of California Press, 1994.

Beattie, Hilary. *Land and Lineage in China: A Study of T'ung-Ch'eng County, Anhwei, in the Ming and Ch'ing Dynasties.* Cambridge, Eng.: Cambridge University Press, 1979.

Bergère, Marie-Claire. *The Golden Age of the Chinese Bourgeoisie, 1911–1937.* Trans. Janet Lloyd. Cambridge, Eng.: Cambridge University Press, 1989.

Bielenstein, Hans. "The Chinese Colonization of Fukien Until the End of the T'ang." In *Studia Serica Bernhard Karlgren Dedicata: Sinological Studies Dedicated to Bernhard Karlgren on His Seventieth Birthday, October Fifth, 1959,* ed. Sören Egerod and Else Glahn, 98–122. Copenhagen: Ejnar Munksgaard, 1959.

———. "The Regional Provenance of *Chin-shih* During the Ch'ing." *Museum of Far Eastern Antiquities* (Östasiatiska Museet; Stockholm), Bulletin no. 64 (1992): 6–178.

Blake, John B. "From Buchan to Fishbein: The Literature of Domestic Medicine." In *Medicine Without Doctors: Home Health Care in American History,* ed. Guenter B. Risse, Ronald L. Numbers, and Judith Walzer Leavitt, 11–30. New York: Science History Publications/USA, 1977.

Borthwick, Sally. *Education and Social Change in China: The Beginnings of the Modern Era.* Stanford: Hoover Institution Press, Stanford University, 1983.

Bray, Francesca. *Technology and Gender: Fabrics of Power in Late Imperial China.* Berkeley: University of California Press, 1997.

Brokaw, Cynthia J. "Commercial Woodblock Printing in the Qing: The Dissemination of Book Culture and Its Social Impact." Paper presented at the conference "From Woodblocks to the Internet: Chinese Publishing and Print Culture in Transition," Ohio State University, Columbus, Ohio, Nov. 4, 2004.

————. "Fieldwork on the Social and Economic History of Chinese Print Culture: A Survey of Sources." *East Asian Library Journal* 10, no. 2 (Autumn 2001): 6–59.

————. *The Ledgers of Merit and Demerit: Moral Order and Social Change in Late Imperial China.* Princeton: Princeton University Press, 1991.

————. "On the History of the Book in China." In *Printing and Book Culture in Late Imperial China*, ed. Cynthia J. Brokaw and Kai-wing Chow, 3–54. Berkeley: University of California Press, 2005.

————. "Reading the Best-sellers of the Nineteenth Century: Commercial Publishing in Sibao." In *Printing and Book Culture in Late Imperial China*, ed. Cynthia J. Brokaw and Kai-wing Chow, 184–231. Berkeley: University of California Press, 2005. "Commercial Publishing in Late Imperial China: The Zou and Ma Family Businesses of Sibao, Fujian." *Late Imperial China* 17, no. 1 (June 1996): 49–92.

————. "Woodblock Printing and the Diffusion of Print in Qing China." In *Higashi Ajia shuppan bunka kenkyū—niwatazumi* 東アジア出版文化研究—にわたずみ, ed. Isobe Akira 磯部彰, 183–97. Tokyo: Nigensha, 2004.

Brokaw, Cynthia J., ed. "Mapping the Book Trade: The Expansion of Print Culture in Late Imperial China." Reports by Cynthia J. Brokaw, Lucille Chia, and Hou Zhenping 侯眞平. 1999, 2000, 2004.

Brook, Timothy. "Censorship in Eighteenth-Century China: A View from the Book Trade." *Canadian Journal of History* 22 (Aug. 1988): 177–96.

————. "Communications and Commerce." In *The Cambridge History of China*, vol. 8, *The Ming Dynasty, 1368–1644*, Part 2, ed. Denis Twitchett and Frederick W. Mote, 579–707. Cambridge, Eng.: Cambridge University Press, 1998.

————. *The Confusions of Pleasure.* Berkeley: University of California Press, 1998.

————. *Geographical Sources of Ming-Qing History.* 2d ed. Ann Arbor: Center for Chinese Studies, University of Michigan, 2002.

Brown, Rajeswary Ampalavanar. "Introduction: Chinese Business in an Institutional and Historical Perspective." In *Chinese Business Enterprise in Asia*, ed. Rajeswary Ampalavanar Brown, 1–26. London and New York: Routledge, 1995.

Buck, John Lossing. *Chinese Farm Economy: A Study of 2866 Farms in Seventeen Localities and Seven Provinces in China.* Shanghai: University of Nanking and China Council of the Institute of Pacific Relations, 1930.

Bussotti, Michela. *Gravures de Hui: étude du livre illustré chinois de la fin du XVIe siècle à la première moitié du XVIIe siècle.* Paris: Ecole française d'Extrême-Orient, 2001.

Cannon, W. J. "Forestry." In *Fukien: A Study of a Province in China*, by Anticobweb Club, 49–51. Shanghai: Presbyterian Mission Press, 1925.

Cao Sibin 曹思彬, Lin Weixiong 林维熊, and Zhang Zhi 张至. *Guangzhou jin-bainian jiaoyu shiliao* 广州近百年教育史料. Special issue of *Guangzhou wenshi ziliao zhuanji* 广州文史资料专辑 (Dec. 1983).

Cao Xianzhuo 曹先擢 and Chen Bingcai 陈秉才, eds. *Baqianzhong Zhongwen cishu leibian tiyao* 八千种中文辞书类编提要. Beijing: Beijing daxue chu-banshe, 1992.

Cao Xueqin. *The Story of the Stone*, vol. 2, *The Crab-flower Club*. Trans. David Hawkes. Harmondsworth, Eng.: Penguin Books, 1977.

Carter, Thomas. *The Invention of Printing in China and Its Spread Westward*. 2d rev. ed., by L. Carrington Goodrich. New York: Ronald, 1955.

Carus, Paul, and D. Z. Suzuki, trans. *T'ai Shang Kan-Ying P'ien*. 1906. Reprinted— LaSalle, Ill.: Open Court, 1950.

Cassedy, James H. "Why Self-Help? Americans Alone with Their Diseases, 1800–1850." In *Medicine Without Doctors: Home Health Care in American History*, ed. Guenter B. Risse, Ronald L. Numbers, and Judith Walzer Leavitt, 31– 48. New York: Science History Publications/USA, 1977.

Chan, Hok-lam. *Control of Publishing in China, Past and Present*. Canberra: Austra-lian National University, 1983.

Chang Chung-li. *The Chinese Gentry: Studies on Their Role in Nineteenth-Century Chinese Society*. Seattle: University of Washington Press, 1955.

———. *The Income of the Chinese Gentry*. Seattle: University of Washington Press, 1962.

*Changning xianzhi* 長寧縣志. 1876. Reprinted—Zhongguo fangzhi congshu 中國方志叢書, Huazhong difang 華中地方, no. 261. Taibei: Chengwen chubanshe, 1976.

*Changting xianzhi* 長汀縣志. 1782.

*Changting xianzhi* 長汀縣志. 1854.

*Changting xianzhi* 長汀縣志. 1879. Reprinted—Zhongguo fangzhi congshu 中國方志叢書, no. 87. Taibei: Chengwen chubanshe, 1967.

*Changting xianzhi* 長汀縣志. 1940. Reprinted—Changting, Fujian: Changting-xian bowuguan and Zhengxie Changtingxian weiyuanhui wenshi bianjishi, 1983.

*Changting xianzhi* 长汀县志. Beijing: Shenghuo, Dushu, and Xinzhi sanlian shu-dian, 1993.

Chao, Wei-pang. "The Chinese Science of Fate Calculation." *Folklore Studies* 5 (1946): 279–315.

Chartier, Roger. *The Cultural Uses of Print in Early Modern France*. Trans. Lydia G. Cochrane. Princeton: Princeton University Press, 1987.

———. *Forms and Meanings: Texts, Performances, and Audiences from Codex to Com-puter*. Philadelphia: University of Pennsylvania Press, 1995.

Chartier, Roger; Alain Boureau; and Cécile Dauphin. *Correspondence: Models of Letter-Writing from the Middle Ages to the Nineteenth Century.* Trans. Christopher Woodall. Princeton: Princeton University Press, 1997.

Chen Jiayuan 陈佳源, ed. *Fujiansheng jingji dili* 福建省经济地理. Beijing: Xinhua chubanshe, 1991.

Chen Jingxi 陈景熙. "Qingmo Minguo ban Chaozhou quce shulu" 清末民国版潮州曲册述录. *Chaoxue yanjiu* 潮学研究 8 (2000): 228–256.

Chen Keng 陈铿. "Lun shijiu shiji shangbanye Fujian de jingji xingtai" 论 19 世纪上半叶福建的经济形态. In *Fujian shi luntan—jinian Zhu Weigan jiaoshou lunwen ji* 福建史论探—纪念朱维幹教授论文集, ed. Tang Wenji 唐文基, 236–56. Fuzhou: Fujian renmin chubanshe, 1992.

Chen Lei 陈雷, Liu Xiangru 刘湘如, and Lin Ruiwu 林瑞武. *Fujian difang xiju* 福建地方戏剧. Fuzhou: Fujian renmin chubanshe, 1997.

Chen Mingguang 陈明光. *Qianzhuang shi* 钱庄史. Shanghai: Shanghai wenyi chubanshe, 1997.

Chen Nengnan 陈能南. "Fujian difang junfa de xingwang he tedian" 福建地方军阀的兴亡和特点. In *Fujian shi luntan—jinian Zhu Weigan jiaoshou lunwen ji* 福建史论探—纪念朱维幹教授论文集, ed. Tang Wenji 唐文基, 163–77. Fuzhou: Fujian renmin chubanshe, 1992.

Chen Yongzheng 陳永正. *Zhongguo xingming cidian* 中國星命辭典. Taipei: Jieyou chubanshe, 1994.

Chen Zhikun 陳志昆, ed. *Fujian Changting zaozhi diaocha* 福建長汀造紙調查. Commissioned by Zhongguo gongye hezuo xiehui Dongnanqu banshichu 中國工業合作協會東南區辦事處. 1946.

Chen Zhiping 陈支平. *Fujian zupu* 福建族谱. Fuzhou: Fujian renmin chubanshe, 1996.

———. *Kejia yuanliu xinlun: Shei shi kejiaren?* 客家源流新论: 谁是客家人? Taibei: Taiyuan chubanshe and Taiyuan yishu wenhua jijinhui, 1998.

———. "Qingdai qianqi Fujian de feizhengchang mijia" 清代前期福建的非正常米价. *Zhongguo shehui jingjishi yanjiu* 中国社会经济史研究 1988, no. 3: 18–25.

———. "Shilun Kangxi chunian dongnan zhusheng de 'shuhuang'" 试论康熙初年东南诸省的'熟荒.' *Zhongguo shehui jingjishi yanjiu* 中国社会经济史研究 1982, no. 2: 40–46.

Chen Zhiping 陈支平, ed. *Fujian zongjiao shi* 福建宗教史. Fuzhou: Fujian jiaoyu chubanshe, 1996.

Chen Zhiping 陈支平 and Zheng Zhenman 郑振满. "Qingdai Minxi Sibao zushang yanjiu" 清代闽西四堡族商研究. *Zhongguo jingjishi yanjiu* 中国经济史研究 10 (1988, no. 2): 93–109.

Chen Zhonglie 陈忠烈. "Ming Qing Gao Lei diqu shangpinxing jingjide fazhan ji qi pingjia" 明清高雷地区商品性经济的发展及其评价. In *Shisi shiji yilai Guangdong shehui jingjide fazhan* 十四世纪以来广东社会经济的发展, ed. Ming-Qing Guangdongsheng shehui jingji yanjiuhui 明清广东省社会经济研究会, 159–74. Guangzhou: Guangdong gaodeng jiaoyu chubanshe, 1992.

Cheng Chongde 成崇德 and Sun Zhe 孙喆. "Lun Qingdai qianqi de xibu bianjiang kaifa" 论清代前期的西部边疆开发. *Qingshi yanjiu* 清史研究 4 (Nov. 2001): 85–96.

Cheng, Ying-wan. *Postal Communication in China and Its Modernization, 1860–1896.* Cambridge, Mass.: East Asian Research Center, Harvard University, 1970.

Chia, Lucille. "Counting and Recounting Chinese Imprints." *East Asian Library Journal* 10, no. 2 (Autumn 2001): 60–103.

——. "Debatable Land: The Fujian-Jiangxi-Zhejiang Border Region During the Song." *Chūgoku shigaku* 中国史学 (*Studies in Chinese History*), no. 8 (Dec. 1998): 1–28.

——. "*Mashaben:* Commercial Publishing in Jianyang from the Song to the Ming." In *The Song-Yuan-Ming Transition in Chinese History,* ed. Paul Jakov Smith and Richard von Glahn, 284–328. Cambridge, Mass.: Harvard University Asia Center, 2003.

——. *Printing for Profit: The Commercial Publishers of Jianyang, Fujian (11th–17th Centuries).* Cambridge, Mass.: Harvard University Asia Center, 2002.

——. "Of Three Mountains Street: The Commercial Publishers of Ming Nanjing." In *Printing and Book Culture in Late Imperial China,* ed. Cynthia J. Brokaw and Kai-wing Chow, 107–51. Berkeley: University of California Press, 2005.

Chow, Kai-wing. *Publishing, Culture, and Power in Early Modern China.* Stanford: Stanford University Press, 2004.

Chu Hsi. *Learning To Be a Sage: Selections from the Conversations of Master Chu, Arranged Topically.* Trans. Daniel K. Gardner. Berkeley: University of California Press, 1990.

Chun Shum (Shen Jin) 沈津. "Guanyu Mingdai Wanli zhi Chongzhen qijian de shujia" 关于明代萬曆至崇祯期间的書價. Paper presented at the conference "Printing and Book Culture in Late Imperial China," Timberline Lodge, Oregon, June 1–5, 1998.

——. "Mingdai fangke tushu zhi liutong yu jiage" 明代坊刻圖書之流通與價格. *Guoli Gugong bowuguan guankan* 國立故宮博物館館刊 1 (June 1996): 101–8.

Clarke, George. "The *Yü-li* or Precious Records." *Journal of the China Branch of the Royal Asiatic Society,* n.s., 28 (Shanghai, 1898): 233–400.

Clunas, Craig. *Superfluous Things: Material Culture and Social Status in Early Modern China*. Cambridge, Eng.: Polity Press, 1991.

Cohen, Alvin P. "Notes on a Chinese Workingclass Bookshelf." *Journal of the American Oriental Society* 96, no. 3 (July–Sept. 1976): 419–30.

Cole, James. *Shaohsing: Competition and Cooperation in Nineteenth-Century China*. Tucson: University of Arizona Press, 1986.

Cooper, Thomas Thornville. *Travels of a Pioneer of Commerce in Pigtail and Petticoats: or, An Overland Journey from China Towards India*. London: John Murray, 1871. Facsimile reproduction—New York: Arno Press, 1967.

Culin, Stewart. "Popular Literature of the Chinese Laborers in the United States." In *Oriental Studies: A Selection of the Papers Read Before the Oriental Club of Philadelphia, 1888–1894*, 52–62. Boston: Ginn & Company, 1894.

Culver, Charles P. "The Lumber Industry of Fukien." In *Fukien: Arts and Industries, Papers by Members of the Anti-Cobweb Society*, 129–39. Foochow: Christian Herald Mission Press, 1933.

Curwen, C. A. *Taiping Rebel: The Deposition of Li Hsiu-ch'eng*. Cambridge, Eng.: Cambridge University Press, 1977.

Dai Yifeng 戴一峰. "Lun jindai Minjiang shangyou shanqu shangpin jingji fazhan de zhiyue yinsu" 论近代闽江上游山区商品经济发展的制约因素. *Zhongguo shehui jingjishi yanjiu* 中国社会经济史研究 1987, no. 3: 89–97.

———. "West Fujian's Rural Society, Economy and Politics in the First Half of the Twentieth Century." In *West Fujian: Land and Migration, 1910s–1940s*, ed. Leo Douw and Dai Yifeng, 23–58. Xiamen: Xiamen University Press, 2000.

Daniels, Christian. "Jūroku–jūshichi seiki Fukken no takegama seizō gijitsu—*Tenkō kaibutsu* ni shōjutsu sareta—seishi gijitsu no jidai kōshō" 16–17 世紀福建の竹紙裝造技術—天工開物に詳述された—裝紙技術の時代考證. *Ajia Afurika gengo bunka kenkyū* アジア·アアフリカ語言文化研究, 30th Anniversary Commemorative Issue II, no. 48–49 (1995): 243–94.

Darnton, Robert. "What Is the History of the Book?" *Daedalus* (Summer 1982): 65–83.

de Bary, Wm. Theodore. *Neo-Confucian Orthodoxy and the Learning of the Heart-and-Mind*. New York: Columbia University Press, 1981.

de Groot, J. J. M. *The Religious System of China: Its Ancient Forms, Evolution, History and Present Aspect*. 6 vols. Leiden: E. J. Brill, 1897. Reprinted—Taipei: Southern Materials Center, 1982.

de las Cortes, Adriano. *Le Voyage en Chine*. Trans. Pascale Girard and Juliette Monbeig. Paris: Chandeigne, 2001.

Defu 德福. *Minzheng lingyao* 閩政領要. 1767.

Deng Liu 鄧旒. *Baochi zhinan che* 保赤指南車. Reprinted—Fuzhou: Fujian ke-xue jishu chubanshe, 1992.

Dennis, Joseph. "The Production and Circulation of Early Ming Gazetteers." Paper presented at the Early Development of Printing in China workshop, Fairbank Center, Harvard University, Apr. 29–30, 2005.

Dietrich, Craig. "Cotton Culture and Manufacture in Early Ch'ing China." In *Economic Organization in Chinese Society*, ed. W. E. Willmott, 109–36. Stanford: Stanford University Press, 1972.

Dore, Henry (Henri Doré). *Researches into Chinese Superstitions*. 13 vols. Trans. M. Kennelly. Shanghai: T'usewei Printing Press, 1917. Reprinted—in 5 vols., Taipei: Ch'eng-wen, 1966.

Drège, Jean-Pierre. *Les Bibliothèques en Chine au temps des manuscrits*. Paris: Ecole Française d'Extrême-Orient, 1991.

———. "Des effets de l'imprimerie en Chine sous la dynastie des Song." *Journal asiatique* 282, no. 2 (1994): 409–42.

Du Xinfu 杜信孚 and Qi Shenqi 漆身起. *Jiangxi lidai keshu* 江西历代刻书. Nanchang: Jiangxi renmin chubanshe, 1994.

Duara, Prasenjit. *Culture, Power and the State in Rural North China, 1900–1942*. Stanford: Stanford University Press, 1988.

Dudbridge, Glen. *China's Vernacular Cultures*. Oxford: Clarendon Press, 1996.

Dukes, Edwin Joshua. *Along River and Road in Fuh-kien, China*. New York: American Tract Society, 1886.

Durand, Pierre-Henri. *Lettrés et pouvoirs: un procès littéraire dans la Chine impériale*. Paris: Editions de l'Ecole des hautes études en sciences sociales, 1992.

Eastman, Lloyd. *The Abortive Revolution: China Under Nationalist Rule, 1927–1937*. Cambridge, Mass.: Harvard University Press, 1974.

Eberhard, Wolfram. *Cantonese Ballads* (Munich State Library Collection). Taipei: Orient Cultural Service, 1972.

Ebrey, Patricia Buckley. "The Early Stages in the Development of Descent Group Organization." In *Kinship Organization in Late Imperial China, 1000–1940*, ed. Patricia Buckley Ebrey and James L. Watson, 16–61. Berkeley: University of California Press, 1986.

Ebrey, Patricia Buckley, and James L. Watson. "Introduction." In *Kinship Organization in Late Imperial China, 1000–1940*, ed. Patricia Buckley Ebrey and James L. Watson, 1–15. Berkeley: University of California Press, 1986.

Edgren, Sören. "Southern Song Printing at Hangzhou." *Bulletin of the Museum of Far Eastern Antiquities* 61 (1989): 1–212.

Edgren, Sören; Tsien Tsuen-hsuin; Wang Fang-yu; and Wan-go H. C. Weng. *Chinese Rate Books in American Collections*. New York: China Institute in America, 1964.

Edkins, J. *Banking and Prices in China*. Shanghai: Presbyterian Mission Press, 1905.

Eitel, Ernst. Review of *Learning to Read in South China*. *China Review* 17 (1888–89): 118–22.

Elman, Benjamin A. *A Cultural History of Civil Examinations in Late Imperial China*. Berkeley: University of California Press, 2000.

Elvin, Mark. *The Pattern of the Chinese Past*. Stanford: Stanford University Press, 1973.

Fairbank, John K. "The Creation of the Treaty System." In *The Cambridge History of China*, vol. 10, *Late Ch'ing, 1800–1911*, Part I, ed. Denis Twitchett and John K. Fairbank, 213–63. Cambridge, Eng.: Cambridge University Press, 1978.

Fan I-chun. "Long-Distance Trade and Market Integration in the Ming-Ch'ing period." Ph.D. diss., Stanford University, 1992.

Fan Jinmin 范金民. "Qingdai Huizhou shangbang de cishan sheshi—yi Jiangnan wei zhongxin" 清代徽州商帮的慈善设施—以江南为中心. *Zhongguoshi yanjiu* 中国史研究 (1999, no. 4): 144–53.

Fan Qilong 范启龙. "Taiping jun sici xia Tingzhou" 太平军四次下汀州. *Changting wenshi ziliao* 长汀文史资料 11 (1986): 16–26.

———. "Yiyi.jiu qiyi—Xinhai geming zai Fujian" 一一.九起义—辛亥革命在福建. In *Fujian shi luntan—jinian Zhu Weigan jiaoshou lunwen ji* 福建史论探—纪念朱维幹教授论文集, ed. Tang Wenji 唐文基, 128–46. Fuzhou: Fujian renmin chubanshe, 1992.

Fang, Xing; Shi Qi; Jian Rui; and Wang Shixin. "Capitalism During the Early and Middle Qing (1)." In *Chinese Capitalism, 1522–1840*, ed. Xu Dixin and Wu Chengming, 165–246. New York: St. Martin's Press, 2000.

Faure, David. "The Lineage as Business Company: Patronage Versus Law in the Development of Chinese Business." In *The Second Conference on Modern Chinese Economic History*, 347–76. Taipei: Institute of Economics, Academia Sinica, 1989.

———. *The Structure of Chinese Rural Society: Lineage and Village in the Eastern New Territories, Hong Kong*. Hong Kong: Oxford University Press, 1986.

Feng Lin 枫林 and Zi Bing 紫冰. "Min, Yue, Gan bian congqian zhuyao hangdao—Tingjiang" 闽, 粤, 赣边从前主要航道—汀江. *Changting wenshi ziliao* 长汀文史资料 8 (1985): 39–41.

Feuchtwang, Stephan D. R. *An Anthropological Analysis of Chinese Geomancy*. Taipei: Southern Materials Center, 1982.

Foucault, Michel. "What Is an Author?" In *Textual Strategies: Perspectives in Post-Structuralist Criticism*, ed. Josue V. Harari, 141–60. Ithaca, N.Y.: Cornell University Press, 1979.

Franck, Harry A. *Roving Through Southern China*. London: T. Fisher Unwin, 1926.

Fu Jianmu 傅建木. "Qingdai minjian kuaiji fushi jizhang gaishu" 清代民间会计复式记帐概述. *Zhongguo shehui jingjishi yanjiu* 中国社会经济史研究 1989, no. 3: 73–77.

Fu, Wei-k'ang. *The Story of Chinese Acupuncture and Moxibustion*. Peking: Foreign Languages Press, 1975.

Fu Yiling 傅衣凌. "Mingmo Qingchu Min Gan pilin diqu de shehui jingji yu diannong kangzu fengchao" 明末清初闽赣毗邻地区的社会经济与佃农抗租风潮. In *Ming Qing shehui jingji shi lunwen ji* 明清社会经济史论文集, 338–80. Beijing: Renmin chubanshe, 1982.

———. "Zhongguo chuantong shehui: duoyuande jiegou" 中国传统社会: 多元的结构. *Zhongguo shehui jingjishi yanjiu* 中国社会经济史研究 1988, no. 3: 1–7.

*Fujian gonglu shi* 福建公路史. Ed. Fujiansheng gongluju, Bianjizu 福建省公路局编辑组. Vol. 1. Fuzhou: Fujian kexue jishu chubanshe, 1987.

*Fujiansheng Longyan diqu gonglu shi* 福建省龙岩地区公路史. Ed. Longyan diqu gonglushi, Bianjizu 龙岩地区公路史编辑组. Beijing: Huayi chubanshe, 1990.

*Fujian tongji* 福建通纪. 1922. Reprinted—Taipei: Datong shuju, 1968. 4 vols.

Furth, Charlotte. *A Flourishing Yin: Gender in China's Medical History, 960–1665*. Berkeley: University of California Press, 1999.

Gallagher, Louis J. *China in the Sixteenth Century: The Journals of Matthew Ricci, 1595–1610*. New York: Random House, 1953.

*Ganzhou fuzhi* 赣州府志. 1873. Reprinted Zhongguo fangzhi congshu 中國方志叢書, Huazhong difang 華中地方, no. 100. Taibei: Chengwen chubanshe, 1970.

*Gaozhou fuzhi* 高州府志. 1889. Reprinted—Zhongguo fangzhi congshu 中國方志叢書, no. 68. Taibei: Chengwen chubanshe, 1967.

Gardella, Robert. "Contracting Business Partnerships in Late Qing and Republican China: Paradigms and Patterns." In *Contract and Property in Early Modern China*, ed. Madeleine Zelin, Jonathan K. Ocko, and Robert Gardella, 327–47. Stanford: Stanford University Press, 2004.

———. "Fukien's Tea Industry and Trade in Ch'ing and Republican China: The Developmental Consequences of a Traditional Commodity Export." Ph.D. diss., University of Washington, 1976.

———. *Harvesting Mountains: Fujian and the China Tea Trade, 1757–1937*. Berkeley: University of California Press, 1994.

———. "Squaring Accounts: Commercial Bookkeeping Methods and Capitalist Rationalism in Late Qing and Republican China." *Journal of Asian Studies* 51, no. 2 (May 1992): 317–39.

Gardner, Daniel. "Confucian Commentary and Chinese Intellectual History." *Journal of Asian Studies* 57, no. 2 (May 1998): 397–422.

———. "Principle and Pedagogy: Chu Hsi and the Four Books." *Harvard Journal of Asiatic Studies* 44, no. 1 (June 1984): 57–81.

———. "'To Be a Teacher Is Hard, and To Be an Elementary Teacher Is Harder Still': The Professionalization of Teaching in Late Imperial China." Unpublished manuscript.

———. "Transmitting the Way: Chu Hsi's Program of Learning." *Harvard Journal of Asiatic Studies* 49, no. 1 (June 1989): 141–72.

———. *Zhu Xi's Reading of the* Analects: *Canon, Commentary, and the Classical Tradition.* New York: Columbia University Press, 2003.

Giles, Herbert, trans. *San Tzu Ching: Elementary Chinese.* Reprinted—Taipei: Ch'eng-wen, 1975.

Goodrich, L. Carrington, and Chaoying Fang, eds. *Dictionary of Ming Biography.* 2 vols. New York: Columbia University Press, 1976.

Gordon Cumming, C. F. *Wanderings in China.* 2 vols. Edinburgh and London: William Blackwood and Sons, 1886.

Gorst, Harold E. *China.* New York: E. P. Dutton & Co., 1899.

Graff, Harvey J. *The Literacy Myth: Literacy and Social Structure in the Nineteenth-Century City.* New York: Academic Press, 1979.

Guan Ming 官鸣. "Fujian Changting zaozhi jishushi chukao" 福建长汀造纸技术史初考. In *Fujian kexue jishushi yanjiu* 福建科学技术史研究, ed. Zhou Ji 周济, 142–53. Xiamen: Xiamen daxue chubanshe, 1990.

Guan Xihua 管錫華. *Zhongguo gudai biaodian fuhao fazhan shi* 中國古代標點符號發展史. Chengdu: Ba Shu shushe, 2002.

*Guangdong shengzhi—chuban zhi* 广东省志—出版志. Guangzhou: Guangdong renmin chubanshe, 1997.

*Guangxi tongzhi—chuban zhi* 广西通志—出版志. Nanning: Guangxi renmin chubanshe, 1999.

Guo Bocang 郭伯蒼. *Minchan luyi* 閩產錄異. 1886.

Guo Shaoyu 郭紹虞, ed. *Qing shihua xubian* 清詩話續編. 2 vols. Shanghai: Shanghai guji chubanshe, 1983.

Guy, R. Kent. *The Emperor's Four Treasuries: Scholars and the State in the Late Ch'ien-lung Era.* Cambridge, Mass.: Council on East Asian Studies, Harvard University, 1987.

Hamilton, Gary G. "Why No Capitalism in China? Negative Questions in Historical, Comparative Research." In *Max Weber in Asian Studies*, ed. Andreas E. Buss, 65–89. Leiden: E. J. Brill, 1985.

Han Xiduo 韩锡铎, ed. *Zhonghua mengxue jicheng* 中华蒙学集成. Shenyang: Liaoning jiaoyu chubanshe, 1993.

Hanan, Patrick. *The Chinese Vernacular Story*. Cambridge, Mass.: Harvard University Press, 1981.

———. "Judge Bao's Hundred Cases Reconstructed." *Harvard Journal of Asiatic Studies* 40, no. 2 (Dec. 1980): 301–23.

"*Hanlin Papers*. Essays on the Intellectual Life of the Chinese. By W. A. P. Martin." *China Review* 9 ( July 1880–June 1881): 109–11.

Hanson, Marta E. "Inventing a Tradition in Chinese Medicine: From Universal Canon to Local Medical Knowledge in South China, the Seventeenth to the Nineteenth Century." Ph.D. diss., University of Pennsylvania, 1997.

Hayashi Kazuo 林和生. "Min Shin jidai, Kanton no kyo to shi—dentōteki ichiba no keitai to kinō ni kansuru ichi kōsatsu" 明清時代, 廣東の墟と市—傳統的市場の形態と機能に關す る一考察. *Shirin* 史林 63, no. 1 (1980): 69–105.

Hayes, James. "Popular Culture in Late Ch'ing China: Printed Books and Manuscripts from the Hong Kong Region." *Journal of the Hong Kong Library Association* 7 (1983): 57–72.

———. "Popular Culture of Late Ch'ing and Early Twentieth Century China: Book Lists Prepared from Collecting in Hong Kong." *Journal of the Hong Kong Branch of the Royal Asiatic Society* 20 (1980): 168–81.

———. "Specialists and Written Materials in the Village World." In *Popular Culture in Late Imperial China*, ed. David Johnson, Andrew J. Nathan, and Evelyn S. Rawski, 75–111. Berkeley: University of California Press, 1985.

He Mingyang 何明扬, ed. *Guizhou banshi yanjiu* 贵州版史研究. Guiyang, 1996?

Hegel, Robert. "Niche Marketing for Late Imperial Fiction." In *Printing and Book Culture in Late Imperial China*, ed. Cynthia J. Brokaw and Kai-wing Chow, 235–66. Berkeley: University of California Press, 2005.

———. *Reading Illustrated Fiction in Late Imperial China*. Stanford: Stanford University Press, 1998.

Heijdra, Martin. "The Socio-economic Development of Rural China During the Ming." In *The Cambridge History of China*, vol. 8, *The Ming Dynasty, 1368–1644*, Part 2, ed. Denis Twitchett and Frederick W. Mote, 417–578. Cambridge, Eng.: Cambridge University Press, 1998.

———. "A Tale of Two Aesthetics: Typography Versus Calligraphy in the Pre-modern Chinese Book." Paper presented at the conference "The Art of the Book in China" (Percival David Foundation of Chinese Art and Archaeology no. 23), School of Oriental and African Studies, University of London, London, June 13, 2005.

Hervouet, Yves. ed. *A Sung Bibliography*. Hong Kong: Chinese University Press, 1978.

Ho, Ping-ti. *The Ladder of Success in Imperial China.* New York: John Wiley & Sons, 1962.

———. "The Salt Merchants of Yang-chou: A Study of Commercial Capitalism in Eighteenth-Century China." *Harvard Journal of Asiatic Studies* 17, nos. 1 and 2 (1954): 130–68.

———. *Studies on the Population of China, 1368–1953.* Cambridge, Mass.: Harvard University Press, 1959.

Hoizey, Dominique, and Marie-Joseph Hoizey. *A History of Chinese Medicine.* Trans. Paul Bailey. Edinburgh: Edinburgh University Press, 1993.

Hou Zhenping 侯真平. "Hunan diaocha lu" 湖南调查录. Unpublished report for "Mapping the Book Trade: The Expansion of Print Culture in Late Imperial China." 2004.

Hsia, C. T. "The Military Romance: A Genre of Chinese Fiction." In *Studies in Chinese Literature,* ed. Cyril Birch, 339–90. Berkeley: University of California Press, 1974.

Hu Shanmei 胡善美. "Changting—Xiamen daxue—Sa Bendong" 长汀–厦门大学–萨本栋. *Changting wenshi ziliao* 长汀文史资料 23 (1994): 1–13.

Huang Guosheng 黄国声. "Guangdong Magang nüzi keshu kaosuo" 广东马冈女子刻书考索. *Wenxian* 文献 76 (1998, no. 2): 266–70.

Huang Junyuan 黄俊苑. *Zhizhai yishu* 止斋遗书. 1875.

Huang Lin 黄霖 and Han Tongwen 韩同文. *Zhongguo lidai xiaoshuo lunzhu xuan* 中国历代论著选. 2 vols. Nanchang: Jiangxi renmin chubanshe, 1982.

Huang Majin 黄马金. *Changting zhishi* 长汀纸史. Beijing: Zhongguo qinggongye chubanshe, 1992.

Huang, Philip C. C. *The Peasant Economy and Rural Development in the Yangzi Delta, 1350–1988.* Stanford: Stanford University Press, 1990.

*Hubei shengzhi—xinwen chuban* 湖北省志—新闻出版. 2 vols. Wuhan: Hubei renmin chubanshe, 1995.

Huc, E. R. *The Chinese Empire.* 2 vols. 2d ed., 1855. Reprinted—Port Washington, N.Y.: Kennikat Press, 1970.

Hummel, Arthur, ed. *Eminent Chinese of the Ch'ing Period.* 2 vols. Washington, D.C.: United States Government Printing Office, 1943, 1944.

Hunter, William C. *Bits of Old China.* London: Kegan, Paul, Trench, and Co., 1885.

Hurlbut, Floy. *The Fukienese, a Study in Human Geography.* Ph.D. diss., University of Nebraska, 1930. Published by the author.

Hymes, Robert P. "Marriage, Descent Groups, and the Localist Strategy in Sung and Yuan Fu-chou." In *Kinship Organization in Late Imperial China, 1000–1940,* ed. Patricia Buckley Ebrey and James Watson, 95–136. Berkeley: University of California Press, 1986.

Idema, W. L. *Chinese Vernacular Fiction: The Formative Period.* Leiden: E. J. Brill, 1974.

———. "Novels About the Founding of the Sung Dynasty." *Sung Studies Newsletter* 9 (June 1974): 2–9.

———. "Review of Evelyn Rawski, *Education and Popular Literacy in Ch'ing China* (1979)." *T'oung Pao* 66, 4–5 (1980): 314–24.

Idema, Wilt, and Lloyd Haft. *A Guide to Chinese Literature.* Ann Arbor: Center for Chinese Studies, University of Michigan, 1997.

Inoue Susumu 井上進. *Chūgoku shuppan bunkashi—shomotsu sekai to chi no fūkei* 中国出版文化史—書物世界と知の風景. Nagoya: Nagoya daigaku shuppankai, 2002.

(*Jiajing Daoguang*) *Qingliu xianzhi* (嘉靖道光)清流縣志. Reprint, 1545 *Qingliu xianzhi* and 1829 *Qingliu xianzhi*. Fuzhou: Fujian renmin chubanshe, 1991.

Jiang Zuyuan 蔣祖緣 and Fang Zhiqin 方志钦, eds. *Jianming Guangdong shi* 简明广东史. Guangzhou: Guangdong renmin chubanshe, 1993.

*Jiangxi sheng* 江西省. Shanghai: Shangwu yinshuguan, Republican era.

*Jiangxisheng chuban zhi* 江西省出版志. Nanchang: Jiangxi renmin chubanshe, 1999.

Jiao Hong 焦竑, comp. *Guochao xianzheng lu* 國朝獻徵錄. Ed. Wu Xiangxiang 吳相湘. Taibei: Taiwan Xuesheng shuju, 1965.

*Jieyangxian zheng xuzhi* 揭陽縣正續志. 1779, Reprinted, 1937. Reprinted— *Zhongguo fangzhi congshu* 中國方志叢書, *Huanan difang* 華南地方, no. 195. 3 vols. Taipei: Chengwen chubanshe, 1974.

Jin Wuxiang 金武祥. *Suxiang sanbi* 粟香三筆. Preface dated 1884. Saoye shanfang.

Jing, Su, and Lun Luo. *Landlord and Labor in Late Imperial China: Case Studies from Shandong.* Trans. Endymion Wilkinson. Cambridge, Mass.: Council on East Asian Studies, Harvard University, 1978.

*Jinxi xianzhi* 金溪县志. Beijing: Xinhua chubanshe, 1992.

Johnson, David. "Communication, Class, and Consciousness in Late Imperial China." In *Popular Culture in Late Imperial China*, ed. David Johnson, Andrew J. Nathan, and Evelyn S. Rawski, 34–72. Berkeley: University of California Press, 1985.

Ju Mi 居蜜 and Ye Xian'en 叶显恩. "Ming Qing shiqi Huizhou de keshu he banhua" 明清时期徽州的刻书和版画. *Jianghuai luntan* 江淮论坛 2 (1995): 1–8 (unpaginated).

*Kang Yong Qian shiqi chengxiang renmin fankang douzheng ziliao* 康雍乾时期城乡人民反抗斗争资料. Ed. Zhongguo renmin daxue, Qingshi yanjiusuo, Dang'anxi Zhongguo zhengzhi zhidushi jiaoyanshi 中国人民大学清史研

究所档案系中国政治制度史教研室. 2 vols. Beijing: Zhonghua shuju, 1979.

"Kanke hangye yuanqi he biange" 刊刻行业原起和变革. Unpublished report by the Chengdushi chengfeng kanke shengchan hezuoshe 成都市乘风刊刻生产合作社. 1963?

Kelleher, M. Theresa. "Back to Basics: Chu Hsi's *Elementary Learning (Hsiao-hsüeh)*. In *Neo-Confucian Education: The Formative Stage*, ed. Wm. Theodore de Bary and John W. Chaffee, 219–51. Berkeley: University of California Press, 1989.

Kingsmill, T. W. "Inland Communications in China." In the *Journal of the China Branch of the Royal Asiatic Society*, n.s. 28 (Shanghai, 1898): 1–213.

Kishimoto-Nakayama, Mio. "The Kangxi Depression and Early Qing Local Markets." *Modern China* 10, no. 2 (Apr. 1984): 227–56.

Ko, Dorothy. *Teachers of the Inner Chambers: Women and Culture in Seventeenth-Century China*. Stanford: Stanford University Press, 1994.

Kohn, Livia. "A Textbook of Physiognomy: The Tradition of the *Shenxiang quanbian*." *Asian Folklore Studies* 45, no. 2 (1986): 227–58.

Kornicki, Peter. *The Book in Japan: A Cultural History from the Beginnings to the Nineteenth Century*. Leiden: E. J. Brill, 1998.

Kuhn, Philip A. *Soulstealers: The Chinese Sorcery Scare of 1768*. Cambridge, Mass.: Harvard University Press, 1990.

———. "The Taiping Rebellion." In *The Cambridge History of China*, vol. 10, *Late Ch'ing, 1800–1911*, Part I, ed. Denis Twitchett and John K. Fairbank, 264–317. Cambridge, Eng.: Cambridge University Press, 1978.

Lacy, Walter N. "Geography." In *Fukien: A Study of a Province in China*, by Anti-Cobweb Club, 3–6. Shanghai: Presbyterian Mission Press, 1925.

Lamley, Harry J. "Lineage Feuding in Southern Fujian and Eastern Guangdong Under Qing Rule." In *Violence in China: Essays in Culture and Counterculture*, ed. Jonathan N. Lipman and Stevan Harrell, 27–64. Albany: State University of New York Press, 1990.

Lan Hanmin 藍漢民. "Tingjiang Shanghang heduan hangyun yu shangsu" 汀江上杭河段航運與商俗. In *Tingzhoufu de zongzu miaohui yu jingji* 汀州府的宗族廟會與經濟, ed. Yang Yanjie 楊彥杰, 493–520. Traditional Hakka Society Series, no. 6, ed. John Lagerway. Hong Kong: International Hakka Studies Association, Overseas Chinese Archives, and Ecole Française d'Extrême-Orient, 1998.

Lao Xiang 老向. "Guanyu kang Ri *Sanzi jing*" 关于抗日三字经. In *Lao Xiang* 老向, 292–93. Huaxia chubanshe, 2000.

Lau, D. C., trans. *Mencius, a Bilingual Edition*. Hong Kong: Chinese University Press, 1984. Rev. ed., 2003.

Lee, James Z., and Wang Feng, with Li Bozhong. "Population, Poverty, and Subsistence in China, 1700–2000." In *Population and Economy: From Hunger to Modern Economic Growth*, ed. T. Bengtsson and O. Saito, 73–109. Oxford: Oxford University Press, 2000.

Legge, James, trans. *The Chinese Classics*. 5 vols. Oxford: Oxford University Press, 1960. Reprinted—Taipei: Wenshizhe chubanshe, 1971.

———. *Li chi: Book of Rites. An Encyclopedia of Ancient Ceremonial Usages, Religious Creeds, and Social Institutions*. Ed. Ch'u Chai and Winberg Chai. New Hyde Park, N.Y.: University Books, 1967.

Lei Hong 雷鋐. *Xiaoshi ou cun* 校士偶存. In the Fujian Provincial Library.

Leong, Sow-Theng. *Migration and Ethnicity in Chinese History: Hakkas, Pengmin, and Their Neighbors*. Stanford: Stanford University Press, 1997.

Leung, Angela Ki Che. "Elementary Education in the Lower Yangtze Region in the Seventeenth and Eighteenth Centuries." In *Education and Society in Late Imperial China, 1600–1900*, ed. Benjamin A. Elman and Alexander Woodside, 381–416. Berkeley: University of California Press, 1994.

———. "Medical Instruction and Popularization in Ming-Qing China." *Late Imperial China* 24, no. 1 ( June 2003): 130–52.

———. "Medical Learning from the Song to the Ming." In *The Song-Yuan-Ming Transition in Chinese History*, ed. Paul Jakov Smith and Richard von Glahn, 374–98. Cambridge, Mass.: Harvard University Asia Center, 2003.

Leung Pui-chee (Liang Peichi) 梁培熾. *Nanyin yu Yueou zhi yanjiu* 南音與粵謳之研究. San Francisco, Calif.: Asian American Studies, School of Ethnic Studies, San Francisco State University, 1988.

———. *Xianggang daxue suocang muyushu shulu yu yanjiu* 香港大學所藏木魚書書錄與研究. Hong Kong: Centre of Asian Studies, University of Hong Kong, 1978.

Li Bingqian 李秉乾, ed. *Fujian wenxian shumu* 福建文獻書目. 1996.

Li Bozhong 李伯重. "Ming Qing Jiangnan de chuban yinshuaye" 明清江南的出版印刷业. *Zhongguo jingjishi yanjiu* 中国经济史研究 63 (2001, no. 3): 94–107, 146.

Li, Chien Ming. *The Accounting System of Native Banks in Peking and Tientsin*. Shanghai: Université l'Aurore; Tientsin: Hautes études industrielles et commerciales, 1941.

Li, Dun Jen. *The Ageless Chinese*. New York: Charles Scribner's Sons, 1978.

Li, Lillian. *China's Silk Trade: Traditional Industry in the Modern World, 1842–1937*. Cambridge, Mass.: Council on East Asian Studies, Harvard University, 1981.

Li Shengbao 李升宝. "Sibao diming kao" 四堡地名考. *Qingliu wenshi ziliao* 清流文史资料 8 (1992): 79–80.

Li Shixiong 李世熊. *Koubian ji* 寇變紀. In *Qingshi ziliao* 清史資料 1, 27–63. Beijing: Zhonghua shuju, 1980.

Li Xubo 李绪柏. "Qingdai Guangdong de shufang ji qi keshu" 清代广东的书坊及其刻书. *Zhongshan daxue shixue jikan* 中山大学史学集刊 1 (Sept. 1992): 130–44.

Lian Lichang 连立昌. *Fujian mimi shehui* 福建秘密社会. Fuzhou: Fujian renmin chubanshe, 1989.

"Liancheng shougong zaozhiye de qiyuan, fazhan he zhanwang" 连城手工造纸业的起源, 发展和展望, by Lianchengxian gongshanglian 连城县工商联. *Liancheng wenshi ziliao* 连城文史资料 8 (1987): 100–107.

*Liancheng xianzhi* 連城縣志. 1938.

*Liancheng xianzhi* 连城县志. Beijing: Qunzhong chubanshe, 1993.

Liang Songsheng 梁松生. "Qingmo Minchu Guangzhou Xiguan sishu gaikuang" 清末民初广州西关私塾概况. *Guangzhou wenshi ziliao* 广州文史资料 35 (1986): 152–56.

Liang Zhangju 梁章鉅. *Guitian suoji* 歸田瑣記. Shanghai: Saoye shanfang, 1918.

Liao Shiyao 廖仕耀. "Anlexiang de chuantong zaozhi yu xushi jingji" 安樂鄉的傳統造紙與墟市經濟. In *Ninghuaxian de zongzu, jingji yu minsu* 寧化縣的宗族, 經濟與民俗, ed. Yang Yanjie 楊彥杰, 745–95. Traditional Hakka Society Series, no. 24, vol. 2, ed. John Lagerway. Hong Kong: International Hakka Studies Association, Overseas Chinese Archives, and Ecole Française d'Extrême-Orient, 2005.

Liao Yuqun 廖育群, Fu Fang 傅芳, and Zheng Jinsheng 郑金生, eds. *Yixue juan* 医学卷. In *Zhongguo kexue jishushi* 中国科学技术史, ed. Lu Jiaxi 卢嘉锡. Beijing: Kexue chubanshe, 1998.

*Lidai jiaoyu lunzhu xuanping* 历代教育论著选评. 2 vols. In Zhongguo jiaoyu daxi 中国教育大系. Wuhan: Hubei jiaoyu chubanshe, 1994.

*Lidai jiaoyu zhidu kao* 历代教育制度考. 2 vols. In Zhongguo jiaoyu daxi 中国教育大系. Wuhan: Hubei jiaoyu chubanshe, 1994.

Lin Shuimei 林水梅. "Shufang yongzhi zhi yi—Liancheng zhiye manhua" 书房用纸之一——连城纸业漫话. *Fujian wenshi* 福建文史 5 (1993, no. 6): 30–32.

Lin Yushan 林玉山. *Zhongguo cishu bianzuan shilüe* 中国辞书编纂史略. Beijing: Zhongzhou guji chubanshe, 1992.

Link, Perry. *Mandarin Ducks and Butterflies: Popular Fiction in Early Twentieth-Century China.* Berkeley: University of California Press, 1981.

*Linting zhi* 臨汀志. Song. Reprinted—Fuzhou: Fujian renmin chubanshe, 1990.

Lister, Alfred. "Chinese Almanacs." *China Review* 1 (1872–73): 237–44.

Liu Haifeng 刘海峰 and Zhuang Mingshui 庄明水. *Fujian jiaoyu shi* 福建教育史. Fuzhou: Fujian jiaoyu chubanshe, 1996.

Liu, James J. Y. *The Art of Chinese Poetry*. Chicago: University of Chicago Press, 1962.

Liu, James T. C. "The Classical Chinese Primer: Its Three-Character Style and Authorship." *Journal of the American Oriental Society*, 105, no. 2 (1985): 191–96.

Liu Ts'un-yan. *Chinese Popular Fiction in Two London Libraries*. Hong Kong: Long Men Bookstore, 1967.

Liu Wenwei 刘文蔚, comp. *Tangshi hexuan* 唐诗合选. Ed. Yang Yerong 杨业荣. Nanning: Guangxi renmin chubanshe, 1986.

Liu Yonghua 刘永华. "Kangzu yu bukangzu: Ming Qing yilai Minxi de diannong, dizhuzhi yu xiangcun shehui" 抗租與不抗租: 明清以来閩西的佃農, 地主制與鄉村社會. Unpublished manuscript.

———. "Shiqi zhi shiba shiji Minxi diannong de kangzu, nongcun shehui yu xiangmin wenhua" 17 至 18 世纪闽西佃农的抗租, 农村社会与乡民文化. *Zhongguo jingjishi yanjiu* 中国社会经济史研究 51 (1998, no. 3): 139–50.

———. "Song Yuan yilai Minxi shehuide tuke zhi zheng yu diannong douzheng" 宋元以来闽西社会的土客之争与佃农斗争. *Zhongguo shehui jingjishi yanjiu* 中国社会经济史研究 1993, no. 2: 36–40.

———. "The World of Rituals: Masters of Ceremonies (*Lisheng*), Ancestral Cultrs, Community Compacts, and Local Temples in Late Imperial Sibao, Fujian." Ph.D. diss., McGill University, 2003.

Liu Zhenbang 刘振邦 and Qiu Hengkuan 邱恒宽. "Jiefangqian Ninghua gongye gaishu" 解放前宁化工业概述. *Ninghua wenshi ziliao* 宁化文史资料 11 (1990): 24–37.

Liu Zongzhou 劉宗周. *Liuzi quanshu* 劉子全書. 6 vols. Daoguang ed. Reprinted—Taibei: Huawen shuju, n.d.

Lockhart, J. H. Stewart. *A Manual of Chinese Quotations*. Hong Kong: Kelly & Walsh, 1908.

London Missionary Society. Annual Reports 105–35. 1900–1930.

Loomis, A. W. "What Our Chinamen Read." *Overland Monthly* 1, no. 6 (1868): 525–30.

Louie, Kam, and Louise Edwards, trans. and eds. *Censored by Confucius: Ghost Stories by Yuan Mei*. Armonk, N.Y.: M. E. Sharpe, 1996.

Lu Xun. *A Brief History of Chinese Fiction*. Peking: Foreign Languages Press, 1964.

Lufrano, Richard. *Honorable Merchants: Commerce and Self-Cultivation in Late Imperial China*. Honolulu: University of Hawai'i Press, 1997.

Ma Chuanyong 馬傳永. "Lianchengxian Sibaoxiang Mawucun minjian xisu" 連城縣四堡鄉馬屋村民間習俗. In *Minxi de chengxiang miaohui yu cunluo wenhua* 閩西的城鄉廟會與村落文化, ed. Yang Yanjie 楊彥杰, 299–343. Traditional Hakka Society Series, no. 4, ed. John Lagerway. Hong Kong:

International Hakka Studies Association, Overseas Chinese Archives, and Ecole française d'Extrême-Orient, 1997.

Ma Jiashu 马嘉澍. "Mawu diaoban yinshuaye chayue ziliao" 马屋雕版印刷业查阅资料. 1996. Unpublished manuscript.

Ma Jixing 马继兴. *Zhongyi wenxian xue* 中医文献学. Shanghai: Shanghai kexue jishu chubanshe, 1990.

Ma Kadan 马卡丹. "Sibao diaoban yinshuaye chuzhen" 四堡雕版印刷业初探. *Fujian wenshi* 福建文史 5 (1993, no. 6): 26–29.

Ma Liwen 马例文. "Minxi Sibao fangke de xingshuai ji qi yuanyin" 闽西四堡坊刻的兴衰及其原因. *Fujian xuekan* 福建学刊 101 (1992, no. 4): 56–60.

Ma Tai-loi. "Novels Prohibited in the Literary Inquisition of Emperor Ch'ienlung, 1722–1788." In *Critical Essays on Chinese Fiction*, ed. Winston L. Y. Yang and Curtis P. Adkins, 201–12. Hong Kong: Chinese University Press, 1980.

Ma Xulun 馬敘倫. *Wo zai liushisui yiqian* 我在六十歲以前. Shanghai: Shenghuo shudian, 1947.

Ma, Y. W. "The Chinese Historical Novel: An Outline of Themes and Contexts." *Journal of Asian Studies* 34, no. 2 (Feb. 1975): 287–88.

———. "Kung-an Fiction: A Historical and Critical Introduction." *T'oung Pao* 65, nos. 4–5 (1979): 200–59.

Ma Yunzhang 马云章. "Sibao yinshuye de xingshuai genggai" 四堡印书业的兴衰梗概. Unpublished manuscript.

Macgowan, John. *Sidelights on Chinese Life*. Philadelphia: J. B. Lippincott, 1908.

Mair, Victor H. "Buddhism and the Rise of the Written Vernacular in East Asia: The Making of National Languages." *Journal of Asian Studies* 53, no. 3 (Aug. 1994): 707–51.

Mann, Susan. "Women, Family, and Gender Relations." In *The Cambridge History of China*, vol. 9, *The Ch'ing Dynasty to 1800*, Part I, ed. Willard J. Peterson, 428–72. Cambridge, Eng.: Cambridge University Press, 2002.

Mao Chunxiang 毛春翔. *Gushu banben changtan* 古書版本常談. Beijing: Zhonghua shuju, 1962.

Mao Shuiqing 毛水清 and Liang Yang 梁扬, eds. *Zhongguo chuantong mengxue dadian* 中国传统蒙学大典. Nanning: Guangxi renmin chubanshe, 1993.

Mao Xing 毛星. "Changting xian gailiang zhi manhua" 长汀县改良纸漫话. *Changting wenshi ziliao* 长汀文史资料 16 (1990): 92–97.

———. "Jianguo qian Changting shangye maoyi linzhao" 建国前长汀商业贸易鳞爪. *Changting wenshi ziliao* 长汀文史资料 12 (1987): 34–39.

———. "Liancheng 'gonghe' zaozhi shihua" 连城"工合"造纸史话. *Zhishi yanjiu* 纸史研究 5 (Dec. 1988): 54–60.

———. "Ning Ting zhiye lishi yuanyuan" 宁汀纸业历史渊源. *Ninghua wenshi ziliao* 宁化文史资料 11 (1990): 73–75.

———. "Sibao guji diaoban de zuihou quchu" 四堡古籍雕版的最后去处. *Changting wenshi ziliao* 长汀文史资料 20 (1990): 98–102.

March, Andrew L. "An Appreciation of Chinese Geomancy." *Journal of Asian Studies* 27, no. 2 (Feb. 1968): 253–67.

Marks, Robert B. *Tigers, Rice, Silk, & Silt: Environment and Economy in Late Imperial South China.* Cambridge, Eng.: Cambridge University Press, 1998.

Martin, W. A. P. *The Lore of Cathay or The Intellect of China.* New York: Fleming H. Revell Co., 1901.

Mazumdar, Sucheta. *Sugar and Society in China: Peasants, Technology, and the World Market.* Cambridge, Mass.: Harvard University Asia Center, 1998.

McDermott, Joseph. "The Ascendance of the Imprint in China." In *Printing and Book Culture in Late Imperial China,* ed. Cynthia J. Brokaw and Kai-wing Chow, 55–104. Berkeley: University of California Press, 2005.

McElderry, Andrea Lee. *Shanghai Old-Style Banks (Ch'ien-Chuang), 1800–1935.* Michigan Papers in Chinese Studies, no. 25. Ann Arbor: Center for Chinese Studies, University of Michigan, 1976.

McKenzie, D. F. *Bibliography and the Sociology of Texts.* Cambridge, Eng.: Cambridge University Press, 1999.

McLaren, Anne. *Chinese Popular Culture and Ming Chantefables.* Leiden: E. J. Brill, 1998.

———. "Constructing New Reading Publics." In *Printing and Book Culture in Late Imperial China,* ed. Cynthia J. Brokaw and Kai-wing Chow, 152–83. Berkeley: University of California Press, 2005.

———. "Ming Audiences and Vernacular Hermeneutics: The Uses of *The Romance of the Three Kingdoms.*" *T'oung Pao* 81 (1995): 51–80.

McMahon, Keith. *Causality and Containment in Seventeenth-Century Chinese Fiction.* Leiden: E. J. Brill, 1988.

Medhurst, W. H. *China: Its State and Prospects.* London: John Snow, 1838.

——— ("Typographus Sinensis," pseud.). "Estimate of the Proportionate Expense of Xylography, Lithography, and Typography, as Applied to Chinese Printing; View of the Advantages and Disadvantages of Each." *Chinese Repository* 3 (May 1834–Apr. 1835): 246–52.

Miao Yonghe 缪咏禾. *Mingdai chubanshi* 明代出版史. Nanjing: Jiangsu renmin chubanshe, 2000.

Miki Satoshi 三木聰. "Kōzo to sobei—Minmatsu Shinshoki no Fukken o chūshin to shite—" 抗租と阻米—明末清初期の福建を中心として. *Tōyōshi kenkyū* 東洋史研究 45, no. 4 (Mar. 1987): 25–57.

———. "Qingdai qianqi Fujian nongcun shehui yu diannong kangzu douzheng" 清代前期福建农村社会与佃农抗租斗争. *Zhongguo shehui jingjishi yanjiu* 中国社会经济史研究 1988, no. 2: 48–56.

Milne, William. *Retrospect of the First Ten Years of the Protestant Mission to China.* Malacca: Anglo-Chinese Press, 1820.

*Minshu* 閩書. Comp. He Qiaoyuan 何喬遠 et al. 1630. Reprinted—5 vols., Fuzhou: Fujian renmin chubanshe, 1994–95.

*Minxi geming genjudi shi* 閩西革命根据地史. Beijing: Huaxia chubanshe, 1987.

Miura Kunio 三浦国雄. "Kaisetsu" 解説. In *Tsūsho no sekkai: Chūgokujin no nichi-erabi* 通書の世界: 中国人の日選び, trans. Miura Kunio and Kato Chie 加藤千惠, 132–59. Tokyo: Gaifusha, 1998. Translation of Richard J. Smith, *Chinese Almanacs,* Oxford: Oxford University Press, 1992.

———. "'Ōkō ki' no Okinawa ruiden" "玉匣記"の沖繩流傳. Paper presented at the Higashi Ajia shuppan bunka no kenkyū kokusai gakujutsu kaigi 東アジア出版文化の研究国際学術会議 conference, Tokyo, Dec. 10, 2001.

Miyazaki, Ichisada. *China's Examination Hell: The Civil Service Examinations of Imperial China.* Trans. Conrad Schirokauer. New York and Tokyo: John Weatherhill, 1976.

Mote, F. W. "China's Past in the Study of China Today—Some Comments on the Recent Work of Richard Solomon." *Journal of Asian Studies* 32, no. 1 (1972): 107–20.

Murakami Kimikazu 村上公一. "Chūgoku no shoseki ryūtsū to taishi hon'ya" 中国の書籍流通と貨本屋 (2). *Nagoya daigaku, Bungakubu kenkyū ronshū* 名古屋大学文学部研究論集 36 (1990): 229–43.

———. "Chūgoku no shoseki ryūtsū to taishi hon'ya—kinsho shiryō kara—" 中国の書籍流通と貨本屋—禁書史料から. In *Yamashita Ryūji kyōju taikan kinen Chūgokugaku ronshū* 山下龍二教授退官紀念中国学論集, 409–74. Tokyo: Kenbunsha, 1990.

Murray, Dian H., and Qin Baoqi. *The Origins of the Tiandihui: The Chinese Triads in Legend and History.* Stanford: Stanford University Press, 1994.

Myers, Ramon H. "Some Issues on Economic Organization During the Ming and Ch'ing Periods: A Review Article." *Ch'ing-shih wen-t'i* 3, no. 2: 77–97.

Nadler, Daniel. *China to Order, Focusing on the XIXth Century and Surveying Polychrome Export Porcelain Produced During the Qing Dynasty (1644–1908).* Paris: Vilo International, 2001.

Nagasawa Kikuya 長澤規矩. *Wa Kan sho no insatsu to sono rekishi* 和漢書の印刷とその歴史. Reprinted as *Nagasawa Kikuya chosakushū* 長澤規矩也著作集, vol. 2. Tokyo: Kyūko shoin, 1982.

Naquin, Susan, and Evelyn S. Rawski. *Chinese Society in the Eighteenth Century.* New Haven: Yale University Press, 1987.

Nevius, John L. *China and the Chinese.* Chicago: Missionary Campaign Library Number Two, 1882.

Nienhauser, William H., Jr., ed. and comp. *The Indiana Companion to Traditional Chinese Literature.* Bloomington: University of Indiana Press, 1986.

Ning Jiayu 宁稼雨, comp. *Zhongguo wenyan xiaoshuo zongmu tiyao* 中国文言小说总目提要. Ji'nan: Jilu shushe, 1996.

*Ninghua xianzhi* 宁华县志. 1684. Reprinted—Fuzhou: Fujian renmin chubanshe, 1989.

*Ninghua xianzhi* 寧化縣志. 1869.

Okamoto Sae 岡本さえ. *Shindai kinsho no kenkyū* 清代禁書の研究. Tokyo: Tōkyō daigaku, Tōyō bunka kenkyūjo, 1996.

Oldfield, W. H. *Pioneering in Kwangsi: The Story of Alliance Missions in South China.* Harrisburg, Pa.: Christian Publishers, 1936.

Ōtsuka Hidetaka 大塚秀高, comp. *Zōho Chūgoku tsūzoku shōsetsu shomoku* 増補中国通俗小説書目. Tokyo: Kyūko shoin, 1987.

Otte, Friedrich. "The Evolution of Bookkeeping and Accounting in China." *Annalen der Betriebswirtschaft* 2 (1928–29): 168–80.

Ouyang Jian 欧阳健. *Wan Qing xiaoshuo shi* 晚清小说史. Hangzhou: Zhejiang guji chubanshe, 1997.

Owen, Stephen. "The End of the Past: Rewriting Chinese Literary History in the Early Republic." In *The Appropriation of Cultural Capital: China's May Fourth Project*, ed. Milena Doleželová-Velingerová and Oldřich Král, 167–92. Cambridge, Mass.: Harvard University Asia Center, 2001.

Owenby, David. *Brotherhoods and Secret Societies in Early and Mid-Qing China: The Formation of a Tradition.* Stanford: Stanford University Press, 1996.

Palmer, Martin, ed. *T'ung Shu: The Ancient Chinese Almanac.* Boston: Shambala, 1986.

Parker, A. P. "The Chinese Almanac." *Chinese Recorder* 19, no. 12 (1888): 61–74.

———. "Review of The Imperial Guide to Astrology." *Chinese Recorder* 19, no. 11 (1888): 493–99.

Parker, Edward Harper. "The Educational Curriculum of the Chinese." *China Review* 9 (1880–81): 1–13.

Pelliot, Paul. *Les débuts de l'imprimerie en Chine.* Paris: Imprimerie nationale, 1953.

Peng Xinwei 彭信威. *A Monetary History of China.* 2 vols. Trans. of *Zhongguo huobi shi* 中國貨幣史, 3d ed., by Edward H. Kaplan. Bellingham, Wash.: Center for East Asian Studies, Western Washington University, 1993.

Perdue, Peter C. *Exhausting the Earth: State and Peasant in Hunan, 1500–1850.* Cambridge, Mass.: Council on East Asian Studies, Harvard University, 1987.

Perkins, Dwight. "Introduction." In *China's Modern Economy in Historical Perspective*, ed. Dwight Perkins and Kang Chao, 1–18. Stanford: Stanford University Press, 1975.

Polastron, Lucien X. *Le papier: 2000 ans d'histoire et de savoir-faire.* Paris: Imprimerie nationale, 1999.

Pomeranz, Kenneth. "'Traditional' Chinese Business Forms Revisited: Family, Firm, and Financing in the History of the Yutang Company of Jining, 1779–1956." *Late Imperial China* 18, no. 1 (1997): 1–38.

———. "Women's Work and the Economics of Respectability." In *Gender in Motion: Divisions of Labor and Cultural Change in Late Imperial and Modern China*, ed. Bryna Goodman and Wendy Larson, 239–63. Lanham, Md.: Rowman & Littlefield, 2005.

Price, Ernest B., and Paul P. Wiant. "Transportation and Public Works." In *Fukien: A Study of a Province in China*, by Anti-Cobweb Club, 72–78. Shanghai: Presbyterian Mission Press, 1925.

Pu Songling 蒲松齡. *Pu Songling ji* 蒲松齡集. 2 vols. Beijing: Zhonghua shuju, 1962.

Qi Yi 齐易, ed. *Guangxi hangyun shi* 广西航运史. Beijing: Renmin jiaotong chubanshe, 1991.

*Qingjiang xianzhi* 清江縣志. 1870. Reprinted—Zhongguo fangzhi congshu 中國方志叢書, Huazhong difang 華中地方, no. 262. Taibei: Chengwen chubanshe, 1975.

*Qingliu xianzhi* 清流縣志. Republican period. Reprinted—Fuzhou: Fujian ditu chubanshe, 1989.

Qiu Hengkuan 邱恒宽, comp. "Ninghua shudian shihua" 宁化书店史话. *Ninghua wenshi ziliao* 宁化文史资料 7 (1986): 89–91.

Qiu Rongzhou 邱荣洲. "Sibao diaoban yinshua suoyi" 四堡雕版印刷琐议. *Longyan shizhuan xuebao (shehui kexue ban)* 龙岩师专学报(社会科学版) 11, no. 2 (Dec. 1993): 57–62; 12, nos. 1–2 (June 1994): 51–56.

Rankin, Mary Backus. "Rural-Urban Continuities: Leading Families of Two Chekiang Market Towns." *Ch'ing-shih wen-t'i* 3, no. 7 (1977): 67–104.

Rawski, Evelyn S. *Agricultural Change and the Peasant Economy of South China.* Cambridge, Mass.: Harvard University Press, 1972.

———. "Economic and Social Foundations of Late Imperial Culture." In *Popular Culture in Late Imperial China*, ed. David Johnson, Andrew J. Nathan, and Evelyn S. Rawski, 3–33. Berkeley: University of California Press, 1985.

———. *Education and Popular Literacy in Ch'ing China.* Ann Arbor: University of Michigan Press, 1979.

Reed, Christopher. *Gutenberg in Shanghai: Chinese Print Capitalism, 1876–1937.* Vancouver: University of British Columbia Press, 2003.

Ren'an 韧庵. *Zhongguo gudai yixuejia* 中國古代醫學家. Xianggang: Shanghai shuju, 1963.

Revel, Jacques. "The Uses of Civility." In *A History of Private Life*, vol. 3, *Passions of the Renaissance*, ed. Roger Chartier, 167–205. Trans. Arthur Goldhammer. Cambridge, Mass.: Belknap Press of Harvard University Press, 1989.

Ridley, Charles Price. "Educational Theory and Practice in Late Imperial China: The Teaching of Writing as a Specific Case." Ph.D. diss., Stanford University, 1973.

Risse, Guenter B. "Introduction." In *Medicine Without Doctors: Home Health Care in American History*, ed. Guenter B. Risse, Ronald L. Numbers, and Judith Walzer Leavitt, 1–8. New York: Science History Publications/USA, 1977.

Rolston, David L. *Traditional Chinese Fiction and Fiction Commentary: Reading and Writing Between the Lines*. Stanford: Stanford University Press, 1997.

Rosenberg, Charles E. "Medical Text and Social Context: Explaining William Buchan's *Domestic Medicine*." *Bulletin of the History of Medicine* 57, no. 1 (Spring 1983): 22–42.

Rowe, William T. "Domestic Interregional Trade in Eighteenth-Century China." In *On the Eighteenth Century as a Category of Asian History: Van Leur in Retrospect*, ed. Leonard Blussé and Femme S. Gaastra, 173–92. Brookfield, Vt.: Ashgate, 1998.

———. "Education and Empire in Southwest China: Ch'en Hung-mou in Yunnan, 1733–38." In *Education and Society in Late Imperial China, 1600–1900*, ed. Benjamin A. Elman and Alexander Woodside, 417–57. Berkeley: University of California Press, 1994.

———. *Hankow: Commerce and Society in a Chinese City, 1796–1889*. Stanford: Stanford University Press, 1984.

———. *Ordering the World: Chen Hongmou and Elite Consciousness in Eighteenth-Century China*. Stanford: Stanford University Press, 2001.

Roy, David, trans. *The Plum in the Golden Vase*, vol. 2, *The Rivals*. Princeton: Princeton University Press, 2001.

Rozman, Gilbert Rozman. *Urban Networks in Ch'ing China and Tokugawa Japan*. Princeton: Princeton University Press, 1973.

Ruitenbeek, Klaas. *Carpentry & Building in Late Imperial China: A Study of the Fifteenth-Century Carpenter's Manual Lu Ban Jing*. Leiden: E. J. Brill, 1993.

Sakai Tadao. "Confucianism and Popular Educational Works." In *Self and Society in Ming Thought*, ed. Wm. Theodore de Bary, 331–66. New York: Columbia University Press, 1970.

———. "Mindai no nichiyō ruisho to shomin kyōiku" 明代の日用類書と庶民教育. In *Kinsei Chūgoku kyōiku kenkyū* 近世中国教育研究, ed. Hayashi Tomoharu 林友春, 25–154. Tokyo: Kokudosha, 1958.

Sawyer, Ralph D. "Military Writings." In *A Military History of China*, ed. David A. Graff and Robin Higham, 97–114. Boulder, Colo.: Westview Press, 2002.

Sawyer, Ralph D., with Mei-chün Sawyer, trans. *The Seven Military Classics of China*. Boulder, Colo.: Westview Press, 1993.

Seaman, Gary. *Journey to the North: An Ethnohistorical Analysis and Annotated Translation of the Chinese Folk Novel* Pei-yu-chi. Berkeley: University of California Press, 1987.

*Shangrao xianzhi* 上饒縣志. 1873.

Shaw, Norman. *Chinese Forest Trees and Timber Supply*. London: T. Fisher Unwin, 1914.

Shen Fu. *Six Records of a Floating Life*. Trans. Leonard Pratt and Chiang Su-hui. New York: Penguin Books, 1983.

Shen Li 沈鯉. "Yixue yue" 義學約. In *Lidai jiaoyu zhidu kao* 历代教育制度考, vol. 2. In Zhongguo jiaoyu daxi 中国教育大系. Wuhan: Hubei jiaoyu chubanshe, 1994.

Shen, Ki-Fein. *Essai dur l'origine et l'évolution des banques en Chine*. Paris: Les éditions Domat-Montchrestien, 1936.

Shi Hongbao 施鸿保. *Min zaji* 闽杂记. Preface dated 1858. In *Min xiaoji / Min zaji* 闽小纪闽杂记, ed. Lai Xinxia 来新夏, 1–200. Fuzhou: Fujian renmin chubanshe, 1985.

*Sichuan shengzhi—chuban zhi* 四川省志—出版志. 2 vols. Chengdu: Sichuan renmin chubanshe, 2001.

Situ Shangji 司徒尚纪. *Lingnan shidi lunji* 岭南史地论集. Guangzhou: Guangdongsheng ditu chubanshe, 1994.

Skinner, G. William. "Introduction." In *Migration and Ethnicity in Chinese History: Hakkas, Pengmin, and Their Neighbors* by Sow-theng Leong, 1–18. Stanford: Stanford University Press, 1997.

Smith, Arthur H. *Pearls of Wisdom from China*. Singapore: Graham Brash, 1988.

———. *Village Life in China*. New York: Fleming H. Revell, 1899.

Smith, Richard J. *Fortune-tellers and Philosophers: Divination in Traditional Chinese Society*. Boulder, Colo.: Westview Press, 1991.

———. "A Note on Qing Dynasty Calendars." *Late Imperial China* 9.1 (June 1988): 123–45.

Snow, Edgar. *Red Star over China*. London: Victor Gollanz, 1937.

Spence, Jonathan D. *God's Chinese Son: The Taiping Heavenly Kingdom of Hong Xiuquan*. New York: W. W. Norton, 1996.

Ssu-ma Ch'ien. *Records of the Grand Historian*. Trans. Burton Watson. 2 vols. New York: Columbia University Press, 1961.

St Clair, William. *The Reading Nation in the Romantic Period*. Cambridge, Eng.: Cambridge University Press, 2004.

Struve, Lynn A. *The Southern Ming, 1644–1662*. New Haven: Yale University Press, 1984.

Su Jilang 蘇基朗. *Tang Song shidai Minnan Quanzhou shidi lungao* 唐宋時代閩南泉州史地論稿. Taibei: Taiwan Shangwu yinshuguan, 1991.

Sun, Ching-chih (孙敬之), ed. *Economic Geography of South China (Kwangtung, Kwangsi, Fukien)*. Trans. of *Huanan diqu jingji dili* 华南地区经济地理 (Beijing: Kexue chubanshe, 1959). Washington, D.C.: U.S. Department of Commerce, Office of Technical Services, Joint Publications Research Service, 1962.

Sun Kaidi 孫楷第. *Zhongguo tongsu xiaoshuo shumu* 中國通俗小說書目. Reprinted—Taibei: Fenghuang chubanshe, 1974.

Sun Wenqi 孙文奇. *Zhongguo lidai mingyi jilu* 中国历代名医集录. Taiyuan: Shanxi kexue jishu chubanshe, 1992.

Sung Ying-hsing. *Chinese Technology in the Seventeenth Century: T'ien-kung k'ai-wu*. Trans. E-tu Zen Sun and Shiou-chuan Sun. University Park: Pennsylvania State University Press, 1966.

Tan Qixiang 譚其驤. "Zhongguo neidi yiminshi—Hunan pian" 中國內地移民史—湖南篇. *Shixue nianbao* 史學年報 3 (1931): 47–104.

Tan Qixiang 譚其驤, ed. *Zhongguo lishi ditu ji* 中国历史地图集, vol. 8, *Qing shiqi* 清时期. Beijing: Ditu chubanshe, 1982.

Tan Wenxi 譚文熙. *Zhongguo wujia shi* 中国物价史. Wuhan: Hubei renmin chubanshe, 1994.

Tan Yanhuan 覃延欢 and Liao Guoyi 廖国一. *Guangxi shigao* 广西史稿. Nanning: Guangxi shifan daxue chubanshe, 1998.

Tang Lizong 唐立宗. *Zai "daoqu" yu "zhengqu" zhi jian—Mingdai Min Yue Gan Xiang jiaojie de zhixu biandong yu difang xingzheng yanhua* 在"盜區"與"政區"之間—明代閩粵贛湘交界的秩序變動與地方行政演化. Taibei: Guoli Taiwan daxue chuban weiyuanhui, 2002.

T'ien, Ju-k'ang. "The Decadence of Buddhist Temples in Fu-chien in Late Ming and Early Ch'ing." In *Development and Decline of Fukien Province in the 17th and 18th Centuries*, ed. E. B. Vermeer, 83–100. Leiden: E. J. Brill, 1990.

*Tingzhou fuzhi* 汀州府志. 1527.

*Tingzhou fuzhi* 汀州府志. 1752. Revised 1867. Reprinted—Zhongguo fangzhi congshu 中國方志叢書, no. 75. Taibei: Chengwen chubanshe, 1967.

Tomasko, Nancy Norton. "Chinese Handmade Paper—A Richly Varied Thing." *Hand Papermaking* 19, no. 1 (Summer 2004): 20–32.

Tsien, Tsuen-hsuin (Qian Cunxun 錢存訓). *Paper and Printing*, vol. 5, part I, of *Science and Civilisation in China*, ed. Joseph Needham. Cambridge, Eng.: Cambridge University Press, 1985.

———. "Yinshuashu zai Zhongguo chuantong wenhuazhong de gongneng" 印刷術在中國傳統文化中的功能. *Hanxue yanjiu* 漢學研究 8, no. 2 (Dec. 1989): 239–50.

———. "Zhongguo yinshuashi jianmu" 中國印刷簡目. *Guoli Zhongyang tushuguan guankan* 國立中央圖書館館刊 n.s. 23, no. 1 (June 1990): 179–99.

Tu, Ching-i. "The Chinese Examination Essay: Some Literary Considerations." *Monumenta Serica* 31 (1974–75): 393–406.

Twitchett, Denis C. *Printing and Publishing in Medieval China.* New York: Frederic C. Beil, 1983.

Unschuld, Paul U. *Medicine in China: A History of Ideas.* Berkeley: University of California Press, 1985.

———. *Medicine in China: A History of Pharmaceutics.* Berkeley: University of California Press, 1997.

van der Loon, Piet. *The Classical Theatre and Art Song of Southern Fukien: A Study of Three Ming Anthologies.* Taipei: SMC Publishing, 1992.

Vermeer, Eduard B. "Introduction: Historical Background and Major Issues." In *Development and Decline of Fukien Province in the 17th and 18th Centuries,* ed. E. B. Vermeer, 5–34. Leiden: E. J. Brill, 1990.

von Glahn, Richard. *The Sinister Way: The Divine and the Demonic in Chinese Religious Culture.* Berkeley: University of California Press, 2004.

von Mende, Erling. "Literacy in Traditional China: A Late Reflex on Evelyn Rawski." In *Autumn Floods: Essays in Honor of Marian Galik,* ed. Raoul D. Findeisen and Robert H. Gassman, 49–60. Berne: Peter Lang, 1998.

Wakefield, David. *Fenjia: Household Division and Inheritance in Qing and Republican China.* Honolulu: University of Hawai'i Press, 1998.

Wakeman, Frederic, Jr. *Strangers at the Gate: Social Disorder in South China, 1839–1861.* Berkeley: University of California Press, 1966.

Waley, Arthur. *Yuan Mei, Eighteenth Century Chinese Poet.* London: George Allen & Unwin, 1956. Reprinted—Stanford: Stanford University Press, 1970.

Wan, Margaret Baptist. "*Green Peony* as New Popular Fiction: The Birth of the Martial Romance in Early Nineteenth-Century China." Ph.D. diss., Harvard University, 2000.

Wang Bin 王彬. *Qingdai jinshu zongshu* 清代禁书总述. Beijing: Zhongguo shudian, 1990.

Wang Fuzhi 王夫之, comp. *Qing shihua* 清詩話. Ed. Ding Fubao 丁福保. 2 vols. Beijing: Zhonghua shuju, 1963.

Wang Gang 王纲. "Qingdai Sichuan de yinshuye" 清代四川的印书业. *Zhongguo shehui jingjishi yanjiu* 中国社会经济史研究 1991, no. 4: 62–70.

Wang Jian'an 王簡菴. *Linting kaoyan* 臨汀考言. Prefaces dated 1699, 1700.

Wang Maohe 汪茂和, ed. *Baihua mengxue jingxuan* 白话蒙学精选. Beijing: Zhishi chubanshe, 1991.

Wang Rongguang 王荣光, ed. *Minxi diming* 闽西地名. Xiamen: Lujiang chubanshe, 1992.

Wang Shimao 王世懋., ed. *Minbu shu* 閩部疏. Preface dated 1586. Ming Baoyan tang 寶顏堂. Facsimile reprint—*Zhongguo fangzhi congshu* 中國方志叢書, no. 243, Taipei: Chengwen chubanshe, 1965.

Wang Shixin 汪士信. "Ming Qing shiqi shangye jingying fangshi de bianhua" 明清时期商业经营方式的变化. *Zhongguo jingjishi yanjiu* 中国经济史研究 10 (1988, no. 2): 14–28.

Wang Tianjiang 王天奖. "Qing Tong Guang shiqi kemin de yiken" 清同光时期客民的移垦. *Jindaishi yanjiu* 近代史研究 2 (1983): 224–41.

Wang Xiaoyuan 王孝源. "Qingdai Sichuan muke shufang shulue" 清代四川木刻书坊述略. *Sichuan xinwen chuban shiliao* 四川新聞出版史料 1 (1992): 43–65.

Wang Xuemei 王雪梅, ed. *Mengxue: qimeng de keben* 蒙学: 启蒙的课本. Beijing: Zhongyang minzu daxue chubanshe, 1996.

Wang Yeh-chien. "Food Supply in Eighteenth-Century Fukien." *Late Imperial China* 7, no. 2 (Dec. 1986): 80–117.

———. "The Secular Trend of Prices During the Ch'ing Period (1644–1911)." *Xianggang Zhongwen daxue Zhongguo wenhua yanjiusuo xuebao* 香港中文大學中國文化研究所學報 (Journal of the Institute of Chinese Studies of the Chinese University of Hong Kong) 5, no. 2 (Dec. 1972): 347–71.

Watson, James L. "The Structure of Chinese Funerary Rites: Elementary Forms, Ritual Sequence, and the Primacy of Performance." In *Death Ritual in Late Imperial and Modern China*, ed. James L. Watson and Evelyn S. Rawski, 3–19. Berkeley: University of California Press, 1988.

Watson, Rubie. *Inequality Among Brothers: Class and Kinship in South China*. Cambridge, Eng.: Cambridge University Press, 1985.

Wei, Shang. "*Jin Ping Mei* and Late Ming Print Culture." In *Writing and Materiality in China: Essays in Honor of Patrick Hanan*, ed. Judith T. Zeitlin and Lydia H. Liu, 187–231. Harvard-Yenching Institute Monograph Series 58. Cambridge, Mass.: Harvard University Asia Center, 2003.

———. "The Making of the Everyday World: *Jin Ping Mei cihua* and Encyclopedias for Daily Use." In *Dynastic Crisis and Cultural Innovation: From the Late Ming to the Late Qing and Beyond*, ed. David Der-wei Wang and Shang Wei, 63–92. Cambridge, Mass.: Harvard University Asia Center, 2005.

West, Andrew C., comp. *Catalogue of the Morrison Collection of Chinese Books*. London: School of Oriental and African Studies, University of London, 1998.

Widmer, Ellen. "*Honglou meng ying* and Its Publisher, Juzhen tang of Beijing." *Late Imperial China* 23, no. 2 (Dec. 2002): 33–52.

———. "The Huanduzhai of Hangzhou and Suzhou: A Study in Seventeenth-Century Publishing." *Harvard Journal of Asiatic Studies* 56, no. 1 (1996): 77–122.

———. *The Margins of Utopia:* Shui-hu hou-chuan *and the Literature of Ming Loyalism.* Cambridge, Mass.: Council on East Asian Studies, Harvard University, 1987.

———. "Modernization Without Mechanization: The Changing Shape of Fiction on the Eve of the Opium War." Paper presented at the conference "From Woodblocks to the Internet: Chinese Publishing and Print Culture in Transition," Ohio State University, Columbus, Ohio, November 3–6, 2004.

Wilkinson, Endymion. *Chinese History: A Manual.* Cambridge, Mass.: Harvard University Asia Center, 2000.

Williams, Samuel Wells. *The Middle Kingdom, a Survey of the Geography, Government, Education, Social Life, Arts, Religions, &c., of the Chinese Empire and Its Inhabitants.* 2 vols. New York & London: Wiley and Putnam, 1848.

———. *The Middle Kingdom, a Survey of the Geography, Government, Literature, Social Life, Arts, and History of the Chinese Empire and Its Inhabitants.* 2 vols. New York: Charles Scribner's Sons, 1882.

Wilson, Thomas A. *The Genealogy of the Way: The Construction and Uses of the Confucian Tradition in Late Imperial China.* Stanford: Stanford University Press, 1995.

Woodside, Alexander. "Real and Imagined Continuities in the Chinese Struggle for Literacy." In *Education and Modernization: The Chinese Experience*, ed. Ruth Hayhoe, 23–45. Oxford: Pergamon Press, 1992.

Woodside, Alexander, and Benjamin A. Elman. "Afterword: The Expansion of Education in Ch'ing China." In *Education and Society in Late Imperial China, 1600–1900*, ed. Benjamin A. Elman and Alexander Woodside, 525–60.

Woon, Yuen-fong. *Social Organization in South China, 1911–1949: The Case of the Kuan Lineage in K'ai-p'ing County.* Ann Arbor: Center for Chinese Studies, University of Michigan, 1984.

Wu Hongyi 吳宏一, ed. *Qingdai shihua zhijianlu* 清代詩話知見錄. Taipei: Zhongyang yanjiuyuan, Zhongguo wenzhe yanjiusuo, 2002.

Wu Hongyou 吳鴻猷. "Lüetan Liancheng tuzhi he dalianzhi ji qi jingying qingkuang" 略談连城土纸和大连纸及其经营情况. *Liancheng wenshi ziliao* 连城文史资料 6 (1986): 81–86.

Wu Huifang 吳蕙芳. *Wanbao quanshu: Ming Qing shiqi de minjian shenghuo shilu* 萬寶全書: 明清時期的民間生活實錄. Taipei: Guoli zhengzhi daxue, Lishixi, 2001.

Wu, Pei-yi. "Education of Children in the Sung." In *Neo-Confucian Education: The Formative Stage*, ed. Wm. Theodore de Bary and John W. Chaffee, 307–24. Berkeley: University of California Press, 1989.

Wu Shideng 吴世灯. "Qingdai Sibao keshuye diaocha baogao" 清代四堡刻书业调查报告. *Chuban shi yanjiu* 出版史研究 2 (1994): 129–61.

———. "Sibao shufang jingying lu" 四堡书坊经营录. Unpublished paper.

Wylie, A. *Notes on Chinese Literature*. Shanghai, 1867. Reprinted—Taipei: Bookcase Shop, 1970.

Xie Shuishun 谢水顺 and Li Ting 李珽. *Fujian gudai keshu* 福建古代刻书. Fuzhou: Fujian renmin chubanshe, 1997.

Xu Baolin 许保林. *Zhongguo bingshu tonglan* 中国兵书通览. Beijing: Jiefangjun chubanshe, 1990.

Xu Ge 徐舸. *Qingmo Guangxi Tiandi hui fengyun lu* 清末广西天地会风云录. Guilin: Guangxi shifan daxue chubanshe, 1990.

Xu Huailin 许怀林. *Jiangxi shigao* 江西史稿. Nanchang: Jiangxi gaoxiao chubanshe, 1998.

Xu Jianqing 徐建青. "Qingdai de zaozhiye" 清代的造纸业. *Zhongguoshi yanjiu* 中国史研究 3 (1997): 135–44.

———. "Qingdai shougongyezhong de hehuo zhi" 清代手工业中的合伙制. *Zhongguo jingjishi yanjiu* 中国经济史研究 40 (1995, no. 4): 125–39.

Xu Ke 徐珂. *Qingbei leichao* 清稗類鈔. 13 vols. Beijing: Zhonghua shuju, 1984.

Xu Tan 许檀. "Dui Qingdai qianqi shangshui wenti de yidian kanfa" 对清代前期商税问题的一点看法. Paper presented at the Guoji Qingshi xueshu taolunhui 国际清史学术讨论会, Nanjing, Nov. 1989.

Xu Xiaowang 徐晓望. *Fujian sixiang wenhua shigang* 福建思想文化史纲. Fuzhou: Fujian jiaoyu chubanshe, 1996.

———. "Ming Qing Min Zhe Gan bian shanqu jingji fazhan de xin qushi" 明清闽浙赣边山区经济发展的新趋势. In *Ming Qing Fujian shehui yu xiangcun jingji* 明清福建社会与乡村经济, ed. Fu Yiling 傅衣凌 and Yang Guozhen 杨国桢, 193–226. Xiamen: Xiamen daxue chubanshe, 1987.

Xu Xinfu 徐信符. "Guangzhou banpian jilüe" 广州版片记略. *Guangdong chuban shiliao* 广东出版史料 2 (1991): 13–19.

Xu Xinwu 徐新吾. *Jiangnan tubu shi* 江南土布史. Shanghai: Shanghai shehui kexueyuan chubanshe, 1992.

Xu Zhengfu 徐正付. "Jinxi shu" 金溪書. *Jiangxi chubanshi zhi* 江西出版史志 3 (1993): 36–39.

Yang, C. K. "Some Preliminary Statistical Patterns of Mass Actions in Nineteenth-Century China." In *Conflict and Control in Late Imperial China*, ed. Frederic Wakeman, Jr., and Carolyn Grant, 174–210. Berkeley: University of California Press, 1975.

Yang Dan. "Le *Classique en trois caractères* ou le passé au service du présent." In *Education et instruction en Chine*, vol. 1, *L'éducation élémentaire*, ed. Christine Nguyen Tri and Catherine Despeux, 179–97. Paris: Peeters, 2003.

Yang Jie 杨捷, ed. *Fujian hangyun shi (gujindai bufen)* 福建航运史(古近代部分). Beijing: Renmin jiaotong chubanshe, 1994.

Yang Lan 楊瀾. *Linting huikao* 臨汀彙考. Preface dated 1878.

Yang Zhengtai 杨正泰, ed. *Tianxia shuilu lucheng / Tianxia lucheng tuyin / Keshang yilan xingmi*. 天下水陆路程/天下路程图引/客商一览醒迷. Taiyuan: Shanxi renmin chubanshe, 1992.

Ye Chunsheng 叶春生. *Lingnan suwenxue jianshi* 岭南俗文学简史. Guangzhou: Guangdong gaodeng chubanshe, 1996.

Ye Dehui 葉德輝. *Shulin qinghua* 書林清話. 1957. Reprinted—Beijing: Zhonghua shuju, 1987.

Ye Xian'en 叶显恩. *Ming Qing Huizhou nongcun shehui yu dianpu zhi* 明清徽州农村社会与佃仆制. Hefei: Anhui renmin chubanshe, 1983.

———. "Qingdai Guangdong shuiyun yu shehui jingji" 清代广东水运与社会经济. *Zhongguo shehui jingjishi yanjiu* 中国社会经济史研究 1987, no. 4: 1–10.

Yin Chengfang 陰承方. *Yin Jingfu xiansheng yiwen* 陰靜夫先生遺文. Yangzhou: Junzhai, 1807.

Yong Ming 詠羹. "Chengdushi de renli chefu" 成都市的人力車夫. *Laogong yuekan* 勞工月刊 1 (Mar. 1935): 1–22.

*Youxue qionglin* 幼学琼林. Ed. Li Shengzhao 李升召. Facsimile reproduction of Li Guangming zhuang 李光明莊 edition—Hainan: Hainan chubanshe, 1992.

Yü Ying-shih. "Business Culture and Chinese Traditions—Toward a Study of the Evolution of Merchant Culture in Chinese History." In *Dynamic Hong Kong: Business & Culture*, ed. Wang Gungwu and Wong Siu-lun, 1–84. Hong Kong: Centre of Asian Studies, University of Hong Kong, 1997.

Yuan Yi 袁逸. "Qingdai de shuji jiaoyi ji shujia kao" 清代的书籍交易及书价考. *Sichuan tushuguan xuebao* 四川圖書館學報 65 (1992, no. 1): 71–80, 47.

*Yuyan wenzi* 语言文字. *Zhongguo dabaike quanshu* 中国大百科全书. Shanghai: Zhongguo dabaike quanshu chubanshe, 1988.

Zelin, Madeleine. *The Merchants of Zigong: Industrial Entrepreneurship in Early Modern China*. New York: Columbia University Press, 2005.

———. "The Yung-cheng Reign." In *The Cambridge History of China*, vol. 9, *The Ch'ing Dynasty to 1800*, Part 1, ed. Willard J. Peterson, 183–229. Cambridge, Eng.: Cambridge University Press, 2002.

Zelin, Madeleine, Jonathan K. Ocko, and Robert Gardella, eds. *Contract and Property in Early Modern China*. Stanford: Stanford University Press, 2004.

Zeng Ling 曾玲. *Fujian shougongye fazhan shi* 福建手工业发展史. Xiamen: Xiamen daxue chubanshe, 1995.

Zhang Guilin 张桂林 and Luo Qingsi 罗庆四. "Fujian shangren yu Mazu xinyang" 福建商人与马祖信仰. *Fujian shifan daxue xuebao: zhexue shehui kexue ban* 福建师范大学学报: 哲学社会科学版 1992, no.3: 105–10.

Zhang Haipeng 张海鹏 and Tang Lixing 唐力行. "Lun Huishang 'gu er haoru' de tese" 论徽商'贾而好儒'的特色. *Zhongguoshi yanjiu* 中国史研究 1984, no. 4: 57–70.

Zhang Hongxiang 張鴻样. "Tingjiang shangye hangyun de diaocha" 汀江商業航運的調查. In *Changtingxian de zongzu, jingji yu minsu (shang)* 長汀縣的宗族, 經濟與民俗(上), ed. Yang Yanjie 楊彥杰, 22–79. Traditional Hakka Society Series, no. 15, ed. John Lagerway. Hong Kong: International Hakka Studies Association, Overseas Chinese Archives, and Ecole française d'Extrême-Orient, 2002.

Zhang Jun 张俊. *Qingdai xiaoshuo shi* 清代小说史. Hangzhou: Zhejiang guji chubanshe, 1997.

Zhang Longhua 张隆华 and Zeng Zhongshan 曾仲姗. *Zhongguo gudai yuwen jiaoyu shi* 中国古代语文教育史. Chengdu: Sichuan jiaoyu chubanshe, 2000.

Zhang Xiumin 张秀民. *Zhongguo yinshua shi* 中国印刷史. Shanghai: Shanghai renmin chubanshe, 1989.

Zhang Zhigong 张志公. *Chuantong yuwen jiaoyu jiaocai lun—ji mengxue shumu he shuying* 传统语文教育教材论—墜蒙学书目和书影. Shanghai: Shanghai jiaoyu chubanshe, 1992.

Zhao Shuiquan 赵水泉. "Jinxi de 'xiao Shanghai'—Xuwanzhen" 金溪的'小上海'—浒湾镇. *Jinxi wenshi ziliao xuanji* 金溪文史资料选辑 4 (1988, no. 12): 44–48.

———. "Xuwan yu muke yinshu" 浒湾与木刻印书. *Jiangxi difangzhi tongxun* 江西地方志通讯 9 (1986, no. 2): 51–55.

Zhao Zhaobing 赵昭炳, ed. *Fujian sheng dili* 福建省地里. Fuzhou: Fujian renmin chubanshe, 1993.

Zheng Guangchang 郑光昌. "Ninghua mingyou techanpin" 宁化名优特产品. *Ninghua wenshi ziliao* 宁化文史资料 11 (1990): 45–53.

Zheng Zhenman. *Family Lineage Organization and Social Change in Ming and Qing Fujian.* Trans. Michael Szonyi. Honolulu: University of Hawai'i Press, 2001.

Zhong Qisheng 鍾其生. "Lun Fujian zongzu tudi" 論福建宗族土地. *Shehui kexue* 社會科學 5, no. 12 (1949): n.p. (7 pages).

*Zhongguo dashudian* 中国大书典. Ed. Chu Zhuang 楚庄, Huang Zhuoyue 黄卓越, and Sang Sifen 桑思奋. Beijing: Zhonghua shudian, 1994.

*Zhongguo gudai xiaoshuo baike quanshu* 中国古代小说百科全书. Beijing: Zhongguo dabaike quanshu chubanshe, 1993.

*Zhongguo guji shanben shumu* 中國古籍善本書目. 10 vols. Shanghai: Shanghai guji chubanshe, 1985–96.

*Zhongguo tongsu xiaoshuo zongmu tiyao* 中国通俗小说总目提要. Beijing: Zhongguo wenlian chuban gongsi, 1990.

*Zhongguo wenyan xiaoshuo shumu* 中国文言小说书目. Ed. Yuan Xingpei 袁行霈 and Hou Zhongyi 侯中义. Beijing: Beijing daxue chubanshe, 1981.

*Zhongguo yiji dacidian* 中国医籍大辞典. 2 vols. Shanghai: Shanghai kexue jishu chubanshe, 2002.

Zhou Lianggong 周亮工. *Min xiaoji* 闽小纪. In *Min xiaoji / Min zaji* 闽小纪 / 闽杂记, ed. Lai Xinxia 来新夏, 1–91. Fuzhou: Fujian renmin chubanshe, 1985.

Zhu Weigan 朱维幹. *Fujian shigao* 福建史稿. 2 vols. Fuzhou: Fujian jiaoyu chubanshe, 1985–86.

Zhu Xi 朱熹. *Huian xiansheng Zhu Wengong wenji* 晦庵先生朱文公文集. 100 *juan*, plus 23 *juan*. In *Sibu congkan chubian* 四部叢刊初編, vols. 1058–107. Shanghai: Shangwu yinshuguan, 1919.

Zhuang Yifu 莊一拂. *Gudian xiqu cunmu huikao* 古典戲曲存目彙考. 3 vols. Shanghai: Shanghai guji chubanshe, 1982.

Zou Chunsheng 邹春生. "*Youxue qionglin* zengbuzhe Zou Shengmai" 幼学琼林增补者邹圣脉. *Liancheng wenshi ziliao* 连城文史资料 11 (1991): 114–15.

Zou Risheng 邹日升. "Sibao Wuge guji diaoban yinshuaye kuibao" 四堡霧閣古籍雕版印刷業窺豹. In *Fanyang Zoushi zupu* 范陽鄒氏族譜, 1: 177–80. 1996.

———. "Zhongguo sida diaoban yinshua jidi zhi yi—Sibao: qiantan Sibao diaoban yinshuaye de shengshuai" 中国四大雕版印刷基地之一——四堡: 浅谈四堡雕版印刷业的盛衰. *Liancheng wenshi ziliao* 连城文史资料 5 (1985): 102–15.

Zou Zibin 邹子彬. "'Lianggong zaozhi Tingzhou fu'" 良工造纸汀州府. *Changting wenshi ziliao* 长汀文史资料 5 (1983): 102–9.

Zurndorfer, Harriet T. *Change and Continuity in Chinese Local History: The Development of Hui-chou Prefecture, 800 to 1800*. Leiden: E. J. Brill, 1989.

# Index

Abacus, primers for, 343–44; *Suanfa cuoyao* 算法撮要, 343–44; *Suanfa yaojue* 算法要訣, 344*n*

Academies (*shuyuan*): business with branch bookstores, 254–56; increased number of, 51–52, 56–57, 322; as markets for educational texts, 80–81, 84, 233, 238, 405; in Tingzhou, 316

Accounting: branch bookstore, 144–45, 262–63, 266*n*; household, 140–45, 150, 262–63, 291; publishing house, 140–45, 291

Acupuncture practitioners, 315

Acupuncture texts, 445–46, 514; *Fazhen du* 發針度, 446; *Tongren yuxue zhenjiu tujing* 銅人腧穴針灸圖經, 446*n*; *Tongren zhenjiu* 銅人針灸, 446*n*; *Zhenjiu daquan* 針灸大全, 446*n*

Adventure novels, 478, 486–87, 492–94, 497, 531–32. *See also* Military romances

Agriculture: crops, 43; double-cropping, 46; glossaries, 337, 339, 341; in Guangdong, 220; manuals, 566; in Minxi, 39, 40, 41, 43; in Sibao, 65; subsistence, 39, 46–47; women's labor, 40, 41

Allusion collections, 309, 399; *Chengyu kao* 成語考, 350*n*; *Jingshi diangu* 經史典故, 311; *Youxue gushi qionglin* 幼學故事瓊林, 165, 255, 260, 307, 311, 313, 349–53, 517

Almanacs (*tongshu*): compilers, 311; *Cui Fu tongshu* 崔福通書, 311; *Luchuan tongshu* 爐傳通書, 311; popularity, 451–52, 469, 471; printed by branch bookstores, 264; *Xiangji [beiyao] tongshu* 象吉 [備要]通書, 454*n*; *Xingping yaojue Bainian jing heke* 星平要訣百年經合刻, 452; *Yuxia ji* 玉匣記, 255; *Zengbu zhujia xuanze guang Yuxia ji* 增補諸家選擇廣玉匣記, 452–54

An Lushan 安祿山 rebellion, 372–73

*Analects*, 332, 333, 365, 377–78, 382, 408. *See also* Four Books

Ancestor worship, 60, 72

Ancestral estates (*zutian*), 69, 70, 76, 276

Ancestral halls, 61, 62, 105, 156–57

Anle 安樂, 119; paper industry, 114, 115, 116–17

Anliuyu 安流圩, 201, 243–49

Anqing 安慶, 12, 539

Anshun 安順, 12

Aofeng 傲峰 Mountains, 58

Astrology, 465–66

Authorship concept, 310, 313, 314

Bai, Limin, 335

*Baijia xing* 百家姓, 321, 326, 328, 349

*Bai tanzi* 擺攤子 (temporary stalls), 238

Bamboo: cultivation, 96; types, 95–96

Bamboo-branch stories (*zhuzhi ci*), 505*n*

Bamboo forests, 95–96

Bamboo paper: availability in southern China, 18; costs, 145*n*; cutting, 121–22; demand for, 120; exports, 44, 95, 120; *lianshi*, 117, 539; *maobian*, 115, 117–18, 121, 519, 537; obtaining, 115–16; page sizes, 118*n*, 119, 121–22; prices, 121; purchased by booksellers, 237; quality, 117–18, 120–21; shipping, 115–16; types, 117–18; *yukou*, 115, 117–18, 121

Bamboo paper-making: materials, 43–44, 95–96; methods, 118–21; outside investment, 46; seasonal cycle, 122; in Tingzhou, 113–15, 120; in Xuwanzhen, 537

Bamboo shoots, 43

Bamboo shoulder baskets (*matuo* or *maduo*), 256

*Banbenxue* 版本學 (study of editions), 5

Bandits, 40, 249–51

Banks, 218

Bao 包, Judge, 486, 488

Bao Xiang'ao 鮑相璈, 441–42

*Baochi zhinan che* 保赤指南車, 442–43

Baojing tang 抱經堂, 12

Baoqing 寶慶, 12, 229

Beijiang 北江, 201, 234

Beijing: book markets, 539; publishing industry, 9, 10, 12

Beiliu 北流, 172, 224*n*, 247*n*

Beituan 北圍, 114, 115, 236, 237

Belles-lettres, 506–10

Benli tang 本立堂, 131, 165, 175, 186, 245, 258

Benzu tang 本祖堂, 239–40

Binding, 109–11; tools, 26

Biqing tang 碧清堂, 261, 397

Block cutters: character-cutting shops, 17, 98, 104; employment relationships, 17; famous lineages of, 15; hiring, 97–99, 100, 104–5; household members, 99–100; itinerant, 17, 98, 99, 542; of local lineages, 98, 100; in Magang, 15, 101–2, 104–5, 133, 536, 545–46; productivity, 103; skills, 14–15; transporting blocks from distant, 17; wages, 15, 17, 102*n*, 146, 541, 546; women, 14–15, 17, 101–2, 133, 146, 545–46; in Yuechi county, 11–12, 14, 17, 536, 540–44

Block cutting: costs, 146; in Magang, 15, 101–2, 104–5, 133, 536, 545–46; preparation, 97, 99, 102–3; process, 14, 97, 102–3; as simple task, 100; as subsidiary craft, 15; in

Yuechi county, 11–12, 14, 17, 536, 540–44. *See also* Woodblocks

Book boxes, 242–43

Book designs, 103

Bookkeeping, *see* Accounting

Book lists, 22–24

Book markets: Jianyang, 294; in Qing, 12; Sibao, 87, 190–92; supplied by Xuwanzhen, 539. *See also* Bookselling routes

Book presses (*shuzha*), 109–11

Book rentals, 518

Books, *see* Sibao imprints

Booksellers, *see* Itinerant booksellers; Sibao publishers/booksellers

Bookselling routes: cities avoided, 199–200, 218, 231, 232–33, 234, 300; cooperation among publishers, 185, 196–97; economic conditions and, 221; expansion, 222, 299; factors in choice of, 206–7, 231–34, 300; local, 193, 236, 237; overseas, 194; relationship to Hakka migration, 211–15, 231–32, 240, 299; scope, 3, 38–39, 194–97; transport networks as factor, 207–11. *See also* Itinerant booksellers

Bookstores: stocks, 123. *See also* Branch bookstores

Bose 百色: bookselling routes, 202, 209, 224, 255; bookstores, 256, 258, 265

Bosses (*laoban*), 101

Branch bookstores, of Sibao publishers: accounts, 144–45, 262–63, 266*n*; assistance to itinerant booksellers, 242, 257; book shipments to, 243–49, 256–57; central control of, 143–45, 261, 264; cooperation among, 257–58; customers, 254; establishment, 191–92, 193–94, 239, 252–53; independence, 145, 262–65; itinerant booksellers based at, 256; locations, 195, 219–20, 231, 234; management of, 143–44; managers, 145, 156–57, 262–63; markets, 254–56; in nineteenth century, 90; opened by itinerant booksellers, 139; orders from schools, 255–56; partnerships, 258–59; printing operations, 263–65; relationship to publishing houses, 253–54, 256–57, 260–62; relations with school officials, 254–55; specialization, 257–58; in twentieth century, 3, 92, 267, 341

Brokerage firms (*yahang*), 298

Brokers (*yaren*), 298

Brushes, printing, 95, 107, 111

Buddhism, 73–74, 467

Burial sites: disputes over, 77, 456; in Sibao, 59–60. *See also* Funeral rituals

*Bushi zhengzong* 卜筮正宗, 462–63

Caishen 財神, 73

*Caizi jiaren* 才子佳人 (talent and beauty) love stories, 488–90, 494, 495, 532; *Diba caizi Huajian ji* 第八才子花箋記, 505*n*; *Erdu mei quanzhuan* 二度梅全傳, 489, 495, 531; *Haoqiu zhuan* 好逑傳, 489; *Jinxiang ting* 錦香亭, 489; *Jiu caizi Erhehua shi* 九才子二荷花史, 505*n*; *Liangjiaohun xiaozhuan* 兩交婚小傳, 489; *Shuangfeng qiyuan* 雙鳳奇緣, 495, 497; *Tiehua xianshi* 鐵花仙史, 489; *Wufeng yin* 五鳳吟, 489, 497; *Wumei yuan*

五美緣, 497; *Xihu xiaoshi* 西湖小史, 490; *Xiuzhen Ba caizi [shu]* 袖珍八才子[書], 505*n*; *Ying Yun meng* 英雲夢, 489; *Zhuchun yuan* 駐春園, 490

Calligraphy: of Zou Shengmai, 311, 507–10

Calligraphy manuals, 336; *Caojue baiyun* 草訣百韻, 344*n*; *Gushu zhuanwen* 古書篆文, 344*n*; *Linchi kaifa* 臨池楷法, 344*n*; *Lishu fatie* 隸書法帖, 344*n*; *Longmen caofa* 龍門草法, 336; *Shizhu zhai shuhuapu* 十竹齋書畫譜, 510*n*; *Zhibi tushi* 執筆圖勢, 344*n*, 345; *Zixue juyu* 字學舉隅, 56

Camphor (*zhang*), 94–95

*Cangban suoyou* 藏版所有 rule, 178–79, 187, 264, 290, 308

Carpentry, 66

Carter, Thomas, 4

Catalpa (*zi*), 94

Censorship, 496–98

Chang Chung-li, 147

Changde 常德, 205, 229

*Changhang* 長行 paper, 117–18

Changle 長樂 county seat, 201

Changning 長寧, 205, 227

Changsha 長沙, 229; book markets, 12, 539; bookselling routes, 205

Changting 長汀 county, 35*n*, 44, 58; bookstores, 264, 267; paper production, 114, 115; publishing industry, 56; rice shortages, 46

Changtingxi 長汀溪, *see* Yin River

*Changting xianzhi* 長汀縣志, 2, 94, 95, 114, 119, 265

Chaozhou 潮州, Guangdong: bookselling routes, 200, 222; bookstores, 82, 200*n*, 219–20; markets, 218; regional songbooks, 505*n*, 557, 558; trade routes, 209

Chaozhou dialect songbooks, 505*n*

"Chapbooks," 490, 495, 526

Character-cutting shops (*kezi dian, kezi pu*), 17, 98, 104

Charitable activities, 155–56, 157, 277–78, 289–90

Charitable or free elementary schools (*yixue*), 52, 322, 324, 405. *See also* Schools

Chartier, Roger, 31

*Che Long gongzi huadeng ji* 車龍公子花燈記, 505–6

Chen Hongmou 陳宏謀, 225, 405

Chen Nianzu 陳念祖, 433–37, 473

Chen Xiuyuan 陳修園, 318

Cheng Dengji 程登吉, 349. *See also Youxue gushi qionglin*

Cheng Yi 程頤, 382, 389

Chengdu: literacy of coolies, 568; publishing industry, 10, 12, 17, 19, 195, 541–42

Cheng-Zhu interpretation of Confucianism, 52–54, 348, 389. *See also* Zhu Xi

Chia, Lucille, 5, 86, 549

Childbirth, 445

Children: moral training, 527; printing work, 109, 132, 288. *See also* Education

Children's textbooks, *see* Primers

Chinese Industrial Cooperative Association (Zhongguo gongye hezuo xiehui), 120

Chongan 崇安, 156, 170, 197

Chongbai tang 崇白堂, 259

Chongde tang, 446

Chongqing: publishing industry, 10, 12, 195, 541–42

Chongwen lou 崇文樓, 253

*Choushi jinghua* 酬世精華, 415–16, 427, 473

*Choushi jinnang* 酬世錦囊, 256, 311, 313, 412–15, 471

Chow, Kai-wing, 5

Chun Shum, 549, 550

Civil service, *see* Examination system; Officeholders

*Classic of Changes*: influence, 525; memorization, 388; number of copies published, 375; use in divination, 450, 451, 462, 464; use in *fengshui*, 456. *See also* Five Classics

*Classic of History*, 375, 388, 391, 395–96, 401. *See also* Five Classics

*Classic of Songs*: editions, 388*n*, 393–94; number of copies published, 375; publications, 307; relative popularity, 387–88; *Shijing niti* 詩經擬題, 312; *Shijing zhu* 詩經註, 165, 307. *See also* Five Classics

Classics imprints, 374–96; compendia, 322; as core texts, 321–22, 375; demand for, 375; paper, 121; prices, 398, 514–15; quality, 393–95; readership, 395; significance, 523–24, 525; study of, in elementary schools, 374–75, 407; unpunctuated, 395. *See also* Five Classics; Four Books

Coir palm, 95, 107–8, 111

Cold damage theory (*shanghan*), 429, 437–38

Collectanea: *Han Wei congshu* 漢魏叢書, 397

Commemorative essays (*shouwen* or *jiwen*), 281–82

Commercial woodblock publishing: absence of scholarship on, 4–5; capital investment, 13, 16; decentralization, 18; demand factors, 18–19; expansion in Qing, 19; geographic extension, 7–13; labor, 17; in late Ming, 8–9; print runs, 16*n*; production costs, 13–14; trade networks, 12–13. *See also* Woodblock printing

Communists, 49, 50, 54

Compendia (*daquan*), 322

Composition, study of, 335, 375

Composition texts, 351–52, 358–66; *Pubian tang xunmeng cao* 浦編堂訓蒙草, 358*n*. *See also* Examination essay collections; Poetry composition

Confucianism: Cheng-Zhu interpretation, 52–54, 348, 389; Fujian intellectuals, 52–54; values reflected in fiction, 497–98. *See also* Zhu Xi

Confucian merchants (*rushang*), 268, 269–75

Confucian writings: *Jinsi lu* 近思錄, 397; *Kunxue jiwen* 困學紀聞, 397; *Xingli daquan* 性理大全, 53, 397; *Zhuzi huowen* 朱子或問, 397; *Zhuzi jingyan* 朱子精言, 397. *See also* Classics imprints; Five Classics; Four Books; Zhu Xi

Con men, 249

Construction crafts, 42, 66

Construction manuals, 423; *Lu Ban jing* 魯班經, 423

Contemporary essays (*shiwen*), 362–65. *See also* Eight-legged essays

Coolies, 568. *See also* Porters

Cooper, Thomas, 149, 195

Copyright rules, *cangban suoyou*, 178–79, 187, 290, 308

Correspondence manuals and collections, 355–56, 414; *Chuxue yingchou shuxin quanji* 初學應酬書信全集, 355–56; *Gujin minggong chidu* 古今名公尺牘, 310; ritual correspondence, 419; *Xinke chidu* 新刻尺牘, 423–24, 427; *Xinzha/Zibian* 信札/字辨, 355–57, 408; *Zhinan chidu shengli yaojue* 指南尺牘生理要訣, 423–24; *Zhushu xingshi* 諸書行世, 310

Cosmology, guides to: *Qinding Xieji bianfang shu* 欽定協紀辨方書, 450–51, 514; *Xieji bianfang shu* 協紀辨方書, 180, 450–51, 469, 472–73, 525*n*

Court-case (*gongan*) fiction, 487–88, 492; *Bao gongan* 包公案, 531; *Longtu gongan* 龍圖公案, 488, 495, 497; *Peng gongan* 彭公案, 488, 494, 531; *Shi gongan* 施公案, 488, 494

Cover pages (*fengmian*), 25, 101, 108, 177–78, 253

Covers, book, 109, 111*n*

Crime: in Guangdong, 221–22; thefts from booksellers, 249–51

Cuiwen tang 萃文堂, 200*n*, 426

Cuiyun tang 萃蕓堂: shipments to bookstores, 244

—inventory, 22–23, 374, 398; Classics imprints, 375, 388, 522; encyclopedias, 422; *fengshui* manuals, 456; fiction imprints, 477–83 *passim*, 488–91 *passim*; guides to good fortune, 469; medical texts, 445–46; painting manuals, 510*n*; poetry collections, 507

Culin, Stewart, 471–72, 511

Cultural integration: of frontier areas, 556; persistence of local cultures, 557–58; publishers' roles, 528–29, 555–56, 559; relationship to literacy, 559–68, 570; role of education, 407–8

Cultural Revolution, 26

Currency-exchange shops (*qianpu*), 218, 240–41

Customary rules: *cangban suoyou*, 178–79, 187, 264, 290, 308; dispute resolution, 187; interlineage relations, 187; relations among publishing houses, 177–84, 290; *suiyi shua xin*, 177–78, 179, 264, 290

Customs duties, *see Likin*

Cutting-and-printing shops (*keyin dian*), 100

Dacheng lou 大成樓, 201

Dafo an 大佛庵, 74

Daguang shuju 大光書局, 267

*Dalian* 大連 paper, 117

Daniels, Christine, 118

*Dao* 刀 (unit of measure), 121

Daoist texts: *Daode jing* 道德經 (*Laozi* 老子), 397; *Zhuangzi* 莊子, 397

*Dapi* 大批 format, 480

*Daquan* 大全 (compendia), 322

*Dasha* 大廈, *see* Mansions

Datong shuju 大同書局, 256

Dawen tang 達文堂, 146*n*

*Da Zengguang* 大增廣, 333

De Groot, J. J. M., 456–57, 461

De las Cortes, Adriano, 323, 560

Demographics, *see* Migrations; Population increases

Deng Lin 鄧林, 313, 389

Deng Liu 鄧旒, 318, 442–43

Dewen tang 德文堂, 201

*Dianpu* 典鋪 (pawnshops), 241–42

*Diben* 底本 (manuscripts), 99, 102–3

Dictionaries, 399–402; *Chuxue zibian* 初學字辨, 355; *Erya* 爾雅, 399; *Erya zhu* 爾雅注, 399n; Hakka dialect, 558; *Kangxi zidian* 康熙字典, 249, 401, 514, 517–18, 551; prices, 401, 551; rhyming, 373–74; *Shiwu yin* 十五音, 531, 558; *Xuanjin Zihui* 懸金字彙, 399–401; *Zhengzi tong* 正字通, 401; *Zihui* 字彙, 399–400

Ding 定 county, Hebei, 530

Dingfu gong 定數公, 62

Ding 丁 lineage, 100

Divination: approaches, 455, 469, 525; manuals, 462–67, 471. *See also* Good fortune, guides to

Division of property, *see* Property division

*Diyi caizu shu* 第一才子書, *see Narrative of the Three Kingdoms*

*Dizi gui* 弟子規, 162, 332–33

*Doctrine of the Mean, see* Four Books

Dongguan 東莞, 209

Dongjiang 東江, 209

Doré, Henri, 462

Dramatic works, 499–500; *Jin pi Xixiang ji tuozhu* 金批西廂記妥註, 499n; in Minxi, 500; *Mudan ting* 牡丹亭, 499; *Pipa ji* 琵琶記, 499; popular, 512; *Xixiang ji* 西廂記, 311, 499; *Yunlin Bieshu huixiang tuozhu diliu caizi shu* 雲林別墅繪像妥註第六才子書, 499

*Dream of the Red Chamber*, 453, 478, 526, 531

Drège, Jean-Pierre, 5

Du Fu 杜甫, 317, 507; "Chun wang" 春望, 372–73

Dudbridge, Glen, 553

*Duilian* 對聯 (parallel rhymed couplets), 311

Dukes, Edwin, 561–67 *passim*

East River (Dongjiang), 209

Edgren, Sören, 5

Education: of boys in late imperial China, 562–63; calculation study, 343–44; in composition, 335, 375; cultural integration through, 407–8; forming characters, 335–36; of publishers' sons, 135, 153–55, 274–75; in Republican period, 54, 57, 91, 92, 260, 530; teaching methods, 322, 325, 374–75, 405–7, 408–9, 527, 561, 562–63; as training for publishers, 137–40, 153–54, 275, 288–89; vocational, 566; of women, 155n. *See also* Academies; Examination system; Schools

Educational texts: capital outlay and production costs, 308; composition guides, 351–52, 358–66; core, 307, 321–22, 403, 554–57, 559, 569; cultural role, 555; demand for, 85, 92, 306–8, 322–24; dictionaries, 399–402; errors, 519–20, 569; as focus of Sibao publishers, 307–8, 321, 324; history texts, 354–55; markets, 80–81, 84, 324, 405; for merchants, 355–57, 566–67; military, 398; modern textbooks, 57, 91, 92, 260, 530; for officeholders, 398; popular textual culture context, 523–25; practicality, 403; revisions, 313; seasonal demand, 122,

123; similarities between Sibao and other imprints, 402–3; supplementary or transitional, 309, 322, 324, 349–57, 365–66; in twentieth century, 92–93, 530–32; types not published in Sibao, 404–5. *See also* Classics imprints; Essay collections; Examination preparation texts; Glossaries; Morality books; Poetry collections; Poetry composition; Primers

Eight-legged essays, 351, 358, 362–65

Eitel, Ernst, 560

Elite readers, 557. *See also* Literati

Elman, Benjamin, 335

Empirical research (*kaozheng*) scholars, 54, 395–96

Encyclopedias, *see* Examination preparation texts; Household encyclopedias; Reference works

Encyclopedias for daily use (*riyong leishu*), 411–28. *See also* Household encyclopedias

Essay collections (ancient-style prose or *guwen*), 358–62; *Guwen xiyi* 古文析義, 313, 358–59, 362; *Tang Song badajia wenchao* 唐宋八大家文鈔, 358; *Zengding Guwen jingyan xiangzhu pangxun hebian* 增訂古文精言詳註旁訓合編, 360–62; *Zengding Guwen xiyi hebian* 增訂古文析義合編, 359–60. *See also* Examination essay collections

Essays: commemorative, 281–82; eight-legged, 351, 358, 362–65

Ethnic conflicts, 39–40, 47, 492–93

Etiquette guides, 414; *Choushi hebi* 酬世合璧, 312; compilers, 310; *Minggong yingchou* 名公應酬, 310; readership, 411, 472. *See also*

Household encyclopedias; Ritual handbooks

Examination candidates, *see* Academies; Students

Examination essay collections, 308, 309, 351; contemporary essays, 362–65; *Keshi lu* 課士錄, 55–56; prices, 514; *Qinding Sishu wen* 欽訂四書文, 364*n*; *Tiegang shanhu sanji xinbian* 鐵綱珊瑚三集新編, 363; *Tongzi wenlu* 童子問路, 364–65; *Xin celun* 新策論, 364; *Zhupi Xiaoti zhenggu chuji, erji, sanji* 珠批小題正鵠初集, 二集, 三集, 365

Examination preparation texts: demand for, 306–7, 308; markets, 84; prices, 515, 517; types, 309. *See also* Allusion collections; Classics imprints; Examination essay collections; Poetry collections; Poetry composition; Reference works

Examination system: abolition, 2–3, 91; changes in requirements, 322, 367, 387–88, 403; curriculum, 52; *jinshi* degree, 50–51, 65, 388, 404; *juren* degree, 65, 388, 404; military, 65; Minxi degree-holders, 50–51; preparation of sons, 135–36, 153, 154; purchased degrees, 279–80; social mobility and, 568–69; Zou and Ma success rates, 65–66, 136. *See also* Education

Eyebrow notes (*meipi*), 365

Families: competition within, 159–60. *See also* Households; Lineages

Family governance (*jiazheng*), 65

Family rituals, *see* Ritual handbooks

Family schools (*sishu* or *jiashu*): establishment, 153, 154, 274–75, 276; increased number of, 52; as markets for educational texts, 84, 324; teachers, 137; texts for, 389, 405, 530; types, 153; in Wuge, 154, 530*n*

*Fanyang Zoushi zupu*, 90, 270–71, 282

Farmers, tenant, 46–47, 70. *See also* Agriculture

Faure, David, 291, 294

Feng Menglong 馮夢龍, 479, 483, 490, 497*n*

*Fengmian* 封面, *see* Cover pages

Fengrao Temple 豐饒寺, 74, 99

*Fengshui*: practitioners, 66, 461; schools, 456–57, 459; siting of gravesites, 77; use of, 450, 462

*Fengshui* manuals, 456–62, 472; *Dili bianzheng* 地理辨正, 458–59*n*; *Dili He Luo jingyi* 地理河洛精義, 459–61; *Dili wujue* 地理五訣, 459, 461; *Luojing jie* 羅經解, 457–58; prices, 514; *Qiandanzi yuanzhu jing* 鉛彈子元珠經, 514

Fenyi 分宜 county seat, 205

Feuds (*xiedou*), 77

Fiction imprints, 478–98; banned works, 496–97; bestsellers, 478; *Chuke Paian jingqi* 初刻拍案驚奇, 478–79; Confucian values in, 497–98; cultural role, 555; *Da hongpao* 大紅袍, 496; demand for, 477; drama, 499–500; *Erke Paian jingqi* 二刻拍案驚奇, 479; *Fengliu wu* 風流悟, 479; *Fengshen bang* 封神榜 (*Fengshen yanyi* 封神演義), 478; *Fu Honglou meng* 復紅樓夢, 478*n*; *Hongwu zhuan* 洪武傳, 495; *Hou Honglou meng* 後紅樓夢, 478*n*; *Hou Shuihu zhuan* 後水滸傳, 496;

*Jinghua yuan* 鏡花緣, 478; *Jingu qiguan* 今古奇觀, 479; *Journey to the West*, 478; linguistic levels, 493–94, 526; literary, 506, 512, 526; *Narrative of the Three Kingdoms*, 478, 479–81, 495, 531; *Nücaizi shu* 女才子書, 479, 495; *Plum in a Golden Vase*, 453, 478, 496; popular, 477, 526; popularity, 498, 511; prices, 491, 495, 514; production costs, 476; *Qian Honglou meng* 前紅樓夢, 478*n*; *Qingshi* 情史, 479, 495; quality, 481; readership, 476, 510–12, 532; regional, 318, 491–93; *Rou putuan* 肉蒲團, 496; *Sanguo yin* 三國因, 531; *Sanyan* 三言, 479; *Shier Lou* 十二樓, 479; *Sida qishu* 四大奇書, 478; story collections, 477, 479; subversive, 496–98; themes, 495–96; in twentieth century, 531; *Water Margin*, 250, 478, 496, 570; *Wu caizi shu* 五才子書 [*Water Margin?*], 522; *Xihu jiahua* 西湖佳話, 479; *Xinke an jian quanxiang piping Sanguo zhizhuan* 新刻按鑑全像批評三國志傳, 481*n*; *Xiyou ji* 西遊記, 237, 478; *Xu Honglou meng* 續紅樓夢, 478*n*; *Yingxiong pu* 英雄譜, 478, 495. *See also Caizi jiaren*; Court-case fiction; Historical fiction; Military romances/adventure novels; Songbooks; Supernatural tales

Financial institutions, 218, 240–41

Fine or rare editions (*shanben*), 5

Five Classics, 387–96; aids to study of, 322; *Chunqiu beizhi* 春秋備旨, 389, 390; *Classic of Changes*, 375, 388, 450, 451, 456, 462, 464, 525; *Classic of History*, 375, 388, 391, 395–96,

401; *Classic of Songs*, 165, 307, 312, 375, 387–88, 393–94; commentaries, 389–95; as core texts, 321; editions, 388, 391–95; *Jianben Shijing quanwen* 監本詩經全文, 388n; *Liji beizhi* 禮記備旨, 389; *Liji jinghua* 禮記精華, 391–93; *Liji zengding jujie* 禮記增訂句解, 393n; number of copies published, 375; *Qinding Chunqiu zhuanshuo huizuan* 欽定春秋傳說彙纂, 390; *Record of Rites*, 332–33, 375, 388, 391–93, 525; *Shijing beizhi* 詩經備旨, 389; *Shijing jianben* 詩經監本, 522n; *Shujing liju* 書經離句, 514; *Shujing pangxun* 書經旁訓, 514; *Spring and Autumn Annals*, 375, 390; study of, 322, 324, 374–75, 387–88; *Taoban Liji huican* 套版禮記匯參, 522; *Taoban Liji shengdu* 套版禮記省度, 522; *Wujing beizhi* 五經備旨, 311, 314, 388–91; *Wujing pangxun tizhi* 五經旁訓題旨, 312; *Yijing beizhi* 易經備旨, 389; *Yijing pangxun* 易經旁訓, 514; *Yuzuan Zhouyi zhezhong* 御纂周易折中, 233, 389–90; *Zuo Commentary*, 374, 375, 391

Fortune, *see* Good fortune, guides to

Foshanzhen: bookstores, 259; publishing industry, 11, 101, 232, 259, 310, 505–6, 545

Four Books: *Analects*, 332, 333, 365, 377–78, 382, 408; commentaries, 321–22, 376–87; as core texts, 307, 321–22; editions, 376–87, 393–95, 531; *Erlun chuanwen beizhi* 二論串文備旨, 381n; number of copies published, 375; prices, 514; published by multiple houses, 179; readership, 376; *Sishu beizhi* 四書

備旨, 99, 165, 307, 389; *Sishu beizhi tiqiao* 四書備旨題竅, 312; *Sishu buzhu beizhi tiqiao huican* 四書補註備旨題竅匯參, 313, 383–87, 394, 514; *Sishu dianlin* 四書典林, 517; *Sishu hejie* 四書合解, 316; *Sishu jianben* 四書監本, 162; *Sishu jicheng* 四書集成, 97–98, 165, 307; *Sishu jizhu* 四書集註 (or 注), 164–65, 180, 385, 387, 514; *Sishu pangyin* 四書旁音, 543; *Sishu shidi* 四書釋地, 396n; *Sishu yizhu* 四書繹註, 376–78; *Sishu zhengwen* 四書正文, 318, 378–80; *Sishu zhu daquan* 四書註大全, 166–67, 307; study of, 324, 374–75; *Xiangdang tukao* 鄉黨圖考, 376n; *Xinding Sishu buzhu beizhi* 新訂四書補註備旨, 313; *Yuanben Erlun qiyou yinduan* 原本二論啓幼印端, 380–83, 408; Yuechi editions, 542–43

*Fu* 賦 (rhapsody) collections, 507n

Fubo 伏波 (Lord Ma), 278, 279

Fujian province: bookselling routes, 196, 197–99; customs houses, 48–49; exports, 44; intellectuals, 52–55, 317–18, 395; publishing industry, 9

Funeral rituals, 418–21. *See also* Burial sites

Funerary dedications (*muzhi*), 281

Fuxing tang 福興堂, 116

Fuzhou 福州: academies, 53; bookselling routes, 236; books purchased in, 237, 260

Gan River 贛江, 205, 208, 226, 227, 234, 247

Gansu: migration to, 19

Ganzhou 贛州 prefecture, 205, 209, 226–27

Gaozhou 高州 prefecture, 201–2, 218; bookselling routes, 222; bookstores, 219, 238, 284; economy, 220–21

Gardella, Robert, 35

Gazetteers: *Da Ming yitong zhi* 大明一統志, 549; *Linting huikao* 臨汀彙考, 56

Gender roles: division of labor, 132–34; of Hakka people, 40, 41, 134*n*; in households, 130, 132–34; traditional, 133, 528

Genealogies, 20–21

Gengxin tang 耕莘堂, 248, 258, 259

Gentry (*shenshi*): management of corporate land, 69–70, 75–76; Zou and Ma lineage members, 275–86

Geomantic texts, *see Fengshui*

Glossaries (*zazi*), 336–42; *Shandong zhuangnong riyong zazi* 山東莊農日用雜字, 337, 566; *Shanxi zazi bidu* 山西雜字必讀, 336–37; *Siyan zazi* 四言雜字, 337*n*, 408, 566; types, 337*n*; *Xinke jujia biyong zazi* 新刻居家必用雜字, 337*n*; *Xinke Siyan zazi* 新刻四言雜字, 337–39; *Xinshou Youxue qimeng tijing* 新授幼學啓蒙提徑, 337*n*; *Xinzeng zazi Renjia riyong* 新增雜字人家日用, 339–42. *See also* Hakka glossaries

Gong 龔江 River, 202, 209, 224, 227

*Gongan* 公案, *see* Court-case fiction

Gongping xu 公平墟 (fair market), 71, 76, 190, 278, 279

*Gongsheng* 貢生 (tribute-student status), 61, 65

*Gongtian* 公田 (public land), 69–71

Good fortune, guides to, 449–69; *Baizhong jing* 百中經, 466, 469; *Bushi zhengzong* 卜筮正宗, 462–63; divination manuals, 462–67, 525; *Liuren shike* 六壬時課, 344*n*; *Mayi xiangfa* 麻衣相法, 465, 469; *Mingshu* 命書, 466*n*; physiognomy manuals, 465; popularity, 469; prices, 514; readership, 463, 469, 471, 472–73; *Sanming tonghui* 三命通會, 465–66; *Sanshi xiang* 三世相, 260; *Shanzeng Yidu liuren ke xuanri yaojue* 删增儀度六壬課選日要訣, 464–65, 469; *Shenxiang quanbian* 神相全編, 465; *Wanfa guizong* 萬法歸宗, 455; *Xinke Guigu xiansheng mingli sizi jing* 新刻鬼谷先生命理四字經, 466–67; *Zhan denghua jixiong* 占灯花吉凶, 344*n*; *Zhouyi meihua shu* 周易梅花數, 463*n*. *See also* Almanacs; *Fengshui* manuals; Morality books

Government books, 398

Gravesites, *see* Burial sites

*Greater Learning, see* Four Books

Guandi 關帝, 60, 73

Guandiba 官地壩, 190

Guangdong province: bookselling routes, 194, 199–202, 217–22; bookstores, 218–19; cultural integration, 556; demand for books, 88; economy, 216–18; financial institutions, 241, 242; Hakka migrants, 41, 211, 212, 213, 214; Hakka-Punti War, 89, 90, 212, 221; local dictionaries, 558; markets, 217–18, 238*n*; merchants, 46; population growth, 216–17; publishing industry, 11; regional songbooks, 557; schools, 323–24; trade routes, 208, 209, 210

Guangnan 廣南 prefecture, 209

Guangong 關公, 60, 73

Guangxi province: bandits, 250; bookselling routes, 199, 202–3, 222–24; bookstores, 254–55; cultural integration, 556; demand for books, 88; Hakka migrants, 41, 211, 212, 213, 214, 223; population growth, 222–23; poverty, 223–24; schools, 323; settlement, 223; trade routes, 208–9

Guangzhou city: avoided by Sibao booksellers, 199–200, 218, 232; foreign trade monopoly, 216–17; Hakka migrants near, 212; publishing industry, 10–11, 232, 545; schools, 530–31

*Guanma dalu* 管馬大陸 (post roads), 207

Guiguzi 鬼谷子, 452, 484

Guihua 歸化 county, 35*n*

Guilds (*huiguan*), 45, 240

Guilin, 202, 213, 223, 232

Guixian 貴縣, Guangxi: bookselling routes, 171, 202, 224; bookstores, 133, 248, 258, 264; transport routes, 248

Guiyang 貴陽, 12, 229

Guiyangzhou 桂陽州, 205

Guizhou province: bookselling routes, 194, 199, 202–3, 225; migration to, 19; schools, 323

*Gulu qian* 賈路錢 (trader's road money), 241

Guo Bocang, 117

*Guoxuesheng* 國學生 (Imperial Academy students), 280

Gutian 姑田: paper production, 114–15, 117, 237

Hakka dialect (*kejia hua*): areas spoken in, 215*n*; development, 40; dictionaries, 558; distinctiveness, 41; Sibao subdialect, 215*n*, 558; spoken by migrants, 214–15; textbooks, 558

Hakka glossaries, 318; *Renjia riyong* 人家日用, 100, 123, 146, 237, 318, 339–41, 558, 566; *Yinian shiyong zazi* 一年使用雜字, 318, 341–42, 558

Hakka heartland, 39

Hakka people (*kejia*): as book buyers, 558; booksellers' use of networks, 85, 240, 299; gender roles, 40, 41, 134*n*; identity, 41, 493; migrations, 39, 40–41, 211–15, 231–32; in Minxi, 39–40; networks, 41, 231–32, 240, 252, 299; peripherality, 41; social customs, 40, 134*n*

Hakka-Punti War (1856–68), 89, 90, 212, 221

Hanbao lou 翰寶樓, 239

Hanchuan 漢川 county seat, 205

Handicraft industries, 41–42, 43, 66, 68–69

Hangzhou: bookselling routes, 199; publishing industry, 9, 10, 44, 80

Hankou 漢口, 228–29, 230, 232

Han River 韓江, 230

Hayashi Kazuo, 217

Hayes, James, 403–4, 414, 451–52, 467, 470, 471, 511, 512, 518, 549–50, 551–52

Health, *see* Medical texts

*Hehuo* 合夥 or *hegu* 合股, 296*n*

Hekouzhen 河口鎮, 203*n*, 209*n*, 537

Hengzhou 衡州, 202, 205, 209–10, 224, 229, 254–55

Heping 和平 county, Huizhou, 213

Heshan tang 鶴山堂, 197*n*

Historical fiction, 481–84; *Da Song zhongxing tongsu yanyi* 大宋中興通俗演義, 482; *Dong Zhou lieguo zhi* 東周列國志, 483; educational purpose, 481–82, 525; *Feilong zhuan* 飛龍傳, 484; *Guiguzi siyou zhi* 鬼谷子四友志, 484*n*; *Kaipi yanyi tongsu zhizhuan* 開闢衍繹通俗志傳, 483*n*; *Nan Bei liang Song zhizhuan* 南北兩宋志傳, 482; *Nan Song zhuan* 南宋傳, 484; popularity, 481; *Sun Pang yanyi qiguo zhi quanzhuan* 孫龐演義七國志全傳, 483–84; *Wudai pinghua* 五代評話, 482; *Xin lieguo zhi* 新列國志, 483

Histories: *Guoce* 國策, 396; *Guoyu* 國語, 396, 398; *Hanshu* 漢書, 396; *Mingshi jishi benmo* 明史紀事本末, 398; *Qian Hanshu* 前漢書, 397; *Shiji* 史記, 180, 396, 397, 398; *Zizhi tongjian* 資治通鑑, 396, 398; *Zizhi tongjian gangmu* 資治通鑑綱目, 396, 397

History textbooks, 354–55; *Dafang gangjian* 大方綱鑑, 354–55; *Gangjian yizhi lu* 鋼鑑易知錄, 397; *Jianlüe tuozhu* 鑑略妥註, 354; *Xinkan Liaofan Yuan xiansheng bianzuan guben lishi Dafang gangjian bu* 新刊了凡袁先生編纂古本歷史大方綱鑑補, 354–55; *Xinzeng Mingji jianlüe wuyan duben* 新增明紀鑑略五言讀本, 354; *Zizhi tongjian gangmu* 資治通鑑綱目, 396, 397

Ho Ping-ti, 226

Hong Kong: educational texts, 403–4; literacy levels, 560; popular texts, 471; small number of books in villages, 549–50, 551–52

*Honglou meng* 紅樓夢, *see Dream of the Red Chamber*

Horoscopes, 465–66

Household-based publishing houses, *see Shufang*

Household businesses, corporate lineage context, 287–93

Household economies, 140–45

Household encyclopedias, 411–28; *Choushi jinghua* 酬世精華, 415–16, 427, 473; *Choushi jinnang* 酬世錦囊, 256, 311, 313, 412–15, 471; *Chuanjia bao* 傳家寶, 422, 527; compilers, 310, 311, 313, 412–13; contents, 412, 426–28; divination sections, 449–50; *Huizuan Jiali tieshi jiyao* 彙纂家禮帖式集要, 316, 317, 416–22, 427, 472, 473, 474; *Jiabao quanji* 家寶全集, 423*n*, 467; *Jiali jicheng* 家禮集成, 414–15; lessons for children, 527; messages, 473–74; popularity, 471; prices, 517; readership, 426–28, 473–74; *Tongtian xiao* 通天曉, 423*n*; *Wanbao quanshu* 萬寶全書, 422, 467; *Wan buqiu ren* 萬不求人, 422; *Yunlin bieshu xinji Choushi jinnang quanji* 雲林別墅新輯酬世錦囊全集, 412–13, 427–28; *Zengding Yingshi bianshu* 增訂應世便書, 421, 517. *See also* Ritual handbooks

Households: accounts, 140–45, 150, 262–63, 291; competition and conflicts within, 159–60; cooperation among, 290; expenses, 150, 291; family relationships, 129–30;

flexible labor assignments, 127, 128, 134, 135, 174–75, 176; gender roles, 130, 132–34; income sources, 127–28; landholdings, 128–29; lineage rules, 140–41; new branch, 163; occupational diversification, 63–65, 173, 287–88; patriarchs, 127, 130, 140, 291; printing rooms in homes, 105–6; printing work, 99, 109, 128, 130; publishing work, 127–31, 134; relationship to lineage, 291–93; sizes, 127, 130, 160, 174; social division of labor, 64, 127, 130; unity, 143, 159, 177. *See also* Property division

*Huaben* 話本 (novellas), 478–79

Huang Bian 黃汴, 208*n*, 247*n*

Huang Fengyu 黃逢玉, 492, 493

Huang Naian 黃耐庵, 492, 493

Huang 黃 lineage of block carvers, 15

Huazhan shudian 華棧書店, 243–44

Hubei province, bookselling routes, 194, 195, 199, 205

Huc, Evariste, 551, 560

Huichang 會昌 county, 209, 251

*Huiguan* 會館, 45, 240

Huilai 惠來 county seat, 201

*Huimo* 徽墨 (Huizhou ink), 111

Huixian tang 會賢堂, 76*n*, 152

Huizhou 惠州 prefecture: block cutters, 15; bookselling routes, 200, 220, 222; bookstores, 219; economy, 220; markets, 218; merchants, 270; publishing industry, 9; trade routes, 209

Huizhou ink (*huimo*), 111

*Huizuan Jiali tieshi jiyao* 彙纂家禮帖式集要, 316, 317, 416–22, 427, 472, 473, 474

Hunan province: agriculture, 228–29; bookselling routes, 199, 205, 225, 228–30; bookstores, 229–30; economy, 229; Hakka migrants, 41, 211, 212, 213, 214, 226, 230; markets, 229; migration to, 228; population, 225, 226, 228; publishing industry, 229; rebellions in, 225–26, 228; schools, 323; trade routes, 229

Huzhou 湖州: publishing industry, 9

Idema, Wilt, 550, 562, 564–65

Imperial Academy students (*jiansheng*), 62, 276–77, 279–80

Imperial Printing Office, 6

Imprints, *see* Sibao imprints

Inheritance, partible, 160. *See also* Property division

Inks: Huizhou, 103, 111; ingredients, 112; pans, 107; printing, 111–13; production, 111–13; tubs, 106

Instruction manuals, 422–23

Itinerant booksellers: books bought from many publishers, 185; contacts with elite members, 284–85; daily sales amounts, 236; dangers, 157, 249–52; early, 83–84, 191–92; earnings, 140, 142–43, 237; education levels, 132; financial management, 240–42; Hakka contacts, 85, 240, 299; ledger books, 23; life on road, 236–40; maintaining ties with home and family, 143–44; marriages, 133, 139, 143–44; number of, 193; returns to Sibao, 156–57, 192, 293; selection, 142–43; selling locations, 238; as stage in career, 185, 192–93; stock transported by, 236, 242–48; texts obtained for publication, 316–17; training, 137–40; travel with family members, 138, 142–43, 192; in twentieth century, 193, 236–38. *See also* Bookselling routes; Sojourning merchants

*Jiali tieshi jiyao* 家禮帖式集要, *see Huizuan Jiali tieshi jiyao*

Jiandao hui 尖刀會, 47*n*

Jiang Haoran 江浩然, 316–17, 416, 426, 473

Jiang Jianzi 江健資, 316–17, 416, 426

Jiang Yong 江永, 376*n*, 391

Jianghu hui 江湖會, 47*n*

Jiang 蔣 lineage, 58, 100

Jiangnan: publishing industry, 8–10, 295–96, 298

Jiangsu: bookselling routes, 199

Jiangxi province: bookselling routes, 195, 199, 203–5, 225–28; bookstores, 226–28; cultural integration, 556; demand for books, 88; Gan River, 205, 208, 226, 227, 234, 247; Hakka migrants, 211, 213, 214; trade routes, 209. *See also* Xuwanzhen

Jianning 建寧 prefecture, 38, 45, 95, 197, 199, 203

*Jiansheng* 監生, *see* Imperial Academy students

Jiantou 梘頭, 60, 131

Jianyang 建陽 county: *Mashaben*, 481; publishing industry, 9, 79, 86–87, 294–95, 298

Ji'ao shanfang 寄傲山房, 389

*Ji'ao shanfang xinji shilian zaojing* 寄傲山房新集詩聯藻鏡, 507, 510

*Jiashu* 家塾, *see* Family schools

Jiaying 嘉應 department: bookselling routes, 200–201, 222; bookstores, 201, 239, 253; Hakka migrants, 213, 220; trade routes, 209

Jiaying city: bookstores, 219; economy, 220; education, 220

Jiayingzhou 嘉應州, 76*n*, 157

*Jiazhang* 家長 (household patriarch), 127, 130, 140, 291

*Jiazheng* 家政 (family governance), 65

*Jiazhu* 加註 (with added notes), 480

Jieyang 揭陽 county seat, 201

Jijin zhai 剞錦齋, 56

Jin Wuxiang 金武祥, 540, 545, 546

Ji'nan 濟南: publishing industry, 11

Jingdezhen 景德鎮, 226

*Jingguan* 經館, 153. *See also* Family schools

Jinglun tang 經綸堂, 168

*Jinpi* 金批 (with commentary by Jin Shengtan), 480, 522

*Jin Ping Mei* 金瓶梅, *see Plum in a Golden Vase*

Jin River 錦水, 205

*Jinshi* degree-holders, 50–51, 65, 388, 404

Jinxi 金谿 county, Jiangxi, 537. *See also* Xuwanzhen

Jiujiang 九江, 12, 205, 208, 226, 537, 539

Jiulong River 九龍江, 38

Jiuxue shanfang 舊學山房, 538

*Jiwen* 祭文, 281–82

Johnson, David, 512, 555

Joke books: *Jie renyi* 解人頤, 497; *Xiaolin guangji* 笑林廣記, 497

Jujube (*zao*), 94, 102

Junior students (*tongsheng*), 375, 475

*Juren* 舉人 degree-holders, 65, 388, 404

*Juxi* 莒溪, 236, 237

*Juxian tang* 聚賢堂, 146*n*, 162, 458

*Kangxi zidian* 康熙字典, 249, 401, 514, 517–18, 551

*Kaozheng* 考證 (empirical research) scholars, 54, 395–96

*Kejia* 客家, *see* Hakka people

*Kejia hua* 客家話, *see* Hakka dialect

*Keyin dian* 刻印店 (cutting-and-printing shops), 100

*Kezi dian* 刻字店, *see* Character-cutting shops

Kulp, Daniel, 451–52

Labor: costs, 124, 131, 288; division within households, 64, 127, 128, 130, 134, 135, 174–75, 176; female, 132–33; gender roles, 132–34; hired, 131; wages, 130, 132–33; woodblock printing, 14, 17, 99, 109, 128, 130. *See also* Block cutters

Laijia market (Laijia xu 賴家墟), 71, 76, 190, 278, 279

Laijiayu 賴家圩, 60

Land: average holdings, 153*n*; concentrated ownership, 46; corporate, 46, 69–71, 75–76, 276, 291; household, 128–29; ownership patterns in Sibao, 58–60; publishing profits used to purchase, 151, 152–53; rental, 46–47, 70, 75–76

*Laoban* 老板 (bosses), 101

Laolong 老龍, 201

Legal texts, 398; *Da Qing huidian* 大清會典, 398; *Da Qing lü* 大清律, 398; *Da Qing xinlü* 大清新律, 398; *Qianlong xinlü* 乾隆新律, 398

Legge, James, 362, 386–87

Lei Hong 雷鋐, 53, 54*n*, 57*n*

Leizhou prefecture, 194, 201, 222

Leong, Sow-theng, 41, 211, 212, 213

Letterpress printing: advantages, 91; development, 2; masters, 265; reprinting, 15; reproductions of woodblock editions, 532

Letters: collections, 310; delivery of, 244. *See also* Correspondence manuals

Leung, Angela, 408, 432, 444

*Li* 梨 (pear), 94, 102

Li Bozhong, 295–96

Li Gao 李杲, 315, 448

Li Guangdi 李光地, 53, 233, 389–90

Li Shihong 黎士弘, 55, 56, 281–82*n*

Li Shixiong 李世熊, 54–55, 56

Li Shizhen 李時珍, 428, 438

Li Ting 李珽, 4, 55

Li Tingji 李廷機, 354*n*, 355*n*, 368*n*

Li Yuxiu 李毓秀, 332–33

Li Zicheng 李自成, 225, 228

Liancheng 連成 county, 35*n*; commercial activities, 43, 44, 45; handicraft industries, 42; paper brokers, 115; paper production, 44, 114; rice shortages, 46; transport routes, 58

Liangyi tang 兩儀堂, 538

*Lianshi* 連史 paper, 117, 539. *See also* Bamboo paper

Lianyuan ge 連元閣, 259, 310

Lianzhou 廉州 prefecture, 201, 218, 222

Liao Tianjie 廖天杰, 316, 317

Liaocheng 聊城: publishing industry, 11, 12

Licheng shuju 立成書局, 258, 264

*Liji jinghua* 禮記精華, 391–93

*Likin* (*lijin* 釐金; customs duties), 48–49, 89, 266

Lin Yunming 林雲銘, 313, 358–59, 362

Lin Zhao'en 林兆恩, 50

Lineage merchants (*zushang*), 4

Lineages: ancestor worship, 60, 72; ancestral halls, 156–57; cohesion, 72; conflicts among, 76–77; control-subordination, 75; corporate landholdings, 46, 69–71, 75–76, 276, 291; corporate property, 291; customary rules regulating relations, 177–85; dispute resolution, 178*n*; heads, 276, 292, 293; household relations with, 291–93; managing competition, 186–88; patronage within, 292, 293–94; relationships among, 71–72; rules, 140–41; socioeconomic differences within, 75. *See also* Ma lineage; Zou lineage

Lineage trusts, 155

Lingnan: bookselling routes, 199; Hakka migrants, 211–12

*Lingnan yishi* 嶺南逸史, 492, 558

Lingshan 靈山: ancestral temples, 263; bookstores, 201, 202, 257, 262, 264; trade routes, 210

Linguistic registers, 493–94, 526

Linlan tang 林蘭堂, 101, 121, 259, 310, 341, 370, 452

Linlan yiji shuju 林蘭儀記書局, 341

Linlan yiji tang 林蘭儀記堂, 100, 116, 131

Linlan zhunji shuju 林蘭准記書局, 123

Linlan zhunji tang 林蘭准記堂, 123*n*

Literacy: benefits, 570; cultural integration and, 559–68, 570; defini-

tions, 563–65; estimated levels in late imperial China, 560–65; of merchants and traders, 565–67; politically meaningful, 569–70; of publishers and booksellers, 137; relationship to social mobility, 568; of women, 527–28

Literary collections, 506–10; *Wenxuan* 文選, 396, 397

Literati: involvement in publishing projects, 315–16; in Minxi, 283; publishers' contacts with, 274, 281–83, 315–16; selling books to, 132, 274, 284

Literature, *see* Fiction imprints; Poetry collections

Lithographic printing: advantages, 91; development, 2; masters, 265

Lithographic texts (*shiyinben*): reproductions of woodblock editions, 264, 532; sold by Sibao booksellers, 237, 260

Liu Wenwei 劉文蔚, 312*n*, 373

Liu Yonghua, 276, 279

Liu Zhong 劉忠, 381–83, 408

Liulichang 琉璃廠, 10

Liu 劉 lineage of block carvers, 15

Liuyiben tang 六宜本堂, 201

Liuyue miao 六月廟, 60

Longchuan 龍川, 209

Longfeng tang 龍豐堂, 245

Longnan 龍南 county seat, 205

Long River 龍江, 209

Longshan Academy 龍山書院, 364

Longxiang hui 龍翔會, 71–72, 278–79

Longzu 龍足 hamlet, 62

Loomis, A. W., 472, 511, 524

Love stories, *see* Caizi jiaren

Lu Xun 魯迅, 491, 531

Lü Zuqian 呂祖謙, 397

Lufrano, Richard, 273, 566

Luojiao 羅教 cult, 47n

*Luojing jie* 羅經解, 457–58

*Luopan* 羅盤 (geomantic compass), 456, 457

Ma Cuida 馬萃大, 168–69, 195, 272–73

Ma Cuizhong 馬萃仲, 106, 151, 168–69, 285n

Ma Dafan 馬大蕃, 164, 175, 307

Ma Dafang 馬大芳, 66, 74–75n, 129–30, 164, 251

Ma Dayou 馬大猷, 312

Ma Dingbang 馬定邦: as boy, 98, 176; charitable activities, 155–56, 157, 290; commercial activities, 67; as itinerant bookseller, 197n; mansion, 190–91; paper transported by, 115; sales at wholesale book market, 190–91; *shufang* management, 151, 163, 165, 166–68, 174–75, 238, 410; social status, 280; sons, 278

Ma Dingce 馬定策, 166, 167, 168, 197n, 280

Ma Dinglüe 馬定略, 138, 139, 141, 166, 167, 197n

Ma Dingtao 馬定韜, 166, 167, 197n, 285n

Ma Heling 馬鶴齡, 315n

Ma Hetu 馬河圖, 61, 62

Ma Jiu 馬就, 167–68, 197n, 281n

Ma Kuanyu 馬寬裕: *shufang* management, 83, 410; texts compiled or edited by, 310–11, 313, 354, 360–62, 469

Ma Lie 馬烈, 161, 168

Ma Long 馬龍, 97–98, 168, 278, 281–82n

Ma Longjin 馬隆晉, 315

Ma Lügong 馬履恭, 168, 197n

Ma Lüzhi 馬履智, 157, 168, 197n

Ma Qian 馬謙, 138, 139

Ma Qilang 馬七郎, 60, 61

Ma Quanheng 馬權亨: family, 164–69; as itinerant bookseller, 197n, 238; *shufang* management, 98–99, 151, 163, 164–66, 175–76, 307, 308, 410

Ma Quanwen 馬權文: death of father, 164; education, 135; inheritance of woodblocks, 163, 165, 175; *shufang* management, 165; social status, 280; support of education, 154, 274

Ma Rixuan 馬日宣, 258, 259, 264

Ma Riyao 馬日堯, 258, 259

Ma Shu 馬恕, 168, 197n

Ma Weihan 馬維翰, 81–82, 84, 96, 97, 269

Ma Xianzuo 馬賢佐, 314

Ma Xun 馬馴, 61, 62–63, 79, 281n

Ma Yuanbi 馬源辟, 314

Ma Yulin 馬玉璘, 202–3, 286

Macgowan, John, 330, 407, 562–63

Magang 馬崗, female block cutters, 15, 101–2, 104–5, 133, 536, 545–46

Magong miao 馬公廟, 73

Ma lineage: ancestor worship, 60; ancestral halls, 61; conflicts with Zou lineage, 76–77, 187, 456; dominance of Mawu, 60; examination results, 65–66, 68n, 136; founding ancestor, 60; genealogies, 20–21, 61, 67, 281–82; generational continuity of publishing, 164–69; gentry status, 275–86; history, 60, 61; lower-shrine, 61; marriage ties to Zou lineage, 58,

68, 186; occupations, 62–67; origins of publishing industry, 79, 81–82; rules, 140–41; social status, 280–81; upper-shrine, 61. *See also* Lineages

Maluowei 馬羅尾: paper production, 114, 116

Mansions (*dasha*), 87–88, 151–52, 190–91

Manuscripts (*diben*), 99, 102–3

Mao Zedong 毛澤東, 570

*Mao* 毛 bamboo (*maozhu*), 43, 95, 96, 117

*Maobian* 毛邊 paper, 115, 117–18, 121, 519, 537. *See also* Bamboo paper

*Maozhu* 貓 or 毛竹, *see Mao* bamboo

Markets: in Guangdong, 217–18; selling books in, 236, 237; types, 238*n*. *See also* Book markets

Marriages: networks, 58; relationship to business arrangements, 186; of sojourning merchants, 67–68, 133, 262; between Zou and Ma lineages, 58, 68, 186

Martial arts, 133, 251

Martial heroes, *see* Military romances

Masha 麻沙, 9

*Mashaben* 麻沙本 (books from Masha), 481

Massage handbooks: *Xiao'er tuina* 小兒推拿, 446

*Materia medica*: *Bencao gangmu* 本草綱目, 428, 438; *Shennong bencao jingdu* 神農本草經讀, 178, 436–39, 519; *Shennong bencao jing jizhu* 神農本草經集注, 437*n*. *See also* Medical texts; Prescription collections

*Matuo* or *maduo* 馬馱 (bamboo shoulder baskets), 256

Mawu 馬屋: Laijia market, 71, 76, 190, 278, 279; Ma lineage dominance, 60; mansions, 87–88, 151–52, 190–91; origins of publishing industry, 81–82; society, 67; temples, 72–73, 155, 278. *See also* Sibao

Mazu 馬祖, *see* Tianhou

McKenzie, D. F., 31

Medhurst, W. H., 13, 548, 560

Medical texts, 428–49; *Baochi zhinan che* 保赤指南車, 442–43; *Caiai bian* 采艾編, 446; *Dongyuan shishu* 東垣十書, 448; *Huangdi neijing* 皇帝內經, 56; *Huangdi neijing: Suwen Lingshu* 黃帝內經：素問靈樞, 429; *Jingui yuhan yaolüe* 金匱玉函要略, 315, 429; *Jingyue quanshu* 景岳全書, 448; *Jiyan yian* 集驗醫案, 315*n*; *Lingshu* 靈樞, 56; *Maijue* 脈訣, 315; *Neiwaike jizheng* 內外科集症, 443*n*; for practitioners, 432–37, 444–48, 450; prices, 428, 432, 446, 514, 517; readership, 448–49, 472–73; *Shanghan lun* 傷寒論, 429; *Shen yanke* 審眼科, 445; *Shishi milu* 石室秘錄, 448; specialized, 442–44; *Suwen* 素問, 56; *Wanbing huichun* 萬病回春, 442*n*; *Wang Shuhe tuzhu nan* 王叔和圖註難, 264*n*; *Xueshi yian* 薛氏醫案, 448; *Yanke jingyi* 眼科精義, 445; *Yanke zuanyao* 眼科纂要, 445; *Yingtong baiwen* 嬰童百問, 442*n*; *Yinhai jingwei* 銀海精微, 445; *Yinhai jingwei bu* 銀海精微補, 445*n*; *Yixue heke* 醫學合刻, 432*n*; *Yixue rumen* 醫學入門, 433*n*; *Yixue sanzi jing* 醫學三字經, 435–37, 519; *Yixue xinwu* 醫學心悟, 433*n*; *Yizong jinjian* 醫宗金鑒, 255, 470,

472–73, 517; *You[ke] jicheng* 幼[科]集成, 442*n*; *You[ke] zhinan* 幼[科]指南, 442*n*; *Yuzuan Yizong jinjian* 御纂醫宗金鑒, 428–32, 514; *Yuzuan Yizong jinjian waike* 御纂醫宗金鑑外科, 278*n*; *Zhenjiu dacheng* 針灸大成, 445–46. *See also Materia medica*; Prescription collections

Medicine: cold damage theory, 429, 437–38; famous physicians, 448; popular practitioners, 444–48, 450; practitioners, 66, 315; training, 566–67; warm factors theory, 429, 430, 448–49

Meiling Pass 梅嶺關, 208

*Meipi* 眉批 (eyebrow notes), 365

Men: occupations, 134–35; roles in *shufang*, 127, 130; as sojourning booksellers, 127, 132; study for examinations, 135–37; training for publishing, 137–40. *See also* Gender roles

Mencius, 329, 348, 385, 386, 387. *See also* Four Books

*Mengguan* 蒙館, 153. *See also* Family schools

Merchant manuals, 273

Merchants: Confucian, 268, 269–75; development of commerce in Minxi, 44–45; educational texts for, 355–57, 566–67; education, 567; encyclopedias for, 415–16; glossaries for, 336–37; literacy, 565–67; middlemen, 297–98, 299; mobility of Minxi, 45–46; morality, 272–73, 277–78; negative views of, 269, 272–73, 280; profits, 68–69; route books, 416; scholar-, 268; skills needed, 357; of Zou and Ma lineages, 66–67. *See also* Itinerant booksellers; Sojourning merchants

Merit accumulation, 277–78

Metropolitan language culture, 553

Middle class, 474, 570

Middlemen, 297–98, 299

Midwives, 445

Migrations: demand for educational texts, 323–24; of Hakka people, 39, 40–41, 211–15, 231–32; influence on publishing industry, 19, 85, 323–24; influence on Sibao bookselling routes, 231–32, 252; of Zou and Ma lineages, 212–15, 230, 231–32

Military romances / adventure novels, 484–86, 494–95; *Da Han sanhe mingzhu baojian zhuan* 大漢三合明珠寶劍全傳, 487; *Fan Tang yanyi zhuan* 反唐演義傳, 237, 486*n*; *Hou wuhu* 後五虎, 531; *Lü mudan* 綠牡丹, 494, 497; *Qian wuhu* 前五虎, 531; *Qixia wuyi* 七俠五義, 531; *Sanxia wuyi* 三俠五義, 487, 494, 529, 531; *Shuo Hu quanzhuan* 說呼全傳, 486; *Shuo Tang yanyi quanzhuan* 說唐演義全傳, 485–86; *Shuo Yue quanzhuan* 說岳全傳, 485, 496–97; *Wanhua lou* 萬花樓, 486, 497, 531; *Wannian qing* 萬年青, 487*n*; *Wuhu ping nan* 五虎平南, 486, 495, 514, 529; *Wuhu ping xi* 五虎平西, 486, 495; *Xiyou ji* 西遊記, 237, 478; *Xue Dingshan zheng xi* 薛丁山征西, 486*n*; *Xue Rengui zheng dong* 薛仁貴征東, 237, 486*n*, 495, 531; *Yinshi* 蟫史, 492, 493, 497; *Zhengchun yuan* 爭春園, 486–87; *Zhonglie xiayi zhuan* 忠烈俠義傳, 487

Military texts, 398; *Wujing duanpian* 武經短篇, 398; *Wujing gaotou* 武經高頭, 398; *Wujing qishu* 武經七書, 398; *Wujing sanshu* 武經三書, 398

Milne, William, 14–15

Minbei 閩北: bookselling routes, 197; paper production, 95; rivers, 38, 42; tea industry, 297

*Ming* 命 (unit of 500 sheets of paper), 121

Min-Gan-Yue 閩粵贛 border region: bamboo forests, 95; bandits, 40; religious sects and secret societies, 47–48; trade networks, 38–39, 45; transport networks, 207

Ming dynasty: fall of, 42–43

Minnan 閩南, 38, 199

Min River 閩江, 38, 236

Minting huiguan 閩汀會館, 157

Minxi 閩西 (western Fujian): agriculture, 39, 40; disorder, 47, 49, 70–71; drama, 500; economy, 41–45 *passim*; ethnic conflicts, 39–40, 47; forests, 94–95; isolation, 35, 37–38; literati, 283; paper production, 95; poverty, 39; publishing industry outside Sibao, 55–57; rivers, 37–38, 42; scholars, 53–55; topography, 37–38

Missionaries, 49, 54, 407, 561–62

Miura Kunio, 453

Miyazaki Ichisada, 285

Model books of calligraphy (*zitie*), 336

Modern textbooks, 57, 91, 92, 530; *Gao[deng] lishi* 高等歷史, 260; *Gonghe[guo] chudeng guowen* 共和國初等國文, 260; *Gonghe[guo] jing* 共和國鏡, 260; *Gonghe guomin duben* 共和國民讀本, 260

Moneylending, 149, 152

Money shops (*qiandian*), 241

Morality books (*shanshu*), 342–43, 467–69; free distribution, 157; *Ganying pian* 感應篇, 343; *Jingshi chuanwen* 警世傳文, 344*n*; *Jingxin lu* 敬信錄, 468*n*; lessons for children, 527; *Quanshi wen* 勸世文, 344*n*; readership, 411, 471; *Taishang ganying pian* 太上感應篇, 467–68; *Wenchang dijun Yinzhi wen* 文昌帝君隱騭文, 510; *Wugong jing* 五公經, 531; *Yifang xunzi* 義方訓子, 342–43, 527; *Yinzhi wen* 陰騭文, 343; *Yuli zhibao bian* 玉歷[曆]至寶編, 468–69

Mote, Frederick, 563–64

Mountain pear (*shanli*), 94

Mountain songs (*shan'ge*), 500, 502

Moxiang shuwu 墨香書屋, 154

Moxibustion: texts on, 445–46

*Muyushu* 木魚書 (wooden-fish books), 505–6, 512

*Muzhi* 墓誌 (funerary dedications), 281

Nanchang 南昌: book markets, 12, 539; growth, 226; publishing industry, 232; trade routes, 537

Nanhai 南海, 220

Nanjing 南寧: book markets, 12, 539; publishing industry, 9–10; Taiping rebels, 48

Nanning: bookstores, 202, 223, 224, 254, 267; Hakka migrants, 211

Nanning prefecture, 223

Nanxiong 南雄 department, 208, 222, 241

*Nanyin* 南音 (southern-pronunciation songbooks), 505*n*

*Narrative of the Three Kingdoms* (*Sanguo [tongsu] yanyi*), 101, 478, 479–81, 495, 517, 531

Nationalist government, 49, 50

Native banks (*qianzhuang*), 218, 240–41

Nevius, John, 351

New Culture movement, 57, 258

Nianzi tang 念兹堂, 169

Ninghua 寧化 county, 35*n*; academies, 57*n*; block cutters, 98; commercial activities, 45; disorder, 47; exports, 43; paper production, 44, 114; transport routes, 58

*Ninghua xianzhi* 寧化縣志, 54–55, 56

North River (Beijiang), 201, 234

Novellas (*huaben*), 478–79

Novels, *see* Fiction imprints

Occupational diversification, 63–65

Officeholders: booksellers' contacts with, 233, 284–85; incomes, 147; language used, 366*n*, 553; relations with Sibao publishers, 280, 281–83; from Sibao, 284–85; of Zou lineage, 275*n*. *See also* Examination system

Officeholders, texts for, 398; *Da Qing huidian* 大清會典, 398; *Da Qing lü* 大清律, 398; *Da Qing xinlü* 大清新律, 398; *Fuhui quanshu* 福惠全書, 398; *Qianlong xinlü* 乾隆新律, 398; *Xuezheng quanshu* 學政全書, 398; *Zhijun shu* 致君書, 398; *Zizhi xinshu* 資治新書, 398

Opium War (1839–41), 221, 250

Oral culture, 500, 527–28, 555

Oral histories, 26–28

Ou 歐 River valley, 211, 212

Owen, Stephen, 526

Painters: in Tingzhou, 55

Painting manuals: *Jiezi yuan huazhuan* 芥子園畫傳, 510*n*; *Shizhu zhai shuhuapu* 十竹齋書畫譜, 510*n*

Paper: availability in southern China, 17–18; materials, 17–18. *See also* Bamboo paper

Paper brokers (*zhihang*), 115, 116

Paper mills (*zhicao*), 114–19 *passim*

Paper nails (*zhiding*), 109

Partible inheritance, *see* Property division

Pawnshops (*dianpu*), 241–42

Pear (*li*), 94, 102

Peasants: glossaries for, 337; literacy, 568; livelihoods, 46–47; renting land, 70. *See also* Agriculture

Pelliot, Paul, 4

Pengkou 朋口, 236, 240

*Pengmin* 棚民 (Shed people), 226

Philanthropies, *see* Charitable activities

Philosophy, works of: *Baizi quance* 百子全冊, 397; *Jinsi lu* 近思錄, 397; *Kunxue jiwen* 困學紀聞, 397; *Xingli daquan* 性理大全, 53, 397; *Zhuzi huowen* 朱子或問, 397; *Zhuzi jingyan* 朱子精言, 397

Physicians, *see* Medicine

Physiognomy manuals, 465

*Pidian* 批点 (with commentary and punctuation), 480

Pine (*song*), 43, 95, 112

*Pinghua* 平話 (simple story), 482

Pingma 平馬, 202, 256

Pingnan 平南, 202

Pingshan 平山 market, 201

Pingyuan 平遠 county seat, 201

Pirates, 221–22, 250

*Plum in a Golden Vase*, 453, 478, 496

Poetry collections, 322, 367–74, 506–7; *fu* (rhapsody), 507*n*; *Guochao biecai ji* 國朝別裁集, 507; *Ji'ao shanfang shiji* 寄傲山房詩集, 508*n*; *Jiyueyun zhai shiti shifu shizhu* 寄嶽雲齋試體詩賦詩註, 373; *Lingtong shi* 靈通詩, 507*n*; *Mingshi biecai ji* 明詩別裁集, 507; *Qianjia shi* 千家詩, 367–72, 514; *Qianjia shi tuzhu* 千家詩圖註, 368–69; *Qingyun shi* 青雲詩, 507*n*; readership, 476; *Songshi biecai ji* 宋詩別裁集, 507; *Tangshi biecai ji* 唐詩別裁集, 507; *Tangshi hexuan* 唐詩合選, 312, 374; *Tangshi hexuan xiangjie* 唐詩合選詳解, 180, 256, 373; *Tangshi heyun* 唐詩合韻, 312; *Tangshi sanbaishou* 唐詩三百首, 372–73, 514; *Tangshi sanbaishou zhushu* 唐詩三百首註疏, 372–73; *Xinke Qianjia shi* 新刻千家詩, 370–71; *Yangyun shi* 養雲詩, 507*n*; *Yongwu shi* 詠物詩, 507; *Yuan biecai ji* 元別裁集, 507; *Zhumingjia baishou shi* 諸名家百壽詩, 371*n*

Poetry composition, 322, 367; *Peiwen yunfu* 佩文韻府, 373; rhyming dictionaries, 373–74; *Shixue hanying* 詩學含英, 312, 374; *Shiyun hanying* 詩韻含英, 312, 374; *Shiyun jicheng* 詩韻集成, 374; *Tangshi heyun* 唐詩合韻, 312; textbooks, 374

Poetry criticism (*shihua*), 367, 374, 506–7; *Shixue jicheng* 詩學集成, 374; *Shixue xinlun* 詩學新論, 374; *Suiyuan shihua* 隨園詩話, 374

Poets: in Tingzhou, 55

Popular genres, *see* Correspondence manuals; Etiquette guides; Good fortune, guides to; Household encyclopedias; Medical texts; Ritual handbooks

Popular texts (*pujiben*), 549

Popular textual culture: alternative cultures, 557–59; availability of books, 548–53, 569; availability to illiterates, 500, 518, 550, 552, 555; as context for Sibao imprints, 523–29, 532–33; homogeneity, 553, 554–55; interaction with oral culture, 527–28, 555; linguistic levels, 526; social impact, 568–70; in southern China, 512, 523, 553–57; variety of ideas, 525–26, 556–57

Population increases: in China, 18–19; expansion of book market and, 18–19, 85, 88, 216–30; relationship to economic conditions, 216–18; of school population, 322–23. *See also* Migrations

Porters, 115, 244, 246

Postal stations (*yizhan*), 207

Post roads (*guanma dalu*), 207

Poyang Lake 鄱陽湖, 203*n*, 227

Prescription collections, 439–42; *Antai baochan liangfang* 安胎保產良方, 445; *Lei Gong paozhi yaoxing fu* 雷公爆製藥性賦, 440; readership, 472, 473; *Shifang gekuo* 時方歌括, 433–35, 527; *Shifang miaoyong* 時方妙用, 434–35; *Tangye* 湯液, 315; *Yanfang huipian* 驗方彙編, 432*n*; *Yanfang xinbian* 驗方新編, 441–42; *Yaoxing fu* 藥性賦, 255; *Yifang jijie* 醫方集解, 440. *See also* Materia medica; Medical texts

Prices of Sibao imprints, 513–18; Classics, 398, 514–15; comparison to other regions, 517–18; dictionaries, 401, 551; examination preparation texts, 514, 515, 517; *fengshui* manuals, 514; fiction, 491, 495, 514; guides to good fortune, 514; household encyclopedias, 517; medical texts, 428, 432, 446, 514, 517; primers, 330–31; retail, 514–15; songbooks, 506; wholesale, 513–14

Primers, 321, 322, 326–49; for abacus, 343–44; *Baijia xing* 百家姓, 321, 326, 328, 349; *Caojue baiyun* 草訣百韻, 344*n*; character formation, 335–36; compendia, 344–45, 348–49, 407–8; compilers, 310; demand for, 123, 237; *Dizi gui* 弟子規, 162, 332–33; *Ershisi xiao* 二十四孝, 344–45*n*, 345; *Gushu zhuanwen* 古書篆文, 344*n*; *Jingshi chuanwen* 警世傳文, 344*n*; *Linchi kaifa* 臨池楷法, 344*n*; *Lishu fatie* 隸書法帖, 344*n*; *Liuren shike* 六壬時課, 344*n*; memorization, 405–6, 527; paper, 121, 330; prices, 330–31; *Qianzi wen* 千字文, 321, 326–27, 328, 330; quality, 330; *Quanshi wen* 勸世文, 344*n*; *Sanzi jing tukao* 三字經圖考, 330–31; *Sanzijing zhu* 三字經注, 514; *Sanzi jing zhujie* 三字經註解, 348; *Sanzi jing zhujie beizhi* 三字經註解備旨, 328; *Suanfa cuoyao* 算法撮要, 343–44; *Suanfa yaojue* 算法要訣, 344*n*; use in twentieth century, 530–32; *Xiaoxue* 小學, 404–5; *Xinke Shenglü qimeng duilei* 新刻聲律啓蒙對類, 370–71; *Xinke zengbu Baijia xing* 新刻增補百家姓, 328; *Xinke zengbu Sanzi jing* 新刻增補三字經, 328; *Xinke zhengzihua Qianzi wen* 新刻正字畫千字文, 330; *Xinzeng youxue* 新增幼學, 310;

*Zengguang zhengwen* 增廣正文, 333–35; *Zengzhu Sanzi jing* 增註三字經, 328–30; *Zhan denghua jixiong* 占灯花吉凶, 344*n*; *Zhibi tushi* 執筆圖勢, 344*n*, 345; *Zhushi San Bai Qian Zengguang heke* 註釋三百千增廣合刻, 344–45, 348–49, 407–8. *See also* Educational texts; San-Bai-Qian; *Sanzi jing*; *Zengguang xianwen*

Print burnishers, 107–8

Printing brushes, 95, 107, 111

Printing ink (*yinmo*), 111–13

Printing rooms, 105

Printing technology: histories, 5. *See also* Letterpress printing; Lithographic printing; Woodblock printing

Printing tools, 107–8; brushes, 95, 107, 111; local manufacture, 111; surviving, 26

Production quality, of Sibao imprints, 519–22; Classics, 393–95; effects on survival, 25; errors, 6, 519–20; fiction, 481; poor, 6, 319; primers, 330

Profits: amounts, 145–47; nonpayment of taxes and, 265; uses of, 149–58, 274–75, 276

Pronunciation guides, 424, 542–43; *Guanhua yin* 官話音, 366*n*

Property division: creation of new publishing houses, 160, 161, 165, 167, 175, 288, 293; disputes, 74; documents, 21–22; equal shares, 162; motives, 159–60; of printing workrooms, 161, 168; relations among *shufang* following, 181, 182–83; of woodblocks, 85, 86, 161, 162, 163

*Pu* 鋪 (roadside or foot-courier stations), 207

Pu Songling 蒲松齡, 337*n*, 491, 493

Public land (*gongtian*), 69–71

Publisher-booksellers, *see* Sibao publishers/booksellers

Publishing histories, 4, 29*n*

Publishing houses, *see Shufang*; Sibao publishing/bookselling industry

Publishing industry, Qing: availability of books, 548–51; book prices, 548–51; core texts, 554–57, 559; distribution of texts, 543–44, 547; in Hunan, 229; in Jiangnan, 295–96; in northern China, 551; official, 283; operational structures, 547–48; prices, 517–18; private, 283; proliferation of operations, 552, 555; specialized local imprints, 557–58. *See also* Commercial woodblock publishing; Foshanzhen; Xuwanzhen

*Pujiben* 普及本 (popular texts), 549

Punti 本地 (original settlers), 89, 252. *See also* Hakka-Punti War

Qiandao hui 千刀會, 47*n*

*Qiandian* 錢店 (money shops), 241

*Qianjia shi* 千家詩, 367–72, 514

*Qianjia shi tuzhu* 千家詩圖註, 368–69

Qianlong emperor, 322, 388, 428, 450

*Qianpu* 錢鋪 (currency-exchange shops), 218, 240–41

*Qianzhuang* 錢莊 (native banks), 218, 240–41

*Qianzi wen* 千字文, 321, 326–27, 328, 330

*Qiaozi xiulin* 橋梓繡林, 317, 426, 428

Qiling 岐陵, 201

*Qinding Xingli kaoyuan* 欽定星曆考原, 450–51

Qing dynasty: censorship, 496–97, 498*n*; industrial-commercial structure, 294, 296–98, 299–300; resistance to, 42–43, 225. *See also* Publishing industry, Qing

Qingliu 清流 county, 35*n*, 42, 45, 58

Qiongji (tang or lou) 瓊記 (堂 or 樓), 260

Qiu Chunsan 邱春三, 284, 286

Qiu Jun 邱濬, 350*n*

Qiu 仇 lineage of block carvers, 15

Qixin shuju 啓新書局, 264*n*

Qiyuan tang 啓元堂, 499

Rawski, Evelyn, 52, 146, 515, 564

Red Army, 50

Red Turban rebellions (1854–56), 89, 221

Reference works, 399–402; *Sishu renwu leidian chuanzhu* 四書人物類典串珠, 401–2; *Tongdian* 通典, 353; *Wenliao dacheng* 文料大成, 353–54. *See also* Dictionaries; Encyclopedias

Regional texts: fiction, 318, 491–93; *Jingfu xinshu* 警富新書, 491, 558; *Lingnan yishi* 嶺南逸史, 492, 558; local writers, 56; *Minting wenxuan* 閩汀文選, 56; songbooks, 318, 502, 505*n*, 557–58; *Yinshi* 蟬史, 492, 493, 497; *Zhangzhou minjian gushi* 漳州民間故事, 531. *See also* Hakka glossaries

Religion: associations, 75; Buddhism, 73–74, 467; publishers and, 278–79; sects, 47–48; in Sibao, 60, 71–76, 278–79; texts, 467, 523*n*

Remittance businesses, 241

Renewal and licensing examinations (*suikao*), 367

*Renjia riyong* 人家日用, 318, 339–41, 558; demand for, 123, 237; production costs, 146; use of, 566; woodblocks, 100

Republican period: disorder, 49, 50; education system, 54, 57, 91, 92, 260, 530; publishing industry, 91, 92; taxes, 266

Revolt of the Three Feudatories, 43, 280

Rhymed couplets collections: *Caiji xinlian tuzhang jiaju* 採輯新聯圖章佳句, 415, 424–26; compilers, 311, 313; *Duilian daquan* 對聯大全, 312, 426; for household use, 424–26; parallel rhymed couplets, 311; *Qiaozi xiulin* 橋梓繡林, 317, 426, 428

Rhyming dictionaries, 373–74

Ricci, Matteo, 16, 548, 550, 551

Rice cultivation, 46

Rice trade, 45, 66–67, 228–29

Ritual handbooks, 414; *Huizuan Jiali tieshi jiyao* 彙纂家禮帖式集要, 316, 317, 416–22, 427, 472, 473, 474; *Jiali jicheng* 家禮集成, 414–15; messages, 473–74; popularity, 471; readership, 411, 421, 473. *See also* Etiquette guides; Household encyclopedias

Rivers: in Minxi, 37–38, 42; piracy, 221–22, 250; trade routes, 208–10, 234; transport of books, 246–48

*Riyong leishu* 日用類書 (encyclopedias for daily use), 411–28

*Rizhi lu* 日知錄, 403

Roads: bridges built by successful publishers, 157, 246, 290; commercial use, 207–8; conditions, 245–46; post, 207; shipping books via, 245–47; in Sibao, 4, 58

Roadside or foot-courier stations (*pu*), 207

Rongxian 容縣, Guangxi, 172

Rowe, William, 225

Ruan Yuan 阮元, 232

Ruijin 瑞金, 205, 209, 227, 286

*Rushang* 儒商 (Confucian merchants), 268, 269–75

Sagely Mother in Heaven (Tianshang shengmu), 71–72

St Clair, William, 532

Sakai Tadao, 411

Salt trade, 45, 147, 258–59, 296

San-Bai-Qian 三百千, 321, 326. *See also Baijia xing*; *Qianzi wen*; *Sanzi jing*

*Sanguo tongsu yanyi* 三國通俗演義, *see Narrative of the Three Kingdoms*

*Sanguo yanyi* 三國演義, *see Narrative of the Three Kingdoms*

*Sanming tonghui* 三命通會, 465–66

*Sanzi jing* 三字經: contents, 327–28; demand for, 123, 179, 237, 326; editions, 328–30, 531; memorization, 527; prices, 330–31; production costs, 145, 146; profits from sales, 147; published by multiple houses, 179; woodblocks, 100

Scholar-merchants (*shishang*), 268

Schools: book orders, 255–56; booksellers' visits, 238; business with branch bookstores, 254–56; charitable, 52, 322, 324, 405; community, 52; county, 52; elementary, 52, 324, 326, 374–75, 403–4, 530–31; government, 284, 285*n*; levels, 324,

326; as markets for educational texts, 233, 254–56; in northern China, 551; prefectural, 52; private, 52; proliferation of, 322–24, 556. *See also* Academies; Education; Family schools

Secret societies, 47–48, 221, 251–52

*Shanben* 善本 (fine or rare editions), 5

Shancheng tang 善成堂, 11, 12, 539

Shandong province: publishing industry, 11

Shangbao 上保 village, 58, 60

*Shan'ge* 山歌 (mountain songs), 500, 502

Shanghai: *Haishanghua liezhuan* 海上花列傳, 494; opening to trade, 221; publishing industry, 91, 532

*Shanghan* 傷寒 (cold damage) theory, 429, 437–38

Shanghang 上杭 county, 35*n*; bookselling routes, 236; bookstores, 239, 264, 267; commercial activities, 45; Communist movement, 54; handicraft industries, 42; paper production, 44

Shankeng 珊坑: paper production, 113, 114

*Shanli* 山梨／橘 (mountain pear), 94

*Shanmu* 杉木 (*shamu* 沙木), 43

*Shanshu* 善書, *see* Morality books

*Shanzeng Yidu liuren ke xuanri yaojue* 刪增儀度六壬課選日要訣, 464–65, 469

Shao Yong 邵雍, 389, 463*n*

Shaowu 邵武 prefecture, 95, 203

Shaozhou 韶州 prefecture, 212, 218

Share-partnerships (*hehuo* or *hegu*), 296*n*

Shaxian 沙縣, 114, 193, 197, 237

She 畬 subgroup of Yao, 39–40

Shed people (*pengmin*), 226

Shegong 社公, 72

Shen Baoshan 沈寶山, 317

Shen Deqian 沈德潛, 358, 507

*Shennong bencao jingdu* 神農本草經讀, 178, 436–39, 519

*Shenshi* 紳士, *see* Gentry

*Shenxiang quanbian* 神相全編, 465

Shi Chengjin 石成金, 422, 528, 543

Shibazhai 十八寨, Yongan county, 145

*Shifang gekuo* 時方歌括, 433–35, 527

*Shihua* 詩話, *see* Poetry criticism

*Shiji* 史記, 180, 396, 397, 398

*Shishang* 士商 (scholar-merchants), 268

*Shiwen* 時文, *see* Contemporary essays; Eight-legged essays

*Shiyinben* 石印本, *see* Lithographic texts

Shizhong chang 時中昌, 117

*Shouwen* 壽文 (commemorative essays), 281–82

Shuangquan 雙泉 village, 58

*Shudian* 書店, *see* Bookstores

Shufang 書坊, Fujian, publishing industry, 9

*Shufang* 書坊 (publishing houses): accounts, 140–45, 291; capital sources, 85–86, 161; centralized management, 143, 144–45, 261, 293; competition among, 160, 177–85; continuity over generations, 164–77; cooperation among, 181, 182–83, 184, 185, 196–97, 288, 290; created after property division, 160, 161, 165, 167, 175, 288, 293; customary rules regulating relations, 177–84, 264, 290; dispute resolution, 187; expansion, 150–51; female managers, 133, 134; hired labor, 131; as household industries, 127–31, 134, 149–50, 287; household labor, 99, 128, 130, 175–76, 288, 300; incomes, 145–49; number of, 86; number of titles on book lists, 86; organization, 127–31; partnerships, 258–59, 298; proliferation of, 85–86, 90, 160, 163–64; proportion of household income, 127–28, 150, 176–77; relations with non-Sibao businesses, 259–60; relative wealth, 151–52; successful, 148–49, 151–52; training of male family members, 137–40, 176, 185, 299; use of profits, 149–58, 274–75, 276; variation in sizes, 162–63. *See also* Sibao publishing / bookselling industry

*Shuhua tongzhen* 書畫同珍, 507–10

*Shuihu zhuan* 水滸傳, *see Water Margin*

*Shunde xianzhi* 順德縣志, 15

*Shuo Yue quanzhuan* 說岳全傳, 485, 496–97

*Shusi* 書肆, *see* Bookstores

*Shuyuan* 書院, *see* Academies

*Shuzha* 書榨 (book presses), 109–11

Sibao 四堡: associations, 71–72, 278–79; economic ties within, 58–60; identity, 58; internal conflict, 74–77; isolation, 35, 58, 309; lack of natural resources, 1; location, 1, 4, 35, 57–58; marriage networks, 58; migration from, 212–15, 240, 252; poverty, 1; roads, 4, 58; social connections, 71–74; villages, 57–58, 60n. *See also* Mawu; Wuge

Sibao imprints: affordability, 513–14, 515–17; bestsellers, 306, 312, 326, 333, 478; categories, 319–20; choice of texts to publish, 305–6, 309; conditions of surviving, 25, 319; core texts, 321–22, 375, 554; editions for specific markets, 522; as historical sources, 24–25; introduction of new titles, 529; overview, 306–9; popular textual culture context, 523–29, 532–33; production quality, 6, 25, 319, 330, 393–95, 481, 519–22; sources, 309–18; southern Chinese authors, 317–18; stability of canon, 529–33. *See also* Educational texts; Fiction imprints; Good fortune, guides to; Household encyclopedias; Medical texts; Prices; Ritual handbooks

Sibao publishers / booksellers: charitable activities, 155–56, 157, 277–78, 289–90; as Confucian merchants, 268, 269–75; education given up for publishing career, 135–36, 137–38, 269, 270; education levels, 137–40, 153–54, 272, 274–75, 284, 288–89, 314; elite social status, 276–84; local leadership, 276, 286, 293; mansions, 87–88, 151–52, 190–91; moral worth, 272–73; purchased degrees, 279–80; relations with local officials, 280, 281–83; self-perceptions, 268; social status, 271–72, 286; texts compiled by, 289, 310–14, 374, 412–13; wealth, 276. *See also* Itinerant booksellers

Sibao publishing / bookselling industry: absence of scholarship on, 3–

5, 6; combined functions, 298–99, 300–301; comparison to other enterprises, 293–301; comparison to other publishing centers, 546–48; decline, 260, 267; factors in demise, 2–3, 90–92, 300; factors in success, 93; income, 145–49; labor costs, 124, 131, 288; in nineteenth century, 88–91; origins, 79–84, 269; overview, 84–93; partnerships, 258–59, 298; peak, 2, 86, 87; production costs, 124–25, 145–46, 300, 519; relations between publishing and bookselling aspects, 185; relationship to government, 265–66; seasonal cycle, 122–23, 244; sources for study of, 20–28; time period, 1–2; in twentieth century, 2, 91–93; value of studying, 6–7; wholesale book market, 87, 190–92. *See also* Bookselling routes; Branch bookstores; *Shufang*

Sichuan province: migration to, 19; publishing industry, 10; schools, 323; Zigong salt merchants, 147, 258–59, 296. *See also* Yuechi county

Simple story (*pinghua*), 482

*Sishu* 私塾, *see* Family schools

*Sishu* 四書 (Four Books), 165, 307. *See also* Four Books

*Sishu buzhu beizhi tiqiao huican* 四書補註備旨題竅匯參, 313, 383–87, 394, 514

*Sishu jizhu* 四書集註 (or 注), 164–65, 180, 385, 387, 514

*Sishu renwu leidian chuanzhu* 四書人物類典串珠, 401–2

*Sishu yizhu* 四書繹註, 376–78

*Sishu zhengwen* 四書正文, 318, 378–80

*Sishu zhu daquan* 四書註大全, 166–67, 307

Smith, Arthur, 289, 407, 528, 549, 551, 555

Smith, Richard J., 463, 469

Social and political criticism, 495–98, 528, 570; *Da hongpao* 大紅袍, 496; *Ershinian mudu zhi guai xianzhuang* 二十年目睹之怪現狀, 494; *Guanchang xianxing ji* 官場現形記, 494; *Hou Shuihu zhuan* 後水滸傳, 496; *Water Margin*, 478, 496, 570

Social structure: middle class, 474, 570; mobility, 66, 279, 568, 569–70; status of book merchants, 271–72. *See also* Gentry

Sojourning merchants: efforts to retain ties with, 67–68; marriages, 67–68, 133; from Minxi, 45–46; separation from families, 67–68; Zou and Ma, 62–63. *See also* Branch bookstores; Itinerant booksellers; Merchants

Song Yingxing 宋應星: *Tiangong kaiwu* 天工開物, 95, 112, 118

Songbooks, 500–506, 512; *Che Long gongzi huadeng ji* 車龍公子花燈記, 505–6; *Che Long xiaojie huadeng ji* 車龍小姐花燈記, 504–5; cultural role, 555; *Meng Jiangnü ku changcheng* 孟姜女哭長城, 501; popularity, 500, 511; prices, 506; *Qin Xuemei zhuan* 秦雪梅傳, 502; regional, 318, 502, 505n, 557–58; *Shili ting* 十里亭, 502; *Shisha ting* 十杉亭, 502; *Xinke Liang Shanbo Zhu Yingtai* 新刻梁山伯祝英台, 500–501; Yuechi editions, 543; *Zhao Yulin* 趙玉麟, 503–4, 506, 557;

*Zhao Yulin changci* 唱詞, 504. *See also* Wooden-fish books

Songs, mountain, 500, 502

Southern-pronunciation songbooks (*nanyin*), 505n

Story collections, 477, 479

Strolling Scholars, 289

Students: affordability of books, 516–17; selling books to, 283–84, 306. *See also* Education; Schools

Study of editions (*banbenxue*), 5

*Suanfa cuoyao* 算法撮要, 343–44

*Suikao* 歲考 (renewal and licensing examinations), 367

*Suiyi shua xin* 歲一刷新 rule, 177–78, 179, 264, 290

Supernatural tales, 490–91; *Caomu chunqiu yanyi* 草木春秋演義, 490; *Jiazhu Liaozhai zhiyi* 加註聊齋誌異, 491; *Liaozhai zhiyi* 聊齋誌異, 491, 495, 514, 522; *Pidian Liaozhai zhiyi* 批点聊齋誌異, 491; *Pingyao zhuan* 平妖傳, 490; *Siyou ji* 四游記, 490; *Soushen ji* 搜神記, 490; *Xu Liaozhai zhiyi* 續聊齋誌異, 491; *Yetan suilu* 夜譚隨錄, 491; *Zi buyu* 子不語, 491

*Suwei shanfang* 素位山房, 116, 242, 258, 531–32, 558

*Suwei tang* 素位堂, 101, 128, 236, 258

Suzhou: bookselling routes, 194; publishing industry, 9, 10, 545

Taiping rebellion, 48, 88–90, 221

*Taishang ganying pian* 太上感應篇, 467–68

Taiwan, Hakka migrants, 212

*Taixuesheng* 太學生 (Imperial Academy students), 280

Talent and beauty love stories, *see Caizi jiaren*

*Tangshi hexuan xiangjie* 唐詩合選詳解, 180, 256, 373

*Tangshi sanbaishou* 唐詩三百首, 372–73, 514

*Tangshi sanbaishou zhushu* 唐詩三百首註疏, 372–73

*Taoban* 套版 (two-color) printing, 522

Taxes: commercial, 265; evasion, 265, 266; *likin* customs duties, 48–49, 89, 266

Teachers: affordability of books, 515–16; booksellers' contacts with, 233, 283–84; books purchased by, 255; competence, 285; in family schools, 137; incomes, 147, 515–16; professionalization, 322; selling books to, 306

Tea industry, 297

Temporary stalls (*bai tanzi*), 238

Textbooks, *see* Educational texts

Textile industry, 297

Textual culture, *see* Popular textual culture

Theater, *see* Dramatic works

*Tiancha* 田茶 hamlet, 62, 131

*Tiandihui* 天地會, 47, 251–52

*Tianhou* 天后, 60, 72–73, 77, 278, 279

*Tianhou miao* 天后廟, 71

*Tianshang shengmu* 天上聖母 (Sagely Mother in Heaven), 71–72

Timber, 43, 94–95

Ting River 汀江, 37–38

*Tingshui* 汀水, *see* Yin River

Tingzhou 汀州 prefecture, 35; degree-holders, 51; economy, 42, 46; forests, 94–95; Hakka migration to, 39; official publishing, 283; paper production, 113–15, 120; writers, 56

*Tingzhou fuzhi* 汀州府志, 281

Tong Ji 童季, 284

Tong Nengling 童能靈, 53, 56

*Tongsheng* 童生 (junior students), 283–84, 375, 475

*Tongshu* 通書, *see* Almanacs

Tongwen tang 同文堂, 168

*Tongzi wenlu* 童子問路, 364–65

Tools: binding, 26; printing, 26, 95, 107–8, 111

Trader's road money (*gulu qian*), 241

Transport networks: axes, 210; development of bookselling routes and, 207–11; porters, 115, 244, 246. *See also* Rivers; Roads

Triads, 221

Tribute-student (*gongsheng*) status, 61, 65

Tsien, Tsuen-hsuin, 4, 6, 8

Tudi bogong 土地伯公, 72

Twitchett, Denis, 4

United States: reading habits of Chinese laborers in, 471–72, 511, 524

Veterinary texts: *Liao ma ji* 療馬集, 446*n*; *Tuojing* 駝經, 446*n*; *Yuan Heng liao niu ji* 元亨療牛集, 446–48

Virtue, 277–78

Vocabulary words, *see* Glossaries

Von Glahn, Richard, 277

Wang Shixin 汪士信, 296–97

Wang Shuhe 王叔和, 315

Wang Yangming 王陽明, 40, 53, 54

Wang Yinglin 王應麟, 327, 348

Wang Ze 王澤 uprising, 490

Wang 汪 lineage of block carvers, 15

Wanjuan lou 萬卷樓, 149, 152, 162, 416, 422, 423, 479

Wanzhu lou 萬竹樓, 81

Warm factors disorders (*wenbing*), 429, 430

*Water Margin*, 250, 478, 496, 570

Water transport, *see* Rivers

Watson, James, 558–59

Weixian 威縣, 433, 434

*Wenbing* 瘟病 (warm factor disorders), 429, 430

Wencui lou 文萃樓, 167–68, 197*n*

Wengyuan 翁源, 245

Wenhai lou 文海樓: booklists, 397; bookstore printing operations, 264; bookstores, 23, 254–55, 257, 261–62, 267; cover page on gate, 178; division of titles, 162; essay collections, 363, 365; fiction imprints, 478, 479, 483, 488, 491, 495; medical texts, 428, 432; in nineteenth century, 90, 261–62; origins, 261; primers, 344; relations with Foshanzhen publishers, 310; relations with unrelated bookstores, 259; seasonal cycle, 123; songbooks, 501; woodblock storage, 103

Wenhai lou account book, 23; Classics imprints, 375, 388; dictionaries, 401; distribution of books to shops, 256–57; income, 147; medical texts, 446; morality books, 468; number of titles, 86, 87; prices, 513–14

*Wenhai lou jiaozheng jianyun fenzhang fenjie Sishu zhengwen* 文海樓校正監韻分章分節四書正文, 378–80

Wenhui lou 文匯樓, 83

Wenjing tang 文經堂, 201

Wenlan ge 文蘭閣, 200*n*

*Wenliao dacheng* 文料大成, 353–54

Wenlin tang 文林堂, 169, 284

*Wenren* 文人, *see* Literati

Wenxiang ge 文香閣, 261

Wenzhou: bookselling routes, 199; bookstores, 174; Hakka migrants, 41, 213; trade routes, 38

Wenzi tang 文玆堂, 169

West River 西江, 208–9, 250. *See also* Gong River

Wholesale book market, 87, 190–92

Widmer, Ellen, 5

Williams, S. Wells, 470, 511, 548–49, 551, 561, 567

Wind and fire walls and rooms, 103

Women: agricultural work, 40, 41; block cutters, 14–15, 17, 146; childbirth, 445; education, 155*n*; Hakka customs, 40, 41, 134*n*; literacy, 527–28; Magang block cutters, 15, 101–2, 104–5, 133, 536, 545–46; managerial roles, 133, 134; printing and binding work, 109, 111, 130, 132, 288; wages, 17, 132–33, 546; *Xun younü ge* 訓幼女歌, 543. *See also* Gender roles

Wood, 43, 94–95

Woodblock printing: dissemination, 542, 555; flexibility of print runs, 15–16; introduction to Sibao, 83–84; labor, 14, 99, 109, 128, 130; output per day, 108–9; physical organization, 105–6; portability, 18; process, 105–9; production costs, 13–14, 17, 18; raw materials, 93–96; technical simplicity, 13; tools, 26, 95, 107–8, 111; training workers,

105. *See also* Block cutters; Commercial woodblock publishing

Woodblocks: destruction, 26; as dowries, 86; durability, 16–17*n*; exchanging with other publishers, 309–10; inheriting, 85, 86, 161, 162, 163; pawning or mortgaging, 179–80*n*; purchasing from other publishers, 97, 101, 104, 179; renting, 163, 179–81, 183; simplified characters, 519; sources, 104–5; storage, 26, 103; surviving, 26; transportation costs, 17, 541, 547. *See also* Block cutters; Block cutting

Wooden-fish books (*muyushu*), 505–6, 512

Woodside, Alexander, 569

Wu Dajin 伍大縉, 316

Wu Sangui 吳三桂, 225–26, 228

Wuchang 武昌, Hubei: bookselling routes, 194, 205; bookstores, 230

Wuchengzhen 吳城鎮, 205, 227

Wuchuan 吳川, Guangdong, 221, 284

Wugang shuwu 梧岡書屋, 154, 530*n*

Wuge 霧閣: fair market, 71, 76, 190; mansions, 87–88, 151–52; origins of publishing industry, 80–81; position relative to mountain, 456*n*; schools, 154, 530*n*; society, 67; temples, 73, 278; Zou lineage dominance, 60. *See also* Sibao

Wuhu 蕪湖, 12, 539

*Wujing beizhi* 五經備旨, 311, 314, 388–91

Wujing tang 五經堂, 253, 265

Wu 巫 lineage of Ninghua, 98

Wuping 武平 county, 35*n*, 45

*Wuxia xiaoshuo* 武俠小説 (novels about knights-errant), 487, 512*n*

Wuyangcheng 五羊城, *see* Guangzhou city
Wuyuan 武緣 county, 255
Wuzhou 梧州, Guangxi: bookselling
  routes, 202, 209; bookstores, 174,
  223

Xiamen University, 50
Xiang River 湘江, 205, 208, 229
Xiangshan tang 湘山堂, 86, 87, 161,
  162, 168
*Xiangsheng* 鄉生 (students), 283–84
*Xiaopi* 小批 format, 480
Xie Meilin 謝梅林, 311, 424
Xie Shuishun 謝水順, 4, 55
*Xiedou* 械斗 (feuds), 77
*Xieji bianfang shu* 協紀辨方書, 180,
  450–51, 469, 472–73, 525*n*
Xingning 興寧 county, Guangdong,
  81; county seat, 201, 209, 219, 222
Xinhua shuju 新華書局 (Fuzhou),
  237
*Xinke chidu* 新刻尺牘, 423–24, 427
*Xinke Liang Shanbo Zhu Yingtai* 新刻
  梁山伯祝英台, 500–501
*Xinke Qianjia shi* 新刻千家詩, 370–
  71
*Xinke Shenglü qimeng duilei* 新刻聲律
  啟蒙對類, 370–71
*Xinke Siyan zazi* 新刻四言雜字,
  337–39
Xinquan 新泉, 236
*Xinzeng zazi Renjia riyong* 新增雜字
  人家日用, 339–42
*Xinzha/Zibian* 信札/字辨, 355–57,
  408
Xiong Damu 熊大木, 482, 484
*Xuan* 宣 paper, 115, 117
*Xuanjin Zihui* 懸金字彙, 399–401
Xuehai tang 學海堂, 232

Xunzhou 潯州 prefecture, 223
Xu River 盱江, 227, 537
Xuwanzhen 滸灣鎮: bookstores,
  105–6*n*, 227, 539; paper production, 537; Sibao bookselling routes,
  205
Xuwanzhen publishing industry,
  537–40; block cutters, 538–39, 546;
  branch shops, 539; markets and
  distribution, 12, 232, 539, 547;
  output, 11, 540; printing rooms,
  105–6*n*; production quality, 519;
  publishing houses, 11, 538; traders
  at Sibao, 191
Xylography, *see* Woodblock printing

*Yahang* 牙行 (brokerage firms), 298
Yamens, 233, 238, 284
Yan Maoyou 顏茂猷, 318, 378
*Yanfang xinbian* 驗方新編, 441–42
Yang Lan 楊瀾, 2, 4, 44, 56, 118, 308
Yangcheng 羊城, *see* Guangzhou city
Yangzhou: publishing industry, 9
Yangzi River, 195, 205, 208, 226, 228,
  230
Yanping 延平 prefecture, 45, 95,
  197
Yanqian 巖前, Yongan county, 145
Yao 瑤 people, 39–40
*Yaren* 牙人 (brokers), 298
Ye Dehui 葉德輝, 17
Ye Mingchen 葉名琛, 560–61
Yesheng gong 葉勝公, 62
Yichang 宜昌, Hubei, 195
*Yifang xunzi* 義方訓子, 342–43, 527
Yijing tang 翼經堂, 115, 117, 245, 248,
  397, 400–401
Yingwen tang 應文堂, 128, 261
Yin-Han River 鄞-韓江, 209
*Yinhao* 銀號 (silver houses), 240

*Yinian shiyong zazi* 一年使用雜字, 318, 341–42, 558

Yin River 鄞江, 37–38, 42, 247

*Yinshi* 蟬史, 492, 493, 497

Yinwu shuwu 印務書屋, 265, 266

*Yisheng* 邑生 (students), 283–84

*Yixue* 義學, *see* Charitable or free elementary schools

*Yixue sanzi jing* 醫學三字經, 435–37, 519

Yiyang 益陽, 205, 229

*Yizhan* 驛站 (postal stations), 207

Yongan 永安 county, 46, 145, 193, 197, 201

Yongding 永定 county, 35n, 42, 45, 46, 54

Yongzheng emperor, 43, 217, 223, 342, 387

Yongzhou 永州, 15

You River 右江, 202, 224, 255

*Youxue gushi qionglin* 幼學故事瓊林, 349–53; contents, 351–52; as core text, 311; expansion by Zou Shengmai, 311, 313, 350, 352; lithographic version, 260; prices, 517; sales, 255; woodblocks, 165, 307

*Youxue xuzhi* 幼學須知, *see Youxue gushi qionglin*

Yu Xiangdou 余象斗, 87, 481–82n, 490

Yü Ying-shih, 270, 274

Yuan Mei 袁枚, 374, 491

Yuan Yi 袁逸, 517, 518

*Yuanben Erlun qiyou yinduan* 原本二論啓幼印端, 380–83, 408

*Yuan Heng liao niu ji* 元亨療牛集, 446–48

Yuan River 沅江, 227, 229

Yuanzhou 沅州, 205

Yu dawen tang 余大文堂, 538

Yuechi county 岳池, Sichuan: block-cutting industry, 11–12, 14, 17, 536, 540–44; introduction of block-cutting techniques, 19; publishing industry, 542–44, 557

*Yukou* 玉扣 paper, 115, 117–18, 121. *See also* Bamboo paper

Yulin 郁林 prefecture, 223

*Yuli zhibao bian* 玉歷[曆]至寶編, 468–69

Yunlong shuyuan 雲龍書院, 57n

Yunnan province: bookselling routes, 194, 199, 202–3, 209, 225; education, 225; migration to, 19; population growth, 224–25; schools, 323

Yunshen Chu 雲深處, 162, 181

Yu River 郁江, 202, 210, 224, 234

Yushan 玉山, 205, 227

*Yuxia ji* 玉匣記, 255, 452–54, 529

*Yuzuan Yizong jinjian* 御纂醫宗金鑒, 428–32, 514

Zaizi tang 在茲堂: fiction imprints, 478, 479, 491; manager, 169; printing building, 106; property division, 162, 169; Taiping rebels and, 89; texts for officeholders, 398; woodblock stock, 86, 87, 151

*Zao* 棗 (jujube), 94, 102

*Zazi* 雜字, *see* Glossaries

*Zazi yunwen* 雜子韻文 (glossaries in rhyme), 337n

Zelin, Madeleine, 296

*Zengbu zhujia xuanze guang Yuxia ji* 增補諸家選擇廣玉匣記, 452–54

Zengcheng 增城 county, 209, 218

*Zengding Guwen jingyan xiangzhu pangxun hebian* 增訂古文精言詳註旁訓合編, 360–62

*Zengding Guwen xiyi hebian* 增訂古文 析義合編, 359–60

*Zengguang xianwen* 增廣賢文: popularity, 123n, 333; price, 124n, 145–46; production costs, 145–46, 308; published by multiple houses, 179; sales in twentieth century, 531; use of, 335, 351; woodblocks, 165, 307

*Zengguang zhengwen* 增廣正文, 333–35

*Zengzhu Sanzi jing* 增註三字經, 328–30

*Zhang* 樟 (camphor), 94–95

Zhang Ji 張機, 315, 428

Zhang Jiebin 張介賓, 438n, 448

Zhang Xianzhong 張賢忠, 10, 228

Zhang Xiumin 張秀民, 4, 9–10

Zhang Zhigong 張志公, 336–37, 368, 371

Zhangshuzhen 樟樹鎮, Jiangxi, 138, 169–70, 171, 172, 194, 227

Zhangzhou 漳州: bookselling routes, 196; bookstores, 199, 242, 257–58, 284, 531–32, 558; local dialect dictionaries, 558; trade routes to, 38

*Zhao Yulin* 趙玉麟, 503–4, 506, 557

Zhaoqing 肇慶 prefecture, 222

Zhejiang province: bookselling routes, 199; Hakka migrants, 211, 212; trade routes, 38

Zheng Zhenduo 鄭振鐸, 3, 486, 540, 546

Zheng Zhenman, 75

Zheng Zhicong 鄭之琮, 364–65

*Zhicao* 紙槽, *see* Paper mills

*Zhiding* 紙丁 (paper nails), 109

*Zhihang* 紙行 (paper brokers), 115, 116

*Zhinan chidu shengli yaojue* 指南尺牘 生理要訣, 423–24

Zhiping 治平: paper production, 114–15, 116

Zhongguo gongye hezuo xiehui 中國工業合作協會, 120

Zhongguo wenhua fuwushe 中國 文化服務社, 267

Zhongtian wu 中田屋, 151

Zhongxin tang 忠心堂, 538

Zhongzhou 中洲 village, 538

Zhou Dunyi 周敦頤, 389, 469

Zhu Xi 朱熹, 348; on *Analects*, 382; association with Minbei, 50; citations of, 469; followers, 52–53, 389; on recitation, 406; works, 385, 396, 397, 404–5

*Zhupi Xiaoti zhenggu chuji, erji, sanji* 硃批小題正鵠初集, 二集, 三集, 365

*Zhushi San Bai Qian Zengguang heke* 註釋三百千增廣合刻, 344–45, 348–49, 407–8

*Zhuzhi ci* 竹枝詞 (bamboo-branch stories), 505n

*Zi* 梓 (catalpa), 94

Zigong 自貢 salt merchants, 147, 258–59, 296

Zi River 梓, 208, 229

*Zitie* 字帖 (model books of calligraphy), 336

Zou Bincai 鄒斌才, 251n, 275n

Zou Bingchun 鄒秉椿, 67, 135, 315

Zou Bingjun 鄒秉均, 128, 156–57, 194–95n, 245, 530n

Zou Boan 鄒伯安, 88–89

Zou Bolong 鄒伯龍, 201, 238, 284–85

Zou Chun 鄒春, 314

Zou Fei 鄒斐, 311, 312

Zou Funan 鄒撫南, 82–83, 154, 280, 530n

Zou Guoguang 鄒國光, 157, 201

Zou Hongchun 鄒洪春, 136–37, 151–52, 154, 274

Zou Hongqi 鄒鋐起, 170, 171, 175

Zou Hongxing 鄒鋐興, 170, 171

Zou Hongyou 鄒鋐猷, 138, 170, 171–72, 175

Zou Huilong 鄒惠龍, 315*n*

Zou Huiyue 鄒徽躍, 315*n*

Zou Jianchi 鄒建池, 90, 195, 258, 259, 261–62, 264

Zou Jinghong 鄒景鴻, 314, 389

Zou Jingyang 鄒景揚, 311, 313, 314, 389, 412–13, 414, 424–26

Zou Jingzhang 鄒景章, 314, 389

Zou Jitang 鄒際唐, 173, 174

Zou Jiyu 鄒際虞, 173, 174

Zou Jun 鄒濬, 151, 205

Zou Kongai 鄒孔愛, 106, 151, 170–75 *passim*

Zou Kongchang 鄒孔昌, 172, 173, 202

Zou Kongchun 鄒孔椿, 171, 175, 176

Zou Kongjia 鄒孔嘉, 102, 171, 175, 176, 250*n*, 251

Zou Kongmao 鄒孔茂, 138, 170–71

Zou Kongshu 鄒孔書, 170, 172, 173, 202

Zou Liulang 鄒六郎, 60

Zou Mengchun 鄒孟純, 81, 83, 84, 96, 97

Zou Ming 鄒明, 149, 152

Zou Mo 鄒謨, 312, 374

Zou Pibin 鄒丕彬, 102, 172, 173, 251

Zou Pihuang 鄒丕煌, 172, 173, 174

Zou Pikang 鄒丕康, 144*n*, 172

Zou Pinghan 鄒屏翰, 312, 426

Zou Pirong 鄒丕融, 172, 173

Zou Qicui 鄒啓萃, 273–74, 317

Zou Shengmai 鄒聖脈: calligraphy of, 311, 507–10; education, 135–36;

family, 265; *shufang* management, 233, 315; social status, 280; texts compiled or edited by, 311–14 *passim*, 350–54 *passim*, 389–90, 499, 508; on value of education, 154

Zou Shengrui 鄒聖瑞, 315

Zou Shilu 鄒什魯, 63, 80, 113

Zou Shuwen 鄒述文, 129, 169–70, 194

Zou Tinglu 鄒廷臚, 314

Zou Tingyou 鄒廷猷, 187, 311, 314, 389, 412–13, 415, 424

Zou Tingzhong 鄒廷忠, 312, 415

Zou Weinan 鄒位南, 23, 255*n*

Zou Weizong 鄒維宗, 80, 83, 84, 193, 249

Zou Xibao 鄒希寶, 315

Zou Xinfeng 鄒新豐, 23, 255*n*

Zou Xiyao 鄒希堯, 23, 255*n*, 271–72

Zou Xuesheng 鄒學聖, 79–80, 83, 97, 269

Zou Yanglu 鄒仰魯, 63, 80, 81

Zou Yuanchang 鄒遠昌, 265, 266*n*

Zou Yuting 鄒裕亭, 315*n*

Zou Zhaomin 鄒兆敏, 157*n*, 290

Zou Zhaoxiong 鄒兆熊, 82, 176

Zou Zheng'e 鄒徵莪, 312

Zou and Ma publishers/booksellers, *see* Sibao publishers/booksellers

Zougong 鄒公, 72

Zou lineage: ancestor worship, 60; ancestral halls, 62; conflicts with Ma lineage, 76–77, 187, 456; dominance of Wuge, 60; examination results, 65–66, 136, 456*n*; founding ancestor, 60; genealogies, 20–21, 62, 281; generational continuity of publishing, 169–74; gentry status, 275–86; history, 60, 62; landholdings, 69*n*; lower-shrine, 62, 69*n*, 82–83; markets, 71; marriage ties to Ma lineage, 58, 68, 186; occupations, 62–67; origins of publishing industry, 79–81, 82–83; rules, 140–41; social status, 280; upper-shrine, 62. *See also* Lineages

*Zoushi zupu* 鄒氏族譜, 276
Zuo Zongtang 左宗棠, 48, 89
*Zushang* 族商 (lineage merchants), 4
Zushu tang 祖述堂, 170, 171, 443
*Zutian* 祖田, *see* Ancestral estates

*Harvard East Asian Monographs*
(*out-of-print)

*1. Liang Fang-chung, *The Single-Whip Method of Taxation in China*

*2. Harold C. Hinton, *The Grain Tribute System of China, 1845–1911*

3. Ellsworth C. Carlson, *The Kaiping Mines, 1877–1912*

*4. Chao Kuo-chün, *Agrarian Policies of Mainland China: A Documentary Study, 1949–1956*

*5. Edgar Snow, *Random Notes on Red China, 1936–1945*

*6. Edwin George Beal, Jr., *The Origin of Likin, 1835–1864*

7. Chao Kuo-chün, *Economic Planning and Organization in Mainland China: A Documentary Study, 1949–1957*

*8. John K. Fairbank, *Ching Documents: An Introductory Syllabus*

*9. Helen Yin and Yi-chang Yin, *Economic Statistics of Mainland China, 1949–1957*

10. Wolfgang Franke, *The Reform and Abolition of the Traditional Chinese Examination System*

11. Albert Feuerwerker and S. Cheng, *Chinese Communist Studies of Modern Chinese History*

12. C. John Stanley, *Late Ching Finance: Hu Kuang-yung as an Innovator*

13. S. M. Meng, *The Tsungli Yamen: Its Organization and Functions*

*14. Ssu-yü Teng, *Historiography of the Taiping Rebellion*

15. Chun-Jo Liu, *Controversies in Modern Chinese Intellectual History: An Analytic Bibliography of Periodical Articles, Mainly of the May Fourth and Post-May Fourth Era*

*16. Edward J. M. Rhoads, *The Chinese Red Army, 1927–1963: An Annotated Bibliography*

*17. Andrew J. Nathan, *A History of the China International Famine Relief Commission*

*18. Frank H. H. King (ed.) and Prescott Clarke, *A Research Guide to China-Coast Newspapers, 1822–1911*

*19. Ellis Joffe, *Party and Army: Professionalism and Political Control in the Chinese Officer Corps, 1949–1964*

*20. Toshio G. Tsukahira, *Feudal Control in Tokugawa Japan: The Sankin Kōtai System*

*21. Kwang-Ching Liu, ed., *American Missionaries in China: Papers from Harvard Seminars*

*22. George Moseley, *A Sino-Soviet Cultural Frontier: The Ili Kazakh Autonomous Chou*

23. Carl F. Nathan, *Plague Prevention and Politics in Manchuria, 1910–1931*

*24. Adrian Arthur Bennett, *John Fryer: The Introduction of Western Science and Technology into Nineteenth-Century China*

*25. Donald J. Friedman, *The Road from Isolation: The Campaign of the American Committee for Non-Participation in Japanese Aggression, 1938–1941*

*26. Edward LeFevour, *Western Enterprise in Late Ching China: A Selective Survey of Jardine, Matheson and Company's Operations, 1842–1895*

27. Charles Neuhauser, *Third World Politics: China and the Afro-Asian People's Solidarity Organization, 1957–1967*

*28. Kungtu C. Sun, assisted by Ralph W. Huenemann, *The Economic Development of Manchuria in the First Half of the Twentieth Century*

*29. Shahid Javed Burki, *A Study of Chinese Communes, 1965*

30. John Carter Vincent, *The Extraterritorial System in China: Final Phase*

31. Madeleine Chi, *China Diplomacy, 1914–1918*

*32. Clifton Jackson Phillips, *Protestant America and the Pagan World: The First Half Century of the American Board of Commissioners for Foreign Missions, 1810–1860*

*33. James Pusey, *Wu Han: Attacking the Present Through the Past*

*34. Ying-wan Cheng, *Postal Communication in China and Its Modernization, 1860–1896*

35. Tuvia Blumenthal, *Saving in Postwar Japan*

36. Peter Frost, *The Bakumatsu Currency Crisis*

37. Stephen C. Lockwood, *Augustine Heard and Company, 1858–1862*

38. Robert R. Campbell, *James Duncan Campbell: A Memoir by His Son*

39. Jerome Alan Cohen, ed., *The Dynamics of China's Foreign Relations*

40. V. V. Vishnyakova-Akimova, *Two Years in Revolutionary China, 1925–1927*, trans. Steven L. Levine

41. Meron Medzini, *French Policy in Japan During the Closing Years of the Tokugawa Regime*

42. Ezra Vogel, Margie Sargent, Vivienne B. Shue, Thomas Jay Mathews, and Deborah S. Davis, *The Cultural Revolution in the Provinces*

43. Sidney A. Forsythe, *An American Missionary Community in China, 1895–1905*

*44. Benjamin I. Schwartz, ed., *Reflections on the May Fourth Movement.: A Symposium*

*45. Ching Young Choe, *The Rule of the Taewŏngun, 1864–1873: Restoration in Yi Korea*

46. W. P. J. Hall, *A Bibliographical Guide to Japanese Research on the Chinese Economy, 1958–1970*

47. Jack J. Gerson, *Horatio Nelson Lay and Sino-British Relations, 1854–1864*

## Harvard East Asian Monographs

48. Paul Richard Bohr, *Famine and the Missionary: Timothy Richard as Relief Administrator and Advocate of National Reform*

49. Endymion Wilkinson, *The History of Imperial China: A Research Guide*

50. Britten Dean, *China and Great Britain: The Diplomacy of Commercial Relations, 1860–1864*

51. Ellsworth C. Carlson, *The Foochow Missionaries, 1847–1880*

52. Yeh-chien Wang, *An Estimate of the Land-Tax Collection in China, 1753 and 1908*

53. Richard M. Pfeffer, *Understanding Business Contracts in China, 1949–1963*

*54. Han-sheng Chuan and Richard Kraus, *Mid-Ching Rice Markets and Trade: An Essay in Price History*

55. Ranbir Vohra, *Lao She and the Chinese Revolution*

56. Liang-lin Hsiao, *China's Foreign Trade Statistics, 1864–1949*

*57. Lee-hsia Hsu Ting, *Government Control of the Press in Modern China, 1900–1949*

*58. Edward W. Wagner, *The Literati Purges: Political Conflict in Early Yi Korea*

*59. Joungwon A. Kim, *Divided Korea: The Politics of Development, 1945–1972*

60. Noriko Kamachi, John K. Fairbank, and Chūzō Ichiko, *Japanese Studies of Modern China Since 1953: A Bibliographical Guide to Historical and Social-Science Research on the Nineteenth and Twentieth Centuries, Supplementary Volume for 1953–1969*

61. Donald A. Gibbs and Yun-chen Li, *A Bibliography of Studies and Translations of Modern Chinese Literature, 1918–1942*

62. Robert H. Silin, *Leadership and Values: The Organization of Large-Scale Taiwanese Enterprises*

63. David Pong, *A Critical Guide to the Kwangtung Provincial Archives Deposited at the Public Record Office of London*

*64. Fred W. Drake, *China Charts the World: Hsu Chi-yü and His Geography of 1848*

*65. William A. Brown and Urgrunge Onon, translators and annotators, *History of the Mongolian People's Republic*

66. Edward L. Farmer, *Early Ming Government: The Evolution of Dual Capitals*

*67. Ralph C. Croizier, *Koxinga and Chinese Nationalism: History, Myth, and the Hero*

*68. William J. Tyler, tr., *The Psychological World of Natsume Sōseki*, by Doi Takeo

69. Eric Widmer, *The Russian Ecclesiastical Mission in Peking During the Eighteenth Century*

*70. Charlton M. Lewis, *Prologue to the Chinese Revolution: The Transformation of Ideas and Institutions in Hunan Province, 1891–1907*

71. Preston Torbert, *The Ching Imperial Household Department: A Study of Its Organization and Principal Functions, 1662–1796*

72. Paul A. Cohen and John E. Schrecker, eds., *Reform in Nineteenth-Century China*

73. Jon Sigurdson, *Rural Industrialism in China*

74. Kang Chao, *The Development of Cotton Textile Production in China*

# Harvard East Asian Monographs

75. Valentin Rabe, *The Home Base of American China Missions, 1880–1920*

*76. Sarasin Viraphol, *Tribute and Profit: Sino-Siamese Trade, 1652–1853*

77. Ch'i-ch'ing Hsiao, *The Military Establishment of the Yuan Dynasty*

78. Meishi Tsai, *Contemporary Chinese Novels and Short Stories, 1949–1974: An Annotated Bibliography*

*79. Wellington K. K. Chan, *Merchants, Mandarins and Modern Enterprise in Late Ching China*

80. Endymion Wilkinson, *Landlord and Labor in Late Imperial China: Case Studies from Shandong by Jing Su and Luo Lun*

*81. Barry Keenan, *The Dewey Experiment in China: Educational Reform and Political Power in the Early Republic*

*82. George A. Hayden, *Crime and Punishment in Medieval Chinese Drama: Three Judge Pao Plays*

*83. Sang-Chul Suh, *Growth and Structural Changes in the Korean Economy, 1910–1940*

84. J. W. Dower, *Empire and Aftermath: Yoshida Shigeru and the Japanese Experience, 1878–1954*

85. Martin Collcutt, *Five Mountains: The Rinzai Zen Monastic Institution in Medieval Japan*

86. Kwang Suk Kim and Michael Roemer, *Growth and Structural Transformation*

87. Anne O. Krueger, *The Developmental Role of the Foreign Sector and Aid*

*88. Edwin S. Mills and Byung-Nak Song, *Urbanization and Urban Problems*

89. Sung Hwan Ban, Pal Yong Moon, and Dwight H. Perkins, *Rural Development*

*90. Noel F. McGinn, Donald R. Snodgrass, Yung Bong Kim, Shin-Bok Kim, and Quee-Young Kim, *Education and Development in Korea*

*91. Leroy P. Jones and Il SaKong, *Government, Business, and Entrepreneurship in Economic Development: The Korean Case*

92. Edward S. Mason, Dwight H. Perkins, Kwang Suk Kim, David C. Cole, Mahn Je Kim et al., *The Economic and Social Modernization of the Republic of Korea*

93. Robert Repetto, Tai Hwan Kwon, Son-Ung Kim, Dae Young Kim, John E. Sloboda, and Peter J. Donaldson, *Economic Development, Population Policy, and Demographic Transition in the Republic of Korea*

94. Parks M. Coble, Jr., *The Shanghai Capitalists and the Nationalist Government, 1927–1937*

95. Noriko Kamachi, *Reform in China: Huang Tsun-hsien and the Japanese Model*

96. Richard Wich, *Sino-Soviet Crisis Politics: A Study of Political Change and Communication*

97. Lillian M. Li, *China's Silk Trade: Traditional Industry in the Modern World, 1842–1937*

98. R. David Arkush, *Fei Xiaotong and Sociology in Revolutionary China*

*99. Kenneth Alan Grossberg, *Japan's Renaissance: The Politics of the Muromachi Bakufu*

100. James Reeve Pusey, *China and Charles Darwin*

# Harvard East Asian Monographs

101. Hoyt Cleveland Tillman, *Utilitarian Confucianism: Chen Liang's Challenge to Chu Hsi*

102. Thomas A. Stanley, *Ōsugi Sakae, Anarchist in Taishō Japan: The Creativity of the Ego*

103. Jonathan K. Ocko, *Bureaucratic Reform in Provincial China: Ting Jih-ch'ang in Restoration Kiangsu, 1867–1870*

104. James Reed, *The Missionary Mind and American East Asia Policy, 1911–1915*

105. Neil L. Waters, *Japan's Local Pragmatists: The Transition from Bakumatsu to Meiji in the Kawasaki Region*

106. David C. Cole and Yung Chul Park, *Financial Development in Korea, 1945–1978*

107. Roy Bahl, Chuk Kyo Kim, and Chong Kee Park, *Public Finances During the Korean Modernization Process*

108. William D. Wray, *Mitsubishi and the N.Y.K, 1870–1914: Business Strategy in the Japanese Shipping Industry*

109. Ralph William Huenemann, *The Dragon and the Iron Horse: The Economics of Railroads in China, 1876–1937*

*110. Benjamin A. Elman, *From Philosophy to Philology: Intellectual and Social Aspects of Change in Late Imperial China*

111. Jane Kate Leonard, *Wei Yüan and China's Rediscovery of the Maritime World*

112. Luke S. K. Kwong, *A Mosaic of the Hundred Days:. Personalities, Politics, and Ideas of 1898*

*113. John E. Wills, Jr., *Embassies and Illusions: Dutch and Portuguese Envoys to K'ang-hsi, 1666–1687*

114. Joshua A. Fogel, *Politics and Sinology: The Case of Naitō Konan (1866–1934)*

*115. Jeffrey C. Kinkley, ed., *After Mao: Chinese Literature and Society, 1978–1981*

116. C. Andrew Gerstle, *Circles of Fantasy: Convention in the Plays of Chikamatsu*

117. Andrew Gordon, *The Evolution of Labor Relations in Japan: Heavy Industry, 1853–1955*

*118. Daniel K. Gardner, *Chu Hsi and the "Ta Hsueh": Neo-Confucian Reflection on the Confucian Canon*

119. Christine Guth Kanda, *Shinzō: Hachiman Imagery and Its Development*

*120. Robert Borgen, *Sugawara no Michizane and the Early Heian Court*

121. Chang-tai Hung, *Going to the People: Chinese Intellectual and Folk Literature, 1918–1937*

*122. Michael A. Cusumano, *The Japanese Automobile Industry: Technology and Management at Nissan and Toyota*

123. Richard von Glahn, *The Country of Streams and Grottoes: Expansion, Settlement, and the Civilizing of the Sichuan Frontier in Song Times*

124. Steven D. Carter, *The Road to Komatsubara: A Classical Reading of the Renga Hyakuin*

125. Katherine F. Bruner, John K. Fairbank, and Richard T. Smith, *Entering China's Service: Robert Hart's Journals, 1854–1863*

126. Bob Tadashi Wakabayashi, *Anti-Foreignism and Western Learning in Early-Modern Japan: The "New Theses" of 1825*

127. Atsuko Hirai, *Individualism and Socialism: The Life and Thought of Kawai Eijirō (1891–1944)*

128. Ellen Widmer, *The Margins of Utopia: "Shui-hu hou-chuan" and the Literature of Ming Loyalism*

129. R. Kent Guy, *The Emperor's Four Treasuries: Scholars and the State in the Late Chien-lung Era*

130. Peter C. Perdue, *Exhausting the Earth: State and Peasant in Hunan, 1500–1850*

131. Susan Chan Egan, *A Latterday Confucian: Reminiscences of William Hung (1893–1980)*

132. James T. C. Liu, *China Turning Inward: Intellectual-Political Changes in the Early Twelfth Century*

*133. Paul A. Cohen, *Between Tradition and Modernity: Wang T'ao and Reform in Late Ching China*

134. Kate Wildman Nakai, *Shogunal Politics: Arai Hakuseki and the Premises of Tokugawa Rule*

*135. Parks M. Coble, *Facing Japan: Chinese Politics and Japanese Imperialism, 1931–1937*

136. Jon L. Saari, *Legacies of Childhood: Growing Up Chinese in a Time of Crisis, 1890–1920*

137. Susan Downing Videen, *Tales of Heichū*

138. Heinz Morioka and Miyoko Sasaki, *Rakugo: The Popular Narrative Art of Japan*

139. Joshua A. Fogel, *Nakae Ushikichi in China: The Mourning of Spirit*

140. Alexander Barton Woodside, *Vietnam and the Chinese Model.: A Comparative Study of Vietnamese and Chinese Government in the First Half of the Nineteenth Century*

*141. George Elison, *Deus Destroyed: The Image of Christianity in Early Modern Japan*

142. William D. Wray, ed., *Managing Industrial Enterprise: Cases from Japan's Prewar Experience*

*143. T'ung-tsu Ch'ü, *Local Government in China Under the Ching*

144. Marie Anchordoguy, *Computers, Inc.: Japan's Challenge to IBM*

145. Barbara Molony, *Technology and Investment: The Prewar Japanese Chemical Industry*

146. Mary Elizabeth Berry, *Hideyoshi*

147. Laura E. Hein, *Fueling Growth: The Energy Revolution and Economic Policy in Postwar Japan*

148. Wen-hsin Yeh, *The Alienated Academy: Culture and Politics in Republican China, 1919–1937*

149. Dru C. Gladney, *Muslim Chinese: Ethnic Nationalism in the People's Republic*

150. Merle Goldman and Paul A. Cohen, eds., *Ideas Across Cultures: Essays on Chinese Thought in Honor of Benjamin L Schwartz*

151. James M. Polachek, *The Inner Opium War*

152. Gail Lee Bernstein, *Japanese Marxist: A Portrait of Kawakami Hajime, 1879–1946*

# Harvard East Asian Monographs

*153. Lloyd E. Eastman, *The Abortive Revolution: China Under Nationalist Rule, 1927–1937*

154. Mark Mason, *American Multinationals and Japan: The Political Economy of Japanese Capital Controls, 1899–1980*

155. Richard J. Smith, John K. Fairbank, and Katherine F. Bruner, *Robert Hart and China's Early Modernization: His Journals, 1863–1866*

156. George J. Tanabe, Jr., *Myōe the Dreamkeeper: Fantasy and Knowledge in Kamakura Buddhism*

157. William Wayne Farris, *Heavenly Warriors: The Evolution of Japan's Military, 500–1300*

158. Yu-ming Shaw, *An American Missionary in China: John Leighton Stuart and Chinese-American Relations*

159. James B. Palais, *Politics and Policy in Traditional Korea*

*160. Douglas Reynolds, *China, 1898–1912: The Xinzheng Revolution and Japan*

161. Roger R. Thompson, *China's Local Councils in the Age of Constitutional Reform, 1898–1911*

162. William Johnston, *The Modern Epidemic: History of Tuberculosis in Japan*

163. Constantine Nomikos Vaporis, *Breaking Barriers: Travel and the State in Early Modern Japan*

164. Irmela Hijiya-Kirschnereit, *Rituals of Self-Revelation: Shishōsetsu as Literary Genre and Socio-Cultural Phenomenon*

165. James C. Baxter, *The Meiji Unification Through the Lens of Ishikawa Prefecture*

166. Thomas R. H. Havens, *Architects of Affluence: The Tsutsumi Family and the Seibu-Saison Enterprises in Twentieth-Century Japan*

167. Anthony Hood Chambers, *The Secret Window: Ideal Worlds in Tanizaki's Fiction*

168. Steven J. Ericson, *The Sound of the Whistle: Railroads and the State in Meiji Japan*

169. Andrew Edmund Goble, *Kenmu: Go-Daigo's Revolution*

170. Denise Potrzeba Lett, *In Pursuit of Status: The Making of South Korea's "New" Urban Middle Class*

171. Mimi Hall Yiengpruksawan, *Hiraizumi: Buddhist Art and Regional Politics in Twelfth-Century Japan*

172. Charles Shirō Inouye, *The Similitude of Blossoms: A Critical Biography of Izumi Kyōka (1873–1939), Japanese Novelist and Playwright*

173. Aviad E. Raz, *Riding the Black Ship: Japan and Tokyo Disneyland*

174. Deborah J. Milly, *Poverty, Equality, and Growth: The Politics of Economic Need in Postwar Japan*

175. See Heng Teow, *Japan's Cultural Policy Toward China, 1918–1931: A Comparative Perspective*

176. Michael A. Fuller, *An Introduction to Literary Chinese*

177. Frederick R. Dickinson, *War and National Reinvention: Japan in the Great War, 1914–1919*

178. John Solt, *Shredding the Tapestry of Meaning: The Poetry and Poetics of Kitasono Katue (1902–1978)*

179. Edward Pratt, *Japan's Protoindustrial Elite: The Economic Foundations of the Gōnō*

180. Atsuko Sakaki, *Recontextualizing Texts: Narrative Performance in Modern Japanese Fiction*

181. Soon-Won Park, *Colonial Industrialization and Labor in Korea: The Onoda Cement Factory*

182. JaHyun Kim Haboush and Martina Deuchler, *Culture and the State in Late Chosŏn Korea*

183. John W. Chaffee, *Branches of Heaven: A History of the Imperial Clan of Sung China*

184. Gi-Wook Shin and Michael Robinson, eds., *Colonial Modernity in Korea*

185. Nam-lin Hur, *Prayer and Play in Late Tokugawa Japan: Asakusa Sensōji and Edo Society*

186. Kristin Stapleton, *Civilizing Chengdu: Chinese Urban Reform, 1895–1937*

187. Hyung Il Pai, *Constructing "Korean" Origins: A Critical Review of Archaeology, Historiography, and Racial Myth in Korean State-Formation Theories*

188. Brian D. Ruppert, *Jewel in the Ashes: Buddha Relics and Power in Early Medieval Japan*

189. Susan Daruvala, *Zhou Zuoren and an Alternative Chinese Response to Modernity*

*190. James Z. Lee, *The Political Economy of a Frontier: Southwest China, 1250–1850*

191. Kerry Smith, *A Time of Crisis: Japan, the Great Depression, and Rural Revitalization*

192. Michael Lewis, *Becoming Apart: National Power and Local Politics in Toyama, 1868–1945*

193. William C. Kirby, Man-houng Lin, James Chin Shih, and David A. Pietz, eds., *State and Economy in Republican China: A Handbook for Scholars*

194. Timothy S. George, *Minamata: Pollution and the Struggle for Democracy in Postwar Japan*

195. Billy K. L. So, *Prosperity, Region, and Institutions in Maritime China: The South Fukien Pattern, 946–1368*

196. Yoshihisa Tak Matsusaka, *The Making of Japanese Manchuria, 1904–1932*

197. Maram Epstein, *Competing Discourses: Orthodoxy, Authenticity, and Engendered Meanings in Late Imperial Chinese Fiction*

198. Curtis J. Milhaupt, J. Mark Ramseyer, and Michael K. Young, eds. and comps., *Japanese Law in Context: Readings in Society, the Economy, and Politics*

199. Haruo Iguchi, *Unfinished Business: Ayukawa Yoshisuke and U.S.-Japan Relations, 1937–1952*

200. Scott Pearce, Audrey Spiro, and Patricia Ebrey, *Culture and Power in the Reconstitution of the Chinese Realm, 200–600*

201. Terry Kawashima, *Writing Margins: The Textual Construction of Gender in Heian and Kamakura Japan*

202. Martin W. Huang, *Desire and Fictional Narrative in Late Imperial China*

# Harvard East Asian Monographs

203. Robert S. Ross and Jiang Changbin, eds., *Re-examining the Cold War: U.S.-China Diplomacy, 1954–1973*

204. Guanhua Wang, *In Search of Justice: The 1905–1906 Chinese Anti-American Boycott*

205. David Schaberg, *A Patterned Past: Form and Thought in Early Chinese Historiography*

206. Christine Yano, *Tears of Longing: Nostalgia and the Nation in Japanese Popular Song*

207. Milena Doleželová-Velingerová and Oldřich Král, with Graham Sanders, eds., *The Appropriation of Cultural Capital: China's May Fourth Project*

208. Robert N. Huey, *The Making of 'Shinkokinshū'*

209. Lee Butler, *Emperor and Aristocracy in Japan, 1467–1680: Resilience and Renewal*

210. Suzanne Ogden, *Inklings of Democracy in China*

211. Kenneth J. Ruoff, *The People's Emperor: Democracy and the Japanese Monarchy, 1945–1995*

212. Haun Saussy, *Great Walls of Discourse and Other Adventures in Cultural China*

213. Aviad E. Raz, *Emotions at Work: Normative Control, Organizations, and Culture in Japan and America*

214. Rebecca E. Karl and Peter Zarrow, eds., *Rethinking the 1898 Reform Period: Political and Cultural Change in Late Qing China*

215. Kevin O'Rourke, *The Book of Korean Shijo*

216. Ezra F. Vogel, ed., *The Golden Age of the U.S.-China-Japan Triangle, 1972–1989*

217. Thomas A. Wilson, ed., *On Sacred Grounds: Culture, Society, Politics, and the Formation of the Cult of Confucius*

218. Donald S. Sutton, *Steps of Perfection: Exorcistic Performers and Chinese Religion in Twentieth-Century Taiwan*

219. Daqing Yang, *Technology of Empire: Telecommunications and Japanese Expansionism, 1895–1945*

220. Qianshen Bai, *Fu Shan's World: The Transformation of Chinese Calligraphy in the Seventeenth Century*

221. Paul Jakov Smith and Richard von Glahn, eds., *The Song-Yuan-Ming Transition in Chinese History*

222. Rania Huntington, *Alien Kind: Foxes and Late Imperial Chinese Narrative*

223. Jordan Sand, *House and Home in Modern Japan: Architecture, Domestic Space, and Bourgeois Culture, 1880–1930*

224. Karl Gerth, *China Made: Consumer Culture and the Creation of the Nation*

225. Xiaoshan Yang, *Metamorphosis of the Private Sphere: Gardens and Objects in Tang-Song Poetry*

226. Barbara Mittler, *A Newspaper for China? Power, Identity, and Change in Shanghai's News Media, 1872–1912*

227. Joyce A. Madancy, *The Troublesome Legacy of Commissioner Lin: The Opium Trade and Opium Suppression in Fujian Province, 1820s to 1920s*

228. John Makeham, *Transmitters and Creators: Chinese Commentators and Commentaries on the Analects*

229. Elisabeth Köll, *From Cotton Mill to Business Empire: The Emergence of Regional Enterprises in Modern China*

230. Emma Teng, *Taiwan's Imagined Geography: Chinese Colonial Travel Writing and Pictures, 1683–1895*

231. Wilt Idema and Beata Grant, *The Red Brush: Writing Women of Imperial China*

232. Eric C. Rath, *The Ethos of Noh: Actors and Their Art*

233. Elizabeth Remick, *Building Local States: China During the Republican and Post-Mao Eras*

234. Lynn Struve, ed., *The Qing Formation in World-Historical Time*

235. D. Max Moerman, *Localizing Paradise: Kumano Pilgrimage and the Religious Landscape of Premodern Japan*

236. Antonia Finnane, *Speaking of Yangzhou: A Chinese City, 1550–1850*

237. Brian Platt, *Burning and Building: Schooling and State Formation in Japan, 1750–1890*

238. Gail Bernstein, Andrew Gordon, and Kate Wildman Nakai, eds., *Public Spheres, Private Lives in Modern Japan, 1600–1950: Essays in Honor of Albert Craig*

239. Wu Hung and Katherine R. Tsiang, *Body and Face in Chinese Visual Culture*

240. Stephen Dodd, *Writing Home: Representations of the Native Place in Modern Japanese Literature*

241. David Anthony Bello, *Opium and the Limits of Empire: Drug Prohibition in the Chinese Interior, 1729–1850*

242. Hosea Hirata, *Discourses of Seduction: History, Evil, Desire, and Modern Japanese Literature*

243. Kyung Moon Hwang, *Beyond Birth: Social Status in the Emergence of Modern Korea*

244. Brian R. Dott, *Identity Reflections: Pilgrimages to Mount Tai in Late Imperial China*

245. Mark McNally, *Proving the Way: Conflict and Practice in the History of Japanese Nativism*

246. Yongping Wu, *A Political Explanation of Economic Growth: State Survival, Bureaucratic Politics, and Private Enterprises in the Making of Taiwan's Economy, 1950–1985*

247. Kyu Hyun Kim, *The Age of Visions and Arguments: Parliamentarianism and the National Public Sphere in Early Meiji Japan*

248. Zvi Ben-Dor Benite, *The Dao of Muhammad: A Cultural History of Muslims in Late Imperial China*

249. David Der-wei Wang and Shang Wei, eds., *Dynastic Crisis and Cultural Innovation: From the Late Ming to the Late Qing and Beyond*

250. Wilt L. Idema, Wai-yee Li, and Ellen Widmer, eds., *Trauma and Transcendence in Early Qing Literature*

251. Barbara Molony and Kathleen Uno, eds., *Gendering Modern Japanese History*

# Harvard East Asian Monographs

252. Hiroshi Aoyagi, *Islands of Eight Million Smiles: Idol Performance and Symbolic Production in Contemporary Japan*

253. Wai-yee Li, *The Readability of the Past in Early Chinese Historiography*

254. William C. Kirby, Robert S. Ross, and Gong Li, eds., *Normalization of U.S.-China Relations: An International History*

255. Ellen Gardner Nakamura, *Practical Pursuits: Takano Chōei, Takahashi Keisaku, and Western Medicine in Nineteenth-Century Japan*

256. Jonathan W. Best, *A History of the Early Korean Kingdom of Paekche, together with an annotated translation of* The Paekche Annals *of the* Samguk sagi

257. Liang Pan, *The United Nations in Japan's Foreign and Security Policymaking, 1945–1992: National Security, Party Politics, and International Status*

258. Richard Belsky, *Localities at the Center: Native Place, Space, and Power in Late Imperial Beijing*

259. Zwia Lipkin, *"Useless to the State": "Social Problems" and Social Engineering in Nationalist Nanjing, 1927–1937*

260. William O. Gardner, *Advertising Tower: Japanese Modernism and Modernity in the 1920s*

261. Stephen Owen, *The Making of Early Chinese Classical Poetry*

262. Martin J. Powers, *Pattern and Person: Ornament, Society, and Self in Classical China*

263. Anna M. Shields, *Crafting a Collection: The Cultural Contexts and Poetic Practice of the* Huajian ji 花間集 *(Collection from Among the Flowers)*

264. Stephen Owen, *The Late Tang: Chinese Poetry of the Mid-Ninth Century (827–860)*

265. Sara L. Friedman, *Intimate Politics: Marriage, the Market, and State Power in Southeastern China*

266. Patricia Buckley Ebrey and Maggie Bickford, *Emperor Huizong and Late Northern Song China: The Politics of Culture and the Culture of Politics*

267. Sophie Volpp, *Worldly Stage: Theatricality in Seventeenth-Century China*

268. Ellen Widmer, *The Beauty and the Book: Women and Fiction in Nineteenth-Century China*

269. Steven B. Miles, *The Sea of Learning: Mobility and Identity in Nineteenth-Century Guangzhou*

270. Lin Man-houng, *China Upside Down: Currency, Society, and Ideologies, 1808–1856*

271. Ronald Egan, *The Problem of Beauty: Aesthetic Thought and Pursuits in Northern Song Dynasty China*

272. Mark Halperin, *Out of the Cloister: Literati Perspectives on Buddhism in Sung China, 960–1279*

273. Helen Dunstan, *State or Merchant? Political Economy and Political Process in 1740s China*

274. Sabina Knight, *The Heart of Time: Moral Agency in Twentieth-Century Chinese Fiction*

# Harvard East Asian Monographs

275. Timothy J. Van Compernolle, *The Uses of Memory: The Critique of Modernity in the Fiction of Higuchi Ichiyō*

276. Paul Rouzer, *A New Practical Primer of Literary Chinese*

277. Jonathan Zwicker, *Practices of the Sentimental Imagination: Melodrama, the Novel, and the Social Imaginary in Nineteenth-Century Japan*

278. Franziska Seraphim, *War Memory and Social Politics in Japan, 1945–2005*

279. Adam L. Kern, *Manga from the Floating World: Comicbook Culture and the* Kibyōshi *of Edo Japan*

280. Cynthia J. Brokaw, *Commerce in Culture: The Sibao Book Trade in the Qing and Republican Periods*